ESCAPE HOME

Escape Home

BY

CHARLES PATERSON

AND

CARRIE PATERSON

DoppelHouse Press | Los Angeles, California

PHOTOGRAPHS, DRAWINGS AND DOCUMENTS from the archive of
Charles Paterson, unless otherwise noted

EDITORS | Hensley Peterson, Carrie Paterson, and Paul Andersen

DESIGN & MAPS | Curt Carpenter

ISBN 978-0-9832540-1-0

TITLE PAGE: *My father Stefan Schanzer and I (age 10), photographed by my sister Doris (age 12), at my father's typewriter in a farmhouse apartment, Saint-Marc-sur-Mer, France, 1939.*

PRINTED IN THE UNITED STATES OF AMERICA

FIRST EDITION

 DoppelHouse Press | Los Angeles, California

In memory of Stefan Bernhard Schanzer

TABLE OF CONTENTS

Prologue

BY CARRIE PATERSON

In 2005, my father Charles Paterson sold The Boomerang, a ski lodge in Aspen, Colorado that he began as a small log cabin, built into a thirty-five unit hotel, and continually managed since he was in his mid-twenties. Upon retirement from over fifty years in business, he began writing a memoir on index cards, episodes he had previously recounted for me in 2002 in a series of video interviews he titled "Short Memories of a Long Life." Our friend Hensley Peterson, after hearing one of his tales around a campfire in 2008, encouraged him to expand his memoir into a larger book. She also began asking questions that led us to look more deeply into the history surrounding his life's events.

And so it began. He started to go through old trunks, drawers, and collections of photographs, commencing to catalog his life. One day I found he had laid out all his hats in an arc by the piano. His efforts were accompanied by the clarity of my mother Fonda's bright memories and research. Over their forty-four years of marriage she has kept her own files filled with articles and references that give context to his stories and those of his father, Steve Schanzer, survivor of two world wars.

Steve, my grandfather, was a legendary storyteller who inspired great affection and was an inspiration to many. When he emigrated to the United States in 1941, he changed the family name from Schanzer to Shanzer. He said he wanted to drop the "c" in order to "get the German out," as if he could banish from sight all the sorrows in his life that had been brought about by the *Anschluss*, Hitler's annexation in 1938 of our family's homeland, Austria. In this book we have replaced the "c" in his name as a kind of restitution and amendment.

My father Charles and my grandfather Steve are the central characters of this book. However, excerpts from the letters of other key figures help to fill its pages, including those from my father's sister, my aunt

Doris Schneider, and a few rare memories from my grandmother Eva Beck Schanzer, who died in 1938.

Midway through writing this book, amongst my grandfather's records, we found one dusty red file that had remained unopened for many years. My father knew the tattered folder contained all the correspondence between my grandfather and members of our family who died in Europe during World War II—my great-aunt Claire Beck Loos and my two great-grandmothers, Olga Feigl Beck and Rosa Schanzer— but he had never looked closely through it. My mother wanted to read the letters. My father protested. Despite my father's misgivings, my mother arranged for them to be scanned and translated. The letters were written in my father's native tongue, German, which he no longer speaks. Many were difficult to decipher because they were penned in *Kurrentschrift*, an old script based on German cursive writing from the late medieval period. My grandfather had kept them laid neatly together in chronological order, like a book he had not written but was responsible for delivering.

With so many contributors to *Escape Home*, this book has become a chorus. The principal voices are a father and son separated by war and reunited, who shared a great love and were lucky to have each other. Some details of these stories have been challenging to write, and others to make sense of because even language can hide what has been lost, buried, or unspoken over the course of time. ▪

Introduction

BY CHARLES PATERSON

At the time of the German annexation of Austria, the *Anschluss,* I was nine years old. Our family lived in Vienna's thirteenth district. As I learn about that year and the violent manner in which the country was transformed almost overnight, I have changed the way I think about my childhood. I have no memory of the day the Nazis marched onto the Ringstrasse, but it altered my family's life forever. We were thrown to the winds. My father Steve, my uncle Max Beck, my sister Doris, and I survived to tell this story.

In this book, we must all turn a page on tragedy, nevertheless, and recognize that vision, intuition, and hope are guides for people in the most terrible circumstances. I am writing our story to give insight to what happened to people like us after our dispossession and to tell how somehow, against all odds, we persevered and even thrived. I believe that young people today, who see other times and their own difficulties, can learn from our challenges, as I did from my father, that it takes courage and tenacity to carry on, while you bring history with you.

When I was born in Vienna in 1929, I was named Karl Schanzer after my grandfather. I am the eighth generation in my family of Viennese. Through many twists of fate and the dramatic world influences that caused them, I became Charles Paterson, a Viennese-Australian-American. For the last ten years I have been rediscovering my past. As I recover memories and letters, I have gained a new perspective on the history I have known, and my life is changing yet again.

Since 1980, I have kept my father's papers and many of his personal effects in an old, wooden filing cabinet in the basement of our house in Aspen, Colorado I designed and built in 1977 for my family. I had rarely opened it since my father's death in 1979.

At the onset of a winter soon after my retirement, I went rummaging through the cabinet. The memorabilia brought back an intense feeling of loss as I began looking through the boxes and files that tell of my father's life experiences first-hand. Old maps of trips spilled forth, photographs, and my father's Masonic vestments. One drawer contained his favorite grey felt hat and a pair of antique Turkish wooden clogs said to strengthen the feet. In another was a box of keys. I also found my Ski Association pins—I was number thirty-one of the first Rocky Mountain ski instructors to be certified—and mimeographed sheets of my father's self-crafted "gourmet" Austrian recipes. Another surprise was the red silk necktie from the early 1930's of a famous Czechoslovak-Viennese architect, Adolf Loos, the husband of my aunt Claire Beck Loos.

Then I found a treasure trove of letters in a stack of old, well-kept file folders. Like puzzle pieces, these letters, many written in German and French, have provided the key to remembrances of a lost time that remain with me still and bring this memoir alive. To my amazement, in addition to these letters, my father also kept all the correspondence I had ever sent to him from my first days in Aspen, Colorado starting in 1949, and from Taliesin in Spring Green, Wisconsin, where I studied architecture under Frank Lloyd Wright in the late 1950's. He also diligently kept copies of all his replies.

The adventures we told each other through the years lay before me undiluted and unedited by memory. I had never thought of that room as an archive for our lives and our relationship. Yet I have been living with it right near my drafting room and my busy life all this time. The discovery gave me great motivation to continue to work on this book, at a time when I felt it was languishing.

Later my daughter and coauthor Carrie and one of our editors, Hensley Peterson, delved a little deeper into the files. In what looked to be a stack of old newspaper clippings, Carrie found my father's journal from 1914-1920 when he was made a prisoner in Siberia during the First World War. Hensley made the important discovery of all the letters sent by my sister and me from Australia to my father in New York when we were separated for over eight years. My wife Fonda had always speculated that since my father kept everything, the letters must be buried, somewhere. That amazing day, we retrieved my entire teenage years. Other exchanges with my father emerged, from and to our foster family, and to advisors who enlightened my father, and now me as well, seventy years later, about the life and trials of children who escaped Europe during World War II.

Our stories are part of a larger history. One and a half million children and teenagers perished in that Holocaust, but thankfully tens of thousands were like us, sent away and rescued. Collectively we are the last remaining witnesses of those tribulations. This book is an expression of my gratitude and, by proxy, my father's, to those who looked out for us and saved our lives. ▪

Wedding of Eva Beck and Stefan Schanzer.
LEFT TO RIGHT, SEATED: *Martha Hirsch, Rosa Schanzer, Liesl Feigl,*
Claire Beck (seated on floor), Olga Feigl Beck, Gertie Weiss (seated on floor),
Eva Beck, Stefan Schanzer.
LEFT TO RIGHT, STANDING: *Baron Felix Pollack-Parnegg, Max Feigl,*
Otto Beck, Wilhelm Hirsch, Richard Hirsch, Max Beck.
Taken in the Beck's Loos-designed apartment, Klattauerstrasse 12 (now
Klatovy Avenue), Pilsen, Czechoslovakia, January 27, 1926.
PHOTO: R. WHITTMANN.

CHAPTER ONE

Foundations

My father Stefan Schanzer was born in Vienna in 1889—as he used to say, the same year as Adolf Hitler—in the last generation of the Habsburg Empire. Vienna, a great mixing ground for ethnicities, religions, and nationalities, was at that time one of the most culturally diverse places in the world. As a destitute artist Hitler lived a miserable life there for five years starting in 1908, and from that experience he formed his political opinions that would change the face and destiny of Europe.[1] But my father never could nor would have blamed Vienna for what transpired in our lives. People, yes, but not the city. It was a singularly special place in his memories, the central jewel in all his stories, and the heart of his identity.

Among my father's collection of items he felt were important to take with us when we abandoned the city after the Nazi occupation, the 1936 phone book demonstrates this fact. An imposing volume with "Habsburg" in white lettering on its red spine, it is testament to the smallness of that area of Europe and to its nostalgia, almost part of the grammar of a city with such historic culture and splendor. After World War II, when my father would meet people from Vienna, he would look them up—much could still be told about someone living in the new world if they used to call his great city home. With such a book published before tragedies and disasters, Vienna—for him a lost love—could be frozen in time.

A point of pride for my father was that our relatives were among a small number of Jewish families, a few hundred people, granted special permission by the Habsburg Monarchy to live in the city during the eighteenth century. We trace our ancestry back through one of the oldest recorded families, the Sinzheims. My third great-grandfather, Abraham Löwy, who married Regina Sinzheim, was born in Vienna circa 1749 and went by the name of Goldstein, as he was a jeweler.[2]

This profession would have uniquely enabled him and his large family to live year-round in Vienna because jewelers were court-appointed to evaluate the worth of items being presented as collateral by citizens who sought loans from the Emperor.[3] This job provided an avenue for a kind of assimilation, possible in the Empire but eventually exposed as a lie only decades after the fabric of the monarchy unraveled in the First World War. When power shifted again in the mid-1930's, people like us, who never considered we could be vulnerable to such charges, were labeled "outsiders."

Even before then, my father's family must have felt our origins were our vulnerability. He never actually mentioned that our direct Schanzer line originated along the western border of Galicia, now Poland. Immigrants from that area came to Vienna in waves, along with the *Ostjuden*—many desperately poor—who were looking for work and fleeing pogroms in the Russian Pale. The Schanzers, I was told by my father, were frequent guarantors for Galician immigrants to Vienna. That Galicians could have been relatives was unknown to me. But in 2011 we found that in Galicia, hundreds of Schanzers populate the birth and death records from the turn of the last century.[4]

When our family recently discovered a gravestone in the Vienna Central Cemetery we learned that my great-grandfather, Bernhard Baruch Schanzer, was born in Lipnik, Galicia in 1833. I like to entertain the thought that our family could have also been skiers from that picturesque region of the Carpathian Mountains; other Schanzers related to us are from the nearby ski town of Żywiec. My father may not have known— he never mentioned it—but I think he would have enjoyed the coincidence; skiing has been a favorite pastime for generations in our family. A *Schanz* is a "ski jump," oddly enough.

Bernhard's birthplace of Lipnik was famous for its textiles and dye works in the nineteenth century. Connected by railway to Krakow and Vienna, it became a major center for the trade.[5] Bernhard started a shipping company, Schanzer Forwarding Co., which he later sold to Schenker & Co., now DB Schenker, still one of the largest in the world. This was an irony for my father, as he liked to point out—a shipping company, and there we were, having been sent by boat, on trains, and under the cover of night in cars, like packages, to fates around the globe.

My great-grandfather Bernhard married Katharina Pollack in

Vienna in 1863. They had a son, Arnold, who died young, and two daughters, Leopoldine (Tina) and my grandmother, Rosa. Katharina died when Rosa and Tina were small children, and with his shipping company perhaps as the explanation for his absence, Bernhard left Rosa and her sister Tina to be brought up by their grandmother, Theresia Pollack. She and her husband Hermann Pollack had started textile mills at the beginning of the Industrial Revolution that became extremely successful while Rosa and Tina were growing into young women.

A brief look at the family at this time shows how lucrative textile businesses were in that transformative point in the nineteenth century. In 1889, by the time my father Stefan was born, his mother Rosa had become an heiress through the Pollack family to a fortune. On his father's side of the family, there was also wealth. My grandfather Karl Schanzer descends from Emma Goldstein and Karl Hirschmann, who was at that time a well-known textile producer and merchant. Although my grandfather went into a different profession—banking—his choice echoes the professional progression of others in the family; Karl's great-uncle Michael Lazar Biedermann, who also married into the Goldstein family, founded a banking empire that grew from humble origins in the wool trade at the turn of the nineteenth century.[6]

My grandfather Karl eventually became the representative to the stock exchange for the Creditanstalt, now known as the Austrian National Bank, where he worked under his second cousin and the general manager, Baron Gustav Springer. With family so enmeshed, it was still surprising to learn a few years ago when we were doing genealogical research that my great-grandfather Moritz, a merchandiser who died of tuberculosis when Karl was only four years old, was the brother of my other great-grandfather Bernhard.[7] It seems that the two Schanzer brothers who came from Galicia to the big city of Vienna and both married into weaving families were destined to have their own family lines intertwined. If their children Rosa and Karl knew about the connection, however, will remain a mystery. According to my father, his mother Rosa told him she and his father Karl were "no relation" and remarked that the coincidence they both bore the name "Schanzer" was at least very convenient, as she did not have to change her name when they married, or, we noticed later, her monogram. Carrying it still is Rosa's ten-foot long Seder tablecloth, a linen jacquard weave of white with blue. It has been at least a generation since our family practiced Judaism, and this cloth is one of the last remnants we have of this complicated and intricately woven history.

My father was born in central Vienna. The first apartment where he lived as a child was located in the block between the Austrian Parliament and the Rathaus (City Hall). This location, one block from the Ringstrasse, was just outside the site of Vienna's ancient fortifications, which had defended the city against the Ottoman invasions of the fifteenth and sixteenth centuries and the sieges in the 1200's by Mongolian hordes. Emperor Franz Josef built the great circular boulevard in 1850 and its construction foreshadowed the steady rise of Vienna as the center of European power and culture.

When my father was a little boy, he would spend time with his mother Rosa or his French governess in the many parks in Vienna bordering the Ringstrasse. He used to tell of being dressed in a sailor's suit, riding in a horse-drawn carriage through the Stadtpark. He remembered seeing other children at play and how he wished to be with them rather than always alone. Sometimes he had to go along with his mother to the famous Viennese café Demel, where she had tea nearly every afternoon with her numerous cousins. Thankfully, there he could always look forward to Ischlerkrapfen, jam-filled Linzer cookies.

He and his parents lived at Schwarzspanierstrasse 4, the street of "Black Spanish Monks," in District IX. He recalled his room had a beautiful view onto a garden with a terrace and tall trees. Adjoining the apartment was the *Bosniakenregiment*—military barracks—housing "Mohammedan" soldiers from Bosnia-Herzegovina, who wore the fez. One of his earliest memories was hearing their Turkish songs. Walking to his kindergarten on Horner Market my father recounted that he passed daily by the excavated site of Roman ruins—the foundations of Vindobona, which was the original settlement of what is now Vienna. Archeological evidence reveals that Jews were present even then, at the founding of Roman Austria.[8]

As a young man, my father continued the family tradition of going to the Opera, where even as a boy his mother Rosa had insisted he accompany her. Whenever he was at the Opera House on his own accord, his relative Countess Amalie Löwenstein would look for him and invite him to accompany her in her box seats. He recounted to me that he was

Wedding photo of my parents Eva Beck and Stefan Schanzer, 1926.

Ich wünsch' dem Bräutlein Evan,	*I wish for the little bride Evan,*
Dass ihrem Gatten Stevan,	*That her groom Stevan,*
Gelinge voll und ganz,	*Can fully and truly*
den Sprung zur Glückes Schanz.	*Leap over the lucky jump.*
Ich ruf mit Kraft mit ganzer,	*I shout with all my might,*
Hoch, immer höher, Schanzer!	*Higher and higher, Schanzer!*

—[UNCLE] ROBERT

perfectly happy to end up otherwise in the high rows on the fourth floor tier. These seats, almost up in the ceiling, were so cheap that the Opera House was accessible to virtually all levels of society, making it a popular venue for a cross-section of Viennese social life.

When my father told his childhood stories to my wife Fonda decades later, he would produce a map of Vienna, which he had specially obtained from his good friend Albin Schwab, who still lived there after World War II. His virtual tours of the city included all the important places in his life marked on the map with small square boxes: where he was born, his last address for his mother, important sites like the Looshaus on Michaelerplatz, and many more—all the memories of a life centered on the Ring.

I grew up quite differently. In 1932, a couple of years after I was born, my father Stefan, mother Eva, sister Doris, and I moved from a central Vienna apartment reserved for Austrian National Bank employees to Lainz, in Hietzing, the thirteenth district at the edge of the city. We had our own house in a small enclave-like village in a new settlement called the Werkbundsiedlung, surrounded by meadows and woods. As a young boy I loved to roam around with my friends in the fields of grass and among the forest pines. Adjacent to the village were the last Emperor's former private hunting grounds in the Wienerwald, the Vienna Woods. All my memories of Vienna date back to this time and place, before I was ten years old.

I remember that when the streetlights turned on in the late afternoon, I was instructed to head for home without delay. This rule was not to be broken under threat of loss of privileges. After my sister and I had accumulated enough stars for good behavior and the satisfactory completion of tasks, we were taken to the Prater, the famous Viennese amusement park on the other side of the city, where there was a huge Ferris wheel.

We often made visits to our paternal grandmother Rosa Schanzer—"Little Omama"—at her apartment, Hörlgasse 16, at the edge of the Ringstrasse near the canal. I remember Little Omama as a woman of diminutive stature, and it was evident she came from a very aristocratic family, always elegantly dressed in black with a hat, veil, and white leather gloves. Sitting primly in our garden, maintaining an upright posture even in a casually slung canvas chair, it seemed she was from an entirely different century. I remember she used to wear on her lapel a little pin in the shape of a fly that I most admired. It was encrusted with precious stones, and one could move its hinged wings.

Little Omama was a very sweet grandmother, always exuding love. She was precious to us, as antique as the apartment where she lived. She had Biedermeier furniture and oriental rugs throughout, and she served the most exquisite little sandwiches and pastries. Even when she visited us at the Werkbundsiedlung some Sundays, she brought the famous little sandwiches; they had no crusts and were cut into small triangles. This style of sandwich was from Venice, where my father said he and his mother visited once for a month either in 1904 or 1905. He would have been a teenager. They stayed at the Hotel Bauer-Grünwald facing the Grand Canal, near St. Mark's Square. Little Omama liked the cuisine prepared by the Austrian chef there. Every day they went on the *vaporetto* (canal boat) to the Lido, an island opposite Venice, to swim in the Adriatic Sea.[9]

On one visit by Little Omama when I was seven or eight years old, we were all sitting in the garden at the Werkbundsiedlung on a fine Sunday afternoon, and I was having difficulties with one of the Venetian sandwiches. I could not chew or swallow the roast beef, as it was gristle. Spotted by my father, an ex-military officer, I was made to stand at attention and chew and chew, because it would be an insult to my grandmother to spit it out. No luck; I could not get it down. Finally, he took me to the backyard, and put the strap to me.

My father was quite embarrassed to find out it was inedible. He apologized and never laid a hand on me again. What I did not know at the time was that my father thought I was unwilling to eat meat anymore because my mother had become a vegetarian and, he thought, had influenced my sister Doris as well as me. He explained his actions as resulting from the fear that not eating meat would limit me in later life and impact my ability to cope with any situation that might arise from being in a different country or culture. I understand he was trying to be a good father despite being gruff sometimes, having learned his own lessons as a young man sent into battle in foreign lands in the First World War. One hard truth in his life was that one must not think of one's surroundings as clearly defined, nor take them for granted.

My father met my mother, Eva Beck, in Vienna circa 1925 at the engagement party for one of my mother's best friends, Hilde Mellion (née Altschul). It is no wonder he was taken with my mother. She was lovely, a dancer, and well educated. She came from a wealthy German-speaking Jewish family of industrialists from Czechoslovakia.

In a letter to me from Hilde in 1995, it was revealed that my father only met my mother by a stroke of fate. He had been reluctant to attend Hilde's engagement party, she said, because he had been working all day on his Folbot, a kayak covered in rubber skin stretched over a wooden frame that could be folded into two large rucksacks and carried onto a train. He was gluing some struts in the boat and the glue affected his senses, making him dizzy. Feeling slightly ill, but a gentleman who kept his promises, he went to the party. There he found about sixty people having a good time, sitting around a big table piled high with Viennese delicacies.

Hilde recounts that my father had been sitting away from the group with a bored or tired expression when he suddenly looked up and saw a beautiful young woman across the room. She wore an elegant white dress with a violet bow at her waist. His demeanor suddenly changed. He walked over and sat next to her, not leaving her side for the rest of the evening. A few days later, Hilde received a phone call from my father to thank her for the wonderful party. He told her that he had received an invitation to meet the Beck family in Pilsen, about five hours away from Vienna by train.

I can imagine the favorable impression left by my father on his future in-laws, Otto and Olga Beck, when they met in 1925. He was older than their daughter Eva by thirteen years, had seen many of the farthest reaches of the world, and carried himself like a gentleman. I think that even as they opened the door to welcome him into their beautiful

My parents (left) with my grandparents Otto Beck and Olga Feigl Beck, and my uncle Max Beck, in the dining room of the Beck apartment, designed by Adolf Loos, Klatovska 12, Pilsen, Czechoslovakia, on New Year's Eve, 1927. PHOTO: CLAIRE BECK.

apartment his strong character would have been clear as well as his sociable demeanor. My parents only knew each other a brief time before they were engaged. They married soon after that, in January 1926, and spent their honeymoon first skiing in the Arlberg, then staying in Venice, still one of my father's favorite vacation spots from his youth.

My father always told me that the forward-thinking nature of my grandfather Otto had impressed him. Otto adopted him in a way, as Karl Schanzer had been lost to a heart attack in May 1919. I was told my grandfather Karl died while telling a joke to his cronies in one of his favorite Viennese coffeehouses; he had leaned back in his chair and asked, "Have you heard the latest story?" and collapsed.

My grandfather Otto was progressive in both his views and his tastes. He embodied what it meant to be an urban sophisticate. He always wore elegant clothes, and his wardrobe consisted of three sections, one for Pilsen and Prague, the others for Vienna and Paris. Like most businessmen of his generation, he was a Freemason, a leading member of the "Piette-Plzen" Lodge in Pilsen. His recommendation allowed my father to join the "Lessing Zu den Drei Ringen" Masonic lodge in Vienna after my father and mother married.[10] These societies were foundational for those of Otto's age, and likewise they would become so for my father, whose Masonic connections, in more ways than one, saved our lives after 1938.

My Beck grandparents lived near the Pilsen Opera House on Klatovy Avenue, the city's main boulevard. They had hired the famed architect Adolf Loos to remodel their apartment in 1909. Loos removed several interior walls in the main living spaces so that a person could stand at one end of the apartment and see all the way through to the far end. The grand and open floor plan gave a sense of spatial continuity. It also reflected the era's most progressive values, what would soon become recognizable as a post-Empire aesthetic defining the Modern period.

The atmosphere of my grandparents' apartment reflected a capacity for assimilation that our people have adopted over centuries for their survival. Loos, who considered himself a philosopher of architecture rather than an architect,[11] was that bridge for my grandparents between the traditional and the new. There are pictures in books on Loos of my grandfather Otto reading next to his fireplace in an inglenook—a seating area typical of the architect—with the family keepsakes, and heirloom menorahs, on the mantle. Otto had come from a Jewish family in the central Bohemian town of Dobříš, Czechoslovakia; he and several, if not all of his siblings converted or were baptized.

My grandfather Otto told his family that he became a great admirer of Loos' radical ideas after often hearing his polemical newspaper articles read aloud in the coffeehouses. Loos espoused views about the way society should be organized and how people should dress and live. One can find among Loos' various writings "The Principle of Cladding," wherein he made a correlation between the exterior of buildings and the first coverings man invented for himself out of "animal skins or textile products;" he wrote, this "covering is the oldest architectural detail." [12] In "Men's Fashion" Loos leveled a critique against frivolous trends, and although "everyone has the right to dress like a king," he advocated for the common man to dress fashionably according to local contexts and in a refined, understated manner. [13] The essay is from 1898, and one can see that his principles of Modern architecture are an outgrowth of this thinking.

There is a picture of my aunt Claire with Adolf Loos attending an opera, perhaps in Vienna, she in a full-length, slim gilded dress with ornamental head cap framing her face, he in coattails and a top hat. They married in 1929, but it was against my grandfather Otto's wishes. Claire wrote a book about Loos after he died in 1933—*Adolf Loos Privat* was published in 1936 and provides an in-depth understanding not only about Loos' idiosyncrasies but also his relationships to friends and clients. Claire interacted with many of them, as he was becoming increasingly deaf and was sometimes in poor health. The book documents Loos' and Claire's lives together, and therefore it also serves as a self-portrait of Claire. [14] I remember Claire from my childhood, but through her book I have come to know her much better—photographer, artist, rebel.

The pictures I have of the Beck sisters are from the early part of the twentieth century. Many show Claire, the younger, with chubby cheeks always next to my mother, beautiful little Eva, dressed as her twin. In a picture shown to us in 2011 by our young Viennese relative Lukas Beck, the great-grandson of Otto's brother Robert Beck, Claire's countenance is like any other child, but my mother's direct gaze, slightly fierce, is striking. Even as a child one can see how sharply she would come to see and experience the world. Lukas also showed us a postcard, now more than a century old, of the young sisters with their father Otto skating on

Adolf Loos and Otto Beck using Loos' ear horn to communicate, circa 1929.
PHOTO: CLAIRE BECK. COURTESY: ALBERTINA, VIENNA.

what we believe to be the frozen Mže river in Pilsen. Otto wears a suit, tie, and bowler hat; Eva and Claire are in winter dresses and earmuffs, and they are all in a line, holding hands. Otto had a sense of humor, as can be seen on this card, which he sent to his brother Robert in Vienna, the director of the Union-Bank. On the back of the card, Otto chides Robert, who was probably working too hard, "Can you do this too?" His signature is extraordinary, stylized after the last "o" with a period and hanging stem. This makes Otto's pen seem musical—DA-da-da-dee-DOM.

My grandfather Otto, who I called Opapa, spent his last years in a wheelchair. I used to sit on his lap when he was wheeled about. The position suited him in a way, as he was used to being chauffeured. He had a large, open touring car that I loved to ride in with him and the entire family. We used to drive in the forest accompanied by our governess and neighbor from Vienna, Mädi Kraus, and our nurse. My grandfather took the captain's seat in the very back and conducted himself like a Grand Marshal, wearing an aviator cap and goggles. Occasionally he allowed his children, and even me, behind the steering wheel. I remember being in great awe and very fond of him.

Professionally, Otto Beck was a wire and steel magnate. He was a partner with his relatives, the Hirsch family, in a factory that by 1938 was

Otto Beck with his daughters Eva and Claire skating on the Mže River in Pilsen. This is the front of a postcard written by Otto to his brother Robert in Vienna, circa 1909. COURTESY: HERBERT BECK, JR. AND LUKAS BECK.

producing over two hundred tons per year of assorted metal products, of which eighty tons were exported annually to America. Since the end of the nineteenth century Pilsen had rapidly expanded economically and become the most important industrial center of Bohemia. Our family tried to trace what happened to the Pilsen factory after World War II. Like our possessions and our lives in Central Europe we thought it too had been dismantled. But it had been nationalized by the Communists and kept intact. My father and my uncle Max Beck died before anyone in our family could have gone looking for it during the window opened for restitution. And we did not, so it was left to the Czechs. The main manufacturing site, located at Cvokařská Street No.1, remained until its demolition in 2002.[15]

Driving in the forest near Pilsen in Otto Beck's touring car.
LEFT TO RIGHT: *Chauffeur, me, our family nurse, Doris,*
our governess Mädi Kraus, and Otto Beck, circa 1934.

On my first return to Pilsen in 1994, we searched for one lost family treasure, just to see it—the Becks' 1928 apartment, the second designed for them by Adolf Loos. We were traveling with my cousin Janet Beck Wilson from York, England—my uncle Max's daughter—and her husband, David Wilson.

From an address on an old letter, we found the apartment building, which faces the park at Beneš Platz, now called the Square of Peace (Náměstí Míru).[16] Together, Janet, my wife Fonda, and I ascended the elegantly tiled staircase to the top floor. I knocked on the door of apartment number two. When a lady in a white coat appeared, I handed her a note in Czech that a family friend from Pilsen, Will Semler, had written out for me. It said that I had lived there with my grandmother in 1938. I didn't explain any further what our circumstances were at that time. She smiled and invited us in. To my shock the apartment interior had been gutted. The space was divided with plywood partitions and was being used as a laboratory.

My grandparents' apartment had been an exquisitely furnished place as one can note from architectural books—as were the Loos apartments that belonged to the Hirsch and Kraus families, our Pilsen and Vienna relatives. It had lacquered white paneling on the walls, fine furnishings,

Second Beck apartment designed by Loos,
Beneš Platz 2, Pilsen, Czechoslovakia, circa 1930.
PHOTO: KAREL LHOTA. COURTESY: ALBERTINA, VIENNA.

numerous oriental rugs, and artwork.[17] In 1994, seeing the bones of the apartment laid bare was, to say the least, difficult. I only glanced in, then thanked the woman, but quickly withdrew and, with a heavy heart, turned away. I could not bear to cross the threshold, and I was almost in tears when I saw what that marvelous space, as I remembered it, had become. ■

CHAPTER TWO

The Werkbundsiedlung
1932-1938

C hildren learn through osmosis. They define home by the way they move through the world, where they go to bed at night, the doors they push open, and the windows they look through. I developed a subconscious connection to architecture and design during my childhood and an attachment to them during a time when everything was being taken away.

Some of the most tangible memories of my early life include the physical environment of our house at the Werkbundsiedlung, Woinovichgasse 46. I remember all my play spots and running in the fields. Our family came to the new progressive settlement from the well-to-do neighborhood of Grinzing, which had typical nineteenth century stately architecture. The Werkbundsiedlung was entirely different. With houses designed by architects of renown, it was a social experiment in Modern living in which my parents considered it a privilege to take part. Each house had its own garden plot and was part of a decade-long program underwritten by the city of Vienna to provide housing and elevate conditions for working families. At the grand opening of the Werkbundsiedlung in 1932, I remember all the banners waving on flagpoles.

The architect Josef Frank was the progenitor of the Werkbundsiedlung in 1928-1929. By the mid-1920's, it was clear the construction of such settlement projects (*Siedlungen*) would be much more expensive than building blocks of tenement apartments (*Gemeindebauten*) on significantly less land;[1] Frank and others understood that the *Siedlungen* would be, however, some kind of a counter-balance in "Red Vienna" to those high-rise housing projects built in dramatically increasing numbers.[2][3] One example of the latter is the Karl-Marx-Hof (1927-1930), which housed thousands of working families in a mini-citadel stretching over one kilometer with its own, clinics, kindergartens, libraries, shops, and cafés.[4]

The seventy homes at the Werkbundsiedlung were built over two years, starting in 1930. Participating architects invited to submit designs included Josef Frank, Gerrit Rietveld, Josef Hoffmann, Richard Neutra, and Adolf Loos among others; there were thirty-two architects in all. Next to our house was the Neutra house and the Loos duplexes were around the corner. Loos' associate, Heinrich Kulka, actually completed Loos' project; during construction in 1931 Loos was traveling in southern France with my aunt Claire, and he became gravely ill.

Loos, as the architectural director of Vienna's settlement housing office from 1921-1924, helped determine the ideological underpinnings of the settlers' housing movement.[5] He envisioned several goals: to uplift and stabilize working families, empower people to become self-reliant and independent, and to create sources of food production during a time of severe economic crisis and near famine after the First World War.[6] Loos reported in a 1921 article in *Die Neue Freie Presse* that allotment gardening in Vienna had produced "one billion crowns worth of food" during 1920; for the *Siedlung* houses, he wrote, "The garden is primary." [7]

Our home was designed by the architect Jacques Groag, a former student of Loos who worked with Loos on the well-known Moller House in Vienna (1928). Groag was also Jewish, and like my mother Eva, came to Vienna from Czechoslovakia. Groag's Werkbundsiedlung allotment afforded space for a front and backyard to the duplex (*Doppelhaus*) he designed. So our home had a large garden and was like a small townhouse that shared a common wall with its mirror version next door, owned by another Jewish couple, two lawyers, Walter and Elisabeth Stricker. We were only two of fourteen families who bought our residences; the other fifty-six houses were leased and gradually became incorporated into the city of Vienna's socialist housing.[8]

Our house had three floors connected by tight semi-circular stair-cases, reminiscent of Loos' nautically-efficient stairways. The small round windows for each floor looked out to the back garden. On the bottom floor we had a living-dining space adjoining a long kitchen. From the elevation of the kitchen we stepped down to the dining area with corner bench-seating and a low hanging lamp. There was a small wood burning stove, an upright Bechstein piano, and large windows facing the front garden and a patio.

The middle floor was for my sister Doris and me, and sometimes a

The duplex (Doppelhaus) on Woinovichgasse at Vienna's Werkbundsiedlung,
designed by Jacques Groag, as it looked in 1932. Left house owned by
Elizabeth and Walter Stricker, the right house by our family.
PHOTO: MARTIN GERLACH JR. COURTESY: WIEN MUSEUM.

maid. I remember the small round table in the center of our room with
four Thonet chairs that were in the Werkbundsiedlung palette of yellow,
green, blue, and rose. Our room was efficiently divided into three smaller
areas by curtains and sliding panels. One of these areas had a built-in
folding table that allowed it to be converted into a sewing room, where a
seamstress made my sister's dresses with fabric from Hermann Pollack's
Söhne (H.P.S.), the textile enterprise owned by my grandmother's family.
Crowning the house, the top floor consisted of our parents' bedroom and
a terrace from where there was an expansive view.

The architectural styles throughout the Werkbundsiedlung, ours
being no exception, emphasized a modern sentiment: utility over ornament, functionality over decoration and luxury. My father told us that he
and my mother bought the Werkbundsiedlung house with help from my
grandfather Otto Beck. At the time those houses, because of their unique
showcase architecture, cost much more than the average home if calcu-
lated by square footage. They were difficult to buy into, but our family
had the opportunity because of the family connection to Loos. My grandfather also wanted to support my parents in their quest for a less formal,

*With my sister Doris in front of our house at the Werkbundsiedlung,
No. 46 Woinovichgasse, Vienna, 1936.* PHOTO: STEFAN SCHANZER.

less urban life. The homes were compact, but with the yards and open space, the feeling in the district was more rural.

At the Werkbundsiedlung our lovely outdoor areas were filled with alpine flowers gathered during trips into the mountains by my parents and placed between rocks as one would find in a natural setting. My parents took great pride in their garden and diligently labored there. They had both come from a city life of apartments, and so they enjoyed the greenery and this opportunity to cultivate an environment in which to raise our family.[9]

My mother Eva, born to more comfortable circumstances and accustomed to living in a city, became a different woman in Vienna "but more beautiful than before," according to her friend Hilde Mellion. In Pilsen she had experienced bouts of depression, and clearly this new life with my adventuresome father improved her outlook. She became an outdoorswoman after she met my father—he was always at the forefront of new sports. They enjoyed many days of kayaking, skiing, and hiking together. During winters my parents would ski the Alps, in the Arlberg. I recall as a six year-old skiing behind my father at a resort and urging him all the time to go faster. In addition to their outdoor life, my parents also maintained a cultural life in Vienna, enjoying many classical concerts and presentations at the Burgtheater.

At the side of the house, our small garage held my father's beloved Puch motorcycle and sidecar. Owning it as a Viennese urbanite signified a break away from tradition. My father went everywhere on his Puch, to work and on vacations with the family. Once, my parents and my sister took a trip to Switzerland and France to visit our relatives, the Langs. To my chagrin I was excluded, as I was too small. I watched the three of them—my mother in the sidecar, my sister two and a half years older than me in the jump seat behind my father, the driver, as off they went. I was left in a home for little boys. I remember the daily tapioca puddings, which I came to hate and which to this day I still abhor.

We did take lots of trips together as a family, however. Our summer days were often spent on the Danube in our Folbot. We would ride the train upstream, sometimes as far as Melk, assemble the boat, and then

Front and back to my mother's Austrian Kayak Club membership card from 1932. An Aryans-only clause was adopted by the club in the mid to late 1930's, but they said they would make an exception for my father and mother.

the four of us would have a great downstream float. I recall being terrified of the big river when I was little and used to hide my head under the front cowl of the kayak.

As athletic people, my parents regularly attended classes for physical conditioning, which included a form of yoga instruction. A certificate shows my mother trained to be a physical therapist. It makes sense to me, as my mother also studied modern dance and was interested in theories of movement, as was her sister Claire. In fact, my mother and a small group of lady friends used the small rooftop balcony at the Werkbundsiedlung to practice the rage at the time—the steps of Isadora Duncan. A pioneer in the history of dance, Duncan incorporated natural movements like walking and running into her choreography of classical poses. One ethereal image of my mother dancing is a studio portrait most likely taken by Claire, a professional photographer, and shows my mother in a static climbing position as if stopped mid-ascent on a ladder, head falling back, eyes closed.

I have very few memories of my mother. One of the last pictures I have of her is under the arbor, a vine-covered breakfast area on the front porch, at her birthday in April 1938. The German occupation had brought an outbreak of scarlet fever, and my mother was hospitalized later that spring.

In the meantime my father was making preparations for us to leave the country, although as children we knew nothing of his plans. Even my mother's physical therapy training certificate was part of the scheme, to show that she could go to work in a new environment in another country. In June, missing our mother from her hospital stay, a fateful event changed all of our lives. My father went to the hospital to pick her up. My sister Doris recalled us making "Welcome home, Mutti" signs with pens and construction paper. We were prepared for her arrival when he came into the house with the terrible news that our mother had passed away due to her illness. We were all devastated. I remember that I had never seen my father cry and was shocked to see such grief in him. It affected me equally though I hardly understood what death really meant, except a great void in my life. My father picked some leaves from the cherry tree on that day and pressed them into his gardening book, which I still have. As a child I could not comprehend how in an instant someone—especially my mother, who I was very attached to—could so completely disappear from our lives.

Several very fond memories I have of my mother are from the winters. She put me on skis when I could barely walk, and taught me skiing on a little hill called the "Flohberg" (Flea Hill) just below our house on the same block. Later I graduated to the larger "Roter Berg" (Red Hill) across the street behind our house to the north.

Walking up to the top of the Roter Berg in 1996, when I returned to Vienna after sixty years absence, I looked out over the city. For all my life I had a recurring dream of a cityscape with a large white building topped by a gold dome, what I only knew as "the city on the other side of the hill." At that moment I realized that the dream was the view toward Vienna from the same place on the Roter Berg where I presently stood. I had not been able to piece together previously either the place or the time. From that vantage point the domed building from my dreams was clearly the Kirche am Steinhof, the famous church designed by Otto Wagner. After seeing this scene again, the dream never returned. In other dreams as well, I have seen my past, but those haven't haunted me because I usually don't remember such specifics. However, my wife Fonda recalls that once in the 1980's, at the time my children were close to my age when I had conquered the Red Hill, she woke up to me crying in my sleep. I told her I dreamed of my aunt Claire and grandmother Olga coming up our street in Aspen, Colorado with the Nazis marching behind them. But I don't recollect that dream at all.

When I returned to the Werkbundsiedlung in 1996 I noticed how tall and expansive the trees are now and how small the houses. In the front yard of our home the huge willow was still there. It is so old now that a hole has opened up in the massive trunk, making a space within the tree as large as for a small child. In the backyard I remember my sister and I used to climb the cherry tree and eat the fruit until we were sick, spitting the pits all around the base. I was surprised that it was gone.

That day we toured the house and had a *Jause*, tea and cakes, with the owner, Brigitte Heinz, and her family. Brigitte, who sadly passed away in 2013, was the daughter of architect Ilse Günther von Hennig, who worked in the atelier of Adolf Loos. Ilse was also my aunt Claire's best friend from school days in Pilsen. In 1938, when we left Vienna under duress, my father hoped to rent the house to someone. By early

1939, Ilse and Oskar von Hennig, who had just married, became his ideal tenants.[10] However, there was no way to send rent checks after we fled the Reich, and under Nazi dictates all Jewish property was to be Aryanized. The von Hennigs watched over our house during the war, though for a period of time no one lived there. It was unsafe so not just the Jewish residents, but later many others also fled.

My father would tell the story that the Werkbundsiedlung had been a target of Allied bombings during the war, because all the flat, modern roofs looked from the air like munitions storehouses. In reality, the planes flew very high overhead and probably did not have that kind of precision, though it is still a local legend. The historical record indicates that the whole thirteenth district was heavily bombed on February 19, 1945—eight large structures fell in the vicinity of a retirement home, the Versorgungsheim Lainz der Gemeinde Wien, just half a mile from the Werkbundsiedlung. That day, over two hundred and fifty bombs rained down destroying many other buildings, and then on February 21, the area was heavily bombed again.[11]

One bomb fell just meters behind our house and destroyed a home owned by the Ternbach family, whose daughter, Inge, was very cute, with pigtails, and was a great playmate of mine. Luckily by that time, the Ternbachs had emigrated to the United States. Another bomb fell to the side of our house and destroyed part of the roof terrace.[12] The Werkbundsiedlung was likely bombed by accident because of several targets including a large Wehrmacht arsenal located a little over a mile away. On the hilltops of the Küniglberg a mile east, and the Maurerberg two miles southwest, were Nazi anti-aircraft artillery FLAK towers and barracks.[13]

In 2011, another visit to the Werkbundsiedlung and the Heinz family revealed that the Werkbundsiedlung housing project, renovated once in the early 1980's, was again in disrepair. Homes stood empty, with plaster and paint peeling. Our former house was in good shape however and remains carefully tended to by Brigitte's husband Raimund Heinz—an architect—and their three sons Philipp, Jakob, and Lukas. It still has flowering plants in the garden and from the dining table one looks out through succulents on the windowsill—echoes of the plants we had there in the 1930's. The old photographs I have are of such a similar scene. Were the images not in black and white, they would look as though they were taken there yesterday.

*Looking out the living room window of our Werkbundsiedlung house,
Vienna, mid-1930's.* PHOTO: STEFAN SCHANZER.

Since 2011 the City of Vienna has been working to restore the Werkbundsiedlung with an investment of ten million Euros.[14] As one of the
few surviving examples of Werkbund housing projects of its kind from
the 1920's and 1930's, it is recognized as part not only of Vienna's but
also Europe's important architectural heritage.[15] After all, it was one of
the most progressive architectural statements made right before everything fell apart. A relic of times before the disastrous war, it should not
just be imagined for what it was by those few remaining who once lived
there, like myself, and the many architecture enthusiasts and students
that yearly pass through to take pictures; it will be a source of great pride.

During our visit in the fall of 2011, as we walked through the narrow
streets, a sadness pervaded me as I remembered my happy childhood
playing in these same places now appearing somewhat reduced and
smaller, but still the same. According to architectural researchers in
Vienna, I may well be the only person still alive to have been part of
the Werkbundsiedlung's first days.[16] When it opened in 1932 during
the summer months, amidst much fanfare, there were roughly twenty
thousand paying visitors who came to see the settlement and took two
hundred guided tours.[17] Even after the initial stampede of visitors, I
remember streams of people continued sightseeing throughout the
neighborhood. The Werkbundsiedlung is subdued now, but it clearly has
a memory—and is still very much alive. ■

CHAPTER THREE

Weaving

After 1938, the Vienna branch of our family's textile firm Hermann Pollack's Söhne (H.P.S.), where my father had been general manager, was in financial straits. Huge losses ensued during the German occupation even though the business had thrived for nearly one hundred years and had grown to incorporate mills all over Central Europe—in Prague, Parník/Česká Třebová (Czechoslovakia); Floridsdorf (Vienna); Braunau (in the Sudetenland); Neurode (Silesia); Schaffhausen (Switzerland); Budapest, Trieste, and Zagreb (in what was then Yugoslavia); and showrooms in Berlin and Paris. At its peak of operations it employed close to ten thousand people. Some of the factories were so big that entire towns cropped up around them. As workers settled the areas, new businesses like restaurants appeared, and the factories provided social benefits such as childcare and fire brigades. Among these types of benefits, the village of Parník, for example, got a new water main, and H.P.S. provided a livelihood for a significant number of people from the surrounding area.[1]

Before the First World War, my father had a position with H.P.S. in the German factory, and afterward, he was a representative for the firm in the Middle East, which allowed him to travel extensively. He used to start in Trieste by ship and make a stopover through Venice on the Lloyd Triestino line on the way to Alexandria.[2] From Alexandria he would travel to Cairo, then Palestine, Istanbul, and Athens.

During World War II, the only industries that thrived in the Reich were those that could be converted to make munitions and war supplies. Even though textile firms were frequently converted to make gunnysacks and other basic supplies for the Wehrmacht, they overall remained on the slide. An audit made in 1941 by the Böhmische Union-Bank of Vienna listed Hermann Pollack's Söhne as one of these, but "not yet Aryanized," though it virtually was. The last Jewish owner, my father's second cousin, Baron Hans Grödel, fled to Canada at the beginning of the war and was forced to

Hermann Pollack's first textile loom, the invention which started the textile empire of Hermann Pollack's Söhne. Photo from a letter sent to Steve Schanzer from Christa Grödel, circa 1950's.

abandon his shares, which totaled sixty percent.[3]

The history of H.P.S. goes back to the early nineteenth century. In three generations it was built from a small weaving operation into a textile manufacturing empire. H.P.S. was founded at the beginning of the 1830's by my great-great-grandfather Hermann Pollack. It was still the early days of the Industrial Revolution, and entrepreneurs taking advantage of new manufacturing processes were cropping up everywhere. The initial success of the business was attributed to Hermann Pollack's invention of a new loom enabling his weavers to greatly increase production. Later he started another process to dye fabrics at a new plant. Soon after that, he expanded the small company by doing different types of weaving. As a result of his inventions and his determination, he became a successful businessman. My father said Hermann spent a great deal of time in his favorite coffee-house however, so it is Hermann's wife, Theresia, who deserves credit for their early financial success. She was reportedly very attentive to the customers of the first small store and carefully managed the books.

Hermann and Theresia had three children, Leopold, Bernhard, and Katharina—my great-grandmother. The Pollacks and their descendants soon populated the ranks of Viennese high society. Leopold and his wife Mathilde had eight children. It was their son, my father's cousin Baron Otto Pollack-Parnegg, who took charge of the factories in the early twentieth century and was referred to as "The Big Boss." He was known to be a *bon vivant*, a wonderful polo player, and friends with the banking family who founded the Creditanstalt, the Rothschilds.

Baron Otto and my father were very close friends. Soon after I was born, Otto asked us to live with him in his castle in Hadersdorf on the edge of Vienna. My parents considered moving there, but wanting to be more independent, and being of a more egalitarian spirit, chose to move our family to the Werkbundsiedlung.

Otto's castle, Schloss Laudon, was originally a fortification. It dates likely back to the 12th century and was purchased by the Austrian Field Marshal Gideon Ernst, known as Baron von Laudon (later Count von Laudon), with strong financial support from Empress Maria Theresa.[4] The castle was Laudon's reward for winning a great battle against the Turks in the Austro-Turkish War of 1787-1791. Schloss Laudon is considered one of ten noteworthy Viennese castles and the most beautiful one with a moat.

Schloss Laudon, Baron Otto Pollack-Parnegg's moated castle in Hadersdorf outside Vienna. DRAWING: CHARLES PATERSON, 2012.

Otto acquired Schloss Laudon in 1925, and when he died in 1937, it was passed to the sons of Otto's brother Friedrich ("Fritz")—my father's cousins, Hermann Johannes Frederick ("Hannes") and Leopold Victor Maria ("Poldo").

In the early 1950's, we discovered that Hannes had emigrated to the United States and was living in Albuquerque, New Mexico. My father and I reconnected with Hannes only by a small town coincidence. When our friends in Aspen, Judge and Dorothy Shaw, mentioned casually to my father that a Mrs. Janee Parnegg had become their tenant in one of the many old Victorian houses they owned, my father suspected a relative. On making Janee's acquaintance a short time later, he found out that indeed she had been Hannes' wife and was looking for a new life in Aspen with their young son, Peter. Discovering Hannes evoked a haunting memory of our past life in Europe as we found out that Hannes himself had skirted disaster during the war and narrowly escaped with his life.

Hannes made yearly ski trips to Aspen with a group of friends and, at first, was hesitant to know any relatives who might lay claim to his inheritance, so he avoided all contact. Years later, in the early 1960's, imagine his surprise as I managed to board the ski lift with him one sunny day after he had been pointed out to me by a mutual acquaintance. I didn't announce my relation to him until we were well above the ski slopes, just in case, as I used to joke, he wanted to jump off. Hannes was at first surprised and shocked, but then delighted when he learned my father was "Steffi," who had been one of their favorite cousins.

From Hannes' memoirs, written in the 1990's, we learned more about H.P.S. and our large family. It was in 1871 that Hermann Pollack's son Leopold took over the company. The next decades saw the business grow into Europe's largest textile concern, known for producing fine cotton fabrics. The material was noted for the high quality of the thread and the density of the weave. I have some men's shirts made out of this fabric that are close to eighty years old, with crown monograms of my father's cousins—Barons Victor and Hans Grödel—and which feel like silk to the touch.

Leopold was also a philanthropist and president of Vienna's Chamber of Commerce, as well as being on the board of other civic organizations, banks, and industrial councils. Hannes related seeing Leopold's portrait displayed in Vienna's Rathaus. Leopold is noted as having been one of the leading industrialists in Vienna for decades spanning the turn of the twentieth century and for his charity work, which included building homes for the elderly and chronically ill.[5] He also built a children's hospital that opened in 1906, the Kinderpavillion at Vienna's Kaiser Franz Josef Hospital.[6] A statue of him was erected there, though later it was removed during the Nazi occupation and never replaced. As recognition of Leopold's efforts the Emperor made him a baron and gave him the Order of Franz Joseph. In fact, he was the last person to receive this imperial honor.[7] [8] The barony then passed through several generations, eventually to Hannes, but in order to become a U.S. citizen, Hannes was required to relinquish the title.

My father always said that Leopold's wife Mathilde Gerstl, who was from Prague, was famous in Vienna for her wit, as well as her *faux pas*. Ribald jokes from and about her were rampant in Viennese society primarily because they were broadcast and elaborated upon by her sons. In coffeehouses and parties in Vienna people would ask, "Have you heard the latest Madame de Pollack joke?" Here is one, keeping in mind that in German and to the Viennese it would sound funnier: One evening, Madame de Pollack was hosting a party. While greeting her guests at the entrance, she inquired as to the whereabouts of one lady's husband. The woman replied, "Oh, he is regretfully unable to attend this evening because he is in bed with angina." Madame de Pollack without missing a beat replied, "What? And you allow that?"

In Leopold's will he implored his five sons to get along and not split up H.P.S. They inherited a lot of money, but not necessarily an interest in weaving or business affairs. One son, Leo, loved horses and just played polo. But the others were at different points directly involved and some lived part-time in Czechoslovakia because the biggest weaving operation was there at Parník/Česká Třebová.

Hannes wrote that his father Friedrich ("Fritz")—second son of Leopold—almost destroyed H.P.S. by gambling away his fortune at Monte Carlo, thus indebting his brothers and H.P.S. as well. The result was his suicide in 1930 to free the family of his astronomical gambling debts. Leopold's oldest son Felix then ran the business, until 1932 when, despondent for reasons unknown, he also committed suicide. Baron Otto, the last of Leopold's sons alive after Felix died, took over H.P.S. company operations.

Baron Leopold Pollack-Parnegg, wearing the Commanders' Cross of the Order of Franz Josef, and his wife Baroness Mathilde (Gerstl) Pollack-Parnegg, paintings circa 1911 and 1908.
COURTESY: PETER PARNEGG. PHOTO: DAVID O. MARLOW.

As Hannes told it, his uncle Otto, whom he and his brother dearly loved, was infatuated with their widowed mother Gabrielle (Ella) Köver, twenty years his junior. After Fritz committed suicide, Hannes relates that Ella was frequently absent, leaving him and his brother practically as orphans at a young age. She had married Fritz when he was forty-five and she, only twenty-three. The story of their marriage, according to Hannes, proceeds from a promenade through the park one day, when Fritz came upon Ella as she was sitting on a bench with a companion. He thought her a remarkable beauty, at once fell in love, and he started to send her roses every day. Ella's family had owned extensive estates in Hungary, and although she had a wonderful title, she had inherited no money, and actually had gone to Vienna to seek a good match.

Threaded through all of Hannes' memoirs is the story of the castle in Hadersdorf. It apparently came into Hannes' hands through a strategic move on Otto's part to keep it in the family after he died. He originally bought the castle for his bride, the Countess Hilda von Auersperg. She was very beautiful and came from one of the finest old Hungarian aristocratic families. (Otto and the Countess later divorced. In 1946, she married Baron Louis Rothschild and eventually they lived in Vermont.)

When Otto died of a heart attack in 1937, while reputedly in bed with one of his mistresses, Hannes was about ten years old. In his will Otto left the castle—not to Ella—but to his nephews Hannes and Poldo, the only heirs of the five Pollack-Parnegg brothers.

The castle of Laudon at Hadersdorf was seized as Jewish property in 1938. It is not clear whether Otto, who was buried on the grounds, still remains in his resting place. The deed for the castle was not restored to Hannes and his brother until 1955. In the interim years after the war, a Russian commander lived there. Hannes recounted that when he returned to the castle the furniture and the interior were nearly destroyed, and he found the large formal portraits of his grandparents Leopold and Mathilde that used to hang prominently had been thrown down the stairs. Soon after Hannes and Poldo were restored the title for the castle, they sold it and subsequently it became a nunnery, government offices, and finally a luxury hotel called Schloss Laudon. It can now be rented for weddings and public affairs, and it has a restaurant. Our Aspen friends, Dr. Bob Oden and his wife Nancy stayed at Schloss Laudon in the 1970's. Dr. Oden told my father of discovering this wonderful hotel in Vienna, to which my father replied, "My family owned that castle before the war." This prompted Nancy to later give us the hotel stationery saying, "I think it should return home."

As for Hannes Parnegg, he returned to Aspen many times throughout the years to visit us and come skiing. He was a colorful character like the rest of his family, and I found him to be a wonderful, expert skier, completely unafraid of the most difficult terrain. He delighted my small daughters on his many visits with an old Austrian nursery rhyme "*Hoppe Hoppe Reiter...*" about a wild ride on a horse.[9] It proceeded in this way: he would bounce a child atop his knees chanting the rhyme with a mischievous grin, his eyebrows arching and eyes popping, finally pretending to drop her to the floor with a shout as the ride came to its climactic end and the rider was thrown. The translation of the rider's fate and premonitions are rather awful, with the rider fearing drowning or being eaten by ravens, but on Hannes' visits our children would insist on this game over and over. It was the source of endless merriment, and they lived the rhyme as purely as children do, always caught in mid-air before anything truly disastrous befell them. ■

CHAPTER FOUR

Childhood

S hots rang out over the Werkbundsiedlung in February of 1934. I was four and a half years old and aware of the "Reds" firing from across our valley to where the "Whites" were holding out. We could hear the shooting from our house. The scene was an awful mess. I will abridge the series of events and try to relate them in an understandable way.

The left-wing Schutzbund had teamed up with the Reds—the Social Democrats. The fascist Heimwehr—the Whites, who wore green and white armbands—sided with the government troops under Austrian Chancellor Dollfuss of the Christian Social Party. From what I've read it seems Chancellor Dollfuss was a little inept chap trying unsuccessfully to keep everything together.

The Heimwehr threatened to join the Nazis if Chancellor Dollfuss did not take "final" action and neutralize the Socialists. The Nazis had been very quiet in the meantime, thinking strategically that the Whites and Reds would eliminate each other. In actuality, all this fighting weakened the Austrian government. On February 12th, 1934 the Socialist leaders gathered at the Hofburg (the Imperial Palace) having been promised immunity to work on a truce. However, treachery ruled the day. They were arrested by government police. What followed was a failed coup by Nazi conspirators who seized the radio station and announced that Chancellor Dollfuss had been deposed. This was supposed to be the signal for a general Nazi revolt throughout Austria, which did not manifest at this time, although a four-day civil war did.

Things really went wrong when the electrical workers went on strike resulting in all the power in Vienna going off, which I remember. Then the Social Democrats tried to print a manifesto for a general strike, but without power, the presses were down, so they defeated their own cause in what my father would say jokingly was typical Austrian fashion. Major Fey, Commisar of Security and Heimwehr commander, ordered a "cleanup," but the Schutzbund decided to hold out in Lainz (the district where we lived) because it was home to a strong number of working class residents. That was when the Heimwehr attacked, which explains the shootings over our house.

Chancellor Dollfuss meanwhile had been looking to Italy for support of his newly formed fascist state (*Ständestaat*), and Mussolini insisted any left-wing Socialist holdouts be liquidated. In the February 1934 uprising, one of the many workers' housing blocks Dollfuss ordered to be attacked was the Karl-Marx-Hof in Floridsdorf, the district where the H.P.S. cloth dying operation was located as well as a huge weapons cache. Heimwehr artillery and mortar rounds fired on the housing project from across the Danube. The building withstood the attack, but the idea it represented for Vienna in the 1930's—social democracy—was mortally wounded.[1]

Then on July 25, 1934 came the horrifying news that eight Austrian Nazis disguised as Austrian Police had entered the Bundeskanzleramt (the Austrian Government Building) and arrested all of the members of the government who were in the building. (Others, who were reportedly out of the building at the coffeehouse, avoided this.) Boldly, the disguised Nazis entered the Chancellor's inner office and shot him in cold blood in another attempted *coup d'etat*. I find it rather sad that at the moment of his assassination, Chancellor Dollfuss thought his own police had turned against him, when they were actually Austrian Nazis in disguise.

Taking Major Fey as hostage, the Nazi ringleader stepped out on the balcony of the Chancellery and negotiated with the rest of the members of government who had been outside. Fey would not let any troops storm the building. However in the end, being surrounded by tanks and Austrian troops and thanks to the Heimwehr, which attacked the forming units of Nazi agents, the coup did not succeed. The Nazis agreed to surrender on the promise of safe conduct to the German frontier. Instead they were arrested. The Austro-fascist government in 1934 was next led by Kurt von Schuschnigg, who became Chancellor at the age of thirty-six. Over the next four years the government, already weakened, began to disintegrate. The *Anschluss* was the final blow.[2]

The Nazi takeover came as a surprise to me in 1938; I was a typical nine year old—not paying attention to politics. By the time of the *Anschluss*, when Hitler's troops walked over the Austrian border, greeted by cheers and by some accounts, flowers, Austria had already been experiencing political turmoil and the force of anti-Semitism for some time. It was with grim resignation on March 11, 1938 that Chancellor Schuschnigg announced via radio broadcast that Germany issued him an ultimatum: the Nazis would only recognize a National Socialist government, otherwise it would invade Austria, which they did anyway. Schuschnigg stepped down and the former anthem of the Holy Roman Empire, *Gott erhalte Franz den Kaiser*, "God save the Emperor," played for one last time. Schuschnigg was sent to the Dachau concentration camp as a political prisoner.

After the *Anschluss*, anti-Semitism was unleashed—endorsed—and the violence was rampant. Jewish-owned shops were looted. There were beatings in the streets. Beginning the very first days of the occupation, Jewish people were not allowed on public transportation, and many, no matter their age, gender, or state of health, were forced to scrub the side-walks clean of pro-Schuschnigg slogans. Still others connected to polit-ical activities were arrested, and thousands of Jews were rounded up and sent to Dachau. Public life for Jews became limited, no longer permitted in public parks or at cafés. Jewish lawyers were debarred and Jews were dismissed from public office, orchestras, and from teaching at schools. The list goes on. I read about this just in 2011 in *The Hare with Amber Eyes* by Edmund de Waal, who is a descendant of the Viennese branch of the Ephrussi family. The Ephrussis suffered much after the *Anschluss*, including having all their possessions stolen, their bank Aryanized, and their palace on the Ringstrasse ransacked. Many just barely escaped the country with their lives.[3]

I had my own experiences with anti-Semitism, which really startled and scared me. I must have been about eight or nine years old when three or four boys older than me overtook me in the small woods where I had taken a short cut on my return from school. They called me a Jew—for them, an epithet—then tied me to a tree and took turns urinating on me. I considered myself lucky after managing to free myself that I was not seri-ously beaten up.

My sister and I also had our bicycles commandeered after some boys saw us tear up a poster of Hitler. One bike was returned to us later, completely destroyed and covered in tar. We never reported this to anyone; we already knew that any resistance to actions against us could endanger our family.

After the occupation, my parents began in haste to arrange for our family to leave the country. My father stood in the long lines to apply for visas and in April of 1938 succeeded in getting our family on the Austrian quota for the United States. By the end of the month he had to register all our assets and the Werkbundsiedlung house with the Nazi authorities.[4] To leave the country we would be required to pay the steep *Reichsflucht* tax.

After my mother died on June 19, 1938, we left Vienna as soon as we could. That August we went to "visit" our maternal grandmother Olga Feigl Beck in Pilsen, with trunks packed and our furniture from the Werkbundsiedlung following, so it could go to storage there. At the railroad station, my father encountered difficulties until the customs official, an older man, recognized my father's appointment papers as an officer in the Austro-Hungarian Army from the First World War and allowed our possessions to pass.[5]

We arrived in Czechoslovakia, still a free and independent country, and were soon settled with our "Big Omama," as we called our grandmother Olga. I remember her as a robust, energetic woman. I know she cared for us deeply. We were happy to see our uncle Max, who was also living in Pilsen, and our aunt Claire, who I believe came from Prague to welcome us. Our father soon took a train to Berlin, a dangerous journey at the time, to see if he could access my mother's trust, which she had inherited from my grandfather Otto Beck. His efforts were unsuccessful. The money, in a frozen bank account there now controlled by the Germans, could have helped us all escape the war, but this last gift from our mother was taken from us.

After my father came back from Berlin, my sister and I remained with our Big Omama for nine months while my father flew to Paris on a work visa through H.P.S. From there he tried to make arrangements for us to leave Europe.

Living in Pilsen was fun for a nine year old. I had a pass for the tram and would spend my days exploring the town from one end to the other on my own or with my sister Doris. I loved my newly found independence! I made a few good friends and even had a girlfriend. On a few occasions we went to Prague to visit our aunt Claire and see marvelous sights such as the medieval astronomical clock, the Cathedral of St. Veit, and the natural history museum. Aunt Claire also came to visit us in Pilsen, and Doris

Parade in Pilsen, 1938. LEFT TO RIGHT: *bystanders including Czech officers, me, and Aunt Claire.* PHOTO: STEFAN SCHANZER.

recounted she was very affectionate toward us, always giving us lots of hugs and kisses.

My sister and I went to a German-language school, but we were also learning Czech, which was quite difficult as I surmise from the school marks I sent to my father. For the most part we liked our teachers, with the exception of one who yelled at everyone and had been a prisoner in Siberia, like my father, during the First World War.[6] We had physical education classes and access to a large swimming pool, where there was a fifteen-foot high dive, which I wrote to my father seemed "like jumping off a church."

Big Omama arranged for a private tutor and charged herself with our education, reinforcing our grammar lessons and behavior. We also had piano lessons, which my sister complained to my father that she found boring. He encouraged us to keep up all these activities, however. My father's original plan in September of 1938 was that we would keep learning German, but soon transfer to a Czech language school in order to blend more easily into our new surroundings.

But Hitler's armies were already close.

The Czechoslovak people had resisted Hitler valiantly for a week before the Munich Accord on September 30, 1938, but without international support, it was impossible to keep the Germans from reclaiming the Sudetenland.[7] The Ministry of Foreign Affairs under Edvard Beneš issued a warning to England and France, that by sacrificing Czechoslovakia to appease Hitler they were also further arming Nazi Germany with "two thousand million crowns' worth of [Czechoslovakian] cannons, machine-guns and ammunition."[8]

From Beneš Platz, where my sister and I used to run around and play, I would ride the tram to the end of the line where there were soldiers' barracks and a border crossing, announced by a banner strung across the road. Pilsen had become a garrison town, and the army was encamped there to patrol along the edge of the Sudetenland. The Czechoslovak soldiers with their small band would march daily down the main street that adjoined Beneš Platz. They always played the same marching song. I remember the tune so well that I can still play it on the piano.

My impression of Big Omama as a child was that she seemed some-what serious and stern. She would insist that we always had good manners and behaved well. My grandfather Otto, who had passed away in 1936 of a blood disorder, had been a bit of a tyrant in the house according to my father, and Olga was made aware by my grandfather that everything, espe-cially the food, had to be perfect. Her seeming toughness perhaps came from my demanding grandfather, but when we stayed with her, as she grieved for her eldest daughter, our mother Eva, certainly from the stress of our current circumstances. Doris wrote in a little journal she kept and later sent to my father that Big Omama was very nervous and as a result was grouchy and scolding everyone all the time. But I can understand her reactions to the sad changes in all our lives and what was rapidly becoming a dire situation in Czechoslovakia.

After the German army moved so close to Omama's apartment, our need to leave the country increased. By the time of the full Nazi occupa-tion of Czechoslovakia in March 1939, we were likely to have been subject to segregation and the beginning of what would become persecutions. For example, there was an edict disallowing Jewish children from Austrian and Czechoslovakian education systems. This law came into effect in Germany and Austria after *Kristallnacht* ("The Night of Broken Glass"), a violent retaliation for the assassination of a German diplomat in Paris on November 7, 1938 by Herschel Grynszpan, a young Polish Jew. In retalia-

"Big Omama" Olga, my father Stefan, sister Doris, and me with Uncle Max's Tatra convertible outside Pilsen, August 1938. My father wears a customary Jewish mourning ribbon over his heart in memory of my mother Eva. The ribbon is symbolic, showing a loved one has been ripped from the fabric of our lives. PHOTO: MAX BECK.

tion, close to a hundred Jews were killed that night throughout Germany, occupied Austria, and the Sudetenland. Plainclothes Nazis burnt or otherwise damaged over two hundred and fifty synagogues, an estimated seventy-five hundred business establishments were looted, and up to thirty thousand Jewish men arrested and sent to concentration camps. *Kristallnacht* is recognized as a flash point of administrative, organized actions by the Nazi regime against Jews. At first the official reports were of condemnation from Nazi government officials, but soon after it was clear the actions were clearly condoned.[9]

A small note I discovered in a letter sent to my father in Paris for his birthday just weeks after *Kristallnacht* says, "Our school may be closed because all the children are going to Germany." I'm not sure exactly what this statement means, but it seems ominous. Perhaps there were threats against Jewish children, or it could be that the parents of my German-speaking, Aryan classmates were encouraged to move a few miles west into the Sudetenland. In any case, this report sent to my father must have added urgency to his quest to find some solution. In addition to the horrific *Kristallnacht* pogroms, our family already knew that things were becoming desperate. In fact, time was running out for all of us, and our attempts to escape the German advance would be frustrated.

Late in the evening of March 14, 1939, my uncle Max Beck, who was also living with us in Pilsen, insisted we leave for Prague immediately because he heard that the Germans were coming over the border that night. The Czechoslovak president Emil Hácha had been summoned to Berlin where Hitler announced imminent Luftwaffe air strikes if Hácha did not cede Czechoslovakia to the German army. Hácha suffered a heart attack and capitulated.

Our grandmother Olga, Doris, and I quickly packed bags with the few things we could and bundled into Uncle Max's Tatra convertible. Aunt Claire was living in Prague, and we thought to reunite the family together there. We drove without headlights because of the blackout restrictions, braving a snowy road. The conditions were extremely dangerous, and one time in negotiating a curve, we almost drove over a steep drop off. I remember thinking we had just missed going over a cliff. The ice on the road contributed to other problems. The small car kept sliding back even on the smallest rise. One time when we just could not gain any traction, we finally all got out and together managed to muster the strength to push the car to the top of a hill.

Arriving in Prague a few hours after we set out we found a hotel and wearily went to sleep, thinking we had escaped. But the next morning we were rudely awakened by blaring loudspeakers and rumbling vehicles on the street below. The Germans had arrived right behind us, and troops in open trucks with guns accompanied by tanks were taking over the streets. Loudly, the Nazis announced that all vehicles were to drive on the other side from thence on, as in Germany. I watched from the window above—it looked like an unending stream. We were trapped. According to witness accounts at the scene, as the Germans rolled into Prague, the Czech people lined the pavements and yelled insults at them. They threatened with fists in the air, and wept bitter tears.[10]

There was nothing we could do. We returned to Pilsen, hoping that our father, now in Paris, would get the papers for our departure and we would be able soon to join him. Big Omama was all nerves.

The Czechoslovak Republic under President Tomáš G. Masaryk (1933-1939) had "gained worldwide esteem as the most enlightened state in Central and Eastern Europe" because of its "philo-Semitic" and "liberal attitude" toward the Jews,[11] and people were on the whole well-treated by a sympathetic Czechoslovak populace.[12] However, with the Nazi occupation came raids and arrests of prominent Jews all over the Protectorate and growing anti-Semitism, even, for example, within the Czechoslovak forces in exile who were fighting with the Allies.[13]

From the start of the occupation, fascist groups felt empowered and held rallies around the country. Terribly, they also burnt several synagogues to the ground. Meanwhile, the Nazis distributed anti-Semitic propaganda and harassed people on the street and in cafés. Jews were disallowed to use the sidewalks, and in Brno, for example, several were attacked in daylight in full public view.[14]

There was an ultimate deadline for Doris and me to leave Czechoslovakia. It had already been decreed at the end of January 1939 that non-Czech Jews had to register with provincial authorities by April 30.[15] An estimated five thousand Jews like us from Germany and Austria had already sought refuge as of October 1, 1938 (when the Munich Accord was signed), to be followed by more than three times that number when Germany took the Sudetenland.[16] The purpose of registration was to identify people to be considered for deportation back to their home countries—an absolute disaster.[17]

Finally after weeks of waiting, at the end of April 1939, Doris and I could leave. Mayor Pik of Pilsen was arrested around this time, along with one hundred and fifty Jews and one hundred and fifty "Marxists" in retribution for a supposed "provocation" against German soldiers on a streetcar.[18] The environment was shifting rapidly into a hostile and frightening one. We felt our family's anxiousness to get us out of the country.

After packing our trunks, we had to have them ready and open for German inspectors to make sure we were not smuggling out any valuables, contraband, or money. Not until then was our luggage to be sealed and our papers stamped. That day, the entire family was standing around the trunks in the living room as the Germans riffled through everything. Everyone was extremely jittery. Unbeknownst to anyone, I had packed with me a little round billiard brush. It was a special keepsake from my father's time in Siberia that he had given me years before, and which I had stowed away with me upon leaving Vienna.

Suddenly one of the inspectors came upon the brush at the bottom of my trunk. It had a false bottom, crammed with cigarette papers, on which my father had written his Siberian war experiences in obscure shorthand. My grandmother blanched and every one of us held our breath. This brush could cost us our lives! On the top paper in the secret compartment, easiest to retrieve, was a map showing coordinates of some strategic point in Galicia, where he was captured in 1914. Numerous times I pried the brush open to proudly show my friends; as a result, the bristles usually came off quite easily.

If discovered, the secret writing and map could mean we would never be allowed to leave, and perhaps all of us could be arrested on the spot. But the many rainy days that week meant the air was humid. The police officer tugged on the bristles and by a miracle, the wood had swelled so the false bottom held fast. He threw it back in the trunk, and our papers were stamped.

At the train station, Doris and I said our goodbyes tearfully to Uncle Max, Aunt Claire, and Big Omama. Before we departed Claire took the diamond ring off her finger and slipped it onto Doris' hand. This was dangerously illegal to take undeclared valuables out of the country, but must have seemed worth the risk. Claire knew that what we carried with us would likely be all we would have to survive the coming days. For my sister, the ring must have seemed a marvelous gift, but it conferred on her a heavy responsibility. We wondered when we would see our family again as we departed from the last familiar place we knew.

In an instant, as sudden as the closing of the train door, my sister and I were alone. Bound for Paris, we were hopeful about seeing our dear father, but frightened. Doris was twelve years old, and I was not yet ten. I remember that on the train German inspectors would come through and search everyone and their luggage. As we were traveling without a chaperone, I kept all our money and our passports. I did not get much sleep as I was fearful we would be robbed, or our documents stolen. The Gestapo came through at all hours to make random checks. We were scared when my sister, then a buxom twelve year old, was taken away for "body searches" to a separate compartment. I witnessed her fear. They pretty much left me alone.

Through my grandmother Olga Beck's letters from 1939-1941, I have come to realize how much she loved my sister and me and how she protected us after our mother died. For the nine months we were in her care, Big Omama worked hard with our father to coordinate our adoption in Australia by Charles Raff Paterson, a lumber industrialist with a strong social conscience who was moved to do something to help the war effort. She made the arrangements through a Pilsen Mason, Dr. Schulhof, who connected her with his brother-in-law, Mr. Julius Rosenfeld of Ivanhoe, Queensland. Rosenfeld, like Mr. Paterson, owned a sawmill operation and was a pioneer in the timber industry in Queensland.[19] After the adoption was confirmed, my father wrote to us from Paris to break the news. In addition to leaving Europe we would also be separated from him.

Paris   April 7, 1939

My dear children,

Omama and Uncle Max have told you that you will be going to Australia and that a nice man, Mr. Paterson, has offered to take care of you.

As you can imagine, it was very difficult for me to make the decision to let you take a trip so far away by yourselves, but I don't dare hesitate for your own good, to send you there, for the sooner and farther away from Europe you are, the better.

I wish I could join you now, as that would be most wonderful for all of us, but it does not seem possible at the moment for me to be able to do so very soon. You can be certain though, that I will do my best to come as soon as possible.

I would like you to tell me if you want to go. Write to me and let me know.

I hope that you will be arriving here soon, and am looking forward to it. We'll discuss everything then.

All my love and most affectionate kisses, from your Papa

A child does not have a choice in such circumstances, but I realize now that my father still provided us with the respect that we would ourselves help make this decision. Our lives and futures were in a state of flux, and we were already accustomed to constantly changing scenes and plans. So we continued to act as most children would—with complete confidence in the decisions of grownups responsible for us. At the same time, our father respected our opinions and continued teaching us to be self-reliant.

I wrote back on April 11, 1939, "Dear Papa, We received your dear letter and absolutely agree that we should go to Australia. The voyage by ship will be very nice. Do you think that Doris and I could take our bicycles? Please answer my question."

Our temporary stay in Pilsen, from August 1938 until April 1939, bonded us strongly to our grandmother. The following letters are from Big Omama to my sister and I while we were in Paris the summer before our adoption. Every time I read them it is clear to me how much she cared for us and wanted us to succeed and become good people.

Olga Beck (Big Omama)
Pilsen   June 1939
Doris Schanzer
Hotel de la Gironde, Paris

Dear Doris,

I have already written you both a long letter and would like you to send me a reply.

The next letter is going to Karli. Don't worry so much when writing to me. You should have the feeling that you are simply talking to me. As you can imagine, I am curious how you are doing now.

You will have to describe your classroom to me and also how you have stored your belongings and clothing, whether or not you always wash your dirty undershirts and wash your stockings after wearing them so that there aren't a lot of clothes lying around and Papa has to pay so much [to have them cleaned]. I also want to know how you like the food and what your daily schedule is like. Such a large city is certainly quite astonishing at first and you want to see so much. Don't wear yourselves out and make sure that Karli in particular gets to bed early. Papa should not force him to eat something if he doesn't want to. He will discover on his own that many things are actually good, even if he thinks that they aren't. You have to try everything.

It is also important that he doesn't get an earache. You know, I always keep him (i.e. his ears) warm either with a compress or cotton and a bandage together with a hot water bottle. You will have to be responsible for it yourself. If you need to know something more, just ask any lady acquaintance, and she will be happy to answer any questions. You don't need to be bashful.

On Sunday, Dr. Pokorny's wife came to visit. She is looking for a boarding house for her daughter Pali in London. If she sends furniture, dishes, and linens to the post office, the child can stay there for nothing. Ask your Papa if he would be interested in that as well. I have all of the linens together and will send them to Paris, if that is what your Papa wants. There are some bed linens and the nice clothes from your Mama. People cannot send dishes. I talk with [your] Uncle Max frequently on the telephone. He still has not arrived [in England].

Read this letter through slowly and then write me back in a relaxed manner, as if you were talking to me. It doesn't matter if there are a few errors, I will correct them.

Give Karli a kiss from me.
A kiss to you,

Your faithful Omama

In a postscript Omama sent her affectionate regards to our father. She added, "He should write and let me know what is going to happen to you. I love getting long letters."

Between the time of the June letter and the next one I have from her on August 19, 1939, Omama's life changed radically. On June 21, 1939, the acting Reich Protector Baron Constantin von Neurath issued an Aryanization decree for all Jewish property; all jewelry, precious metals, bonds, money, and foreign currency were required to be registered.[20] This was the beginning of a systematized pauperization, where Jews would eventually have to sign over everything they owned.

That summer Adolf Eichmann was transferred to Prague from Vienna to oversee the emigration process of Jews from the Protectorate. He issued a decree making it illegal for Jews to remain in the provinces, requiring them to move to the capital.[21] We believe Olga was thus forced at this time to move out of the Pilsen apartment, the second one designed by Loos that had been her family's home for over ten years. Like many Loos apartments in Pilsen, it became the home of a high-level Nazi.

Olga rented a place to live in Prague and put many items aside for us, should she be able to ship things out of the country. The civil rights of Jews were being diminished day by day since the Nazis seized Czechoslovakia in March, starting with exclusion from business activities and certain public places, as well as segregation. By the end of November 1939, Jews were not even allowed to have or buy newspapers, except for the *Jüdisches Nachrichtenblatt*, which was censored by the Gestapo.[22]

Olga Beck

Prague   August 19, 1939

My dear *Schneckerln* [little curly heads],

I was in Pilsen for an entire week, as I just now completely cleared out the apartment. It was a lot of work, but everything is ready now so I can send it off if I am granted permission. Upon my return I found your dear letters. Karli wrote such a nice letter this time, which pleased Miss Paukner [the tutor] greatly, although there were a few mistakes with the plurals, such as *Erdepfel* [potato] from the root word *Apfel*, should be written with an *ä*, and *fersammeln* [gather] should of course be written with a *v*, *wier* should be written only with an *i* not *ie* [we], *schleft* [sleeping] should be *schläft* and a couple of others, but I don't want to be irritating. Just write again and I can make the corrections. I sent you an extra letter, which I registered on account of the big stamp and sent several small stamps on a second letter and will send you more if you want.

[Doris' good friend] Peter is coming to Prague to attend a preparatory school for Palestine and may be living close by. He was very happy with your letter.

I'm interested to hear the way everything is organized for you two. [Your nicknames] Karli *"Hirondelle"* ["Swallow"] fits him very well and as *"Etoile de mer"* ["Starfish"] Doris will feel like a star [in the sky]. Papa wrote me today with the happy news that he will be traveling with you to Australia. I am very glad to hear that of course, as I was always afraid that you would have to go alone. Although I find it terrible that you are leaving, I am relieved now to know that Papa will be going with you. Karli's wish that we [Aunt Claire and I] might also come may perhaps come true, but it is unlikely to happen very soon, and I only hope that you two will not have forgotten me by then. The things you are going to see on this big trip should be at least as much as one would find in an entire geography book, and you won't even have to read a book to learn about them, which is certainly very nice!

I bought a whole set of Czech stamps [at Karli's request], with *Czech Moravia* printed on them. They will be very rare, since they were only available for a short time. I will send them as well—be sure to take good care of them—they cost 80 crowns.[23] I thought you might draw me a picture of the ocean when you have time—or don't you have pencils? Uncle Max is quite busy in London. He makes his own drawings of machines, has them constructed in iron and then gets them up and running. I am certain that Karli will also learn how to do this, as Mr. Paterson is an engineer and is looking forward to having Karli work with him since he doesn't have a son.

It isn't at all nice in Pilsen right now. [Great Aunt] Elsa [Klinger] and [her daughter] Edith [Kafka] will be leaving soon,[24] and then I will be alone—but I will still have my many lady friends.

So, many kisses from

Your faithful Omama ■

Eva Beck, circa 1921.
PHOTO: JAN F. LANGHANS STUDIO, PRAGUE.

Stefan Schanzer, prior to the First World War.

Our grandmother, Rosa Schanzer with Doris and me in the garden of our Werkbundsiedlung house (other neighborhood children, left and right), circa 1933. House in background destroyed by a bomb in World War II.

My parents, Stefan and Eva Schanzer on their Puch motorcycle in the Böhmerwald on the border of Czechoslovakia and Austria, 1931.

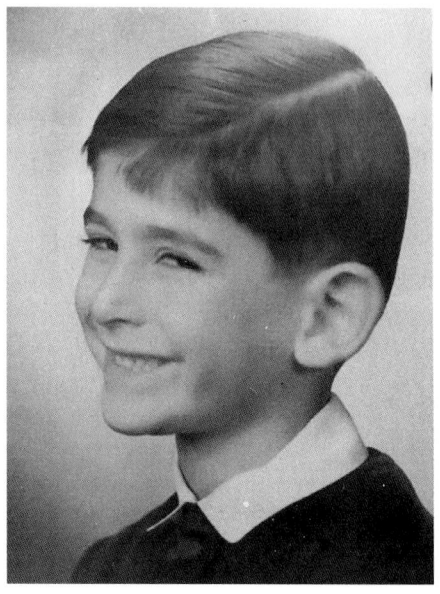

Me at five years old, 1934. PHOTO: "WÄHLE DEIN BILD," VIENNA.

My collection of "Böhmen und Mähren/Čechy a Morava" stamps issued after July 1939 in the Nazi Protectorate of Bohemia and Moravia. Depicted are linden tree leaves with closed buds, a view of Zlín (3K), the Iron Works in Moravská Ostrava (4K), Hrad Zvíkov (40h), Hrad Karlštejn (50h), and St. Vitus Cathedral in Prague (1K), among others.

*My grandfather Otto Beck reading in the living room inglenook of the Loos-
designed Beck apartment, Klattauerstrasse 12 (now Klatovy Avenue),
Pilsen, Czechoslovakia, 1928.*
PHOTO: CLAIRE BECK.

*My grandparents Rosa Schanzer, circa 1930's and Karl Schanzer,
circa 1910's.*

CHAPTER FIVE

Mutti

I t was my father's intuition, and my grandmother Olga Beck's, that saved us. They were determined to get us out of Europe against all the odds. I certainly knew and felt some of the dangers as we fled, but I see now that my father sensed what was coming long before the *Anschluss*. He even considered leaving Austria earlier with our family and was willing to give up our entire life in Vienna. Only during the research and reading of many letters for the writing of this book can I clearly understand the events that led him in 1938 to take the necessary brave steps.

I had always known that my mother was reluctant to leave, even while my father was arranging for our emigration as a family. Living in Vienna had changed her life in so many positive ways. Several letters saved by my father, however, bring to light that at the end of 1937 my mother was realizing emigration might be necessary as she wrote to ascertain whether there was a community of Pilsen émigrés in New Zealand. Something familiar, anywhere, seems to have been more palatable for her than a blank slate. In the mid-1930's my father considered moving us to South America to be a representative there of Hermann Pollack's Söhne, but my mother did not want to take that opportunity, and later, my father said, she expressed her regret.

In April 1938, shortly after the *Anschluss,* my father wrote to relatives of Olga's brother, Max Feigl, who lived in the United States, to try to get affidavits of support for immigration. We were on the Austrian quota but needed someone to sponsor us in America. We would be leaving Austria with almost no money. As of April 26, 1938 it was required, under orders of Hermann Göring, that all Jewish assets over 5,000 Reichsmarks be reported to make them available for any use deemed necessary for the German economy. And if our money wasn't to be stolen outright, we would still not be able to take anything with us.

These relatives, the Rieses, wrote to seven other of their relatives.

My mother's last birthday at our house in the Werkbundsiedlung with Doris and me, April 4, 1938. PHOTO: STEFAN SCHANZER.

My father included a business plan for a scarf enterprise to show how he would be able to support us with business connections from the textile industry. But as of the beginning of June, no one could provide the documents or had yet replied to the Rieses about the crucial affidavit. Besides guaranteeing that children would go to school until the age of sixteen, the documents committed the signer to supporting all members of a family until they were financially self-sufficient, which would have been an unknown and perhaps protracted amount of time considering how severe the depression was in the United States.[1]

I realize that with emigration avenues suspended, my father decided he must take matters into his own hands and get us out of the Reich himself. It wasn't until some forty years after we left Vienna, after my father's death in 1979, that I found out how my mother, already in a very fragile mental condition, actually died. I'm not sure she was ready to leave the hospital, or had the strength to make such a difficult journey. My wife Fonda, my daughter Carrie, and I have been able, with letters and documents found by the Beck family in Vienna, to piece it all together during the writing of this book.

I knew my mother had been sick with scarlet fever. The contagion was feared to be as virulent as the Spanish influenza that ravaged Europe and killed millions twenty years earlier. One generation is not enough time

Mutti's birthday breakfast. PHOTO: STEFAN SCHANZER.

to forget such a pandemic, and she suffered as people's precautions accumulated and mixed with hatred. She had been isolated in a ward behind a glass partition completely cut off from the world. But she was also being harassed by anti-Semitic comments from other women at the hospital. According to my father, they told her it didn't matter if she got well, and they taunted her saying the Nazis "would get her anyway" when she was released. Behind the glass wall she must have felt great alienation and despair—the lack of contact with everybody, trapped, ill, and away from her family. Perhaps thinking of being a burden due to her illness, already depressed, and fearful and that in her weakened state she would not be able to make a long and emotionally arduous journey, she took her own life, and hung herself.

I cannot imagine her desperation and resolve.

It was my sister Doris who first learned of my mother's suicide. In 1976 she traveled to Vienna with her family and visited Anna Hirtringer, the maid of my paternal grandmother, Rosa Schanzer. Rosa—"Little Omama"—stayed in Vienna during the war, hidden in her own apartment. Anna had been extremely loyal to my grandmother and had come to work for her as a teenager. Over tea with Doris, Anna mentioned in passing what a tragedy it was that our mother killed herself in the hospital. To Doris, this came as an enormous shock and surprise.

Between 1938-1939 in Austria, suicides by Jews increased by roughly twenty-fold after the occupation.[2] Another of our relatives also took this path. Days before Eva, a Mrs. Pollack-Parnegg threw herself out a window in Vienna. From the corresponding death dates we believe her to be Gertrude, the wife of Baron Otto's older brother Walther.[3]

When Doris found out the truth about our mother's death she said she cried during the opera she attended that evening with her family and throughout the night. Later Doris said that she always had some level of apprehension about what might have become of our mother and perhaps, in some way, knew the truth. Big Omama had made our father promise that he would never tell his children about the circumstance of our mother's death. He was a man of his word, and he never spoke of it. In 1979, my sister finally told me his long-guarded secret, which had become her own responsibility. On the day we went to pick up my father's ashes, riding in the car, she could not hold back any longer.

I was quite taken aback by my sister's admission, but it was somehow healing to consider why this piece of my family history had been kept from me all these years. Perhaps my father had thought to protect Doris and me from the harming effects and the burden of this shocking truth. Now

Mutti hiking in the Alps, circa 1934. PHOTO: STEFAN SCHANZER.

Gravesite of my grandfather Otto and my mother Eva in Pilsen's Jewish cemetery, discovered in the summer of 2011. A memorial plaque for my grandmother Olga and my aunt Claire was added to the right side in October 2011 when the stone was refurbished. PHOTO: CARRIE PATERSON.

with hindsight, I am not sure how I would have handled it if I had known; it certainly would have been much more difficult to adjust to the new life that was an inevitable unknown before us.

After my mother's death, my father truly abandoned his life in Vienna. Even though he traveled the world in his seventies and eighties, he never went back to his birthplace, where he and my mother had lived together so many happy years.

In early November of 2011, during a visit to Pilsen on a cold autumn morning, four of the Beck descendants entered through the massive gates of the small Jewish cemetery. I was together with my cousin Janet, my wife Fonda, daughter Carrie, and Janet's daughter, Amanda Wood. Accompanying us was a new friend, an art historian and curator, Petr Jindra, who had hurriedly arrived to meet us there on his bicycle.

Leaves in waist high mounds greeted us, but the back portion of the cemetery remained unraked. We searched among the graves as if walking across a lush golden carpet. At the end of a row next to an open green space, an area had been cleared around a beautiful, modern granite headstone[4] bearing the name of my grandfather Otto and my mother Eva in large gold letters.

It was an emotional moment, particularly for me. The site of my mother's burial, together with my grandfather's, had been discovered only a few months previously by architectural historian Petr Domanický.[5] He had been researching the Beck family for the exhibition "Loos-Pilsen-Connections" at Pilsen's Západočeská Galerie, which focused on Adolf Loos' first architectural clients. Until that time I had no idea where my mother had been buried and always presumed it was in Vienna though I could find no trace. In 1938, my sister and I were told we were too young to attend her funeral, and in subsequent years I never asked my father about it, preferring to leave unspoken that moment of grief.

Before our arrival, with Petr Jindra's kind coordination, the Pilsen Jewish community organized for the headstone to be cleaned, polished, and re-set. We had requested that a new inscription be added for my grandmother Olga and aunt Claire. As I stood at the site, tears began to well in my eyes. It had taken such a long time for the sadness to reach into my soul—seventy-three years. We followed the traditional Jewish custom of placing small stones on the grave, to mark our remembrance of our family. We also placed stones for each of the twelve living Beck descendants, now three generations.

There were no dry eyes as we departed, knowing that our Beck grandparents and their daughters are now memorialized together, in Pilsen—just as it should have been. ■

CHAPTER SIX

A Boy of Ten
Is Already Grown

When my sister and I arrived in Paris at the end of April 1939, we continued to correspond frequently with our Big Omama, Aunt Claire, and Uncle Max—who was himself about to emigrate. Two letters in particular usher in a sense that my sister and I were not only going to leave Europe, but that we were suddenly about to become adults.

An illustrated postcard sent to me for my birthday shows two birds caring for their nest. It is spring, and the eggs are ready to hatch. I imagine my artistic Aunt Claire chose it for us, intuiting that the image spoke both to our family's intentions and to the fortitude my sister and I would need for our coming journey. The card is an emblem of the prudence and care with which our family prepared us for new lives.

I returned my family's birthday wishes with a long letter narrating a week or so of my life and everything I noticed. I was quite wordy for a ten year old. My father typed it out for me and kept a carbon copy. Through a child's eyes, one can see war is already underway and its impact imminent—the distance from our family, being in strangers' hands, the explorations of two children left to experience and under-stand the world by themselves. Like allegorical stories that I can only understand now, over seventy years later, I can read them as indications of what I felt about our condition of being refugees and foreshadowing what was later to come.

For Big Omama, I narrated the day my sister and I spent at Versailles. We were visitors to royal grounds, already dispossessed of empire. A violent thunderstorm with pouring rain passed over us and we crawled into a tunnel, soaking wet, until it left. When the sun came out, it brought with it hope and the possibility we could again be simple children. Yet, the loss of our mother hangs in the air like a question.

Still to this day, I am unable to answer why she left us, or to remove from the image of my childhood its indelible mark.

Karli, Paris   July 15, 1939

Big Omama, Prague

Dear Omama,

I had a very nice birthday. Doris made me a big, beautiful cake that tasted very good and [I was given] a stamp album, which is much bigger than the one I had in Pilsen. I have already collected a lot of stamps again and will soon have as many as in my old collection. I would like to take this opportunity to ask you to send me some Czech, Austrian, and possibly some pretty German stamps. I recently saw a censored letter that a lady received containing many beautiful stamps which was sent from Czechoslovakia. I will need all the beautiful stamps to trade in Australia where I may be able to get a lot of very pretty stamps in exchange.

The next day, we took a trip by bus and drove all day with a nice group of Papa's friends. Unfortunately, Papa was busy and could not come along. We also took a walk and saw a lot of things. It was nice, especially since there were two boys on the bus who I played around with. There was something in the back of the bus to stand on, where we had a very good view. We drove a lot through the forest. We also went to Mulan and ate so much there that we all got terrible stomachaches. We ate lunch from 2-4 and dinner from 8-10. We didn't get home until midnight. I could hardly drag my stomach home it was so full.

I got a letter of greetings from [my future adoptive sister] Mary Paterson in Australia with her picture and a newspaper clipping with a picture of her sister [Joan], the older one, who seems to be quite famous, whereupon we sent her a picture of Princess Plump, who has gotten much prettier and the story is also much better now.[1]

Yesterday, we were at the Celebration of the Republic parade on the Champs-Élysées. I pushed my way into the front row and was able to see a lot. The people were dancing in the street. In the evening, there was a fireworks show and they shot something like rockets into the air that made a terrible racket but then turned into flower bouquets, circles, hands, and other beautiful things. It went on for quite a while, with something different every time. On a bridge that no one was allowed onto, there was a waterfall, only made of fire, and some kids had some shavings that sprayed something like sparks and then made a huge noise.

Yesterday we were at Versailles. There were a lot of interesting things to see, so much that I can't even describe it all. We went out shopping at noon and took what we bought to a big, beautiful lake where a couple of tents stood. We ate everything [until it was] all gone, and because the weather was so nice, went for a hike deep in the woods. We walked and walked, and then it started to drizzle. We thought it would stop soon, since we couldn't feel much because of the trees. All of a sudden there was a downpour, but Doris had a raincoat along and we used Doris' coat to cover our heads. Suddenly, there was a clap of thunder, and we thought there would be a thunderstorm, so we ran quickly away from the big tree. We ran so fast, through so many puddles, that we got very dirty. We ran to a tunnel, and when we got there we were soaking wet. Karel Bondy was along, and he also only had a windbreaker. We thought we would have to go back to Paris to dry off, but decided it would be a waste of our train tickets, so we stayed and sunned ourselves when the sun came out again at the palace. Everything that had been totally drenched soon was dry again.

When we had dried out, we went into the palace grounds. The water fountain show began. We looked at all the fountains. Then we went to the palace of the princess, but since I don't know the story, I don't know how it came to be that a princess lived there. It is called Trianon. We walked on and looked around. There were also houses with straw roofs and a lot of fishes under a bridge where many people were standing throwing bread to them and finally, at the very end, came a big swan that ate all the fish food and always wanted more. There were small swans too, which were looking everywhere for their mother, but the mother didn't care about them, but rather ate and ate, and let them look for her.

We walked on through the park. It finally got quite late, and they began to close, because at night they have colored water fountain shows that cost 10 francs for admission, but luckily we were able to get out in time and went home. Our shoes were so dirty from the slosh we ran through in the forest, and when I took off my shoes I was shocked to see that my feet were as dirty as my shoes, because everything went through my shoes. I had to really scrub my feet and even used a brush, but the dirt remained.

Karli

Just a few weeks after I dictated that letter my father enrolled my sister Doris and me at a *Colonie de Vacance* [summer camp] on France's west coast hosting refugee children. I remember the water there was frigid, and I needed to wear a swimming cap because I used to get frequent ear infections and my ears were very sensitive. My father saved a newspaper clipping, which pictured dozens of us, and indicated himself—"ich"—under a wide-brimmed hat. I can't see my sister, but I'm in the center of the photo, marked also by my father, with an arrow— "Karli"—staring straight at the camera. I look quite dour in a raincoat with tiny legs and stiff arms.

The article comments that among the refugees are children from Austria "who still bear on their young faces the marks of their recent vicissitudes." With great compassion for our situation, the article also salutes the Parisian organization of Freemasons, UJM Clarté, for sponsoring "this humane gesture of solidarity."[2]

When our father went back to Paris, we wrote to him often, keeping him in our thoughts and telling him about our daily experiences. We kept asking him to come, and tried to be persuasive that the seaside would be much nicer than Paris. It must have been an anxious time.

French newspaper article announcing arrival of refugee children in Saint-Nazaire at the Jean-Macé school, summer 1939.

Title page of "Princess Plump" written and illustrated by Doris and me with our aunt Claire while living in Pilsen, 1939.

Princess Plump.

Girls at the Jean-Macé school, St. Nazaire, 1939.
Doris, top row, third from left.

Boys at the Jean-Macé school, St. Nazaire, 1939.
I am in a white shirt, fourth row, third from right.

Initially it was difficult for me to make friends at the camp. I wrote to my father, "The boys are not so nice to me. Pjer Brun is especially nasty." In another letter I compared his behavior to the *Hitler Jugend* and had told the boy so.[3] By the end of the month, however, Brun was my good friend. As he himself attested in French at the bottom of another letter, signed officially P. Brun, "Karli is getting better at bonding with other people. We get on well and are on full friendly terms." He signed the letter giving his "amités" to my father, just as if he were an adult, my father's equal, entrusted with the care of a child. The rest of the letter details fun activities, a huge pillow fight (*riesen Pöllsterschlacht*), and a dance.

The summer camp allowed me to be a young boy growing out of his innocence in a typical way. Picking my way along the rocks on the beach one day, I saw a lovely looking girl, and with my eyes on her instead of my feet, I slipped and fell, landing on my front tooth. I wrote to my father about it, which must have worried him. I tried to put his fears to rest. "My tooth is doing great, my lip is totally healed. You don't see anything anymore. My tooth is not loose—I was mistaken—and it also doesn't hurt." Emphasizing my independence, the letter showed my father I was becoming impermeable to life's small troubles. He would not have to worry about me being on my own.

In the meantime, my father received word that Mr. Paterson and Otto Pick—the husband of my grandmother Rosa's cousin Käthe Pick, both Austrian émigrés to Canada —would be facilitating all of us coming to Australia together. My father sent a letter to Doris and me on August 17, 1939 that he received a telegram from Mr. Paterson. "He informed me that the permits—yours as well as mine—would be sent to me on the next plane out. If the situation concerning the disembarkment fee goes as planned for me, it may be possible that we could all three take the lovely trip together." My father, very protective of us, clearly set the tone in his letter that we were still children and needed him. He wrote, "I am so relieved to be at this point. I was happy to hear that the boys are so nice to you now, dear Karli. Hopefully, it will stay that way. I am very happy to be here [in Paris] so that I can get right to work on plans for our departure together."

Meanwhile, we were relocated a few miles away to an orphanage in Saint-Marc-sur-Mer as French soldiers moved into our camp in Saint-

Writing letters in the farmhouse apartment, Saint-Marc-sur-Mer, circa 1939.
PHOTO: STEFAN SCHANZER.

Nazaire. A French naval base for submarines and destroyers was located there, which I remember had concrete bunkers facing the sea. We pleaded with him to join us. I wrote, "Our trip to St. Marc was very difficult. We rode in a truck because there was no bus. I want most of all for you to come soon. Find a train and come. I'm sure it is not nice in Paris. We have made a new dining hall because the old one was too small. The food is still very good. Many, many kisses, from Karli."

My father's next short letter is dated on September 2, 1939—a day after Hitler invaded Poland and a day before France, Britain, and the British Commonwealth, including Australia, declared war on Germany. The possibilities for getting ship's passage to Australia had drastically changed.

September 2, 1939

Dear Doris, dear Karli,

I got your sweet card. You are quite right that I was supposed to come to you immediately. But since I have to take care of an important matter on Monday regarding our trip to Australia, I will simply have to be brave and wait here. I do not know for sure, but I will try to come to you either Tuesday or Wednesday.

Doris and I with our landlady and chickens. PHOTO: STEFAN SCHANZER.

There won't be any ships in the near future, since they are all currently being used to transport troops. That is another reason for me to stay here to (try to) get a spot. Be very good and take care. I have received no more news from Big Omama.

Lots of kisses and all my love,

Your Papa

Most likely following this letter Doris wrote, "Last night, the sirens were howling in Saint-Nazaire. You could hear them all the way here. I do not know if we will be able to go to Australia at all now. I, too, want most of all to see you here. Maybe you can come with a private car. Maybe someone can drive you here. Or you can go directly if and when the trains are running again. Many, many kisses from Doris."

Our father shortly joined us in Saint-Marc-sur-Mer. He took us out of the children's home and sublet a small apartment above a farmhouse on the property of a kindly dairy farmer named Perrin. The apartment was quite stark with hardly any furniture in it. I recall food was very scarce, but Perrin and his wife always supplied us with eggs and some vegetables from the garden.

Doris and I attended school in nearby Saint-Nazaire. My sister and I were fascinated to see our fellow pupils drink red wine with their lunches. Our French skills were already good by this time. In addition to speaking French at home with us, my father encouraged me to read the French comics, and quickly my vocabulary improved.

All my life I have been a real pack rat just like my father, and I still have those old French comics, mostly Mickey Mouse, Donald Duck, and Popeye. In one, *"Papa Retombe en Enfance"* ("Papa Returns to Child-hood"), the father of Popeye masquerades as a child in a pram to get the attention of a lovely lady walking in the park; to do so, however, he has to release the pram's proper occupant—his grandson—behind a tree.

While Doris and I went to school my father worked diligently at his typewriter corresponding with the Australian embassies, with Otto Pick, Mr. Paterson, and the Australian immigration offices at Canberra. I remember him in our upstairs apartment in the farmhouse, always typing away. His English helped him enormously in this correspondence with Australia and Canada. My father in fact knew five languages—German, French (from his governess as a child), and Italian from all his travels as a representative of Hermann Pollack's Söhne, as well as Russian, and a functional English he learned in Siberia from a Hungarian he met while a prisoner of war.

My father was also making applications for his mother Rosa as well as assisting his brother-in-law Max Beck—already then in England—to make applications for Omama and Aunt Claire. Olga's sister, my great-aunt Elsa Klinger, had already succeeded in getting papers to go to Melbourne. She was followed to Melbourne soon after by their other sister, my great-aunt Luise Glässner.

Most of the applications for immigration from "German" countries needed to go through the Department of the Interior at Canberra, a noto-riously bureaucratic office.[4] Our files show that my father's permit was in fact held up there. Starting in 1938, the Australian Cabinet established a quota to stem the flow of refugees.[5] The country was heavily Isolationist due in part to having suffered the heaviest proportional human casu-alties of all the Allied countries in the First World War.[6] Yet Australian newspapers sympathetically covered the plight of the Jews in Europe, and subsequently many citizens were moved to help in any way they could.[7] Mr. Paterson was clearly one of these.

To facilitate my father's visa application, Mr. Paterson provided him with a guarantee of support, and Otto Pick sent money to a holding company for the disembarkment fee. But in the end neither man could help him. The permit would only be granted for my sister and me. Government policies starting in mid-1938 in reaction to the *Anschluss* included "special precautions" against Jewish immigration.[8] However, an exception for children seems to have been made, because children could more easily assimilate.

To make our life easier with our new parents in Australia, we were baptized before we left.[9] My foster mother, Eileen Paterson, was Roman Catholic, and Mr. Paterson was Protestant. One of my father's Viennese Masonic friends performed our baptismal ceremony, a Lutheran pastor named Dr. Frederick J. Forell. Like my father at the time, Dr. Forell was a member of the "Mozart" Lodge in Paris. Dr. Forell was, according to a letter from my father to Otto Pick in March of 1941, "a very nice man, who did his best to help all emigrants." In a coincidence, my wife Fonda would later take history of religion classes from Dr. Forell's son, Dr. George Forell, at the University of Iowa in 1968, before she met me.

In the spring of 1940, as the Germans were sweeping across northern Europe, Doris and I took an express train with our father out of Paris. We arrived in Marseilles after two days travel on March 22, 1940. She and I were about to embark alone on the long voyage to Australia. Even though my father had tried for nearly a year to arrange his own visa, it had still not come through.

On our sail date, we found ourselves with our father on a dock with our luggage, teary and very sad. He brought us over the gangway of the British ship the *P.&O. Strathnaver* and stayed with us until the last moment before the gangplank was pulled up. In later years he said he was tempted to stow away on board with us, but feared he would have been sent back.

The *Strathnaver* was the last British passenger ship to leave from France before the country was occupied. Already the ship had been requisitioned by the British government as a troop ship and was bringing Australian soldiers to Europe on all of its return trips.

My sister and I realized that saying good-bye to our father might mean we would never see him again. He told us, "You are going to your new family now." As children we had little concept of my father's feeling

Doris and I, Saint-Marc-sur-Mer, 1939.
PHOTO: STEFAN SCHANZER.

of loss and his actual sacrifice of shipping us off to a far land with little knowledge of how this might turn out. In his documents I found that he had sent to Mr. Paterson all the data for a life insurance policy held in his name in Trieste, Italy. On May 24, 1940, he wrote, "Later on this indication may be of some value for the children and for you."

When I was a little older I came to realize that without the adoption all three of us might have easily perished. The scenario that crosses my mind is how our father could ever have led our little family through France after it was occupied, traveling by any means at our disposal—on foot, by bicycles, walking through fields and forests, and even over mountains, to reach a safe haven. We were far safer on that ship, as history would soon confirm.

The journey from France to Sydney was a full month—and most memorable. A composition I wrote for a school exam in March 1941 noted, "My sister and I left France at about five o'clock in the after-

Birthday postcard sent to me in Paris by my grandmother Olga, my aunt Claire, and my great-aunt Elsa Klinger on my birthday, July 7, 1939, after my sister Doris and I left the Nazi Protectorate of Bohemia and Moravia.

noon with heavy hearts and woke up in the morning when the steward knocked on the door and brought two apples and two oranges. I got up and went to the dining room, where I saw my sister already at the table trying to make the waiter understand what she wanted for breakfast."

Doris and I were on our own with a new language and culture to learn. But a stroke of luck put our family friends' son on the same ship with us—Will Semler, who was fifteen years old and also emigrating to Australia. As he boarded the ship, someone with a German accent told him there were two Austrian children on board, and asked him to look out for us. What a surprise for him to find that we already knew each other, and that we were the grandchildren of the Becks.

Oskar and Jana Semler, Will's parents, were industrialists in lumber and metal fabrication in Pilsen. I visited them when I lived there, and remembered that the Semlers' apartment was in what seemed like a mansion. Loos' former student and collaborator, Heinrich Kulka,[10] designed the apartment after some of Loos' last sketches in the year before he died, and its features echo one of Loos' last and most famous works, the Villa Müller in Prague.[11] The Semlers' home used to have multiple floors, but has since been broken up into separate private apartments. It also has the unfortunate distinction of having been taken over by the Gestapo and used as headquarters—at the end of World War II, an SS officer is said to have shot himself inside.[12]

When I visited Pilsen in 2011, it was not possible to see all floors of the Semler apartment but we were able to explore the grand room of the living and dining areas with its parquet floor and stunning black and white wall panels of veined marble and stippled maple. We also toured another Loos apartment close by belonging to Vilém and Gertruda (Taussig) Kraus. There the architect included large mirrors over marble banquets at either end of a large extended room, so when you stand in the middle of the space it reflects around you as if into infinity.

My sister and I were grateful to have found Will Semler with us on the *Strathnaver* in 1940. He could speak English very well, having learned it by reading funny passages from P.G. Wodehouse over and over. Will had come from England with his older brother Štěpán. They were on their way to join up with their parents who were sailing separately from Italy to Melbourne, Australia. In Marseilles unfortunately, Štěpán was taken off the boat by the Foreign Legion and conscripted to fight with the French army. They had no uniform for him so they put him into war with an 1870's German uniform, according to Will, "one leg green, the other red, wooden clogs instead of boots, and a wooden gun."[13]

Will had a lighthearted way about him and a sense of humor. Doris and I spent a lot of time with him on the ship. He helped us talk to other people and taught Doris how to iron a shirt (his shirt!); when I was older, this skill for ironing she then taught me.

Prompted by my daughter Carrie, Will sent an email at the beginning of 2012 about his own escape from Czechoslovakia in 1939: "It is all so very simple," he wrote, proceeding then with a complicated story. Will's father, Oskar Semler, suggested Will try to go north through German lines and to England. "I did," he wrote, "and finished up in a German prison. Very comfortable. They even had the forethought to make a step in the concrete floor as a cushion at night." More people were captured and put in prison—soon came Will's two cousins Honza and Petr, sons of Hugo and

My P.&O. Strathnaver *card for "Child Schanzer," 1940.*

Helena Semler, who had lived just across the street from the Becks' first Loos apartment in Pilsen on Klatovy Avenue.[14] "Some weeks later, a tall SS man arrived—of course you could have used our [knocking] knees as metronomes. Well, not so, he came to see how he could help us! First he smuggled out one of my cousins who came back with a wheelbarrow with half a horse on it. Where or how he obtained it I never found out but we found an old wash boiler and cooked it in that. Best meal of the century." [15]

Will wrote that to get to England all the Czechoslovaks in the prison, about one hundred by that time, pooled their money and sent cables "via the SS man to the King of England, the British prime minister, the Prime Minister of France, the Pope, as well as President Roosevelt.... One day the British Embassy in Cologne received a cable back from Lord Halifax: 'Semler to Britain'.... Halifax had a withered arm, always wore a bowler hat, had been Viceroy of India, and was then Foreign Secretary. That is how all three cousins got [to England]." [16]

On the *P.&O. Strathnaver* in 1940, Doris developed a crush on Will and enjoyed dancing lessons with him. Many years later, Doris confessed to him that she really had fallen in love with him. As she left Europe, she was becoming a young woman and Will was familiar—he knew our grandparents, Uncle Max, and Aunt Claire, now so far behind. Will wrote to me that he remembered seeing Aunt Claire and Loos in Marienbad, where we have a few remaining pictures of our family on vacation, as the near-deaf architect talked with clients using his iconic ear horn.[17] Will has written his own memoir—*The Family Paperweight*—a kind of mad hatter's tale of his relatives and Pilsen mores, told with ironic wit and humor.

Doris and I must have heard some of Will's stories on the *P.&O. Strathnaver*, and in his 2012 email he told me more. Will remembered that in Pilsen, "There was a funny incident when the Germans sent the 'Protector' of Bohemia, Baron von Neurath to arrive standing up in the typical open Mercedes. School kids were commanded to greet him with swastikas. When he came within sight the kids stripped the swastikas and just held up the sticks shouting, 'Neurath the Shithead' (the nearest translation)." At his British school, Will had to recite some Czech poetry for a Christmas party, but he could only remember "an absolutely filthy long ditty.... I stood on the stage hoping that none of the three hundred parents would understand." [18] Neither Will, nor other Czech-speaking acquaintances, thought it appropriate to translate the song for this book. Instead he suggested another: "*Bejvavalo dobre.*"—"It used to be fine, it used to be fine, when we were young, the world was like a blossom." [19]

On the *Strathnaver*'s journey through Egypt we encountered miles of sand, a sight absolutely foreign to Doris and me. We were amazed to see our first camels and nomads in the desert when we shipped through the Suez Canal after traveling southeast from Malta. I wrote, "We stayed about four hours in Port Said, then moved into the Suez Canal from where you could see the desert and on the other side, mud for miles. The next morning we came to the Red Sea. A long way from there you could see mountains and hills, and then we went out to sea, without land in sight." We came to the Yemeni port of Aden in a few days, and then on we went through the Indian Ocean to Bombay (Mumbai).

The scarcity of food in France had given Doris and me quite an appetite. We used to order the entire menu from top to bottom and sometimes back up to the top, even though we had no idea what we were getting, since we did not understand any English. We ordered the meat, the fish, all the appetizers, the pasta, and one of each dessert. It was delicious food and came in large quantities. I wrote a letter to my father that was later mailed from a waypoint, "I like the English meals better than the French. I never ate bacon before."

Most of the children were leaving the ship in Bombay, and so the Captain decided to have a big costume party for us. Since we had no costumes, we made our own. I decided to be a Turkish Prince, using my sister's dressing gown, which had Turkish colors. Doris made balloon trousers out of it, then took a towel and made me a turban. I wore her slippers, and she helped me draw on a moustache with an eyebrow pencil.

Doris wrote to our Big Omama on April 3, 1940, "The day before yesterday there was a party for the children. I didn't like it all that much because it was too babyish for me. When they started handing our prizes, I ran away because everyone would be staring at me. The whole crowd, I mean tourist class. I didn't want that. They looked for me all over the ship. Karli finally found me. I went back. The group had already dispersed, 'Thank goodness.' I was given a bracelet with sailors on it and a roll of candy.... Write your next letter to me in Australia. You know the address. Two married couples are traveling with us and taking care of us."

We were not allowed to disembark in Bombay. We witnessed the poverty there from the ship. I remember seeing Indians sleeping on coiled ropes on the dock. In Ceylon (Sri Lanka) the ship docked at Colombo, and I tasted my first mango, but wrote that I had to spit it out. My Viennese taste buds, and all my sensibilities, had not caught up with my geography. As we traveled across the Indian Ocean and around the southern edge of our new country Australia, we wondered how we would manage to adapt. We missed our father and had no idea what our lives would be like there, or with our new family.

We landed in Adelaide, then Melbourne, where we bid good-bye to Will Semler and met up with our great-aunt Elsa Klinger. We had managed to send her a letter from Bombay so she would know when our boat would arrive. She took us to her home, cooked us our favorite foods, and showed us around Melbourne and the Royal Botanical Gardens, where I saw bamboo for the first time and kangaroos. From Melbourne, we went north along the coast to Sydney. There we were met by our neighbors from the Werkbundsiedlung, the Strickers, who had managed to emigrate to Australia via Haiti. After a two-day stay with them, we took another smaller boat for two days up the coast to Brisbane to meet our new family.

Mr. Paterson—Charles—was a tall handsome man of reserved demeanor, and his wife, Eileen, was pleasant looking in her mid-forties.

Their daughters, Mary and Joan, were older than me by six and eight years. I remember thinking, when they greeted us at the station, that they were both pretty. They drove us to our new home in a suburb called Graceville on the banks of the Brisbane River. The front yard was edged by large pine trees, and the attractive one-story house with gabled roof was spacious due to the balconies that had been recently enclosed to create more bedrooms for us in anticipation of our arrival.

On the boat I had developed an acute earache during the journey from sleeping out on deck. When we left India the cabins were too hot to stay inside, so we camped out in the moist evening air. This resulted in a mastoid infection and an emergency surgery on my right ear soon after we got to Brisbane. The operation was botched, which rendered me half-deaf thereafter—this presented a difficulty that for the rest of my life I have been loath to admit. Upon later discovery of other letters, I learned that it had been a more serious operation. The doctors had to remove a bone in my nose that would have pressed on my brain, which resulted in a six-week stay at the hospital.

Charles Raff Paterson and Eileen Paterson at the Graceville house
in Brisbane, 1940.

Mary and Joan Paterson, Brisbane, 1940.

Doris and I began school that spring, but both of us had to start in second grade because we spoke no English. We spent four months in the second grade, three months in the third grade, and then two months in the fourth grade. It was quite embarrassing to be with younger kids, when we felt and looked so grown up, so we learned quickly and advanced. The other kids always wanted to hear stories of Europe and how we escaped. But I often felt isolated and lonely. We seemed like the only "foreigners" around, oddities from an unknown land. As I learned English and tried to meld in, it became much easier for me. I strived to become Australian and to put my European background behind me. ◼

My Dear Children

During the time my sister and I were in transit and then getting used to our new Australian surroundings, my father's life became even more complicated. He had started a class to become a driver for heavy trucks at the beginning of April 1940, which necessitated he go back to Paris. Previously in Saint-Nazaire he also looked into doing this kind of work, but could not afford the fifty francs per lesson. In April, however, he made a connection with the Jewish Assistance Committee, which was financing the classes for refugees, and he hoped this way to save a little money while waiting for his visa to Australia.

On the *Strathnaver*'s first port of call in Malta on April 2, 1940 a letter from our father was waiting for us from Paris. "Your letters are very sweet.... For now I guess that it will be at least two more months until my departure. But you can be sure nothing will stop me from following you as soon as possible. Since both of you left, nothing makes me happy here.... Regarding Big Omama, I'm waiting for news from Uncle Max that she and Aunt Claire are supposed to leave in two months."

I can imagine our father back in Paris in a small hotel, sitting in a lonely place and typing industriously with two fingers. He wrote to us in French as we were now used to speaking together. The following letter was probably one of the first we got from him after we arrived in Brisbane.

Paris   May 16, 1940

Dear Doris,

Finally the letters from you both, for which I have been awaiting impatiently, have arrived, as well as this pretty photo, which pleases me so much and which I show to everyone who knows you. I'm very happy that the welcome everyone has given you,

My sister and I soon after arrival in Graceville.
Brisbane, Australia, 1940.

especially Madame Paterson's, was so good. Also the description of the house gives me great pleasure, because it seems to be the same type as ours. I hope also that you will easily overcome the small misunderstandings that will occur due to the language, because it's extremely essential that you are friendly and kind toward everybody, for all the people who are now around you are your definitive surroundings, and they have welcomed you in the nicest way.

On the subject of your remark that you can wear the blue dress that was too small here in Paris, I'm not very happy about that, for you know that in my opinion you shouldn't lose weight. So I advise you not to make any effort in this direction, because for a little girl of your age, the figure isn't yet very important. You must reach the age of the princess [Princess Plump] when she talked with the witch. Just yesterday I was looking with joy at the little book [about Princess Plump] that you two drew together. Have you found the copies that you sent to the Patersons? In what condition did the cognac and the sausages arrive?

I am also very happy that you have the opportunity to speak French, but you should also do dictations to learn spelling well. I remind you also to see if it would be possible to begin to play the piano again, for with some practice you would play well in order to be able to dance. Please write to me about this.

I hope to receive your news soon. I embrace you with all my heart.

Papa

Below is the second half of the same letter, almost exactly equal to the number of words as the letter to my sister on the top half of the page.

Dear Charlie,

I was very happy with your letter, for which I waited impatiently. The descriptions and locations of the places that you saw are very interesting. I'm also glad to hear that you and Doris are well settled, and that the troubles have finally disappeared. I would love soon to be able to say the same for me also, but I don't think it will be possible in the near future. Concerning my trip to Australia, the chances diminish from one day to the next, and I don't know what I will do. We have to wait.

In any case I congratulate myself every day for having sent you both to the Patersons, and all my friends feel the same way. The children of Montmorency [outside of Paris] will soon go to Bordeaux, but I hear at the same time that it must not be as lovely [there]. You both must be very glad to have arrived at your place of destination.

I told Lowum that you have a new friend, also a brown dog. He wasn't very happy that you are forgetting him so quickly.

I hope that in taking horseback riding lessons you won't fall off, but I'm very pleased that you are beginning so young. When one begins at your age one learns to ride well. I hope, also, that you will talk often with this nice French woman who invited you [to speak with her], so as not to forget what you have learned. Also I ask you to write to me the names of the people to whom you have written, for according to this list I will tell you whom you have forgotten.

Write to me again very soon, and I embrace you with all my heart.

Papa

My father's own story unfolds here, told primarily through one letter he wrote to my sister and me when he had virtually only the clothes on his back and had made a dramatic three-month escape by foot and bicycle from occupied France. Reading like a chronicle, this letter from Lisbon of dozens of pages describes the events ensuing from his capture by German soldiers on June 19, 1940. It was delivered to us in Australia via a ship's captain nearly a year after it was written.

The letter took my father nearly three weeks to compose. He first sent it to Dr. (Pastor) Forell, who by January 1941 was in the United States, and Dr. Forell shared it with our relatives in Canada, Otto and Käthe Pick. On February 1, 1941, Otto detailed for my father his receipt of the manuscript from Pastor Forell after paying him a visit in New York City at his home. "He seems to be a very nice man," Otto Pick wrote. "I told him that if I can be of any service to him, I will be glad to do so. I will give a copy of your very interesting diary to our relatives when we return home [to Vancouver], and as soon as we have an opportunity to send the original to your children, we will certainly do so."

My father wrote his original story in German, envisioning his intended audience of émigrés and relatives, and in order to tell the story most expediently and in all its detail. Meanwhile my sister and I began to lose our German and our French, necessitating that the letter be translated into English in Canada by another relative, Tommy Wiener, who was just "released from a concentration camp," according to a letter from Otto Pick. Tommy was saved from uncertain fate and had emigrated to Vancouver thanks to the Picks' nephew—a cousin of my father's—Martin Mandl. Of Tommy's past or future life we know not much, save that he joined the Canadian Artillery in 1942. For the following translation of this valuable letter, by way of which I can still reflect in amazement on my father's fortitude, I am eternally grateful.

Lisbon   September 27, 1940

My Dear Children,

After I left you [on the ship in Marseilles] the French Ministere de
l'Armement [War Department] arranged a job for me as a driver
of heavy trucks, and I was supposed to take over my new occupation as soon as possible in Nantes....

My father needed to get a "Sauf Conduit," permission to pass from
one town to another, but a June 1st air raid on Paris disrupted his plans.
Upon fleeing west to Brittany during the evacuation, he was conscripted
into the French army and assigned to work at an Army camp in Audierne, in the province of Finistère. He proudly noted that he was elected
group leader. "Knowing my cooking ability, I was requested to take over
the camp kitchen," he wrote. They built a fireplace and cooked goulash
for five hundred French and otherwise conscripted soldiers.

The German advance "was frightening," he wrote, and quickly they
had to face the fact Brittany had been cut off. Knowing the Germans
would arrive any day and hoping to stay a step ahead, they were
preparing to decamp, when suddenly three German soldiers appeared
on a hill nearby. Fifty French soldiers in the camp all threw down their
arms and surrendered.[1] In a few minutes the camp was occupied and
everyone taken prisoner. The first order that followed was to separate
Aryans from non-Aryans,[2] who were then put under closest observation.

This story begins at the critical moment when German soldiers
turned their backs on their new prisoners momentarily in order to look
for water for the camp.[3] From our father's letter to us:

Two hours passed, when suddenly I noticed that a few people were
climbing over the seven-foot wall of the camp by means of a table.
They were escaping behind the corner of a house approximately
a hundred feet in front of a German machine gun that had been
set up. The German guards were looking the other way, so I didn't
hesitate. I went as I was, without possessions or baggage. Over the
wall... and I was outside.

How desperate the situation seemed. I was without resources and without documents hundreds of miles behind the front. I didn't even know where the front was, or if there still was a front. I had a little cash, at least something, so I set about getting far away from the camp. I walked for the whole afternoon following the beach towards the south. I knew about two nearby fishing villages and had hopes to leave for England on a fisherman's boat, because I wanted to join [my brother-in-law] Max [Beck] who was already in London at this time. I walked the whole night, toward Guilvinec, led by the stars.

In the morning I rested in heaps of dried pea-leaves. There it was at least warm as the hours before dawn are usually the coldest. I went without a path, straight over fields. At eight that morning I came to a lonely, beautiful old church and one house with a store. There was a woman there who gave me breakfast and soap. The woman advised me to go to Guilvinec or to Loctudy, at the mouth of the Pont-l'Abbé river estuary, where there would be an opportunity to get away. I walked to Guilvinec, but heard from two women

French coastline looking south from Audierne.
PHOTO: CARRIE PATERSON, 2011.

that the village had already been occupied, so I decided to go to Loctudy, where I arrived that evening. I had a shave and hoped to gather some information. There were fishermen loitering in the village, but I learned that they were not allowed to go out to sea.

I realized that it was impossible to get to England, so I decided to continue on south. Two straits had to be crossed, and since the ferry [to Île-Tudy] was just about to leave, I decided to set off immediately. I boarded the ferry and crossed the strait without challenge. By then I had been twenty-seven hours on the run, and I was very tired. When evening came, I sauntered alone on the deserted beach, heading further south. I was very desperate and filled with doubts that I could get through the German lines unobserved. I did not dare to go to a hotel.

At eight o'clock that night I reached the second strait and was exhausted. I could not go on. I decided to risk the hotel in the village of Sainte-Marine where, to my great relief, I was cared for in a charming manner. There was hot running water, and I could wash my laundry. After I was properly cleaned up, I felt better and had enough courage to go on.

The next day, June 21, at 6 a.m., I went down to the bank of the strait and found a woman who was busy loading crabs and shrimps into a boat. I helped her load the boat and was allowed to come with her. Soon I was on the other side. I met a machinist, who showed me a good route on a map that he gave me. I wanted to buy a bicycle to get on faster, and he told me about a friend of his who could help. I continued walking and saw nobody on the road or on the path he showed me, and then came to La Forêt-Fouesnant, where I met the engineer to whom I had been referred. For 400 francs I put together old parts, and soon I had a fine bike. I ate in a small pension, mounted my bike, and felt strengthened and adventurous. ▪

CHAPTER EIGHT

Prisoners Don't Ride Bicycles

It was very important that I always had good maps. The French farmers gave them to me from the calendars in their farmhouses, and they were good for every region. Now that I had a bicycle and could cover some distance, I decided to visit our old friend Perrin the *fermier* [farmer] in Saint-Marc, from where I somehow hoped to go to England.

On the way I came to Baud. This village was not occupied. I stayed in the hotel 'Cheval Blanc', where I met a manufacturer of preserves and advised him about fruit preserves without oil, as oil was very scarce at the time. He was excited by this information and immediately wanted to engage me as a collaborator. He visited me twice. Unfortunately, I could not explain my sad situation. I went on early the next morning.

I now entered a very dangerous zone of Lorient, where it was already known that people had been gathered and put into internment camps. I read placards saying that Germans, Czechs, and Poles had to report immediately. Any person helping anyone to get into the unoccupied zone from the occupied zone would be put before a court of war—court-martialed. The news was not at all encouraging, and I often thought of giving up and reporting myself to the authorities.

I went on and on, pedaling many miles. The further I got the more I met willing and nice Frenchmen. I always went through very small villages, and my intuition was right; I never met any German troops in the villages. I was strengthened by this good fortune and had courage enough to go on.

Then I had a very disagreeable adventure in Pont-Scorff.

Farmhouse in Brittany, France, 1940. PHOTO: STEFAN SCHANZER.

On approaching the village I realized immediately that heavy fighting had taken place. There was barbed wire at the entrance to the village and, on turning the corner, I saw Frenchmen being led away by Germans as prisoners. I turned immediately and rode along another street and onto a path that crossed a field, where I stopped to consider the situation. A farmer and his son approached me, and when the farmer saw me studying the map, he knew what I wanted. He informed me that I was about five hundred yards from the internment camp where everyone was being kept. He showed me which way to go and how to dodge all the guards. He said I had to ride up almost to the source of the river, as all the bridges were heavily guarded. But there was a great obstacle just before I reached Saint-Marc. It was the river La Vilaine.

The bridges were watched by Germans. So, I had to see about catching a ferry. Studying the map, I rode to a point where I assumed there would be one. I saw a car driving in the same direction and followed. Soon we approached some buildings along the river, which I could see was quite broad. Just before I reached the village a nail punctured my back tire.

A farmer who helped me repair the flat tire confided to me: "The whole day long my deaf son and I have helped people cross to the south. Just now my son has set off with five French soldiers. It takes fifteen minutes to be on the other side." The situation seemed favorable because the crossing was on a bend of the river that was hidden from view. The farmer himself took me across the river, and there were the French soldiers. They told me that this was the only point to get over from the other side. The Germans had occupied all the other boats, but apparently had forgotten about that place.

Now I was on the other side, and I hoped to be in Saint-Marc by evening. I was forced to ride on the main road since the country around Saint-Nazaire was impassable because it was full of salt swamps. Fortunately, I did not meet anyone. Before I reached Pornichet, a German plane saw me and flew twice overhead, trying to get a glimpse of me. Knowing the country, I rode hard toward Sainte-Marguerite, passing the former British Camp where the Germans now kept prisoners. This was the saddest part of my journey, traveling alone on the paths we used to stroll along so often. It all seemed like a dream. I went through the little wood and turned at the end of it to visit the farmer Perrin.

The farmer was very surprised to see me. He invited me for dinner and wanted me to stay overnight. I also visited our former landlady and her old mother, who were very frightened because there were one hundred and fifty Germans in the castle and in the hotel nearby. I departed at 5 a.m. the next morning and went back the way I had come. I dared not pass through Saint-Nazaire because of the German garrison there. I did not want to visit my friends there for fear of endangering them with my presence.

Now a new problem arose—crossing the Loire River. I heard that all the bridges were heavily guarded and that you had to produce papers at the bridgehead because only twelve miles south from Tours was the unoccupied zone. I knew that Buzançais, where the shop of Les Fils de Reviron is located, must be all right, and my hopes rose for meeting my cousin Raoul there.[1]

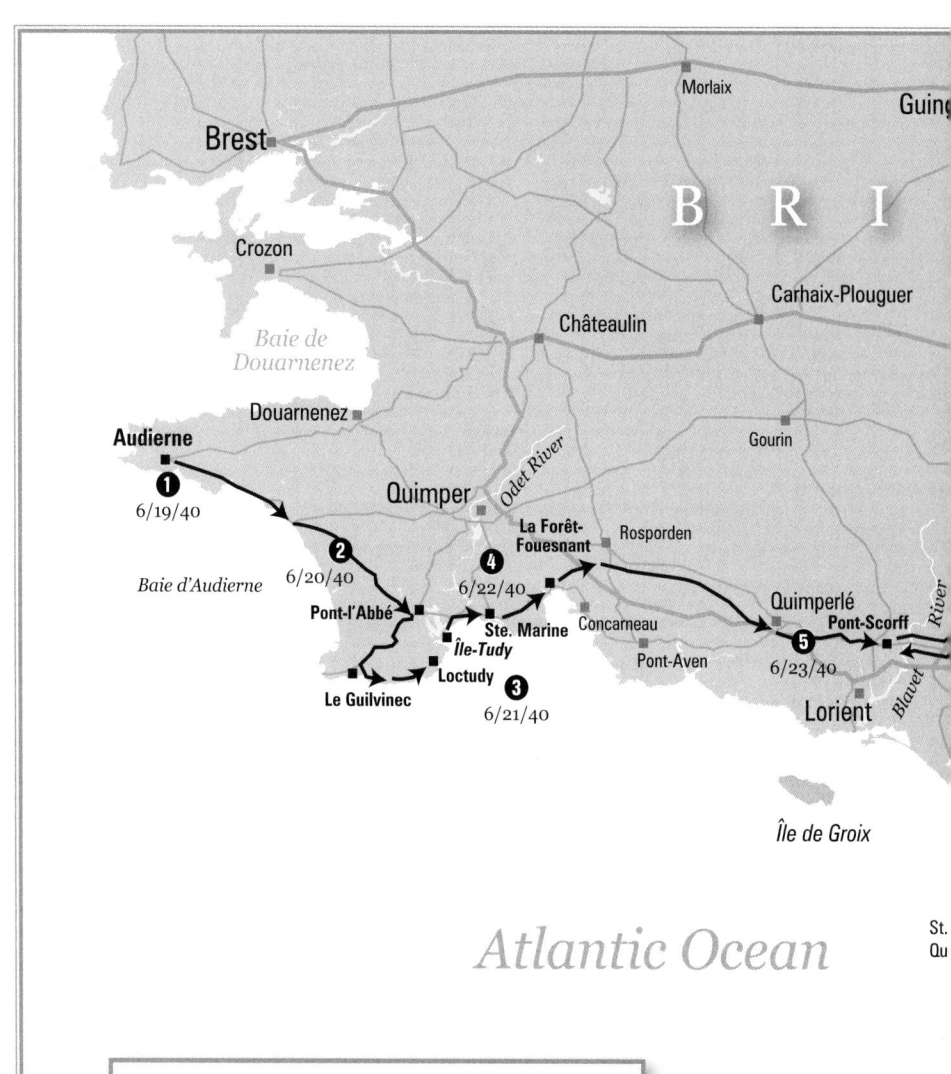

STEFAN SCHANZER'S
Escape from Nazi-Occupied France

JUNE 19–SEPTEMBER 21, 1940

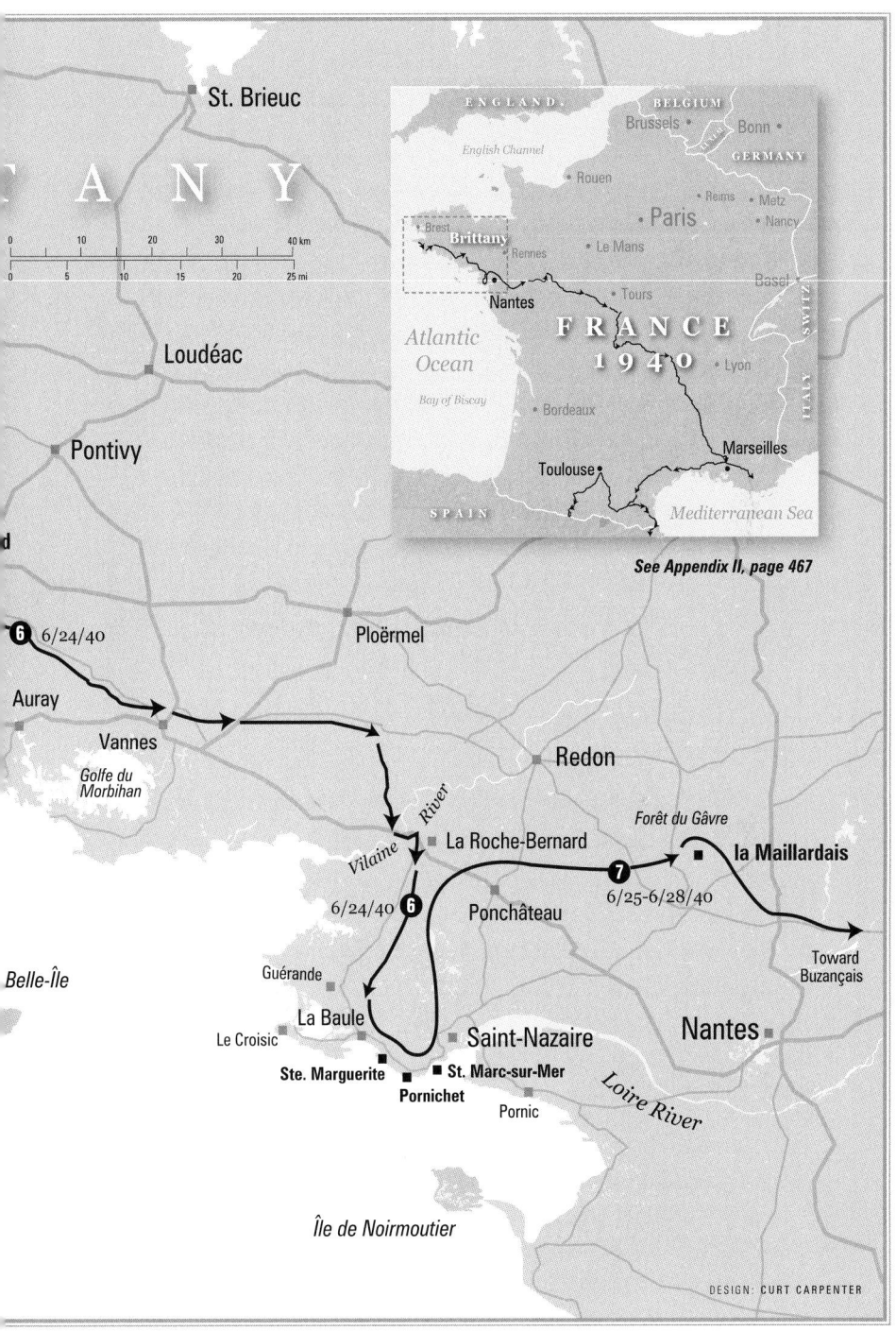

St. Brieuc

ANY

0   10   20   30   40 km
0   5   10   15   20   25 mi

Loudéac

Pontivy

d

6 6/24/40

Auray

Vannes

Golfe du Morbihan

Belle-Île

Ploërmel

Redon

Forêt du Gâvre

Vilaine River   La Roche-Bernard

6/24/40 **6**   Ponchâteau

■ **la Maillardais**

7 6/25-6/28/40

Toward Buzançais

Guérande

La Baule

Le Croisic

Ste. Marguerite   ■ St. Marc-sur-Mer

Saint-Nazaire

Nantes ■

Pornichet

Pornic

Loire River

Île de Noirmoutier

ENGLAND.   BELGIUM
Brussels ·   · Bonn ·
English Channel   GERMANY
· Rouen
· Reims   · Metz
· Brest   · Paris   · Nancy
Brittany   · Le Mans
· Rennes
Nantes   F R A N C E   Basel
· Tours   1 9 4 0
Atlantic   · Lyon
Ocean
Bay of Biscay   · Bordeaux
· Marseilles
Toulouse ·
S P A I N   Mediterranean Sea

See Appendix II, page 467

DESIGN: CURT CARPENTER

I had heard that Nantes had been occupied, as well as Angers and Saumur. I estimated that the occupation was still about twelve miles away, and my assumption was right. All of the villages in the circuit around those towns were occupied.

To avoid an occupied town, I had to go through the large wood of Maillardais [Forêt du Gâvre]. I was told that the British had been there. But they had left in haste when the German army took the area. I approached the wood through tiny villages, all of which had been evacuated. I found myself on a very bad road as I came to the edge of the wood. There the road improved and, riding a few hundred yards, I saw English posters and ammunition and bombs. I rode very carefully, being afraid of land mines, which may easily cause an explosion. I was also afraid of the Germans, who were guarding the camp in an area which extended for about six miles. But I had luck and crossed through the woods to the other side.

But that was not all. There was more to come. I reached Joué-sur-Erdre, which is on a little river. Crossing a bridge I saw French soldiers, whom I greeted. I then rode toward the middle of the village, when suddenly I recognized some trucks with Germans on them. I waved quickly, warning the five French soldiers, then turned, riding into a field where I hid and waited. A farmer appeared on a horse and said, "I saw how you saved the French soldiers from being captured. What about you? You prob- ably would like to stay here overnight, wouldn't you?" He invited me to dine with him, and he also gave me breakfast. The next morning he advised me to cross the Loire at Ingrandes. I rode on and that day saw many beautiful castles along the road, all of which had been taken over by the Germans. I had to be very careful, and only reached the Loire late in the evening.

I met a woman who advised me to ride to the Château du Vauboisseau. She said there was a farmer there who had boats and crossed the river frequently, so I went to him. I found him busy unloading hay. He explained that the Germans had taken his boats that were on the other side of the river because they saw him taking over passengers. His wife arrived and said she observed Germans marching in front of the Château. That was far too much for me, and I rushed away.

I met another farmer, who put me up overnight. The next day I decided to cross the Loire between Saumur and Tours. Judging by the map, I knew there were small islands in the river that could facilitate a successful crossing. I detoured around Angers and had to cross three rivers in my circuit. Since my twelve-mile estimation at Nantes had proved successful, I applied the same concept and assumed that the three bridges north of Angers would be unoccupied.

The town of Grez-Neuville, which I reached at 3 p.m., was unoccupied. Here I took a refreshing bath in the river and washed my laundry, which dried almost immediately in the hot sun. Towards evening I reached the town of Écuillé, where I stayed overnight in the Accueil des Réfugiés [Refugee Shelter]. Even the mayor of the town encouraged me in my journey.

When I reached the second river the next morning, I saw three French soldiers on bicycles. They were Savoyards, who served in Norway. They, too, were not able to cross the Loire at Ingrandes, so they had the same plan as I. They had already waited for two hours because the ferry was on the other side, and there was no one to take them over. They were swearing about this. But I was there only a few minutes when the ferry suddenly started moving. Once there, we rode on together all day until we reached Saint-Philbert-du-Peuple, where we stayed overnight.

We approached the Loire the next day. One of the French soldiers said he was unhappy because I determined the route and the other soldiers always went along with my suggestions. When we reached the main road on the Loire, we saw German reconnaissance planes flying overhead and German motorcycle formations on the road.

We went into a café where Parisian refugees were seated, and the situation became disagreeable. The complaining soldier ranted:

A bridge in Joué-sur-Erdre, France.
PHOTO: LINDA ENGLE, 2006.

"Je m'en fous! Je m'emmerde! J'irai par le pont au risqué de me faire pincer." [I don't care! I don't give a damn! I will go over the bridge at the risk of getting caught.] I told them that I would go down to the river to consider the situation, and the soldiers followed me.

We reached the Loire on a small path and saw two boats fastened on the bank. I decided to wait until the owner appeared and meanwhile, took a bath. During the time I took the bath I checked how the planes went. They were punctually every thirty minutes. So I knew that we could cross immediately after the plane flew and that we had half an hour time, and that was time enough.[2] When a man appeared, I spoke to him because the soldiers were very shy. The man said he had a boat one mile below, but for one person only. I told him that all three had to go over. He agreed to inform the owner of a bigger boat, who arrived half an hour later, but said that he had to *déjeuner* [eat] first. This took an hour, and the soldiers grew impatient. At last the boatman arrived. He looked at us and asked if we were prisoners. I asked him whether he had ever heard of prisoners riding bicycles. He took us across. Everywhere there were posters indicating that prisoners were not allowed to communicate with the civilian population. In fact, this was prohibited by threat of death penalty.

The boatman took us up the river about a mile and then through small islands, hiding us from reconnaissance planes. The soldiers said they wanted to be let off in an occupied town, fearing they would lose their way in the woods, but I declared that I would go through the woods. Again the soldiers followed.

The crossing was easy, and we reached the other side at a huge shooting range named "Camp Militaire du Ruchard." Later, we reached Avon-les-Roches, where one of my brake cables broke. While I was repairing it, the three soldiers left me, and I never saw them again.

In the evening I came to Saint-Épain, where I found accommodations with a young lady and her parents. From then on, I always had to ride through villages occupied by Germans. The hills were taken over by the German Cavalry, and it was frightfully difficult to get through. Many times I had to cross through fields in order to dodge the Germans. I often rode in a zig-zag pattern so that they could not determine from which direction I had come. In the late afternoon I reached a lonely road in the direction of Petit-Pressigny. Suddenly I saw a German newspaper, dated June 19, 1940, right in front of me in the field. It contained the celebration of Hitler's occupation of Paris and the festivities in Innsbruck and Munich. After I read this, I was so desperate I did not want to go on. I lay down in the field, feeling very unhappy, alone, and deserted.[3]

I mounted the bike and rode toward Preuilly-sur-Claise. I knew that there was a German checkpoint up ahead, but I didn't care. As I came down the mountain road I realized that this was suicide. I swerved to the left and came down a lane to a lonely farmhouse. The peasant there saw that I was a refugee and gave me wine and bread. He told me he could show me the way to Azay-le-Ferron.

He said, "I am going into my field now to mow hay. Please come with me." We went out into the meadows with scythes, and he showed me the way to Azay by passing a castle that was occupied by Germans. I had to go through a ditch to safely pass the castle. There I heard swearing in German and the lashing of a whip. But the Germans were too occupied with their horses to notice me.

On the other side of the ditch, I saw the road to Preuilly, but I could not pass through the thick hedges. At last I found a hole where I could push my bike through to get on the road. Soon I came to a fork in the road where I saw two men on guard with a noncommissioned officer. This is the end of my journey I thought, but I didn't hesitate. I rode on toward the men. I even stopped pedaling to salute them. The soldiers carried on with their conversation, not even bothering me. Later, I discovered the reason why. There had been a long train with French peasants returning from the occupied zone into the unoccupied zone with permission from the *commandanture* [Headquarters]. These peasants had horses and carriages, so the German soldiers thought that I was with the group and that all the formalities had been arranged.

I rode past, but didn't know exactly where I was. I went over to the first peasant I saw and asked for a drink of water. There was a young girl there who I asked if there were Germans in Azay. She was astonished by the question. "There are no Germans here. You are in the unoccupied zone!" You may imagine my pleasure when I received this information, after the anxiety of twelve days on the run. It was now July 2, and I rode happily into Azay, where I found good accommodations in the Centre d'Accueil [the local shelter]. I was asked what it was like "over there."

The next morning I rode via Mézières-en-Brenne to Buzançais, where I met Mr. Luquet and employees of Lang Company. My cousin Raoul was still in the south, in Luchon with his parents [Clementine and Paul Lang]. I had hoped that my luggage had been forwarded from Paris to Buzançais but heard that everything was still stored in the Paris shop. Raoul arrived a few days later. Everyone was happy to see me. They had worried so much about me. ■

CHAPTER NINE

Sauf Conduit

The days in Buzançais were nice and agreeable, and I began to recover from the exertions of my tiresome journey. I had slimmed down a great deal. The food question was very complicated. I ate in the inn together with the employees of Lang Company, but despite *hors d'oeuvres*, the *entrée,* and the *dessert,* we could not eat well. In fact, there was so little to eat that I had to go to the nearby farms to get hold of some fish or meat. I lived in the Lang office and slept on the Siberian bed I had made.[1]

I had read an article in the *Paris-Soir* about the crossing of refugees into Spain and Portugal. I then decided to go to Portugal as well. I knew that remaining in unoccupied France would only mean internment. My cousin Raoul was not of my opinion. He advised me to stay.

During this time in Buzançais, I had a lot of conversations with French soldiers who came over the border between the occupied and unoccupied zone. They complained about the faulty ammunition they were issued, and I always had the impression that government circles tried to frustrate their efforts of resistance. All agreed that the French leadership, the officers, and also the high staff, were absolutely incapable of doing anything to stop the occupation for reasons nobody knew. They had a lot of weapons. But they did not use them, they just surrendered; they threw the weapons down, and the Germans marched on.

As I naturally could not risk applying for a "Sauf Conduit," I decided to ride my bicycle to Marseilles. In my opinion this was the safest way. Police never bothered about cyclists.

I started off in the middle of July. The first night, I stayed with farmers, and we had a long discussion about my journey. I will never forget the hospitality of the French people. They were charming in every way and sympathetic to my plight.

The next morning I reached the village of Pontarion, where the family d'Aussy [2] was very nice in taking care of me. After a too-brief visit I rode on that afternoon to reach my destination where I met Mr. Österreicher [3] in Aubagne, near Marseilles. In getting there, I rode over the entire plateau of the Auvergne. Normally, this is a beautiful journey, but I always had the feeling of Hurry! Hurry, or you will be too late! Soon, my visa for Spain would expire, and there was a long way to travel before entering that country, if that were even possible.

The journey went smoothly. I crossed through various roadblocks, where police ask for papers, without being challenged. I took a shower in Riom, this time in a garage. I was lucky because I was allowed to travel in a bus up the steepest part of the Massif Central, up to Alleuze, some fifteen or sixteen miles. It took me one day to ride from Alleuze to Saint-Rémy-de-Provence. I crossed the wrong bridge over the Rhône at Tarascon. On both sides were *gendarmes*; one was speaking to a girl and the other was busy controlling a car. I rode across the bridge without challenge. I would have wanted to stay overnight in Tarascon, but had to go on to Saint-Rémy where for the first time I had courage enough to stay in a hotel. The landlady forgot to give me the register to sign, and thus I escaped the peril of being identified by the police.

The next morning I wanted to go via Aix-en-Provence to Aubagne. I came to a street crossing below Saint-Rémy and was informed about a bus to Aix-en-Provence. I wanted to gain some time, so I went to a café and began talking with the driver of a truck going to Marseilles. He invited me to ride with him for fifty miles. I could not tell him that I had no "Sauf Conduit." He put my bike on the truck, and we started off. There was a French soldier riding with us. My view was toward the rear, and I could not see what was happening in the front. The truck was stopped at least six times, but only the papers of the driver were checked. Just before we came into Marseilles the truck was stopped by a *gendarme*, a policeman, who inquired about the bags. *"Qu'est ce qu'il y a dans ces sacs la?"* What do you have inside the sacks? I replied: *"C'est pour l'exportation."* Those are for export. That seemed to satisfy him. *"Alors, c'est bien,"* he said, and we drove on towards Marseilles.

I thanked the driver, who refused to take any money, not even an *aperitif,* knowing that I was a refugee. I got back on my bike and rode ten miles to Aubagne, where the people I met were amazed that I did not have a "Sauf Conduit," because they themselves needed one going even to Marseilles, to town.

The days that followed in Marseilles belong to the darkest I ever went through in my life. I had to go on, but how and without a passport? I did not know. Daily, many hundreds were arrested. Cars were stopped, only they didn't stop cyclists.

I tried twice to conform with "rules and regulations," but the various officials always referred me to another department. The Commissioner of Police sent me to the Avenue du Prado. None of them could understand how it was possible for me to get into Marseilles without a "Sauf Conduit." *"C'est incroyable! Il se balade par toute la France avec son velo."* [It's incredible! He crossed all of France on his bicycle.] "Oh, I can't believe it," they said again and again. "If we Frenchmen want to go ten miles out of Marseilles, we must have a 'Sauf Conduit.'"

The Commissioner threatened me: "I will have you arrested and will put you in the custody of the Sécreté [Secret Police]." [4] I appealed to him, we talked about politics—he realized that only Hitler was to be blamed for my misfortune, and he advised me to get out of town quickly.[5] He showed me a map of Marseilles, "Take this road, it's not guarded. Go to a mayor near Marseilles. He will provide you with a 'Sauf Conduit,' and then I will put you 'en règle' [officially on record]."

I thanked him profusely for his advice, didn't do anything, and instead stayed for three more weeks in Marseilles! [6]

I spent the whole day with émigrés on the Rue de Convalescence. I knew that only there I could learn something, if I wanted to go on. There I met an employee of H.P.S. Floridsdorf,[7] who introduced me to a friend at the Czech Consulate. Unfortunately, the Czech Consul was in Vichy north of Riom, the seat of French government collaborating with the Germans under the occupation, and I had to await his return.

Meanwhile, I often went to Aubagne to the Österreicher family. I greeted the *gendarme*—he knew me already. Or at least it seemed to me that he knew me. Anyhow, I think he was convinced of the uselessness of his business. "It's very strict now, but you needn't have a 'Sauf Conduit.'" At least, that's what he told the Österrichers. "You should go via the Route Libre [free route]," he told me. "But how is that possible?" I asked. "Foreigners," he said, "have the right to get into the adjacent municipality without a 'Sauf Conduit.' Aubagne is on the boundary with Marseilles along this road and that's why you can go to town. But on the other roads there is regular control because two other municipalities are lying in between." Everyone followed his advice, and that's why the *gendarme* never bothered me.

On August 19, I had all the necessary visas to go to Portugal through Spain. These included a Chinese and Siamese visa, plus Portuguese and Spanish transit visas. On August 23, I received my replacement Czech passport and had to go to the Prefecture for verification. But instead of the prolongation of my papers, I was ordered to report immediately at Les Milles for the consideration of my position. The official in charge assured me that it was only a *little* formality, but I knew about these formalities and knew that if I reported as directed I would never get out.[8]

On August 24, at 11:30 a.m., I queued up at the Spanish Consulate together with Mr. and Mrs. Wolff (Ellen Richter, the famous film star). Then I went to Aubagne, to the Österrichers, where I was safe for at least twenty-four hours from any control. I had all the visas and only needed a "Visa de Sortie de la France" [French exit visa], which I hoped to get in the province, in one of the little villages. It was impossible to get one in Marseilles, but

In the high mountain village of Graissessac, France.
PHOTO: LINDA ENGLE, 2006.

I had only thirty days on my Spanish visa. How was I to travel without a "Sauf Conduit?" Always the same problem.

After studying the map, I decided to travel to see a friend of mine in a village in the mountains—Graissessac near Bédarieux. I decided to go by train from Aubagne, via Marseilles, to a station toward Bédarieux. This way I did not have to go through the control, as I would not have to leave the station in Marseilles. I started off on August 25 in the evening and arrived at a little station at midnight. The stationmaster was kind enough to let me sleep on a bench in the waiting room until 4 a.m.

When the morning came, it was a beautiful, but hot day. Besides bread and fruit, I did not get anything to eat. I arrived in the village of Graissessac very late, where my friend already expected me with his relatives, who were H.P.S. clients. I had to report to them fully about what had happened to me. They all wanted to go the way I was going to escape, but so far nobody had made it. They have wasted time, and now it's too late.

The next morning, my friend and I went to the mayor, who said I could stay if I wanted to because of my Czech passport. The mayor said I should report to the Police. The *gendarmes* approved my passport with the Chinese visa and said I did not need a "Sauf Conduit." As long as my transit visa was valid, I could move toward the Spanish border unhindered. I asked for a confirmation, and the *gendarme* wrote it in my passport. At least I had a "stamp," but there was no hope for a Visa de Sortie.

I departed the next morning to see my Uncle Paul and Aunt Clementine Lang, who were in Bagnéres-de-Luchon, ten miles from the Spanish border at the foot of the central Pyrenees. For the first time, I felt safe. Eighty miles from Carcasonne a driver gave me a lift over the big mountain ranges. Two days saved! He said that he also had "demobilized," i.e. escaped, and had marched for days. Toward evening, I reached Limoux, where I stayed, this time *"en règle"* [on the record], in a hotel.

In the morning I rode my bicycle toward Luchon, passing Saint-Paul-de-Jarrat. To the south the Pyrenees were already visible. I rode for a while with a priest, and we spoke about a lot of things. A patrol of *gendarmes* passed us on bicycles and greeted us with friendly salutations.

When I reached the train at Saint-Paul, I discovered that in order to reach Luchon I did not have to go via Toulouse. I could change trains one station before. I got into the crowded train with my bicycle at 6:30 a.m. All stations were watched by *gendarmes*. Everything was controlled.

While traveling on the train to Toulouse, I overheard a conversation between a lady and an officer of the French police. First they spoke about the most important question, the *ravitaillement* [transport of food]. Then, passing some barracks, the lady asked: "How is it that there are still prisoners? I thought there had been a German Commission to free these people?" "Yes," said the officer, *"Ce sont les Allemandes dont Hitler ne veut pas"*—"It's the German-speakers [refugees] Hitler doesn't like. We have to hold them prisoners." That was another strong signal that I had to go twice as fast. Anyway, I felt good—better to be here on the train.

Around ten o'clock I rode on the street to Saint-Gaudens. In Saint-Gaudens there was the usual control maneuver. The *gendarme* was busy controlling a car, so he just waved me through. I had a cup of coffee at a café, consisting of brown water with saccha-

rine, then started off for the last thirty miles. The journey was
very tiresome, the road always going uphill. Thus I came into
the valley of the Garonne. At Labroquère two *gendarmes* were
visible. I was just then riding with two girls, and he wanted me to
stop, which I did. But everything was fine, and he said, "*C'est bien,
Monsieur*," and we rode on.

I had to pass another control in the valley to Luchon near Cierp-
Gaud, but I knew all about this from Raoul, who went from
Luchon to Buzançais. I rode again with some girls. This time
we were actually halted by the *gendarmes*, who wanted to see
our papers. "Are you French?" they asked me. "*Non*," I replied,
to match my passport. "*Je suis Tchécoslovaque.*" [I am Czech.]
"Well," he said, "you will meet many of your people." He glanced at
my passport and said I could go on. I mentioned also that I went
to see Mr. Lang, who he knew quite well was the father of Raoul,
the owner of the factory in Mulhouse near Basel, Switzerland.
This was the first control, just six miles from the Spanish border.

Thus I arrived in Luchon and hoped to get quickly into Spain.
Uncle Paul and Aunt Clementine Lang were astonished that all
went well. Uncle Lang advised me to apply for a Visa de Sortie,
but I knew this was impossible, as I only would have been
rejected in Vichy.

I did not know how to go forward. We had no reports about the
crossing of the border, as mail was censored in Spain. My uncle
and I went to the mayor of Luchon, who was also my uncle's
doctor. The mayor gave me a letter of recommendation, and I set
off for Saint-Gaudens to see the Sous-Préfet [local administra-
tion] about a Visa de Sortie. He said it was impossible, though I
informed him that I was over military age, over 50, and that I was
Czech. He said there were no Visas de Sortie for Czechs.

I waited a few more days, but knew that way would never work.
So again, I looked at the map and decided upon a route. The days
in Luchon were lovely, and I enjoyed my time thoroughly. I was
so fully convinced that I would succeed in crossing the Pyrenees,
that I even sold my bicycle for the same price that I had bought it.

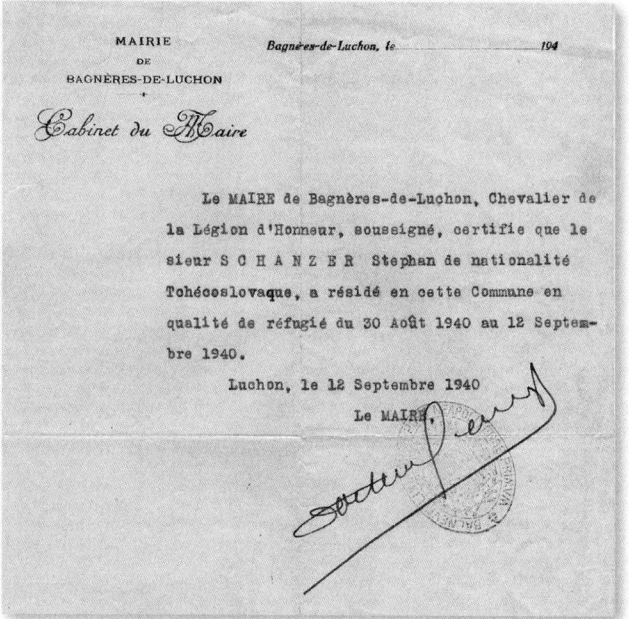

Letter from the Mayor of Luchon attesting to my father's refugee status.

On the evening of September 5, I walked to the Hospice de France.[9]

There were many French tourists from Toulouse at the Hospice de France. I had to sleep in the hay again as there was no vacancy. I did not sleep well that night. The tourists talked the whole night about the terrible conditions in Spain during the Civil War.

I started the next morning at 5:30 a.m. The Port de Vénasque, 8,000 ft. high, was right in front of me. I said at the Hospice that I would come back in the evening. But I didn't know that I actually would be coming back that night.

At 8:40 a.m. I reached the Port de Vénasque and crossed the French-Spanish border. In front of me was the glacier range of the Maledetta, and not a soul was to be seen. I walked downhill for some time, when suddenly two men approached me. They carried rifles. They were Spanish border patrolmen. I went toward them and showed my Spanish visa. I understand a little Spanish, and they said that I should not have gotten into the country that way and therefore I had to go back. But as they were not quite sure about it, they told me they would take me to their commanding officer, and he would decide what to do. But first we had to patrol the mountains until 11 o'clock.

The C.O. [commanding officer] glanced at my passport and said I should go back to my point of entry. But before that he invited me for lunch. We had port and *côtelettes* [cutlets], and fruit, coffee, and cigarettes. The border patrolmen tried to talk their C.O. into allowing me to proceed, but he was not convinced. After some time I discovered the real reason why I had to go back. There was a 10-day *grenzsperre* [closure of border traffic], and that was why the C.O. did not want me to proceed.

Turning back, I first reached the Hospice de France then went back to Luchon. The Langs were all very disappointed about my failure, and so I decided to try once more.[10][11] This time I was advised that in Fos there was a certain Inspecteur des Douanes [Customs officer] who was supposed to be able to provide the necessary stamp on my passport. I met with him, but the gentleman did not know anything about that business and advised me to go to the Special Commissioner. But the latter informed me that he was not allowed to give stamps to Poles, Czechs, Germans, or Austrians. And thus, the bus for Spain departed with one passenger only, a Hungarian who had his Visa de Sortie and all the other necessary papers.

The customs officials suggested I go to Cerbère or Le Perthus. He said the trains were cheaper in France than the expensive bus ride to Lerida, Spain. It was also rumored, he said, that fifty emigrants were kept back from entering Spain at Les. I decided, instead, to go back to Perpignan. I asked my friend Glaser to join me, but he did not want to go that way, so I went to Toulouse and took the train from there. Again I traveled with a French officer. He swore about the Vichy administration and said he was for De Gaulle.[12]

I arrived in Perpignan at 9 a.m. I was all alone and had to find out how to cross the border. I strolled through the city until I found a young refugee who told me where to find fellow emigrants. He directed me to the Café Palmarium. There I met my old friend from the French camp in Audierne, Mr. Fischer from Vienna, who had jumped over the wall as I did. He had been for several days in Perpignan. His family was in Porto, Portugal. We discussed the matter of getting across the border and decided to go by bus to Le Perthus, which is in the Pyrenees, a village in both French and Spanish territory.

For me, time was growing very short. On September 22, my Portuguese visa would expire, and the next day, on September 23, so would my Spanish visa. It was already September 14, and I had to include at least four days for the journey through Spain. I was very worried about staying in France, where it would have meant internment to be without papers. I was told that typhoid fever was raging high in these camps, and to me the prospect was not at all agreeable.

The bus ride went smoothly, and our papers and passports were found to be in order. At the Café Palmarium, we made inquiries and were told to find a man in a leather jacket. We found the man, who demanded $50, plus 2000 French francs. We threatened to go instead to the competition in Cerbère, and only then did he agree that it should be 2000 francs only.

After, we went directly into a hotel where the restaurant down-stairs was full of French *gendarmes* and customs officers. It was very hard to go through a line of your enemies into your room.[14] We waited for twenty-four hours in the hotel. The man told us we were not to take any luggage. I had only a small rucksack, but I was forced to leave even it behind. At 8 p.m. sharp we were told to wait on a bench until our "guide," the one with the leather jacket, returned. He would light a cigarette to show that every-thing was okay. Then we should follow him from a distance of ten paces. The man had taken note of our names for the Spanish border patrol.

A *gendarme* passed as we were sitting on the bench. He went into the café opposite the hotel. Then our guide appeared and

Visas issued to my father by the Siam, Chinese, Portuguese, and Spanish consulates in Marseilles, August 20-24, 1940.

also went into the café. Suddenly he appeared, lit a cigarette, and walked off. We followed him along a small path.

We went along for only a few yards when, suddenly, the guide stopped and turned. "*Messieurs,*" he said, "*vous êtes en Espagne.*" [Gentlemen, you are in Spain.] We handed him the 2000 francs each, and he said that soon there would be another guide to take us to the border patrol. We walked on for one mile until we came to the customs station and the official, a very nice young man, gave us the stamp we needed. He wanted us to take the bus and to reach Barcelona at 4:30 a.m. Two miles ahead was the Aduana, the Spanish Customs, but he said that we need not fear anything as we were now legally in Spain. At the Aduana they already knew about us, the paying foreigners. We waited for the two employees of the Banco de España, who changed our money into pesetas. Meanwhile, I spoke to a Spanish captain, but we had to be very careful with our conversation not to reveal too much.

We marched the whole night. Twice we were controlled, and in the morning we finally came to the railway station at Figueres, where we boarded a train. At 8:40 a.m., we arrived in Barcelona. Everyone was carefully controlled in the train. There was only one official checking the train, and this was far more effective than the dozens of French *gendarmes* who did the checking on French trains.

We spent the whole day in Barcelona, where we were shown around by the agent of Mr. Fischer. In the evening we boarded the crowded train for Madrid, where we arrived at 12 midnight. Again we had to get new train tickets, and at 8 p.m., we departed for Badajoz, on the border with Portugal. We couldn't get into Badajoz because a car was derailed somewhere on the track. It was only September 19, so we were in time though only just— there were three days before my visa would expire. The frontier control went fine on both Spanish and Portuguese soil. The officials from both countries were very kind and invited us for coffee while checking our passports. We arrived in Lisbon after four nights on the train.

Now I am safe, and I would like to know whether I will be allowed to remain in Lisbon for the next fortnight.

In ending, I would like to tell you something that shows the willingness of the French people to help. Before I could travel to America, for the American Consulate I needed a "Certificat de bonne vie et de bon moeurs" [literally: "An attestation of good manners and of not being a criminal"]. This was an easy thing to get in France, but difficult to get here in Portugal. So, I went to the French Consulate and asked for such a report. I produced my Czech Passport, and the official said I would receive the wanted document that afternoon. They could gather from my passport that I had left France illegally and that I had surely taken money across the border without the consent of the Banque de France, more than the allowed 500 francs. Despite all of that, for four Portuguese escudos, I received that afternoon the "Certificat de bonne vie et de bon moeurs." We spoke at length about the present conditions of France and departed the best of friends.

Ça, c'est la France...........
Many kisses from your loving
Papa   Lisbon, October 16, 1940 ■

CHAPTER TEN

Australia

My letters from Australia to my father mark the beginning of my life, not only in a new country, but in the English language as well. For the first year my sister and I lived there, I was still scheming our reunion, little aware of the difficulties that lay ahead. The war meant no travel between countries for passengers, no money, and an escalation of the war in the Pacific. Because of the dangers of Japanese submarines in the waters separating Australia and America, starting in 1941 the shipping lanes were routes of particular contention. Not knowing any of this, I held onto the hope we would all be together soon.

Both my sister and I missed our father, who was only available to us now through writing across an unimaginable distance. Often our letters to him were delayed by months—his letters back to us as well. It must have been bittersweet for him when something from us did arrive, and without much news between us there was a constant anxiety on all our parts. In a letter to Otto Pick on February 2, 1941, my father writes, "From my children I had news indirectly, from my brother-in-law, Max. The news is from the 22nd of October 1940. They know only that I am living." When my father was still in Portugal I sent the following letters to him.

Brisbane   March 20, 1941

Dear Papa,

I know Mr. Paterson is trying his best to get you out of Europe.
One night I woke up and thought I was in France in the
Boarding School and I heard a Boat Siren and thought it was an
Alarm and was just going to jump out of bed half asleep, when I
remembered where I was and went off to sleep again.

The last letter I got from you is from November 1940, so I am a little bit worried. I hope you are able to come here to Australia soon. That would be the happiest day in my life.

So I close my letter with loving wishes from your always loving son,

Charlie

March 30, 1941

Dear Papa,

I just received a letter from you from January 10, 1941. It was hard for me to understand the Austrian, so will you please write the next letter in English if you can. I was full of joy when I knew that you were all right. I will be very interested in the book you wrote about your adventures in France. I am very glad to hear that you have a chance to go to America where it will be much easier to come to Australia. I think you will be able to come with some American troops if you can't come otherwise from America to Australia.

Many kisses and "Good Luck" from your always loving son,

Charlie

In this last letter, I also wrote about my new environs. I have no recollections of this entire time, perhaps because of the language transition. "I am in a very nice boarding school now. I have forgotten all my French and Austrian language, but I tried to keep it up as long as I was with Doris, but now I am only speaking English all the time so I will forget everything. Doris is in another boarding school, but I am writing her a letter nearly each week. I am between fourth and fifth grade because I am doing fourth grade for arithmetic and fifth grade in other subjects. Mr. Paterson has gone to Sydney now."

Through the letters, how much clearer to me our situation in Australia has become! It seems our foster father left Brisbane for Sydney within a year after our arrival, and he and my foster mother Eileen placed my sister and me in Catholic boarding schools two miles away from each other. Separated from Doris, I was apart from everything I knew of home.

But from what I can tell by our letters, my sister and I seemed happy at boarding school. Among my first English letters was one to my great-aunt Elsa in Melbourne. The date is cut off. I recounted: "I go to a very fine college, they have a very nice boat, we had a good ride on Friday and I was driving the boat a little bit. I was first in the second class [second grade] to learn English, but by exam I came second and was too good for this baby class so they put me in the third class [third grade]. It is hard for me because I can't do the money sums. We play cricket and I am a Captain. Last day the ball hit me in the eye and I still got two black eyes. Now I started to play tennis and it is very easy for me. I like school very much. I go some Saturdays skating on rollers. It is very much like ice-skating. I have a very good time here and go every Friday and sometimes Saturday to the pictures. I go every Sunday playing with my friends. I remain your loving nephew, Charlie."

The positive aspect of the boarding school environment was that Doris and I were no different than the rest of the students—all of us were away from home, living without parents.

These experiences were valuable, and the Patersons must have paid a dear tuition for us to be at these schools. Before finding these letters, I didn't consider how much they had to organize for us. The lasting impression that has stayed with me all these years is something more of the challenging circumstances of our arrival and attempt to be integrated into the family.

From the beginning I found my foster mother difficult to get along with. She showed signs of an uneven disposition, and I was a typical growing boy. I was scheduled for chores and sometimes they were not finished properly. I was often restless and bored and would slip away to read, so, in this, Mrs. Paterson's criticisms were partly justified.

My foster father was a distant personality and was much wrapped up in his business, a timber concern called Hancock Brothers. He came home, read the paper—often even at the dinner table—and said very little to anyone. Our interaction with him was minimal.

We missed our real father, who had always been a bubbling, interesting personality. Nothing can substitute for the warmth of real parents who have been lost. There were no hugs in the Paterson family; the British stiff upper lip was the norm. I recall that in Vienna both my parents always came to our room to tuck us in and hug us goodnight.

But Doris and I didn't write to our father about any unhappiness, instead keeping it to ourselves, perhaps to protect him from worries.

Instead of writing to him about these things, I kept a diary in a little black book my father had given me, covered in leatherette and embossed with a small insignia on it of his treasured motorcycle, Puch. On one of the diary's first pages, I wrote in German script only months after arriving in Australia. When translated it caused a flashback of memories I had repressed, which illuminated the challenges of the next seven years.

SATURDAY July 6, 1940

My birthday [party] was nice. 23 children invited. Lots of presents and a very lovely day.

My ear very good; the doctor very good. I only have cotton in and behind my ear now.

SUNDAY July 7

Father said yesterday he is going away on the 19th for a week to a hotel in the city.

The girls and mother are jealous because he loves us.

Mother not very nice. Outing from 9 to 7. In the evening she still was not nice.

MONDAY July 8

Father not at home. Father said last night that if everything wasn't better in a week he will sell the house. We'll go to a school where you are there all day long like a boarding school.

TUESDAY July 9

When I came home from studying I rode [a bicycle] into the little gate (in our front yard) and immediately someone came out and yelled at me that I was told (supposedly) yesterday to use the big gate. But I remember very well that no one told me anything.

The seeming harshness of my new family has been a lasting memory. Luckily having my sister Doris with me helped; she always supplied an ample amount of motherly affection. Doris shouldered much of the responsibility for our wellbeing after we left from France. All those subsequent years in Australia we looked out for each other, Doris and I. But truly she became my mother after we left Europe, and in doing so, she—even more than I—lost her childhood.

There were many fights and disagreements in the Paterson household. I realize now, as I probably did then, that Charles and Eileen's marriage was in distress even before our arrival. My sister and I only added to the contentious situation, but for years we felt that we were the cause. The feeling of not being wanted persisted with us and caused our continual discomfort.

I remember some very spirited discussion in the household about the wisdom of adopting two foreign children. And I, for one, was constantly being picked on for the smallest of things. I was trying to make the best of this disharmonious situation, but it seemed I was subject to constant harassment. I remember that my foster sister Mary and I fought one time very seriously, after some infraction I can't recall. She threatened me and gave chase but could not catch me because I ran down to the riverbank, where I knew she would not follow. The back of the house led to a lower elevation with a tennis court, which then sloped down steeply, with a path through the scrub to a jetty.

The riverbank was my escape in more than one way. It was wild, overgrown with bushes, and I spent a lot of time on the jetty fishing and reading in the sun. I loved to spend solitary hours at the river when I wanted to disappear. No one bothered me there. It was a typical young boy's adventure spot. My friends and I would often hang out by the water's edge or go swimming. Our two dogs would often accompany us, and Caesar—my brown, short legged, curly haired retriever who loved the water—would swim with me. I had to be cautious always, to keep him to my side or else lose the skin off my back, since he would try to get behind me to follow. My other dog, Darby, who was older and wiser, would sit patiently on the jetty and watch us.

Once I was fishing from our jetty with a heavy line and a piece of rotten meat attached to the hook and sinker. Suddenly there was a great

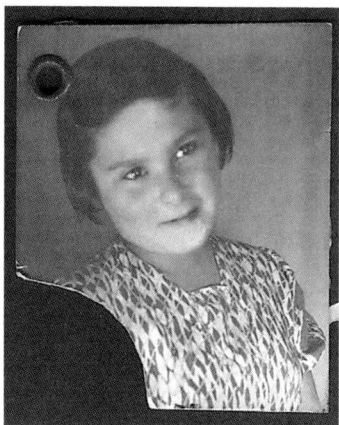

Our 1940 passport photos with Nazi swastikas cut off.

tug on the line, almost pulling me into the river. A friend who was with me helped me reel in my catch. It was a three and half foot shark. We were so proud that we put a stick through its gills and slung it over our shoulders, dangling the body between us as we paraded through the neighborhood to show it off.

A day I remember quite well, my sister and I took our Austrian passports with the Nazi swastikas on their black covers down to the riverbank and decided to have a ritual with incantations to destroy Hitler. We built a small fire, and chanting damnation to the Germans, we burnt our passports. However, first we had the presence of mind to remove and save our pictures, excising the swastikas from their corners.

Starting my first years in Australia, I became involved in the Boy Scouts, and being naturally ambitious, found great challenge in earning as many proficiency badges as were available. Soon my sleeves were covered in badges, and I became a King's Scout, equal to an Eagle Scout in the United States. I then led the Kingfisher Patrol and was responsible for seven or eight scouts. Learning leadership skills and making decisions in my teens served me well in later times. Building bridges with ropes, like the American Indians, was a skill we learned from our scoutmaster who had lived with them for four years.

Frequently we made trips into the bush—not far out of Brisbane—and learned good camping skills and bush lore. I recall one particular trip when we took the rail line to the hinterland, so to speak. The train compartments were quite interesting as each section of a dozen seats facing each other had their own exits to the outside, and there were about twenty of these to each rail car. Someone in our group started chanting "Did she fall or was she pushed," and before long the whole rail car was chanting this over and over for what seemed like hours on end. That it was a chant about a woman's accidental death, or murder, perhaps made it stick in my head.

As the war progressed in 1942, we came back from our boarding schools, and my foster father, Charles, returned from Sydney to live with us full-time at Graceville. I began to call him "Dad." He was very inventive and entrepreneurial, and I admired him, the way a son takes to his father to learn about life and how to be a man.

Dad decided to turn the tennis court in our backyard into a chicken run. Together, we cobbled together chicken coops for almost four hundred birds with lumber from his yard. I recall it was all hardwood, and one would have a devil of a time to drive in a nail on the framing. I spent quite a bit of time straightening out large nails since there was a wartime shortage. It is ironic to think that my maternal grandfather and uncle were in the business of manufacturing wire and nails in Czechoslovakia before the war and exporting them around the world. Could they have been the same nails in Brisbane I was at that time saving?

The chickens became my responsibility: feeding, caring for them, raising baby chicks, gathering the hen's eggs, washing the eggs, and crating them for sale. I also had a couple of ducks and loved the large duck eggs, which I always kept for the family. At this point I was about fifteen, had a salary of twelve shillings and six pence a week (which seemed like a fortune to me), and was on my way to becoming a farmer-entrepreneur. I saved every penny. I wrote to my father in New York, "I'm standing up to the Scout's motto: A scout is thrifty. I have already saved 7/10 schilling and bought two 'one pound' war saving certificates." On weekends, I would clean out the pens and dump wheelbarrows full of chicken droppings over the grassy edge of the riverbank at the back.

I washed all the eggs by hand at first, but it was an enormous job—we collected as many as two hundred per day. Then I used a contraption that Dad obtained and which he very likely adapted. I wrote to my father in New York, "Yesterday we tried out our new egg washing machine. It is worked by handle, which is pushed to and fro. The eggs are placed on [the machine] at the top end and are chaffed and turned by moving strips of rubber [through a water trough]. The machine is 5-foot long and 1-foot wide and is placed by certain stands on a slope and the eggs slowly travel down as they are turned and rubbed by the wet saturated strips of rubber. About 2/3 of the machine has the rubber, and the rest are strips of flannel which dry the eggs. There are two persons needed, one turning the handle and feeding the machine and the other packing the eggs into a 30-dozen box as they come down clean and dry at the bottom end." This ingenious invention saved me a lot of time at night, as egg management was an evening task.

Dad was an engineer and had invented improvements to the machinery used to cut wood veneers; it was a new method at the time to cut these straight from large logs. These special veneers were manufactured at Dad's plywood factory in Cairns, Northern Queensland. Because the veneers were extremely thin, the wood was used efficiently resulting in a cheaper product much appreciated by contractors and builders. Dad

At the Queensland Boy Scouts' Easter Camp,
Yandina, 1944.

also bought a spark plug factory, where I worked part-time during holidays, on the assembly line. He later slowly converted this factory to manufacture hollow core doors and plywood bathtubs. The bathtubs perhaps didn't last very long, but they were beautiful—sprayed in the colors of blue, yellow, or rose enamel—and they sold well because there were no steel tubs available during the war.

There was also a shortage of petrol, as it was rationed. This made driving almost impossible, so to get to work everyday, Dad came up with a new rig for the Chevrolet, comprised of a frame on the back of the car to hold a large tank, which held charcoal. He would start the car with petrol after lighting the charcoal, which produced carbon dioxide and would mix with the fuel to run the vehicle.

The Patersons were right up with the technology of the time, and then ahead some. I remember a kind of Rube Goldberg machine in their bedroom on a tray that had cups and was a combination alarm/lamp/clock/electric teakettle, called a "Teasmaid." Before it was time to get up in the morning, the kettle would turn on, boil the water, and under pressure, a spout would fill the teapot, which sat on a platform that would then drop down, setting off a buzzer, turning on the light, and waking up the sleeper. With this time-saving but bizarrely complicated automatic apparatus, tea could be poured moments after you awakened.

The hollow core doors manufactured at the converted spark plug factory were quite inventive too. We made them from two plywood sheets by placing struts that glued into the hollow doors. These strips of wood came from deconstructed gas mask crates that Dad bought from the war surplus along with many other items. We also unpacked the gas masks and stripped the trunks from the face of the masks to sell as grips for bicycle handles. This was recycling and economy at its best. I even got the idea to build my own bicycle accommodating these grips, so with the pocket money I had, I bought a frame, painted it a bright blue, found wheels and the rest of the parts in a bike shop, and assembled them.

The crates were stored in an open paddock across the street from the factory, where later a new large building was built and the doors and other furniture were made. This lot was behind an American war surplus warehouse, so people thought it was a dumpsite. The first weekend the gas masks were there, some people broke open a lot of the cases and had strewn the gas masks around in order to remove the rubber hoses. Another fellow and I had been hired to unpack the gas masks and strip them. I was then also assigned to guard them. But soon this became too large of a burden for me to handle as I became paranoid that everyone was trying to "get" me as well as the masks.

Consequently, I felt too much pressure and life seemed to be falling apart around me. Stress at the Paterson home did not help my frame of mind. I remember sitting in the kitchen watching the clock tick. It was like a time bomb. I felt like something was going to explode. But my sister Doris intervened and took me to a small inn at the seaside for a week. Soon I felt better. At that time, Doris and I were very close. We talked a lot and walked on the beach. These were difficult times for me, and I felt grateful for her warmth and support, which I did not feel I had at the Patersons. She was the only one who could help me get my equilibrium back, so we could return to Graceville.

After a few years with the Patersons, Doris and I made contact with relatives of my grandmother Olga who had emigrated to Brisbane in the winter of 1939, Felix and Erna Popper. Felix was also a Mason. My father had tracked down his address through a mutual friend and had sent it to Doris, who insisted the Patersons take her there to visit the family. Throughout our years in Australia, my sister and I turned to Felix and Erna Popper for advice, and they became increasingly important to us.

Mr. Popper wrote an affectionate and reassuring letter to my father on October 18, 1942. "It was arranged for Doris to spend the weekend, and so we are delighted to have her with us just now, and hope that she feels comfortable and happy. To celebrate that event, Mrs. Popper cooked some favorite dishes for her that she might have missed for some time." Attached to this letter with a straight pin is Doris' account: "I am getting all the good things which we used to get to eat a long time ago, and I like them very much. I feel as though I have known Mr. and Mrs. Popper all my life. Many, many *busserln* [kisses], Doris."

The Poppers lived only a short train ride away and they continued to look in on us. It has been surprising for me to learn about all the watchful eyes and caring gestures of my father's friends. I remember we felt so all alone.

The Paterson house was in the suburbs of Brisbane, beyond the beautiful Indooroopilly Bridge that spanned the Brisbane River. I went to high school at a Christian Brothers private Catholic school called St. Joseph's Gregory Terrace located in town. The train was only a few blocks from the house, on the Ipswich Line. We had to wear uniforms—black shorts, white short-sleeved shirts, black and red ties, and felt hats with black and red headbands. The curriculum was rigorous and scholarly, including Latin and college preparatory courses similar to British education.

The Christian Brothers all wore long black cassocks and were very strict. When we did not get all our homework done or we misbehaved, our teacher would line us up against the wall and produce from his voluminous robe a leather truncheon, which was about eighteen inches long and a full inch thick. Holding out our hands, we would be meted out a number of whacks, depending on the seriousness of our misdeeds. One of the brothers, who I admired because of his methodical teaching of mathematics, actually would froth at the mouth when doing so.

We all got to be quite clever to minimize the pain of punishments by dropping our hands at the moment of impact. This had to be done carefully so the teacher would not notice. Another trick was to coat your hands with mustard before leaving home when punishment was anticipated, for example, if one did not do one's homework the night before. The mustard would harden one's palms and lessen the pain of impact—at least so we thought. In grade school we had another trick. The teachers used to use a cane about four or five feet long, which stood near the teacher's desk and would be employed quite often. Before class, some of the fellows would get a hold of the cane and use a pocketknife to make a small slit in the business end, inserting a nearly-invisible horsehair. This would have the stunning effect of splitting the cane on the first impact with the unfortunate student's hand. However, this method had limited applications since the teachers might get wise to it if used too often.

It's clear now, as I write this in more modern times, that I had truly been sent to a penal colony! ■

CHAPTER ELEVEN

War Cry

O ur suitcases were unpacked, our language now English, and our faces graced by the strong Australian sun. But just as our shadows traced our steps on the macadam as we walked down the street to school, our memories of the disaster unfolding in Europe constantly followed us.

Many of our classmates were interested in what events transpired to necessitate the Australian adoption of two Viennese children. Perhaps because of their curiosity, or the idea of a wise adult who thought it better that children like me share rather than repress our circumstances, I was asked to write a serial column for the student newspaper at Gregory Terrace in 1944.

As a fifteen year-old reporter, I tried to engage my audience with suspenseful details about the war and elements they had heard of—gas masks, concentration camps, the evil Nazis, and their weaponry. But with these images, how could I convey to my teachers, friends, and other boys at school the unimaginable times and trials experienced by my family? I was unhappy at home; Doris and I missed our father; we had lost our mother in a tragic way and were uncertain about our future. Doris, meanwhile, kept sending inquiries through the Red Cross: where were Aunt Claire and Omama?

Reading over the old newspapers now I realize that without personal testimony from children like us who had experienced mortal danger, the war in Europe could have remained an abstraction for Australian kids my age. But for us to bear witness to what was happening on the other side of the world gave a wider context as to why Australians themselves were at war—my classmates' uncles, fathers, brothers, and the women, like Joan Paterson, who were proud members of the WAAF (Women's Auxiliary Air Force). Testimonies like ours imparted an emotional content to facts, announcements, radio reports, shortages, and to the air raid drills we did at school.

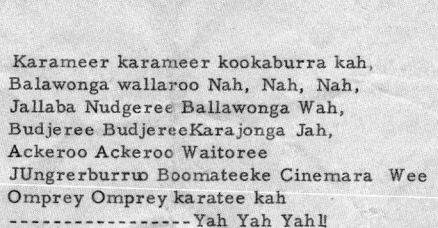

Karameer karameer kookaburra kah,
Balawonga wallaroo Nah, Nah, Nah,
Jallaba Nudgeree Ballawonga Wah,
Budjeree BudjereeKarajonga Jah,
Ackeroo Ackeroo Waitoree
JUngrerburruo Boomateeke Cinemara Wee
Omprey Omprey karatee kah
----------------Yah Yah Yah!!

Aboriginal "War Cry" used at
St. Joseph's Gregory Terrace
High School in Brisbane
at sporting events,
circa 1944.

The harrowing moments recollected in my column take on a second meaning to me now, about how my first-hand childhood experiences were subsequently transformed into narratives. I note how I put different emphases on things, where episodes are omitted, and where I skipped over my fears, showing the strength and character of an adult who handles situations for younger people. I am surprised to read my full and blunt cognizance of the dangers we faced and my memories of Jews being persecuted in Vienna before we left, which in my older years I had ceased to remember.

I sent the following columns to my father in America and then to my uncle Max in England. Max wrote back to me that when I graduated I should consider being a reporter, or a writer. I never thought of myself that way, nor do I remember having fully related my early experiences fleeing from Europe when I was younger. But as all of these letters and memorabilia have surfaced, it has become clear that I have always wanted those around me to recognize what really happened.

In writing out our stories I think I was strongly influenced by my father's 1941 letter about his perilous journeys through France. His exciting descriptions colored terrifying experiences, transforming his escape into something novelesque, allowing his young readers to make it all the way through to the end.

1944

The editor of this paper has asked me to write of my adventures overseas, and so give you an idea of conditions in Austria, Czechoslovakia, and France when I was there. I shall begin with "My adventures while I lived in Austria."

It was seven years ago, and I still remember it as though it all happened yesterday, and how peaceful Vienna was in 1937. Then quite suddenly, on the eve of the 13th of March 1938, the Austrian president, Schuschnigg, gave his last speech over the wireless. He told us that it was useless to shed any blood by opposing the German army, which had overrun part of Austrian territory.

Next day, the Germans had full control of Austria. Jews were persecuted in many ways, such as being stopped in the streets and made to wash the German cars, or wash the footpaths. It was not uncommon to see painted across a shop-window—'Do not buy here, the owners are Jews'—and a German soldier guarding the front door, forbidding anyone to enter.

I remember the day when [my sister Doris and] I tore down a large picture of Hitler pasted on the wall in a street. Next day, two of the 'Hitler Jugend' (Hitler's youth movement) called at our house and demanded our two bicycles, or we would be reported. We were afraid that my father might be put into a concentration camp, and so we had to comply with their wishes. A month later one bicycle was returned all smashed up and partly covered in tar. The other, we never saw again.

It took three months to get our passports and papers to be able to go to Czechoslovakia. Meanwhile my mother died from scarlet fever, which the Nazi troops brought into Vienna and which was more or less sweeping the country.

When we got our papers, my father, my sister, and myself were ready, anxiously awaiting the train, which was to take us to Pilsen, in Czechoslovakia, where my grandmother [Olga] lived at the time.

Next week I will relate to you "My Journey and Of Czechoslovakia."

The train, which was carrying us to Czechoslovakia from occupied Austria, was nearing Pilsen, and the border, when suddenly the train was stopped, and some Gestapo men boarded.

They went from compartment to compartment, checking over papers and searching the luggage of all the passengers. The reason for this was that people leaving Austria or Germany were only allowed to take a certain sum of money with them.

Coming to our compartment, they opened our suit-cases, took half of the clothes out of them, and having searched them thoroughly, stuffed the clothes back any-old-how, not worrying how crushed they would get.

About an hour later the train was on its way again, and soon we arrived in Pilsen. There we stayed [with our grandmother Olga] for about nine months. Meanwhile the Germans had slowly and surely moved the border of Czechoslovakia further and further towards Pilsen. When they arrived at the outskirts of Pilsen, about two miles from where I lived, they stopped, having put a sentry box on a bridge with a German soldier on guard. Across the road was a large notice suspended from tree to tree saying that was the new border.

I often went to the border, and once I saw two old Czechoslovaks coming up the road into Pilsen having all their belongings in a little cart, pulling it behind them. Their home had most likely been taken by the Germans.

I think that the main reason for the stop was that there was a large Czechoslovak military camp, and a small airport, near the new border. But there were no fighter planes, only small sports planes and trainers at the airfield.

While all this was happening, my father flew to Paris alone, from where he was arranging our departure from Czechoslovakia.

Next week, "The Air-Raid Alarm" and "From Pilsen to Prague."

I was still living in Pilsen when one night, suddenly the alarms went. I was rudely awakened from my slumbers and told to get up quickly for there was an Air-Raid.[1]

We were quite alarmed as we had not yet received our Gas Masks and were expecting Gas raids. We had not been instructed about Air Raids and had no Air Raid Shelters, except cellars. A lot of people were out in the streets, some with Gas Masks on, others with none. The suspense lasted approximately half-an-hour, during which time a few bombers flew overhead. But as no bombs were dropped, I take it they were not German planes.

A few months after that incident, one night when my Uncle Max came home he informed us that he had heard from a very reliable source that, on that night, the Nazis were going to occupy Pilsen. We at once secretly packed our clothes, and having told no one, except to say we were visiting Prague (Capital of Czechoslovakia), set off in my Uncle's car.

It was a pitch black, wintry night and the roads were frozen over with ice. No lights were on as there was a black-out, and snow was falling heavily so that the driver could only see a few yards in front of him.

At one stage of our wintry midnight drive, we could not climb a very slight hill because the road was all ice, and when we were about halfway up, suddenly the car would slide backwards down the hill again. Eventually we got to the top, but all had to get out and push, which was very hard. All this delayed us about half-an-hour.

Another incident was when my Uncle drove straight off the road, as he could not see the road. We nearly went over a cliff, had it not been for very skillful driving, and we halted only a few feet from the cliff. We did not arrive in Prague till well after mid-night.

Next week's chapter, "The Nazis arrive in Prague."

We arrived in Prague at about 2 a.m. where we spent the night at a hotel. Next morning, as we had a wireless in our room, the announcer's voice was just warning all vehicle drivers to drive on the right-hand side, not the usual left, because the Nazis were coming through the city in full force. (In Germany cars are driven on the right hand side and in Czechoslovakia on the left.) I found out later that Pilsen was occupied by the Germans almost at the same time as Prague.

About thirty minutes later, I could hear the low rumble of heavy tanks and soon, sure enough, they were passing through the street below. There were quite a lot of them, followed by army trucks filled with German soldiers armed to the teeth.

Quite a few officers passed by in smaller cars, with swords dangling from their belts. Incidentally, later I heard that these swords were made out of wood, and only the sheath was steel. I take it that this was to save steel, as at that time Germany was very short of iron and steel. Then followed armored cars and heavy guns. Also there were open trucks with a machine gun in the middle of each and a crew, ready for a fight, if need arose.

Our attempt to escape the grasp of the greedy, blood-thirsty, and ruthless Nazis had been frustrated again. Our only hope now was from my father, who had gone ahead to Paris to arrange our passports and papers to leave the country.

As we had no chance of escape, we went back to Pilsen to await patiently a letter to say that all had been arranged for us. At last a letter arrived and soon the papers came through for my sister and [me] to leave the country, for Paris.

We soon had all our things packed, and that same week a German examiner was sent to examine and search our ports [luggage] and seal them, to see that we smuggled no money away, as we were only allowed to take about ten shillings with us. Luckily, when my father left Czechoslovakia he smuggled some money to France, or we would have had hardly a cent to live on.

While the Nazi snooper was searching my port, he came across a little brush, which was given to me by my father, and the lid of which could be pulled away and then a small piece of wood has to be removed. This discloses a little hollow space crammed full of cigarette papers, covered with a lot of shorthand writing. This was written by my father in the last world war and was a sort of diary. He wrote it when a prisoner of war [in Siberia], and with that diary he later escaped.

My heart was beating hard as the Nazi was examining the harmless looking brush. He tugged at the hair but luckily the old glue stuck well and did not come off. I regretted then, that I did not put a high valued money note into it and smuggled it over the border. Anyway I have still got this brush and if any of you like to see it, I'll bring it to school someday and show it to you.

Soon we were on our way. To go to France from Czechoslovakia, we had to cross through the heart of Germany. As me and my sister, who is only two and a half years older, were traveling by ourselves through Nazi Germany, you can imagine that we did not feel too good, at the ages of 9 and 12 years, and were a little frightened.

Next week, "Traveling through Germany."

The billiard brush with false bottom containing my father's Siberian diary.
PHOTO: CARRIE PATERSON.

The train pulled out of Pilsen and my sister and I said a last farewell to our relatives there. We were all by ourselves, as we knew no one on the train.

When we arrived at the German border, there was another search. They went through our ports, which had not been sealed by the other German in Pilsen. Of course we were searched too. I heard later that some people smuggled out a lot of money by putting it all into a hollow doll, others by putting high valued money notes between the soles of their shoes, and so on.

Most of the way through Germany we saw nothing but fields. We traveled all day, and our papers were checked a few times during the journey. When night came, we had the compartment to ourselves and were able to make ourselves quite comfortable. I was looking after our papers and passports and had them in my coat, which was hanging up near my head. In the middle of the night, a man came in and sat in the far corner. I was pretending to be asleep, but with one eye half open I watched his shadowy form lest he might creep up and steal our papers. I stayed awake, though since the lights were dimmed it was rather hard to do so. After about an hour's traveling the man left the train.

I was much relieved and immediately transferred the papers under my head. Then I slept till morning. In the morning, we arrived at the border of France, where the papers and tickets were checked as well as another search of our ports. At last we were in France, but alas, a new difficulty arose. We could not speak French, except to say *"Oui,"* and *"Non!"* So you can imagine what happened when a French-man started to talk to us on our way to Paris.

We were standing in the corridor of the train carriage when a Frenchman, who had been standing nearby, looking at the fields flittering past, approached us and started to tell us about the river, which we were just then crossing.

I knew that he was talking about the river by the way he motioned with his hands, as all Frenchmen do, and also about some battle

*Postcard showing Pilsen circa 1938, sent by my grandmother Olga Beck
to my father in Paris.*

which was fought on its banks. I knew this by the way he was
jumping about, and pointing here and there. Every now and again
we would just mumble "*Oui, oui,*" in a sort of understanding way.
He talked and talked; but at last he stopped and looked at us. I
realized he must have asked us a question. What could I say? So
I shook my head gravely and said, "*Non.*" I don't know what he
asked, but he just looked at me, and then I think he realized that
we could not speak French, and looking rather apologetic (so I
thought) he retraced his steps down the corridor, shrugging his
shoulders as he disappeared into a compartment.

At last we were thundering through Paris and soon arrived at the
station. There was great hustle and bustle with ports, etc. At last
we had all our luggage out on the platform, but we could not see
our father anywhere. I left my sister with the ports and went along
the crowded platform in search of him. I had walked about half the
length of it when suddenly I saw him among the crowd. I gradually
worked [my way] up to him through the crowd, and after a happy
reunion, led him to my sister and the ports.

Soon we were leaving the enormous railway station in a taxi,
which was taking us to our hotel.

Next week's chapter, "Lost in Paris."

Three days after our arrival in Paris my father told me that he had a very good friend [named d'Aussy] who owned a large picture theatre, and that we could go there sometimes. I wanted to go that day, and at last persuaded him to allow us to go, although he could not come with us. He gave us directions to follow, and saw us off on an under-ground electric train called the "Métro."

We got out at the right station, and soon found the theatre. Naturally we got in for nothing, and before the picture, my father's friend showed us all the machines.

After the pictures, which I thoroughly enjoyed, though I could hardly understand a word, we proceeded back to the "Métro." Unfortunately we got lost in all the underground passages leading to the numerous platforms, and after going this way and that, I thought we had at last found the right platform. We boarded the train and counted the stations. When the sixth station had flittered past and our station, which should have been the fifth, did not show up, we realized that we were on the wrong train and probably were somewhere on the other side of Paris.[2]

We got out at the next station, and when we reached the street again by way of moving steps, we did not know where we were and had never seen the place before.

How were we to get home? We could not ask anyone where to go or where we were, because we could not speak sufficient French. Near-by flowed the mighty Seine River, which also flows near our Hotel. So we decided to follow it.

Suddenly I stopped and told my sister that I had a brilliant idea and thought of a way by which we could get home without having to walk and take a great chance of losing our way again. What was this idea of mine?

Next week, "I solve the tricky problem."

My sister and I were stranded on the outskirts of Paris and we were evidently lost. When I asked for suggestions from a number of boys at school as to what they would have done in such a predicament, I got replies such as these: Ask a policeman (but I could not speak French, all I knew was my address), hitch-hike, swim down the river, make a raft, look up a directory, look for someone speaking your language and ask him, and so on. At last one bright chap said, "Why hail a taxi of course;" and he was right.

Well I hailed a taxi which was not very hard to do, as there were plenty of them around (not like Brisbane), and after stuttering with a terrible accent "Hotel de la Gironde, 42 Rue de Rivoli" I tumbled in, followed by my sister.

After traveling awhile we noticed that the surroundings were familiar, and in a few minutes the taxi pulled up. We got out, and the driver put his hand out of the window and mumbled in a deep tone, "*Dix francs, s'il vous plait.*" I soon realized what that meant and stood there dumbfounded for a few seconds, because I thought it would have only been two francs and that was all I had. Now, we were in trouble. I pulled myself together and got to work immediately trying to explain with shrugs and grunts and pointing, to the coin in my hand and to the hotel opposite the road that this was all the money I had, and I would get some more from my father, at the hotel. He looked at me and then at my sister, suspiciously, and so I bade my sister stay in the car as a sort of hostage until I brought the money.

But, another shock was in store for me... my father was not at home. What should I do? In sheer desperation I ran to the Hotel owner's office and again with grunts and pointing (as if I were dumb) showed her from the door, the taxi and my sister in it.

She soon realized what had happened and kindly lent me ten francs with which I paid off the taximan and then hurried upstairs with my sister leaving the explanations for my father, when he should return to the hotel. ■

*Watercolor self-portrait in Paris waiting to cross the street
outside the Pont-Marie Métro, 1939.*

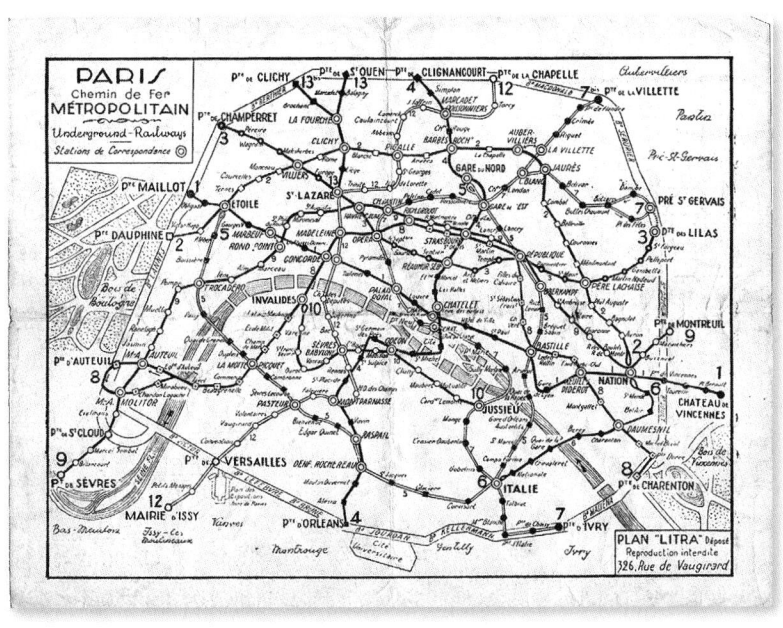

Paris Métro map, 1939.

CHAPTER TWELVE

Resurfacing

A question emerges while digging through files and writing this book. I am constantly wondering why my father kept copies of all of his correspondence. It is said survivors never throw anything away. But even without that truism to bear on his recordkeeping, the mere fact of his diligence illustrates how much he wanted order in his life.

Perhaps my father thought he would need to refer to the circumstances over the years that were part of my sister and me being adopted by a foster family, which had been a kind of formal arrangement. In business matters and accounting, as in other aspects of his life, my father was always meticulous. But maybe he thought I would someday learn something I had not known before. I had no inkling until his letters surfaced that during the years we were apart he knew more about what was really happening to my sister and me than what we wrote to him.

My father had made his way from Lisbon to New York on a ship called the *Njassa* on May 18, 1941. This was difficult to achieve and timely, as his visa was nearly expired and to overstay the term would mean prison, or running again. He had lived in Portugal for nine months by that point, making his living teaching English to groups of other émigrés using the Berlitz method, even though he was still not entirely proficient. In later years, he would say, "I stayed one chapter ahead of my students." On November 10, 1940, he wrote to his cousin Käthe's husband, Otto Pick, in Canada, "I have English lessons from morning till night with very much pupils, who are beginning now already to speak a little. So I am able to earn my living. But nevertheless, I would be very glad to leave for U.S.A. because I could not sustain once more all the adventures I lived through the months of June, July, August, and September."

Otto Pick helped my father get a political affidavit through lawyer connections in the States and wrote many letters on his behalf for an "emergency visa." The political affidavit was finally secured in April 1941

Leaving Lisbon on the Njassa, *May 18, 1941.* PHOTO: STEFAN SCHANZER

with several letters of recommendation. One came from my father's old friend John Baruch—a fellow Viennese Mason who had also escaped Europe through Lisbon and was the nephew of the famous U.S. statesman Bernard Baruch. Another important testimony came from the musician and composer Eugene Riese in Los Angeles, the same young man who two years previously had been unsuccessful in lobbying any of our American relatives for an affidavit of support for us to emigrate from Vienna to the United States. The last requirement for immigration was financial solvency, proven with $5000 transferred by Otto Pick in my father's name to a U.S. bank. This generous effort by Otto Pick above all was crucial. My father wrote to my sister Doris on November 12, 1943, about Otto Pick, "He saved my life, a fact I will never forget."

The American Consul confirmed that my father had permission to immigrate into the United States because our number on the Austrian quota had already been called up previously in 1938, after we fled. But visas were then being limited because of lack of space on ships sailing to New York. There is more to this story on the American end; visas were being limited to ten per cent of the allowable quota,[1] a fact that has only recently become widely known. In the end, my father secured a place and the Hebrew Immigrant Aid Society (HICEM) in Lisbon paid the passage.

He set off on the trip wearing a new suit, now his only one. It was a gift from his students, of a light color, so he looked very upbeat in a photo we have from him as he stepped onto the ship. Another photo he took is off the boat's prow, as it cut swiftly through the water.

After my father had gotten settled in the United States, he received a letter from our relative Richard Hirsch in Australia, who had been in touch with my sister and I and had read my father's chronicle of escape from France. Richard was a cultured man, intelligent, and kind. His father Wilhelm and my grandfather Otto Beck were first cousins and partners in the nail and wire factory in Pilsen before Richard and my uncle Max took the reins in the mid-1930's.

Sydney   December 18, 1942

Dear Stefan,

We all have read your letter of your adventures in Europe with much interest, and we can fairly well imagine through what kind of feelings you must have gone, before reaching a place of safety. Are you about to write a book about all you have seen? I believe it would be interesting for thousands of people to read it.

From [your brother-in-law] Max I get news, on very rare occasions, after all he seems to be getting on quite well. A few other friends in England I hear [about] are quite happy too, whereas the news trickling through from Europe is appalling.

Doris makes in her letters the impression of a grown up girl, very business-like, and self-conscious. I believe that the education of youth in this country is much more efficient than it was in Europe, the education of school itself giving a very solid foundation for their future, being much more practical.

Charles has passed his examinations—which means quite a lot— and is the sort of boy one wants a boy to be. I am sure Mr. and Mrs. Paterson understand how to handle the children, as in general, it is amazing how well people in this country understand how to handle other people, and what good psychologists they are. I think it is the perfect country for children to grow [up in] and be educated.

We all should be very pleased to have some news from you if you can spare the time to write.

Best regards from everybody.

Sincerely yours,

Richard Hirsch

For architectural history it is interesting to note that Richard's Loosian apartment in Pilsen on Plachého Street was only re-discovered in 1987; details about it are still coming to light.[2][3] The entire living and dining room interiors were in disrepair at the end of the Communist era, but they were bought and restored by Vladimír Lekeš, an art and antiques dealer in Prague. Lekeš reassembled the interior in 2010 in a Prague apartment of similar dimensions overlooking the old Jewish Cemetery in Josefov.[4] Richard's parents, Wilhelm and Martha Hirsch (of the well-known Oskar Kokoschka portraits), had an apartment just below Richard's, which is considered one of Loos' finest early interiors with its garden room walls of green marble and black lacquer.

As our English progressed, we wrote long letters to our father close to once a month. I imagine sometimes they arrived in bundles. By the time seven years had passed, the letter collection he amassed was huge. When we found them all in Aspen in 2011 I was rendered speechless. I had to stop writing this book for a while in order to read all the letters and absorb their contents. My letters totaled some forty-four pages. My sister's, more like diary entries, were even more expansive than that. I spent three days looking through them all, from early morning until night, and they sparked vivid memories of the incidents retold. When I read the letters of my sister, who passed away in 2004, it was as if she were sitting across the table from me, as she was then as a teenager, telling me about her boyfriends.

From the letters, I know now that as early as the fall of 1943 my father had conflicting reports of how well we were getting along with the

Patersons. Mr. Julius Rosenfeld of Brisbane—the original contact made for the Patersons to adopt us—told my father we were well adjusted and happy. But Fred Beauchamp, my father's friend in Sydney, disagreed. A very complete and serious report came to my father through our relative Felix Popper, who had also been an advisor to Doris as our situation in the Paterson household became progressively more difficult. On April 14, 1944, my father wrote to Felix eliciting the full story, "Through different letters of Doris and Charlie I see that they found a second home in your house and I thank you for it very much, as well as your wife. Some days ago I got a letter from Doris [who refers] to an incident, which she promised to Mr. Paterson not to write [about] to me. At the same time she is saying that you know everything about this incident.... She is saying she and Charlie would like to come to New York.... I am delighted to have the hope to have the children again with me.... My only worry is the thought of ungratefulness towards the Paterson family, who in reality saved us by their action from a certain death. Please write me also your opinion about this. I would also like to know if the behavior of my children [has been] correct. This would clarify the situation."

My father in New York, 1942.

The reply came back a month later, and it was a real revelation for me to read the background to our adoption and have my impressions about our lives with the Patersons confirmed. "Dear Friend, It is a hard task to deal in a letter with as difficult problems as set out in your letter of April 14th, however I do not wish to delay my reply...." Mr. Popper pointed out that from the start Mrs. Paterson was against the adoption, but Mr. Paterson went ahead despite her expressed wishes. The disagreement resulted in us going to boarding school shortly after our arrival. But also there was another complication. Apparently, shortly after we arrived Mr. Paterson decided to live apart from his family, having a personal attachment to a lady friend. This affair meant we only seldom saw our adoptive father, though Mr. Popper said on occasion we succeeded in meeting him secretly in town. I assume the affair must have fizzled, and that's why Mr. Paterson returned home.

Mr. Popper continued to assess that Mrs. Paterson was a woman of rather narrow outlook who always treated us more or less as intruders into her family. He said Doris had been suffering under those conditions more than me. It is true we did not feel welcomed as adopted children. Rather, Mrs. Paterson treated us as boarders. Doris did all our washing and, as well, she cooked my breakfast. The situation at the Paterson home also unfortunately resulted in Doris leaving school at age fifteen. (She eventually got her G.E.D., went on to Rutgers, and graduated from University of Colorado in her forties.) She stopped going to school in Australia to become, in her words, "financially independent" to escape the difficult relationship with Mrs. Paterson. But Doris was unsatisfied with the jobs available to her with her limited education.

When Mr. Paterson left a second time and communications with him were severed, we lost an anchor, and this, Mr. Popper related, affected Doris especially. After requesting to meet with Mr. Paterson, and waiting several months for a reply, Mr. Popper finally succeeded in having a frank discussion with him in February 1943, when Mr. Paterson had again returned home. As a result of that conversation it was decided Doris should resume her education by attending evening classes (at one point she joined a drawing class, and later a secretarial course), and the atmosphere at the Paterson house became friendlier.

Mr. Popper became an arbitrator and helped my father retain his composure in his communications with Mr. Paterson, the man to whom he had entrusted so much. In the end, Mr. Popper only faulted Mr. Paterson once in a letter dated January 28, 1945, for his "liberal conception of life," which made him "reluctant to interfere with the affairs of others," and for treating me and my sister "as grown-up people, respecting fully [our] opinions, but forgetting that children, although they should learn to think and act under their own responsibility still require advice, control, and guidance." The effects of Mr. Paterson's ongoing extramarital affair on his own family, or what secondary effects it must have had on me and my sister, remains unstated in the letter.

By May 11, 1944, Mr. Popper advised my father on how to best proceed extracting us from Australia. "Take all necessary steps now to procure all documents and permits so that the children may have the opportunity of uniting with you as soon as you deem it advisable or necessary. By that means you will give the children something to look forward to, and this chance before them immediately will make them happier and more contented.

"When everything is fixed, you may write to Mr. Paterson the following lines: 'Recognizing that my children and I owe you our lives and everything we have, I feel I cannot evince my gratitude better than by relieving you at the first possible moment, when by strenuous efforts I have attained a position which enables me to care for my children, from your great responsibility.' ... There is no need to precipitate decisions that will have far reaching consequences. Think things over, discuss them with reliable friends, and should you require further information or assistance in any shape or form, I shall be only too glad to respond. Yours fraternally, Felix Popper."

My father brought Mr. Popper's report to the American Friends Service Committee (the Quakers) in New York where he had several friends. He responded to Mr. Popper on July 12, 1944 that the Quakers felt we were "not in a physical need, but in a moral need" to leave Australia and we had to come to the U.S.A. as soon as possible to join our father.

The two big obstacles for our immigration into the United States were first, the visas, and second, the impossibility of travel across the Pacific while there was still a war. Our quota numbers for the United States from Austria in 1938 would also take at least a year to be transferred to

Brisbane, and new quota numbers would need to be obtained before any possibility of an exit visa. Then, before entry visas could be issued, my father needed to produce the tickets, already paid for, and have affidavits. On these matters, he began to work immediately.

He closed his letter to Felix Popper with thanks—"It was very kind of you and your dear wife to offer your home to my children in case of emergency, but let's hope that it will never become necessary. I thank you and your wife for this big sign of friendship. It comforts me a lot about the sad situation."

Then my father wrote a somber reflection—"It [makes] no sense to look back to a time [when] Mr. Paterson was writing a lot of letters to me in France before the children started to Australia. But I can't understand a man, on bad terms with his wife, who invites into his house two more children, who apparently knew at this time that he will leave his family. And how does it come that I got a letter of welcome from Mrs. Paterson, from Joan and from Mary, before the children started to Australia? These are questions I never will be able to understand."

Perhaps no one, including Mr. Paterson, really believed my father's immigration into Australia would turn out to be quite so difficult. Mr. and Mrs. Paterson were left with my sister and me in their care as only a tiny part of the world's humanitarian crisis and as constant and close reminders that the accelerating war would alter everyone's lives, irrevocably, around the world. ∎

CHAPTER THIRTEEN

The Goldens

As Nazi Germany fell, we knew it would only be a matter of time before we could see our father again. Then came the end of the war, to the joy of all the Allied countries. On August 10, 1945—the day after the second atomic bomb was dropped on Japan at Nagasaki, I started a letter to my father and halfway through wrote in capital letters, "STOP PRESS." I continued on Saturday, August 11, "This morning we received the great news of the Japanese [offer to] unconditional surrender if they can keep their Emperor. It looks as if this great war is finished ... and there will be no more horrors and sufferings when this world is at last at peace again."

Ten days later on August 21, 1945, my sister wrote to my father, "On V-P day [Victory in the Pacific, August 15, 1945] everyone here in Brisbane celebrated in marvelous sort of way. People going up and down the main streets banging kerosene tins, blowing whistles. About eleven other girls and I formed a group and just went mad for about two hours. We boarded trams, ferries, and trucks (anyone's truck), and had rides. After about two and a half hours of this we were tired out and dragged our weary bodies home. I will never, as long as I live, forget that day.... Hoping you are as well as ever, I remain, your loving daughter, Doris."

To be fair to the time that Doris and I spent in Australia, I should emphasize that the majority of my memories from my teenage years, apart from the central Paterson-family conflict, were basically happy, with many pursuits and adventures.

Doris and I spent all our Christmas holidays and January with the Paterson family at Surfers Paradise, the famous Queensland beach with miles of fine golden sand, surf, and crystal waters. During the 1940's, it was still a sleepy coastal village with only one hotel—a single story Spanish colonial that had gardens filled with parrots and cockatoos. My friends and I would body surf from morning to night and spend our days

LEFT TO RIGHT: *Three friends with Mary Paterson, Doris, and me,*
Surfers Paradise, circa 1945.

otherwise under a huge umbrella. I loved hanging out at the beach with
my sister Doris and her glamorous girlfriends. Other times would find
me in the shallows of the river, which meandered near the beach, where
we would lay covered with a thin sheet of water in the sand for hours on
end. Such were the simple pleasures of this new, non-European life.

In the summer of 1945, in January, my best friend from grammar
school who was also at Gregory Terrace with me, John Golden, had come
to stay with the Patersons at Surfers Paradise for a few weeks. John and I
shared the same birth date, July 7, 1929. He and I used to spend all day on
the beach and in the surf. We ran with an older crowd, loved to dance, and
even though we were still teenagers, we were allowed into the nightclubs.

John's parents owned a twenty thousand acre cattle station in the
Australian outback. I first visited them there in summer 1942 before I
turned thirteen and remember well the long train-ride out there with
his sisters. After John spent time with us at Surfers Paradise, he invited
me to come home with him the rest of our two-month break from school,
so I spent the remainder of the summer of 1945 and the following one in
1946 in "the bush" with the Goldens.

It was quite an adventure just to get out to the cattle station. First
we traveled by the Western Line Train for three hundred miles, almost a

Entertaining my friends, Brisbane, 1946.

day, to get to Yuleba (pronounced "YULE-ba"). This was a small outpost, consisting of a general store, post office, and pub, with a few small, dusty houses scattered around the dry land. Once a week, I recall it was a Thursday, the mail truck went out to the outlying cattle stations, and you had to coordinate with the truck to get a ride.

Our route to John Golden's family station called "Spion Kop,"[1] Dutch for "spyglass hill," was by a bumpy dirt track, and the truck would stop along the way at every station to deliver the mail. We made our way over rutted, rain-scarred roads for some sixty miles. I remember vividly when suddenly we came to a section where a bush fire was raging. Without hesitation or concern, the driver continued into this inferno of burning trees on both sides of the track in his small pickup. I could hardly believe it and was scared out of my wits. Trees full of flames were falling across the road behind us, but he managed to come through unscarred and without burning up the mail and us. It took us almost a full day to reach the homestead gate, which was still removed about half a mile away from the house over a treeless grass-covered expanse.

The homestead was located in the center of a man-made plain where the vegetation had been cut back all around to protect it from the bush fires that raged periodically. The nearest neighbor was five miles away, so it was quite isolated.

Large verandas surrounded the house with overhanging eaves. The corrugated tin roof was built with gutters so that all the runoff water during the "Rainy" could be caught in tanks placed strategically around the building. There was no other source of water and no electricity. The shortage of water during the "Dry" was such that one bathtub full of water served at least three or four of us—not all in one tub at the same time, of course. The house was beautifully built and very comfortable. To one side was an elegant tennis court. On Sundays, neighbors from all around would arrive in old Model T Fords and engage in tennis matches, decked out in white shorts, and we would drink lemonade on the cool verandas. Transported away from the rough life of the cattle station in the middle of the Australian bush, these afternoons would evoke a genteel British scene.

On arrival, I was warmly greeted by John's mother and father and made at home in their guest room situated off one of the balconies. I slept well and deeply on my first night there. On awakening, I found I could not move. What was going on? Well, I soon discovered that both my big toes were tied to the bedposts. This practical joke was a ritual in their family for all new guests. The Goldens would sneak up early in the morning, lasso the big toes of their unsuspecting guest, and tie them to the bedstead with string. When they heard the sounds of dismay and the struggle to get out of bed, they would gather around and have a good laugh. There were many practical jokes in that household. I remember also that the old fashioned, hand cranked phone on the wall was a party line, and a certain number of rings would be the signal it was a call for you. Of course the whole vast "neighborhood" knew everyone's business, as people sometimes would listen in on the calls.

As the new "Jackaroo" I was assigned my own horse—a small chestnut mare. We made friends immediately, except one day I was angered when she threw me over her head as I was chasing down an errant heifer that had broken ranks from the lot we were droving. I went into the bush after the heifer with too much abandon. As I leaned left to miss a tree, the mare decided to veer right. Luckily, all that was bruised was my pride as a result of this—my only disagreement I ever had with my horse. An immediate lesson was to let horses decide the route in the future, which they knew much better by instinct than the rider.

While running cattle we wore khaki shirts and shorts—blue jeans were uncommon at this time. Wide-brimmed bush hats protected us from the brutal Australian sun. Our saddles were "English," which differed from the American western version, as they had no front horns for roping. We would spend all day in the saddle, rounding up cattle and transferring them from one huge paddock to another to rotate the grazing. Riding through the bush, we would see king kangaroos as tall as horses, which easily bounded over fences in full flight.

We camped in the bush when we were too distant from the homestead. Near a billabong, we would set up, sleeping under the stars with dingoes serenading us throughout the night. On those occasions we would be out for days at a time rounding up cattle to put them through the "dip," a long narrow wooden trough filled with a noxious black liquid, which smelled of creosote. The cattle would be driven and prodded into the trough and made to swim through, so they completely immersed themselves in this foul smelling stuff. The procedure was done yearly to protect them against a deadly disease, called red water. These were exciting times, especially for someone my age, and I added a lot of knowledge to my bush lore and riding skills.

At the house there was a piano in the living room, and often when one of John's sisters played we would notice emus coming right up to the wire fence, close to the house, enraptured by the music. To me this seemed quite miraculous. As for other birds, we would hear the kookaburras who would start with first a loud gurgling in their throats and then erupt into a laugh-like raucous call. Often we would startle a flock of white cockatoos while riding through the bush and they would launch into the air filling the sky like a white cloud—a sight to see! Fascinating to me were the giant lizards we often saw that looked like they belonged to prehistoric times and the sleek yellow-brown iguanas totaling often six feet in length with their tails. Of other animals, we heard more than we saw, like the wild yelping songs of packs of dingoes, or calls of other night creatures.

One evening after dinner, it was nearly dark, with light reflecting off the verandah, when we heard a frog's pitiful noises sounding in great distress. John and I rushed off the veranda, barefoot, to see what the problem was. A snake had taken the unfortunate frog and was dragging it out of the bushes. John grabbed a stick and started to poke the snake causing it to let go of the frog and make a dash for our unprotected bare legs. We ran like hell back up the stairs of the veranda, because those snakes—it was either a brown or a death adder—were deadly poisonous.

The food at Spion Kop was beef and more beef. A steer would be shot periodically and quickly skinned. The meat was cut into large sections right there on the ground, and most of it salted down to preserve it, then shared with the neighbors who had driven for miles for the event. Since there was no refrigeration it was necessary to swap meat quickly between stations after a kill.

A letter reached me in 2010 from Auchenflower, Brisbane. It was from Irene O'Sullivan, none other than John Golden's piano playing sister of my summer days in the outback some seventy years before. Only eighteen months older than we were, she remembered me fondly when friends of mine discovered and contacted her in Australia. The sad news in the letter was that John had contracted an allergy to cattle and had to sell Spion Kop in 1975. Soon thereafter his wife and family left him and it was a low blow for me to learn he had died at the early age of forty-seven. This explained why he had not answered my correspondence over the years.

John's grandfather and brothers had pioneered the area since the early nineteenth century and owned other cattle stations in the vicinity of Yuleba. One of these owned by his uncle, called Bundi, was described in an article included by Irene in her letter. The following is an edited selection by its unknown writer, a woman only listed as "A Brisbane Reader." [2] Her experience, from 1913, very closely mirrors my life at Spion Kop in the 1940's and shows how little over the first part of the last century in that vast country really changed.

BY TRAIN AND BUGGY TO 'BUNDI' STATION, IN 1913

A boarder at the Brisbane Grammar School invited me to her station home, 'Bundi', for the Christmas holidays. At last the day arrived and we set off in the Western Mail for Yuleba. I was a town girl and this was my first journey to the outback. How I remember that journey by train over the Great Dividing Range, the train twisting and turning, and the engine pulling manfully. It was grand.

John Golden with friend Melva at Surfers Paradise, circa 1946.
PHOTO: CHARLES PATERSON.

When we got to Toowoomba it was raining hard. All through
the night we traveled over the Darling Downs and at 2 a.m. had
a beaut hot pie at Chinchilla. We arrived at Yuleba at 5.30 a.m.
and it was raining in torrents. The hotelkeeper came to meet us
and said he had a message from 'Bundi' that all the creeks were
'bankers.' We were to stay at the hotel till they could get in for us.

On the sixth morning, we set off after breakfast and all of Yuleba
came to see us off. One old shearer, 'half shot', followed us down
the street, waving his hat and calling out, 'it's grand to be like
this.' I waved him goodbye, I was so glad to be on my way. He
and his mates were celebrating Christmas and the wonderful
rain after a grievous drought.

A forty-five mile drive lay ahead and we passed only one
homestead all day. At eleven o'clock we were on 'Bundi', but did
not reach the homestead till six at night. I said to Julia, 'You do
live a long way from the front gate.' The creeks had very high
banks. We tore down and the impetus sent us tearing up the
other side. One hung on for dear life. It was good to get to the

journey's end and have a clean up. One of Julia's brothers was waiting for us with a change of horses. He had made a damper and some good billy tea. Julia had seven brothers, all six feet and over. I told her she had forty-two feet of brothers.

At 'Bundi' the nearest neighbor was eighteen miles away. The mailman came once a week and the rations by bullock team once every six months.

Once, I was taken mustering and given a safe place at the rear. At midday a halt was made and five or so quarts of that delectable tea was brewed to wash down the bread and bully beef.

We had a very happy Christmas and soon after, Julia and I went to visit two of her brothers who had taken up land twenty-four miles away at 'Spion Kop'. The day before we left 'Spion Kop' to return to 'Bundi' was very hot, 118 degrees, so next morning we made an early start.

While we boiled tea for lunch, we could see great black storm clouds banking up, and we hurried on. Never will I forget the fury of that storm. The lightning fairly sizzled and thunder came right on its heels. The gullies quickly became bankers and Charles let the horses out of the buckboard and we set off to walk eight miles to 'Bundi'. The rain came down in torrents and among all that timber and wet horses it was terrifying. When I was at 'Bundi' and introduced to people they would say, 'Oh, we heard about you. You are the girl who came with the rain.'

After the storm it got cold and my teeth chattered. The horses had to swim across the creek below the homestead, but we arrived safely, and, oh, the bliss of the warm kitchen and mugs of hot cocoa. The day came to say farewell, but I will never forget that holiday in the golden west, away back in my radiant youth. ■

CHAPTER FOURTEEN

When War Is Over

In 1945 when I was almost fifteen, I sent several letters to my father in New York, and they were returned. I mistakenly had been using the address of 47 West 75th Street instead of 43 West 75th Street. Upon my return from the outback on the third year, in 1946, I was looking forward to going back to school. I had passed the Junior scholarship exams that entitled me to two more years, tuition free, at our private high school Gregory Terrace. But when I came back to Graceville, a strange and unfriendly feeling emanated from the household. My foster mother's greeting was frosty. What had I done? I had a foreboding of disaster.

That evening, on my foster father's return from work, I soon found out what was wrong. He insisted I was not to return to school that week, because he had been told by my foster mother that during my absence out west the previous year, a letter I had written to my father had been returned to Brisbane, had been opened by the postman since it had no return address, read to determine its owner, and then brought to my foster mother. Mr. Paterson was told the letter contained disparaging remarks about the family and informed me I was not welcome in the household any longer, and from now on, I should start to earn my own living. I asked to see the letter, because I did not think it was all that bad—and after all, it was written more than a year before—but was told that Mrs. Paterson and their daughter Mary had burned it and that he did not see the letter either.

When confronted about the letter, to keep things straight, and to get help in clearing my name, I said Doris felt the same way and that she had also written letters from work. I suggested Mr. Paterson read the letters from my father that she had in the office of her workplace. The next morning he did just that, which caused my sister consternation, but he found nothing supporting the idea that she had written anything awful. Doris wrote about the incident to our father, explaining that my letter contained many "childish and not so nice things," and told him that his letters in reply to her complaints were at safekeeping at the Poppers.

For all the letters we have in our files, two of the most important in my life are lost forever: my mother's suicide note and this letter, destroyed by Mrs. Paterson. Not knowing what they said is a considerable omission in my personal history because they both meant for a child the unfathomable loss of home.

I was devastated at the thought of moving out of Graceville and felt an injustice had been done. My sense of fair play and confidence was shaken. I had tried valiantly to get along and felt the privacy of my correspondence with my father, a diary of my thoughts and feelings, had been violated. Perhaps I was misguided by my frustrations about our situation as adopted children when I vented to my father. I was still pretty young, after all, and the world must have seemed cruel, my emotions just always under the surface. Schanzer—no longer welcome, Paterson—no longer welcome. Who would I become?

A few days later, Mr. Paterson was going to Sydney on business, so Mrs. Paterson and Mary decided to join him, leaving Doris and me staying alone upstairs in the house. Joan, with her husband and new baby, were in their apartment off the tennis court, and we rarely saw them. Doris and I enjoyed our time together for those last two weeks I remained at the house as this affair cooled down. We made ourselves at home and cooked all our favorite food.

When the family returned from Sydney, it was time to make myself scarce. I packed up and went into the city. I found a single room at Kangaroo Point that I could afford with my meager savings. I could not return to the house or to school, however I managed to make the most of my newly found independence. I was sixteen but felt quite grown up and was determined to make it on my own. Life's paths take strange twists and turns, and one often wonders how everything might have been different, but for small things that happen.

I began a methodical existence, working for a living and eating in cheap cafés frequented by "wharfies" and other working people. I spent my Saturdays and Sundays either roller-skating or hiking with my friends. The Poppers often had Doris and me over for dinner; I managed well with corn flakes in the morning and making my own sandwiches for lunch. Saturday nights were reserved to go dancing so my social life would not be neglected. Although I was lonely at times, it made me grow up and strengthen my resolve to reunite our real family.

I kept my departure from Graceville from my father for over a year. It was Felix Popper, acting as our second adoptive parent, who wrote to him to tell him about it soon after it happened. This set off another firestorm of letters between him and my father to strategize about the best way to get us to America.

On July 4, 1946, he wrote to Mr. Popper, "Doris was forced by Mr. Paterson to show her private correspondence with me to Mr. Paterson. I was more than astonished about this fact. On the other hand, the idea of Mrs. Paterson to destroy a letter that didn't belong to her and to speak about this letter after [a year] on such an occasion proves only one thing: she wants to get rid of the children by any means and as quick as possible. Furthermore, Mr. Paterson...[by allowing the interruption of Charlie's] education proves that he has not the intention [to give him] any responsible position in his enterprises. It would have been only in his personal interest to have a highly educated man on his side. I see therefore no more chances for Charlie in this surrounding and I ask you to tell me frankly if my conclusions are right."

The overall tone of my father's exchanges with Mr. Popper suggests that he continued to be upset and wanted Mr. Popper to step in. Mr. Popper, on the other hand, was reasoned, calm, and emphasized that we were not in any danger, and in fact, according to Doris, things had improved.

My father considered with Mr. Popper our second option for reuniting, whereby my father would come to Australia. But at the time, the Australian government did not have a definite immigration policy and had not been granting any landing permits, except in one case when, according to Mr. Popper, two thousand permits for relatives of Jewish displaced persons were issued. Mr. Popper indicated this was quite a charitable gesture on the part of the Australian government, and then on the next line, a shocking revelation. Except for the Poppers in Australia and Mrs. Popper's brother who had immigrated into Australia on one of the two thousand permits, their whole family in Europe had perished in concentration camps.

Mr. Popper only included this single brief line, and then continued his letter, listing the difficulties my father might have upon immigration to Australia. His final strong advice for my father was not to contact Mr.

Paterson until my father was in possession of the relevant immigration papers either way. My father heeded this caution well, which explains the relatively sparse communication between him and Mr. Paterson.

Doris remained with the family despite the fact it was still a dysfunctional household. It was clear Doris would never be an equal to Mrs. Paterson's child. Mary thought herself a painter, so when Doris wanted to go to art school, it was refused on the contention that two artists in the household was too many. Mrs. Paterson insisted Doris continue secretarial studies. At the time she was working as a secretary and seamstress for a skirt manufacturer called River Frocks to earn her keep. And there was still the central conflict—Doris had written in one of her letters to our father that she was not comfortable anymore in a household where her brother was not welcome. On December 7, 1946 she wrote she had the chance to go to Sydney to work with a Mr. Evans to help his dress designer and cutter, "I showed [him my] drawings and he appeared to like them, because he offered me a job," but the expenses to move would be steep, and Mr. Paterson discouraged her, offering a job with his company instead. Doris continued, "I would not like to do something [Mr. Paterson] would not approve of, so I will probably end up doing office work again, after all these wonderful dreams of becoming a first rate designer and cutter." But with determination she concluded, "Someday I will do what I have always wanted to and what looked [to be] almost in my grasp."

In defense of my foster father, he displayed concern for my sister and me, and a conscience about my departure from the house. He gave me a job, for one. Perhaps he disbelieved the severity of "the letter" and used his own judgment.

After I left Graceville, I started to work full-time for him on many different projects. I was constantly shifting from odd jobs to the Mayne Spark Plug factory. Mr. Popper's opinion of this work as preparation for my future: a complete waste of time. Then Dad, as I now called him, offered to hire me for a more serious position at his Northern Plywoods mill at Bungalow in Cairns. He was leaving for Cairns in three days, but I hesitated to leave all my friends in Brisbane at such short notice and be displaced still one more time. The opportunity did not present itself again.

Instead, I began learning the building trade using my own hands. Dad started to buy real estate properties, one of these nearby, in hilly

St. Lucia where he decided to build a house for his daughter Joan, her new husband, John Connolly, and their baby daughter Elizabeth. Dad thought I could learn carpentry and with a carpenter crew of two we began building their house. I was glad to be included in this work. I rode my bike to the job and was hired on as an apprentice carpenter. One of my responsibilities was to "boil the billy" for morning tea. Tea was expected on every job site and consisted of building a small fire in the yard and boiling water over it in a can hung on a wire between two sticks. I would throw in a handful of tea leaves, and we would have our morning break with tea that was black and powerful.

A year later would find me at our favorite resort, Surfers Paradise, where Dad bought a piece of land near the beach. There I helped build another house for the Paterson family. I was happy to be back at the beach and learning a lot more about house construction from the ground up to the finish. We lived on the site, which had been our holiday house for many years, in a caravan Mr. Paterson had custom built at his factory.

The construction of the house went well. When the family was expected to arrive at the new Surfers house for vacation, I transferred back to Graceville to avoid any family conflicts. Dad needed my help in Brisbane, and so I returned to work in the Mayne spark plug factory, where Dad was building an additional new factory across the street in which he planned to build furniture.

My father became an American citizen on September 15, 1946. On November 2, 1946, my father wrote to Mr. Paterson that he would finally be able to offer us the possibility of a new life with him in the United States. "So the time has come now to reconsider the entire question of the children's future." Mr. Paterson was in the opinion of Mr. Popper and had suggested to my father for years that he consider immigrating to Australia. But my father felt strongly about his new country. "I appreciate your reasons for suggesting that the children remain in Australia, the country [that] offered them shelter, when such shelter was of vital importance for them.... [But] I feel greatly indebted to the United States as my new homeland, in which I found refuge and in which I have made a relatively happy readjustment." The word "homeland" is striking to me here, as it recalls a concept available in the German language only, *Heimat,* to describe all that we had lost and the security that for generations his ancestors strived

My adopted magpie, who fell out of a nest and broke his wing, 1947.

to establish in Vienna. Clearly he had irrevocably transferred his allegiances and thought we should as well.

Mr. Paterson wrote back on his factory stationery on December 12, 1946, one of the only letters I have from him. This document, which surprised me greatly when I found it, illustrates a concern for us he never expressed directly to us in words. I don't believe he wrote regular progress reports during the war or had much other communication with my father about us. His formality belies the type of business relationship he seems to have had with my father, and it is clear they did not write to each other often.

"Dear Mr. Schanzer, I must apologize for not replying to your letter relative to Doris and Charlie going to America, but I have been away from Brisbane most of the time for the last two months.... [I] would offer no objection to Doris and Charlie proceeding to America as soon as possible.... I might add that the children would prefer to stay in Australia if you could come to this country, and it seems to me that they would be sacrificing a good deal in leaving here for the United States where they would have to start life afresh after becoming used to conditions [here]."

My father's age—57 years old—was also a consideration, wrote Mr. Paterson. "Furthermore in view of your getting on in years ... it would be better for you to settle down in [Australia] where the children would be in a better position to look after you.... I do not want you to think that I am putting any obstacle in their way of going to America, my only consideration being the welfare of the children. I trust you are keeping well and that your business is prospering. With kind regards from my family and myself. Yours sincerely, Charles Paterson."

A letter soon after in March 1947 from my sister to our father provided the catalyst for him to obtain visas for our exit from the country. She wrote that I had been exiled from the Paterson house, which he already knew from Mr. Popper, but had been asked to keep this in confidence. This provided the opportunity for an indignant response in a letter to me on March 28 wherein my father requested I permit him to write to Mr. Paterson directly. "That you can't return to Graceville anymore ... is very grave and I have a right to know what happened between you and Mrs. Paterson. It is not right if this incident is not a real obstacle for your staying in his house, to put you on the street, which is really the fact.... I wonder how it happens that Mr. Paterson doesn't interfere, because by your adoption he has certain duties to perform or if he is not willing to do so, to inform me directly, that I may take steps to care for you as a father. This is my duty."

Our immigration, the operation he had been preparing—unbeknownst to us—for nearly three years was now made to be imminent. He stated firmly, asserting himself as our only true parent, "I will do everything in my power to get you and Doris as quick as possible out of the situation. Nothing else will be considered any more.... With many many kisses to you both I am, your loving Dad."

I wrote in defense of Mr. Paterson, but still my father pushed his point that an intervention by Mr. Paterson to keep me at home in Graceville should have been possible. "What I don't understand is the attitude of Mr. Paterson in this case. He has to supervise you till to your majority.... It is not so simple for a man like him to get rid of a responsibility he assumed. He could have written me that since a long time and we could have reached a decision much sooner. But it seems to me that it is working out that way to make the decision for you easier." It was not an easy decision, but Doris and I together, with confidence in our father, were ready to take the next step, to another identity, in a new land.

On July 7, 1947, my eighteenth birthday, our visas were issued by the American Consul. Mr. Paterson had applied for British passports for us, as otherwise we would have had to wait until Austrian and Czechoslovakian quota numbers for the United States were issued to us. I would have been able to travel because of my age—I had time to wait. But for my sister, born in Pilsen and issued a Czechoslovakian passport, the matter was urgent because in November she would turn twenty-one, and my father would no longer be able to apply for her as a dependent, meaning it could have been many years for her to leave Australia.

The fare for our voyage—which my father could barely afford—was offered to be paid for by Otto Pick, who insisted in a letter of July 29, 1947 that my father not pawn anything, but should rather let him know if he needed any additional funds, which he would be glad to lend. However my father, being very proud and correct, declined the assistance. He had a small amount saved, and it would be enough. It amazes me to keep reading Otto Pick's offers and his generosity. He was a very kind man, and I never so clearly understood until these letters surfaced how much he was an aide to my father during this time. On August 12, 1947, another letter from Otto Pick repeats, "I am at your disposal whenever the need arises. In any case, I do hope your children will arrive safely and in the near future."

To get our places on board a ship bound for the United States was another matter. Finding out that we had no confirmed accommodations after the ship's passenger list was chosen on August 4, my father wrote to my sister on August 11, 1947, "I hope that you will realize it will be a fight.... Only those will get on the ship who have the best connections. If you do nothing, you will not go.... I know how it is from [being in] Portugal and how I got my ship tickets. There was the same fight, perhaps worse, because everybody was in danger."

The same day my father petitioned a lawyer in New York named Abraham Felt to help us. An active Mason who lectured on the history of the Masons and composed poetry and Masonic hymns, Felt was also the representative of the Grand Lodge of Vienna.[1] He had already provided an affidavit for our immigration visas, but at my father's urging, Mr. Felt then wrote directly to the Matson Line at Rockefeller Plaza in New York to put in a personal plea for us to be able to depart on September 20 on the *Marine Phoenix*. This would be our only opportunity to leave before Doris' birthday, explained Mr. Felt, and if Doris could not go "it may mar her chances from coming to our country for a long time." Thanks to Mr. Felt's kind letter and his influence, our passage to America was confirmed.

My father wrote what seems to have been his last correspondence to

Mr. Paterson about us leaving, to thank him for his generosity, on July 14, 1947. "The visit you made to the American Consul was a help to them … because they received British passports and the name under which they will travel is Paterson formerly known as Schanzer. I have to thank you with all my heart for this final assistance you gave to my children. It is my wish that they will wear this name of Paterson here in the United States with your permission. This will be in remembrance that you saved all our lives during the most critical moments of our existence and for all you did for the children during their stay in Brisbane." This in fact answers another question I have had all my life and which people, including my children, have asked me. My very name is a tribute to this man whose actions saved us, though the price for him was much added internal strife with his own family.

I have a lot of respect for my foster father. Even though he was a man of few words, he was fair, and I had a genuine affection for him. He was always very considerate of me; he never raised his voice at me, or put me down, even when we had our conversation in the house before I was asked to leave. He was, however, always very involved in his business and never talked much to any of us at home as I remembered. This emotional distance did not indicate what kind of man he was.

I was never notified when my foster father died on March 5, 1968, though I learned recently from his granddaughter Katy that they tried to contact us. It saddened me to find out about it in the early 1970's through good friends of mine, Nancy and Bob Oden, who went to Australia and tried to trace the family for me. From them I learned that soon after Doris and I left Australia, my foster father had divorced Mrs. Paterson and married his young secretary, Joyce Baker. The new Mrs. Paterson was reluctant to speak with our friends. We assume the reason she was hesitant was a fear that Mr. Paterson's adopted children would try to make a claim on his estate, which was then in a protracted probate.

There was a son from this second marriage, named John Charles Paterson. In 2010, he was fifty years old and a marine biologist. I exchanged a couple of emails with him, until mine stopped going through. Reportedly he still lives on Magnetic Island, where Captain James Cook was thrown off course by mysterious effects in the late 1770's. In our emails he told me he was following his father's great love of the ocean and marine life, of which I never knew.[2]

Doris and me upon our departure with Eileen, Mary, and Charles Paterson, Brisbane, September 1947.

On September 19, 1947, the Paterson family and many friends gathered at the rail station in Brisbane to give us an emotionally charged farewell. It was friendly in the end. We chose to not speak about anything in the past that had caused ill will. We left gratefully, but also grateful to them.

Mr. Popper's final advice to my father on September 22, 1947 after seeing us off: "You have to face the fact, if you like it or not, that those two children, though your children by birth, are practically unacquainted with the conception of having a father. They have grown into independent human beings unaccustomed to accepting any restricting authority. You will have a job on your hands that will require a very careful handling, any amount of patience, and psychological insight."

He continued with observations about our character: Doris had a lot of common sense but was an emotional teenager who could sometimes "fly off the handle." She had an obvious artistic talent that could further be developed. His assessment of me: "very sensible" and "honest, full of the best intentions." He thought being on my own had actually done me a lot of good. He wrote, "I'm sorry Mrs. P. kicked him out so late." ▪

CHAPTER FIFTEEN

To America

Doris and I set sail on the *Marine Phoenix* on September 25, 1947 to the United States. Spring stayed behind us in Sydney, and three weeks later we would arrive in America where it was already autumn.

The first day on board the ship nearly everybody was sick. I have to admit that my sister and I were among them, but only for a day and a half, after which we were accustomed to the ship's continual roll. The second day was much better because people began to make friends, and that night we had a dance on board. To dance with the ship tossing under your feet is an art all its own, but very soon we had mastered a method to keep our balance.

A party of six of us went ashore at Auckland, New Zealand and had a look around the city. When we got on solid ground we found ourselves still with sea legs, swaying with the motion of the boat, the ground seemingly rolling underfoot. Sometimes it seemed to become so rough that we had to hold onto something to prevent from toppling over. An onlooker would have thought us slightly drunk.

After we left New Zealand, the weather cleared up, and the sea became much calmer. Four or five days later, we arrived in Suva in the Fiji Islands where my sister, friends, and I again went ashore, and as it was very hot, went straight to the swimming pool. In a diary I wrote an impression of the policemen directing traffic that I also remember because I took a picture. "The policemen looked very *drôle* [peculiar]. They were barefooted and wore dark blue tunics [with gold buttons], a white skirt with a zig-zag bottom which was held up by a red sash and belt." We were last to get back to the ship that day, and just after we boarded, they pulled up the gangplank.

From Fiji we went by many other tropical islands on our way to Pago-Pago in American Samoa. Soon we passed the International Dateline and consequently had two Fridays—October 3, 1947 West and October

Policemen in Suva, Fiji, October 1947. PHOTO: CHARLES PATERSON.

3, 1947 East. All through the trip we advanced our watches half an hour every second day.

Pago-Pago was the most beautiful place we had yet seen, with the hills right up against the natural harbor. The island was covered with palm trees and tropical vegetation. We took a car trip all around the island with a local interpreter, admiring the native huts built out of timber and straw. I bought a shell necklace at the marketplace that twenty-some years later I gave to my wife Fonda. On the other side of the island we went for another swim. The water there was the most extraordinary light blue we had ever seen and very salty. We stayed nearly for an hour diving and swimming.

The goodbye band on the wharf saw us off. Pago-Pago was our last stop before San Francisco. The next twelve days were long, but certainly not trying or boring. On a floating hotel, with four hundred and eighty passengers, there was plenty to do. Three times a week movies were screened, the second session of which finished at 11 p.m. when a late dinner was served. Our breakfast was not until 9 a.m., so we were always able to sleep in. We used to have horse races for an hour and a half after tea with six of those wooden creatures. They were advanced by throwing six dice, each representing a number on a horse. After the races, we danced until midnight. On our ship, we had a lot of young war brides who were

Upon our arrival in San Francisco, October 1947.

joining their American husbands (MacArthur's headquarters had been in Brisbane), so as I loved to dance, it was great—I always had a partner. The people who were not tired by then used to sit around the piano and have a sing-along for a few hours or stroll around the decks in couples, in the moonlight. On the third to the last night our friends got together for a real party, with beer and Coca-Cola. We finally went to bed at 3:30 a.m., when the seas got rough, with beer and cola bottles flying around.

The food, I remember, was excellent. I saved the menus, they impressed me so much. Two share the same dates in October—when we had two dinners, on either side of the dateline. For the rest of my life I have loved ships and traveling on the water, but the foods are often too rich these days on luxury cruises, so I have to be more careful now to avoid sodium not to stress my heart. My sister adored cruises too,[1] and she went by ship on many trips later in life—including to the Galapagos Islands, Alaska, and the Franz-Joseph-Land archipelago, frozen in the Arctic Ocean.

After the roughest two days at sea, on the 14th of October at around 5 a.m., we dropped anchor in the San Francisco Bay. We docked beside the Bay Bridge, which was very famous then at an astonishing span of eight and a quarter miles, and then the boat started to hum with activity. The immigration officials came aboard, but we had to wait until another ship with nine hundred passengers from Shanghai was cleared. Consequently we did not get off the ship until the afternoon and then spent the rest of it in customs clearance.

We were met by Ricky Sommers, the daughter of my mother's friend, Hilde Mellion. Ricky was my age and brought us to meet her father, Curt Sommers and his wife, who had offered my father to have us stay with them until we could leave for New York. Curt was a waiter. It had become a fact of life that so many highly educated and sophisticated people, some of whom had been executives in Europe, were thrown into the New World by the war and were now in simple jobs. My father started in a chocolate, marshmallow, and candy factory, the result of which was he could never eat hard candies again.

The next day we took a thirty-mile Greyhound bus tour around beautiful San Francisco, and three days later we were in Los Angeles to see the film city. I recall a performance with Jimmy Durante at the Hollywood Bowl and all the Hollywood stars' footprints in the concrete outside Grauman's Chinese Theater. I was surprised to find on a backstage tour of the movie studios that the houses constructed for Westerns and mystery thrillers were actually only fronts and made out of timber, plastic, and cardboard. Such different places, and a person could move from one to another in just paces. I wrote back to friends, "One minute we were in a Brooklyn street, with cobblestones and all of a sudden there in front of us was the most vivid snow scene." Later that day my sister and I visited the beaches of Santa Monica, which though nice, could not compare to the breathtaking Queensland South Coast we had just left.

From California, Doris and I took the streamlined *Santa Fe* train bound for New York via Chicago. I wrote back to an Australian friend how impressed I was with it, being nothing like the trains rattling through the Outback on much narrower rails, or the European trains on which we had traveled during the most anxious days of our childhood. These American trains didn't have any compartments, but instead had rows of two seats separated by an aisle down the middle. The seats could be individually adjusted in four positions, and had built-in ashtrays. Under each seat was an adjustable extension padded with foam rubber just as the seats were and which were covered in the same wine-colored cloth. I remember how luxurious it felt to stretch out my legs completely. It was possible to recline fully and sleep nearly as comfortably as in a bed.

The carriages also had soft wall-to-wall carpet and were air-conditioned, which seemed to purify the air. They were almost soundproof, so that there were no outside noises as we floated over the American landscape. An individual light at each seat allowed me to read until lights out at 10 p.m., and after that point, if I wanted to stay up, I went to the lounge car where there was a radio at the bar. Just before bedtime, attendants came by to give out pillows for the night at twenty-five cents each. The seats were so soft, and the train ran so smooth and silent, that at seventy or eighty miles an hour it was hard to determine whether or not we were even moving.

In the morning at 7 a.m., waiters brought morning coffee to the seats. Attendants came through the coaches every half hour or so with fruit, sandwiches, soft drinks and milk, ice cream, chewing gum, cigarettes, and reading material. The dining car also served three meals a day. America was a land of plenty, and I was very impressed.

Our fare—one of the cheapest—with all the above comforts was

With the Santa Fe *train bound for New York via Chicago,*
October 1947. PHOTO: DORIS SCHANZER PATERSON.

Doris and I in Central Park, 1948. PHOTO: STEVE SCHANZER.

$52.00 each for the complete trip from San Francisco to New York. Of course there were much more expensive trains with berths upstairs and a seating area downstairs, and also special luxury trains, whose coaches were like living rooms. The latest trains at that time even had glass roofs and telephones.

In Chicago Doris and I missed our connecting train. I was again the document and money keeper, and I carried what I thought then to be a considerable sum. We wanted to see the city, but I certainly did not feel like walking around dark streets. I had seen too many gangster movies featuring Chicago, and I was not about to give up all the "chicken money" I earned gathering eggs on the Patersons' converted tennis court. So we went to a movie instead—perhaps according to my tastes, something with a John Dillinger character.

We arrived in New York the next evening. Our trip in total took three and a half days, not including breaks at Los Angeles and Chicago. Because the train was late, we missed our father as he had gone to a different station. We phoned his landlord and then took a taxi to his address. It seemed an echo of our adventure in Paris, when we were only kids—in a new city, in a taxi, but now assured that when we were delivered to the address, it would really be ours where we could stay.

My father's one bedroom apartment was in an old brownstone on West 75th St., between Columbus and Central Park West. When we got there he was waiting for us on the street. It was an emotional meeting. We had been separated for eight years. To describe in words the tenor of that impactful moment is difficult for me. I remember its poignancy but no specific details other than the first embrace. He showered us with the affection he had been denied as a parent for so long, and we stayed up very late in the night talking. The first time we had heard our father speaking English to us was by phone from San Francisco, and we had been charmed by his accent. It must have felt strange for him to hear us speaking this new foreign language also, and with the Australian intonation, as we told him about our trip. The whole reunion was wonderful and bizarre. We listened to each other's stories for hours with the fascination that deep feelings bring.

October 20, 1948 | Western Union Telegram

To Patersons: Arrived well and safe after wonderful journey and happy reunion thanks to your help during most critical time. Love, Doris, Charlie.

With our arrival in the U.S., Doris and I were very happy to be together again with our father. But despite the joy of reunion, we both felt heavy at heart leaving behind our Australian experiences and the friendships we had formed. I tried not to think of our difficult times with the Paterson family and instead reflected on their hospitality.

My father had not changed a bit and did not seem to look a year older than when we last saw him. All that time we were apart just seemed to slip away. In those long war years my father had become an American. He changed his name to "Steven B. Shanzer" to Anglicize it. I have often thought about the fact that the three of us lost our names while we were apart. I had decided, as our father suggested, that I would indeed keep my last name as "Paterson." Under this moniker I had transformed from boy to man, not any longer "European" or "foreigner," but someone from the young country of Australia, and now America, who could see a bright future ahead.

New York   November 16, 1947

Dear Mr. & Mrs. Paterson,

The children are here and fine and you can imagine how happy
I am to have them with me. You may read the report of their
journey, which is enclosed. Their trip was a very happy one and
they saw a lot.

Now that a few weeks have passed, I can only say that the education you gave them for all these years was really excellent and I
couldn't expect it to be better. Everyone who meets them admires
them and tells me that they are very nice well-mannered children.

I thank you once more very much for all you have done for us
during all the years my children were with you, and I hope to have
the opportunity of seeing you someday to thank you personally.

With my best regards to you and your family.

Very sincerely yours,

Steven B. Shanzer

Even though my father never did meet the Patersons in person, and
nor did my sister and I see Charles and Eileen again, I am happy to say
that we have stayed in touch with their family. Joan's children Michael
Connolly and Katy Common came to Aspen to live and work at The
Boomerang, my ski lodge, in the 1980's, and Katy's children Amy and
Christopher and her husband Tod have been close to us ever since. In
fact, the Patersons' great-granddaughter Amy came to visit us in Aspen
just in December 2011. She is a lovely young woman in her mid-twenties starting her own business in graphic design. As for Katy and Tod,
they came to be with us in Hawaii in 2007 at our younger daughter
Jenny's wedding to a New Zealander, Evan Rose.

I sent these chapters on Australia to Katy in January 2012 for her
review, with a little forewarning. I hoped it wouldn't pain her to read these
stories of her grandmother Mrs. Paterson. We had never talked about that
past. Katy's response to me was beautifully considerate, full of emotion,
empathetic, and forthright. With her permission I include a few details

here so that the character of Mrs. Paterson, of whom I only saw one side, can be given posthumous justice. She was an important figure for Katy, her sister and brother, and her cousins. They called her "Nor Nor," and she was a stabilizing force who shepherded her family through cycles of trauma and abusive treatment of which I had little knowledge.

Eileen Paterson was born in 1894, one of three children, to Irish immigrants. Her father abandoned the family when she was ten years old to marry the housekeeper. Throughout her life, Eileen was a talented seamstress and quilter. When her second daughter Mary's third child was born, and Mary was ill, Eileen moved in with the family and looked after everyone. She transformed after her divorce from Mr. Paterson, who was considered by the rest of his family to be distant, rather self-serving, and uncompromising. No longer in that marriage Eileen recuperated her sense of self that was lost in her silent rage against him. "Nor Nor" is remembered as a warm and caring grandmother, who made ragdolls with red hearts sewn on them that said, "I Love You" for all her granddaughters. Katy's mother Joan relied on "Nor Nor" when Joan was virtually a single mother raising three children, as her husband was an alcoholic. "Nornie" would look after the children on weekends and was "a lifeline of support" for all six grandchildren.

Joan came once to Aspen to visit us and was happy at my success and my ski lodge. Mary is still living north of Brisbane with her two sons, while her daughter Jane Wyatt Holmes is married with three children. Jane's son, Paul, now a solicitor in Brisbane providing legal aid for the economically disadvantaged, came to work for me for a short time in Aspen in 2002.

Charles Raff Paterson's obituary written by his son-in-law, John Wyatt, was attached to Katy's email. I was surprised to see that among his many accomplishments is an entire paragraph devoted to our adoption. "During the early stages of the Second World War [Charles Raff Paterson] and his then wife Eileen already having two daughters, adopted two Austrian Jewish children, Karl and Doris Schanzer, to enable these children to escape from Nazi-occupied Europe and come to Australia. [The children] rejoined their father Mr. Schanzer in the United States of America shortly after the end of the war." Charles Raff Paterson died in 1968 at the age of seventy-three. I wish I had seen him again.

Darby the dog, me, Doris, Eileen, and Mary Paterson,
Surfers Paradise, 1941.

Eileen passed away in 1976. She was eighty-three years old. I wrote
to Katy that I also wish now I had returned to Australia in my late
twenties or early thirties and met her grandmother Eileen, "Nor Nor,"
again. She was really "nor this nor that" as I remembered her, and I
was unaware of the larger circumstances she faced. I vividly recall my
sister and I wanted so desperately to be part of the family. When we left
Australia I was eighteen, and I had chosen independence over attempts
to fit in. ▪

CHAPTER SIXTEEN

Finding Home

I went back to high school in the winter of 1947, starting shortly after my arrival in New York, in order to complete the education I missed for two years in Australia while I was on my own. I swam on the swim team, as I had before, and graduated in less than a year in spring of 1948 from Textile High. I continued my education the following year as an engineering student at New York City College. But soon, I became bored and restless and, wanting to earn some money, I left school for the second time and had a short stint on Wall Street—not as a banker or clerk, however. I went back to what I knew best and joined a crew as a carpenter. We built partitions in a financial office, which was my introduction to "American high finance."

Next, I worked on a large skyscraper apartment building just off Fifth Avenue as a field engineer. Our group of three was responsible for the

Me working on a survey crew in the Bronx as a field engineer for Cauldwell-Wingate, 1950.

layouts of each apartment and the framing of the concrete floors for the next story. This was accomplished by readings with a surveyor's instrument. We had to check carefully and often walked along on the edge of the building in the narrow forms for the next floor, with a twenty-story drop on one side and the cold concrete below on the other. In the dead of winter it was sometimes a challenge with the freezing wind blowing through the open buildings. Later, we worked on a huge housing project in the Bronx consisting of a cluster of more than a dozen multi-storied buildings. Finally, my job ended after our company, as general contractor, was struck by a carpenters' and masons' strike. At first we crossed the picket lines, branded as "scabs," but with those taunts and then the seriousness of the strike as it evolved, we decided not to cross over anymore. However, when the strike was finally over, so was our employment.

New York had a record snowfall in the winter of 1947-48, and it was then that my sister and I took up skiing again. We practiced with my father in Central Park on a small hill. Soon we had people joining us to learn to ski from around the neighborhood of Central Park. Before long, every Sunday we began to give ski lessons on the little hill just off Fifth Avenue. Soon the group became too large and proficient, so we moved to a bigger hill in Van Cortlandt Park, just a subway ride away in the northwest part of the Bronx. Before we knew it, we were teaching skiing and leading bus trips on weekends out of New York for the American Youth Hostels.

Doris and her future husband, Herb Schneider, got to know each other on these many ski trips.[1] She was working as a dressmaker/designer at the time, and Herb was an Austrian-born, MIT-trained electrical engineer. His family back in Austria distantly knew ours, living just forty miles south of Vienna in Wiener Neustadt, where his father Dr. Sigfried Schneider, an M.D., had a dental practice. Just before the war, Herb's maternal uncle, Pali Tolnai, funded and arranged for him to be a boarding student at Robert College, an American boarding school in Istanbul. He finally was able to emigrate to join his family in the summer of 1940. He got to the U.S. via a long and hungry trip on the Trans-Siberian Railroad, followed by a boat from Japan. Later, as a member of the U.S. Army Corps of Engineers, Herb was in Tokyo after the Japanese surrender, and he learned skiing on his free time, traveling to the snows in northern Japan.

My father giving ski tips to a friend, Doris, and me in New York's
Van Cortlandt Park, winter of 1950.

All of us were part of a skiing diaspora and got out of New York at every opportunity. New England was good skiing on weekends. However, the icy ski slopes were sometimes discouraging, and when in early February of 1949 the snow began to melt on one of our trips to New Hampshire, we began to look at a map to see where there would be better skiing. My father pointed at Denver and said that this was the gateway to the Rockies, where the skiing would be more like it was in the Alps. As I was free of any job and school responsibilities at the time, it seemed a perfect chance to travel, so I gathered all my ski gear and, with a bus ticket and $35 to my name, I took off for the mythical West.

While making bus connections at the Greyhound station in Albany, I spotted another skier on the other side of the waiting room with all his gear and began a conversation with him. It was raining heavily, and we both looked and felt equally out of place with our forlorn equipment. His name was Chuck Colletti. He was a big fellow from the Bronx of Italian parents who had just quit college, had been a carpenter as well, and was headed for New Hampshire. On learning that the snow was melting in New England and I was headed for Denver and better skiing, Chuck changed his ticket in a matter of minutes and joined me on my Western adventure.

We headed toward the snow, and flurries of postcards were sent back to my father and sister. We traveled to Buffalo, stopped to see Niagara Falls, then over the next three days made stops in Cleveland, Chicago, St. Louis, journeyed across the plains of Kansas, and finally arrived in Denver, Colorado. The date was February 25, 1949.

Even though we only got into Denver at 6 a.m., Chuck and I immediately went to all the job agencies in town. They had nothing at ski resorts. But not dismayed in the least, I wrote to my father, "The weather is beautiful and so is the town. We watched the sun play on the mountains as it rose this morning. We are now on a train to the mountains—to Winter Park—70 miles west of Denver. From there we will go to half a dozen ski resorts personally."

We stayed in Winter Park that weekend for seventy-five cents a night. I only took my backpack and skis along, leaving my suitcase at the Greyhound station. I wrote to my father and sister, "I expect to stay here for the weekend and if unsuccessful go back to Denver where I can get a job easily. I am feeling wonderful and still have plenty of money (sixteen dollars to be exact). Everything is perfect."

My father's letter of March 19, 1949 shows his excitement and ongoing encouragement of me, and the beginning of many business schemes he would dream up over the next years for skiers that could involve us. This new industry was booming in the sport's still vastly uncharted Colorado territory. He wrote, "I am very happy that you are making a survey of the country there and I will tell you now what ideas I have concerning these mountains ... where there seems to be nothing for the comfort of the skiers.... Ski lifts are unpractical and old fashioned, because the distances from the valley seem to be too great and also the capital investment.... The only solution for the Rockies would be helicopters, which could lift a big number of skiers from the valley and deposit them on the mountaintop they choose for the day." This was the very idea that became popular with the high alpine heli-skiing in the Canadian Rockies, years later. He continued, "Moreover these helicopters would have a summer use in spraying insecticides, so that there would be a year round use for the investment. What I ask you now to study in Denver are the possibilities of such an enterprise.... If somebody should be interested, he needs experienced skiers to work all the plans out. And for that he needs us. Please write me how you like this idea."

Concerned about my money situation, my father wanted to wire me more cash on the spot. Doris knew me better and was of the opinion that he wait for my call, should this be necessary. He finished his letter with sweet words and a conspiratorial tone, "Doris and I are missing you very much. But we both agree that it was very necessary you went ahead to explore the situation. Hilde and Fred [Mellion] are sending you their best regards. He told me that I am a bad father to allow you to go away instead of inducing you to go right away to college and to study to be a contractor. He is disappointed. I did not tell them about our new ideas. Love, Pop."

Over the next weeks, I wrote almost daily reports back to New York on postcards and complemented those with descriptive letters of the skiing out West.

Denver   March 2, 1949

Dear Doris and Pop,

I hope you received all my cards. The reason why I am writing so
often is that every day something new happens and one day seems
like a week. We spent all day Saturday going around to lodges and
places in the vicinity, but although people were nice, they could
not help us and had no work. So on Sunday morning we tried
again and hitchhiked in an open utility to Berthoud Pass—some
12 miles away—at 10 degrees above zero. Well, it sure was cold, but
a beautiful morning and the scenery on that ride absolutely unsur-
passable with the road winding through the mountain. Anyway,
we didn't get a job there either and hitched back so that we could
spend the day skiing at Winter Park, which was superb. It was
as high as Mt. Cranmore [in New Hampshire] and the snow was
powder on a 45" base. They had two T-bar lifts, which took you to
the very top. It took nearly half an hour. It was a difficult and challenging decent and I took quite a lot of punishment until I gained
enough confidence to grit my teeth and not be afraid to gain a lot
of speed, continually checking right and left through hundreds
of small hillocks [moguls]. Anyway I am still in one piece and
went to the top about seven or eight times. We checked our skis
there—as we intended to go back on weekends at least and caught

the Sunday night ski train back to Denver, after a day of the best skiing I had yet.

I hope you are fine. Everything is dandy with me.

Love,

Charlie

The next few nights Chuck and I stayed at the Denver YMCA and looked for jobs. I was energized and at no time discouraged, probably because people were so nice. Finally I asked for a carpentry job at the state employment agency. All they had was for the Denver Rio Grande railroad—bridge building at $1.20 an hour for six days a week. I dragged Chuck, now weary, to the rail yard office of the B&B (Bridge-Building) section, and we secured our places. I helped Chuck to secure a job, as contrary to me he had no tools with him. We had to do a complete physical check up and spent a day filling out a stack of papers, which I reported to my father was almost worse than leaving Australia. I had a grand total of $3 left when I started; Chuck, $13.

One beautiful sunny Sunday, late that winter of 1949, my fate took a significant turn. I was skiing on the upper wall of Arapahoe Basin with Chuck at over twelve thousand feet altitude. He and I had stopped for a breather before plunging into the snow bowl and were chatting away, when I spotted a green aspen leaf patch on the yellow jacket of a nearby attractive blonde. Naturally gravitating to her, I skied over and asked her what the green leaf was. She replied that this patch came from a fabulous new resort called Aspen. Chuck and I had never heard of it. Curious to discover new skiing territory, we managed to hitchhike there the following weekend, which at the time was a good six-hour drive from Denver over the twisty two-lane Route 6.

The North American Ski Championships were being held that weekend, and the town was packed with racers and onlookers. Chuck and I applied for our free ski tickets upon being hired on as packers for the racecourse. The first ride up Ruthie's Run was an eye opener—at this time the single lift was touted to be the world's longest. At the top, a patroller handed me a shovel and told me to follow him as he barreled down the slope.

Chuck Colletti on Aspen Mountain, 1949. PHOTO: CHARLES PATERSON.

As a skier most recently accustomed to the ice and short slopes of the Northeast, I was not prepared for the amount of snow and moguls on Aspen Mountain, and it felt like survival skiing at best. I was scared, but managed to hang on. After working the course, we became gate-keepers for the race, which was a great thrill. One of the racers was Toni Matt, who was a legend for schussing the nearly sixty-degree pitch of Tuckerman's Ravine on Mount Washington in New Hampshire and surviving. The story goes that he caught an edge on one of his first turns at the top and, recovering, had little choice but to go for broke.[2] Toni was U.S. downhill champion in 1934 and 1941. During the race in Aspen, I was a bit too excited when Toni Matt whizzed by my gate. When I stepped slightly forward to snap a photo, I recall him swearing at me as he came by. This was embarrassing, and I hoped nobody noticed.

On previous ski trips in Colorado, unplanned as they were, Chuck and I never encountered problems finding inexpensive places to stay. However, Aspen at that time was different, and we seemed destined to freeze to death on our first night, as the town was jammed full for the races. Accommodations were very limited in Aspen in those days, and during big events like this one, none were available. About midnight, we were still wandering around town, knocking on doors.

We encountered a little old Victorian house on the east side with a glass entry door covered with a frilly white lace curtain. It was memorable because the door was opened by a lovely young woman who was stark naked except for her long blonde hair to her waist. We were understandably startled, but managed to ask if we could bunk down in her house. There were people in sleeping bags all over the small living room. She apologized as she shaded her eyes, saying that she had gotten a bit snow-blind, but that there really was no more room on the floors.

Disappointed, we wandered back to town and found an open building. It turned out to be the Elks Building. The heat was on, which helped our half-frozen condition, and on the second floor, as we walked through the dusty hallways, we found unlocked offices and a room at the end of the hallway containing a billiard table. It had a corner window with a built-in bench. What luck! Chuck stretched out his six-foot-plus body on the billiard table, and I retired to the cushioned wood bench, pulled my leather jacket over me, and slept undisturbed.

After spending another day on the mountain and working the snow packing crew, I was sold on Aspen. We managed to find a couch for $2.50 in the living room of the SkiMor Lodge situated at the foot of the jumping hill. That afternoon after skiing, I decided to look for a job so that I could stay longer in town. I was an impressionable nineteen-year-old and my experience with skiing Aspen Mountain and the encounter with the naked young woman certainly had an influence on me wanting to stay around. I thought this was heaven! At the Hotel Jerome, I was interviewed by a Mrs. Edith Seibert, a kind lady and as it turned out, the mother of a famed young racer and then Aspen ski instructor, Pete Seibert, who would in 1958 find the location for the Colorado ski resort of Vail, which he founded and opened in December of 1962. Mrs. Seibert offered me a bellhop position at the hotel to start in a few days.

Before starting my prestigious new job, however, I had to go back to Denver to get the rest of my belongings. Chuck and I asked for rides at the Hotel Jerome, and as luck would have it, a man and his girl-friend were going back to Denver and offered us a lift. He turned out to be a State Senator, Donald P. Dunklee, and off we went in the back seat with his large St. Bernard in the center. In the old town of Dillon he bought us dinner at what became my favorite restaurant, where I would always stop while driving that stretch of Route 6. It was inexpensive, with good food, and the wood-paneled walls were adorned with memorabilia dating back to the mining days as well as trophy heads of big horn mountain sheep and elk bucks. Old Dillon later disappeared at the bottom of Dillon Reservoir in 1963. In my imagination I can see the old western town there, under water, complete with houses and stop signs.

I hitched back to Aspen a few days later to begin my new career as a Hotel Jerome bellhop and "ski bum." Chuck stayed in Denver, continued working with the railroad, and then joined me in Aspen, where he found a job as a busboy. He soon returned to New York, however, to make more money as a carpenter. I, on the other hand, was very happy in my new position in which I was able to ski five days a week. I paid $1.50 per day for my chairlift ticket instead of $4 and got all my food for half price at the cafeterias owned by the Hotel—one in town, the other at the top of the mountain. Staff housing was provided for us in bunk accommodations, first at the lodge called Roaring Fork and then in the Wheeler Opera House, where there was a wonderful hot shower— in Denver we only had a bathtub—so I could shower in the morning and then after skiing, before work. It was a sweet setup!

Aspen   March 26, 1949

Dear Doris & Pop,

There is a lot to tell you. I am getting accustomed to my new job as a bellhop. There are three of us, and we wear Tyrolean jackets (somewhat like you have at home). I like my job extremely well; it is very interesting, besides of course quite profitable.[3] You see, the hotel owns practically the whole town— not literally, of course, but besides the hotel, they also own about twenty large houses which are each a little hotel of their own, controlled from the main hotel where I work. The result is that we have to take people all over town, deliver their luggage, etc.; for this purpose the bellhops have exclusive use of a jeep.

This morning I went for my Colorado chauffeur's license test and it is now practically in my pocket—I am waiting for them to send me a Photostat copy. The test was as follows: I went to the town's hardware store [Tomkins Hardware]. There a young fellow [Hod Nicholson] handed me some twenty printed questions to answer, of which I was allowed to get four wrong. He then filled out the forms; I signed, thanked him, walked out and drove back to the hotel in the jeep. He didn't even test my driving ability.

The town is full of people (and nice girls) from all over the country and a lot from the east. It has been snowing all week up to this morning and the skiing is superb, with about six inches or more new powder (very light) on the mountain every day. Without conceit, I think I'm getting to be quite a fair and good skier now, and I even ski the French method [with parallel skis] when conditions permit. I also do quite a few jump Christies, which are done as you hit a bump, put down one pole in the snow, lift the skis up about six inches, and then turn them in mid-air. This is best on a steep hill, as you cut right and left very quickly all the way down.

This town used to be a big silver mining town, which became a ghost town for a while 'till they started this ski and summer resort business here. In my opinion, it needs a lot of development, is full of opportunities and, after the F.I.S.[4] World Ski Championships meet [in] February [next year], this is going to be THE place in the U.S. In fact, I am thinking seriously that we should settle here.

Doris, I find that there is no dressmaking shop in town. I think custom sports and dress attire might make a good show. If you could build up a little business here, I think people would even buy or order your stuff from Denver. Pop, for you there are numerous [possibilities], besides the fact that there isn't any jeweler or watchmaker in town to my knowledge. I am even thinking about the helicopter for Aspen. There is also plenty of work in the hotel business, besides the fact that this hotel is planning to build another new hotel in the vicinity. Another of the

many things I like about this town is that most of its people
are from somewhere else; the visitors, etc. make it very broad-
minded and cosmopolitan, while yet it remains a small town.

Anyway, I am sitting tight on a wonderful job. I talk to people
and meet a lot of the big shots. In fact, yesterday I was introduced to Mr. Paepcke.[5] He is the millionaire from Chicago who
owns practically the whole outfit here. He is a very nice fellow
of whom you would never suspect the power he has in this
town—just a fine bloke, as friendly and genuine as anyone.

Well, it's about time for me to get off duty now, 11 p.m.
Tomorrow, I'll be skiing again from 8:30 a.m. to 2:30 p.m. so
I think I'll toddle off to bed. Last night was my night off, so I
went to a movie and then came over here to the hotel to smoke
my pipe (I bummed some pipe tobacco off my newspaper
friend) in an easy chair and dance a little in "the blue room" to
their four-piece band.

How true are the words: "Skiing is not only just a sport—but a
way of life." This sure is the life!

Love,

Charlie

One day I was stationed in the lobby of the Hotel Jerome wearing
my Tyrolean bellhop uniform, when the film star Gary Cooper appeared
on the stairs, six-foot plus in his Stetson, carrying his suitcases. I was
in a panic as I watched him descending. That was my job! As he hit the
bottom step, I rushed over and tried to take the bags to carry through
the lobby. He would not let go, however, and we tussled for possession. Here I was, this slip of a bellhop trying to wrest two large suit-
cases from the hero of countless Westerns. It was like the standoff at
"The OK Corral." I was determined enough to win the battle, however,
and proudly carried his bags through the lobby and to his jeep parked
at the entrance. A fifty-cent tip at the time was great, but it seemed he
was not too happy about giving it. I heard stories later that he would
pay his bill at the gas station next to the Hotel Jerome by check, so they

Gary Cooper entering the Hotel Jerome, 1949.
PHOTO: CHARLES PATERSON.

would never cash it with his famous signature. Perhaps he knew this was the way to get free gas, and was a bit frugal, like me!

Soon, it was late spring, and all the roads off Main Street were mud tracks. I was asked to drive Mr. Paepcke to a house owned by the hotel called the "Gay Nineties" in his big Buick. I had to negotiate the car through quite a quagmire. Mr. Paepcke was very gracious as I slid all over the place, and asked me where I was from and about my family. I thought, here is this great man showing an interest in a lowly bellhop, and it was touching. He said to me, "Why don't you bring your father and sister to Aspen. We need people like your family here." Entrepreneurial people were highly sought after to bring new vitality to the old town, which had been all but abandoned after the mining days.

By April of 1949, I started seriously to consider Aspen as the future home for my father, Doris, and me, and began looking at real estate. I had no real money—just everything that I could save and still a bit of my "chicken money" from Australia. The weather was turning warm, and the snow was melting through the streets. The puddles everywhere were reminders about how much snow used to be on the mountain and that next year, it would be there again. I was full of plans and not a bit discouraged by the land rush mentality that seemed to be everywhere that year as Paepcke's intentions to rejuvenate the old silver mining town of Aspen became more and more clear. Unlike the veins of silver ore that used to run through the mountains and were now mostly depleted, snow was a renewable resource, and the town had it in spades.

Ever since the war, accelerating land development had begun raising the stakes for would-be real-estate moguls like myself. Initially what I found out about the rapidly rising prices made me choke! My sister and father thought we might rent some place to stay together during the next year, but I considered that to be much more expensive than the idea of buying some land and building our own house.

One of the two real estate agents in Aspen was Jim Moore. He ran a small motel, Moore's Court, near the Hotel Jerome and was also the town barber. He would tell people about which lots were available in town while cutting their hair. He also tried to recruit me for the high school, even though I was already a graduate and nineteen years old, because they needed more people on the roster in order to get funding and teachers from Denver.

When I ventured out with Mr. Moore to see what was for sale, he showed me a few plots in the range of $600 to $900, usually clustered together in two or three lots. There were three corner lots near the Hotel Jerome—just two blocks from the lift, for $850—but they were sold by the next day. Others sold for many thousands. So I decided to quickly buy three middle lots at the foot of Shadow Mountain. They were priced at $750, and because of their beautiful location only eight blocks from the single ski lift for Aspen Mountain, I decided this would be a great spot for a future home. I immediately communicated to my father my desire to make the purchase. I wrote one letter on April 20, 1949 asking for his opinion and agreement, but for fear of losing the deal, by the 21st I had already committed a 10% non-refundable deposit—$75 of the $85 I had—to the owner Leroy Waterman. He was in fact the fourth owner in this accelerating chain of land speculation.

I was playing for keeps, however. I wrote to my father and Doris on the 22nd, "I hope you will not judge me too rashly on my snap decision to buy that land for $750.... I took a picture of it with my camera, so you'll see it when I come home—I am sure you'll like it.... The money we are going to put into this is actually better than in the bank, because

I feel that in a year's time if we don't want it, we could sell it at a few hundred dollars profit. But I am sure we won't sell. You know it isn't like me to make snap decisions, but when I see something good, I don't want to miss out, and so without any outside influence to persuade me to buy, I took that decision into my own hands.... A little while ago, I spoke to a lady who owns a shop here [Terese David]. I was helping her with some luggage as she had just come back from New York. I happened to mention that I bought some land a little way up from her home.... She was so surprised when I told her the price. 'Why,' she said, 'someone offered me an old shack on about half a lot the other day for $6,500.'... She told me what a wise move I had made."

The day after I bought the land, April 23, 1949, two fellow bellhops and I headed across country in a La Salle owned by one of the boys. I wanted to go back to visit with my father and Doris, put my affairs in order, and return to Aspen as soon as possible. By sharing costs and the driving, the boys and I made good time back to New York almost non-stop, changing drivers and eating sandwiches on the road.

I now recall an uncharacteristic remark made at the time by my father, that as our wonderful life together in Aspen through the years unfolded were hard for him to live down. I had purchased a piece of paradise; his first reaction was, "What? Are you crazy, buying land in the wilderness?" ■

CHAPTER SEVENTEEN

Summer of '49

B y the summer of 1949, I made a decision to return to Aspen, this
time with a friend, Herbert Kellman. The Kellmans were another
immigrant family, who lived downstairs from us in the brownstone on
75th Street. Herbert was about my age and was a music student. We
heard him practicing the piano for hours on end. He was delighted with
the prospect of a new adventure.

With Herbert helping, I began to homestead and build a little cabin
on my new land. Herbert proved to be a good construction helper and an
even better friend. We spent the entire summer in Aspen building the
cabin in our time off from doing odd jobs to support ourselves.

Aspen would not only get on the map as a great new ski spot in the
West, but also as a place where European culture could flourish again
after the disasters of war. That summer of 1949, Walter Paepcke ushered
in the Goethe Bicentennial Convocation and Music Festival to celebrate
the great philosophy and humanism at the core of Germanic literature
and culture. It seemed there would be no better time for my father to
reinstate himself as the cultured man he was than to be part of this
renaissance. I thought he could be hired as an interpreter or translator,
considering his linguistic skills. Nevertheless, he did not move to Aspen
that summer, but continued his line of business with an export/import
company, Fordom Trading, in New York.

For the Goethe Bicentennial Convocation and Music Festival, Aspen's
first music tent was designed by architect Eero Saarinen, an American
transplant from Finland. With tangerine colored walls and a white top, it
looked much like a circus tent and is considered an early example of the
architect's fascination with vaulted forms. The immediate mental association one makes with the tent is of flying acrobats. Saarinen later worked
with the concept of weightless structures in other works like the Jefferson
Memorial Arch in St. Louis and the TWA terminal at La Guardia. The

Aspen tent had a diameter of one hundred forty-seven feet and sat two thousand people. At forty-five feet high, the canvas structure was asking a lot of gravity to stay up for the events and needed people working daily to keep the ropes taut.

When I was hired onto the tent crew, I had my first taste of what would soon become Aspen's hallmark international culture. I observed all of the events for free. Many famous people presented, like humanist Dr. Albert Schweitzer, who came all the way from Lambaréné in what is now Gabon, Africa; José Ortega y Gasset, the Spanish philosopher; Gregor Piatigorsky, the cellist; writer Thornton Wilder; pianist Arthur Rubinstein; and Dimitri Mitropoulos, conducting the Minneapolis Symphony. For me it was the inspiration for a lifelong love of classical music and dedication to what later became the Aspen Music Festival and School. Future years found me serving on the Board of Trustees for decades, and then I was named a lifetime trustee. My wife Fonda has served three terms on the board as vice president as well as on the executive committee.

The Goethe Bicentennial lasted three weeks—from June 27 to July 17— and I was fully employed during this time, first on the tent crew for two weeks and then as an usher. It was thrilling to see people streaming into the tent to hear the lectures and listen to the concerts, of which we partook fully. Herbert and I became very friendly with conductor Dimitri Mitropoulos. We would see him in the Hotel Jerome lobby and chat with him at length. It seemed he liked to talk to the local people and especially to Herbert as a music student. He was very accessible, not as one would expect of a famous conductor. The whole town was choked with people and the hotel lobby jammed with attendees, professors, lecturers, and musicians. Herbert and I enjoyed mingling with these intellectuals and celebrities.

That summer Herbert and I lived for a while in the Hotel Jerome employee housing, although we did not work there anymore, which caused some complications. He wrote his depiction of Aspen and of our antics to a friend, Madeline Day, who made a copy for me in 2009.

Aspen   August 10, 1949

Dear Madeline,

After the festival most of the hotel-help [except us] were laid off

Festival attendees and the first Aspen music tent designed by Eero Saarinen. Goethe Bicentennial, 1949. PHOTO: CHARLES PATERSON.

and there were only about eight people sleeping in the dorm. Consequently, the hotel decided to close down the dormitory. All the "inmates" were ordered to move out by a certain day. One by one they left; all except us. Here is the reason: we decided to build ourselves a cabin on Charlie's land. Of course we had been living under a false security and we had put off preparing for an emergency like that from day to day. But now the time had come and by the [time the] deadline for moving out came, we had only put up one wall and the roof.

[But] one night we came home and found the place padlocked. The janitor must have realized that we were putting one [over] on him, got fed up, and locked the place up. Not to be beaten, we went round the back, swiped a huge ladder from an adjoining restaurant, put it up to the first floor where there was a roof, and entered hence into our accommodations.

This was our entrance and exit from then on. But what a bother! To climb up this damn great ladder carrying groceries in our arm was no joke, besides, there was the danger of being seen and/or mistaken for burglars. One night we went to a nightclub and had to climb down the ladder in our good clothes. When we got down we found that we were filthy. Also, imagine us creeping back up there at one o'clock in the morning. It's lucky that the [one] town cop didn't shoot at us. Neither was it pleasant for us inside the place. The two of us were alone in this room of 80 beds, all of which had been stripped (we had to sleep in our sleeping sacks) and we were even afraid to put on the light for fear of being seen from the outside. Then, after two days of this misery came the pay-off. One of the hotel officials saw Charlie climb down the ladder.

I was still on the roof and could see what was happening below. The guy didn't see me, but took one look and then hurried away. In hastily getting off the roof and hurrying down, I accidentally knocked off a brick from the roof. The damn thing hit Charlie right on the head. It's lucky he wasn't killed, for when I got down to the ground he was clutching his head with blood gushing from it. I examined the wound (call me Dr. Kell from now on) and found to my utter relief that it was only a surface cut. The brick must have just glanced him on the corner. After a minute or so the bleeding stopped and, as Charlie didn't seem any the worse for it, we set off for work. When we arrived, we found that we had been laid off.

You see, all the troubles come at once, because the next day saw the triumph of justice. The guy who saw Charlie on the ladder spilled the beans and the manager of the hotel (the big wheel) told us in so many words that the dormitory was closed—even for ladder-climbers. We had to get out—pronto. That evening we paid good hard cash for a night's lodging in the hotel—the first time since we arrived here.

The next day, we felt it was time to move into our cabin, although we only had the back, the roof, and one side finished. We moved all our luggage (enough for a whole family) into the new "home," improvised a third wall of clothes, made up our beds on the ground, and went back to town to a party which some of the boys were giving. Some party!

Anyway, to put it in a few words, we completed our cabin while we were in the ranks of the unemployed. After a week or so of

The Aspen Times *announcing the arrival of Albert Schweitzer from Lambaréné, Africa, July 7, 1949.*

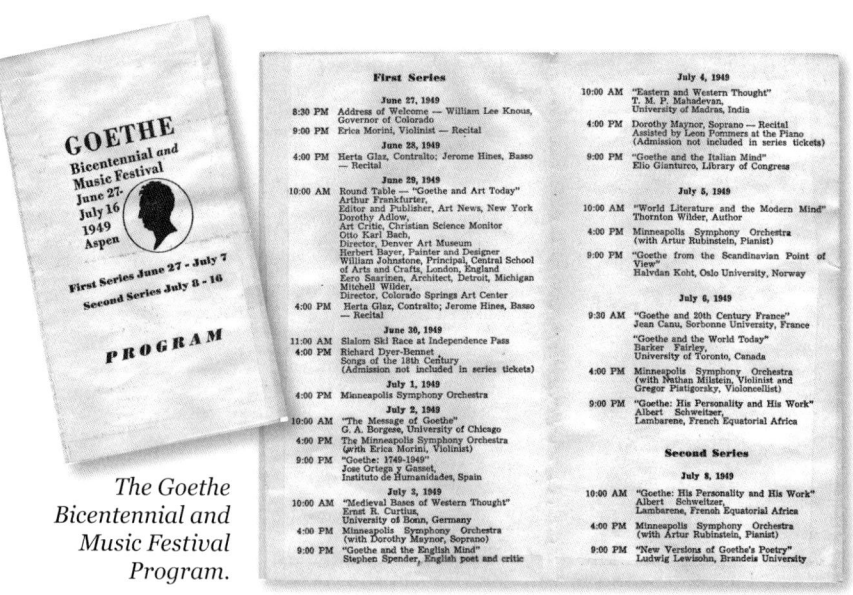

The Goethe Bicentennial and Music Festival Program.

sleeping on the floor, somebody managed to get two army cots for us from Denver to make things more comfortable. It was quite a time, though, before we had all four walls up, and we had gotten quite used to sleeping, for all purposes, under the stars.

Out here, the temperature at night often drops to the freezing point and we often have ice on the window in the morning, and so you can imagine that our nights are not too pleasant, although we "borrowed" a couple of blankets from the hotel. For water, we go to a little mountain stream a few feet away.

Otherwise, the place is quite like home. We have made the cots into a double-bunker bed, also built two tables, some chairs, a cupboard, etc. Real cozy. Now all we need are some women to make it really habitable. See you soon.

Love,

Herbert

P.S. Yesterday I was invited up to the Richard Deyer-Bennet School of Music here in Aspen, sat in on one of their composition classes. They played through some of my stuff and sang a few of my rounds. Went over quite well.[1]

After the Festival was over and everything quieted down, I got a new job as a carpenter at $72 a week. The fact I was living on about $7 a week for food, and had free lodging now in my cabin, made this a great deal. Herbert and I did all our own cooking on a little hot plate.

I wrote a six-page report to my father on July 29, 1949. "We really eat like kings almost, and I assure you that I haven't lost any weight—in fact I gained some." My father was always obsessing that I did not eat enough, therefore the assurances. "This is my second week as a carpenter. I earned $176 up to the end of the last week and was able to start a bank account with $140. However, I was held up for timber at my cabin as I could not obtain 12" planks to finish one side but was hoping to buy some left over planks at the Hotel [Jerome] pool for three and a half cents per foot, where they were building a shower shed and solarium.... Right now we are living in the cabin with the back and north wall finished and the other two sides still open to the air only with the studs. I built the cabin back and to the side of the three lots so it won't be in the way if we ever build a house."

My father had feared I had ruined all my chances to be a respected fellow in Aspen because Herbert and I were caught making illegal use of the Jerome's employee dormatory. On August 8th, I wrote: "I don't think I disgraced myself too much in the eyes of the Hotel, and they treat it as a great joke, because they all are exceptionally nice to me, except Fred and Elli Iselin who I think told the management and won't even bother to greet me anymore on the street."

In retrospect, the last part of this letter amuses me because later I established myself successfully as a ski instructor. Aspen Ski School's Friedl Pfeifer,[2] along with Fred as co-director, chose me to teach the top class on Aspen Mountain for my last eight years out of a seventeen-year career. Over that time Elli and I also became good friends.

In the winter of 1959-1960, Fred recruited from the Aspen Ski School for a made-for-TV movie he directed for H. J. Heinz Co., *Little Skier's Big Day.* I skied for the film with a formation of "rescuers" looking for a six year-old girl named Susie (named after the real Susie Wirth), as she had gotten lost in a snow slide when skiing down to school from the top of Aspen Mountain at the Sundeck, where she lived. Fred made several movies and was a town character with a wonderful, light sense of humor and a real panache, both in front of the camera and behind it.

As for Friedl, he was also a magnetic personality as well as a strict, fair boss. I did an interview with Marie-Claire Messinger of Austrian Public Radio in 2010 for a feature about Friedl and noted, "I enjoyed working for Friedl because there was never a doubt about where you stood [with him]." He kept everybody on his toes. I remember that the ski trails on Aspen Mountain and Buttermilk Mountain were designed with Friedl's special touch. "Friedl had a real knack for laying out trails," I told Messinger. "They all had a romance to them, and a rhythm, and it was almost like skiing in a song." At the beginning of the Aspen Ski School, according to Friedl's son Peter Pfeifer, in the same radio feature, Friedl used to offer "free skiing lessons for housewives" on Thursdays as his "marketing plan." Before long, Peter said, the husbands were skiing, the children were skiing, the town, and then the whole state was skiing.[3]

*Herbert Kellman and I taking a break from building the cabin
in Aspen, summer 1949.*

After the tourists and visitors for the Festival had gone, the summer was still far from over. MGM, Metro Goldwyn Meyer, then came to town to film a Western, *Devil's Doorway*, with Robert Taylor. Paula Raymond was the romantic female star and Louis Calhern cast as the villain. I was hired on as a carpenter at first, along with eighteen others and a dozen laborers, to help build the sets consisting of some log cabins at a location a couple miles down from Maroon Lake. I had expected two weeks' work of ten- to eleven-hour days and overtime at the fabulous regular pay of $2.40 an hour.

On August 8th I wrote, "We are building two log cabins with interiors and four other ones with false backs—in other words, only front and side walls. I expect we will start on other things such as sheep wagons soon. We are working in a beautiful setting at about 9,000 feet. About a mile away the wonderful series of mountains [called] the Maroon Bells rise up to 14,000 feet [where] it snowed today when we had rain and hail at the location. In this same valley are camped a tribe of Native Americans from South Dakota, well out of view of the movie set, who have been hired for the battle. [Herbert and I] are pretty well settled now at the cabin and got up our curtains last night. About a hundred yards away from our land is an old mine in which there is still solid ice inside, and which we are using as a refrigerator, which comes in very handy."

The building job with MGM finished in record time, and when I was laid off, I became a driver for the Hollywood cowboy who was in charge of the livestock for the movie. I picked him up daily in a jeep at six-thirty in the morning at the T Lazy 7 Ranch, owned by Lou and Had Dean, and then spent most of the day watching the shooting sequences. One day, Gary Cooper came up on location and shot some of the scenes with his own camera. When that job ended—as my boss transferred to Grand Junction for the next shoot with the cattle, and my jeep was decommissioned along with me—I was hired on as an extra, riding in the posse dressed disreputably and then subsequently, in the cavalry with a splendid uniform. Stunt men were falling off their horses during the battle, some of them into a pond in front of the cabins. In one scene I had to fall down dead, shot by a fusillade from the Indians and their chief, played by Robert Taylor, who were defending their little fortress settlement, which was going up in smoke and flames.

When I went to the movie in New York at the Capitol Theater I was very excited to see myself on the silver screen, but alas could not, as the shots moved too quickly. We had worked for more than a week on these scenes. But the paycheck was great, and we always ate meals on location, being fed royally just down the road at the T Lazy 7. It occurs to me now that there is a parallel between my Aspen cabin with only two sides built and the partly built movie cabins—a real Potemkin village—except my walls were there to stay and theirs, only "smoke and mirrors," were to disappear completely from the landscape within a short time.

A few years after *Devil's Doorway*, Hollywood again came to town, looking for extras. This movie was *Cheyenne Autumn* and was about the Cheyenne, dispossessed of their lands by government edict, who were being marched from Wyoming to a reservation by the U.S. Army under stressful conditions. No one was told where the movie was being made, and we all got into a bus, five hours later landing in Monument Valley, Utah at a small tent city. We were issued cavalry army uniforms and spent the next three days doing drills out in the field, but with no cameras, nothing. It felt like we had been shanghaied back into the army, only it was 1885. Finally, we were transported to a remote site, with the Monument Valley formations all around us, and instructed to march in formation toward the cameras. Though we were roasting in our uniforms in the summer heat, the hillsides had been sprayed with a coating of white, to make it look like early fall snow. Alan Ladd was one of the officers and John Ford was the director, for whom we spent an awful lot of time

*Riding with the cavalry in the Maroon Creek valley
during the filming of* Devil's Doorway, *1949.*

Robert Taylor.
Devil's Doorway, *1949.*
PHOTO: CHARLES PATERSON.

Me with homestead in
Devil's Doorway. *Maroon Bells
formation in background, 1949.*

waiting. He was always cavorting around with a patch over one eye and a large red kerchief hanging from his mouth, with which he would continually wipe the perspiration from his face.

Due to the generosity of people then living in Aspen, I had a lot of encouragement and help to build my cabin. By the end of the summer of 1949, it ended up being eight by sixteen feet, and was built out of leftover lumber with railroad ties as a foundation and covered with asphalt "brick like" roll roofing on the outside. The inside paneling was slab lumber with the bark still on it, which was usually cut up for firewood, but it turned out to be quite handsome.

Tom Sardy, who owned the Aspen Lumber Company, contributed to my project by extending me credit for all the insulation. He told me "pay me when you can"—no paper work or even an IOU. I heard later he helped many people this way. Three windows I found at the dump had been in an old barn. I obtained some of the leftover lumber from a house I had worked on with Andy Beusch, an executive with Sears Roebuck in

John Ford (center, behind cannon) on location filming Cheyenne Autumn. *Kayenta, Arizona, 1953.* PHOTO: CHARLES PATERSON.

Chicago, who was building that house himself. He was gracious to give me all the planks from the foundations and other leftover lumber at a cheap price. The foundation boards were still encrusted with concrete and were riddled with holes from the bailing wire ties, but they were right for my needs.

I went looking for curtain material at my friend Terese David's store in an old Victorian house on Main Street. She was a sophisticated lady who had Parisian fashions and beautiful fabrics. The original mover and shaker of Aspen's "Bastille Day," she yearly became the pied piper and paraded with a group of small children in their latest French outfits. She was also my neighbor on Hopkins Avenue and owned a hand-adzed log cabin on the next corner, which was reputedly one of the oldest buildings still standing in town. When I told her what I was doing, she donated the curtains. The material was a heavy-striped, vivid-colored fabric hung from rollers and small aluminum tracks.

Soon, the cabin was most cozy and livable. I had worked on it every spare moment in order to finally have a place to live. With bunk beds on one end and a couch opposite with a table, it was complete. The hot plate next to the couch was the kitchen. Building the humble little cabin had not been easy, and I loved it all the more for that.

"My social life here seems rather colourless and a little disappointing," I wrote to my sister in upstate New York, where she was working as a waitress in a Catskill hotel. However, there were "a few bright spots— one recently in a date with a good looking blonde at the Four Seasons Club, and then the other night Herb and I had two girls here at the cabin after a dance, for a hot dog, cup of tea, and a little necking. Unfortunately they were not inclined to stay the night and keep us warm—it gets awful cold here at nights. Sometimes I even get a little lonely, as there weren't a terrific lot of young people in summer as I had hoped, and I really miss the good old family life with you and Pop even more so."

At the end of that memorable summer, I padlocked the door of the cabin and returned to New York, where I went back to City College to continue my education with civil engineering courses. February of 1950 was the F.I.S., World Ski Championships, which really helped put Aspen on the map as one of the world's great skiing places. There was a tremendous shortage of beds for the F.I.S., and my cabin stood empty because I was back in school.

Outside my cabin, 512 West Hopkins Avenue, Aspen, 1950.

When I received my electric bill at the end of that month, I noticed that there was a reading on my electric meter. Obviously someone had broken into the cabin and was using it. Whoever it was, they were respectful of my property. When I returned to Aspen in the spring, I found everything intact, without any loss to any of my belongings, as if no one had ever been there. People living in Aspen then never locked their houses, and it was everyone's habit to leave their car keys in the ignition.

Even though the little cabin had been very comfortable for me and Herbert the first summer, I began laying the foundation for a real log building during my second summer, 1950—again with Herbert—and by the end of 1951, it was complete with a living room, kitchen, and bath adjoining the original eight by sixteen foot shack, which I converted into a bedroom. The expanded log cabin was then my home, and soon also my father's, for the next twenty-five years. ▪

CHAPTER EIGHTEEN

Manna from Heaven

In my first days in Aspen, when my father was still in New York, I used to write very detailed descriptions back to him of the skiing conditions, the state of my skiing, my adventures, and my equipment. In one letter I narrated for him a memorable trip I took at the end of the ski season in 1951 to Montezuma Basin, a high-altitude valley about seventeen miles out of Aspen that stretches up and back from the valley floor where the ghost town of Ashcroft now sits. Writing it out for him wove my life together with his, like two skiers' tracks cutting back and forth across a fresh powder slope, one having made his descent before the other in time.

"We left Aspen on Sunday morning, April 22," I wrote. There were six of us—three boys and three girls: Julius, a Czechoslovak friend from New York; Jack McTarnaghan, a friend from the ski patrol; Nanette, a tall, good-looking blonde from Hollywood who worked as a reservation manager in the Hotel Jerome; attractive Joyce; and Ann, a handsome brunette from Stonesthrow, a bed and breakfast in Aspen at the time.

"One can imagine what a jolly crowd we were. We drove to Ashcroft in Jack's '46 Plymouth and had to put on chains about half way of the twelve-mile trip. We were off in a snowstorm about 10 a.m. with our packs on our backs and our skins on our skis." On the way up, we first met five fellows coming down from Tagert Hut and then two couples coming back from the "Mill," an old mine building which had been converted for ski touring guests. The Mill was operated by Stuart Mace, the owner of Toklat Lodge, who also had Husky sled dogs and was caretaker of the other huts in the backcountry.

"Seven hours later," I wrote, "we arrived at the 'Mill' and—as Ann could go no further—Julius and Ann stayed overnight there, while the rest of us climbed on to Tagert, where we arrived at about 6 p.m. It was a distance of about five miles, climbing from Ashcroft at 9,500 ft. to Tagert Hut at [11,240] ft."

Setting out for Montezuma from Ashcroft in a spring snow storm, April 1951.
PHOTO: CHARLES PATERSON.

Tagert Hut was built with massive logs. The snow was so deep on our trip—even in the spring—it was all the way up to the eaves, with about four feet on the roof. There was only a little passageway leading through the snow to the door. Inside, there was a little wood stove and two double bunk beds pushed together. Each bed had a mattress and heavy quilt. All eating and cooking utensils were there, as well as a table, chairs, and plenty of food left over from people who had been there before us. Wood was always kept piled high inside, and there were axes and saws to cut down dead trees for firewood, which you were expected to replace.

We were soon settled comfortably and slept very well. My sleeping bag and the quilt enabled me to sleep warmly in my underclothes. I wrote, "Actually, I had the lightest pack because I had brought only an extra pair of socks, undershirt, and shirt, besides my share of the food." I remember the others staggered under tremendous loads. Consequently, on the trip up, "I had to exchange Joyce's rucksack for mine." Unfortunately, my great sealskins, which at first stuck well onto my waxed skis, started to come off after about six hours of climbing. So, I changed to some army-issued skins, and the difference was like black and white. They turned out to be much heavier, and I had to lift my skis at every stride, while the sealskins had just glided over the snow. "I immediately grew tired," and from there on, with Joyce's heavy pack, had a fairly tough time.

"The next morning," I continued, "the four of us left the hut at about 8 a.m. and started up above timberline for some touring. It was just gorgeous, and we returned before lunch because, after that time, the snow was too soft and treacherous. All that morning we heard and saw avalanches and, being on safe ground, we would start slides on the opposite mountain just by yodeling."

We spent our afternoons and evenings very delightfully, telling stories, gossiping, and most all the time, roaring with laughter. Nearly every evening we had a little party.

On the second day, we were up bright and early and climbed to the Montezuma Mine at about 12,500 feet. We were forced back mid-morning because of a blinding snowstorm, which kept up all day and half the night. But on the third day, we had wonderful powder snow and sunshine, and we climbed way into Pearl Basin, which "was just out of this world at about 13,000 feet with the peaks under clouds hanging at 14,000 feet," I wrote. "We called this place 'Shangri-La,' and it was just like climbing up into heaven. I never thought I would enjoy touring so much. On the lightweight sealskins, I even enjoyed the climb. The skiing down was of little consequence, because it was so short and the scenery can only be appreciated on the ascent. I was surprised how well the stick-on wax worked on the descent after I had corked it down and put a little 'A 24' downhill [wax] on top of it."

The last morning, Thursday, "we were on our way home in a blinding snowstorm with thunder and lightning. There were about four inches of new snow on a well-settled base, and we had wonderful skiing all the way back into Ashcroft." It was the end of four wonderful days and a new experience for me. "The trip cost us $4 each for the overnights at Tagert and $4.50 each for food. When we got back into dead Aspen, it was raining. We sat down in Mathew's Drug Store and, over our parting friendships from the wilds, all buried our sorrows in huge 35-cent banana splits."

I recall eight years later I returned to Montezuma with friends—a charming couple prominent in Cincinnati and eventually some of the first home owners in the new ski resort of Vail, Irma and Fred Lazarus.[1] Along were dazzling Trish from London, who I was madly in love with, and her friend Margaret, as well as Aspenite Waddy Catchings. We

Our jolly group at Tagert Hut on our Montezuma trip, April 1951.

Removing my climbing skins on top of Pearl Pass, April 1951.

stayed at the Mill and had our gear packed in by Stuart Mace's sled dog operation out of Ashcroft. What a luxury compared to my first tour.

One evening the girls decided to make lasagna, a meal made unforgettable when Margaret dropped the dish while removing it from the oven, and it ended all over the floor. With great merriment we scraped it up inch by inch and ate every scrap we rescued. We all agreed it was the best meal of the trip.

As a resident in Aspen, life was good, but in the summer of 1951, to earn savings I had a self-imposed schedule of working some fourteen to sixteen hours a day. During the day I helped build a barn/studio for the artist and architect Herbert Bayer on Red Mountain, and in the evenings I began a job at the Golden Horn. This was a popular—and actually, the only—restaurant and nightclub combination in town. Guido Meyer ran a Swiss restaurant in this space until nine o'clock; then it morphed into a nightclub run by Steve Knowlton. Steve, a U.S. Army Tenth Mountain Division veteran and Olympic skier, had the funniest show, which included miming from records with two other clowns. People packed the place nightly. He always told a joke of being on the Italian front in World War II, advancing on the Germans. Steve's platoon took over a line of defense, finding soldiers in their foxholes. They thought they told the soldiers, "Surrender or we'll shoot!"—"*Verzicht oder wir schießen!*" But instead it came out as "scheiße"—pardon me, "Come out or we'll shit!" Over the years Steve and I became good friends. One of his ambitions was to eventually build a ski museum with his great collection of ski memorabilia. As we grew older, whenever he came to town and visited me, we used to scheme how to go about creating such a museum.

I enjoyed the Aspen restaurant business. I met a lot of people, saw the entertainment, and ate for free. Not only the shows were comical at the Golden Horn. I wrote to my father on July 15, 1951: "I had a stroke of luck last Wednesday. I went from dishwasher to waiter in almost the blink of an eye. Here's what happened: Guido, who runs the restaurant, fired John, the waiter. A few minutes later Jack McTarnaghan [from the trip to Montezuma] quit from behind the bar. Then Steve Knowlton, who owns the nightclub, hired John back to work as a bartender. So I quit my dishwashing and took John's place as a waiter and Guido got a new dishwasher. Consequently everybody was happy again."

Steve Knowlton and Bob Knight doing a skit at
The Golden Horn for Knowlton's night club act, 1950.
LOEY RINQUIST COLLECTION: ASPEN HISTORICAL SOCIETY.

The other waiter at the Golden Horn, Turvy (his sister's name was Topsy), offered to help me expand my cabin as he wanted to get some experience in log construction. He had worked with the Wright-trained architect Fritz Benedict a couple of summers previously and was very handy, so I thought he would be perfect as an assistant. Unfortunately for me, this didn't pan out, and I was left on my own to find people to work as hired hands.

By the time I settled in Aspen, my former life in Australia seemed like it had belonged to another person, and I was almost entirely disconnected from it. In 2011, I was interested to read a letter from Felix Popper to my father, dated September 22, 1947, in which he relayed his strong opinion of how we should transition from that country to the United States. My father had promised to return with us to Australia if we did not like living in America. For Mr. Popper, this offer was a mistake. The only way to settle in a new country, he said, was to forget everything of the past and start life fresh. The sentiments expressed are similar to the way many Jewish émigrés like my father also dealt with leaving Europe. Mr. Popper wrote to my father that he did his best to convince us that we should forget Australia and that we would never come back.

Mr. Popper wrote, "Needless to say that all of us will miss your children, there were many wet eyes when they left. We have loved them dearly and wish them every success and happiness over there." Felix Popper extended his enduring friendship to my father, which they maintained the rest of their lives, along with the mutual hope: "May you be happy after all the tribulations and nightmares of the last years."

The war years were harder for my father than I could possibly have imagined. As a teenager I was trying to cope with my new life in another country and culture and to be an Australian; as a young man I was becoming an individual and an American. Meanwhile my father was forging a new life but not forgetting us, or anyone: my mother Eva, my grandmother Rosa, the Beck family, his Viennese friends.

The Czech steel enterprise belonging to the Becks and Hirschs, my mother's family, was lost to the Third Reich and its war machinations. All Jewish employees and owners of the textile factories belonging to my father's family firm Hermann Pollack's Söhne—H.P.S.—had been dismissed, their pensions and shares stolen, and the enterprises thus taken over by the remaining employees and their Swiss or Austrian creditor banks, who facilitated the Aryanization.

My father lost all his possessions except what was contained in two trunks stored in the Paris shop of Les Fils d'Emanuel Lang Co. Miraculously these items, including his beloved typewriter and his skis, were able to be sent back to him in New York in 1942 with the help of the Lang family, the American Friends Service Committee (Quakers), and also Otto Pick. A third trunk came, but we don't know what it originally carried, as it arrived empty. My father wrote once that he was thankful the other two that were not ransacked on their journey from Paris had carried his winter clothes. Later from the Langs, after the war, came a handmade little wood box, which we treasure and still keep on our bookcase. It is made of rough pine, was hand-addressed and sealed with wax and string; in it was sent back to my father the family jewelry including my mother's favorite bracelet and her wedding ring.

In the early 1950's, my father was working as the office manager at Fordom Trading Company. One focus of the company was exporting ship tankers to South America, to carry oil. It was a good job, certainly better than working in candy factories, summer camps, and restaurants,

My first cabin with Shadow Mountain Lodge and Mesa Store in the background. Aspen, 1949. PHOTO: CHARLES PATERSON.

though he made less money at this job than as a jeweler, but the executive position had been an important step to getting us back from Australia.[2]

I worried about my father's health and that living in New York as he was, without extensive means, would shorten his life.

Then he wrote me a frank letter—he was on his last dollar. This had never happened to him before. He had left Fordom Trading because he feared a pending scandalous divorce case would require him to testify, and to keep his job it was clear he would be asked to lie under oath. He refused the only other work he could get—to show apartments for rent. The job came with the stipulation that if the interested person were dark-skinned, he would be required to tell the person the apartment was already rented. A man of honesty, and one who recognized prejudice, he could not work for such employers.

I always wanted my father to come live with me in Aspen and knew we had to take action to get him out of financial straits. It occurred to us at the same time that the mountains and fresh air would be a good move for him and that he might live a healthier and longer life. Years later, when his old friends in New York were ailing in their health, we commiserated and often remarked about how wonderful it was to live in the West, in the mountains. He used to tell his friends in New York, "Charlie has a little cabin in the mountains with running water—straight from the roof!" The essence of my lifestyle was not lost on him. Everything I needed was right there at the cabin I built for myself. What came from the sky, as non-religious as we were, appeared like manna from heaven.

So, my father and I concurred that at his age, sixty-two, he should finally leave New York. He made the break from the big city and came to Aspen. We were reunited again, and I was delighted to have him with me. It was in my effort to introduce my father to Aspen that I arranged to lease a small lodge called the Holiday House from Margaret and Frank Day Sr.—Frank was the manager of Sears Roebuck's shoe department in Chicago, and Margaret was in advertising.

In a letter of December 1951, my father's first winter in Aspen, he wrote to Käthe Pick in Vancouver, "Since fall my life has changed completely." Our little business at the Holiday House was going strong and had advance reservations. I was building another addition on the cabin, and our plans for a two-car garage included workbenches—carpentry for me and jewelry making for him. He intended to create sure sellers in the West—silver belt buckles.

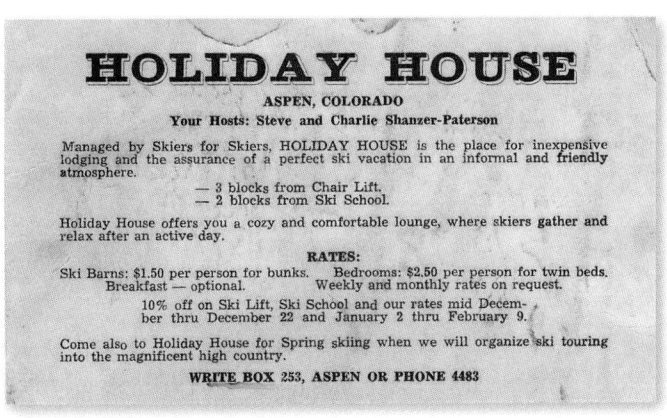

Holiday House promotional postcard, 1952.

Doris stayed in New York following her career aspirations to be a dress designer. It was only with regret that she had turned down an offer to work with a dress designer in Sydney after the war and, at one time, had dreams of going to Paris to study there. She wrote to the Langs for advice, but after she met Herb Schneider and was hired as an assistant designer in New York in 1952, it was clear she would be staying on the east coast of the United States.

Years after my father settled into his new Colorado life he would tell the story that upon arriving in Aspen he thought me crazy to settle in such a small and undeveloped town. But then he would add that after skiing for the first time down Ruthie's Run on Aspen Mountain, he understood everything and agreed wholeheartedly with my choice. He acclimatized easily to the idiosyncrasies of Aspen's small town life, with which he found parallels to Vienna, where he had enjoyed a robust social scene and almost everyone knew each other. As well, the surrounding Rocky Mountains, the snow, and the pines reminded him of the Austrian Alps that he had loved so much.

Aspen in the early 1950's was almost like a retirement for my father though he was never going to stop working and seeing the world. He had come through an extraordinarily difficult period in his life, but it is remarkable that he never spoke of any sense of loss with me. It was a guarded, deep wound in his heart, scarred over purely by his own will to go on.

His motto had always been to live life to its fullest, which implied not dwelling in a past he could not change. ▪

CHAPTER NINETEEN

Dispossession

From Pilsen in September of 1938 my father wrote to his friend Albin Schwab, "As you know, I am the sort of person who, when hurting in particular, am able to muster up the strength to never look back." I realize, however, the letters my father kept for me and his grandchildren to tell our story ran counter to this stated impulse to never look behind. Like the white pebbles in the German children's fairy tale of Hansel and Gretel, they return me home, trailing across the years of my most frightening experiences.

Included in the many letters my father saved are those from my grandmother Olga and my aunt Claire, perhaps some of the most important testimonies we have. I cannot take the readers of this book through them in all their detail. They are too long, and it would be too difficult to live 1940 and 1941 together with them, step by step. The writing of this part of our story has been hard on me, so I have relied upon others to translate, organize the letters, and provide supporting research for context.

One might ask why or how my father became the record keeper of that time. The archives of my uncle Max Beck, the lone survivor from the Pilsen Beck family, contain almost no correspondence with his mother Olga and sister Claire. Mail between Nazi-occupied Czechoslovakia and England was sporadic, and progressively more censored and disallowed, so the most assured point of relay for the Beck family was the neutral country of Portugal where my father was waiting for a visa. Thus, their letters were a surprise for Max's daughter Janet to read when they were translated from German in 2010, just as much as they were for me.

We proceed into this part of our story backward, retracing steps. At the end of February 1942, Max and my father were hoping their families were still alive, trying to wait out the war. Nothing had come from any efforts to obtain visas for Olga and Claire to leave. Max had been making claims with the Czech Refugee Trust Fund to get some funds for Olga and

Claire's applications, but for the last few months emigration visas for the two places that seemed most likely, Cuba or Ecuador, had been impossible to obtain. The last preceding correspondence between my father and Max before the United States entered the war was in November of 1941, when panicked telegrams and letters arrived from Olga and Claire. Both Max and my father were frustrated and helpless to do anything, but they continued to try to make contact with people and agencies that might help. The mass deportations of Jews from Czechoslovakia to ghettos and concentration camps had started in the middle of that October and, unbeknownst to my father and my uncle Max, the Nazis had already closed all Jewish emigration from Europe.

In 1942, Doris and I inquired about Olga and Claire through the Australian Red Cross. We may have done so many times. It seems my sister led in this correspondence from her business office at Rawlings & Son, and she sent copies to my father. In 1946, Doris wrote to the Red Cross that the last telegram we received stated Claire and our grandmother "were being sent away." Then on May 1, 1947 the letter from the Red Cross Bureau for Wounded, Missing & Prisoners of War in Brisbane sent Claire's deportation dates, with her transport numbers to Terezín on December 10, 1941 and to Riga, Latvia on January 15, 1942. Claire was thirty-seven years old when she was murdered and Olga, who was also sent to Riga, but on August 20, 1942, was sixty-three.[1]

This last fact about Olga was only ascertained recently. It was my cousin Janet who went to Terezín in 2006 to see if she could find out anything about our grandmother. The information was hard to find—an Olga Beck had died there, but her birth date was not the same as our grandmother's. Finally, the correct record was sent to Janet. At the end of 2008, architectural scholar and writer Ivan Margolius[2] confirmed the details.

The last telegram from Olga came through the Red Cross and is dated May 13, 1942. It was restricted to thirty words. She wrote to us that she was healthy but would be changing her address soon. She sent kisses to us. Ten weeks later, on July 30, 1942, she was transported to Terezín.

In the months after Claire was deported from Prague, Olga was never able to communicate with her son, my uncle Max, or my father about it, and she herself may not have known what had become of Claire. Olga's letters would have been censored like all international mail, made even

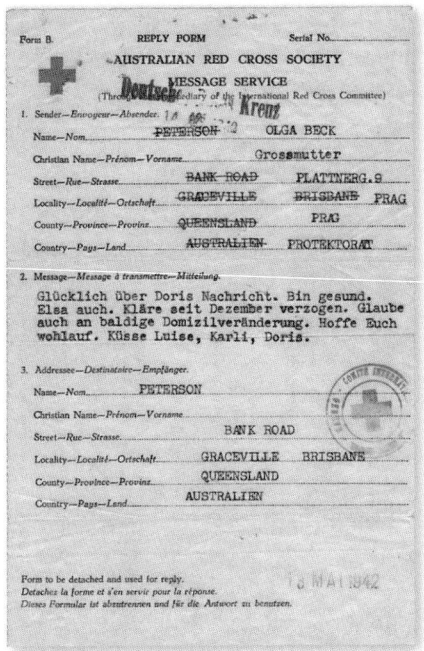

The last communication Doris and I received from our grandmother Olga
in Prague before her transport to Terezín, May 13, 1942.

more difficult by the United States entering the war at the end of 1941. As for Claire, any outgoing mail from Terezín was forbidden during the time she was there, under penalty of death.[3] Even earlier, starting January 1941, Jews in Czechoslovakia, with few exceptions, could not have telephones, and by January 1942, use of any telephone by Jews was forbidden.[4]

Terezín (Theresienstadt) was the principal ghetto where Jews from the Protectorate of Bohemia and Moravia were interned. The Nazis' total plan was kept secret not only from the public, but was also unknown to Jews both outside and inside the camps.[5] Hiding as much as they could from the general public, the Nazis sent transports at night or in the early morning. At these times, there would be fewer witnesses, and they wanted to avoid the public spectacles that had caused outrage and weeping by Prague citizens upon seeing the prisoners pass.[6]

Terezín was established on November 24, 1941 in an 18th century fortress town less than forty miles north of Prague. The conditions were horrible, on the level of actual concentration camps in its first year. Through the fall of 1942, people who were strong enough to work at Terezín were put into positions of manual labor; but they lived without adequate clothing or food, and the elderly or sick starved or died of disease because the rations were assigned to those who were strongest. Many thousands died at the camp itself. By the end of the war close to an additional one hundred and fifty thousand people had passed through Terezín's gates, sent to death camps in "the East." Czechoslovak Jews were some of the first deported, and nearly all had gone by the end of 1942.[7] Tragically, during the course of the war nearly eighty percent of the Jewish population of Czechoslovakia had been killed.[8] [9]

At the end of 1942, the Nazi SS set up Terezín as a propaganda camp. For a few short months in 1943 there was thus a brief respite in the conditions as the Nazis feigned that people lived a semblance of normal life in the "ghetto." [10] [11] After this period, a cultural life defiantly persisted.[12]

Numerous intellectuals, as well as artists and musicians were "residents" at Terezín, and amazingly over two thousand three hundred lectures—more than one a day—were reported to have been given by people there.[13] The Zionist youth leader Willy Groag was also interned there—he was the nephew of Loos' student Jacques Groag, the architect for our house at the Werkbundsiedlung. Willy Groag managed to save poems and stories written by children in Terezín during their time there; many times these children were alone and wrote hopefully about returning to be with their families.[14] They are displayed at the ceremonial hall next to the Klausen Synagogue in Prague, where Fonda and I saw them.[15] Many of the letters are included in the book *I Never Saw Another Butterfly* and the musical work "The Song of Terezín" by Franz Waxman.[16]

At the Aspen Music Festival in 1995, its forty-seventh season, Music Director Ara Guzelimian, Provost and Dean since 2006 at The Juilliard School, invited the Hawthorne String Quartet to play an entire program of music composed by Jewish prisoners at Terezín in the 1940's: Hans Krása, Viktor Ullmann (a student of Arnold Schoenberg), Pavel Haas, and Gideon Klein. In effect, that program of poignant, uplifting music started some of the research for this book project. The evening was a beautiful memorial and dedicated in the program book to Olga and Claire. Janet from England, my sister Doris, her husband Herb, my wife Fonda, and I attended.

Portrait of Olga Beck, mid-1930's.
PHOTO: CLAIRE BECK LOOS. COURTESY: JANET BECK WILSON.

The program book featured an article about the Beck family. Some of the best photographs we have of Claire and Olga were printed there. My cousin Janet found them among her father Max's papers. From Claire and Olga's physical appearances, it appears the photographs were taken in the later 1930's. It is unclear whether the photos were sent to Max in England, or whether they came with him from Czechoslovakia in his solitary brown suitcase when he fled. We believe Claire, a writer and photographer, produced the images. My wife Fonda took one look at Olga's soft and confident, loving smile and said, "That's a mother's gaze—I think she is looking at Claire in this picture." In Olga's eyes I can also see home.

The letters from Olga and Claire in Prague, translated from German in 2010 by Constance Pontasch, help draw a picture of their lives in 1940 and 1941. They were so proud of my father, and of Doris and me. It is bittersweet for me to read of the positive outlook they communicated about us.

In 1940 Olga Beck lived in an apartment in Prague's seventh district, a jutting thumb of land surrounded by the Vltava River. Close by, the beautiful green and forested hill of Letná rises. At the foot of the hill was a river town, with some housing but also smoke stacks and industrial areas. This was Olga's second apartment in the district,[17] a few blocks from the riverbank on the main avenue leading from St. Anthony of Padua's church on Strossmayer Square onto the Letná Plain. She wrote to my father as soon as she had an address for him.

Olga Beck   October 16, 1940
Sonnenbergstrasse 6, Prague VII

Mr. Stefan Schanzer c/o Mme. Bergler
Rua Santo Antonio de Capucho 2B.4D, Lisbon

Dear Stefan,

I was so happy to get your card, after waiting so long. I just knew
you would make your way and hope, that you will see the children again soon. I often long to see [them], but am glad to know
they are being well taken care of. Please congratulate Doris for
me on her 14th birthday—a young little lady. I would like to know
about her life and Karli's. [Your] Mama [Rosa Schanzer] wrote
me about your card, and I will send her [your] news immediately.
She, too, is living in the sole hope [that all goes well].

I heard from Max that he is in good health and working. He is
[slow] to write, but I am used to waiting, also with regard to the
future. I am healthy and am having no stomach pains despite
a heavy workload, and am not keeping any special diet.... Klär
[Claire] looks well and is in Tábor [at/near her friend] Anča's. She
was with Franz too. [I] hope that will end soon, since he will be
leaving.

Please write again. I can then write you in greater detail, since
you will have to be staying there longer. With warmest greetings,

Your devoted Olga

I am glad you are staying with nice people.

Parts of the letter above also appear on a postcard sent by Olga the
next day, October 17, 1940. Both communiqués received Nazi censor
stamps. It is clear Olga was not sure which words, if any, were going to
get through, so she doubled her efforts and would often ask my father
which letters or cards he managed to receive.

Eleven days later, Claire sent a letter to my father from Tábor, a city
to the south of Prague, where she had been visiting for some amount of
time we cannot determine.

Claire Loos   October 28, 1940
Budějovická 800, Tábor

Dear Stefan,

We were very happy to hear from you. One of your acquaintances
wrote her relatives here several times, so we knew that you were
doing fine, but nothing more. I am glad that you are in good health;
one cannot ask for more these days. Mother is doing well. She still
works hard, cleans her little apartment herself, cooks, and bakes
Oblaten [traditional Czechoslovakian wafer cookies].

I have taken a room at Rise Gutenstein's [at Zelená 4, Prague VII],
with whom I get along quite well. Aunt Elsa[18] lives downstairs, but
we will probably all move in together. At least one can save a lot on
expenses.[19] We [can afford] two years here. It would be better for us
if Eva's brother [Max][20] were with you, but we are glad that he is well
and healthy, more than that we do not know, but God willing, we
will all be united together again, and that will be the best.

I am trying hard to earn some money, which is very difficult. I have
been making flowers out of leather, quite pretty, but cannot get any
materials for it now. What can one do? We are happy to be healthy
and not starving. There are shortages of this or that on occasion, but
they are short-lived. Due to the terrific organization of the Germans
here, I am sure that no one will go hungry, even though the crops
were not good this year.[21] There is a lot of snow right now, and the
temperature is -4° below 0° [Centigrade]. But it is so beautiful at
Tábor in the snow that we are not cold. We are also heating already.
You there, in beautiful Spain, will not know any cold. We just want
to stay healthy and keep our nerves.

Please write us very soon. We often see Elly's sister. She visits her
mother in Yugoslavia, since she is Yugoslavian. Her common-law
husband does not want to give her and the children up [because
they are going to be separated]. There are sad family circumstances
everywhere. One must persevere.

Warm regards,
Claire

Claire Beck Loos, possible self-portrait, circa late 1930's.
COURTESY: JANET BECK WILSON.

While it is true the Germans were "organized," by that time in October 1940 food ration cards were not given to Jews for various items like sugar, vegetables, nuts, cheese, meats, and many kinds of fruit, and as well, basic supplies were made available in unequal quantities.[22] Jews were also, by some eye-witness accounts recorded in Ivan Margolius' book *Reflections of Prague*, bullied and pushed to the back of the line by Gestapo or SS.[23] The Prague municipal administration prohibited clothing ration cards for Jews as well. They were not allowed to buy many consumer items. The identification cards that would have allowed access to unrationed provisions were also not issued to them.[24]

On November 15, 1940, Olga wrote to my father that she and Claire registered for a visa for Shanghai, which was accepting virtually all applications from Jewish asylum seekers, and she had been granted four hundred dollars as a travel stipend from the Jewish Religious Council of Prague to be paid out in crowns. This amount could be transferred to Ecuador, and Olga was hopeful she could also get a grant for Claire so the two of them could make the trip to Lisbon together and sail to South America. However, my father would need to obtain the visas for them. Many other relatives and friends had already made the trip and were reportedly doing well; one even owned a restaurant. Olga wrote,

"A person could get along well in Ecuador on $400. Perhaps a [money] transfer from the frozen [bank] account would be granted for Claire, too, in the same amount, if it were requested for emigration...."

At the beginning of 1940 the Nazis put strict limitations on how much money Jews could transfer out of bank accounts; as well, none could be wired in.[25] By March 1940, all jewelry, securities, and objects made of precious metals were required to be deposited in sealed safety deposit boxes.[26] Starting in October 1940, no items could be sold or given to non-Jews for safekeeping either.[27] This planned process of pauperization left everyone pooling their meager resources and asking family members overseas for help, many of whom, like my father and Uncle Max, were refugees themselves with little means. Another avenue, which it seems Olga took, was to apply for assistance from the Jewish Religious Council. Early in the German occupation the Council was given the impossible task of raising funds for all Jews in Prague to emigrate.

Olga continued in the same letter, "Claire will be writing to you separately. She is starting a job with a photographer on Monday, in order to get back into practice, and recently took a course in advertising photography. I am learning to make small baked goods. My apartment [in Prague] is being demolished now, and I will have to look for a room. It is not easy to undertake such big changes. But everything can be survived. It doesn't worry me, just makes more work.... Lots of love from your devoted Olga."

In Claire's next letter from November 17, 1940, it appears my father encouraged her to keep up with her photography. Perhaps he sensed that staying busy in a time of anxious waiting would be of some comfort. We do not know, though it is intriguing to speculate, just upon what Claire focused her camera's lens. She wrote, "Dear Stefan, ... Your letter encouraged me to start right away using my abilities as a photographer again. I begin work on Monday as sole assistant to a young photographer. I am looking forward to it very much."

Her letter also solves one mystery for us about our furnishings from the Werkbundsiedlung. She wrote, "I almost lost [the] furniture [you gave me], which you brought from home and put in your name by mistake. Can't do anything about that, but will try to get it back.[28] Unfortunately, we cannot travel much right now and are sitting here quietly hoping to soon be reunited with everyone." By this point Jews were not allowed to leave the region where they resided—temporarily or permanently—

without written permission from the *Zentralstelle* (Central Office for Jewish Emigration).[29] So in the matter of whether Claire was able to go to Pilsen to retrieve the furniture, the affirmative is unlikely.

We know the furniture came with us to Pilsen because it is reported in a letter that has recently come to light thanks to Peter Csoklich. My father wrote to his friend Albin Schwab, Peter's grandfather, in September 1938, "As far as the [Werkbundsiedlung] house is concerned, I simply left it as it was. All of the furniture and belongings are already here in Pilsen. Mrs. Elli [Löwasser, Rosa's friend], with whom you are surely acquainted, would actually like to put the house up for rent. I do not think that is a long-term solution."

Years later, in 1947, as the Patersons were preparing to build the house at St. Lucia in Brisbane for their daughter Joan Connolly and her family, my sister Doris was going through a stack of magazines the Patersons had collected to give them ideas about what to build. She found *Ideal Home*, a publication from England, and was surprised to find pictures of our own living room, and other rooms from the Werkbundsiedlung house in Vienna, featured inside.[30] The house appeared unlived in, like a showcase, empty of people.

We sent the magazine to our father in New York, with the architect's name, Jacques Groag, circled and note next to it, "Who is he?" Groag, a Czechoslovak Jew, had fled to England with his wife Jacqueline, a textile designer. This article about the Werkbundsiedlung appeared in 1947 as part of a larger feature on Groag's architecture practice before his exile. The pictures of our house were taken before our family first moved in. It was eerie for my sister and me in 1947 to see our house without us but with all the furnishings, as if we had never been there.

Around the same time, Jacques Groag collaborated on a small book with Gordon Russell for Penguin Books, *The Story of Furniture*. They write an uncanny first line to the introduction, "Have you ever thought how odd a house is without furniture? For it is the people and things in a HOUSE which make it into a HOME." [31]

Our house stood empty when we fled, and like so many buildings in Austria, became a symbol of a glaring vacancy rendered by the banishment and murder of the Jewish population.

Interior photos of our Werkbundsiedlung house featured in the British magazine Ideal Home, *March 1946.*

From Olga Beck   November 13, 1940
Prague

Dear Stefan,

On Saturday, Claire brought me, beaming with joy, your dear letter from the mailbox and we read everything together with immense interest. I immediately reported to Mama Rosa [in Vienna], who loves to hear my latest news as much as I do hers. We live with you in spirit and follow each of our relatives with great interest, especially when there is something positive. I am happy you are able to put your chess skills to such good use. It is quite a bit of good luck. I am learning [new things] too, but it takes a while to sink in. Some of it sticks though and may be of use sometime. Our prospects are few. One either has to have a visa or a pre-paid destination or guarantor before one can try to get an identification card. Claire will write you too, but you can find out for yourself what the possibilities are.

I'd like to get a few lines from Doris and Karli, and long to hear from them.

Warmest regards,

Olga

It touches me deeply that our grandmothers and Claire wanted so much to hear from us. I have a lingering memory that we did not send letters to them often because we thought writing was futile, as the addresses given us by our father were care of contacts in Sweden and Hungary. My sister and I, assimilating into English, had also begun rapidly to forget our mother tongue. We were able to send our news, however, through our father in Portugal, at least through the first months of 1941. In an undated letter from that winter Olga writes, "I was tremendously happy to get the letters from the children, even if they did not write anything about their foster parents. School and sports are more important to them. And also the news about [the son of our Pilsen friends,] little Willy [Semler]. It is more important that they are healthy and being well taken care of." After this, the only indication that Olga received word from us is her telegram in May 1942, where she wrote she was happy to get a letter from Doris. My sister seems to have remained tightly connected to the women in our family, and remained so, despite the losses that were to come. ■

CHAPTER TWENTY

What Traces Are Left

During 1940 and 1941, my father's mother Rosa, our Little Omama, wrote to him on small black-bordered cards, filled front and back. We have thought perhaps they were the last spare cards she had in her Vienna apartment and she was being frugal, because a card with this black ink on the edges was normally used to send condolences or notices of deaths. On November 11, 1940, she sent to my father in Lisbon his birth certificate and birthday wishes. The love exuding from her writing contrasts so much with the black border. I can feel her motherly affection, across time.

> My dearest Stefan,
>
> Enclosed I am sending you the birth certificate you requested.
> I wish you, my dearest, all the very best possible on your birthday.
> You should soon be able to hold your sweet children in your arms
> and be able to find a job that fits you perfectly. Unfortunately, I am
> not able to congratulate my dear Doris on her birthday,[1] but if you
> get in touch with her, please do that for me. Our dear [Olga] also
> wishes you all the best on your birthday and sends best regards.
>
> Sending you my love and thousands of kisses, I remain
>
> Your Mama,
>
> who will love you forever.

In December my father sent my grandmother Rosa more news of himself, and gifts of chocolate and coffee for the New Year. On December 14, 1940, she wrote an emotional card. "Dearest Steffi, ... This morning I received a package from you.... It touched me to tears. I hope you did not have to do without just to send it." This appears to be only the second time she had heard from him since his escape from France a few months before.

"Little Omama" Rosa visiting at our Werkbundsiedlung house, Vienna, circa 1935. PHOTO: STEFAN SCHANZER.

Just as in the Protectorate, the censored mail in Austria was highly unpredictable. "I have only received one card from you, and dear Mother Olga wrote me everything that you had written her. You have unfortunately had to endure some very difficult times; hopefully you will be able to get by well, doing the tutoring." Her next words are like a little prayer. "May dear God let you and the dear children be together again soon and help you make a living there." She signs it, "With affectionate kisses, dear Steffi, I remain, Your Mama, who loves you very, very much."

In Lisbon, my father was trying to find work doing whatever he could. He asked Olga to send him any photos she and Claire could find of our garden at the Werkbundsiedlung—I think as proof that he knew how to maintain a landscape. He also asked for his gardening book, within it the leaves he had picked from the cherry tree the day my mother died.

On December 15, 1940, Olga moved to a shared apartment at Plattnergasse 9 in Prague's old town, one block from the Vltava in the first district, of Staré Město.[2] My father sent packages ahead of her so she would have a little housewarming gift upon arrival. She wrote back to thank him. My mother Eva was on her mind too. Because of her moves and regulations, my grandmother had been forced to give up more and more of her possessions, including all the little house wares like dishes and linens she still had of my mother's. Likely she sold them discretely, since such economic activity would have been illegal, though it would have allowed her some money in hand.

From Olga Beck c/o Liebig   December 17, 1940
Plattnergasse 9, Prague I

Dear Stefan,

I was going to answer the letter you sent to Claire and me immediately. I am glad to have waited. I received one package in the mail today and picked up a second at the customs office. Thank you for both. I enjoyed the special treats, but regret that you are spending your hard-earned money on me. I will send the photos too, but can't find the ones from the Werkbundsiedlung. The many pictures have gotten all mixed up and difficult to sort out. There would, of course, only be very few shots of the garden.

I moved a few days ago and am now living with some very nice people. My room is <u>one corner</u> of a large white room, but it is enough for me. There is one big advantage, and that is that I am by myself, and have to keep my household reduced to the bare necessities. I often think of dear Evchen [Eva].[3] Many of her things are finding good use, since it doesn't make sense to save them. It would have been better if I followed this rule from the beginning.

I think about the children quite often and would be happy to get a few lines from them, but children don't think about writing. They think you know what they are doing and how they are.

The matter concerning our trip to Ecuador is certainly problematic and may not be necessary. Still, it is better to have everything ready, just in case they need it, since everything often takes months to finalize. It is possible to go either in a group or as an individual from here, but the snag is usually the transit visa for Cuba, which is almost impossible to get. The cost of the trip is quite high. Luggage is easy to transport, since there isn't much.

What is the climate there like? Klaus [Max-Klaus Beck] ... doesn't discuss his plans with Claire. He is very conservative and believes

Eva Beck Schanzer, 1938. PHOTO: CLAIRE BECK LOOS.

that it is better to go with a sure thing than with something uncertain. It's hard to tell what he has in mind. If he would at least talk to [you,] his brother-in-law, about it!

I wrote to [your] Mama Rosa. I was astonished to hear that you had no news from her. She only writes me once in a while and keeps it short. I always fill her in on all the details. She recently wrote me that she had finally gotten rid of a stubborn cough. It is a good thing Anna [her longtime maid] is with her—she is a good person. I am looking forward to further reports from you and thank you for your sweet thoughtfulness. Enclosed are a few small, older photos. Claire will send you [the] pictures of the garden.

Love, Mother

Warmest regards and wishes for the New Year.

Olga only sent a few photographs to my father—probably whatever she had. The photos of the garden include one of the only I have of my Little Omama, taken by my father, sitting in a lawn chair surrounded by our Loos *Stockels* (three-legged stools). I rescued most of the rest of our small archive on the eve of our departure from Vienna when I was nine, and now the archive is as much a survivor as me. Our manner of collecting these photos explains why some are so posed, others seemingly removed from vignette frames, others with pencil marks. The only picture I have of my grandfather Karl is only half a photo, the other person having been cut off. A few others appear to be haphazard.

Two underexposed snapshots of my mother, sister, and me upstairs at the Werkbundsiedlung house have light pouring in from the window behind us. My daughter Carrie brought to my attention a famous quote by Susan Sontag, "Photography makes us feel that the world is more available than it really is." Even though our faces cannot be seen well, I love the pictures—they show how much light was in our house. Another picture of my mother is hauntingly beautiful, taken by Claire. In the developing process it seems Claire left her thumbprint on the left side. I imagine the chain of gestures starting with Claire holding the image of her late sister, and then giving the photograph to her mother Olga, who then enclosed it for my father in a letter.

On New Year's Eve, December 31, 1940, Olga wrote to my father that Claire "works every day at a photographer's shop, but is rather out of practice. He likes to work using modern methods and only takes Leica[4] pictures, which he then enlarges. The photos are similar to the *Bewegung*." The *Bewegung* was a group of artists who promoted a style of art that likely influenced my aunt Claire as a young artist. This photography was linked to the contemporary dance of the time, and realism, where body gestures and poses were as natural as possible.[5] With a Leica camera, Claire's employer was likely doing street photography. This might have been a way for Claire to learn new methods, as her surviving photographs are primarily portraits taken with a larger format camera in people's home environments.

Claire's time with the photographer in Prague lasted only a few months. Olga wrote on April 9, 1941 that Claire was now learning to cook pastries and confections. At that time we know she was living at Zelená 4, located up the Letná hill in Prague's seventh district. But she did not give up photography. According to Olga, Claire wanted "to try going it on her own." She wrote, "We are buying everything [Claire] needs for her photography, using money we obtained from selling some furniture. My landlord is an excellent photographer and is happy to help her get the rest of the necessary equipment."

Claire was a somewhat known photographer at that time because of the portraits she did of her late husband, Adolf Loos. She had studied at Graphische Lehr- und Versuchsanstalt in Vienna, an art school with a well-respected photography program,[6] and from where she graduated in 1928. The fact that Olga's landlord would help Claire get what we can assume to be developing equipment and chemicals, perhaps even donate space for a darkroom, shows some level of interest in her work. And yet, post-1938, no other photographs by Claire have been identified. Possibly they were lost or destroyed. Some of them, as well as negatives of her Loos portraits, may have been deposited in a bank (the Escompte- und Credit Bank) in Prague on October 4, 1939, which was later liquidated by the Nazis.[7] Some photographs may have been confiscated with the rest of her belongings when she was sent to Terezín. If she gave her photographs to people, another strong possibility, they have been absorbed into the large archives of Holocaust documentary images, or if they were portraits—for she may not often have been able to use her camera in public—perhaps the work survives in another family's collection somewhere of their own loved ones, who were killed in the war, or who luckily survived. We have a small hope that some of Claire's photographs exist in an unknown repository, and for these traces of her, we continue searching.

At the end of 1940 and the beginning of 1941, Olga lived "quietly alone at the home of a young married couple," as she wrote to my father at the turn of the year. She continued, "I would be happy if I could stay here a long while. Claire is level headed, and I will see to it that she is taken care of, if anything should happen to me. Otherwise she would be left empty-handed. She has had no news for two years now as to the whereabouts of her trust officer, whether he is in New Zealand or South America." [8]

We can see now there were other mitigating circumstances that prevented Claire and Olga's emigration in 1941. They reported that to obtain papers for Ecuador it was much easier for women who were married. In a letter on January 20, 1941, Claire asked my father if he knew anyone. "I wouldn't insist on much, just that he is decent." On February 8, 1941, she was more insistent. Olga wrote, "[Claire] wants me to tell you that she would not be adverse to marrying your business partner there now, and if you wouldn't put in a good word for her." One month later, their predicament was clearer. Olga stated the fact frankly to my father on

March 11, 1941, for he had misunderstood what Claire was really asking. "Single women are not allowed entry into the country (Ecuador)—one has to be included with a family or be married."

In an undated letter at the beginning of 1941, it appears that this added complication was taking its toll on Claire. Olga wrote that Claire started cooking lessons to keep her nerves from being frayed. "A famous restaurateur is the instructor. [Claire] is much less anxious and distracted now.... Everyone is astonished that such a lovely person hasn't managed to do better for herself. The F. [Franz?] is still quite attached to her, and it would be good if she left. She doesn't want to though without [me] and as long as Klaus [Max-Klaus Beck] doesn't have a secure job." Perhaps other opportunities for Claire to leave were presenting themselves, but without Olga, she would not go.

Olga wrote also in this letter that in order to secure a visa to Cuba a $2000 bank account balance had to be shown. "I do not know if it will be possible to pay for all of that and ship's passage as well. Perhaps Klaus [Max-Klaus Beck] will be able to report to you soon what [he] finds out. What did you learn from the Committee? Claire thought it would be better if she were to marry, but if emigration is possible for a single woman, that would be fine too. [Her brother Max] would approve at any rate!"

My father, meanwhile, had clearly been working on some scheme to get Claire and Olga to Ecuador, evidenced in a cryptic note kept by my father from Walter von Schuschnigg, former Austrian consul (and the brother of the deposed Austrian Chancellor Schuschnigg), who became a leader in the Allied war effort to liberate Austria.

Lisbon   Feb. 12, 1941

The Ecuador operation has reached a critical phase.

You are hereby requested to appear at the office located at Avenida da Liberdade 164, on the 5th floor tomorrow, Thursday the 13th, either in the morning between the hours of 9:30 a.m. to 1 p.m. or in the afternoon between the hours of 3:00 p.m. and 5:30 p.m.

Failure to appear will be interpreted as a lack of desire to participate in the afore-mentioned operation.

Sincerely, Walter von Schuschnigg[9]

From England my uncle Max was trying to get visas for his mother and sister, but was running into dead ends. He writes on April 21, 1941, "I was at the Committee and also at the Czech Ministry for Social Welfare. They both told me that there is nothing to be done from here. I don't know if you know that I already had everything ready for Olga and Claire for Tangier. Today I am glad they did not go there." The German-Italian offensive in North Africa started in February 1941, and the spreading war—should Claire and Olga have managed to leave Czechoslovakia—would have engulfed them again.

Max continued, "I also made enquiries at the Home Office but there is nothing to be done. You say that it is possible to get visas to British India. That may be possible when the people concerned are in Portugal. You say that the whole matter [with Schuschnigg] has been postponed; well I think at the moment they are on the safest spot at home. You know what it means once you start moving, and then there is still the problem of supporting them. I am keeping an eye on the matter but at the moment I really don't know what I could do as long as I am here."

Throughout April 1941, Olga continued selling off their possessions to have a little money. One has to wonder what short-range security the items were able to bring when sold as cheaply as they would have been. Olga wrote of various upcoming expenses—passport photos, physical examinations, application fees—and that she was willing to risk everything to get out of the country.

On April 18, 1941, Olga reported that they were no longer baking *Oblaten*. Instead Claire was pursuing another avenue to try to make some small money as a photographer, in advertising. Later that spring, Olga and Claire worked making belts, handbags, and luggage. Also, to be prepared for South America, in spite of the fact that emigration looked impossible, they began learning Spanish and continued to work in whatever different capacities were available to them in order to be employable abroad. Olga wrote on June 11, 1941, "Claire is now going to a lady who owns a small catering service. Such a small business could serve as a springboard for doing something similar over there with you. She is trying very hard! I am now working in belts and handbags, but I am really better suited to keeping house and could still work at a job doing that. Claire is always saying that she is amazed at how agile I am. Her arms and legs ache because she is not in shape."

Then, that month saw a drastic turn for Jews in Czechoslovakia still trying to emigrate. In what is known as Operation Barbarossa, Germany turned on its former ally Russia on June 22, 1941 and invaded with full force and a blitzkrieg. According to historian John G. Lexa, "Following the outbreak of war between Germany and the Soviet Union in June 1941 emigration from the Protectorate became increasingly difficult." [10]

Starting September 1, 1941, Jews in Prague were required to wear the Judenstern, the Yellow Star of David. At all times in public the star needed to be visible and was indicated to be stitched onto coats on the left side, just over the heart.[11] As if that were not marker enough, the Nazi-issued stars also had bold black letters, "Jude," reminiscent in their letterform of Hebrew characters. Even the alphabet was segregated. Olga wrote on the third day after this new law, "Dearest Stefan! ... We are having cool fall days here already. Summer is over. I am sure you will not be able to do anything about getting us out, as it is useless, especially since Claire would not be able to come on account of her age [and not being married]. [Our neighbor] Mr. Taussig also cancelled his departure on account of his daughter."

The tone of Olga and Claire's letters to my father had significantly changed at this point. A negative outlook prevailed. By October 11, the Nazi policy was that all Jews would be "resettled" outside of Europe. People were still trying to hope for emigration and escape from what had become a smaller and smaller prison of laws, regulations, and bureaucracy. But they saw what was happening around them. People started disappearing, and no word would be heard from them. It was difficult to deny the grim reality of the times and the imminence of deportation.

Triangulating between documents, we can point to moments in Claire and Olga's lives in October 1941 using other testimonies of the time. Ivan Margolius' mother, the writer Heda Margolius Kovály, tells a story of a Mrs. Taussig, perhaps a relative of Olga's friends, or the woman who lived next door. In Kovály's poetic memoir *Under a Cruel Star: A Life in Prague 1941-1968*, she writes that in the assembly ground barracks of the Trade Fair Palace, where people were required to gather for transport to Lodz Ghetto, Mrs. Taussig flew into a rage and tore out her false front teeth, throwing them at the Lieutenant Colonel (*Obersturmbannführer*) Fiedler overseeing the operations.[12]

Olga and Claire's letters do not indicate anything about their observations of Prague Jewish life or how their liberties were being constrained more with each passing week. Instead, we found mostly a record of daily life. The letters appear to show they were living day to day because of the uncertainty, and they crafted their words to pass the censors.

In her letter from September 3, 1941, Olga wrote, "Claire has moved [to the house of Professor Meyer, Korngasse 47],[13] but spends most of her time at my place and eats here too. Today we had mushrooms with *Liwanzen*[14] for dessert. I eat mostly vegetables and soft *Mehlspeisen*[15] as I have to be careful with my stomach. Aunt Elsa visits often. There are actually a lot of our friends still here. You see quite a few in the building when the [designated] afternoon shopping [time] is over. Everyone has family in the U.S.A. and is interested in how they all are doing. Claire is working doing photography and now will also start learning to sew. Whatever a person is able to do is useful, if not at the moment, then later. I don't have anything else to report. Our days are all pretty much the same. Sometimes there's a [civil] disturbance, and other times things go along fine. You simply have to stay healthy, and then you can get through most anything. I hope you will write again soon. We are always happy to hear from you. Affectionately, Olga."

A note at the bottom of the letter is from Claire. "Dear Stefan, Thank goodness we are doing well. I am happy with my new apartment (I am sleeping with an old lady in one room) and go to Mother's afterwards to tidy up her place in the morning, etc. I am busy with photography again, but was only able to get a low-quality camera; still, being able to practice is the important thing. Write us right back and tell us what you are doing. Regards, Claire."

In September 1941, my father started getting cards from Vienna written by his mother Rosa that were melancholic. She was obviously lonely, and was confined to her apartment for her safety. As of February 1941, we know from Olga's letters that she began sleeping in a room next to her parlor. Gestapo raids through the city to find Jews were occurring with frequency, and this must have been horrifying. My father had written to Otto Pick on April 14, 1941 relating one of these experiences, about which we have no details, where Rosa presumably was nearly deported to a concentration camp. "[About] my mother I had news that was extremely bad. She was threatened to be transferred to Poland. But finally she was able to arrange the matter and is staying for the moment again in Vienna.... After this incident you may imagine that I will do my best to bring her as quick as possible to the U.S.A., because from [what I understand] this transferring to Poland means death."

In Little Omama's card dated September 16, 1941, it is clear things had also changed in Prague for the worse. Olga was not writing, or perhaps could not. When I read Little Omama's sadness I understand how this must have pulled at my father's heart—her wishes for his future, her desire to see him again.

Vienna   September 16, 1941

My dearest Steffi,

A couple of minutes ago your sweet letter, for which I had been anxiously waiting, arrived. Why didn't you write for such a long time? You should give me this pleasure more often! Thank you very much, too, for your sweet birthday wishes. Hopefully, we will be together soon. My longing grows from day to day; there is no sacrifice too great to keep me from coming to you. I feel so alone and lonely; hopefully, I will still live to see the day when we will be together again. Thank God, you have also had direct good news concerning the dear children, [that] they are doing very well there and are with good people. Please write soon as to which of the [job] offers you will take of the ones you received and also write more often. Unfortunately, since it has turned cold and rainy, I have been coughing more again. A change in air would do me good. I haven't heard from dear Mother Olga for quite a while and don't know why she hasn't written…. I will close for now and wish you all the best for your future.

1,000 affectionate kisses from your Mama, who loves you forever.

Best regards from dear Anna.

Among all the turmoil of that era, all the women in my family were still thinking about Doris and me. In their correspondences with my father they were able to change the subject and meditate on the good that had come to pass and the luck that we had been able to arrive in Australia with hope for new lives. Olga wrote to my father on October 3, 1941, "I got your card a couple of days earlier, which Mama Rosa and I had anxiously been awaiting. Now we know how the children have adjusted and are being cared for. It's truly lucky that they are being looked after so well. I really don't think we could have come up with anything better. It would be a stroke of luck for them to see the two grandmothers and their father all in good health again, but there is really no chance of that, unless some unforeseen solution comes about for travel later."

Of their lives, Olga continued, "Claire is very diligent. She is sewing at a tailor's and helps with the housework 2-3 times a week at a couple's home. It does her good, and you never know what may be of use. Between times she [visits] me. I found a nice place to live with good landlords, and she sleeps at the home of a very good family. It is so strange how everything has changed. One forgets that one once [lived] in a totally different manner.... When she is done with sewing, Claire goes next door to Aunt Martha [Hirsch]'s sister, where [Mr.] Popper often stops in for a pleasant visit. He envies you! I hope your next letter is full of good news, although I would prefer to hear it from you personally! Many affectionate regards to you and indirectly to everyone you care about, your devoted Olga." The letter also has a simple addendum from Claire, "Affectionate regards."

The next communications from my father happen all on the same day. They are neither sentimental nor emotional but extensively logistic, the result of a notice from an agency "Čedok" informing him that Claire and Olga would have the chance to emigrate. The telegram in question arrived on October 22, 1941. We have just recently put all the puzzle pieces together and realized this telegram was sent the day before the Nazis closed all Jewish emigration from Europe, a fact, as has already been mentioned, that my father could never have known. It seems that neither Claire, nor Olga, nor any of the people in Prague still working to help them knew this fact either.

My father wrote on November 2, 1941, "Dear Mother and Dear Claire, ... You can imagine how I felt when I got [your] telegram, especially since it is impossible for me to pay the necessary large sums in order to obtain visas to Cuba. Beyond that, thousands of telegrams similar to yours have been arriving here, and the aid societies are only helping those who have special connections. I know this from personal experience, only all too well." Nevertheless, he wrote to them, he would still implore the aid societies. He then swiftly telegraphed Max that he should also try to arrange visas from England, and wrote Max another letter expressing regret they had not been able to do any more for Olga and Claire by this point. He then wrote Olga's relatives the Rieses, who had pledged their support in July 1941, to get the affidavit of financial support.

My father's measured responses in his three separate letters that day are telling. To my aunt and grandmother, fearing imminent deportation, he sent accurate information and asked them to think positively. To Max, his letter was urgent to inspire action. To the Rieses, he sent a final, desperate, and clear plea for help: "I include a letter from Simmons tours by which you may see how difficult and costly the conditions of such an emigration are. The worst of it is that we all here have the impression that it is the last moment to help them. Without this help they are lost." But it was too late—the conditions were already so advanced beyond reason.

In January 1942, my father received Claire's last letter. We looked at the multiple postmarks over and over again in disbelief. The last postmark is January 22, 1941, and by that point days had passed since her death. The postmark from the Protectorate was November 24, 1941. In between those dates, the letter had been opened and read by U.S. Examiner 378, who affixed another seal. The echo of Claire's voice finally arrived after passing between censors in two countries at war and after bouncing between New Jersey and New York, the letter having been forwarded as my father again changed his place of residence.

My aunt Claire's last letter, sent from Prague to my father in New York,
before her transport to Terezín in December, 1941.

From: Claire Loos   No date
c/o Professor Meyer
Korngasse 47, Prague II

To Steven B. Shancer [Schanzer]
82-35 Lefferts Blvd., Kew Gardens, N.Y.

Dear Stefan,

I wrote you several letters but tore them all up again. Now yours of
November 2 came and confirmed [that you are working on] everything. I also went straight to the Jewish Culture Society, which is
helping me in my quest and was told that they will make a deal
with the Joint [Committee] to help me with the ship's passage since
my account was hardly sufficient to get one. Hopefully it isn't too
late. I know that it is asking a lot of you to request everything from
there and how difficult it is to get it, but when you are desperate,
you have to try everything.... As you know, I was registered for
Ecuador since there weren't any other possibilities, but was not able
to get anywhere. I wrote you about it back then. There was no help
coming from abroad and nothing doable from here.

It is wonderful that the children are doing so well. I did not forget
Doris' and your birthday and am sending you many best wishes for
that. I believe it is Doris' 15th. I imagine she is quite the young lady.
I certainly would love to see her and Karli again. I am very glad that
you have been able to find other interim employment. You aren't
overly selective, and yet it seems you are capable at every job. I will
write Mama Rosa too, so that she can try initiating something. Elli
will surely give her a hand. I'm sorry, but I cannot help you with the
money. Since she is over 70, it is not so pressing.

I just hope to find a solution and thank you so much for your efforts.

Love,

Claire

Dear Stefan, I hope that we will see each other again!

Happy Birthday to Max, too. Olga.

Stefan and Max
1939-1947

My father's arrival in the United States in the spring of 1941 was a small triumph. However, it must have been overshadowed by the reality of the war in Europe and the hardship of losing family, friends, acquaintances, and his homeland. For Jewish would-be immigrants and refugees like our family, one wonders what kind of empathy Americans had. How could Americans have fathomed the desperation of the times in Europe without messengers like my father arriving on the shores to give testimony as to the dire circumstances abroad?

The official policy of Isolationism in the United States still had advocates even when the country entered the war in 1941. There remained a minority of outspoken members of Congress and citizens more concerned about the American lives that would be put at stake than about European matters. But President Franklin D. Roosevelt's executive orders and proclamations of neutrality between September 5, 1939 and November 15, 1940 make clear how the swell of war in Europe started to engulf the world and how it simply could not be ignored.[1] Among these documents, a cablegram sent to the Premier of France on June 15, 1940 reveals Roosevelt's true sympathies and the predicament he faced with a non-interventionist Congress.

Roosevelt wrote these lines to the Premier the day after the Nazi invasion of Paris, during the time my father had been conscripted into the French army. "In these hours which are so heart-rending for the French people and yourself, I send you the assurances of my utmost sympathy and I can further assure you that so long as the French people continue in defense of their liberty which constitutes the cause of popular institutions throughout the world, so long will they rest assured that materiel and supplies will be sent to them from the United States in ever increasing quantities and kinds. I know that you will understand that these statements carry with them no implication of military commitments. Only the Congress can make such commitments."

Roosevelt, however, soon introduced the Lend-Lease Act in January 1941, which was ratified by Congress on March 11, 1941 and authorized the extension of military aid.[2] American Navy war ships began to move into the Atlantic in the spring of 1941, and American aid to Britain and France became, in effect, a kind of proxy war with Germany already brewing. After Pearl Harbor on December 7, 1941, Congress could no longer maintain its Isolationist stance. The United States had been attacked, and there was no longer any doubt that the war in Europe and the Pacific required American intervention. Four days later, Hitler declared war against the United States to resounding applause from members of the Reichstag gathered for the announcement.[3]

Responses to Hitler's war of aggression had varied throughout the world, from the Soviets, who at first collaborated in Hitler's invasion and partitioning of Poland but then became enemies of the Nazi state, to Europe's initial appeasement of the dictator with the signing of the Munich Accord and the sacrifice of the Sudetenland, to the emergence of new Fascist regimes and various forms of collusion, neutrality, or resistance to the occupations. By the end of 1941, crucial years had already passed.

Historians have shown how high-ranking Nazis cloaked their plans for what has become known as "The Final Solution to the Jewish Question" in "sophisticated methods of deception—fraud, camouflage, and circumlocutory, innocuous language." [4] Many people since the end of the war have tried to quantify evidence discovered about Hitler's overarching plans and the effects of his lieutenants' goals—like those of the murderous Heydrich, vying for Hitler's approval—to try to comprehend the Western response to reported atrocities in order to settle what is really an existential problem that has no simple answer. How could this genocide happen? Circumstances for Jews in territories that came under Nazi occupation, like Poland, the Soviet Union, and Czechoslovakia had changed quickly for the worse in 1941.[5] My father's correspondence with Claire and Olga that year demonstrates just how difficult it was to communicate needs and find assistance.

Throughout 1940 and 1941, my father and my uncle Max had been in

My uncle Max at a resort in Czechoslovakia, 1938.
PHOTO: STEFAN SCHANZER.

close contact and had written much to each other when they had active hopes. But after it seemed impossible to get Claire and Olga out of the Protectorate, my father and my uncle Max stopped communicating for a time. It must have been difficult to confront the absence of letters from Prague.

On February 24, 1942, Max wrote to my father, "The last letter I received from you was dated the 2nd of November 1941. I have not written to you since that date which is certainly a long time but you may understand if I just tell you that I did not want to worry you too much with my worries. I presume you received all my cables, but after all, everything has changed and it is no good discussing the past. Last week I heard that Olga and Claire are well and still living at the same address. It may interest you to hear that I received some money from the Czech Claims Office. When I received the money I was glad and sad at the same time. Sad, because it would have been enough to help my family."

Before the Nazi occupation, according to Max, Czechoslovakian gold had been smuggled out of the country—we know not by whom—and he said that this money may have been all that was necessary to save Olga and Claire's lives.[6] But perhaps it would not have been enough. Max had submitted a claim for his portion of the Beck and Hirsch factory, but he received what was in reality only a paltry sum. The money from the Czech Claims Office only made a small difference in 1942 for Max, who now had nothing else left.

To tell Max's story, we must go back to his escape from Czechoslovakia in the spring of 1939, when my father arranged for false papers that indicated Max was traveling to France as a photojournalist with a press team. My father told me that when he met Max at the Paris train station, Max was visibly shaken by his journey through Germany. This was soon after my sister and I left Czechoslovakia, and I imagine the controls were just as stringent if not even more so for a man Max's age, twenty-nine years old, than they were for us.

Max traveled toward the Dutch-German border, but he was detained by the Germans at Rheine. There he was held up for what may have been weeks, while in the meantime, my father and some of my father's other connections tried to find a way to help him. One friend in Australia, the Pilsen Masonic connection facilitating our adoption, Dr. Hugo Schulhof, wrote in an undated letter to my father, "We have received your letter and much as we were happy about having yet again a sign of life from Europe, we were very upset about the precarious situation of your brother [in-law, Max]." At the beginning of the war, Max had planned to set up a branch of the Beck and Hirsch families' wire and nail factory in England, and found a partner in London who was interested in combining business interests. But Max's original guarantor in England withdrew his offer of assistance upon finding out the guarantee needed to be unlimited.

Luckily Max found another guarantor in a man, a possible relative, living in Birmingham, Mr. F. Fourer. With this support the British Committee for Refugees from Czechoslovakia successfully petitioned the Passport Control office in Cologne for Max's immigration. He set sail for England from Hamburg.

Max entered England on May 3, 1939, registered as a Social Democrat, with an indication of his refugee status being "racial." His only possessions of some clothes and family photographs were stowed in a lone brown suitcase. After months in England, Max was employed by the F.N.P. Manufacturing Company, where he was offered a job drawing wire. The owner, Mr. Vale, who was a friend of Max and Richard Hirsch, sent Max an official letter soon after he began his job, saying he hoped to start "a plant for the manufacture of metal pot scourers" in conjunction with Max and Richard.

Mr. Vale wrote, "We would be prepared to make an installation of 20 knitting machines and 15 semi-automatic sewing machines of your own design and construction, which should be sufficient for the production of 200 gross per day and provide additional work for 34 hands working in two shifts." Business and export contacts from the Pilsen factory would be combined with F.N.P.

After Richard Hirsch and his family fled Czechoslovakia in 1939, the Hirsch/Beck factory in Pilsen was taken over by the Prague Iron Company.[7] Any business venture with F.N.P. Manufacturing Company became impossible, and Max had to accept the reality that he was no longer a business magnate in exile, but a true refugee.

Even though Max had practically nothing when he left Czechoslovakia, he was generous to my father. Max cabled the maximum amount he was allowed to my father's first address in Lisbon—£5—so he had something to live on, and then offered in a letter dated October 14, 1940 to send £200 more, presumably by check, which was then two-thirds of all Max had left to his name.

Max also had given a loan to my father earlier in 1939 for my father's Australian immigration, which I learned might have actually been possible were it not for an emergency request by Max from England to transfer the money back so Olga and Claire might obtain visas for Morocco. My father, years later, wrote to my sister in Australia on November 12, 1943 to explain why he hadn't been able to follow us to Australia from France in 1940, "I didn't hesitate one moment and sent [Max's] check back to England.... I couldn't go to the consul in Paris to press for my renewal because I had not the money complete." With his landing permit secured, would my father have been able to emigrate and join us? From what I understand, the ship we were on was the last to depart from France before it was occupied.

In the letter of October 14, 1940 Max offered my father advice and support, suggesting he still try to go to Australia to join us. "I think you should write to the Australian authorities ... telling them how much you have already experienced and mentioning the fact that you are one of a million people who has succeeded to escape the hell and that you expect that after all you have the right to some humanity. Make them the proposition of bringing £200 as landing money, ... that you know different proceedings from your textile business and that you are anxious to do your bit in the national war effort."

My father had earlier written to Max he would consider joining the Australian army, but Max checked at the Australian consulate and replied that only natural born citizens of Australia could serve. My father also inquired with Max in 1941 about joining the Czech army—was he crazy? Perhaps this was the way he could most see himself being useful to society, even at his age then, fifty-one.

Luckily my father never went back into an army. Max planted the idea that he instead should become a teacher. On December 14, 1940 Max wrote, "I am very pleased to hear that you are earning your living by giving lessons, maybe you will remember that I encouraged you to develop your capacities as a teacher when I saw you last."

In letters starting the beginning of January 1941, one can clearly read the congenial relationship developing between Max and my father. Max wrote on August 5, 1941, as my father started a new life in the United States, "Remember it is three years now that we lost dear Eva and three years it took you to find a new home where you can work and be a free man. You have struggled very hard and only people of your kind who have will power, endurance, and a bit of luck can stand up to all this strain and be successful." Max was two decades younger than my father and seemed to look up to him.

That summer of 1941 it appears that Max was overwhelmed with the task before him to try to get his mother and sister to safety. He had neither the means nor power to change the circumstances for his family, and became dejected. "I appreciate very much that you would like to help Olga and Claire, but to be quite frank I don't see my way how I could be of help to you or them, as any application for sending money abroad would be rejected." Most clearly the transfer of money was one of the biggest obstacles.

Documents in Max's archive explain further. A letter from Barclays Bank on June 3, 1941 shows the Bank of England returned his cashier's check for £25 intended for my father's arrival in the United States with the note "Application not allowed." An earlier letter on May 5, 1941 from the Money Order Department in Bournemouth gives more detail about why. "Under Treasury Regulations remittances by means of the International Money Order Service may not be sent for the benefit of persons who have taken up residence in that country [U.S.A.] since September 3, 1939." He also tried to send money on May 14, 1941 to Portugal, where my father was about to leave on the *Njassa* for the United States. Simply, money could not be sent out of England to persons displaced because of the war.

Max wrote to my father on February 24, 1942, "You asked me to make enquires about immigration to the U.S.A. There are now required two sponsors who have to [get] in touch with the Department of State directly. If you could find two sponsors for me I would be grateful.... If I leave this country now, I would be only allowed to take £10 with me." Should he emigrate, Max would again be left with nothing, but he was willing to start again from the bottom to work his way up. He was interested in attempting to emigrate, at the very least for some sense of family. Olga and Claire expressed several times in letters they wished for him the same.

He continued, "It would be nice if [you and I] could be together again. I have no doubt I would find my way in the new surrounding.... I wonder if you have still the job in the candy factory? How are you getting on? Hoping to hear soon from you, I remain sincerely yours, Max."

But after Claire and Olga disappeared under a curtain of silence, my father didn't write to Max for some time. The winter and spring of 1942 passed. The summer passed. Max's Czech passport would only be valid until May 20, 1942, and it seems that by that time he would have had to make a decision about applying for British citizenship. On August 23, 1942 Max tried to contact my father again. "Dear Steven, It is over a half a year that I have not heard from you. I presume the last letter I wrote you must have been lost." Clearly, the letter had not been, but perhaps it was delayed? "In any case the content of the letter is no longer of any interest as I have decided to stay here. I have no news from my family. To my last letter, which I wrote through the Red Cross, I have not yet received any reply. I wonder if you regularly get news from Doris and Charles? ... I wonder what you are doing? Do you get news from your mother? I would be really glad to hear from you soon, so please write without delay. Sincerely yours, Max."

In the meantime, over the summer my father received very sad news via Lisbon. On June 20, 1942 a letter was written by a Viennese relative we cannot trace for certain.[8] The letter is not signed, and the envelope is missing. The letter is addressed to "Steffi," my father's nickname from his youth in Vienna. It reads, "Dear Steffi, ... You are probably surprised to get a sign of life from Papa and me after so long. This time though my letter has a very sad purpose as I have to inform you of some very depressing news that I just received. Your dear mother, our much beloved and adored Aunt Roosa [sic.], passed away about a month ago. Not long before that, she had applied to be taken in to a pensioners' home in the Seegasse⁹ where my father visited her. Soon after we received the unhappy news. I don't know that all the old people who stayed behind there aren't rather to be envied though when they leave this valley of tears, since the destitution and humiliation they have endured is beyond description. Therefore, dear Steffi, do not be too sad to read this."

My father wrote back to Max in the spring of 1943 and informed him of Rosa's death. I can find no answer from Max in return until over a year later. He was still trying to find news about Claire and Olga. In a letter to Richard Hirsch in Australia dated June 3, 1944, Max wrote, "I have no news of my family. All I could find out about them through the Red Cross is that they are not on the list of the people deported."

Max's next letter to my father was on May 5, 1944. "My dear Steven, A few days ago I got a letter from [our family friend] Mr. Furst, informing me that you are anxious to know what is the matter with me. Well I use this reminder as an opportunity to start writing again. Actually, to be quite frank, I did not feel like writing as the correspondence with you reminded me always of the past. I think the last letter you wrote to me was over a year ago. You wrote me about the death of your mother. I was very sorry to hear about it. I think it was also the last time that I heard about my family. I wrote them a letter [at that time] through the Red Cross, which did not come back but remained unanswered."

Max's letter suggests the ripple effects of World War II and the grief that penetrated his life and the life of every refugee globally. To Richard Hirsch he wrote an undated letter at the end of summer 1945, "The war in Europe is over but this has not brought me much changes personally. There is no news from my mother and sister and my hopes are fading.... Pilsen is at present in American hands, but the rumours go that it is only temporarily." Perhaps the only relief was that even though "the housing problem is a bit of a worry, otherwise we have plenty of food and thank God the bombing [by the German Luftwaffe] has stopped."

Richard's reply on September 23, 1945 is sympathetic in the way only one can be who is living through the same circumstances. "Dear Max, We were very sorry to hear your sad news about your relatives in Europe. We all knew that the report will be that way but once the news relates to one's relatives and friends, you have to go through the same emotions over again, and it is doubly hard. Our news, apart from my parents-in-law, [the Ruedingers], are on the same lines.... We are here still more or less cut off [from] the rest of the world. We have no direct news at all from CsR [Czechoslovakia]. We are refused passports, involving loss of citizenship and loss of all claims in true Nazi fashion. Don't you over there know a bit more of the affairs? We have sent a memorandum to our Government in Prague, in June, [but] didn't even get a reply."

In his letters from 1941–1945 to my father and Richard, Max also tells more about his circumstances, providing a window on the life of someone surviving such incomprehensible events and losses. He began working at an engineering firm at the end of 1943, earning "his living but not much more" and had begun to adapt to English society. Max also wrote of a wonderful new friend in his life, Elizabeth (Betty) Houdret, who would in short time become his wife and the mother of my cousin Janet Beck Wilson. To my father on May 5, 1944, Max wrote, "My chief friend is Betty who looks very much after me. She often brings me cakes, which she makes, and even does some mending for me.... After having lost so many friends it does you good to have somebody who looks after you. She is 26, her mother of Italian origin, and her father English and of Belgian origin."

Max's physical health was sound thankfully, and he had the rest of his life to look forward to. "As far as my health is concerned I am very fit. I have put on another twenty pounds since I am in England, have some more grey hairs but otherwise I feel quite enterprising.... Excuse this short letter after such a long time. I only thought, I let you know that I am still alive. Sincerely yours, Max."

To this long-awaited letter my father wrote back from a new address in Long Island on July 21, 1944, "It was really a big pleasure for me to get a letter from you after such a long time.... At the same time as I got your letter, I got also news from Australia, concerning the children." Relating our troubles with the Patersons to Max, my father also attached the assessment and report from Felix Popper, so that Max could be fully

Max Beck and Elizabeth Houdret, circa July 26, 1946.

apprised about us and about my father's plans to bring us to the United States. He writes to Max, "You may imagine how happy I feel to have the hope to be with my children together after so many years." Max, Doris, and I were his only connections back to a family life. It seems from the tone of this letter that something had broken through for my father, so that he could again reach out. "I am glad to hear that you are not alone any more, and I am happy about that." But he also had hard news. My father closes his letter to Max, "About your mother I heard a very uncertain and unconfirmed report that she should be in Theresienstadt [Terezín]. About Claire this source didn't know anything only that she is not together with your mother. I am always looking through the lists appearing here, but till now I have no definite result." [10]

After that letter, Max and Steve remained connected, though they would not see each other in person for nearly thirty years, until 1972. With the war over, and their bonds renewed, Max felt close enough to my father to confide in him. On May 27, 1946: "I have had a very tough time for the last year.... I [have] great doubts that I will ever get my fortune back and realize that my life here has nothing to do with the past and that I am quite a different person.... The Czech elections have given me the best incentive to apply for English naturalization. I have decided to stay here and not go back anymore."

But resigned to his new life, Max could also look forward. "I am still a bachelor but I don't think for long. I am now for the fourth year friendly with [Betty Houdret] an English girl of good family, she is not rich but very affectionate and looks after me well." Half a year later, another letter announced that Max and Betty married, and they were expecting a child. She would be called Janet Evelyn, her middle name a tribute to my mother.[11] In the wedding photo, Max looks much like my grandfather Otto. He wears a suit and a big smile, and has the dapper appearance of a young sophisticate. "I dare to say that I have built up a certain amount of happiness and have also restored my mental and physical balance. One of these days I hope to become again my own master, but it all takes time."

Max spoke many languages—Czech, German, English, French, and others. He had apprenticed in France, and had traveled to England, America, Austria, and Germany when he was in his twenties. A worldly man, he was also clever. He quickly moved from running a wire-drawing machine when he first arrived in England to then become a mechanic for F.N.P. and eventually an engineer.

Janet told us that after the war Max was in novelties—games—and starting in the late 1940's, he became self-employed and started a business as an agent for watch materials. He traveled extensively around the UK to jewelers supplying watchstraps and anything needed to repair the wind-up watch of that day. His work in this regard was almost metaphorical—Max started his life itself over again.

Max and Betty lived a middle class English life, but Max still used to dress to the nines—even, as Janet reports, wearing a suit while working in his garage. When questioned about his rich choice of clothing, that he could not actually afford, Max used to reply to his daughter, "Let them think!"

It was surprising for me to know that Janet only found Max's small family archive in 1988, when her mother Betty passed away. It was only then she saw all that he had saved, including the letter from 1982 that informed Max of his sister Claire's death. Describing her feelings about this, Janet wrote a letter on March 25, 2010, a thoughtful consideration of the father she had known, and addressed it to him. "Knowing this was so final for you, I cried, you had been so brave all that time, you kept your emotions to yourself, I wish you had been able to talk about your past…. I am thankful that although those days were so sad and lonely for you, you picked yourself up and started again, you were a very proud, smart gentleman."

Janet told us that during the time Max would visit his watch clients, he recognized a gap in the market for jewelry displays. He then devised and patented a self-adhesive velvet that could cover the pads upon which necklaces, rings, and bracelets sat in rotating and lighted displays. He had at one time six lady home workers making these pads. Max subsequently pursued this line of work until he died of cancer in 1984. Janet still has photos of her father's innovations. The empty, purple velvet pads had been photographed by Max proudly from the street, after working hours, never matter that the jewels were gone. ▪

Aspen, Early 1950's

My father had already been in America ten years before he joined me in Aspen in the fall of 1951. Several facets of my memories of that time have been altered by what I have recently learned about my family in Czechoslovakia and what was happening in the world when I was just a child of eleven. Placing Rosa, Claire, and Olga centrally in this book makes the rest of my life with my father have new resonance, and it is more clear to me why he remained with me, so close. We were bachelors together for eighteen years, until I married Fonda in 1969, and enjoyed each other's company like friends, often eating dinner together on cozy winter nights in our cabin. In Aspen we found a true paradise where nothing evil could ever touch our lives again.

My father was sixty-two years old when he came to Colorado, and we began in earnest to build our new life together. He was physically strong and as healthy as he had ever been. The clean mountain air made him even more vigorous and adventurous. One of the things he enjoyed most was the influx of tourists and local characters—meeting all the new people.

The first job my father and I worked on together when he arrived in Aspen was to finish the final details on my cabin, which would become the heart-center of our home together for many years.

In September of 1951, my father and I went up above the old mining town of Lenado to search for lumber with John Strong, a logger who operated Strong Lumber, a small sawmill at the end of West Hopkins Avenue. We easily found an appropriate pine and cut down a long, straight tree to make the cabin ridge pole. My father took photos, which later appeared in a book of Aspen history, *The Quiet Years*.[1]

Another logger in Lenado named Flogaus delivered the rest of the logs for the cabin. All summer he'd been on the lookout for good material for me. The very straight and evenly sized trees he selected were then

*John Strong and I hauling down the ridgepole for the Aspen cabin from
Lenado, Colorado, 1951.* PHOTO: STEVE SCHANZER.

Aspen log cabin and fireplace under construction, fall of 1952.
PHOTO: CHARLES PATERSON.

cut flat on the top and bottom. I had then to take off the bark. This was a big job, but I somehow managed it by myself. I remember sitting on the logs placed between two carpenter's horses, straddling the logs for weeks on end, using a two handled draw knife. Next the logs for the walls were stacked on top of each other with one by four-inch, rough-sawn planks between each course, driven through with a huge ten or twelve-inch spike every three or four feet. Each log was cut to length, with an extension of about eight inches at each corner. I built up the walls when they got higher with various friends helping to lift each new course into place. For a cabin of this type the logs are interlaced, the way fingers of two hands can be.

I still had a lot of work to do to get the cabin ready, and my father helped building the most important element, the fireplace. It was a labor of love. This hearth, I dreamed, would be at the heart of the living room, and around it my own ski lodge, The Boomerang, would later grow and thrive.

I wanted an unusual type of stone for the fireplace, and I found it in a big meadow on the Maroon Creek Road where the local high school football field is now. There was a pit about seven feet across, full of hard and rough, reddish-pink stone. What it was from, I'm not sure, maybe pieces from a foundation, something from the mining days. There was no timber around, just the stones, in this odd hole in the middle of seemingly nowhere.

I carted the stones home in the trunk of my car with half a dozen trips. They were a beautiful color with very irregular, sharp shapes, and they turned out to be tremendously difficult to lay up. The stone was so hard you couldn't break or shape it—you just had to fit the pieces together somehow, like a puzzle.

My father and I worked for weeks to get the face of the fireplace completed. Then the logs I planned for the walls had to become an integral part of it. They were inserted into the masonry mass behind the stone façade. I laid up the back of the fireplace that was visible from outside the cabin later—another foot and a half of masonry, which contained the flue. For this, I cemented on larger, lichen-covered, burnt orange stones to cover it, all of which I gathered from the rockslides along the east base of Red Butte on the outskirts of town.

The cabin was located only a few blocks away from the Holiday House, where my father lived and which we were managing together. Of all the jobs my father worked after the war, he was especially fond of the two winters we ran that little bed and breakfast.

The Holiday House was an old Victorian with a few rooms and, in a cabin out the back, bunkrooms separated into "girls" and "boys." We charged $1.50 for breakfast and dinner and $2.50 for the night. I ran the books, fixed things, and was on Aspen Mountain every day of the winter with the ski patrol. He was the *chef extraordinaire* and the resident manager. I kept my private room at the small cabin. It was the perfect father/son business partnership.

The hospitality business came naturally to my father as a transplanted Viennese. The fact that he liked people, enjoyed telling his stories, and loved to cook all worked together in perfect combination to make him a delightful, welcoming host. He possessed his own sincere brand of *Gemütlichkeit* and was warm-hearted, genuine, and open to people. No matter who was at the door, he would invite them in for food and cheer. His Viennese dishes were very popular and in later years, that is how many people would remember us. He always cooked for those at his table with great aplomb and joy.

My father and I cooking up a storm at Holiday House, 1952.

A favorite dish was Hungarian Goulash, which he cooked in large quantities for friends and guests. After being the French army camp cook in Audierne, faced with the hunger of five hundred French soldiers, he could certainly handle some hungry skiers. All of my father's recipes were quite unique. He compiled them into a cookbook for his cooking classes at Colorado Rocky Mountain School in Carbondale where he taught for over twenty-five years. For the school's fiftieth anniversary, my wife Fonda and I republished it for them as a tribute to him. I've included some of our favorite recipes as an appendix to this book.

One story of his cooking comes from Susan Dean Weissberg, a long-time friend. As a teenager she used to love to spend time with my father, hearing his tales. He invited her over to dinner one night and accidentally dumped a can of prunes instead of tomatoes into the goulash. Suzy was taken aback when he turned the dish into a new recipe—goulash *à la prune*. I'm not sure she enjoyed the taste as much as the performance. My father's motto was "Basic cooking leads to creative cooking," and he rarely gave any quantities for recipes or anything but the basic ingredients and procedures. Much like his life, which was long and generous, his philosophy in cooking was to make the best of what was at hand. There was no roadmap for success. One must learn to think on one's feet.

I built the cabin in much the same manner, with no formal architectural plan, but much energy and some spontaneous ideas.

One winter evening, with my new, adjacent log structure closed in from the elements, the roof on, the windows in, and the floor still a rough sub-floor, I decided to have a chinking party to finish off the inside. In the early days of Aspen all you had to do was tell a couple of people that there was a party and hordes would arrive. No one expected a formal invitation. At the annual Aspen "Old Timers'" event on Labor Day, I still have people reminding me about this party. It must have been as memorable for others as it was for me.

The fireplace going, we mixed the mortar in the middle of the floor. I supplied everyone with trowels, set up the *glüwine*—heated red wine with cloves and other spices—and cooked hot dogs over the fire in the finished fireplace. The mortar for chinking was a special mixture that I devised consisting of sand and vermiculite, a mineral product made from mica that served as a substitute for sawdust, which people had used in the mining days. After a good crowd arrived, we all got to work, partying at the same time. The entire cabin was chinked by the end of the evening.

The next winter, I recall another party at my cabin. In 1953, after I left the ski patrol and became a ski instructor, I would on occasion attend afternoon dances at the Hotel Jerome in the ballroom, called the Blue Room. We would meet a lot of nice people there, ski instruction clients and otherwise. At one of these events, I was dancing with Norma Shearer, the famous silent film star. I recall being flattered when she complimented me on my dancing, which I followed up with mention of a small party at my cabin the following evening. Never giving it another thought, the next night I was surprised to see a cab pull up and Norma, in a mink coat, negotiating the small path to my cabin with snow up to her elbows. My guests—fellow skiers—were quite astounded at her grand entrance, and she seemed to have a great time with us all.

This star-studded event was a forerunner of things to come. Soon Hollywood descended on Aspen and helped make it a famous place. The actor Jack Nicholson bought two houses, one of which belonged to our old friends Judge and Dorothy Shaw. Actress Jill St. John built another house, also Goldie Hawn and Kurt Russell. Actor George Hamilton renovated several homes. Other frequent visitors were John Wayne and Rock Hudson. Gary Cooper's ranch house on Red Mountain, after he sold it, had a sign out on the road—"hedoesnotlivehereanymore."

In the early 1950's, one of the assistant directors of *Devil's Doorway*, Frank Meyers, fell in love with Aspen and bought the land across the alley from my cabin, on Main Street. At the time the corner lot was empty, and the middle lot had a shack where an old blind woman tended to her flock of pigeons. The following summer, Frank built Shadow Mountain Lodge on that property and moved in with his family. The blind woman and her pigeons, an image of Aspen before skiing, were gone.

Years later, the lodge was bought by the Sanderson family, who called it Aspenhof. The name changed again to the Christiania when the Danish Gantzel family[2] became the next owners, and I was commissioned to do its redesign. The roof's prominent feature, reminiscent of Frank Lloyd Wright's Unitarian Church in Madison, Wisconsin, was an Aspen landmark for decades. The Christiania, like many lodges and hotels from the early days, was eventually sold and torn down. In the 1990's it became a cabin-condominium complex.

In 1953, at the end of our second winter in Aspen together, my father and I decided to go into the restaurant business. We leased a space in a broken down bar called the Ski and Spur. Someone had removed the "S's," so on the east concrete block wall it read "ki and pur." The place had been badly neglected by its then owner/manager. When we were setting up our restaurant, I opened a wall closet and out tumbled a cascade of bills that had never been paid.

Nevertheless, we were very brave and opened with a Viennese menu: Wiener Schnitzels, goulashes, and Kaiserschmarren—a sweet egg dish served with raspberry syrup, plums, and raisins. We only had half a dozen tables. Our staff of three consisted of my father, cooking; our waiter, Neil Handelman; and me, taking care of the rest of the details. Neil was from New York and had wandered into Aspen early that winter after his army stint, on the recommendation of a New York friend from the American Youth Hostels. He settled in with my father and me in the cabin. He lived in what we then called the "silver room"—another small addition to the original structure, which had no paneling, only aluminum-sided insulation. On a visit fifty years later, Neil reminded me that he bought the lumber to finish the room so he could live there rent-free.

Word soon got around that we were running the restaurant, and our friends started to show up. Some of our regulars were the Sampsons, who built a log home in the next block that was designed by Elizabeth Wright-Ingham, Frank Lloyd Wright's granddaughter. (It later became a restaurant, the famous Chart House restaurant, but is now demolished.) Judge Shaw and his wife Dorothy would also often be our guests. Next to Walter Paepcke they were the largest Aspen landholders at the time and were special friends of my father's, the Judge being a fellow Mason. He was also a coffeehouse crony just like my father and my father's Viennese friend Kurt Bresnitz, the jeweler. Kurt had arrived in Aspen in 1950 and did watch repair in the window of his Mill Street shop "The Alpine Jeweler" to showcase his skills. He and his wife Lotte were neighbors of ours, renting a small Victorian cottage from Judge and Dorothy Shaw on Main Street, and they became friends for life.

At the Ski and Spur, my father and I found the restaurant business to be hard work and not terribly rewarding. We broke even at the end of the season. This made our decision—we had enough sense to quit and leave the restaurant business to others.

Seasonal spring sheep drive through Aspen to the high country down Hopkins Avenue in front of the cabin, 1953. PHOTO: CHARLES PATERSON.

Our first and only restaurant operation—The Ski and Spur—during its interior remodel (carpentry assistant unidentified), fall 1952. Now the location of the Limelight Hotel.
PHOTO: CHARLES PATERSON.

Aspen was still like the Wild West when I arrived to town. In the early days, Aspen's police force consisted of one police officer, Kralicheck, who was summoned by a unique method when he was needed at night. On the Hotel Jerome's rooftop there was a searchlight. When he was required, one would call the hotel's front desk, and the clerk on duty would throw a switch for the light on the roof. This spotlight then shone on a large rock outcropping on Shadow Mountain directly in front of my cabin. The police and I were the first to know if there was any problem in Aspen after dark. The practice was finally discontinued in 1960.

Then there was the two-vehicle taxi service, Little Percent Taxi, run by Natalie Gignoux, consisting of one jeep and one car. Natalie asked me to take care of the business for her one spring in the early 1950's while she went on vacation. In those days everyone left town for Mexico when the lifts closed. The communication system for taxis that were needed at the airport was that when a private plane came in, the pilot would fly low over Aspen, revving his engine thrice if they needed a lift to town, and on hearing this I would drive out to the airport to pick them up. It was very basic, but it worked.

Everyone loved Aspen in those early days. Just a few years ago, on June 2, 2009, I received a wonderful letter from one of the great friends my father and I made through The Holiday House. Betty Moore reflected almost sixty years after she met us how my father in particular played a major role in the life choices she and her husband, Ken, made when they decided to settle in Aspen.

Dear Charlie,

I saw your recent letter to Ken and am glad you are writing a book [that includes] the early days of Aspen. We came in 1952, and the trip changed our lives. On that first visit, we ran into George Garfield [one of President Garfield's grandsons] in the Jerome bar, and we were wondering where to stay. He steered us to the Holiday House where we met Steve and you, and right away we were installed in comfort and good cheer, in the dorm cabins out in back. For 2 or 3 weeks we lapped up the fabulous goulash dinners, huge breakfasts, and listened to Steve's stories of his and your escape from Europe. What a very dear man he

My father at Holiday House, Aspen, 1952.

was! We had stopped in Aspen en route to Sun Valley—but it was another 30 years before we ever got there. You and your father convinced us that Aspen was "where it was at" and we stayed part of it for 50 years.

Betty

At the time we met him, by Aspen standards, Kenny Moore was a rich man. In subsequent years, besides buying prime real estate, including a lot east of the Hotel Jerome and a silver mining building called the Tippler at the foot of Little Nell on Aspen Mountain, he began taking apart old abandoned mining structures for their huge beams, which he would sell to building contractors. I always admired him for doing this alone and considered him to be somewhat of a superman to accomplish some of these feats by himself. Ken and Betty built and ran the Tippler Inn for many years with the Tippler Bar adjacent. The businesses were very fancy for the times, especially the gourmet Copper Kettle restaurant,[3] where diners sat next to massive concrete pyramidal piers excavated by Ken that had underpinned the Tippler mine structure.[4]

The son of the owner of the Holiday House, Frank Day Jr., also enjoyed my father's stories and spent a lot of time with him. He was on summer break from college at Harvard where he studied journalism, and in the summer of 1952, managed to elicit the full gamut of exciting adventures from my father about his experiences in the First World War. Frank's enthusiasm and ambition were clear to my father and myself, and was later realized when he became a real estate mogul in Boulder, Colorado. Not only did he buy the lovely old Hotel Boulderado,[5] he started a chain of breweries catering to his restaurants, including Old Chicago, which still exists.

Frank became captivated by my father's whole world, which epitomized chivalry, honor, and triumph over adversity. I saw in Frank an aspect of myself—as a little boy I used to go upstairs to my parents' bedroom and open their closets to find my father's elegant blue uniform, with gold buttons and cuffs that he had worn for ceremonial dress as an army officer. In 1914, my father became a first lieutenant in the Jäger Battalion #4, the mountain troops of the Austro-Hungarian army. His record of service, now in the War Archives (*Kriegsarchiv*) in Vienna, notes that he was stocky and strong, listened well to his superiors, was worldly and knowledgeable, and had a good sense of humor. He was twenty-five when he was promoted to officer's rank, just slightly older than young Frank and I were in 1952.

Frank conducted a series of interviews with my father at Holiday House. My sister Doris' son, Tom Schneider, tape-recorded my father reading the transcript over several days in December 1970 and January 1971, so it is still possible to hear his voice recounting the tales that follow.[6] ∎

Prisoner of Fortune, Prisoner of War

It is hard to imagine the scale and intensity of the First World War. There were more men fighting and more casualties in combat than in any other human conflict to date. About seventy million soldiers took part in the war; sixty million of those were Europeans.

When the First World War broke out, my father found himself in Rouen, the capital of Normandy, in the north of France. He had been sent there by the family textile company H.P.S, along with his cousin and best friend, Otto Pollack-Parnegg, to study a new weaving method at one of the factories belonging to Les Fils d'Emanuel Lang.

The Lang factories and H.P.S. at that time together formed the largest textile conglomerate in Europe. This was the result of an arranged marriage between my father's cousin Clementine Pollack-Parnegg and Paul Lang, the great-grandson of the founder of the French factories, Emanuel Lang. Their wedding took place in Vienna and was a huge society affair. She and Paul at first lived in the region of Alsace in northeast France, on the border of Switzerland and Germany, until they moved to Paris.

Paul and Clementine's son Raoul was one of my father's favorite friends. The filial bond between them was the basis for a lifetime of close comraderie. In the better days between the two World Wars, my father would take his Puch motorcycle to visit Raoul, driving through the mountains and quiet valleys of the Alps, or the lowlands of southern Germany into France.

In 2011, I visited Raoul's daughter Marie-Claire and her family at Clementine and Paul's beautiful estate only a few miles from the first French factory in Waldighoffen, in Alsace. The factory was built at the time of Paul and Clementine's marriage in 1892. At that time they lived

Clementine, Raoul, and Paul Lang with Stefan, Eva, and Doris Schanzer at the Lang estate, circa 1935.

just next to the factory. Up until World War II the Langs had twenty-eight thousand people working for them. On our visit to Alsace, Marie-Claire's husband Renaud de Foestraets kindly toured my wife Fonda, my daughter Carrie, and me through some of the area's medieval villages. It was a beautiful crisp fall Saturday, and I could imagine my father driving along the small winding roads on his Puch.

Just down the road from Waldighoffen is the old Jewish cemetery at Durmenach. Renaud and Marie-Claire have one of the only keys to the gates, and so we were able to enter and see the four identical granite sarcophagi of Clementine, Paul, and Paul's parents, Rafaël and Rosalie, all of which are devotedly polished and cleaned of moss every year. Down-hill from the tombs is a large empty swath of grass plots that remains empty. Jewish families from the area owned the plots, but many people in this community never returned from concentration camps. Raoul's sister Yvonne Sauphar had a son, Etienne, who was one of these. Yvonne tried to get him out of occupied France, but he was caught by the Nazis and sent to Auschwitz. He was only sixteen. Marie-Claire and Renaud have a beautiful black and white picture of him, smiling and freckled, in a frame on their sitting room table.

The sitting room has green velvet wallpaper, a baby grand piano, and a beautifully rendered pastel portrait of Clementine's father, Leopold. A portrait of Raoul, just as I remembered him in Paris in 1940, hangs on the nearby wall. All other art is overshadowed by one large portrait hanging above the sofa of Clementine in her early thirties. She is lovely and regal, with a soft smile and brown eyes, pale skin. Her dark dress seems to be of satin, lace, and sequins with a camellia brooch the size of a tea cup, fastened at the cleavage. On her head balances a large sloping black hat with imperial white ostrich feathers.

In the summer of 2011, before we visited the Lang estate and just when we thought we had already found everything we needed for this book, we discovered my father's journal documenting his life in Siberia, dating from his capture in 1914 through his return to Europe in early 1920. There are songs, poetry, and some of the speeches given in the camp by others, as well as addresses in Vienna where fellow captives

Portrait of Clementine Lang (Pollack-Parnegg), circa 1900.

used to live. Much of the later part of the journal is in shorthand, perhaps to avoid punishment if it were found. We have not translated the journal yet, save for the first few pages.

As a child of privilege, my father said that in his youth he was a "spoiled Viennese brat." His military service in the First World War, as a result, must have been transformative.

His Siberian story begins in France, in the Norman coastal resort town of Deauville as Austro-Hungary declared war on Serbia July 28, 1914. My father recounts walking along the seashore with his cousin Otto, as they discussed what to do. Otto suggested they go to America to avoid the conflict, which he himself did (though he returned to Austria after the war), but my father said that he felt a commitment to return to Austria and fight for his country.

Like many of his generation, my father entered the war out of special fealty toward Emperor Franz Josef, whose successor and cousin Archduke Franz Ferdinand had been assassinated on June 28, 1914 in Sarajevo. Many Jews in the Austro-Hungarian Empire felt indebted to their Kaiser for the laws he passed in the nineteenth century extending equal economic and civil rights to Jews for the first time in history. The July/August 1914 newsletter for The Israelite-Austrian Union stated, "In this hour of danger we [Jewish Austrians] consider ourselves to be fully entitled citizens of the state ... [and] want to prove to the state that we are its true citizens, as good as anyone.... After this war, with all its horrors, there cannot be anymore anti-Semitic agitation.... We will be able to claim full equality."[1] The hope was pure if not idealistic.

It must have been in the first days of August that year that my father took a train from Paris east. The train stopped in Nancy and did not go further. He walked at least fifty miles to reach the German border, which had been closed following a declaration of war between France and Germany on August 1, 1914, and crossed the frontier during the night. He enlisted, but later called that action "the biggest mistake of my life."

The start of the conflict had a domino effect and soon most European countries would become embroiled. My father said, "I joined my 'Hunter' [*Jäger*] Battalion in Galicia (Poland) to the dismay of my father, who was pro-Allies. After much combat, my men, who were Poles and Ruthenians, went over to the Russian side."[2] They were fifteen or twenty men advancing an attack for General Dankl's army against an entire regiment of Russians who mounted a counter-attack. It was on September 2, 1914 that he was captured, and my father became a prisoner of war in Siberia for the next five and a half years.[3]

Considering the massive casualties of the First World War (for Austro-Hungarian infantry a staggering rate of eighty-two percent)[4] perhaps my father was lucky at first to have been spared an awful death in the trenches. In the first weeks of fighting he must have seen the bloody action up close—I have the gold buttons he cut off the uniform of a dead Cossack, who were rumored to be some of the most brutal fighters, using torture methods on their prisoners and cutting out tongues.[5] But there was still a certain civility in that war at the beginning that is hard to imagine now. My father loved to tell the story of the Russian officer who captured him, greeting him like a gentleman and speaking to him in French. He offered my father a cigarette, and then told him calmly and without malice, as shrapnel burst over their heads, "Come with me, you are now my prisoner." This type of cordial behavior rapidly evaporated as prisoners were taken from the front to the Russian interior.[6]

I thank our young relative Lukas Beck in Vienna for helping us read my father's first journal entry to illuminate what happened after his capture.

September 3, 1914

We left our rooms at dawn. The ground was wet, because it had been raining at night. A Russian [military officer] demanded the Russian coat I had tied onto my backpack. We marched toward Piaski with officers leading the way; behind them a group of approximately 100 men.

I remember an old windmill at the right side of the entrance to the town where I discovered a lot of Russian portable camp kitchens. Everyone was dejected and walked silently. When we arrived in Piaski, we were brought to some other men who were in a house by the street beside the river. There I met Lt. Zdenko Steidl of the [detachment] FJB4. We greeted each other and decided to stick together in this miserable captivity. The Russians took away my torch, my films and my Kodak camera, and of course my shoulder loops with ammunition. They also took away my documents, my certificate of appointment, and my pipe, but they did not take my money. At midday we marched [over sixteen miles] from Piaski first to the west and then northwest to Lublin. Steidl and I marched ahead.

Behind us, when we turned back, we saw a regiment captured by Russian soldiers. We were really depressed after that. We walked through a very monotonous landscape. I was feeble because I hadn't eaten anything since the evening of August 31st. I wasn't hungry because my stomach was weak. My left knee was hurting terribly. During the march a Bosniak died because he was heavily wounded. Behind drove a cart with seriously injured people in it. I placed my backpack on this cart, but Steidl and I had to walk on foot to Lublin.

POWs captured in Galicia at that time could expect several months' hardship. Wounded and exhausted they had little food in the "march toward the rear." They averaged over fifteen miles a day, with extremely arduous marches of up to twenty-eight miles in one day, before they entered internment camps. Prisoners who could communicate in Hebrew or Slavic languages reported they were able to ask for aid occasionally from people in the countryside and towns. [7]

My father's next entries in his journal are four months later, from a camp in the most eastern part of Russia, after having traveled for weeks across the country on the Trans-Siberian Railroad. New Year's Day, 1915: "New Year's Eve was very sad. Some songs were sung. I went to bed pretty early. Tea was my New Year's drink. Lt. Jellinek recounted for us [the story] 'A patriot tells his adventures,' which ended with a 'hipp hipp hurray' to both [Austrian and German] emperors. Today we heard rumors about a further transport. January 2nd: Our oldest men were taken to another camp. They were sad when they had to go...."

In 1952, telling young Frank Day the story of his years in Siberia as a prisoner of war, my father was an older man himself. Having survived World War II, memories of the misery evident in his youthful journal from the First World War had been varnished over. His World War II experiences put all of it into perspective, and he never told me anything about his suffering as a prisoner. Additionally, the experiences of the average infan-

Billiard brush with false bottom concealing Stefan Schanzer's First World War POW diary from Siberia written in shorthand on cigarette papers.
PHOTO: CARRIE PATERSON.

tryman, compared to that of the officer's life, differed dramatically and conditions initially were decent enough for him, though stark. [8]

My father's attitude about his circumstances remained that they were fortuitous—he was not one to take anything for granted. "I was lucky," he said. "The Hague Conventions of 1899 and 1907 stipulated that POW officers were to be treated on the same footing as officers of the army that had captured them. They were to be given superior lodgings, paid a monthly salary by the captor state, and were to be exempted from any work.[9] One of the great fortunes of the Austro-Hungarian POW officers was that the officer provisions of the Hague Conventions were generally respected by the Russians, at least until the Bolshevik Revolution in November 1917."

While this was true for the majority of his stay in Siberia, my father only took exception to his own statement in regards to the timeliness of the salary payments, which were missing or delayed by months when certain Russian officers found they could pocket the money if they just shipped their prisoners to another camp right before the payments were due to arrive. For this reason among others, my father spent the first several years as a POW in various camps. His prisoner group was first sent from Lublin, Poland through Moscow and Samara, then over the Ural Mountains to Omsk, where they went upriver on a flat-bottomed riverboat three days to Pavlodar. My father was one month in Pavlodar, "a pretty wild" place he said, but where nevertheless he had a fairly pleasant stay as he became the translator for the prisoners through the charming wife of one of the Russian officers. She and my father spoke to each other in French and became friends.

But abruptly in November 1914, the Austrians and Hungarians were separated from the Czechoslovak prisoners and sent back to Omsk on the riverboat. They traveled with Cossack guards who slept outside on the freezing upper deck in their fur coats. The Trans-Siberian Railroad was their next home, for weeks and weeks. *Teplushki*, the railcars—barracks on wheels—had coal burning stoves and three tiers of bunks; my father said, "Those on the bottom froze, those on the top suffocated." [10]

He then was interned in Nikolsk-Ussurik for December 1914, then at Khabarovsk (Krasnaya Rechka) until October 1915. Finally in November, 1915 he was sent to Dauria, a town in the region of Trans-Baikal, which he called "a wild and fertile domain." This is where his Siberia stories recorded by Frank Day begin. He told them with aplomb, focusing on the unique experience of life in a prison camp. I quote from his transcript, with slight editing modifications to help it read more smoothly and with valuable additions from research and interviews done by my niece Linda and nephew Tom.

Our prison camp in Dauria was in a region stretching along the border between Siberia and China at the northern edge of the Gobi Desert. Some made attempts to escape the seven miles to China, but all were failures because the Russians had an agreement with the Tungsé, a desert tribe. The Russians paid fifty rubles for every officer they brought back. Escape was impossible without a guide through the Gobi Desert, the only way out, where it was necessary to travel from one water hole to the other. One of the Chinese smugglers that frequented the camp would offer to guide an escaping officer for one hundred rubles. Then, at the first water hole, the Tungsé robbed the officers, returned them to the Russians, and collected their reward.

The prison camp held six hundred officers and four thousand soldiers, all from the Austro-Hungarian Army. We Austrians had a strong sense of honor that was sometimes displayed among the professional officers, many of whom had quarrels. Normally, these would have been settled by a duel, but since we had no arms, a protocol was made. All duels would be settled when we got back to Austria. This entailed written agreements that were signed by high-ranking officers.[11]

In 1915, during my first winter in the Siberian prison camp [in Dauria], men in the barracks died of asphyxiation when carbon monoxide seeped from the big heat stoves. These cast-iron monstrosities reached to the ceiling and were lodged in the wall between two rooms. The stoves were started with wood and then filled with coal. When there was no longer a blue flame, the flue was completely closed, and the stove would stay hot for twenty-four hours. The windows were sealed off against the cold with

Former POW barracks in Dauria built in the late 1800's.
PHOTO: LINDA ENGLE, 2007.

strips of old newspapers cemented with a flour paste. Just one small window was left open for ventilation. The problem was with the flue. If it were shut too soon, carbon monoxide would enter [into the room]. You couldn't smell it or taste it, and men died in their sleep.

In 1916, my father sent a postcard from Dauria to Vienna through the Red Cross to Dr. Fritz Boschan. His son Fred sent my father's Dauria postcard back to him in 1959.

Dauria   January 14, 1916

Dear Fritz,

Your dear card, which I received today, gave me great pleasure. I have been here since the first of November, and I am feeling better than in Krasnaya Rjetschka [Krasnaya Rechka]. Dauria lies 60 versts [the Russian equivalent of a km] north of Mandchouria [Manchuria], (a border post with China). The present winter is significantly less glacial than last year. Always clear air [and] blue sky. The whole region is empty, without trees, as it is already near the Gobi Desert. I work on my languages and the guitar. But this is only to pass the time, to forget the long wait for peace. On the whole, because we have been prisoners for so long, all of us have become sad and apathetic. I envy your fate very much. You must have done many interesting things. I hope, dear Fritz, that we will see each other soon and in good health.

Your friend,

Steffi

My father and his cohorts at the camp tried to keep afloat mentally by teaching each other lessons about various subjects. This included languages primarily, and my father became proficient in five. It is new information to me that he was also learning guitar—I never saw him pick up a musical instrument. Perhaps it would have reminded him of those long boring days in Siberia. My father said all the prisoners lived in barracks, but there were no fences to keep the prisoners in. There was simply nowhere to go, a true purgatory. They had freedom of movement, but without freedom at all.

For their own entertainment, "the men had started a theater company, and there was a regular theater performance of Franz Lehár's *The Count of Luxembourg*, staged by a group of Austrian prisoners. This operetta was performed in two acts, complete with orchestra. All of the instruments, from violins to trumpets, were handmade by the men. Costumes were made from flour sacks." When the Bolsheviks took over the camp in 1917, the prisoners performed the play twice in one night—first for the Semenovs,[12] then for the new occupying army. This came about because the armies, who were fighting each other in the Russian civil war, would not attend the same performance. My father would say, "It was the only entertainment for miles around, and rather than a 'captive audience,' it was a captive theater company!"

From my father's journal I can see the prisoners were quite talented. They taught each other songs and gave speeches. One of the songs has verses written along with musical notations. One can almost hear it as sung by all the men in the battalion together marching along. It starts with a verse saying that when a man is twenty and a young woman is eighteen, he is "*ready to row, ready to set sail.*" It is the time "*to be at the helm for the tra-la-la, tra-la-la.*" There is another verse for each decade of life until the man dies at age ninety. My father also recorded poems. It's not clear, and I may never know, but perhaps he even composed some of them. Not only did he never reveal himself as a musician, but my father as a poet is hard to imagine. Perhaps in the bleak surroundings with nothing to do, there would have been solace in letting one's mind wander into the more fertile space of language and rhyme.

My father appreciated the bizarre turns of history, and he enjoyed recounting what he knew of the swings of power and intrigue he witnessed in Siberia. Some of our friends and guests never heard enough of these stories, which often presented side avenues. But when another fork in the tale presented itself, he would say, "Ah, but zat is another story...." No one ever got all of the stories at once, but instead they were apportioned like little morsels to his listeners.

The guards at the prison camp changed according to who was in power at the time. At first, it was the tsarists; then, after the abdication of Tsar Nicholas II on March 15, 1917, the prisoners were guarded by troops

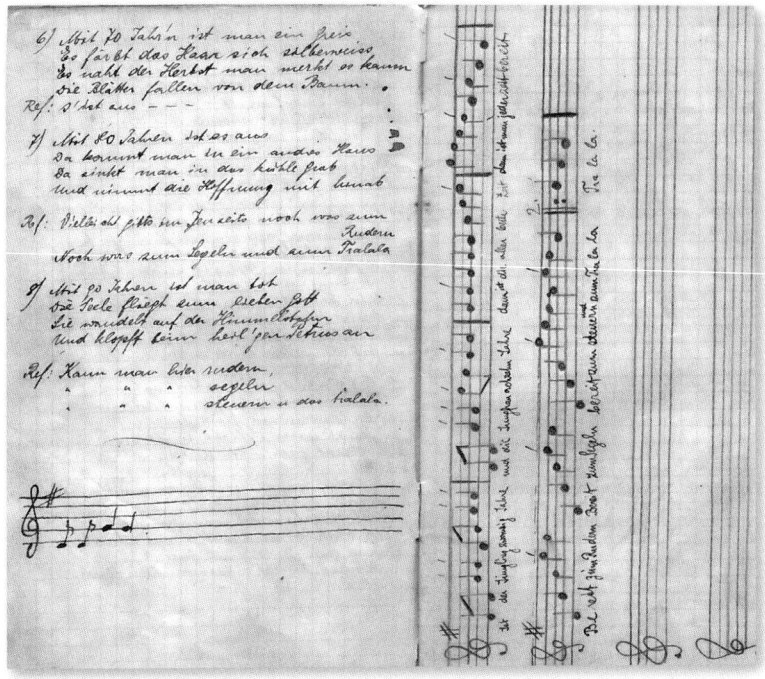

My father's POW journal from Siberia.

of the Kerensky regime; then after Kerensky, by the Bolsheviks.

The collapse of Imperial Russia meant the end of the three centuries of Romanov dynasty rule. There were food shortages and widespread inflation, both of which contributed to the Russian Revolution in 1917. The Tsar was replaced by a shaky coalition of political parties that declared itself the Russian Provisional Government. Prince Lvov, the non-communist Russian Provisional Government leader, was succeeded by Alexander Kerensky, who himself took power after the unrest of the "July Days" when soldiers and industrial workers rioted between July 3rd and July 7th, 1917. My father recounted several related events that affected his prison camp.

Kerensky faced numerous challenges, most of them related to the war. Heavy military losses were being experienced on the front, and thousands of dissatisfied soldiers were deserting. Kerensky was expected to move quickly to deliver on his promises of jobs, land, and food, but there was a great shortage of food and supplies, which was difficult to remedy in wartime. Other political groups were doing their utmost to undermine Kerensky, and they soon succeeded after the Petrograd revolution, when workers revolted in the factories in October 1917. After Kerensky came the Bolsheviks, or "Bolsh," as we Austrians called them. We knew the Bolsh were coming to our prison camp because the Kerensky troops gradually sifted out until, one day, our camp was deserted.

After the Bolsheviks took over in 1917, they brought in trains to get rid of us Austrians. We, of course, thought only of going west, toward home, and to our great relief, that was the direction our train went. It was a slow train that took twenty-four hours to reach Chita, a [Russian] city of approximately one hundred thousand, with unpaved streets and wooden sidewalks. To everybody's astonishment, we were [not taken back to Austria but were] put in nice officers' barracks in Antipikha, a small village east of Chita. We arrived in April when there were no leaves on the trees, but azaleas were in full blossom in the woods, and it was a really marvelous sight. There was a river below the bluffs, the Ingoda, which flows into the Amur River. The Trans-Siberian Railroad cut through the valley, and there was a scattering of huts that belonged to railroad workers. There were also a few miserable farms and peasant hovels. On Easter Day, some friends and I were invited by the railroaders to partake in the Easter feast, which involved eating, eating, and more eating, which was more than welcome to hungry prisoners of war.

Life was not bad for me. The Bolsh were not so strong. They did not know what to do, and also did not have men to watch us, so we were relatively free. The fifty rubles the Bolsh paid us to live on were nearly worthless, but there was a Czechoslovak brewer in Chita who thought that the signature of an Austrian officer was better than rubles for the promise it made to pay him eventually in Austrian crowns. We lived on his money and survived nicely on his beer. During those easy days we made big hikes through the marvelous woods and ate potatoes roasted over fires.

About this time I met a theater girl, Ducia Soleviewoj, who lived in Chita. She was a Menshevik[13] schoolteacher, extremely charming, blue-eyed, and blonde. We had dates outside the camp, mostly near the river Ingoda, where we picnicked. Any date with Ducia meant a considerable risk, and as I walked beyond the barracks I was often shot at by the Internationalists,[14] another warring group, who had camps in the area. Ducia also came to my room, which was not without danger.

On one of my jaunts from the camp to see Ducia, I stumbled into a mushroom patch that filled an entire ravine. The mushrooms were growing from horse manure that had been dumped there in peacetime. I notified the others at the camp, and many of our men made trips to gather mushrooms, which were prepared in all possible manners. These mushrooms helped to bring back strength to the men.

Because of Ducia, I missed an opportunity to go home.

One day I was watching Bolshevik soldiers dance the Kolomejka[15] in the Antipikha railroad station when a train pulled in. At this time many prisoner trains came from the east via the new Amur Railroad, which was completed during the war. Two of my old friends (we had been prisoners together in 1915) were on that train. The train prisoners had money, and they had paid the trainmen and engineers to take them on. They told me to jump in, but I did not, because I had a date with Ducia. Also, there were rumors that our whole camp would be transported soon to the west. I didn't feel any urgency, so I said good-bye and watched them pull out. I would never get such an opportunity again.... ■

At the End of Empire

For all the adventurous stories my father told of his time in Siberia, there were also very difficult times with pervasive hunger, illness, and brutality. My father said sixty percent of the men died from starvation, spotted fever, cholera, and pest—bubonic plague.

Starting in 1917, matters in the prison camps were complicated by the appearance and influence of the Czechoslovak Legion, characterized in the 2012 book *Prague Winter* by Madeleine Albright as "a ragged but intrepid band that [had] fought bravely and well against the Germans" for the Russians, after switching allegiances from the side of the Central powers.[1] One of my father's favorite books dramatized this time and is still a classic piece of literature about the First World War, Jaroslav Hašek's *The Good Soldier Švejk*. The hapless Czechoslovak soldier's continuously comedic episodes can be read two ways. On the surface, the stories portray the experiences of an infantryman whose fate and circumstances always lead him to absurd situations that the reader is allowed to laugh at because of the soldier's seeming stupidity. But contrarily, Švejk can be seen as a figure of passive resistance to the Habsburg Empire, the war itself, and the Catholic Church. The humor in *Švejk* results from the way the soldier manages to "accidentally" insult all authority figures. My father consistently recommended the book to anyone interested in that historical period.

As my father related, "In 1917, the Bolsheviks stated that if the Czechoslovak Legion remained neutral and agreed to leave Russia, they would be granted safe passage from Siberia en route to France via Vladivostok." So the Czechoslovak Legion traveled in that direction on the Trans-Siberian Railroad.[2]

> Soon Czechoslovak trains, not at all welcome, began appearing near our camp, moving east as prisoners of war were moving

west. Each Czechoslovak regiment had ten rifles and one machine gun in the last train car. These men were traitors to the Austro-Hungarians. They were one of three parties in the Dauria region that hated each other: the Czechoslovak Legionnaires, the Austro-Hungarians (mostly officers), and the Internationalists (Austro-Hungarians who had joined the Red Army as the only way of getting food and women). The Russian presence had faded at this time to a seemingly minor power. They were not even able to run the waterworks or the electric plants. Those had been turned over to Austro-Hungarian prisoner specialists throughout the length of the Trans-Siberian Railroad.

The situation, which was really explosive, got rapidly worse. The Internationalists began to rebel against their officers. They even coerced the Soviets into letting them guard us, their own officers. One day, I spoke to an [Internationalist] Austrian soldier from Vienna who was guarding one corner of the officer's camp in Antipikha. He said, "I will explain to you what Bolshevism is: What you have belongs to me, but what I have does not belong to you."

Soon the Czechoslovaks advanced from Irkutsk towards Chita, and the Bolsh retreated. The explosion of relations finally came and there was shooting at the railroad station between the Japanese, who came in on trains through Manchuria to Chita, the Mensheviks—aligned with the Russian Provisional Government [in 1917 before the October revolution], and the Czechoslovak troops. I went to the station the next day and the dead still lay around in heaps. The station was in shambles.

By the end of 1917, my father's camp in Antipikha was even more isolated. No humanitarian assistance was getting through after the Kerensky troops left. Christmas Red Cross packages were looted by Bolshevik officers, who when asked about it would just say, "*Nietschevo!*" My father said this word, "nothing," carried with it the full meaning "I don't know! And I don't give a damn!" He said that these Russians "didn't care about anything but vodka, women, cards, and horses." They were gruff in comparison to the Austrians, who kept up appearances and persisted in very strict disciplines of dress, speech, and behavior. Even after the Treaty of Brest-Litovsk ended the war between Russia and Austro-Hungary on March 13, 1918, Austrians dressing in uniform continued. My father said, "It was a way of life."

Unfortunately, the Treaty of Brest-Litovsk did little to change our predicament. On March 18, 1918, more Bolsh appeared on a train but were challenged by the Semenovs, a rebellious band of loyalists. The Bolsh used the railroad to transport them into battle, often relying on the same trains and trainmen as the Semenovs. The trains would pull up from opposite directions, the troops and equipment would unload, and there would be a battle. They fought under only one agreement—not to destroy the railroad and not to harm the trainmen. Once the battle ended, the losing party got on the train and went away.

On the day the Bolsh came, their trains stopped outside of town and unloaded. The Semenovs were there, and the Bolshevik cavalry came sweeping in, their light artillery pulled by horses. The Bolsh regiment was made up of Burjate. These were Mongols with red faces, giving them the appearance of American Indians. The Burjate lived around Lake Baikal, where they raised herds of cattle on the steppe. These Burjates were a regiment who had fought from the front in Europe all the way through Siberia, commanded by Bolsh commissars.

The last stand of the Semenovs was near our camp. Some of the Austrian prisoners stood around and watched the battle, and some were wounded by stray bullets. While I was watching, my dog was shot right next to me.

The Semenovs fled on horses, and the Burjates pursued them to the heights of the Daurian range. Some Austrian officers went along with the Bolsh to see what was happening, so the newspaper in Manchuria wrote that the Bolsheviks were commanded by Austrian officers.

But instead of pursuing the Semenov troops to the Chinese frontier, the Bolsh returned to the Semenov barracks, stole their personal belongings, and disappeared in the desert. This left no one at the camp except for the Austrians and a few Chinese and Russian smugglers, but there was nowhere to go and no way to get there, so we stayed put. The Semenov troops came back several days later on horses and a train. They instituted harsh rules, and nobody liked them.

A week later, the Bolsheviks returned. They came again on a train and stopped at the top of a hill in the west. There were cavalry and infantry, and as many as two thousand men. The Semenovs were mostly officers, with no men other than several hundred hired Chinese. The Bolsh had artillery, and the Semenov troops were beaten, so they loaded up and left on their train. Still, it was not over. The Semenovs came back now and then, crossing from Manchuria across the Chinese frontier. They would storm Dauria and kill a few Bolsheviks.

On October 28, seven months later, Czechoslovakia declared independence from Austro-Hungary. By October 31, the mighty Austro-

A Japanese and an Austrian officer, Siberia, circa 1919.

Hungarian Empire had dissolved. From my father's accounts, all of these events conspired to make misery for the thousands of men in his camp.

By October 1918, we Austrians were in the hands of the Czechoslovaks. The Austrians saw the Czechoslovaks as traitors, and they, in turn, disliked the Austrians. A month before the Czechoslovak takeover, the prisoners had been transferred by the Bolsh into one camp to economize on the number of prison guards. When the Czechoslovaks seized control, conditions were very over-crowded. Many of us were on the point of starvation, and many couldn't even walk.

Soon the Czechoslovaks were attacked from the west by strong groups of Bolsh. The agreement between them had collapsed, and fighting erupted in May 1918. We received news that the Allies had started landing at Vladivostok. The Czechoslovaks loaded us Austrians onto a train because they were afraid of an uprising in the event of a Bolsh return. Our train stood for twenty-four hours without an engine on it, and no one knew on which end the engine would be attached. Everyone hoped to go west, but the train finally went east. It was early November, and it was cold, with much snow. We had no warm clothes, and our uniforms were worn out and threadbare.

The train rolled through the night and the next day, only to return to Dauria, where it stood another twenty-four hours at the station. Morale was extremely low. The Czechoslovak commander in charge of us had been an Austrian Officer aspirant, and he treated us poorly. There were riots, bad words, and mistreatment. The professional officers rebelled most, and there were a lot of clashes and beatings. Hope was fast disappearing that we would ever return home. Fortunately for us, the Japanese had taken over our barracks, so an arrangement was made with the Semenovs, and the train headed off for Manchuria, China. The only bright spot was cheaper food there.

The trip from Chita to the East was arduous. The guards were Serb soldiers, uneducated, rough, and cruel. Among them, a

Captain Wik was the worst of the worst. Some Austrians hatched a plan to escape south from Harbin, China, to get away from the Czechs and the Serbs who were guarding our transport. But I fell ill with the grippe, Spanish influenza, which killed thousands at this time. The cold was intense. The plan to break at Harbin fell through—I was more or less the leader of the whole thing, it was my idea, but I was so feeble that I could not even move. So the whole thing collapsed—none of them had the guts to go alone, and not one of them left.

News of the armistice came when we pulled into Manchuria. This was a terrific blow because it meant the end of the Austrian-Hungarian monarchy, but it also meant the end of the war and whatever that would bring. The train moved again very slowly east. One day Vladivostok was reached at the end of the line.

But the Czechoslovaks still controlled the Austrians. The Bolsheviks dismissed us as bourgeois, but the Czechoslovaks considered us as their former oppressors and enemies. The Austro-Hungarian officers considered the Czechoslovaks enemies and traitors only worthy of being hanged after returning home.

I was in our new camp near Vladivostok for over a year. It had been taken over by the Americans. Since the Allies had the actual power in neighboring Vladivostok, and they wanted to stop the mistreatment of prisoners by the Czechoslovaks, they decided that the Japanese would take over our camp. Relations between the Japanese and the Austrians were good. They even had a professor from the University of Tokyo as a translator.

Vladivostok in November 1918 was swollen to six times its normal size by refugees and foreign troops, so there were people of many nationalities. Our change of guards was the biggest stroke of luck for us because it meant that as Japanese prisoners of war, our worthless fifty rubles pay was changed to fifty yen (twenty-five dollars) per month.

There were no lights in our barracks, but some of our engineers discovered an old dynamo and steam engine on a nearby hill.

POW barracks near Vladivostock, circa 1919.

Unfortunately, everything had been dismantled. The Austrian engineers got the outfit working, but the wires were bad and not the right kind. A line of one-and-a-half miles was laid using "Siberian cement" to hold up the poles. But when spring came, the poles fell down because the cement was mostly frozen water. The system eventually got up and running, and we had lights, but it never worked very well.

In Siberia, it was common to build a little house over open wells and heat them with stoves in the winter so the wells would not freeze. There was such a well a half-mile from camp, and that was our water supply. The Russians used to bring water in horse carts, but this ceased, so we had to haul water ourselves. We learned that there were small rails lying around and little mine cars that had been used in building the camp and the fortress. We decided to use the mine cars to carry water barrels to camp. We found the rails near the sea and tore them out from the frozen ground. And that's how we made a railroad.

When summer arrived in 1919, we went swimming at the so-called "Korean Gulf," named after a village of Korean fishermen living there. Discipline was light, so we prisoners enjoyed things like that. A Japanese soldier accompanied our small groups to the beach, but wearing normal European shoes that he was not accustomed to, he had a tough time keeping up. The Austrians even had to carry his rifle. The Japanese military were really ineffectual. I often watched the Japanese troops training, which was very old-fashioned in the old German style. The Japanese were very hard to train, especially when it came to bugle signals, which they simply could not learn. One unhappy bugler had to blow from early morning till late at night, to learn just a few notes.

We officers were invited in the spring to the Japanese barracks for the traditional cherry blossom festival, but not much resulted from this. Then one day, the Japanese commander decided to improve the relations between the prisoners and the Japanese soldiers by organizing hikes that were called "Friendship Marches." The landscape was beautiful, and we Austrians loved to hike, but the Japanese could not keep up with us, even though we were emaciated prisoners. These friendship marches were soon dropped by the Japanese commander.

For future political reasons, which at this time nobody understood, the Japanese tried hard to get on excellent terms with the Austro-Hungarians. The Japanese soldiers were always in the barracks talking to us, always questioning and trying to learn. They made us very nervous by that. The Japanese command instituted Japanese language classes, but only the Hungarians could learn it. Hungarian is grammatically similar to Japanese and also similar to Finnish, Turkish, and Lithuanian. The Hungarians progressed so quickly with Japanese that the Austrians had to give up and drop out of the classes.

The Japanese venerated the German officers. They thought they were gods, even after their defeat in the war. The Japanese officers somehow had this implanted within them. Since the Austro-Hungarians hated the Germans, this fawning by the Japanese disgusted us. The Austrians never had a real dislike of the Allies, and it was a mistake for the Austro-Hungarians to ally themselves to the hated Germans. We paid dearly for that.

During our last winter under the Japanese, I tried to ski. I had no other wood than pine, but I shaped a pair of skis with the help of a Turkish carpenter. To bend the wood, so the ski tips turned up, he had to cook the wood for twenty-four hours. The only means to cook the skis was in a big teakettle they had for the men. He did that overnight, and the next day everybody complained that the tea water tasted of resin. Once the skis were finally finished, I tested them on a very thin layer of dry snow. Since there were no good bindings for the skis and I did not have any good shoes, the test was very discouraging. I even thought that I was too old ever to ski again, so the whole experiment ended in a big disappointment.

At this time a telegram came from Ducia in Chita saying she was well and was still alive. I wrote back to her, but never heard from her again. Soon another letter arrived bearing the sad news about the sudden death of my father, Karl. This letter had come through the Red Cross. I had been cut off from home since the start of the Bolshevik Revolution in 1917. None of my letters had gone through, and everybody in Vienna thought I was dead. My first card that I sent from Vladivostok arrived two weeks after my father Karl's death.

Returning to Vienna, my father found his old life completely gone. He grieved for his father. As a veteran who fought for the Emperor, my father felt he had no place in what was now a disintegrated Imperial realm. "I had difficulty adjusting myself to my new life," said my father, "and it was several years before I could again feel settled. I would not advise anyone ever to return home after such experiences as I had, but to look ahead rather than back."

As I reflect on this statement he made in the early 1950's to young Frank Day, I recognize my father's strong will, above everything else, to move forward in life. In hindsight, the Siberia stories my father told show a lot about his character and his ability to survive trying circumstances. He was lucky to not having succumbed to influenza or starvation, and there is a suggestion that he suffered beatings at the hands of his Czechoslovak commanders like the other officers. But he never spoke of that sort of thing, or of fears he may have had during that time, but rather converted everything from that era into a tale of luck and fortitude.

After the First World War, my father experienced more disappointments, starting with learning of the total loss of his inheritance from his father. The considerable fortune had disappeared due to mismanagement and the banking crisis. It was difficult to find work, and he was underemployed.

For decades in Aspen, my father was able to live a life that he had only enjoyed before the First World War. Skiing was solace for heart and mind, as evidenced even in prison camp when he did whatever he could to make skis. Early pictures I have of him circa 1910, when he was a very young man growing his first moustache, show him with his dog skiing across an alpine snowfield scattered with young pines. In another he is enjoying what looks to be a high-altitude lunch with friends, perhaps on a peak's summit. In the 1920's and 1930's my father also spent a lot of time with my mother Eva traversing the peaks of the Arlberg. We have a picture of them together in what looks to be a vast and pristine winter paradise on a sunny day with a few high clouds. She is following the tracks he is breaking, traversing a moderate slope through powdery snow. My father had such youth about him, even into his last years—he was still skiing at age eighty-six.

I always recognized my father's *joie de vivre*, against all odds, but not in the way I do now, looking back and understanding how this attitude expresses itself over a lifetime.

Late in the writing of this book, a detail came to light that makes clear my father's observational capacity to understand world events and trends. My father recalled his boat trip back to Europe from Vladivostok at the end of the First World War, "When we docked in Shanghai, we went ashore and walked along the Bund, the main street along the river. We passed a park, where I saw a sign that at the same time amazed and depressed me. It said: 'All Coloured People, Chinese Included, Are Forbidden to Enter the Park'.... It appalled me that white people had the audacity to forbid the Chinese from their own territory.... People there

My parents ski touring in the Arlberg region of the Austrian Alps, 1935.

expressed themselves freely toward me because I had been a prisoner, and they talked [openly] about the political situation and especially about their hatred for the English, which at this time was already very great. They said they would no longer stand white oppression."

My father realized that this segregation and disenfranchisement meant China was ripe for a revolution, which indeed occurred six years after he stopped through Shanghai. After seeing the stark contrast between Bolshevik propaganda and the reality of life under Communist rule, he could understand what "opportunities [were] afforded the 'Bolsh' [Communists] by this [park] sign." He said, "I was convinced that no army could withstand [Communist] propaganda, for every enlisted man was made to feel that they were the victims of the bourgeois officers who were driving them for their own interests.... In 1920, the picture was already clearly painted, but most of the world did not yet understand it."

After Shanghai, my father's ship docked in Singapore. He observed, "The weather was very hot. I saw that no white man went on foot; all went in rickshaws. I had felt in Shanghai that rickshaws were degrading for the Chinese, and I refused to be drawn around by another human being. Anxious to see how a man could stand up under the heat, I took a short hike on the outskirts of Singapore in the midday heat. There was no ill effect. Again, I saw golf courses, etc. all restricted. Everywhere there were signs 'For White Men Only.' There was also a shocking difference between the luxuriant white quarters and the native slums. The white quarters were full of trees and nice houses, similar to American suburbs, while the natives lived in crowded, flimsy, wooden houses. When we docked in Colombo, it was similar to Singapore. I talked to different people around town, among them a jeweler. When he found out that I was from Vienna he invited me to dinner. He was native, and he talked very freely about the English oppression. His people had hoped that the war would weaken the English so that the Indians could gain independence. The picture was again apparent: the English must go."

The collapse of all empires is inevitable, as my father learned after the dual monarchy of Austro-Hungary disintegrated. Although my father sometimes seemed nostalgic for Austro-Hungary's Imperial days, because his family's life in Vienna was peaceful, after 1920 he clearly saw war's roots in colonial oppression. ∎

One of the Japanese cargo ships that left Vladivostock
with returning POWs for Europe, 1920.

CHAPTER TWENTY-FIVE

Money Matters

In the spring of 1953, my father was looking for a summer job. Meanwhile, I had moved to Rockford, Illinois for a few months' stint helping the office manager at our friend Harry Espenscheid's lumber company. I was in a cast and healing a broken leg I incurred at the end of the season on Aspen Mountain while skiing on Spring Pitch too fast and recklessly.

My father's first idea for work was to apply at the Hotel Colorado, a large hotel in Glenwood Springs, about forty miles northwest of Aspen. But it was a bureaucratic operation, and he did not appreciate the red tape or the reply he got with a stamped signature of the manager. In Europe he had connections but in Colorado—none. He expected the job would not be forthcoming and instead began to lay the groundwork in Aspen for a truly Viennese café.

He wrote to me on May 15, 1953, "We are working on a new idea, to serve coffee, tea, etc. at Shaw's mining museum next to the Wheeler Opera House. The name of the enterprise will be Café Museum, the same name as the Café Museum in Vienna, built by your uncle Adolf Loos. Arlette will bake the pastries. Mrs. Shaw will build a small kitchen and all the facilities. At the same time everybody can visit the museum and read and look at the pictures. The whole thing will be unique."

Loos' Café Museum in Vienna is near Karlsplatz, and was never literally attached to a museum. It still does good business, though it is without much of the original interior, has gone through several different hands, and was decrepit for several decades before its recent refurbishing. Unfortunately to some, all Loos' original furnishings such as cane chairs have been replaced with tourist-friendly red velvet booths. I was there with my wife Fonda and our daughter Carrie in 2011 and found the environment to be quite cozy. But two generations of Viennese with whom we were there found the redecoration a travesty and said they would not frequent the establishment again!

My father used to say that in his generation it was a standard procedure to make a joke out of the classical Viennese pessimism, so when someone asked him how he was, he would reply, "From bad to worse, as usual." But not just Viennese anymore, and now an American, these traits became fodder for the reservoir of humor my father possessed.

My father's letters were full of jokes and gossip, like conversations we used to have over dinner, or what I have heard from his friend Kurt Bresnitz they used to talk about when they met for their daily coffee klatch at The Epicure on Aspen's Main Street. Kurt and my father had a pact to tell each other a new joke every day. Other opportunities were my father's visits to Kurt's store Alpine Jeweler. My father would ask, "How's business?" Kurt's reply was a standard complaint in typical Viennese style about how bad it was. To match this retort my father had an old saying that also appeared in the Marx Brothers' *Duck Soup* from 1933: "*Ah, Der Pleitegeier*! The vulture of bankruptcy is circling!" This Yiddish-Viennese from the turn of the last century is a word play on the German Bundesadler Eagle, sometimes caricatured as a vulture in the context of Germany's economic depression. Kurt's shop actually did quite well; he was in business for thirty-six years, from 1950 until 1986.

Like us, Kurt escaped Vienna in 1938. He was just weeks away from graduating from the Commercial Academy (the equivalent of college). He served in World War II for the Americans as a translator, was at the Battle of the Bulge at the end of 1944 in Belgium—one of the bloodiest in the whole war—and was present at the liberation of Dachau and among the first to enter Hilter's mountaintop retreat, the "Eagle's Nest." In 2010, he was awarded an honorary diploma from Aspen High School—making him the oldest graduate, in his nineties.

From my father via letters to Rockford I got all the Aspen scuttlebutt. I read the latest on May 15, 1953 that our popular Hotel Jerome manager, Chuck Bishop, had been treated badly by Mr. Paepcke and a rumor was circulating that Paepcke was thinking about closing the ski lifts, "because he does not like skiers," supplanting all the tourist activities with the Aspen Institute. Today this seems absurd.

My father also informed me, "There is a rumor that Friedl Pfeifer [founder with Paepcke and others of Aspen Skiing Corporation] is fed up with Aspen and is going [back] to Sun Valley. Judge Shaw says Paepcke is a very hard man to deal with. So Judge Shaw wants to open the area in Lincoln Gulch. I think I will go pretty soon there to look at the region." This was serious news from our small town and reason for alarm. Would our skiing have to move elsewhere? Or did there just seem to be so many other opportunities in that excellent terrain? Lincoln Gulch was another old mining area, but about ten miles out of Aspen up Independence Pass Road, a thin winding ribbon that would have been, at the very least, treacherous for winter travel. Luckily for Aspen, downhill skiing developments stayed fairly close to town.

I found a letter from the fall before, September 9, 1952, where my father tried to talk our friend Harry Espenscheid into starting a high alpine lodge. The Espenscheids had been great guests of ours at the Holiday House and became enamored with Aspen. We helped them look for land and close the deal, after which time my father schemed a way for the three of us to start a business together.

Informally surveying the land one day while up on Taylor Pass with Frank Day Jr., my father came upon his newest idea. They were up at an elevation of twelve thousand feet to rescue Frank's jeep that he had gotten stuck. My father wrote to Harry about the adventure, "Now as you know, the jeep road to Taylor Pass and Taylor Lake passes through the hinterland of your property. I was really amazed about the possibilities your location has.... In winter this is a ski terrain above the timberline of extreme beauty similar to the Arlberg formations. But nobody ever skis there.... It would be easily reached in winter with a snowcat ... and then after skiing they could spend the night at a cabin on your property. [It] would also be a wonderful starting point for all tours to Montezuma and Mt. Hayden. There is also from Taylor Pass a ten-mile hike possible [along Richmond Ridge] to the Sundeck [at the top of Aspen Mountain]."

The mountains made my father dream up yet another new chapter in his life—running a ski touring lodge. He continued, "I saw one mile up the jeep road to Taylor Pass on the left side a whole big mountain slide of stones, the same moss covered type as we built our outside fireplace, ready for use in the size of bricks. You need only cement to build a house on your location. You just have to truck them down the jeep road."

While my father was always thinking of new opportunities, his ideas were often too grand, and he never had the money to get them started. Running even a small lodge in town was hard enough as we found, and the Espenscheids thankfully never took him up on his idea. Most of his other business schemes never materialized either—helicopter tours, a corporation with his friends the Ortmans to own a gasoline station and a grocery story with a dozen cabins at the edge of town, a jewelry room in the back of our cabin, the import of European handkerchiefs, jet planes, perpetual motion by magnetism, pantyhose so that ladies didn't have to use garter belts, self-cleaning public toilets.... Some of these, of course, came to exist. My father was a visionary, but without funds.

Instead, he continued to be a teacher of languages as he was in Lisbon during World War II. With pupils for French and German, and a cooking reputation to back up the conversational exchanges, he was never short on people in Aspen who wanted to learn from him. He wrote on June 18, 1953, "My French pupil Eleanor Birkholz, the nurse, left for the summer but I have four new ones. They are all now coming at 8:30 in the morning and I have nearly every day a lesson."

In his letters to me in Rockford, my father told of various romances between people we knew. He always had an opinion and was good at getting the scoop. "Every time Jo Culloden sees me she is asking about you. I heard that the story with Chuck is off and she was seen with the new Swiss cook from the Hotel Jerome. She said that she will go home for two weeks and then probably return again for the summer as a publicity woman. So Lenny Woods'[1] hand is still to be felt above her, nevertheless the new colonel [the manager of the hotel] is firing all of the old personnel. I have the details from Barbara Zuger, my new pupil."

The Hotel Jerome management was drawing ire from all around town. My father continued, "The colonel is instituting a sharp regime. He just fired Barbara because she talked to the guests and ate her breakfast with another girl in the dining room after the hours. No ski bums anymore, only professionals. They have to work from eight to six every day, six days a week, they have to not mingle with the guests and only use the back door entrance. No swimming pool any more for them. She told me the cook asked for wine for a pot roast, he said use pepper and salt, that is enough."

As observed at the Jerome, Aspen was changing in what, to my father, were almost offensive ways. He naturally would be the first person to sense things "going downhill," particularly when it came to food. In this same letter he also told me the traditional Hospital Benefit dinner was horrible, spoiled by bad cooking. My father wrote with indignation, "First fruit cocktail out of the can. Then a turkey which was hard meat, nearly no stuffing, dry, no gravy, and on the side some whole small onions with the famous, starchy white sauce over it. You could not eat them; they were out of a can too. Then came an ice cream, as bad as possible with a very tiny little bit of cookie. And coffee. This was the famous dinner. There were so many complaints." As a result, the "colonel" had to back off his militaristic style of management and apologize for the bad dinner because he upset so many people.

On and on it went: if it weren't for my father being Viennese one might think Aspen was going to the dogs. But no, he was enjoying himself writing this all down. He continued, "I described this so thoroughly because I wanted to show you the new spirit Paepcke introduced at the hotel. There will be no more credit at the bar, not even to the Smiths, those rich people who run big bills monthly. You may imagine the talk in town." It seemed that Paepcke was suffering too many losses and was clamping down on everyone's lax attitudes. He was apparently trying to get the hotel to be more business-like. But this German efficiency offended my father. It was not very *gemütlich*, hospitable.

Then my father reported running into Fred Iselin, the ski school co-director, who seemed only warm on the idea of me returning to work for him. He told my father that I should stay in the construction industry, as "there is no future in ski teaching." But the bottom line was that I was determined to return to skiing after the summer, no matter what—it was a joy, a lifestyle. So I sent a letter to Iselin immediately to make sure I had a place. I needed to secure that job, future in it or not. I had planned my life in Aspen to be spent on skis.

My father encouraged me and concurred that it was a good thing to pursue, at least for the next winter—and he missed me. "I myself am looking forward to seeing you again. It gets sometimes very lonely without you. Love, Pop."

Back in Rockford, I had just moved out of the Espenscheid's house, having found something suitable to rent in town. Harry and his wife Dorothy had been very good to me, and they had put me up when I first arrived. Their three small children, two boys and a girl, were delightful and always came running out the door to hang onto my hands or hug me when I returned from work. They had a nice house on the golf course, two cars, a horse and pony, and a huge new television set in anticipation of television coming to Rockford. An industrial city with a healthy economy and a predominately Swedish population, Rockford was a growing city. I observed, however, that the houses being built were conservative and mostly ranch style. Nevertheless, the old part of town was quite lovely with huge elm trees lining the streets in the stately neighborhood.

I got paid at $60 a week working at Harry's "City Lumber" and found him to be quite an entrepreneur. He had his hands simultaneously in a lot of businesses, which guaranteed him to be a person from whom I could learn key traits. His myriad enterprises besides the lumber yard included building houses and housing developments, a lease deal with Piggly Wiggly supermarkets in a new mall he had developed, and investing in a few new oil wells. He reminded me of my Australian foster father, Charles Raff Paterson, who had the same entrepreneurial spirit and took me under his wing when I was seventeen, involving me in his businesses in a similar manner.

In the middle of summer I checked out an old book from the local Rockford library, *How to Plan a House: A Book for All About to Build* by George Gordon Sampson, from 1910. I made lots of notes and read assiduously while redrawing floor plans for the future lodge I wanted to build in Aspen.

The lodge idea was a moving target, which was constantly reviewed and changed as I learned more and more about construction problems. I was envisioning starting to build in the fall of 1953 and being ready by the winter ski season. To do this, I hoped to get a railcar load of lumber through my great-aunt Käthe Pick from her family's lumber company, Canadian Forest Products Ltd. in Vancouver. It was already a good-sized operation at that time, but later it grew into a huge enterprise, CANFOR, and became the largest lumber conglomerate in Canada. In 1953 I was a dreamer—perhaps influenced by my father's wild ideas— when I planned to ask them to gamble on Aspen and invest lumber in our lodge. The Picks had helped my father already extensively in our quest to emigrate to Australia and later to the United States, so I felt they were a good connection. But I was so ambitious about the lodge that I was not

City Lumber in Rockford, Illinois, 1953. PHOTO: CHARLES PATERSON.

even realistic, which my father rapidly pointed out. His own relationship with the Picks was familiar and friendly—they had also seen each other in France in 1938 and later in New York—but it was delicate. My father no doubt felt indebted to them beyond what I possibly understood. This made my intentions a little tricky for him to navigate. However, I continued my campaign.

Rockford, IL   July 29, 1953

Dear Pop,

You see why I'm so hyped up about the lodge, since I figure I could build it by the winter season if I go at it like hell in Sept., Oct., Nov., and Dec. If I get a loan, I could go ahead and hire the necessary help. I don't think I could spend the next months more profitably. I feel very strongly that I should go ahead right away and at least write Aunt Käthe a letter about the lodge, etc. If I don't get a reply in two weeks, I'll write another and call her up on the phone.

Today after work, Harry Espenscheid and our Super came by, since I was late getting away [from work, as a carpenter on one of the houses]. I stayed while they looked around. Harry complimented me on a nice job, which pleased me a great deal. I pointed out that the [house] blueprint should be changed a little to save material and make things more workable, and Harry immediately turned around and said he'd pay me for my time to redesign the plan a little and make some changes. I think I'll take him up on that and work on it nights.

Love,

Charlie

My father was not in as much of a rush as I was to see the lodge built. On August 18th, 1953, he wrote with much gentleness and understanding, "I want as much as you that we build a lodge for ourselves, but I think that it will be premature to try to finish a lodge this fall. We certainly would not be ready in time and would lose a lot of money, and get into a terrible situation. I would perhaps advise a middle way. First, secure an option on the land to the right and left [of the cabin]. Then quiet the titles. Then perhaps make a ski barn out of the back room and the garage. This would start us in the lodge business again and would not involve too much capital. And when we are again established in the lodge business, then we could perhaps go ahead next spring in building. When we both work very hard in this small addition and cook meals in winter for the ski bums, we could make a living. We could also rent to the weaving people, who would like to use the space for looms."

While my father was very clear that we needed to be careful financially, I felt like I was living in a silver rush. But for him, a lodge in a young ski town was potentially a money pit. Our friend Judge Shaw advised my father against taking on more debt. My father's idea was to ask the Picks for a long-term credit on lumber and then ask Harry Espenscheid to finance the building.

Meanwhile, my father's Café Museum was becoming a business of its own. "Mrs. Shaw has the intention to build into the museum a heating plant," he wrote, "and we could run [the Café Museum and make] meals for people who order in advance there. We have only been open three days and we did not have any advertisement whatsoever, not even a sign outside, but today a lot of people came to buy the pastry that I made, Linzertorte and Ischlerkrapfen, to take them home, because they said it is much better than The Epicure."

Viennese cookbook, 1925.

Still, my father reported, there were other exciting opportunities. "The day of our big opening at the Café Museum, which was a big success, the whole town was here. There was a gentleman asking me how is Charlie? He came just now from Graz [Austria] from the Puch-werke, for Puch motorcycles. Sears Roebuck will import all the Puch products into [the] U.S. I told him right away that I would like to have the representation in Aspen and surrounding towns, and he said that this is very interesting to meet a Puch man, and he will keep me posted. I close this letter to bring it to the post office. Love, Pop." This man was no other than Andy Beusch, who helped me get cheap materials for my early cabin, and for whom I had worked building his house on West Bleeker Street. To my father's dismay, the Puch distributorship never materialized, but with cooking, baking, and language instruction, he had enough to do.

Shortly after writing his letter to me, my father received word from his old friend Albin Schwab about our ongoing restitution claims against the Austrian government. The results were not positive. The Austrian government was compensating Wehrmacht soldiers and their families first, those conscripted to fight with the Nazis, before they dealt with claims by Jewish concentration camp survivors or émigrés.[2] Schwab was not able to achieve any results, despite a great effort.

My father continued to file claims up until 1977, two years before his death. Some of these were about my mother's inheritance that disappeared in Berlin at the start of the war. He also encouraged me to apply for my own pension, which I am due by right of my Austrian birth certificate. When I applied, one request was for documentation of school attendance, of which I had none. However, Doris and I looked at the map of Vienna that Schwab had sent my father, and on it we retraced the route we walked to school. We remembered all the street corners, and the school buildings showed on the map. We then made a copy of the map to include with the application, with our route to school highlighted as part of our testimony.

By retroactively paying Austria several thousand dollars, I became eligible to receive a life pension. This is part of a larger reparations program under the U.S.-Austria International Agreement on Social Security for people who were persecuted for religious or political beliefs during World War II.

There is much more to be written about restitution, since it was only toward the turn of the twenty-first century that the Austrian

Albin Schwab with granddaughter Birgit and piglet, late 1940's.

government created a commission to look more closely into the appropriation of Jewish assets and property. In 1998, an investigative journalist named Hubertus Czernin exposed Austria's collusion with Nazi plundering.[3] In the face of Czernin's reporting and other negative press, Austria made the commitment to fully restore all property, including furniture and artworks that were stolen from Jewish families during the war.

The return of stolen artworks in particular was contentious. One famous case is that of a Gustav Klimt painting, the 1907 portrait of a woman related by marriage to Otto and Käthe Pick, Adele Bloch-Bauer. The painting was returned to her niece Maria Altmann in Los Angeles after a long lawsuit.[4] The painting was one of Klimt's signature works, and claimed by the Austrians to be a national treasure and part of their cultural heritage, even though it was ill gotten. Four other Klimt paintings were also returned. The case of the Bloch-Bauer portrait is the subject of a 2012 book, *The Lady in Gold* by journalist Anne-Marie O'Connor. It is a timely story about Nazi plunder told at the same time Austria declared 2012 to be "the year of Gustav Klimt around the world."[5]

On April 14, 2005, a *New York Times* article by William Glaberson detailed Käthe and Otto Pick's own efforts at restitution for the loss of the Bloch-Bauer-Pick sugar refinery, one of Austria's largest in 1938. The claim recuperated $21.8 million of the refinery's significant total worth. Eight days before the *Anschluss* in March 1938, the Picks had set up a trust account in an unnamed Swiss bank to protect their ownership, but according to Glaberson, "The attempt quickly unraveled. Within months the bank had violated the terms of the account, and the business was Aryanized.... In a letter dated December 22, 1938, a bank officer provided an explanation as blunt as it was chilling: 'The situation has changed.'" The new owner was a Nazi sympathizer.[6]

Out of the $50 billion in restitution programs undertaken since the end of WWII, the Pick claim is one of the largest awards. The Swiss banks alone have had to pay out $1.25 billion as a result of a class-action lawsuit filed in 1998.[7] The number is a shocking revelation, to think about the economics of Nazi Germany alone—and how Europe's road to ruin was financed with all these stolen industries and money. And beyond that, it wasn't just that the war that was underwritten, but the pleasures and refinements of life itself were transferred into Nazi hands.

The cruel irony is that while Nazis espoused a socialist view and promised to lift up the German working class, they saw themselves as heirs to a great kingdom, with palaces, artwork, and all the trappings of a ruling class. For example, Nazi Hermann Göring, commander of the Luftwaffe, Reichsmarschall, and at one point Hitler's intended successor, talked openly about his intention to plunder treasures from occupied territories.[8] Reinhard Heydrich even confiscated the beautiful castle of Ferdinand Bloch-Bauer in Panenské Břežany, fifteen miles north of Prague.[9][10]

As Glaberson concludes, "In a way, to the living descendants of [the Pick and Bloch-Bauer] families and to a world where the number of surviving victims of the Nazis and their collaborators is dwindling, the huge award [from the Swiss bank] is more than that. It provides a detailed trip back to a dark time, showing exactly how the banks' actions helped the Nazis, how lifetimes' achievements were lost in days, and how the process was masked in the language of ledgers, legalisms, and banking."[11]

While I was in Rockford, my father wrote to Doris, Herb, and me about our own restitution efforts. He was grateful that his friend Schwab "did a tremendous lot of work for us, [more than anyone] ever did before. He went right to the source of things, and by his letter you see quite clearly that the Austrian Government owes us the money. We know now also where to address our complaints. It is the '*Finanzlandesdirektion, Dienstelle fur Vermögenssicherung*' [Provincial Finance Directorate, Department providing asset protection]." He joked, "You could better call this '*Vermögenssicherung* (Fortune Securing)'— '*Vermögensunsicherung* (Fortune Unsecuring)' because there the money disappeared." Writing this book, I paid a visit to my father's old friend Kurt Bresnitz—well into his nineties—to check a few translations. When he read this letter about the Unsecure Bank, Kurt laughed, "Oh, my father must have deposited his money there too!" ▪

CHAPTER TWENTY-SIX

Basic Training

By October 1953, I was ready to return from Rockford to Aspen. However, I was about to be ensnared by the U.S. Army. I wrote to my father that I had to go to Chicago for a whole day to get my physical examination and to Freeport, a town about thirty miles west of Rockford, with my two witnesses to meet with the Army examiner. To my disappointment, they passed over my recently broken leg and my chronic ear problem caused by the botched operation in Australia. I was found "fully acceptable for induction into the armed services." They noted the damage in one ear, but it didn't faze them a bit. Soon after, an article appeared in the paper that the November draft would be the largest since spring, with forty-two men drafted from Rockford, even though the Korean War was already over in July. This concerned me especially because my plans to return to Aspen to start building a lodge were completely frustrated.

My father wrote back sympathetically on October 24th, 1953:

Dear Charlie,

I am very sorry to hear that the Army is closing in on you. Fortunately, it's after the armistice in the Korean War. In army matters it is an old rule that you have to take it as it comes and never protest too much. But you have to make the best out of it. Perhaps you could get into the building corps and you would learn very much by it. Everything is better than the infantry. That, you have to avoid. The idea to come back to Aspen is good, because it disturbs the bureaucrats and delays everything, and perhaps you will have better luck in Denver than in Chicago. Anyway, I look forward to seeing you here soon.

Love,
Pop

I got home to Aspen from the Midwest and was greeted shortly thereafter by the long arm of the draft. I was sent off to Basic Training at Fort Ord in Monterey Bay, California, to be followed by an unknown assignment, in an unknown place determined by the Army. I had just become a United States citizen a few months before on July 24, 1953, and now it was my turn to serve my new country.

By this time it was well into the 1953-54 school year, and my father had been hired as a language teacher and silversmith instructor by John and Anne Holden, the founders of Colorado Rocky Mountain School (CRMS) in Carbondale, Colorado. The school was modeled on Holderness in Putney, Vermont, an experiential education that involved a lot of hands-on work and outdoor education trips.

My father was a great role model for the teenagers at CRMS. Having come through so much, he fascinated them with his stories and put the difficulties of their developmental years in perspective. My wife Fonda pointed out that he must have also loved being there because the children's ages at CRMS coincided with the years he was deprived of parenting my sister and me.

He also made a big impression on several of his students. One of these was Robin Perry. At this writing Robin is the Director of the Ski Patrol at the Buttermilk Ski Area. This was fortuitous in 1999, when my daughter Jenny applied to work there. Robin was surprised and delighted to find out she was the granddaughter of one of his favorite teachers. He hired her as an Emergency Medical Technician (EMT) on the patrol, and in 2004 she went on to become a paramedic. She was the sole female paramedic on the mountain through her career, and she remained there for ten winters. She credits her start and continuance to all the patrollers in our family. My sister, her husband Herb, and I were the examples, but my father's legacy helped get her in the door.

At the end of January 1954 my father hosted the entire CRMS junior ski team at our cabin. They stayed overnight on the floor of the living room and on the built-in Siberian beds that served as our couches. This was during the annual winter carnival, Wintersköl, where the ski team placed "not so badly," as he wrote, considering they all had just started racing.

This must have been on a weekday, because apparently later my father participated in more festivities and even the Wintersköl costume ball on the weekend, where he had signed up as a volunteer. He wrote in a letter

At Fort Ord basic training, 1954.

to me at Fort Ord (many of these are not dated), "The ball was nothing special, but I was there in my Arab costume and I had a good time selling the soft drinks." This "costume" was something he had in his trunk from his travels to the Middle East—his white, Egyptian cotton, full-length nightshirt.

If this seems strange, one must imagine what Aspen was like in those days. My father concentrated his life on the light-hearted spirit that flowed through the place. In one letter he wrote about a dinner party at his good friend Mary Lib's house followed by charades with a newly founded society, the "Red Underwear Society."

The story of this society must be told in his own words. "The proponents were Mary Lib, Mrs. von Fumetti, and Mrs. Snobble. At first I was very reluctant to appear, but Mrs. Snobble talked so much, that finally I conceded. The red undershirt and the famous trousers with the design in the back that you bought at [Aspen's] Thrift Shop were just the right thing to wear at this party. I arrived at Mary Lib's house and there were: Mr. and Mrs. Snobble, Mr. and Mrs. Thatcher Shaw, the Craigs, Mr. and Mrs. von Fumetti, Arlette [Lawyer], Langen (the nudist), a girl who lives with Mary Lib named Carmen, a man I do not know his name but apparently from ski school, and Mrs. Seibert. The dinner was excellent and a punch served. Everybody was really in underwear. The first prize was awarded to Mrs. Shaw. She got a wonderfully wrapped package with fancy ribbons on it and in it was a pair of completely torn under trousers, which she put on right away."

He wrote that photos were taken, unfortunately none of which I have. "It really was a funny evening. Loey Rinquist was there to take shots with her camera. I was photographed with the Shaws, but only from behind, with the wonderful design of your trousers. So you know that can only happen in Aspen or on Montmartre in Paris. Anyway they plan the next meeting at our house, with a special initiation of all the members through the proponents of the Arlberg skiing method. Also a parade is planned in red underwear down the mountain."

The Arlberg ski technique was developed and taught by Hannes Schneider at St. Anton, Austria (no relation to us as far as we know, even though, interestingly, his son was named Herbert and wife Doris, same names as my brother-in-law and sister). It was originally brought to Aspen by Friedl Pfeifer, Schneider's protégé and then the director of Aspen's Ski School. The technique started with the snowplow emphasizing safety and control and progressed through the stem turns to parallel skiing. Schneider was jailed by the Nazis shortly after the annexation of Austria by Germany but was "sprung" in 1939 by a North Conway native, Harvey Gibson, who built Mt. Cranmore ski area and hired Hannes to run his ski school.

Another funny note from my father caught my attention about a concert at the Aspen public school. He wrote the concert was "very good," but it seems he was being generous about the orchestra. "The band played in their new Alpine uniforms (they cost $1800). Anne Hollenbeck was very good as usual, and Sigrid [Braun Stapleton] accompanied the chorus very well on the piano. She is going to study to teach music at the college in Gunnison. She directed *The Merry Widow,* only the merry widow must have been very sad because the orchestra got sometimes completely out of her hands. But it was not her fault they played wrong. It was too difficult. They can only play marches well." My father knew this opera and other Lehár compositions not only from the Vienna Opera House, but his Siberian prison camp where prisoners did renditions of *The Count of Luxembourg.*

The annual Wintersköl meant that college kids arrived in Aspen, and of course there was lots of drinking and merriment throughout town, including in our cabin. But not by my father! The following story about this wild weekend arrived in a newsy letter to Fort Ord dated February 9, 1954. It also related the story of a car accident he had on Highway 82 outside of what is now called Old Snowmass—he went off the road in a snow storm nearly into the river, hitched into Aspen, but forgot his keys in the car and had to spend the night in our unheated concrete storeroom on a bench, no blankets. I am reminded that my father, age sixty-five, was very tough.

In many ways the following Wintersköl incident is a great illustration of how my father and I learned to run a ski lodge, and also of the early environment in Aspen where we, father and son bachelors, found ourselves. He wrote,

> I came home a little tired and I decided to go to bed very early at 8:30 p.m. and suddenly the telephone rang at what I thought was two or three in the morning. But it was Fred [Braun] from Holiday House who asked me if I could take some guests. I asked him how late it was and he said only 11 p.m. Now as I was half awake I couldn't say much and he said [he would] send them over. So a man and a girl arrived and I said to them, you [can] have the cabin with a double bed. But the man said: "The trouble is I have a whole 'harem' outside in the car." I said as this was the case it would probably be only a theoretical harem. He said unfortunately that's the case. So he came in with four girls and the problem arose how to fix them up. Finally as I had not enough sheets and blankets for all of them we settled on a price of $1.50 a night per person and they wanted to stay for two nights…. The man turned out to be a professor of psychology at a university in Colorado (I promised not to divulge the name of the university on account of the subsequent events) and the girls, students there.
>
> We had a very nice morning, but they apparently had not enough money for breakfast. They went right away to the lift and skied all day long. I was on the mountain too with the Rocky Mountain School, but I did not see them ski. Finally they came home completely exhausted and I made them some tea. They stayed and we had a very nice afternoon. A teacher of Rocky Mountain

A Wintersköl parade marching band turns the corner in front of the Hotel Jerome, 1950's. COURTESY: ASPEN HISTORICAL SOCIETY

School was there too, because he wanted to stay overnight in the outer room. So stories were told and we had a big discussion about politics and psychology and started together with back-rubbing of the girls by us three men. But they had eaten nothing and wanted to go to eat a pizza pie (the cheapest). They wanted me to go with them to Mario's Restaurant—where [the owners] Tish and Mario sing arias with the opera-singing waiters—and I promised to see them there later or at the Golden Horn. But at 10 p.m. I did not see them at either place so I went home and got to bed.

At around 12 a.m. the door opened and the psychologist and one girl came in and said to me, "Steve, have you some black coffee? One of the girls is not completely 'well.' So the other girl came in "under her own steam" (as you say at the American Youth Hostels) and sat on my bed. She was very tipsy. The first girl was the only one who was sober. The psychology teacher was also a little tipsy. (The fourth girl of the harem he had lost for the evening to another man who called up. She said she did not like the man but a dinner invitation is a dinner invitation. Before she left all four girls danced for their pasha lying on the couch and for the CRMS teacher and me to the tune of a Mozart Minuet.)

Anyway finally the psychologist brought her in on his arms and she collapsed completely on the bathroom floor. Now I got a little bit angry with them, as it was already late at night and I broke up all hilarity and asked to be quiet and go to bed. Finally I got everybody to bed and I had a big discussion with the psychologist about moral standards of college kids, etc. You know my ideas. I even told him, that if he or one of the girls would have come home with a lover, I would have considered it as completely moral and natural and I would have given to their disposal the cabin, but this I consider as an evasion tactic of the real issue [being so drunk] and completely immoral. He agreed that my point of view is right from the modern point of psychology, but not after the moral code of the colleges. He had a lot of excuses.

Next morning everybody was very tame and they went off skiing. The not-drunken girl, who agreed completely with me and with my views, wanted to meet me at the Sundeck, and as promised, she really was there, and we skied down Spar Gulch. Finally she asked me the favor not to divulge the name of the university. But it really was a bit too late, because the teacher who witnessed all that had already told the story to the staff at the Rocky Mountain School. Nevertheless after this rough treatment they all asked, very shyly, if they could come back again the next time they will be in Aspen. I said yes if I could lay down certain laws. And on that they agreed.

It pleased me that my father had so much social activity in Aspen, though I can imagine my own eye-rolling about the gossip. Reading about this hullaballoo now, however, is quite amusing, and it reveals how we often spoke together as bachelors and friends. I'm glad I saved these letters—of course, like my father I have my own file cabinet!

I remember how my father's letters always contained little notes from people I knew, sometimes on old menus and very often on scraps of paper from people thanking him for his hospitality. Obviously he was very busy inviting people for dinners, and I always encouraged him with his social life. "Good work and keep it up," I would write. I think it was his intention to keep me well informed of Aspen events so I would not be homesick or feel like I missed something. He was so thoughtful in that way. The letters had the opposite effect, however; in reality they made me miss him.

I was also going to miss skiing. My father noted the Aspen Skiing Corporation was raising funds to build its first double chairlift that summer, "from the dam in Spar Gulch to the Sundeck," by selling bonds to Aspen locals to raise an extra $25,000. So there was going to be excellent congestion alleviation for skiers that winter. But, my father added, "The only loser will be our 'friend' Howard Awry [at the other lift] because no long lines will wait at his Coney Island stand any more. So everybody will be happy but he will not be *glücklich* [i.e. very pleased]." Not attempting to write this word in English, the particular reversal of fortune for the hot dog stand owner was clearly for my father a specifically Viennese condition.

Life at Fort Ord was demanding and boring at the same time. Midwinter I had strep throat, which was making its way around the units. Almost all the troops had a continual cold and cough. The worst trouble of course was that we were confined in close quarters, and the lack of rest and sleep lowered our resistance.

On our first weekend pass, we went into Monterey and had dinner there. I was very disappointed because there was nothing but soldiers. The lack of women, to even talk to one, was a worthless situation, and sitting in a bar never has appealed to me. Three of us were going to go to a USO dance that evening, but the fellows had to stop off first and guzzle beer, so I went off alone. I waited till 9:15 p.m., but when only two women had turned up by that time, I decided that the best place was bed for me and get some rest, so I caught the first bus back to the base.

At least I got my leg back to normal a few weeks into my army training and was able to march in formation without limping. In the beginning, however, there were many times when I could not do any "double-timing" and went behind the formation with the first aid man when we ventured into the field. Even though basic training was rough in spots, it was also quite interesting. We were kept busy with firing machine guns at targets and running through the woods with only compass bearings, sometimes maneuvering backwards through the course with gas masks.

I read in a long letter back to my father about one time we spent all day up in the hills working on camouflage and concealment exercises. We had to crawl through a course and stay late into the night, then crawl back through again with flares going off and blanks being fired at us. In this second pass we had to go over two barbed wires, one of which had a booby trap connected and flares. After, we were up past midnight cleaning our rifles, which were full of sand and grit. We had about four hours sleep that night. At rifle inspection the next day they told us the whole company had dirty rifles, so that night we worked many hours to get our rifles completely disassembled and on display for one of our Second Lieutenants to inspect. I doubt if we got much sleep that night either. Reveille was always at 4 a.m.

We used to fire on two different types of ranges. One had pop-up targets with cardboard silhouettes that would suddenly jump out of a foxhole next to the path we walked along. We would have about four seconds to aim and fire before they dropped the lever control and the target disappeared. There were about a dozen of these mechanical targets, some with two or three men each, and we had to try to hit them all.

On the other range they had a similar set of challenges, only you had to move sideways on the firing line along about a dozen positions— behind a pile of rocks, into a foxhole, through windows of a building, then over a roof-top, a log, and finally crawling on the ground behind sand bags. In front of each position were two targets several hundred yards away, and at the order from the commanding officer in a tower each target would pop up for twenty-five seconds, during which we could fire two shots. If someone hit the target in the first shot he got ten points, if in two shots only five points.

I wrote to my father, "I passed O.K., with two hundred and fifty points." To qualify on those two ranges you had to get one hundred and sixty-five. I tried to impress my father so! But I was honest. When learning about night vision we actually had to fire at black silhouettes about thirty-five to fifty yards in front of us in the complete dark. I wrote back to my father, "Although I practically couldn't see anything I got three hits out of four—I suspect though that the next man on the range was firing at my target."

My letters are excellent reminders of the training required of soldiers at that time. What it could have been like to do these maneuvers during a war, however, makes me shudder.

I wanted my father to be proud of me. I thought he was sure to be interested in how the modern Army of 1954 was training its soldiers, especially how to respond in the event of a poison gas attack. Tear gas was first used in 1914 by the French and the Germans for incapacitating the enemy. By 1915, chlorine gas was developed, causing an extended agonizing death for people caught in trenches on the Western Front.

The Army had special chambers to train us to deal with these types of attacks. For tear gas, they had us enter with masks on and then remove the masks and sing "Jingle Bells" as we walked around in a circle. It was difficult to experience the tear gas, stumbling along and singing that silly tune five times before they let us out, with stinging eyes and tears running all over our faces. Luckily, when the fresh air hit us outside, it brought us back to normal fast. After this we had to go into another chamber with deadly chlorine gas while holding our breath, and then after a minute or so, we were allowed to put on our gas masks. We were not surprised to see an ambulance parked outside, in case of a mishap.

As part of the gas mask training we also ran an obstacle course, at the end of which we had to crawl about fifty yards with barbed wire overhead, over trenches, built-up mounds, and sandpits, while explosives went off on each side of us, completely enveloping us in artificial smoke. While we were crawling this course, they let off a tear gas grenade, and we had to put on our masks. During one drill, a fellow right in front of me was on his back under the barbed wire when the tear gas went off. He fumbled his mask, got panicky, dropped his mask, rifle, and helmet and ran. For this (mainly because he left his rifle) the cadre and officers took his rifle and threw it in the sand, then told him to get it clean, keep it absolutely spotless, and carry it with him from then on until told to stop. It was two weeks before they let him off, and we could see him carrying his rifle even to the mess hall.

Later that spring we went on a three-day bivouac. A torrential rain caused the original area to be flooded out, so they moved us to another location. Soon we were sent off with fifty-pound packs, gas masks, rifles, and blankets. All day maneuvers taught us squad tactics and how to attack enemy positions, and when attacked, how to fight the aggressors. This carried on into the night. But finally we got a cease-fire order, because our line hit the enemy much too late due to the rain, so not even a shot was fired.

The next day after a brisk march, we reached another bivouac area and were supposed to put up tents. Some of the troops were too tired by this time, since it was already dark, and planned to rough it outside. However, it rained again, and everyone who was not prepared had a soggy wet morning. I escaped that fate by applying my old boy scout knowledge from Australia: to undress and keep everything in the sleeping bag with a watertight poncho covering me. Many had just rolled up in their blankets with their clothes and boots on, and they were completely soaked when it started to rain heavily in the wee hours of the morning.

Reveille at four in the rain, and we were on the move again with a pretty miserable group. Reconnaissance patrols were sent on a difficult route through the scrub with compass bearings, in groups of ten men. The nearby mountains were covered in snow. Even after these long maneuvers we could still appreciate their beauty on our six-mile march back to camp.

As for my father during this time, toward the end of my basic training he sent me a clipping on May 6, 1954 from *The Aspen Times* about an ambitious cleanup effort around town sponsored by the Aspen City Council and the Chamber of Commerce. "But unfortunately it was a flop," he wrote. Only a few people came out for the event. There were only five people plus the president and "Magnifico with his broken leg.... You see, a very heavy force." My father worked with Henry Stein, "the richest man in town," picking up all the rusty beer cans and papers.

Compared to Stein, my father called himself the *"Schnorrer,"* a word from Yiddish that can mean a beggar or freeloader, who is distinguished by his extreme chutzpah. In this case, my father used the word's other meaning as a funny backhand self-congratulation for being someone poor but thrifty who, through perseverance, gets along in any circumstance. He continued, "We did a very good job but I could not refrain from thinking that Stein could have hired a whole gang of workers instead of doing that himself. At noon we were both disgusted, and it started to snow-rain. So he invited me to his house and gave me a lot of trout." ▪

CHAPTER TWENTY-SEVEN

The *Tachinierer*

Rather than let the Army decide my fate, I began a campaign at Fort Ord to become an army ski instructor. These were elite positions that would get me out of the trenches.

My father organized that a letter from Bob Craig, a well-known Colorado mountaineer, was to be sent to the colonel at Camp Carson in Colorado Springs on my behalf. Craig was later a member of the ill-fated 1953 K2 expedition where many were caught in a major avalanche and three died.[1] His letter was a very excellent reference, and I quoted it proudly back to my father: "This man Pvt. Charles Paterson US 554 was formerly an instructor in the ski school here and is an unusually fine type. He has a great deal of intelligence, ability to instruct and to lead, and can handle responsibility." If not a ski instructor, I would possibly be sent to officer's school, but that was the least attractive option since I really did not want to serve for the required three years. I had too much to accomplish if I was ever to get the building of my lodge off the ground. I wasn't meant to be a military man—my only enemy was time lost.

At the end of eight weeks of basic training, I still had no success in getting transferred out of the Army's boot soldier regiments. My father sent consolations in his last letter to me before I came home, and told me to keep trying.

Aspen   March 28, 1954

Dear Charlie,

I am very sorry to hear that you had bad luck with the Mountain Troops. I think myself, that they could only use very able-bodied men and not men with any restrictions like you with your leg. It was wrong from the beginning that they drafted you. Now you could only try to make the best side of it and try to serve in

Colorado and take out next winter all the superior officers as a private ski teacher. If you succeed in this, it would give you a very good life in the Army. We called that in the old Austrian Army *"tachinieren"* and such a fellow a *"Tachinierer."* So that will be what you will become.

Love,
Pop

When I first read this letter, I naturally assumed *"Tachinierer"* meant something like "mountain soldier," and he was bestowing upon me a title of honor. Years later, doing fact checks for this book, we found my father was actually joking with me, and this is an Austrian slang word of obscure origin first used in the First World War to refer to someone evading military service or leaving the front. An online dictionary enlightened us that the word has an etymology through the Czech word *"tachni"* to someone missing his thumbs, which explains why in my father's time the word was understood to mean a shirker. Without thumbs, no work![2]

In my last days at Fort Ord I continued to work on my transfer to Colorado Springs to complete my service. I went to the adjutant's office and showed them Bob Craig's letter. They were going to prepare my transfer papers right away until the Sergeant discovered on my file that I was a C profile. Right away he turned around, went back to his desk, and told me that I had no chance. Since I was a C profile, I would have eight weeks of basic and then go into specialized training. For Camp Carson in Colorado, I would need sixteen weeks of basic, so the Sergeant said it would be a waste of time to talk to the transfer officer again. "Sorry— can't do another thing for you."

Well that's that, I thought. But there was still a chance, since Bob had already written a letter, and the next day I got the other references for the colonel. One of them was from my Ski School boss Friedl Pfeifer, a former member of the 10th Mountain Division, 87th regiment. This was the famed 10th Mountain Division, which fought so valiantly toward the end of World War II in the 1945 Italian Campaign and forced the surrender of the Germans in the Po Valley.[3]

I wrote my appeal for a transfer despite the negative opinion of the adjutant's office, thinking perhaps it would go through different channels and at least I would still have a small chance to transfer. And suddenly my fortune changed.

Much to my surprise, at the end of basic training special orders came through for me to go immediately to Camp Hale in Colorado to join the ski troops. Almost as if my father had pre-envisioned it, they needed instructors, they said, for an elite group called Mountain and Cold Weather Training Command (M&CWTC). I would now become one of them. The Command consisted of about sixty men stationed at Camp Hale near Leadville in the winter and Fort Carson in Colorado Springs in the summer.

Camp Hale had been built during World War II for the explicit purpose of training ski and mountain troops with special operational skills adapted to mountain terrain. The camp became the winter training center of the 10th Mountain Division, which was disbanded after the war and the original Camp Hale built in 1942 was torn down. In the early 1950's, during the Korean War, the M&CWTC was born in Alaska as an outgrowth—or you may say, the second generation—of the 10th.[4] Our mission as instructors was to teach skiing and mountain climbing, rescue operations, and cold weather survival. The people brought in for the outfit were an extraordinary bunch with whom I was more than honored to be serving. Most were college educated, officer material.

The Command also attracted the best skiers and mountain climbers in the country. These included Keith Wegeman, a Colorado native who was on the national championship ski team and an American Olympic ski jumper. He was a great guy, with a body like Schwarzenegger, and was the model for the "Green Giant" peas; in the early 1960's he hosted a television show called "Ski Tips." Another, Ralph Miller, had been captain of the Dartmouth ski team. During his army stay in 1955, he became the world speed record holder while training in Chile for the winter Olympics to be held in 1956 in Cortina d'Ampezzo, reaching 109 m.p.h. on a pair of Northland wooden skis, wearing only ski pants and a T shirt—no helmet. The M&CWTC also included Buddy Werner, who was then America's premier racer. Unfortunately, a few years after Buddy got out of the army he was killed in an avalanche in Europe while being filmed in a ski movie directed by Willy Bogner, Jr., son of famous skiwear manufacturer. There were many other M&CWTC draftees who were recognized in their fields.

In the Command we taught Special Forces, Green Berets, and others who would go back to their own units as instructors. In our blue scarves and blue helmets, we outranked all officers in the field. Officers would often get irked after saluting us in camp—thinking we were majors and outranked them—because we always wore our mountain sheep pins on our caps. In fact, we were only lowly privates or corporals. After a few officers complained, we were ordered to take the pins off our caps.

In the summers, our training took place in Cheyenne Canyon, and we would be trucked up out of Camp Carson in Colorado Springs into the mountains every day. I was on a demonstration team, which twice a week put on a show for the public in the Canyon. There were bleachers built into the side of the mountain for the spectators, and it was very well attended. My job was to rappel down a sheer rock wall, which I usually accomplished in three jumps. Until then I waited for my cue tucked away in my rocky niche, always with a soft cover book to read that I could easily stash in my fatigue pants.

Across the way, the Whittaker twins, of mountaineering fame, would climb a sheer pinnacle of rock in their whites. We would do a suspension traverse, which consisted of a high wire strung across the canyon with one of the boys sliding across on a carabiner. Jim Whittaker would later be the first American to summit Mt. Everest in 1963. In 1965 he guided Robert Kennedy up the newly named Mount Kennedy (elevation 13,095 feet) in the Saint Elias Mountains in Yukon, Canada. Later, as CEO of REI, Whittaker built the company into a national chain. His twin brother Lou ran the climbing guide service for Mt. Rainier.

Another part of the demonstration would have two guys bringing someone down the sheer rock face in a stretcher as a rescue operation, with another guy on belay at the top of the rock face. One of our exercises during a climb was to leap off the rock, calling out "falling!" The partner on belay would let us run a few feet before snugging up on the rope to arrest the fall. In the beginning it was a bit hair-raising, but after a while we got used to it. We much depended on our climbing partners, who were usually on belay, either above us or below. Men of higher rank were usually on the end of one of our ropes, so we never had any trouble from them.

We were told never to climb alone. One morning, when practicing rock climbing on our own time, one experienced climber fell, but he was on his own, and no one had seen him. Suddenly, someone came across his body at the foot of a cliff. The fall was fatal. I will never forget when the civilian instructors gathered us around his body and proceeded to lecture us on the rules of climbing in the middle of our grief and horror at the fate of our companion.

As winter came, the M&CWTC was transferred to Camp Hale, and our army-issue white skis took the place of our ropes. There we taught skiing and cold weather survival.

We were billeted in eight men "Jamesways." These were insulated canvas half domes, similar to Quonset huts, with a small kerosene heater at each end. This fuel created a layer of smog-like smoke, which persistently hung in the valley throughout cold days and had everybody coughing. The Jamesways had been reactivated after World War II to replace buildings that were torn down in 1946. But they only served as temporary shelters, and the entire camp lasted less than a decade before it was torn down once more.[5]

We took turns every morning to relight the stoves in the Jamesways at least a half-hour before reveille, usually at 5:30 a.m. At fifteen below zero, this was not a popular duty. We slept in double down sleeping bags on canvas cots. Although the temperatures would drop well below zero,

Assembling a Jamesway at Camp Hale, Colorado, 1955.
PHOTO: CHARLES PATERSON.

it was against regulation to run the heaters after lights out for fear of carbon monoxide poisoning.

It was always dark when we would "fall out" in front of our James-ways in the snow. Some of us creatively acquired sheepskin-lined Air Force snow boots to slip on instead of our regulation, stiff cold ski boots, which also took valuable time to lace. Unfortunately, Master Sergeant Bill Brown,[6] a decorated veteran who had also been in the 10th and was always on someone's case, discovered our trick one morning and put a whole bunch of us on KP duty, kitchen police.

While I was stationed at Camp Hale, one day my father drove over from Aspen in his beloved, dusty blue Oldsmobile sedan. Stationed at the gate, Sergeant Lash Laursoo had been clued in to his arrival. He was a friend of mine, from Estonia, and had served for three different armies in World War II. When my father arrived Lash saluted him and let him into the camp. Things were so relaxed at Camp Hale that my father ate the evening meal with us and stayed overnight, even having breakfast with us the next day. My father was impressed. One of our cooks had been a chef on the Queen Mary, and with double rations for the cold weather—special troops that we were—we had the best cuts of beef, ample butter, eggs, and bacon.

How different than my father's was my own army career, replete with the opportunities, freedom, and democracy of this country. Like so much else in my life, I was aware even in the Army that I had many privileges he did not, and that our relationship would have this consis-tent theme—that I would live a better life than he, that I would be safer, stronger, and not have to suffer like those of his generation, so many of whom, like himself, were survivors of multiple wars, economic depres-sions, trauma, and upheaval. I admit that at that time I knew of his expe-riences only in the most peripheral way, as stories told by a man who could spin a great tale, and I thought of myself as self-made and lucky, feeling optimistic always.

But things could have easily been different. My luck was not just dependent on political systems in America, but the time period in which I served in the Army—the brief quiet period between the Korean War and the war in Vietnam. After being drafted it was clear to me how little choice people had in these matters. I learned that during World War II all Austrian non-Jewish males between the ages of eighteen and sixty were drafted into the Wehrmacht. None could escape the draft without risking the penalty of death. What Austrians had to go through by virtue of this situation is something I had not considered until late in my life.

Among those conscripted was one of our Beck relatives, Herbert Beck Sr., the son of my grandfather Otto's brother Robert Beck. Robert and his wife Friederike da Lezze[7] raised their family in Vienna. My mother, my aunt Claire, and my uncle Max knew their younger cousin Herbert Sr.— but I do not remember him. From the *Anschluss* forward, under the Nazi Nuremburg Laws, Herbert Sr. and his sister Ilse would have been categorized as "Mischlinge of the 1st degree," meaning that as half-Jews with at least two Jewish grandparents, they would have faced certain restrictions in attending higher education and would not be allowed to marry Christians—even though baptized and not having a Jewish mother.

Herbert Beck Sr.'s grandson, Lukas Beck, told us his grandfather was spared from much of the war itself. We learned more of the details from Lukas and his father Herbert Beck Jr. upon finding a small reference to the Viennese Becks in a letter from my grandmother Olga dated September 3, 1941. Olga wrote to my father, who apparently inquired about them, "Herbert has a job and Ilse is studying at the university." By 1942, Ilse would have been disallowed this opportunity.[8] She told my daughter Carrie in 2010 that she felt during the war it was only a matter of time before the Nazis would come after her.

Herbert Beck Sr.'s letters reveal he had to partake in the German invasion of Czechoslovakia, and then he was in a car accident early in 1941 in France. He spent three months there and in Magdeburg, Germany in a hospital with a broken arm. On June 22, 1941, Germany attacked Russia in Operation Barbarossa and Hitler's brutal "War of Annihilation" on the Eastern Front began. However, the Nazis considered Herbert Sr. "unworthy to do military service" in Russia. So instead of sending him to fight they put him in the Organisation Todt, a construction and engineering division, and he was able to work a desk job. Initially he worked for a shipping company that supplied the German army, and after he left the Organisation Todt—ironically—he was employed at the Creditanstalt in Vienna, where my grandfather Karl Schanzer and so many people in his family had worked. After World War II, Herbert Sr. remained at the Creditanstalt for the rest of his career.

My U. S. Army buddy Lash Laursoo, on the other hand, was drafted by the Estonian Army in World War II to fight the Russians, but soon the Germans took over the country, and he was forced to wear a Nazi uniform. The Germans sent all the Estonians to Denmark as occupation forces, but Estonians worked with the Danish underground. The Germans then decided to send all the Estonians back to the Eastern Front. But after three days of travel by train, Lash surrendered with other Estonians to the British, and he spent the next eleven months as a prisoner of war. Lash kept no secrets about having been in the German army. He knew my own story, and still it did not affect the way we formed an alliance at Camp Hale. There is something about being in the Army with someone— you recognize your shared fate and your dependence on one another.

Later Lash went off to a new career as a cook and then became a chef at the Red Onion in Aspen. After that, he was a ski shop owner and a condo manager in Frisco, Colorado. Many years later, just before retirement, he came back to work for me as a handyman for a stint at the Boomerang Lodge, then the Mountain Chalet. In 2011, when he was eighty-four, he told the story of his World War II experiences as an Estonian soldier in a book titled *The Barn Keeper's Son*, written by Kristin Carlson. The book has been endorsed by the Estonian government and will be part of their national archives along with other donations from Lash including photos and memorabilia. His POW photos and wartime passports are now in the national War Museum in Tallin, Estonia.

In January 1955, the Mountain and Cold Weather Training Command was sent to test our equipment and skiing skills with a four-day trip from the east side of Independence Pass over to Aspen. One early morning, we were trucked over to Twin Lakes and up the Independence Pass road as far as the gate where snowplowing stopped. The troops made ready to climb the pass with sealskins, packs, and sleeping bags. The idea was to bivouac, build snow caves for the overnights, and finally ski into Aspen. Rations were to be dropped on the pass by plane.

This trip was done by the 10th Mountain Division in World War II, but had not been repeated since. The ski team was chosen as the advance group to break trail. I only recall spending one night in the snow, but at subsequent reunions, the boys told me it was three. Our last night the group camped at Lost Man Campground on the west side of the pass after a great powder run, down the steep. I recall building my shelter out

A climbing demonstration on The Wheeler Opera House by M&CWTC in Aspen, circa 1955. PHOTO: PERRY CURTIS.

of pine boughs and being very comfortable.

The following morning, we skied the rest of the way to Aspen and straight to the Red Onion, where the boys did not hesitate to lift a few beers. I, however, went home to my cabin, had a hot shower, shave, and put on a white shirt and black ski pants. I had also taken a couple of civilian instructors over with me to clean up, as everyone was unwashed and unshaven. When I returned to the Red Onion, Colonel Link took one stern look at me and said, "Paterson, you're out of uniform!" Hoisting a beer, he then laughed and proceeded to give me a weekend pass saying, "I guess you are home anyway, so you might as well stay." After many beers, the rest of the crew was routed back to Camp Hale in buses through Glenwood Canyon, singing and having a merry time.

In the summer, the owner of the Red Onion, Werner Kuster, made a special appearance with our troops in Aspen in a demonstration of climbing and rescue maneuvers on the historic Wheeler Opera House. (Werner had been in the M&CWTC before my time.) We rigged up a suspension traverse from the third floor out of a window to the ground.

Training ice axe technique to chop steps. Gannet Peak Glacier in the Windriver Range, Wyoming, 1955. PHOTO: CHARLES PATERSON.

I was assigned to come down off the building on a carabiner to simulate an evacuation off a cliff. Two troopers drove pitons into the grout between the stones of the front wall, which may very well still be there. They quickly ascended the building to the roof, with one guy on belay. Another couple of troopers lowered a litter from the top of the building off the west wall with Werner Kuster as the "evacuee." Then I descended via the same route by rappelling, which I managed in three leaps.

Another highlight of my army career was a special trip to climb Gannet Peak, the highest mountain in Wyoming, at 13,804 feet. Our group was flown to Riverton in an army DC-3, from which we disembarked with all our gear, ice axes, and crampons. We were to train on one of the glaciers, and had a long hike into a valley filled with high grasses and wildflowers. There we bivouacked for a week, setting off daily over the rocky ground and small icy streams. It was summer, but the mountain was covered in snow and ice.

One day we left camp very early to ascend the peak, encountering crevasses and steeper pitches where many times we had to rope together in the event someone fell or slipped. At the top we were greeted with a fantastic view of a panorama of mountains, reaching all the way to Yellowstone. The most fun was glissading down the vast stretches of snowfields off the side of the mountain. This is accomplished on your ski boots in a skiing position with your ice axe to the side for control, or to be used to go into a self arrest, if need be, because of an obstacle or if you were picking up too much speed. It is a very fast and efficient way to descend, almost like skiing.

In May of 1954, repositioned for the summer at Camp Carson (now Fort Carson), we prepared for a climbing show in Cheyenne Canyon to be held in conjunction with a big parade for Armed Forces Day, an annual event in the military center of the state, Colorado Springs. We had two platoons marching in the parade. One was a winter platoon, complete with skis, ski boots, "over whites" (the camouflage uniform), and ruck-sacks. I was in the other, representing the summer mountain troops, with ropes, rucksacks, and also army ski boots. One of our most impor-tant demonstrations was for General Collins, the Commander of Camp Carson, and his invited guests, who consisted of dignitaries, a number of active and retired generals, other high brass, and their wives. There was much pomp and circumstance with a band playing, and General Collins was very pleased. His charming, blonde wife thanked us by calling from the stands and waving to a group of us standing there.

I didn't go back to Aspen much that spring because of classes like "Military Justice" and some ski instructing. Willy Schaeffler, the director of the ski school at Arapahoe Basin, had approached me to teach for him as they were holding special classes that people could sign up for, through the *Rocky Mountain News*. He agreed to pay me $15 a day even though I was still not fully certified, and also hired my friend Max Good, who had taught in California and later had his own ski school.

It was a nice deal for us to be able to come over to teach skiing on weekends and good money. In one of those classes I met Dr. Bob Dean and his wife Mary. Dr. Dean was an intern in obstetrics at a Denver hospital and had been recently discharged from the Air Force. He came well prepared for ski lessons in his flying suit with large pockets, where he carried a bottle of whisky and paper cups. He snowplowed awkwardly and when he fell down, he would burst out in uproarious laughter, pull out the bottle and offer drinks all around. It was one of the most unorth-

With Bob Axtell at Camp Carson, Colorado in M&CWTC
winter and summer outfits, 1954.

odox and jolly classes that I ever had. The Deans and their children Janet, Bob, and Susan became lifetime friends after I encouraged them to buy a house in Aspen and, many years later, Dr. Dean saved my father's life during an operation at a Denver hospital.

Around this time I also met a beautiful young woman, Vera Fusek, through my Corporal and friend, Meta Andel. Meta and Vera were both from Czechoslovakia. Meta's father had clothing factories, and I had a hunch, the way you do about people you feel comfortable with, that his father and my father must have known each other when my father was the manager in Vienna of Hermann Pollack's Söhne. I quickly became enamored with Vera, who was an aspiring actress and studied in London, twenty-two, and a very beautiful brunette. Vera's father was formerly in the Czech parliament, had escaped from the Russians, and then moved to Washington. Vera and I got along great, but as she put it, she was "in the middle of an unfinished affair" with a Czech boyfriend. I thought perhaps I would just bide my time, and she could finish it up.

On her last weekend in Denver, I went to see Vera unannounced. She had sent me a very nice picture and letter, and I was rather impetuous, arriving suddenly on a Saturday night without knowing her plans. It shouldn't have been a surprise to find her unable to break a dinner date. She was going out with some fabulous guy who had flown his own plane from Washington State to see her, knew Howard Hughes, and perhaps could help her in her movie career. On Sunday night when I talked to her on the phone, she told me of having a "horrible" experience with this guy, when he wouldn't drive her home, but attempted to drive with her out of town. She almost jumped from the car and finally persuaded him to take her home.

After that I never got to see Vera again but received news that she began her acting career and was filming in Kenya, East Africa. Vera appeared in a number of TV series throughout her career, including *BBC Sunday Night Theater* and a stint on *Doctor Who*. Vera also narrated a documentary titled *The Doomed City: Berlin* and in 1980 starred in the movie *Treasures of the Snow*. ◼

Breaking Ground

Finally, in March of 1956, my army career was over. It had been a good two years, and I considered myself lucky. The training would serve me well for my future life in the mountains, which I had every intention to follow. In addition, the skiing at Camp Hale in the winters was mostly fun for me, never a hardship. The most advantageous aspect of it all of course was staying in Colorado, in the mountains, and being close to home. I was honorably discharged and came back to Aspen to rejoin the Aspen Ski School and continue what was to become a seventeen-year career as a ski instructor on Aspen Mountain.

My ambition to build a lodge was not diminished, and I decided to finally go to Vancouver to see my great-aunt Käthe Pick. Sadly, her husband Otto Pick, so helpful to my father and to us during the war, had died on March 20, 1950. I was not able to personally thank him for his generous efforts.

Getting to Vancouver turned into another adventure.

One of my buddies from the army, Dave Olson, was discharged from M&CWTC the same time as I was. He had traded his Plymouth for an "Ercoupe," a two-seater aircraft, and was planning to fly home to Tacoma, Washington. I decided to join him and cross the Canadian border into Vancouver. There was a small delay, however, while Dave changed his Chinese pilot's license to a valid American one. At the time, Dave was a bit of a mystery since he had only been in our outfit for three months. As it turned out, his time at Camp Hale was his only military duty. Years later, he told me he had been a C.I.A. agent, and they were training him in mountaineering and winter survival.

Dave picked me up in Aspen, and we set out with a feeling of high expectations, pointing our little plane to the west. As we flew over Idaho we encountered heavy thunderclouds and experienced nearly zero visibility. The Ercoupe had no instruments, save an altimeter, and luckily,

Dave, a highly skilled pilot, was able to execute a 180-degree turn to land us safely at the Boise airport in a driving rain.

After resuming our trip, Dave let me fly the plane sometimes. We sat side by side with a plastic bubble over our heads like being in a fighter plane. I recall seeing the massive formation of Mount Rainier to my right as we stepped up altitudes with the air currents. It was lit by brilliant sunlight, and we took photographs. I remember the feeling of exuberance during this highlight contrasting with the harrowing experience over Boise.

Dave wrote up the following account of this trip for me with the astute eye of an outsider.

From Dave Olson   May 10, 2005

In 1956 Charlie wanted to reconnect with his Aunt Kaethe [Käthe]. Knowing I was on vacation at home, he asked if I'd be interested in flying to Vancouver to share his visit there. This would allow him to casually call Aunt Kaethe indicating he and a friend were barnstorming around the Pacific Northwest. Would it be convenient for him to fly up and see her with friend Dave

Dave Olson and I arriving in Vancouver, spring of 1956.

En route to Tacoma and Vancouver in Dave's Ercoupe with Mt. Rainier beyond, spring of 1956. PHOTO: CHARLES PATERSON.

in Dave's small plane? She said, Yes, to plan staying with her for a couple days, and to call her for pick-up on arrival at the Vancouver Airport.

A day later we flew to Vancouver. Shortly after clearing customs, Kaethe arrived with her chauffeur, Clarence, all spiffed up in his fancy uniform. She appeared to be a prim and proper 70-80 something, friendly, and unpretentious. Her car was a snazzy silver Jaguar. Charlie rode in back with Kaethe and I in front with Clarence. Proceeding up the highway along the Fraser River, passing a large timber operation dominated by a tall chimney emblazoned with ten foot high letters "CFPL" (Canadian Forest Products, Ltd.), Kaethe pointed it all out and said, "This is one of our mills." Entering a posh section of Vancouver, Clarence took us up a long circle driveway to the front entrance of a rather forbidding stone Tudor mansion.... Left alone [in my room], I laid down, basking in this new experience, mindful of my serendipitous good luck buying the airplane, partnering with Charlie, and his creative thinking, which led to where I was now.

After dinner in jackets and ties, Kaethe adjourned the three of us to her TV den. When the program proved dull, Charlie pulled the drawings of his proposed lodge out of his pocket to pour out his dreams and show Kaethe what he hoped to build in Aspen.... Kaethe turned to me for review of the TV program guide, leaving Charlie with no move but to pocket his plans.

[We] motored by a few of Vancouver's vistas and sights the next morning, ... followed by a tour of a huge plywood mill managed by Kaethe's son-in-law, [Leopold Bentley,[1] formerly Bloch-Bauer], who acted as our personal guide. Most impressive was how machinery was shut down as we passed by....

Kaethe took us to lunch at an upscale Vancouver restaurant. After being seated and ordering, Kaethe turned to Charles (she never called him Charlie).... On cue, Charlie began his account of how far he had come, the future he visualized for skiing and Aspen as a world-class, year-round resort, and where he wanted to go as a player in that picture. He went over his plans for the first units he foresaw to be the beginning of the Boomerang Lodge. He needed financing and lumber to proceed with the project. Kaethe gave him her rapt attention. I was impressed with his quiet details, conviction, and determination, like I was seeing a man I hadn't met before.

When he finished, Kaethe gave him a look reflecting perhaps sadness and a desire to support him.... She explained that all of her side of the family fortune had already been distributed through gifts and trusts so she was effectively living on family support.... Neither Charlie nor I needed a crystal ball to know [the] answer. Charlie graciously hid his disappointment so we could enjoy small talk and lunch. On the flight back to Tacoma, a somber Charlie's wheels were already turning and exploring other options to build his lodge. Don't think I've ever seen anyone move-on so quickly—from keen disappointment, as if it were just another speed bump in the road of life, to 'where do I go from here to make my dream come true?'

We had a brief stop at Seattle-Tacoma Airport to clear U.S. Customs. On landing we were directed by the tower to taxi and park close in, front and center, outside the main terminal surrounded by major airline monsters coming and going. The tower powers had my total attention. How insignificant I felt sitting there in our forlorn and decrepit little Ercoupe waiting for the Feds to arrive and welcome us to the U.S.A. Thirty minutes later we were back in Tacoma.

Charlie stayed an extra day so we could go up to Seattle and reconnect with Jim and Lou Whittaker, his buddies from M&CWTC days. We were shown their ratty second floor mountaineering equipment store off Pioneer Square. Then we adjourned to a nearby tavern for a couple beers. Here the Whittaker twins [of REI] expounded on their enthusiastic vision for the future of mountaineering in the Pacific Northwest. I had been witness, back-to-back, to young men's dreams for their futures. With no vision of my own, I thought probably none would succeed. How wrong I was!

I said good-bye to Dave Olson and the Whittakers and on my bus trip back to Colorado, stopped in Portland, Oregon. I suddenly realized how close this was to Mt. Hood. I changed my plans and took a shuttle the sixty miles to Timberline Lodge, which was built during President Roosevelt's "New Deal" in the 1930's. The lodge was located within the Mount Hood National Park. The manager's wife knew me from Aspen Ski School, and they treated me royally with ski equipment and accommodations. I recall the spring skiing was fabulous.

I remember being disappointed at the time about my trip to Vancouver to see Aunt Käthe, but the silver lining to this story is that if I had obtained the lumber from Canadian Forest Products, Ltd., I would have built the wrong lodge. It took me another seven years to find the means and to create the proper design. My big plans had included a ten-unit lodge, very typical in style, and were drawn out in section by our architect friend Fred Mellion, the husband of none other than the famous matchmaker for our family, Hilde Mellion. Even though my big plans were delayed, I was still determined to get going somehow.

Returning home to Aspen, I decided that building three new units would be a start, so I went down to talk to the local banker.

Getting a loan at that time in Aspen was an interesting procedure. Lucas Woodall, owner of Pitkin County Bank, was an old-timer and known to be a skinflint who would never lend out money. He was always seen in town in the same brown suit, fedora hat, and cigar in his mouth. I made an appointment to see him and was told I could have an audience after the bank was closed.

Duly, I was let into the bank after hours and ushered into a bare back room with rough floor boards, a small table in the center of the room, two chairs, a whisky bottle, and a couple of glasses. Mr. Woodall was seated at the table with his feet up and the usual cigar in his mouth. His friendly greeting to sit down and join him in a drink seemed a little unorthodox to me, so I sat, but declined the drink. After pleasantries, I told him I wanted to borrow fourteen thousand dollars. I said I needed it to start construction on a three-unit building attached to my log cabin, which would be called the "Boomerang Lodge." It seemed he took a shine to me, as I was just out of the army. I was surprised that he agreed to make me a loan—I heard this was a rare occurrence. But the banker was in turn quite amazed when I repaid the loan early.

I broke ground in September 1956 with the help of my friend Lash Laursoo, who I had persuaded to opt out of re-upping for another tour of army duty. Soon, we had the concrete slab in, although I recall that it was hunting season, and there seemed no one available to get anything done. But Lash and I struggled ahead, put up logs, and finally a roof before the winter weather hit us.

Even though the trip to see Aunt Käthe had put a damper on bigger dreams, I was able to start a business. The small lodge was successful. After its first year, in the fall of 1957 when it was quiet in Aspen and there were no tourists, I closed the doors to drive cross-country to visit my sister Doris and her husband Herb Schneider. I also wanted to see their two small children, who were growing up fast—Tom, born in November of 1955, and Linda, born a little over one year later in December.

On my return from my sister's home in Millington, New Jersey I decided to stop in Freeport, Illinois to see a ski pupil of mine, Bob Kimes. His family owned a lumber yard, and he was designing houses for the company, much as I had done for Harry Espenscheid only a few years earlier. So I stayed to help with some drafting, and one weekend, he suggested we drive up to Spring Green, about forty miles northwest of Madison, Wisconsin to see Frank Lloyd Wright's Taliesin, about which I knew little to nothing.

Bob and I both had a common interest in architecture. But my eyes opened to a new vision. I was so fascinated with the Fellowship and Taliesin that during our tour that weekend I surprised myself and asked if I could interview with Mr. Wright for an apprenticeship. Being there, I suddenly had an urgency to start an architectural career, imbue myself with the spirit that pervaded the place so strongly, and participate in the life of the Fellowship.

The word came back quickly. Yes, Mr. Wright would see me the very next morning.

I could hardly believe that this world famous architect would have the time or interest to meet with me. I set off early from Bob's house in my little Chevrolet convertible the next day for the Hillside School, where I was to meet Mr. Wright in the drafting room, at ten o'clock.

I was nervously waiting at the appointed time, but when Mr. Wright had not shown up by noon, I decided to make inquiries at the house. I was told Mr. Wright had gone for a drive that morning. Sorry! I remember seeing his Bentley, earlier, in the driveway. Later, I found out that Mr. Wright usually did not keep first appointments with potential apprentices to see if they were really serious.

Well, I was serious, and I waited around until he showed up in the drafting room at about two in the afternoon and began walking around the apprentices' desks. I quickly approached him and told him I had made an appointment at ten o'clock in the morning. He made no comment or apology, but walked me over to a little seating alcove by the fireplace. We sat down for a chat. In his late eighties, he was very sharp and had an acuity that impressed me. He inquired about my background. I told him about my building experience and mentioned that the architect Adolf Loos married my mother's sister Claire in 1929, and that our family had been clients of Loos. Mr. Wright was aware of Loos' controversial philosophies and architecture practice in Europe, and he may have taken my relationship to Loos into consideration. I also told him about my lodge and that I built it from the ground up, starting with a little cabin.

After my short interview with Mr. Wright, he said yes, he would accept me and I should go see his secretary, Gene Masselink, who I had met earlier to schedule my appointment. Gene was a very nice man, an artist and graphic designer, who had his office at the main house. When I sat down to talk with him, he mentioned they could accept me on the G.I. Bill, to which I was entitled after my army service to pay for higher education. At that time I also told him that I planned to return to Aspen every winter to teach skiing and run my small lodge, and hoped that this was acceptable to Mr. Wright.

I returned home as the snow began to fall. Soon it was several feet deep, and I was back on the hill teaching skiing. However, I had not stopped thinking about Mr. Wright and Taliesin, and so I went to one of Wright's former students, Fritz Benedict, to learn about his own experiences attending Wright's school.

At that time, Fritz's architectural office was in a converted Victorian building—the Bowman Block—in downtown Aspen. He later moved to a reclaimed mining era building set among Aspen trees at the edge of town. He designed many beautiful projects inspired by his Wright training. Fritz (known at Taliesin as Frederick) had been one of Wright's earliest apprentices, leaving only to serve in the famed 10th Mountain Division troops in World War II. He originally went to work at Taliesin in Wisconsin as a horticulturist and landscape designer. Fritz revered Mr. Wright and his work, and he became one of his strongest disciples of "organic architecture" in the region. He significantly impacted early development of Aspen along with his brother-in-law from the Bauhaus, architect and artist Herbert Bayer. One of the strongest legacies Fritz Benedict left when he died in 1995 was on the face of Colorado skiing itself, as he also did the master planning in the 1960's for the new ski towns of Vail and Snowmass Village, as well as the plan for thirty backcountry huts in the 10th Mountain Division Hut Association, connected together by three hundred and fifty miles of trails.

My talk with Fritz was reassuring and encouraging. I then crafted the following letter to Mr. Wright.

Aspen   December 9, 1957

Mr. Frank Lloyd Wright
Taliesin West, Box 157, Scottsdale, AZ

Mr. Charles Paterson
Box 253
Aspen
Colorado

Dear Charles Paterson: I am very sorry you have had to wait so long for an answer to your letter. Since we heard from you we have received, from VB 7-1993 from the Veterans Administration... VA Center Denver.

So far as we know now - you are welcome to come on to Taliesin next May. We are terribly over-crowded but I think we shall have room for you. We will be back in Wisconsin and I hope settled down for work by the 15th of May. Just let us know a week or two in advance when you arrive.

TALIESIN WEST

Meanwhile I hope you have a fine winter in the snow - and my best to Fritz - Fred Benedict . . .

Sincerely,

Eugene Masselink   January 9th, 1958

*My acceptance letter to Taliesin from Mr. Wright's
private secretary Eugene Masselink, 1958.*

Dear Mr. Wright,

After my return to Aspen, I had a long conversation with Fritz Benedict, who studied under you from 1940-1943, and who was very interested in my short visit to Taliesin. On the wall above his desk was a very good color picture of you. He was very happy to hear of your good health and reciprocates your good wishes. Having known me for many years, also as an employer when I worked for him on a few of his construction projects, he thought that I would get along very well in the Taliesin Fellowship.

Certainly Taliesin was most interesting, and a highlight for me was our short chat in the studio. Mr. Masselink was most helpful in answering my eager questions on the school and I submitted my application for enrollment in the Fellowship while there. I was very heartened in your indication of acceptance.

I remain very sincerely yours,

Charles Paterson ■

CHAPTER TWENTY-NINE

Taliesin

"A building is not just a place to be. It is a way to be."

—FRANK LLOYD WRIGHT

I arrived at Taliesin the end of May 1958. I was now twenty-eight years old. Immediately I felt that this green valley with its gentle hills was a special place, and I experienced the comfort of knowing that I would like it there and feel at home.

I drove my car up to an open court, behind which stood the imposing building that had been designed by Mr. Wright in the early twentieth century for two of his maternal aunts, Jane and Nell Lloyd Jones. Originally called the Hillside Home School, it was an expansion of their progressive co-educational boarding school and one of his first commissions. Later it became part of the architectural school of Taliesin with an adjoining drafting room and a theater.

Three quarters of a mile away, over the hill, was the Wrights' beautiful home, named "Taliesin" after a famous sixth-century Druid bard,[1] and also meaning "Shining Brow." Aptly named, the house hugs the crest of the hill. One of the Wrightean principles is to integrate the building with the site, so it is "of the hill" instead of "on the hill." The house, appearing from a distance as one approaches on the road, is mirrored on the water of a beautiful man-made lake with a waterfall cascading at its edge. Wright's genius in planning is evident everywhere.

At the base of the way leading to the house at a fork in the road from Highway 23 is an enormous triangular and multicolored bed of flowers, giving the approach to the Wright home a magical quality. Mrs. Wright designed the garden, and soon I found out it was cultivated by the Taliesin apprentices.

Located between the house and the school is Midway Farm, with its long, low horizontal barn and roof—both red—and, atop the lime-

Midway Farm, Taliesin East, 1958. PHOTO: CHARLES PATERSON.

stone milk house, a striking red spire that can be seen from the highway. Elegantly proportioned, this arrow pointing into the sky punctuates the terminal of the agricultural buildings. Bolted to the weather vane, the decoration Mr. Wright specified in detailed drawings is made from common materials. These were twelve W.C. floats,[2] as one finds in toilet tanks—but one would never know it.

Taliesin is no ordinary farm. It is an estate, hundreds of acres, comprising a home, school, and working farm, as well as woodlands and the Wisconsin River. The extensive buildings are—like the Wright's home—carefully sited along the rolling hillsides, making discreet pods of activity connected by softly curving roads. The garden layout also follows this soft grid, with semi-circular arcs that echo the curves in the landscape. I remember a rhubarb patch, vineyard, apple orchard, strawberries, and vegetables beds, all planted to encourage Taliesin's self-sufficiency, and with an equal eye toward artistry.

In the morning of my first day, a Saturday, I was assigned to my new quarters in one of the outlying houses named "Aldebaran," located a mile from the school. Formerly, Aldebaran was the farm of one of Mr. Wright's maternal uncles, James Lloyd-Jones. Mr. Wright's grandfather, Richard Lloyd Jones, was a Unitarian minister who emigrated from Wales seeking religious freedom. He and his wife Mary arrived with six children and were settlers in 1840 of the wooded Wyoming Valley, where they developed farms that would later become Taliesin. Known for their oratory and passionate beliefs, the valley was soon to be named by neighboring settlers "the valley of the God Almighty Jones." [3]

There were six of us at Aldebaran. Mrs. Wright's widowed son-in-law Wes Peters had an apartment downstairs, and upstairs two older apprentices lived down the hall from the large, attractive room I shared with two other fellows. There was quite a bit of privacy because the room was L-shaped and I had the small leg of it to myself. The room had built-in dressers made of warm wood and a large mirror that gave it a spacious feel. Drop-down, square ceiling lights added a comfortable and relaxed feeling at night.

My desk in the drafting room was already determined and was located in the center of the room; and quite an incredible room it was—an airy open space with natural light flooding the long continuous tables from clerestory windows. A lattice of dark wood and large triangular trusses with "Taliesin red" pin stripes accentuated them. Mr. Wright was known to describe the drafting room as a light-filled forest, while my father, upon visiting years later, noted it was like a cathedral.

I learned that following afternoon tea everyone was encouraged to work in the drafting room on his own projects. I hoped to get started soon on plans already materializing in my head. From the beginning at Taliesin, I was thinking about designing my future lodge to be built in Aspen.

There was a core group of apprentices who were making the architectural practice at Taliesin their life's work. Some had been there since they were teenagers. They idealized the Wrights, as I also came to do. The senior apprentices like Wes Peters, John "Jack" Howe, Tom Casey,

Jim Pfefferkorn, Ling Po, John Rattenbury, and many others, were also our teachers, even though at this time there was seldom any formal instruction. The Taliesin motto was "learn by doing."

There was a lot of work to be done at Taliesin and yearly turnover, thus there was an ongoing need for new apprentices. Some left disillusioned with the non-academic format. Others left to pursue their own careers. Many of the latter included Mr. Wright's international students. Apprentices came from all over the world. During my years, Egypt, China, Japan, India, Canada, and Switzerland were all represented. Nari Ghandi from India, for instance, whose work has been compared to Antonio Gaudi, was at Taliesin then. Apprentices from India could relate to the Fellowship as a type of 'Ashram' experience where work and study take place in a secluded community with a guru.

Our daily and weekly schedules were structured. After our breakfast, apprentices would go to their assigned duties. The roster was made by Mrs. Wright (Olgivanna),[4] and was always posted in the drafting room. Mrs. Wright was from Montenegro, formerly married to the Russian architect Vlademar Hinzenberg, and was a disciple of the mystic George Gurdjieff, with whom in the 1920's she studied the art of what he called

Apprentices working in the garden triangle at the entrance to Taliesin East, 1959. PHOTO: CHARLES PATERSON.

Hillside, Taliesin East, 1959. PHOTO: CHARLES PATERSON.

"The Work"—sacred dance movements and ways "to awaken people to their higher selves." [5] Having expanded her own artistry and creative practice through a mentoring relationship, it was her idea initially to create the Taliesin Fellowship.[6] With a few followers, the founding of the Fellowship was a natural outgrowth of the Depression where self-sufficiency was paramount. At that time, Wright's architectural commissions were almost non-existent.

The list of duties that made the Fellowship function included construction, tending the garden, working on the farm in a "collective" fashion, harvesting, kitchen detail, or working in the drafting room, where we would draw on details of current architectural commissions under the supervision of Jack Howe and older apprentices. We would work until lunch on our chores, break, and then continue again until afternoon tea. One of us was responsible for preparing the daily tea every week, which varied from location to location and went from simple to elaborate, depending on the host's inspiration. Very often there was even a cake made for the occasion. Afterward, we went back to work in the drafting room, or at our chores, for a few hours until dinnertime. At Taliesin the system of breaks during the day and week was well designed for a rounded experience and for the Fellowship to come together.

Taliesin felt democratic, and sometimes people would not show up for their assignments, even though the expectations were clear. No one seemed to mind, at least not outwardly, although I think it was somehow always noted. For me this life was perfect. I liked the construction-related work to which I was first assigned, learning new innovative methods and using my past-learned building skills. My time in the drafting room was equally engaging, watching the work of others, noticing new designs, and then doing the actual drawings.

New apprentices were often heard to grumble that they were not assigned to the drafting room for months, and instead were put in the field and on construction. We had nearly an hour of gardening every morning. Certainly not all of our tasks seemed directly related to architecture. One week, we planted the entrance triangle with hundreds of red, pink, and white petunias.

The physical work we did on the farm and high expectations in the drafting room, assignments to which did not materialize immediately, were difficult for some apprentices to accept. However, those of us who stayed and went along with the program of the Fellowship formed a fast core of friendship and camaraderie.

In principle, Wright avoided modifying surrounding environments to suit his buildings, but rather designed them to work in harmony with existing natural features. He tried to incorporate local building materials and created spaces that were open and airy. Light was of critical importance. Indirect and diffused light was accomplished with clerestories or upward deck lighting. One of the signature Wright elements was creating corner glass windows; by mitering the glass, the solid corners created by posts or walls are eliminated.

Mr. Wright was an amazingly youthful man in his late eighties. For all his years he ruled his domain with a firm hand. Life at Taliesin revolved around him including what time we ate, since the food was not served until he and Mrs. Wright arrived at Hillside from their house. During the weekday they ate upstairs on a balcony overlooking the dining room, while on Saturday we would dine with them in the reception foyer of the theater.

Our evenings during the week were free. Some apprentices would go to Spring Green, but I usually stayed late in the drafting room to work on plans for my lodge. Some of us also studied Mr. Wright's drawings and architectural plans—his life's work—which were available in the waist- high flat files lining each side of the drafting room. We treated the drawings with utmost care and respect, knowing we were privileged to touch the works of the Master. These same drawings are now priceless museum pieces, which have been kept in climate-controlled vaults at Taliesin West in Arizona and will now be archived at Columbia University and the Museum of Modern Art in New York.

The founding director of the Frank Lloyd Wright Archives at Taliesin West in Arizona—Bruce Brooks Pfeiffer—was an apprentice during my time. He is still there as a senior fellow and is also the author of many books on Wright including *Frank Lloyd Wright: The Masterworks*.

As an illustration of the way our education at Taliesin was designed around the human experience, our weekends were always special. Dinners, lectures, free time, and occasions for the Fellowship to foster social bonds were all important.

Mr. Wright enjoyed movies, often Westerns, so Saturday nights would be reserved for showings in the Theater at Hillside. The Theater is a wonderful space. Originally the gymnasium of the Hillside School, Wright redesigned it in 1933. It was first named the Playhouse, a new space for musical and theatrical performances. The seating, with red velvet cushions, is steeply raked to the stage, like a miniature Greek theater. The rows are broken so there is eye contact between members of the audience, who then enjoy the musical performances together. Mr. Wright rebuilt the space in 1952 following a fire and designed a modern patterned curtain as a backdrop to the stage. The curtain has vivid red, green, and yellow geometric forms, with gold accents. An abstraction in felt, yarn, and black cording, it is a mosaic of the surrounding rural landscape, representing Taliesin overlooking the Wyoming Valley and the Wisconsin River.[7]

Sunday mornings were reserved for a formal breakfast with the Wrights, at which time Mr. Wright would give a talk, attended by all. Recognizing we were hearing the Master, the mood seemed to change in the room as we listened in awe, straining not to miss a word. These talks were frequently recorded and during the early 1950's, a few of the talks to the Fellowship were made into a series of three LP records, which are now collectors' items. This series also includes Mr. Wright reading fragments of Walt Whitman and improvising on the piano.

Sunday dinners, which were formal dress up affairs, usually were held at the main house after cocktails with the Wrights, to which a select group was invited. Much time and effort would be spent on these occasions, requiring a lot of work to be done beforehand. It was a privilege to be invited to serve the dinner, as much as it was to attend. The apprentices always wanted to please the Wrights and knew because of their encouragements that they appreciated our extra efforts.

After Sunday dinners, we would have a musical performance, usually a quartet played by the most gifted apprentices, with the Wrights in attendance. Mr. Wright loved music, as he said it was structured similar to architecture. In his autobiography he noted, "Bach and Beethoven are invariably inspiration, even information, to me." [8]

Mr. Wright used to play classical music privately on his grand pianos, one in the living room and another in the studio of the house. Music was an important thread throughout the Taliesin life, and we had some very good musicians in the Fellowship. I remember a chamber music trio with John Armantides on the violin, Vern Swaback on the trumpet, and Bruce Pfeiffer on the piano. Our choral group was also very active, and in later years was under the direction of Effie Casey.

Many weekends were set aside for special events. Often, notable people—friends of the Wrights—would be invited. One summer we saw and heard the poet Carl Sandburg, and on another occasion, we had a visit from Adlai Stevenson, twice the Democratic candidate for president (1952 and 1956). For these celebrations we would decorate in a manic fashion, and everything was dropped to make events both meaningful and aesthetically attractive. Freshly cut boughs from deciduous trees were placed on all the rooms' interior decks, which are a Wrightian signature design feature. Flowers were everywhere. These occasions were memorable, and apprentices were always invited to participate. We would show up in full force and in our best finery.

The second week I was there, Taliesin celebrated Mr. Wright's eighty-ninth birthday. We spent days getting ready for the big event, which was also being filmed for television—*The Voice of America*—to be shown around the world. The day began with Mr. Wright opening his "birthday box." At this annual event apprentices in the Fellowship presented to Mr. Wright recent, beautifully executed plans of their own designs. He gave a critique of each one as the apprentice explained the plan. A few

*Mr. Wright giving his critique at a box presentation on his birthday,
June 8, 1958.* PHOTO: CHARLES PATERSON.

of the apprentices stayed up many nights working on their projects. I
remember some would also make exquisite architectural models.

In the afternoon after the presentation, the Wrights had a cocktail
party in the house for the Fellowship and their many guests. It was fascinating to see the Wrights' home on the inside and wander through the
open rooms. Mr. Wright looked very dapper in a white suit and chatted
cheerily with everyone. Then came a big banquet-style dinner. I was
assigned to serve it with six others. The table was beautifully decorated,
and everyone had wine. Again, the movie cameras were busy. After this
there was supposed to be a dinner dance, but we never had time because
a concert was starting in the Theater. Late at night, after the concert,
we adjourned to the lake located below the house, where fireworks were
already in progress. They were being shot off the miniature galleon, a
scale model built by the apprentices that was floating in the water. The
ship was lit up with lanterns, and hundreds of small candles bobbed
around it in little paper cups creating an enchanting scene of lights
drifting across the lake.

The way Taliesin had evolved, it seemed like a royal household,
where Mr. and Mrs. Wright were the king and queen, attended by senior
apprentices and the new apprentices, like myself, as the rest of the court
and the worker bees. Some might wonder why everyone at Taliesin would

The Wrights en route to Hillside from their house at Taliesin East, 1958.
PHOTO: CHARLES PATERSON.

address the famous architect as "Mr. Wright." This was the outgrowth of the way he was known to quote Mark Twain, who said, "Familiarity breeds contempt." However we referred to him, he was still a father figure for everyone at Taliesin while Mrs. Wright was like a well-loved and feared mother. We really were similar to a family—albeit a bit large, with some sixty of us.

One of the few restrictions at Taliesin (besides no whistling in the drafting room) was that Mr. Wright would never allow anyone to smoke in his presence—he felt strongly that it was a personal and private, unhealthy habit that should not be shared. So people were known to hide from him when the urge to smoke overwhelmed them. There was a famous live television interview with journalist Mike Wallace where Wallace began to smoke and Wright did not allow it. A photograph of Mr. Wright from his early days appeared in publications with his own cigarette airbrushed out. I have a copy of an original, with the cigarette held between his fingers.[9]

Mr. Wright's public presentation was so different than his persona around us. In public he could be a tremendous showman, carrying his cane and wearing his cape and porkpie hat. A photo comes to mind of Mr. Wright dressed in such a way. Pictured at the building site of the famous Johnson Wax building in Racine, Wisconsin, he stands with his

Mr. and Mrs. Wright joining the apprentices at a Sunday picnic on the grounds at Taliesin East, 1958. PHOTO: CHARLES PATERSON.

client S. C. Johnson. One of the three-story lily pad inspired columns is loaded with tons of cement bags in the background, to disprove the engineers who said it would collapse with even a third of that weight placed on them.

To the apprentices, I never heard Mr. Wright utter an unkind remark. Yet he was known in the public realm to make sometimes outrageous and provocative statements, even insulting ones, likely recognizing the value of these remarks in the media to promote a point of view. He was, in fact, infamous for his acerbic remarks in public. One day Mr. Wright was giving a talk at a college in Minneapolis. When he was asked after his lecture what he thought of a new building on the campus, of which he did not approve, he replied, "Dynamite it." Often retold, this tale sits among another famous story about a roof leak over a client's grand piano; when the client reported this in a histrionic phone call, Mr. Wright's reply was to simply move the piano.

The Taliesin life was imbued with the learning process. It expanded and fixed in one's unconscious as long as one kept an open mind. We learned how to look at details and how important "terminals" were, where each line ended. Mr. Wright had us look at the structure of flowers for instance—the extension and harmony in living growing things.

Mr. Wright also followed this principle in his faultless attire and would always appear in suits with starched collars and cuffs. He had an elegant wood cane, and his shoes were always polished. Mrs. Wright wore colorful dresses, and they both wore hats when we saw them outside. I have a picture of Mr. Wright with Mrs. Wright at Taliesin West in Scottsdale, Arizona wearing his light-colored porkpie hat with a cream colored suit. The photo was taken by one of the apprentices, and the slides were shared around. I also have a slide I took of the Wright family enjoying a picnic with us on the grounds at Taliesin in a secluded spot. The couple and their daughter Iovanna sat in chairs and on sheepskins placed on the long grass under a leafy tree, with their finery and Taliesin-red teacups in noticeable contrast to the natural setting.

I enjoyed the intensive schedule of life at Taliesin. I even liked doing the varied chores. In fact, they took my mind off things. I had been very social in Colorado, and met a girl named Dana at the wedding of a Denver socialite the prior fall. Dana came to Aspen to work for the winter and had become my fiancée. She was accepted by the Wrights to live with me at Taliesin, but had ended our engagement through a letter I received my first week there. It was a nice letter, but I was disheartened.

Toward the end of the ski season in 1958, Dana and I had traveled to Taliesin West in Scottsdale, Arizona, where the Wrights and the Fellowship spent their winters. We flew down with Bill Roosevelt, piloting his plane to visit his father, Elliot. Bill was the grandson of our wartime President and a past ski pupil of mine. Dana and I had a charming interview with the Wrights. It was not unusual at Taliesin for apprentices to be there with a partner or spouse, who were integrated into the Fellowship.

However in the end, Dana expressed misgivings and though assuring me there was no one else, she feared it just wouldn't work out. I wrote the news to my father on July 11, 1958. He was understandably disappointed since my sister had already started a family. I continued in my letter to him, "Dana feels that her parents' objection ... will never change and the little issues like religion, etc. will take on greater proportion later. Perhaps she is right—perhaps not. The best thing to do for me is exactly to do nothing. In the meantime we remain friends."

A month later I got a letter that pinpointed the situation more clearly. She had met someone else in the middle of May, a cadet at the Air Force Academy, and started going steady with him a few days after I last saw her in Denver on my way to Taliesin. They planned to marry that September, and she was really sure about him. Among other things, I wrote to my father, he was "a devout Episcopalian and both families were heartily in favor of the union." Dana had originally pressed me for marriage, but it was clear her father, who had urged us to wait a year, had a lot of influence on her decision. Her mother was against the marriage from the outset. As I read the letter again, I heard an echo of my father's letter to my sister and me from Lisbon after his daring escape through France. *"C'est la France!"* he had written at the end. "Well," I wrote, seemingly with a shrug, *"C'est la vie!"*

In the winter of 1957 I had made a connection with the young *Playboy Magazine* through friends and my ski teaching in Aspen. I thought it might be good for my fledgling ski lodge if I nurtured a relationship with the promotion director Vic Lownes. He and *Playboy* literary editor and author A.C. Spectorsky had come to Aspen that winter to research lifestyles in the emerging ski town, but upon their return to Chicago, they realized they didn't have enough details about the town and tourism information as the article developed into the lead story. Lownes needed names of restaurants, shops, and other things to do in Aspen, and asked me to write something up. I provided a long letter, which was then reproduced in full on pages 67 and 74 within the article, which was attributed to Spectorsky and Fred Iselin, co-director of Aspen Ski School. This peeved me a little at the time, but I was too unknowing in such matters to do anything about it.[10]

Due to their bad conscience I was treated extremely well at the Playboy Mansion, which I visited in Chicago when I was in residence at Taliesin East in 1958. Thus I reported to my father from Taliesin on September 25th that year, "I was introduced to some glittering nightlife [in Chicago] by Vic Lownes who fixed me up with a batch of telephone numbers in the model category. Seems there are nothing but beautiful and available

Playboy Magazine's *promotion director Vic Lownes with
unidentified models outside Elli Iselin's Ski Shop in Aspen, 1958.*
PHOTO: CHARLES PATERSON.

young women around that *Playboy Magazine*. We had a delightful (and
expensive) dinner at a flashy restaurant and night club (on the *Playboy*
account), and Vic was a charming host." I also got to meet Hugh Heffner,
publisher and owner, when we passed him in a hallway at the offices of the
magazine. A very busy man, I was lucky to get a few sentences from him,
before he rushed off.

In and around Chicago I had "three very exciting and interesting
days" as I had also seen "twenty-five to thirty of Mr. Wright's other
houses" in Oak Park. I wrote, "I'll spare you the details—but all I can say
is that my impression of Chicago sure has changed [from my first visit
in 1948]." When still a teenager fresh off the steam-liner from Sydney, I
feared even to depart the train in Chicago for the gangsters my sister and
I might encounter.

The same weekend I went to visit the Playboy Mansion, I also spent an
evening at Wyatt Jacobs', a lawyer who wanted to invest in my lodge. He
lived in a Mediterranean mansion on the North Shore thirty miles from
Chicago. He and his wife took me to dinner at a country club and were

very nice, though I wrote to my father, "Only I was rather sorry because I gave up a date with a beautiful model since I didn't have time to do both. I don't know when I'll learn. Sometimes I feel like a country boy." I was in the company that weekend of older experienced people, so no wonder I felt that way and was so impressed. I continued in my letter, "You ought to see this fellow Vic operate! He is fantastic. He plans to spend a week in Aspen early December when he has to fly out to Denver to give a speech or something. Plans to stay with us at The Boomerang—I hope I'll be home."

As the fall of 1958 progressed, my father worried that I had not promoted our lodge nearly enough to *Playboy*. Vic had written to me on September 10, 1958, "I checked with Spec to make sure there was mention of The Boomerang in the article, and he said that there certainly was, but that your letter did not emphasize it too much. I think you missed a bet not laying it on just a little bit thicker." Neither Vic nor my father understood my logic. I purposefully did not wax fantastic about The Boomerang—after all, it was still only a three-unit lodge.

At Taliesin, I had wasted no time starting my plans for an expansion of my little ski lodge. I felt that I had limited time and much to do, so kept at it ambitiously. I was in the drafting room at every opportunity, sometimes for an hour in the mornings and three to four hours in the evenings or on my lunch hour. Drawing the lodge was an application of the Wrightean motto "learn by doing." The fact that Mr. Wright's life's work was so available to us gave me much inspiration and confidence. The danger was always for new apprentices to be overwhelmed by Mr. Wright's genius, which could easily discourage the humbleness of one's ideas.

Soon, I started a new concept to put the lodge on a 30- and 60-degree modular hexagonal grid system. The layout was a lattice of diamonds. I was learning this method from Mr. Wright's work, where the lines of the building and the partitions fall within the grid creating harmonious spatial relationships. By the beginning of July, I completed the ¼" scale plan of the lodge with all furnishings and then started on elevations. I kept in mind the economy of the plan and thought it very workable—certainly for the circumstance of being a ski lodge and its location. An unintended consequence of following the hexagon grid was that the final site plan of the building became fortuitously shaped like a boomerang. ▪

CHAPTER THIRTY

A Critical Mix

At Taliesin, construction projects were going on everywhere. Word traveled that I was a good plasterer, due to the fact that I had mastered cement finishing during the previous summer when I did the floors on my three-unit lodge in Aspen. So I was put on the job. It was told that one time Mr. Wright did not like some plastering work and took a hammer to it. Thankfully, this did not happen to me.

The plastering method we employed was actually outmoded at that time because of the innovation of drywall, but at Taliesin everything had been wood, glass, stone, and plaster, so they continued with the same technique. I soon found myself with an assistant, repairing all the Taliesin soffits that had been damaged by roof leaks. The state of disrepair had become so desperate that Mr. Wright had even considered hiring professional plasterers and, so I heard later, he thought I was one of the pros. Finally, after a few weeks he realized I was one of the new apprentices. I suspect a senior fellow cleared up the misunderstanding— no, they weren't paying me, I was "learning by doing."

As I related in a letter to my father, I heard that when Mr. Wright saw our work, he told someone that he wanted "those two boys to do the chapel," referring to Unity Chapel (1886) that was next to Taliesin and was the Lloyd Jones' private family chapel. Members of the family were buried in a small cemetery adjoining it. The Chapel was one of Mr. Wright's first drafting jobs while a young man working for the architectural office of Joseph Lyman Silsbee in Chicago, before he went to work for Louis Sullivan. Outside the Chapel the soffit plaster was falling away.

However, we were never assigned the task at the Chapel, but were instead put on a project in the Wrights' home. Joe Fabris, a senior apprentice who had been there already at least eight years—and of this writing over sixty years later—is still at Taliesin—was in charge of the construction at that time and good to work for. When he found out how

At the Wright house, plastering the newly remodeled bedroom addition for Mrs. Wright, Taliesin East, 1958.

much I knew, he showed me all the different things they wanted done, then left us completely alone. Joe would tell me to do the work the way I thought best, and then my assistant and I wouldn't see him for a couple of days.

Besides plastering and painting, we built an addition to a roof overhang in my first couple weeks. The nicest thing was not being pressed for time. If we didn't get it done the first day, we would get to it the next.

I also worked on a remodeling project for Mrs. Wright's room. It was to be completely modernized with Danish furniture. I was in and out of the house constantly, passing through the logia and "blue room" as it was called, as I had to stucco a wall just outside on the balcony. Mrs. Wright was quite positive about what she wanted. If there was a discussion with Mr. Wright about how things were to go for her room, she always carried the day.

Someone took a picture of me during this job, spreading dark stucco on a wall perpendicular to a series of half a dozen thin French doors and windows. This must have also been where we did the overhang addition because one can see that a window in that wall just has the framing and the roof overhang is open, only studs. My tools are gathered around me and white dust covers the flagstones.

What was most interesting about this project was getting to know the beautiful house better. There were many details to absorb in Mr. Wright's work. I was allowed to wander through the house, a special privilege, and so was able to admire the Wrights' treasure trove of art including Japanese screens and vases. The grand living room was filled with Wright designed furniture. A cream and blue Asian rug covered the floor.[1] Wright's barrel chairs enclosed the rectangular dining table, and exquisite art objects were visible on the overhanging decks that surrounded the rooms. Everywhere one looked was a new vista and discovery. It was a constant wonder and education for me to be in these intriguing spaces.

I worked the remaining summer of 1958 as a plasterer and always arrived at teatime, my clothes splattered with white. I used to tell my daughters that my plastering was the true beginning of my architectural career. I would describe how Mr. Wright found me working one day on a ceiling and said, "Come with me, and I'll make you an architect!" But that's just myth, the kind of thing you tell young children to get their eyes to pop. Nevertheless there is a grain of truth in the story, about the power Mr. Wright had to redirect someone like myself, who had been thrown about the world and was still looking for my place.

With our rotating shifts of duties at Taliesin, it was inevitable that I would be transferred out of construction eventually, if only temporarily. Joe Fabris was quite unhappy about this and wanted me to stay with the building projects when it came my turn that summer for kitchen detail. I demurred because I thought it would look bad if they gave me special considerations. Actually, Joe did succeed in getting me a week off "vegetables" because of the plastering, but then I went back to the kitchen. I reported my experience to my father in a letter sent around my twenty-ninth birthday, July 7, 1958.

"This week finds me on as kitchen helper—Taliesin's K.P. I am up at 5:45 a.m. and work through till 2 p.m., when I go down to the river for a couple hours, where we also have a beautiful [little] beach. There I swim, read and soak up the sun. Back in the kitchen for another hour before dinner and I am through. It isn't a bad schedule and I get along well with the cook—Donald Brown—who is also my 'house mother' as we call him because he is in charge of [Aldebaran] where I live. Yesterday I talked him into letting me make the spinach, which is usually served in the worst possible way. I made creamed spinach.[2] He spoilt the cabbage, which was supposed to be 'Bohemian' but tomorrow I won't let him ruin the rice!" When I could that week as a kitchen helper, I tried to make a difference in what was served, adding Austro-Hungarian cooking flair.

In general at Taliesin, the food was fine—after my tastes—but I did miss eggs in the mornings and meat in the evenings (which we did not get on weekdays). Also we did not drink any coffee or tea with our meals. On weekends, however, the menu was lavish. Still, I noted to my father, for me the food usually was just not quite enough—a lifelong refrain from memories of lean times as the war broke out in Europe.

On July 29, 1958, my "official day off" after another week in the kitchen, I wrote to my father from the riverbank beach while sun tanning. Even though the Fellowship apparently "raved" about the Viennese creamed spinach I made, I was ready to get back to my lodge plans in the drafting room and to go back to plastering. I had "parried off inquiries" about the extent of the Austrian recipes I knew in order that they didn't "try to make a cook out of me."

My last day on kitchen duty had been hectic. It was the first time that Mr. and Mrs. Wright had come over for Sunday breakfast in weeks. "To begin with—the breakfast cook decided to make waffles. As the first batch was ready—and since they did not grease the waffle irons—every one of the six waffles stuck like mad. At this point the phone rang, which I answered. Mrs. Wright was on the phone that she and Mr. Wright would be over in five minutes for breakfast. As this was announced in the kitchen, everybody got jittery, especially the waffles which still refused to part from the waffle irons." Can food be jittery? My father thought so. This letter brings to mind that whenever he encountered the famous American dessert, Jello—for example in the CRMS cafeteria line—he would stop and with a solemn nod, formally address it, "Do not tremble. Do not vorry. I vill not eat you."

After breakfast, Mr. Wright gave his customary informal Sunday talk, which was full of wit and wisdom. You could have heard a pin drop in the dining room it was so quiet, though filled with nearly eighty people.

During preparations for Sunday dinner, to which I was also assigned, the kitchen misadventures continued. My father must have found especially funny the dilemmas of the cook. We had roast beef, creamed spinach, and baked potatoes, but got off to a late start and

The Wrights, bottom left, at Sunday breakfast, Hillside, Taliesin East, 1958.
PHOTO: CHARLES PATERSON.

had only served about fifteen people when the phone rang. The message came down that the family would be over in a few minutes to see the film made at the beginning of the summer on Mr. Wright, his work, and the Fellowship.

Everybody went to the theater and took their seats, but only the first part had been shown when another call came that we should go ahead with dinner. Everyone hurried back to the dining room, and we started serving dinner again. After about twenty more plates went out, Mr. and Mrs. Wright arrived in the theater to see the film. I wrote, "Everyone (but a few hardy individuals) left their dinners [for the second time] and rushed back to the theater. At this point the cook threw up her hands and left for the evening." She then "proceeded to get drunk." After the film we had a belated dinner and went back for another film, a Western.

Liberated from the kitchen after that, I arranged for a small beach party to celebrate with counselors from a girls' camp nearby that was owned by one of Mr. Wright's apprentices from the early thirties, Herbert Fritz. I wrote, "Needless to say a couple of the counselors are very cute.... We had a nice time and had cake and pop and had the girls home by a respectable hour—everything on the up and up. One blonde beauty interests me particularly—as you can guess. Won't let it interfere with my work though. Love, Charles."

In August 1958, I started my new permanent assignment in the drafting room. One design project I was given was a fireplace in a recently built Wright house that had been causing problems because the builder did not follow the plans in regards to the chimney flue and it had been smoking when lit. I found a practical solution by redesigning the interior of the firebox.

When I wasn't working on projects such as these, I focused very seriously on the lodge design for Aspen. My plans were taking shape, and the diamond module was forcing me to think 'out of the box' and 'in the grid.' I had to keep adjusting the drawings, however, because changes were constantly occurring with new Aspen zoning codes, even over the course of one summer. I was doing presentation drawings as well as perspectives; the latter were in colored pencils, the way we were learning from Mr. Wright's commissions. As apprentices we were encouraged to copy detailed drawings of current projects, in order to learn the elegant solutions employed by Taliesin that also simplfied construction.

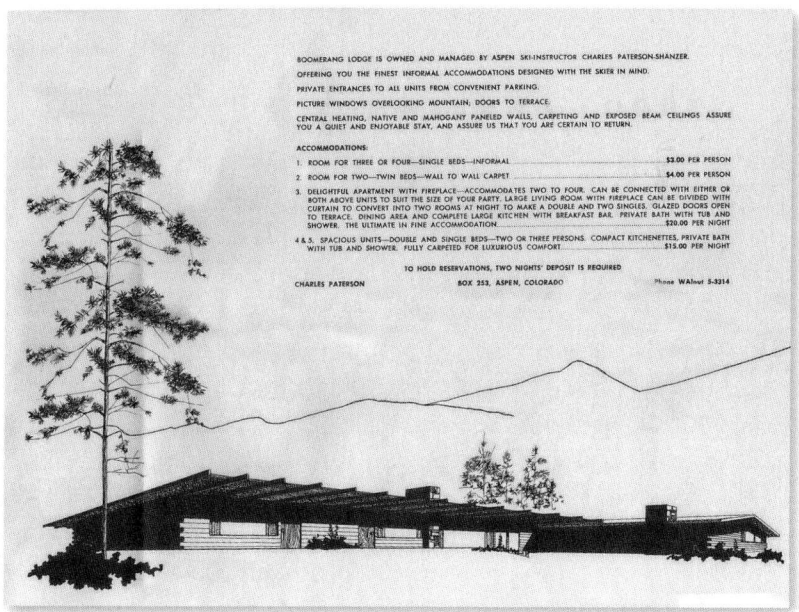

The Boomerang Lodge brochure, 1959. Rendering by Art Dyson.

I noticed that over the course of my first summer as this plan evolved, I started to design and draw better. I had help and encouragement from a new apprentice who had his desk next to mine. This was nineteen-year-old Art Dyson, somewhat of a young prodigy, who later became dean of the Taliesin School and an internationally renowned architect. Currently based in California, he practices a very futuristic and visionary architecture. His talent was recognized early in his apprenticeship by Mr. Wright, who had him work on the renderings for the Guggenheim Museum in New York City, which opened its doors in October 1959. Art showed me how to draw figures, trees, and cars in perspective for presentation drawings, and even designed a modernist style cover for one of my early Boomerang brochures when I still only had three units. I printed the brochure the following winter on buff paper with brown text and Art's drawing of the building.

Despite all my work over that summer, I did not neglect my social connections with the outside world. I felt that at Taliesin we tended to concentrate on our inner life, and sometimes it was much like a monastic experience. So, in my little convertible, I would occasionally take weekends to visit friends from Aspen who were scattered across that area of the Midwest.

One such friend, Barbara Elsner, a former ski pupil, owns a Frank Lloyd Wright house in Milwaukee. The "Bogk House," as it is still known, was built in 1916. It is a narrow, two-story urban house in the center of a block of other residences, with a hipped roof and stone steps leading up to its understated main entrance. The living room has exposed brick walls and was richly decorated with Wright custom designed furniture and rugs accented by persimmon colored velvet draperies. It is one of Mr. Wright's few non-"Prairie houses" from that time period. It stands out among his projects because it shows his solutions to condensed city living. It also reflects a Japanese influence and is considered by the owners to be a work of art. Interestingly, because of the small urban lot it has similar design constraints and solutions as were used in our Werkbundsiedlung house in Vienna. However, the Bogk House is much more elaborate. The *Milwaukee Journal* described its exterior: "Tapestry brick with precast concrete ornamentation restates some of Wright's favorite themes—deep-set windows, overhanging eaves, and a decorative frieze reminiscent of Mayan temple architecture." [3]

Almost eighty years after the house was built, my wife Fonda and I were standing with Mrs. Elsner at the November 1997 reunion at Taliesin West in Scottsdale, Arizona and had the pleasure of meeting Santiago Calatrava, a guest speaker at the event. He remarked to us that Mrs. Elsner's home is one of his favorite Wright houses. Calatrava, the Spanish architect, structural engineer, and sculptor, is world-famous for his creative and graceful design aesthetic, many times manifested in elegant bridges and museums. A recent *New Yorker* feature on Calatrava reveals his understanding of architecture as a form of communication between people and a social medium through which we build societies. "I think it is important to build for people, and to deliver this message of hope: through good construction and a sense of progression, a better under-standing of each other can be achieved."[4] To me, this statement has clear resonances with Wright's philosophies.

For Wright, social patterns and lifestyles resulting from the era and people's expectations for living were as equally important as the archi-tecture. He tried to understand his clients' desires for living with nature and appreciating the unique features of a particular landscape. However, he was unyielding about changes to his plans and was known to disavow a building where alterations had been made to the design without his permission. He could also be tyrannical with his clients about their personal accoutrements and the placement of his self-specified furniture.

When I visited Mrs. Elsner in 1958, the Taliesin Fellowship had just completed a kitchen remodel for them. She invited me to stay the weekend, and I was in awe of the wonderful spaces of the house. The reflections and play of light coming from the window placements, along with other inte-rior details, made even some of the smaller rooms feel spacious. To be in a Wright house and see how people lived there was a continuance of my Taliesin education. The night I got back to Taliesin after visiting the Elsners, I thought to reciprocate Mrs. Elsner's hospitality by suggesting that Mrs. Wright invite the couple for dinner. Soon afterwards, Mrs. Wright hosted a nice dinner party for them at Taliesin.

I enjoyed seeing how the Wrights continued their friendly relation-ship with their clients. From this, I learned that an architect should endeavor to understand his clients by spending time together with them in pleasant company. The way to achieve harmony in a building is to first meet their needs as people. Later when I started to practice architecture,

*With Kay Comfort and friend on the Comfort's Chris Craft
at Torch Lake, 1959.*

a number of my clients came from friends I had made over the years, and many of us shared the love of skiing and the sense of freedom and joy it brings.

Some of these friends in the Midwest, the Comfort family, had also been ski pupils of mine, and they became quite important in my life during this period. Hartley Comfort owned a printing business in St. Louis and later became an investor in the Holiday Inn at Buttermilk, a ski mountain for beginners and intermediates just outside of Aspen. We stayed in touch for most of our lives. He and his family loved to ski and were frequent guests at The Boomerang starting in the mid-1950's.

I wrote home to my father on August 20, 1958 about a fabulous summer get-away week at the Comforts' house on Torch Lake. They owned twelve pairs of assorted water skis and one of the best sailboats as well as a twenty-six-foot Chris Craft that could seat eight people and do forty-five miles an hour. Kay Comfort's brother also had a small two-seater speedboat. I wrote, "The canoe and rowboat on the beach didn't look like they had been used all summer."

The first day I tried my hand at water skiing. I caught on easily and

*Summer house for Kay and Hartley Jr., the Comfort children,
designed by Charles Paterson at Taliesin, 1958.*

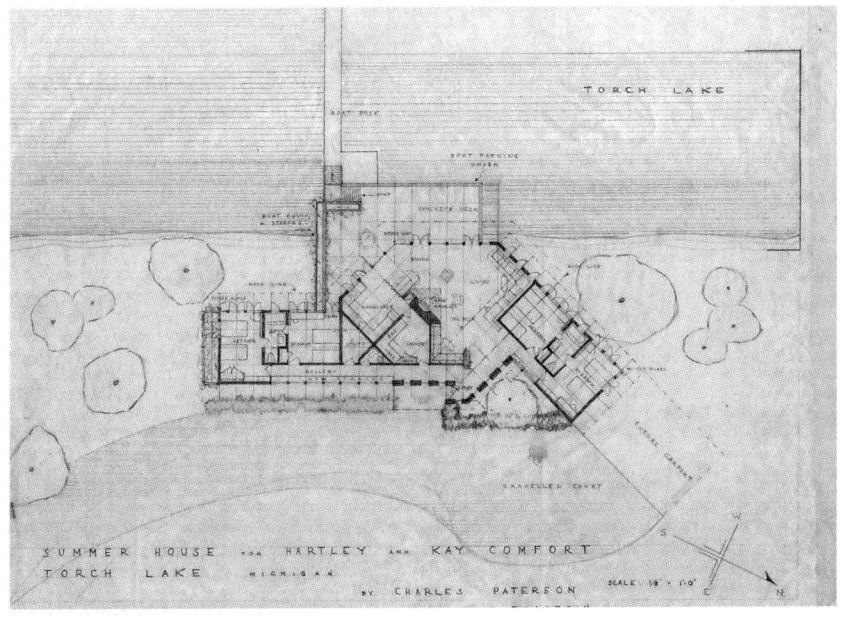

Comfort house plan, 1/8 inch scale.

found it a lot of fun. That afternoon we took out the beautiful E sailboat, which the Comforts raced every weekend against all the other boats on the lake. They needed me to crew for them, so with the four of us, we won the Saturday race against twelve other boats, which was quite a thrill. My job was to keep the boat from tipping over, and I spent most of my time "riding the boards," hanging on the outside of the boat to balance it as it keeled sharply in the wind. The following day we had a more blustery day and came in third.

I remember the Comforts were wonderful hosts. One evening, "family night" as it was called—since the cook and the maid were off and the Comforts ate at a buffet at the yacht club—I showed my slides from Aspen, being an enthusiastic proponent of Aspen and the Skiing Company. I reported, "The Comforts were thrilled I had [the slides] with me." I was in my element talking about skiing and sharing the pleasure of our outdoor experiences in Aspen.

During that time I looked at some property that Mr. Comfort was thinking of buying and building a house on for his son and daughter, right on the lake. I wrote to my father, "The lake, by the way, is one of the most beautiful I have ever seen. The water is a fantastic light blue and as clear as a bell. If I had more money I would buy some property there myself, since it hasn't been too developed yet. I am doing a drawing for the Comforts for exercise on what the house should look like."

I designed a four-bedroom house for them. In addition to preliminary drawings I also did a color perspective, which showed the house as seen from a bird's eye view. I oriented the house to the lake in such a way that the lake became almost a part of the living spaces. The house was set on a square eight-foot module, with a glass front that angled outward forty-five degrees. It had French doors leading from the living room to a large concrete deck over the lake that extended out with steps down to a long wooden jetty. The flat roofs had large overhangs for summer shade and passive solar gain in the cooler months. My drawing shows the house as it would be seen from out on the water. I imagined this approach to the front of the house would be the one most used and enjoyed by both the Comforts and their neighbors.

We were motivated by the Wrights to lead a full and well rounded life at Taliesin, as can be illustrated by the breaks in work for tea-time, the special weekends, and events for which everyone dressed formally. Sometimes Mrs. Wright even encouraged a romance here and there. But I avoided entanglements, for the most part, because I felt they could weaken my concentration on learning and capturing the essence of Mr. Wright's architecture, devoting myself instead to my studies. However, the small group of "vacation" letters in my father's file, like the one above, suggests that in addition to my studies I retained the free spirit that inspired my life in Aspen. I realize now that this, in addition to Mr. Wright, would be the influence that galvanized my own architecture.

When I got back to Taliesin from my weekend with the Comforts, I found a note from an Aspen friend, Barbie Gallun, who had visited. I wrote to my father, "She turned up with a group of tanned girls and had the boys set on their ear in the drafting room asking for me. When someone told her that I had gone with my sister she laughed and proclaimed, 'I know better!', to the merriment of the entire drafting room. At least a dozen people told me the story and I am jokingly accused of having a harem—the boys now call me 'The fabulous Mr. P.' Anyway, I went right back to plastering and everyone seemed glad to see me back (nobody wanted to do any plastering in my absence). Lots of love, Charles."

As I applied myself diligently to my work at Taliesin, I found myself fully committed to that new lifestyle. To work alone in the immense drafting room at night was strangely eerie. Often this was the case as I was there almost every night working on my plans. One night I felt a strange sensation, almost an out of body experience while thinking about the design. It seemed that everything was suddenly clear and that I understood deeply the principles of organic architecture. It was a mystical and fleeting feeling, but it reinforced for me that the immersion of one's mind into a state of concentration has a spiritual effect on the psyche. This state was amplified by my efforts to comprehend the balance in Mr. Wright's architecture.

"Every great architect," said Wright, "is—necessarily—a great poet. He must be a great original interpreter of his time, his day, his age." This aphorism reflects on the intangible quality of life at Taliesin, where Mr. Wright had not only become a father figure to most of us but even more so, a mentor. The expression Mr. Wright had used to describe Louis Sullivan, "Lieber Meister," was now, in turn, how I and others felt about Mr. Wright. ▪

*Frank Lloyd Wright with Carl Sandburg entering the
Taliesin Playhouse Theater, Taliesin East, 1958.*
PHOTO: CHARLES PATERSON.

A Sympathetic Chord

During the fall of 1958, my father visited me at Taliesin on his return from staying with my sister Doris and her family on the East Coast. He was welcomed by the Wrights and given guest accommodations. In late September, upon his return to Colorado, he gave a short speech at Colorado Rocky Mountain School describing his experience. I have the transcript of his lecture only because my father sent a copy to his friend Albin Schwab in Vienna, and the letter was given back to me at the end of 2011 by Albin's grandson, Peter Csoklich.

My father prefaced his talk to the students and faculty at CRMS with an aside that he had no difficulties finding his way even though people told him they could never find Taliesin even during the day. "I reached Taliesin around 12 p.m. As there are no indications [in Spring Green] whatever where the school is located, ... I followed the very accurate map my son had sent me," he said.

"I got an excellent room at Taliesin itself ... underneath [the Wrights'] living room, called the 'Silver Room' ... with a wonderful looking fireplace and a wonderful view overlooking the artificial lake. Charles first of all showed me the designing room [drafting room], which looks like a big church.... In the right hand corner next to an enormous fireplace Frank Lloyd Wright has his designing desk. He is there very often during the day looking over the latest creations of his students and correcting them. Also here he discusses new projects, nevertheless he has in his house, a private studio.... All over the designing room are models of his works, also models of new projects.

"Some of the most interesting things I saw there were the birthday boxes ... on display in the big designing room. For Frank Lloyd Wright's birthday the Fellows usually give him a plan of some project ... and when he opens the box, he [critiques] all the plans therein. This happens also at Christmas time."

Taliesin East drafting room. Alvin Louis Wiehle in foreground,
Nari Ghandi, background, circa 1959. PHOTO: CHARLES PATERSON.

My father then talked about all the encompassing arrangements at Taliesin—the fenestration, roof overhangs, patios, interior decks with leafed branches, etc. "Nature is always coming into the rooms by floral or leaf decorations.... I was amazed by the beauty of [Wright's] living room and other parts of the house because the books I studied about his architecture don't give the right idea. I always thought that his interiors were not so warm, but they are."

Making an observation about Taliesin that only few dared to say, my father continued, "Mrs. Wright and also Frank Lloyd Wright's pupils created a sort of, let's call it, 'Imperial Court' around him.... It was interesting to watch ... how everything revolves around the two principal persons."

The Sunday my father visited, there was a lunch given by the Fellowship on top of a hill near Taliesin. "A terrible wind blew and everybody felt the oncoming of a thunderstorm," he said, but the lunch was a feast. "A whole lamb was barbecued in a pit similar [to the way] we have a whole ox barbecued on Potato Day in Carbondale. Both Mr. and Mrs. Wright and family were at this lunch, but as good and nice as it was, it interrupted the regular Sunday Schedule." Because of the barbecue my father unfortunately missed hearing Frank Lloyd Wright's usual Sunday talk.

The following morning, my father and I were summoned to an audience with the Wrights. I was quite nervous, but my father on the other hand was most relaxed as we were ushered into their living room. My father described our meeting with the Wrights for his CRMS audience as a lively discussion. "Together with Charles, I had a long talk with Mr. and Mrs. Wright in their living room. We talked about Aspen and also about the latest events in the Middle East."

My father's experience of that part of the world was as the Middle East sales manager of the family textile company Hermann Pollak's Söhne (H.P.S.). He felt he knew the area and the people well and said, "Mr. Wright was concerned about the fate of his big Baghdad project, and told me that the new [revolutionary] government had partially approved it." As it happened, when the commissioning Hashemite monarchy in Iraq was overthrown,[1] no work had yet been paid for, and within a year, the new government abandoned Wright's plans as "too grandiose." The plan by Wright for Greater Baghdad included a civic center, opera house, two art museums, botanical gardens, a telecommunications tower, and a new university campus. But after the coup it was not the time for extravagant architecture, which in Mr. Wright's plans called forth the city's thirteenth-century glories and Orientalist images from *The Arabian Nights*.[2]

"Then we talked about Charles," my father reported, "and [Mr. Wright] said: 'Charles is a very good plasterer now, but we will make an architect out of him.'" I remember that as the conversation drifted to my progress, and Mr. Wright was complimentary, I thought I would sink through the floor.

My father continued, "At the latest, Charles was transferred permanently to the drafting room and is working now on one of Frank Lloyd Wright's projects under the supervision of the head designer. If I compare Wright's work with that of my late brother-in-law, Adolf Loos from Vienna, who led in Europe ... a similar fight for good architecture, I must say now that Wright's work [has] reached a much higher perfection [than Loos]. The reason is that Loos died in 1933 and all he would have created between 1933-1958 was not done." Wright's most productive years and some of his most interesting projects were developed in his seventies and eighties, years that Loos, who died at age sixty-three, never saw.

"I finally left [Taliesin] for the West," concluded my father, "mentally totally exhausted from everything I had seen and experienced, and I hope one day to return to Taliesin for further studies." When my father came back to visit Taliesin again the following summer of 1959, Mrs. Wright remembered him well and again gave him a room in her house, usually reserved for visiting dignitaries.

The comparison between Loos and Wright is fraught with dangers— differences in culture, clients' requirements, and environments—but as my father noticed and often discussed with me, looking at the two together brings out many interesting parallels. Despite what appears on the surface to be great differences in architectural styles, the approaches of Loos and Wright resonate for me in a sympathetic chord. Loos wanted to teach people "how to dwell," not just in his homes but also in the world.[3] Wright famously said, "I don't build a house without predicting the end of the social order."[4] Like Loos, Wright saw his buildings as transformative, which would alter the way that people lived and usher in a new era.

The two architects were certainly aware of each other. In the summer of 1932, Loos wrote the unusually high compliment in a card to Wright's apprentice George Kastner, "Frank [Lloyd] Wright is the best architect of the Americas."[5] In 1933, Wright extended an invitation to Loos to participate in a traveling exhibition to be first seen at the Chicago World's Fair. That year the Fair's theme was "A Century of Progress." In Wright's words, the exhibition would feature "organic architecture" from around the world, and the materials would be cataloged in the Taliesin archives.[6] Unfortunately, Loos was nearly on his deathbed and could not participate.

In the 1987 *Guide to the Musée d'Orsay* in Paris, which my wife Fonda recently found on our bookshelf, Loos and Wright are paired because they both created stunning and original examples of ways to filter space in their vast and open interiors. Wright notably broke up his open floor plans into semi-private spaces with his stained glass and his chairs, the backs of which were designed often as partial screens—for example, in Wright's house for Isabel Roberts (1908). Similarly, Loos' use of a mirrored partition with beveled glass for the apartment of Gustav and Marie Turnowsky [7] in Vienna (1900) is an example of a "transparent, reflective fragmentation of space" created for his clients to emphasize the different patterns of their lives and their individual requirements.[8] The examples given are significant because at that time—the beginning of the twentieth century—it was unlikely the two architects knew of each other yet. Their common reference was the Japanese pavilion at the 1893 Chicago World's Fair, which made a significant impression on both.[9]

While I was away on a weekend break that summer of 1958, Mr. Wright autographed several books for me. When Gene Masselink reminded him that I was the nephew of Adolf Loos, he wrote at the front of his autobiography, published in 1932, "To Charles Paterson in memoriam Frank Lloyd Wright."[10] Oddly phrased, this was in fact a reference to Loos, and through this dedication Mr. Wright was paying his respects. In another book of Mr. Wright's that he signed for me, *A Testament,* published just the year before, in 1957, he lists architects in Europe who were revolutionizing architecture at the turn of the twentieth century: "the Mackintoshes of Scotland; Van de Velde of Belgium; Berlage of Holland; Adolf Loos, and Otto Wagner of Vienna."[11] I was intrigued to see Loos in this list, as was my father. Wright was in some senses revitalizing his name; when Loos died in 1933, his work fell into obscurity for decades.

And in a second book on Wright: "Until Loos appeared on the scene just after 1900, advances in domestic planning were almost all English and American as they had been for a generation," observed architecture historian Henry Russell Hitchcock in his foreword to *Frank Lloyd Wright to 1910: The First Golden Age,* published in 1958. Hitchcock continued, referring to Wright's interior work, "the houses of Voysey in England and of Loos in Austria had doubtless as much influence [in their own parts of the world]."[12]

When I told my father about these mentions of Loos in books by and about Wright, it became of interest to my father to pursue getting an English translation done of my aunt Claire's 1936 book, *Adolf Loos Privat.* Losing Claire as we did, tragically, this was one small way my father thought to keep her voice alive. Her intimately recorded tribute to Loos is a lively encounter with both of their characters and with the time period itself. Reviewers and historians have compared Claire's writing to her photography and portraiture of Loos in his later years; [13] to read her book is not only to encounter Loos, but also her, the woman behind the camera.

I remember during the time of my apprenticeship at Taliesin I felt a need to correct the record about Loos to Mr. Wright when in my first year there, Mr. Wright came across me working and exclaimed: "I don't know why your uncle started all this Bauhaus stuff!" which actually he did not—but at the time I didn't dare say so.

The timing of this comment is important. As discussed by Adam Cohen in the *Wall Street Journal,* "The Baghdad commission likely increased Wright's concern about the spread of the [Bauhaus] International Style. The Iraqi government had invited Wright as one of a 'panel of architects of world fame' to modernize Baghdad. Wright called the other architects, including Le Corbusier, Gio Ponti, and Walter Gropius, 'those glass box boys.'" [14] Certain Loos exteriors can be compared to the Bauhaus, being blank, white, and boxy, though Loos' intentions were totally different from those Modernists. The outside came only as a second consideration after the interiors and feeling of the domestic spaces were well-conceived. Loos was still also invested in wood and stone as his primary building materials, as was Wright.

Loos was opposed to the primary Bauhaus inspiration—the influence of the machine—and instead was a proponent of craft and the hand-made. This ethos is similar to Wright's. The Imperial Hotel, Wright's magnificent building in Tokyo that withstood both earthquake and fire, is said to be the last hand-made building of the twentieth century. [15] Loos also advocated for craftsmen and that they be paid their proper wages to make durable goods. In Loos' view a pair of shoes or an item of furniture should be useful and desirable for the lifespan of the materials, rather than disposable according to fashion. In his infamous polemic titled "Ornament and Crime," Loos railed against superfluous architectural ornamentation, like carved plaster flourishes on public buildings, which, he argued, were paid for by the Austrian government at the expense of Austrian society. It's hard to believe now, but when Loos presented these ideas in a lecture in Munich in 1909, people rioted. [16]

Loos and Wright seem to me similar in character, though I think neither of them would have admitted there was an equal anywhere in the world. Each was an eccentric, bombastic, and certain that his philosophy was the true way of architecture. This alienated some and caused

Adolf Loos with ear horn, circa 1930.
PHOTO: CLAIRE BECK LOOS. COURTESY: ALBERTINA, VIENNA.

Adolf Loos in his Vienna apartment with his dog Beau-Beau, circa 1929.
PHOTO: CLAIRE BECK LOOS. COURTESY: ALBERTINA, VIENNA.

Adolf Loos in his Vienna apartment, circa 1929.
Apartment interior now in the Wien Museum.
PHOTO: CLAIRE BECK LOOS. COURTESY: JANET BECK WILSON.

Adolf Loos in his Vienna apartment, circa 1929.
PHOTO: CLAIRE BECK LOOS. COURTESY: ALBERTINA, VIENNA.

conflicts on certain jobs; however, each was the kind of dynamic person who could galvanize truly dedicated followers. For Loos, architecture could be polluted and made dilute by excessive design. Wright understood himself to be a modernizing force, a bringer of sense and reason to American architecture, which had lost itself in turn-of-the-century Greek revival and still suffered from acute Victorian fecundity.

Two notable architects, Rudolph Schindler and Richard Neutra, form a bridge between Loos and Wright, and one can see that relationship clearly looking at their individual architectural styles. Often paired together and compared by scholars, Schindler and Neutra were both United States immigrants of secular Jewish heritage, who became friends and worked together briefly in Los Angeles. Each spent time working with Loos in their home city of Vienna, and later each found his way to study and work with Wright. Neutra's work on Frank Lloyd Wright commissions with Rudolph Schindler while living with Schindler at his King's Row house in Los Angeles was the beginning of their long California careers.

While Schindler and Neutra's relationships to the architectural masters were quite distinct, still some comparisons can be made. More time would be required to do so, however, and to adequately address the large volume of Neutra and Schindler works in Southern California, let alone their impacts elsewhere, is not a task for this book. Worthy of brief note for the comparison, nonetheless, are Schindler's unique perspectives on coloration, which compliment those philosophies of light and color developed by Loos and Wright, as well as Schindler's original concept of Space Architecture, in part inspired by Loos' complex arrangements of interior space.[17] Suffice it to say, those interested in the juncture where the architectural legacies of Loos and Wright meet have two extensive bodies of work in Schindler and Neutra to examine further.

At Taliesin, I found other resonances between Loos and Wright. Both architects had a respect for raw materials and took inspiration from natural processes. Wright's plans for Taliesin included using the native limestone in Wisconsin, and at Taliesin West in Arizona, desert stones from the site were incorporated into the walls.[18] Natural forms—hollyhocks, lily pads, rushing streams, snail shells—all became part of Wright's vocabulary.

In his interiors Loos used richly veined and contrasting marble and travertine, mahogany, and cherry. The visible patterns present in materials were decoration enough. Specifying directional cuts in richly textured woods with burls and knots, Loos allowed the materials themselves to form subtle punctuated patterns. In the Villa Müller, fish tanks and green marble visually rhyme to create the living room landscape. Loos' buildings and interiors, like Wright's, reflected the truth of the Earth, even at their most fantastical.

Above the mantle at Taliesin was carved the Lloyd Jones' family's motto, "Truth Against the World." Wright expounded in 1939, "Organic architecture [is] the modern ideal ... holding no 'traditions' essential ... nor cherishing any preconceived form ... but—instead—exalting the simple laws of common sense—or of super-sense if you prefer—determining form by way of the nature of materials." [19]

Rather than designing 'with' materials, Loos also allowed his architecture to arise 'out of' the materials. This also means there is a surprising permanence to his work. His interior marble and wood paneling in many of his Pilsen apartments, for example, survived war, Nazi occupation, and years of neglect under Communism. That an apartment's walls, like mountains or other natural features, can remain virtually unchanged through destructive episodes and human dramas is remarkable.

Loos' favorite materials, from marble to silk to rich veneers, made an apartment a world unto itself. In *Adolf Loos Privat* Aunt Claire quotes Loos criticizing architects of his time, "I don't understand architects! They're always afraid of using strong colors beside each other. I find that a meadow full of flowers is very beautiful, and yet every flower is a different color. Colors can be used together in a room in exactly the same way." [20] Loos' sense of nature invoked its innate sensuality.

Also in my aunt Claire's book is the story of how Loos solved the problem of one client's apartment, which was located overlooking the Škoda factory in Pilsen. Jan (Hans) Brummel,[21] who also became a Beck friend, had "a depressing view, particularly from the dining room. Loos put up sheer golden yellow curtains at the windows which when drawn drench the room in sunlight." [22] Loos used fabrics and surfaces to create atmospheric effects, choosing the most appropriate locations for them. This was also true of my grandparents' 1928 apartment, which I remember had diaphanous curtains and light pouring through the large windows that overlooked a park.

Perhaps this explains why I sought out someone like Mr. Wright. I felt so inspired being around him and the environment he created. It was totally different than my European upbringing, yet familiar, and felt true to my new home under Colorado's expansive skies. Wright believed in bringing the outside in, and oriented his buildings toward natural features. In Wright's work the use of materials bled across the borders to create what he called "integral" design.

While Loos conceptualized buildings in terms of a clearly defined exterior/interior binary—almost to an extreme—and Wright favored the illusion that the interior was not limited by walls, but rather flowed into the outdoors, both architects, as with many modernists, relied on this essential relationship to structure their spatial thinking.[23]

I have reflected many times on the mutual influence both Wright and Loos have had on my life in terms of my lifelong interest in design and architecture. Knowing so much about Loos through Claire, the Beck family, and my father, in a way had brought me to Taliesin. But my interest in architecture, not just building, really started in America because of my father. Even in the early days of designing my cabin, he made suggestions about how things should be done according to what he had seen Loos achieve. For him there was only one right way to build— and that was following Loos. He told me, "I did not understand architecture until I met your mother." If it weren't for Otto Beck following Loos, perhaps none of this would have come to be.

When I was contemplating where to put the dining table in my cabin, for example, my father suggested an inglenook—a Loosian small benched eating area with table—that would separate the kitchen from the living room. He also gave me an idea to make a cozy atmosphere with intimate table lighting, much like one can see in Loos apartments, and which can be observed in Claire's photograph of a 1927 New Year's Eve dinner at the Beck apartment in Pilsen. The lamp in my cabin sat at the end of the table and consisted of a large branch cut on the wider end to make a natural base. I ran a hidden wire up its twisted form to a lamp fixture inserted in the top end. The lamp's angle was naturally leaning, like someone taking a bow. Its single bulb we covered with a parchment lampshade. I made several of these types of lamps, including a floor lamp. They went well with the cozy log cabin feeling and were part of my method of building from local materials.

*My father Steve in the living room of our 'bare bones' cabin, showing the
windows behind the seating corner and a table lamp made
from a tree branch, 1954.* PHOTO: CHARLES PATERSON.

Other details from Loos I incorporated in collaboration with my
father: built-in cabinets and closets with sliding drawers that required
no hardware, and room dividers. When I did a master bedroom expansion years later, after Fonda and I married, we created a kind of half level
with a two-step drop down to the bed, a lowered ceiling, and built-in
bookshelves on each side.

My father was actually so strict about his aesthetic principles he was
gruffly insistent about how I would proceed in that expansion. To achieve
it we had to take down the wall that separated the cabin from the garage,
which presented the opportunity for an arched beam. I remember my
father holding his head, "No, there will be no Fischer von Erlach in this
house!" Architect Johann Bernhard Fischer von Erlach was a designer
of Schönbrunn Palace and the large Karlskirche (St. Charles Church)
in Karlsplatz—and my father would not suffer another moment of the
flowery Viennese Baroque style in the new lives we were making.

In the cabin living room I built two "Siberian beds" for our couches
and placed them below long windows, so light would pour in behind
you as you were seated. The apartment Loos designed in 1929 for the
Becks' Pilsen acquaintances Jan and Jana Brummel and the 1928

Moller House in Vienna both feature similar seating against a window. Architecture historian Beatriz Colomina writes about these spaces, "The position of the sofa, and of its occupant against the light, produces a sense of security."[24] The couches were intentionally low so we had a separation from our guests who roamed outside in the garden, though we could be looking up and enjoying the mountain view. The Siberian beds were placed at right angles. The space left in the corner at the heads of the beds soon became a raised, square planter. My father recalled Loos doing something similar and suggested that the plants be Loos' signature red geraniums.

I also remember an incident when my father actually stomped out of the cabin in a huff after seeing my cabinetmaker improvising a round corner at the base of a new cabinet next to the built-in desk in the living room. It should be a right angle! He put me in my place—"How can you call yourself an architect and allow this?"

All of these stories came to mind upon the surprise of finding a Loos house plan while going through the drawers in my father's filing cabinet. I was reminded that my father's attachment to Loos was not superficial, or anecdotal, or nostalgic for times in Europe before the war. Our family was part of the "Loos community," comprised of Loos' loyal clients and friends.[25] For my father, the plan held a special emotional connection to my mother. Perhaps my father was also keeping Loos' ideas close in a practical way—to refer to, as one does with a letter, in order to keep facts straight after the people, witnesses to the time, are gone. He did not actually need the plans for a building, because Loos had inspired many stories, and his architecture had become oral history.

The unrealized Loos house plan, an emblematic symbol of home, of Vienna, of my mother, and the Becks, survived the journey to the United States in a thick envelope with Claire's writing and French stamps. The plan was sent from Kniže men's haberdashery at Champs-Élysées 146, Paris on August 26, 1930,[26] a little more than a year after I was born. An enclosed letter signed "Claire and Adolf" described the plan, which had been originally drawn for another (unknown) client. I can only imagine the envelope was in one of my father's trunks that had been stashed at the Paris offices of Les Fils d'Emanuel Lang, which were shipped to my father in 1942. The envelope, in exile with my father, was a small part of the life he had intended to take with him and to rebuild.

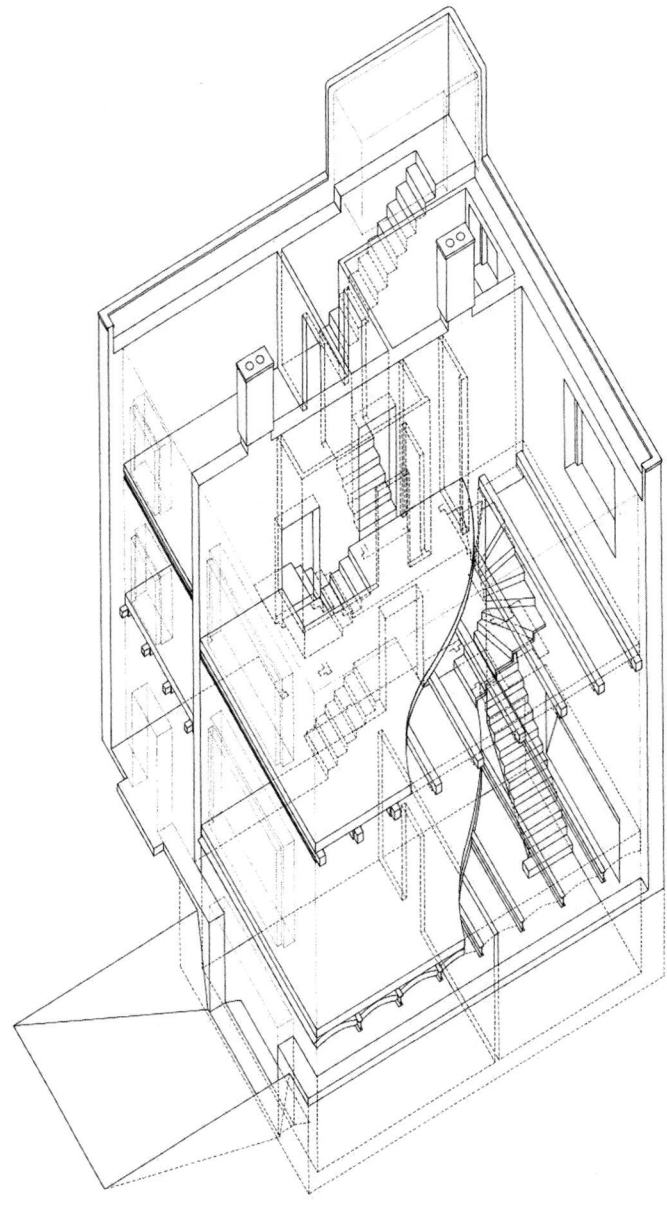

Adolf Loos: 9 x 9 meter Einfamilien(doppel)haus, 1930. Spatial reconstruction and axonometric drawing by Univ. Prof. D.I. Arch. Hans Puchhammer, Univ. Ass. D.I. Dr. Sigrid Hauser, Christoph Karl, and Gerhard Kienesberger. (Adolf Loos als Konstrukteur. *Vienna: Institute for Architecture and Design, Vienna Technical University, 1989. 32.)* COURTESY: HANS PUCHHAMMER.

Looking at the Loos plan in its axiomatic perspective, it is a fabulously complex puzzle, with six half-levels and a flat roof. Each level has a different ceiling height than the one before it, with bedrooms more intimate than the living spaces. One must try to visualize walking through this house that only exists on paper, for an undetermined site. The entrance level and the garage, below grade, form the first floors. "From the anteroom," Claire wrote, "one could access a cloakroom, restroom, and kitchen, and from there get to a pantry, a garden, and [down] a staircase into the laundry room, basement, and garage." The next four levels are alternately stacked and spiral upward around a central, continuous sheer wall,[27] with the living and dining rooms on the half-level above the entrance; the next half-level up, a maid's room and a guest or craft room; then on the next half-levels above, the family bedrooms. The children's room and bathroom are located at the very top, where there is also access to the roof.

This unbuilt house, rendered in what is known as "the 1930 Paris plan," is important architecturally because it features one of the only examples of Loos' "split level" design.[28] It has resonance with Loos' more complicated *Raumplan* idea of interlocking cubic spaces one sees in his later masterwork, the Villa Müller in Prague, but the 1930 Paris plan is simpler—more like Loos' split level Moller House—because the spatial shifts only happen along the vertical axis. My father noted the connection between the Moller House and the plan Claire and Loos sent him, and that like himself, Moller worked in textiles.

I assume my father recorded this information on the plan because the architect for our eventual Werkbundsiedlung home, Jacques Groag, realized the Moller House with Loos, and this would have been a good credential for Groag. The 1930 Paris plan actually has several features similar to the house by Groag we moved into, though the 1930 Paris plan would have been larger. With a footprint of 9 x 9 meters it is not large, but tall—equal to three stories. Claire wrote, "The house can be made smaller if we adjust a wall. Loos says that it would be cheaper but not by much. I am sending you the plans anyway, which Loos estimates at maximum ... 20,000-25,000 [Austrian Schillings]. The house can also be made out of wood.... This house is planned for a corner lot, but with minor changes it can be built as a row house or a duplex."

Where did my parents intend to have the house built? This question was a key to unlocking a small secret held in the Adolf Loos archives at the Albertina in Vienna—yet another trace of our family, as light as the pencil with which it was drawn on translucent paper.

In the spring of 2012, Professor Otto Kapfinger was researching the Werkbundsiedlung houses and my family involvement there for the 2012-2013 Wien Museum exhibition "Werkbundsiedlung Vienna 1932—Manifesto for the New Dwelling." Several hypotheses about Loos' and Claire's letter to my father had been exchanged with my daughter Carrie, and Otto Kapfinger took it upon himself to investigate. He recalled in an email the day he went to the Albertina archives with Dr. Andreas Nierhaus, Curator of Architecture at the Wien Museum. With their white gloves on, they found a plan signed by Loos amongst his original vellum paper drawings bearing a note in pencil on the back, "Haus Schanzer." It was not the 1930 Paris plan, but one very similar, showing a scheme for a small row house intended for the Werkbundsiedlung.

While based on the 9 x 9 meter 1930 Paris plan we have, the house plan in the Albertina is scaled down to 8 x 6 meters.[29] The history of the 8 x 6 meter plan was known only somewhat. It had been elaborated with the help of Kurt Unger while Loos and Claire were with Unger in the French Riviera from April to June of 1931.[30] The small notation in the Loos archive involving our family went undetected before, so the 8 x 6 meter plan, discussed in various architectural books including the massive compendium *Adolf Loos—Leben und Werke,* was never previously connected to the Werkbundsiedlung or to our family.[31]

A description found by Carrie in the Albertina's Loos archives in November 2011 explains that Loos had asked his student Kurt Unger to use the 1930 Paris plan to draw up a scheme for the Werkbundsiedlung duplex, because it had a good solution to building on a small lot. But construction had already begun on Loos' Werkbundsiedlung project, which was being managed by Loos' collaborator Heinrich Kulka—foundations had been laid, and it would be impossible to adapt the 1930 Paris plan to the site after all. A letter to Loos from his housekeeper, Mitzi Schnabl, dated September 30, 1931, recounts that my father went to the housing authority (GESIBA) and filed a complaint against Kulka.[32] Before the research for this book, it remained difficult for us to imagine what dispute had transpired.[33] The unpleasant feelings between my father and Kulka created by these events are unfortunate, to say the least. Kulka

Ein Schatz für Loos-Forscher

Adolf Loos als Hochzeiter: Selbst engagierte Loos-Forscher haben bisher nichts von der Existenz dieses Dokumentarfotos gewußt, das der KURIER hier exklusiv veröffentlicht. Das Bild entstand wenige Jahre vor dem Tod des weltberühmten Architekten, nachdem er sich 1930 entschlossen hatte, ein viertes Mal zu heiraten. Zu sehen sind: Loos' legendäre Haushälterin Mitzi, Loos-Schüler Heinrich Kulka, Braut Claire, Bräutigam Adolf, ein (unbekannter) Trauzeuge und Loos' neue Schwiegermutter.

Das Bild hatte sich über 50 Jahre im Besitz des in London lebenden Bruders von Claire Loos befunden, der es nun dem Herausgeber der neuen Loos-Bücher (siehe Samstag-Buchseite), dem Wiener Regisseur Adolf Opel, überlassen hat.

"A Treasure from Loos-Wedding"
This family photograph was lost to history until my uncle Max Beck
allowed Adolf Opel, the editor for the 1985 edition of my aunt Claire's book
Adolf Loos Privat, *to publish it in the 1980's.* LEFT TO RIGHT: *Mitzi Schnabl,*
Loos' housekeeper; architect Norbert Krieger; Claire Beck Loos; Adolf Loos;
architect Heinrich Kulka; and Olga Feigl Beck, July 18, 1929.
COURTESY: JANET BECK WILSON.

was friendly with the Becks and appears in Claire and Loos' wedding photograph from 1929. There are only three other people, Mitzi Schnabl, architect Norbert Krieger, and my grandmother Olga, all smiling, as Loos and Claire pose for the newspaper camera in overly dramatic style. Loos stands in the center with his ear horn in one hand, and shows off his new ring, held over his heart, with an expression that seems to say guilelessly, "Me?" Claire tilts her head, a small bouquet pressed to her chest, and looks upward in an equally conspiratorial manner, performing a romantic pose reminiscent of ladies being wooed in silent movies.

I remember my father remarking that Loos' Werkbundsiedlung houses would have been too small for us, but never knew anything more. It may be that my father simply didn't want to talk about bad memories. We realized Loos' 1930 Paris plan, and the outgrowth into an 8 x 6 meter plan, was the first Werkbundsiedlung house he had been forced to abandon because of circumstances beyond his control. When we had to leave Vienna, the 1930 Paris plan became more than an architectural plan; it was a symbol and a referent. He kept the letter from Claire and Adolf Loos, a memory of people lost, together with the unbuilt plan, which could also represent hope for the future. ■

Architecture in Evolution

I was home teaching skiing again in the spring of 1959. It was the end of the season, and I was preparing to make my next sojourn to Taliesin. One beautiful day, with blue skies and brilliant crystals glistening on the snow in the warm sun, my life changed suddenly in a manner I will not forget. I was lunching with my ski pupils at the Sundeck, a hexagonal building designed by Herbert Bayer, perched at the top of Aspen Mountain with views of the surrounding Elk Mountain Range. It was then and there that the news of Mr. Wright's death reached me. A few days later, the following sad letter arrived from Taliesin West written by my fellow apprentice and friend Vern Knutson.

As apprentices, we idolized Mr. Wright. I grieved deeply.

Taliesin   April 16, 1959

Dear Charles,

We have laid the Great Master to rest. He drew a peaceful ending here to the stormy scene of his battles and triumphs.

Mr. Wright had been feeling very well all winter and was extremely active and happy. The Saturday before his death he complained of a stomach ache and that evening was taken to a hospital and had quite a bit of pain at the time. He had minor surgery Monday for an intestinal blockage. Although he appeared to be recovering well he succumbed early Thursday morning.

Mrs. Wright returned at breakfast, calling us all into the Garden Room to tell us. It all came so quick and quiet that it still seems hard to believe. We had never connected death with him.

Upright stone marker with circle of flowers and bench (foreground) at the original grave site of Frank Lloyd Wright, adjacent to the Lloyd Jones' family Unity Chapel at Taliesin East, 1959. PHOTO: CHARLES PATERSON.

Late that afternoon (Thursday) Mr. Wright was returned to Taliesin West. We made a beautiful simple mahogany box to place the (awful looking) casket in, placing it in front of a backdrop of red velvet covered with bougainvillea flowers, which we loved so much, hiding all the pitiful, mournful flowers that had been sent by the dozens.

That evening at sundown we had services for him in the Garden Room, for the family, Fellowship, and a few close friends. It was very beautiful and simple, as he would have wanted it. Mrs. Wright opened by reading from the Bible, Job, standing beside [Mr. Wright] and holding his hand as she read. Then Gene read a beautiful poem about him. Iovanna played a harp solo, then Brandock a cello solo, John A. [Armantides] violin, and finally the chorus sang the mighty "Ave Verum" by Mozart, all music that Mr. Wright loved so much. Our good-byes lasted throughout the evening and night.

Mr. Wright was taken to Wisconsin by Wes & Ken the following day. Mrs. Wright, Iovanna, and Gene flew up Saturday. Final services were held for him there and burial was at the family graveyard. At the same time as the funeral there, we who had to stay in Arizona had a concert of his favorite music in our Garden Room, so we could be with Mr. and Mrs. Wright in spirit at least.

At first we had all planned to return immediately to Wisconsin, but after trying to get packed and organized, we realized that there just wasn't time. The cold weather did not sound welcome either. Mrs. Wright, Iovanna, and Gene flew back Monday, and we will probably all remain here until nearly May 1.

We are a pretty lonely people now, like sheep without a shepherd I guess. The camp reeks with emptiness; his presence, however, remains in the prophetic strength and beauty of his work, the clarity and boldness of his thought.

To those of us who knew him personally, I believe, his rank as the world's greatest architect often seemed incidental to the vast range of his thought upon the panorama of human works and ideas. His was a truly universal mind, fed and enriched by the philosopher's insatiable curiosity. He kindled man's hearts, was and is a titanic force.

There will never be an equal to Frank Lloyd Wright.

Sincerely,

Vern

Now that I am approaching the same age that Mr. Wright was when I knew him over half a century ago, I recall gratefully how his influence and generosity of spirit has been a strong force in my life. His bright light truly was a spiritual guide, and it has not diminished in time.

The first weekend I was back at Taliesin in the summer of 1959 was the anniversary of Mr. Wright's birthday. Relatives of Mr. Wright's, many former apprentices, and intimate associates came from all parts of the country to commemorate the anniversary. Even though, as I wrote to my father, the Master was not with us anymore, the crowd was enormous, and his presence could still be felt.

There were so many guests that I slept on a mattress on the floor at

Hillside, being unable to find a bed elsewhere. A half hour after I arrived, I was already at work, since there was so much to do for the upcoming celebrations. Saturday night was a banquet for over two hundred people, and the whole drafting room was turned into a banquet hall.

The weekend was quite hectic, but things soon settled down in the following weeks as we got back to work.

I was again living in quarters at "Aldebaran" but really wanted my own room. After a few weeks I was allowed to move to "Tan-y-deri," Welsh for "under the oaks." This house was designed in 1907 by Mr. Wright for his sister Jane Porter and her husband, but was later used for members of the Fellowship. Other occupants that year were long-time apprentices like Bruce Pfeiffer. The house was simple, but quite lovely. It was a square two-story building with a hip roof, shingle siding, and a front porch. We lived below the oldest existing Wright building in Wisconsin, "Romeo and Juliet," the famous 1896 diamond and octagonal windmill tower with observation deck. It was a beautiful daily walk on the path over the hills through majestic stands of trees to go to work in the drafting room and shared meals at Hillside. No longer was I reliant on a car, as I had been during residency at Aldebaran.

I looked forward to beginning classes in engineering, scheduled twice a week, as well as talks by Gene Masselink on "Abstraction." Jack Howe's class on design was fascinating. After Mr. Wright died, they were having more formal classes at Taliesin. Mrs. Wright would now speak at Sunday breakfasts and also read from former talks by Mr. Wright. I imagine it was trying for her then to suddenly head up the architectural practice. However, she and the others seemed to keep things running smoothly. I wrote to my father on June 12, 1959, "Everything seems to run as before, except no more changes are to be made—only those which Mr. Wright planned before his death."[1] Mrs. Wright had become the representative for Mr. Wright on all his projects, which included several houses that were still on the boards, as well as the final detail drawings for the Guggenheim Museum in New York City, and the Marin County Government Center in California, just being completed.

That summer of 1959 I began engineering classes with Tom Casey and Jim Pfefferkorn. I started working on a complex, soaring roof structure for the Boomerang upper lounge that floated above ten-foot high corner-glass windows. I also had my first client job, calculating the beams for the unusually long span of a flat roof, which would receive heavy snow loads where the house was located, back in Colorado.

These first architectural clients were Leroy and Martha Waterman from whom I bought my original three lots in Aspen. In the old days, the Watermans kept horses on that lot and installed a barbed wire fence with dry aspen saplings for posts around the property. Before 1949, they even considered having a trailer court of mobile homes there, but thankfully that never materialized, and until my cabin sat upon it, the land was kept wild.

Leroy talked to me after he had seen a slide presentation on Wright's projects that I showed in the winter of 1959 to a gathering at my father's Masonic "Spar Lodge" in Aspen. I could not have imagined when I bought the Aspen land from the Watermans in 1949 that I would be their architect some ten years later. The Watermans were consistent in hiring Wright-trained architects: in the 1940's they hired Fritz Benedict to remodel their gas station and grocery store at the entrance to Aspen, which was flanked by a dozen small tourist cabins.[2]

The Waterman commission was for a major redesign of a modest, late-nineteenth century brick home originally built by an Italian rancher. The house I designed for them still stands in the midst of the Roaring Fork Club, a golf development with hand-hewn log cabins located eighteen miles northwest of Aspen. The Waterman house remained in the hands of its original owners for sixty years, resisting the inevitable turnover of property and redevelopment that occurs in the valley.

Leroy Waterman was a fantastic craftsman. He did all the woodwork in his house out of solid walnut, which he had acquired from Lucas Woodall, my first banker, who had a garage full of rough-sawn walnut planks. Leroy planed these boards and used them on the entire interior of the building—on cabinets, doors, stairways, interior balconies, twelve-foot high French doors, and the living room floor. He converted a barn on the ranch into an extensive carpentry workshop to accomplish this feat.

I designed several Wrightean features in their home, including a stairway with long steel poles at every step. The poles reached from floor to ceiling and had small square walnut blocks every two feet along their vertical axis to act as a screened decoration. The stair led to bedrooms with canopied interior balconies overlooking the living room, which had

The Waterman house in Basalt, Colorado that I designed at Taliesin, 1959.
North-east corner of living room.

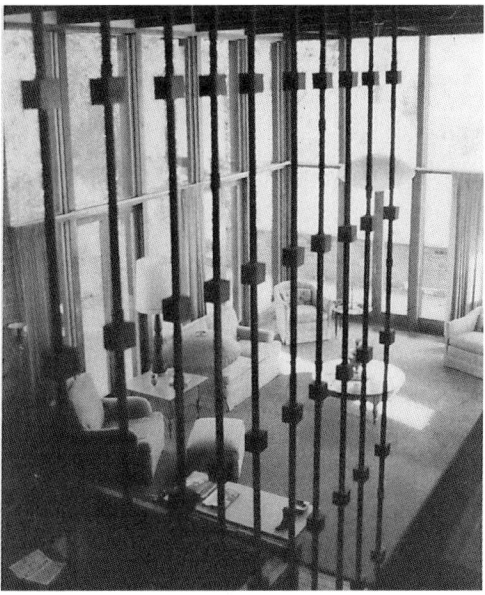

Stairs hung on vertical rods. Waterman's handcrafted walnut blocks
were used as both a design and screening element.

Waterman house after redesign, south-east corner, circa 1960's.
PHOTO: CHARLES PATERSON.

Waterman house before redesign, east view, circa 1950's.
PHOTO: CHARLES PATERSON.

a fireplace reading nook and opened out onto a deck through the tall walnut French doors. One of the client's requests was a living room large enough to hold square dances, so all the furniture had to be able to be moved out through those doors.

The flat roof of the house with large beams and overhangs gave it a sense of sturdy shelter among the trees. The galley kitchen had windows that reached countertop to ceiling, overlooking a meadow. After Leroy's death, Martha ran the house as a bed-and-breakfast called "Altamira."

My father came to Taliesin the second time for a short visit in September 1959. After he left, Mrs. Wright insisted he come back soon. I was invited to dinner at the house a few nights later. We were a small group of ten altogether, and it was very pleasant and formal, with hors d'oeuvres and cocktails before the dinner with Mrs. Wright. It was a special occasion to be invited to dine with her, and I came to the realization the Fellowship wanted me to remain at Taliesin much longer than I had planned.

The following day, eighteen of the long-time apprentices left for Philadelphia, where Mrs. Wright was to give a talk at the opening of the Beth Sholom Synagogue in Elkins Park, Pennsylvania. It is the only synagogue Mr. Wright built and features a dominant, glazed glass pyramidal structure reminiscent of a temple and a mountain.[3] From there Mrs. Wright and the apprentices went to New York to see the Guggenheim Museum for an inspection tour before it opened in October.

I was lucky enough to be Mrs. Wright's server at the house upon her return from the East coast. It was a prestigious job, because at meal times the family server was the only person to have direct contact with Mrs. Wright and her guests. The other people (usually about five) prepared things and generally hovered around the kitchen. Mrs. Wright was of course very gracious—but everything had to be just right. The table had to be set perfectly, wine was served with almost every course, and usually there were half a dozen chosen people in for dinner from the Fellowship.

On a different occasion, when Mr. Wright was still alive, I was serving a small dinner party attended by Alicia Patterson Guggenheim, publisher of *Newsday*, and Bruce Brooks Pfeiffer, one of the senior Fellows. I was in the kitchen when I heard an aria, sung by Alicia, followed by uproarious laughter. When I entered with the next course, there was a silence, and everyone just looked at me before resuming the conversation. The next day, Bruce told me he had been recounting a story for the table that came from my father. I could see why they didn't acknowledge it at the time; it was a kind of gossip spread Viennese-style, as my father's sense of humor was passed around Taliesin. The story was about Jennie Tourel, the mezzo-soprano, who had been a tenant for a couple of months during the summer Music Festival in one of our three Boomerang units in Aspen. She had complained to my father that—among a litany of other things—a spider had come down from one of the beams over her bed. When Bruce told this story, it prompted Alicia to sing out in Jennie Tourel's operatic style, elaborating on Jennie's surprise at finding such a companion in her bed.

In serving dinner for Mrs. Wright, one had a chance to see more of her, which subsequently meant that if you wanted an audience with her, it would be more likely. I wrote to my father, "You know, it sounds strange—but it is quite hard to get to talk to Mrs. Wright. If one goes through 'channels'—it usually is impossible."

In my second year I wanted to talk to her about my stay, and so she asked me to join her in a little morning walk. On this occasion, we had a pleasant stroll around the grounds of Taliesin. I told her I wanted to come the following year even though I was going back to Aspen for the winter to teach skiing and run my little lodge. She stopped and said to me: "Charles, you know you are the only one we let come and go like this. Why don't you just stay?" I was surprised by what I took as a compliment—many people, after all, left Taliesin under duress, or because they were unable to adapt to the system. Mrs. Wright then told me that they had never before allowed a six-month apprenticeship as I had done the year before. But Gene Masselink and Mr. Wright had agreed to let me come and go when I had spoken with them for the apprenticeship originally, and so she kept their word. I was perhaps the only one with such an arrangement throughout the years.

The last couple weeks in October of my second year, Mrs. Wright talked on several occasions about the whole Fellowship going to Europe for a month the following May. It was going to cost around a thousand dollars per person because they were planning to fly each way—probably with forty or fifty people. It was an exciting idea for me, and if they really were to go, I planned to come back to Taliesin from Aspen earlier and join them for the trip, even though I had no idea how I was going to afford it. One of the compelling aspects of the proposed trip was to return to Europe for the first time since I had left twenty years before.

I wrote to my father about the trip the Fellowship would make in 1960 and my desire to join them, but that I didn't want to "jeopardize" my education or completing my working drawings for the lodge. I wonder now about the instinct I had back then. The way to go back "home" to Vienna would have been ideal under these very circumstances—as a future architect, as a planner, as someone within the bonds of friendship and fellowship from America, and wrapped in the magical cloak of Mr. Wright's influence—not to return to Europe as a dispossessed individual, or seeking the remains of my former life, which I could by then only partly remember.

The trip to Europe never took place that year, and I stayed in America, returning to Taliesin in the spring of 1960 as planned.

It was my third year and I moved to an apprentice room next to the main drafting studio at Hillside. This was another definite step up for me in terms of the location of my housing. There were six private rooms on each side of the studio. My room had recently been rebuilt by a former apprentice. With a few additions I made it my own, including a picture on the sideboard of me skiing on Aspen Mountain. We were encouraged to change these rooms to our own specifications and to add personal design touches.

I remember being awakened daily at 6:30 in the morning by the ageless Ling Po, walking through the hallways calling "Garden!" in his Chinese accent, to summon us to the daily task. He was one of Mr. Wright's skilled renderers in the drafting room and a fantastic artist. We would gather in the vegetable garden or the strawberry patch at Midway for the first hour to pull weeds under the watchful guidance of Ling, whose duty it was to keep the gardens in top shape.

In the spring of 1974, on one of Ling's early visits to Aspen, we had an opening on a trip river rafting through some of my father's favorite areas on the Yampa and Green Rivers in Utah. We asked Ling to come along. This was an unexpected chance for travel and adventure, riding rapids. First, Ling called and received permission to delay his arrival at Taliesin East. We hurriedly outfitted him for outdoor adventure, including

Carrie, Ling Po, and Nutzi on The Boomerang lawn, 1974.
PHOTO: FONDA PATERSON.

retrieving my long-idle, small wicker box with watercolor supplies. He took the opportunity to renew his passion for the medium and each night as we made camp on a sandy beach, he would paint one solitary vista. He came home with six small portraits of life in the canyon, in contrast to others on the trip who shot hundreds of photos. For years afterwards, friends from that trip would ask about him, and he was known to visit and encourage several of the artists who had also traveled with us.

Later in my life during his many Aspen visits, Ling Po would sketch in pastels and oil sticks Colorado's vast assortment of interesting land-scapes—mountain views, wildflowers, and the Roaring Fork River. Once we went for a picnic with my family at the Grottos on Independence Pass, and Ling spent an hour observing and drawing close to the rushing water as it crashed and fell over the rocks in a cascade.

Ling gave us several of his beautiful artworks, and we have them all around our house. He did a rendering for me of the Boomerang Lodge as well as a portrait of my younger daughter Jenny for my birthday in July 1983 when she was seven years old. He also made a birthday card in September 1981 for my daughter Carrie, a geometric abstraction of a grasshopper on a zinnia. All of his creative works we treasure. One of these is from September 1974—a thank you for the river trip three months previous—a Wisconsin landscape, a "gin color." Because of the slow speed at which watercolors dry, he experimented successfully with gin to speed the process in the humid atmosphere of the Midwest.

On his visits to Aspen, Ling Po also taught me the daily discipline of T'ai chi exercises, which I have done every morning for the past thirty years. I think of him often this way. "Slower movements," he would say. "More deep breathing." I would follow him making circles with my arms in the air. His suggestion was to practice T'ai chi in front of a mirror to make the movements more dance-like and graceful.

In the 1990's a major change occurred in Ling's life when he joined a Buddhist monastery in California after devoting over fifty years of his life to Mr. Wright and Taliesin. This remarkable event came about shortly after one of his visits to Aspen when we lent him a book, *What The Buddha Never Taught* by Tim Ward, an account of Ward's time at a Buddhist monastery in Thailand that centers on laughter, which Ward found to be the most healing practice of the Buddhists, though it was not part of the formal education.

Following Ling's years in the monastery, he moved to Texas to live with his sister. We learned in 2012 he was in his nineties, but we think of him as timeless and for years never knew his exact age. We have saved each of his letters to us, as well as the several cards he sent to my father, all in beautiful, calligraphic penmanship. We miss his visits with us and think of him often.

After Mr. Wright's death, the wonderful annual tradition of the birthday box presentation continued. Mrs. Wright and Taliesin's senior fellows gave their critiques, including Wes Peters, chief architect, and Jack Howe, who had always been at Mr. Wright's elbow and was in charge of the drafting room.

My box presentation of the Aspen lodge in my last year was unusual in that it was for a realizable project on an existing piece of land, so I was pleased when the panel of judges approved and praised my work. I remember Jack Howe told me I had improved greatly from the previous year. When I started at Taliesin, I remember struggling at first. Two months after I arrived in my first year, July of 1958, I wrote to my father

Birthday Box project at Taliesin East.
LEFT TO RIGHT: *David Dodge, Kamal Amin, Dick Clark, Jim Pfefferkorn,*
Wes Peters, Richard Carney, Cornelia Brierly, Jack Lee,
Joe Fabris, and Richard Miller, circa 1958.
PHOTO: CHARLES PATERSON.

that my first attempts at the lodge design had been on the wrong track. "My interest in my drawings seemed to diminish when I began on small detail work—also because I am fairly slow. The reason is that every time I start another section[4] ... of parts of [the] building like [a] steel beam and roof or fireplace, I have to make a regular research project out of it and study from another drawing how it is done here so well.... It is amazing how Mr. Wright has simplified the integral parts of a building." I continued, "Certainly this is not standard construction as I am used to seeing it. The important thing, of course, is to draw and build enough so that you get used to the system and retain the knowledge."

During my third Taliesin summer, at the end of August of 1960, my sister Doris and her family stopped to visit while on their trip cross-country back to New Jersey from Colorado.

They appreciated their weekend at Taliesin, meeting everyone and seeing all the work there. Herb, my sister's husband, wrote in a note to my father that they had the opportunity to take full advantage of the grounds for walks and swam in the river with their children, Tom and Linda. They enjoyed a tour, as well as an elegant dinner on Sunday night

My living quarters off the drafting room at Hillside, Taliesin East, 1960.
PHOTO: CHARLES PATERSON.

with candlelight, served on Wright's Taliesin-red plates. We enjoyed being together as a family and wrote back to my father of their visit. Oddly, he did not return our letters right away, as was his habit. Soon we found out the gap in our communications was due to him being hospitalized in Denver after routine surgery for what we all thought was appendicitis. At the end of the summer, he was still not well.

In mid-September 1960, a letter had arrived at Taliesin from my father that created concern. I had been writing to him at CRMS where he was teaching, but the letter was postmarked from Denver. I wrote back, "I was surprised to get your letter today and find that you are still in the hospital. Thought that you would be out a few days after [your second] operation and have been writing you in Carbondale all this time. I am most sorry to hear that you are still in Denver and imagine it must be pretty grim for you in the hospital—especially since you are so unaccustomed to it, after all these years of perfect health."

My father's hospital stay was the result of an operation for a blockage in the urinary tract and gallstones. But initially he thought he might be there for complications from another condition, which he did not inform me of at the time. Apparently his skin had turned yellow while I was away that summer, and his physician told him that he had cancer with probably less than a month to live. But in his typical optimistic fashion, he continued on with his life as if nothing were different. My father's friend Kurt Bresnitz has a story about this time, told to me on my eightieth birthday in 2009, at which time Kurt was ninety-two years old.

After my father was given the diagnosis that he had a terminal illness, he called Kurt and proposed that they go on a big trip around the southwest so that my father could see all of his favorite places one last time. After the trip he began counting down the days: five days left to live, four, three, two, and on the last day he bid good-bye to Kurt. The next day, he called Kurt to go have a cup of coffee. "Kurt, I am on day zero," he said. On the next he called Kurt again, "I've got minus one day to live." And so he kept counting down until it seemed absurd. He lived almost another twenty years.

I missed my father when I was at Taliesin, even though I found the work there fascinating. I had also made my commitments to Aspen, to skiing, and to build the lodge. After my father was out of the hospital I still continued to worry about his health, but was happy to learn he had lost eighteen pounds. One thing that can be said for delicious Austro-Hungarian cooking is that it is not spare in calories. He loved his goulashes and Kaiserschmarren, which had not helped his weight in later years. When I wrote home the rest of the fall, I kept my father informed about the progress of the lodge project in anticipation of its realization, now that the working drawings were nearing completion. This would be yet another new phase of my life and of our lives together.

My last days at Taliesin were bittersweet, and when I departed I told everyone they were always invited to stay at the new Boomerang Lodge on their twice yearly migrations either to Taliesin East in the spring or Taliesin West in the fall. For the next fifty years, apprentices, some of whom came with Ling, made Aspen a stop in their travels, and they were always welcome.

Having the Boomerang Lodge fortuitously located on the migration route between Spring Green and Scottsdale was a wonderful way to stay in touch with friends and hear news of Taliesin.[5] I have kept strong memories of my time there. I learned the principle from Mr. Wright that designs and building ideas must always adapt. This kept me occupied in future years as I was always building and rebuilding the lodge. Something could always change, something be improved. More light, more elegance, more units, until I simply couldn't do it any more.

From Taliesin I solidified an idea that is the silver nugget of all my experiences growing up in the circumstances that I did. Nothing is ever static; change is inevitable. Embrace it.

I recall vividly the time when I was working in the house at Taliesin and Mr. Wright decided that a stone wall just off the living room needed to be replaced with glass to bring in more light and a view of a new flower garden. Within the hour, two apprentices were there with sledgehammers to knock the wall down.

Mr. Wright would appear in the drafting room unannounced except for his signature alert on entering, by clearing his throat. One time, Mr. Wright appeared behind my desk early in my Taliesin career as I was working on a project. I jumped up, and he peered at my drawings. It was a symmetrical elevation, which showed a door in the center. Looking at the drawing, he pointed and said, "Never put the nose in the middle of the face," and then, chuckling, continued on his rounds in the drafting room. What came to mind for me later was the Winslow House in River Forest, Illinois, which Mr. Wright had designed in the 1920's. This was a very beautiful building, but the main front door was precisely in the middle. Oftentimes Mr. Wright's singular statements were made with a twinkle in his eye, and no apprentice ever forgot them. ▧

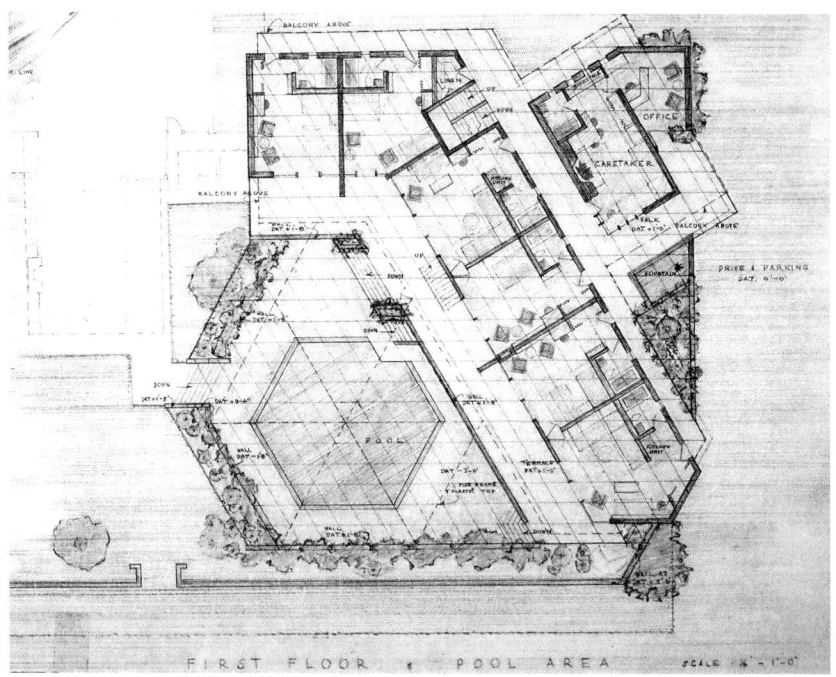

Diamond-grid plan of the Boomerang Lodge by Charles Paterson, 1960.

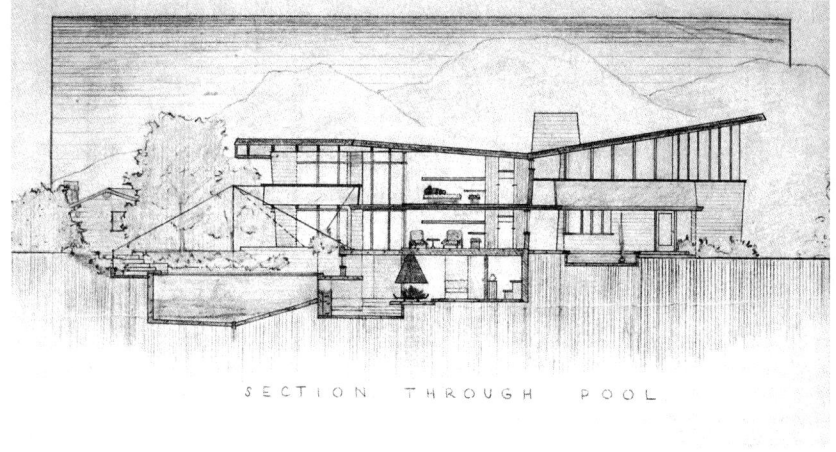

Boomerang Lodge cross-section for Taliesin box presentation, 1959.

Building

I was ready to break ground for the new Boomerang Lodge in the fall of 1961. I was ambitious at thirty-two years old, and I attempted to secure financing for the expansion at various financial institutions in Denver, without much luck. Finally, I found myself in the offices of a fairly new government agency called the Small Business Administration (SBA), which had been formed in 1953. I entered the building with all my presentation drawings and renderings from Taliesin, and I must have made a favorable impression on the director, Mr. Biggs, because they gave me a loan, though it was only approved after a lot of paperwork and a couple of months of anxious waiting. It turned out the agency was a bit nervous about loaning money in an "unproved" resort town. And in fact, I was the first to bring a SBA financed project to Aspen.

With an optimistic attitude and confidence in the future of Aspen, I began building before the loan was approved, which was risky at best. I felt I had little choice in the matter but to start the project, as winter was approaching, and I had to lay the foundations as soon as possible.

That winter was a record early snowfall. We had twelve inches of snow on my foundations on Labor Day.[1] During that late fall and winter, my crew and I spent hours every morning shoveling snow out of the building. As architect, general contractor, and manager of the new lodge, I had many moments of trepidation. It didn't help that I had already accepted reservations for February.

One day as a joke—that I did not take well—my lead carpenter and several of his cohorts jacked up the back of one of the workers' trucks and then asked him to run an errand. When he tried to drive off, the back wheels spun, and he went nowhere, causing everyone to stand around and guffaw. It made me angry that this nonsense went on during working hours. I was already nervous about getting finished in time, so I told my foreman and lead carpenter off in no uncertain terms. The lead

Boomerang Lodge south-east corner with two-story, battered block wall and pool area wall, left. Me on my bicycle with my dog Nicky, 1962.

carpenter promptly offered to knock my block off. Suddenly my father, always looking out for me, came out of nowhere and stepped in front of him. Standing nose to nose with the carpenter, he told the guy to strike him first. My father, well into his seventies, was formidable in his fury, and the carpenter quickly backed off.

The construction of the lodge was unique enough that it caused some consternation for the block layers; the "battered walls" for the ends of the building and the upper lounge were meant to step outward so the concrete blocks had to be offset a half inch on each course. The engineering and steel reinforcements had to be exacting or the walls would have collapsed. Mr. Wright had done battered block walls on several single-story buildings, but rarely on taller structures. It turned out to be quite an accomplishment when the walls held up successfully according to my design and did not tumble down. Using masonry in this way was a new look that made the building special and much admired at the time.

The magazine *Modern Concrete* interviewed me for their January 1965 issue about The Boomerang. The article explains, "The [masonry] method, which Mr. Wright named battered block construction, consists of offsetting each course to create horizontal shadow lines and applying a heavy wash of Portland cement and sand to strike out the vertical joints and give an interesting rough-texture finish. The changing play of light and shadow that results on both sides is an integral ornament of the wall itself." [2]

We worked through snowstorms and other tribulations. Sometimes it was so hectic I thought I would lose my mind. In the early winter I despaired that we would ever finish, even though I had done my homework diligently, choosing fabrics and furniture, and meeting payroll. Despite everything, we prevailed, the job got done, the furniture and carpeting were installed, and my first guests arrived as planned. Up to the time of their arrivals, we were continuously shoveling snow until it piled around the building as high as the second story balconies. It had been a lot of work but in the end, everything came together. My new guests liked the lodge, and its reputation was made.

Traditional hotels had interior hallways, which I disliked. My design incorporated separate exterior entrances to the rooms, either on the ground floor or from exterior balcony walkways on the second floor. The Boomerang distinctly felt like a lodge with its homey atmosphere, large grounds, and access to nature. All the accommodations had French doors leading to large private balconies or pool terraces, which were to be extensions of the rooms and had dramatic, unobstructed views of Shadow Mountain. In the summer, the sun would set over the cottonwood trees at the other end of the property and bathe the rooms in a golden light.

My idea to have a unique lodge in Aspen, incorporating Wrightean design and a modern approach, worked well. Our guests came back for years, as our brochure assured—"The Boomerang Lodge: Where you are certain to return." We had several write-ups early in the game. *Life Magazine* came to town in 1964 and did a photo shoot at the nascent lodge, featuring yours truly with Jeff Glen, the son of a ski pupil of mine, Stanley Glen, and blonde Norwegian Greta Evenson, all riding a surfboard down a snow ramp into the new hexagonal pool. Between 1969 and 1972, *Town and Country* named us as the only Aspen hotel in their list of the top one hundred and twenty-five best resorts in the world. Kudos from the *New York Times*, *Ski Magazine*, and others followed.

We completed the pool in the spring of 1963, a little over a year after the new building opened. One of the pool walls was thick plate-glass, forming an underwater window to the downstairs lounge. It was quite sensational. Children especially liked to watch the swimmers from the sunken hexagonal-shaped viewing area with its built-in surround seating. Light would filter through the water creating "a shimmering rainbow on the window" by day, as noted in the *Modern Concrete* article, and by night the circular, underwater floodlights would cast the area in an aqua green hue. The article continues, "Two special features of the downstairs fireplace lounge are its hexagonal shape and a large underwater observation window into the pool outside. Seven feet long and nearly three feet high, the window is flanked on each side by a mirror mitered in at a 60-degree angle. The mirrors reflect the pool, and the viewer is presented with three images instead of one." [3] Often we had a roaring fire going in the open copper-hooded fireplace that crowned the small flight of stairs leading down to the window, so the firelight was also refracted through the mirrors and the room.

Originally I had planned an aquarium as well in this location, where the fish would be reflected through mirrors to the sides of the underwater window. I always thought that at some angle the fish and the swimmers would be combined in the mirror, but instead the aquarium ended

The Boomerang pool with swimmers, mid-1970's.
PHOTO: CHARLES PATERSON.

up as a planter with ivy growing to the ceiling. It was all for the best. As I knew nothing about fish, I might very well have had a lot of dead ones on my hands.[4]

The underwater window and the fireplace were part of the larger Lower Lounge, where we served afternoon tea, and there were changing rooms and a sauna. Kids had dominion over this space many times. They would rush down into the sunken area, dripping wet from the pool to watch their siblings make funny faces under the water. My children and their friends, of course, used to lead in this activity. Many years later, in the year 2000, my daughter Carrie and her then husband, Charlie Eckart, immersed themselves underwater in front of the window for a wedding picture. For their wedding announcement photo, they clinked champagne glasses and blew bubbles, he in a white shirt and tie, and she in an Aspen Thrift Shop lace dress.

While running the new lodge I continued my career as a ski instructor, and by the early sixties was leading the top class in the Ski School on Aspen Mountain. Skiing is a very straightforward activity. It frees you of all worries. You must concentrate on what you are doing and put everything else out of your mind. By the beginning of each winter season, I

Underwater pool window with Boomerang guests and me (right), 1965.

Me in high gear teaching the top class on Aspen Mountain, winter 1965.
PHOTO: BOB KRUEGER.

would be so tense about The Boomerang, but then I would go skiing. For me it was a release from stress, as I imagine it has been for many others through the years.

I had a few well-known people in my ski classes. Back in 1957, there was one whose identity was kept secret. I only knew her as Anne Scott. She was a charming lady in her early fifties. I found her very interesting, as we had lively discussions, so I managed to always ride the lift with her. One day on the No. 5 double-chair, she waved to someone below who she said was her daughter. She noticed my puzzled look, because I had recognized her daughter. Anne had to confess that she was in Aspen incognito with her husband and family. She asked me to keep her identity a secret and, at the end of the day, introduced me to her husband, who was skiing on Little Nell.

Anne's husband was a tall and distinguished-looking gentleman, who dressed in dark blue ski pants and a well-fitting jacket. He was none other than Charles Lindbergh, the aviator, author, inventor, and explorer who became world famous in 1927 when he piloted solo the first non-stop transatlantic flight from New York to Paris in the single-engine mono-plane "Spirit of St. Louis." The family was known to try to be completely secret wherever they went. Almost no one ever knew the Lindberghs were in Aspen, but there had certainly been rumors.

At the time, I had no knowledge of Charles Lindbergh's isolationist political stance during World War II, which I would have found diffi-cult to understand.[5] On the ski slopes, in any case, one can choose to suspend judgment of a person, and it was my great pleasure to teach Anne Morrow Lindbergh, a delightful personality.

A few weeks after having Anne in my ski class, I received a package. It was a book entitled *North to the Orient*. The inscription on the flyleaf from the author was flattering. "To Charlie Paterson, who also flies in another element—this book is about some very early flying from a grateful pupil. Anne Morrow Lindbergh. Christmas 1957, Aspen."

One of my favorite ski pupils was Robert McNamara, then Secre-tary of Defense during the Vietnam War. He took private lessons from me exclusively. I was always impressed how frank Mr. McNamara was in our conversations on the lift, especially as the escalating Vietnam War continued on a more and more disastrous course.[6] One day I led McNa-mara down North Star, which had a very steep pitch and was marked as a double black diamond run. He caught an edge at the top of the slope and somersaulted the entire way down. Standing below, horrified as I watched this unfold, I thought that if there had been Secret Service with him, they would have surely accused me of trying to harm the Secretary of Defense. At the bottom he picked himself up, unhurt and laughing, with his glasses still on his head.

By 1965, The Boomerang Lodge was so successful that I needed more rooms. So I designed six more units to be built over my original three that adjoined the log cabin, with which I had started the lodge a decade before. These were much smaller and simpler to construct than anything I had done before and were soon completed. With smaller balconies, they afforded the same views, but could be more economically priced.

I continued to teach skiing and to bring my ski pupils in to join us for afternoon tea, which had become a tradition at The Boomerang, as it was at Taliesin. Tea was served in the Lower Lounge, where the underwater window made for a lively scene. On Thursdays, the new Aspen Highlands

Steve telling stories in the Boomerang Lodge upper lounge, early 1970's.

Ski Area would show ski films in the lounge on a projector that popped up between the built-in seating I designed for these types of events. There was a movie screen across from a large, low hexagonal table that could easily seat a dozen people around its perimeter. In addition to a choice of teas, we served spiced cider, hot chocolate, nuts, and various other snacks and cookies. In the afternoons the lounge was full of activity.

After skiing, people especially enjoyed the heated pool, coming inside lobster-skinned to get cups of ice from the ice machine, or to go into the eucalyptus-scented sauna that was angled between the men's and women's changing rooms. I created the sauna in an intimate trapezoidal space that otherwise would have been underutilized, installing the heating element on the small end and stadium type redwood benches along the back wall that could seat six people. In the 1970's, we added the latest craze, a Jacuzzi, increasing the pool area's popularity. Amidst the clatter of the Coke machine, the laughter, and the conversation, tired skiers also inhabited the space, cozying up in one of the small reading nooks with an assortment of paperbacks and magazines, or playing board games.

A continental breakfast was served daily in the sun-drenched upstairs lounge with panoramic views of the mountains. The guests loved gath-

Boomerang Lodge upper lounge, 1990.
PHOTO: DAVID O. MARLOW.

ering there to chat with others about their plans for the day. The environs encouraged mingling and interaction between guests. This was accomplished in a subtle way by having one long wrap-around bench of built-in seating under the eight-to-ten-foot high windows, with low tables. These were exciting days, and I much enjoyed my time with all of Aspen's interesting visitors.

In a basket on a bench at the entrance to the breakfast lounge I kept a number of scrapbooks. One contained a history of the architecture of the building. Others featured photos of Aspen's early days and press clippings about The Boomerang, including interviews that were done through the years. These were natural conversation starters.

My father used to join us at breakfast, and the guests enjoyed his delightful stories. In this way he was able to continue his involvement in the lodge and with the guests into his later years. Like his "Campfire Talks" he was accustomed to giving at the Colorado Rocky Mountain School, he would expound on his experiences in Siberia in particular. This episode in his life was of great interest to people. He would never offer up stories of the Nazi occupation of Austria, although he would talk freely about the duress and success of our escape from France at the onset of World War II.

The backdrop for our continental breakfast was one of the most important features of the lodge—the high fireplace in the center of the back wall.
Its opposing battered walls built of concrete block stepped up and out to
echo the walls of the building. The hood was also concrete block masonry,
which sloped down and out into the room. On the floor we used to have a
large Navajo rug that my father brought back from one of his many trips
around the Southwest. On snowy mornings we would have the fireplace
going, and the lounge was very cozy. I used to stack the wood out on the
balcony and arrive before breakfast hour to start the fire.

In the early sixties I acquired the andirons and grate for the fireplace
from an elderly lady who lived in a small Victorian house in Aspen. I found
her on the recommendation of Aspen hardware store manager Bernie
Popish. On arriving at the house, I told her of my mission, and she was
very kind and happy to have me look at them to buy. In the center of the
kitchen floor was a small trapdoor. We lifted the panel and descended a
rickety old wooden stair into an earth-floored root cellar to extricate them.
In the daylight these andirons were beautiful. They stood almost three feet
high, were obviously from a grand old Victorian house, and were made of
heavy, twisted wrought iron. The lady was happy to sell these antique treasures to me for twenty-five dollars.

Above the fireplace eventually came to hang a huge boomerang about
three feet across, hand-carved out of hardwood. It previously belonged
to an aboriginal tribe and was sent to us by a well-liked former employee,
Andrew Joseph, who was a houseman and driver in 1971. By the 1980's
when he visited he had become a very successful Sydney commodities
trader and hotelier. The history of the boomerang remains elusive, as its
large size is very unusual.

Through the lodge, my family gained a whole new group of friends
and acquaintances. Ironically, we even discovered by chance old-world
friends, like my piano teacher from Vienna, Mr. Freund, or a woman
named Anna, who after a few days with us told my father in a shy manner
that she thought she was a distant relative of my mother's.

Over the years we had all kinds of people returning year after year.
They came from all over the world and from every state. Many became
good friends and are still in touch with us. We receive a great number of
Christmas cards from former guests, and this is a nice reminder that the
impressions left by a vacation in a comfortable, peaceful hotel can create

bonds of friendship like no other.

Just as in every Aspen establishment, The Boomerang also saw its share of interesting and famous people. One of our most eccentric, famous guests included a Rockefeller who carried no money or credit cards and came to the Upper Lounge in his bathrobe with a can of sardines and a Lindbergh-type aviator's cap. His room bills were sent directly to an office in Rockefeller Center and were always promptly paid.

The Viennese-born philosopher, social critic, and Roman Catholic priest Ivan Illich also stayed with us. He came into the breakfast lounge and introduced himself individually to each guest before having his cereal. There were also several U.S. Senators: Floyd Haskill, Tim Wirth, Ben Nighthorse Campbell, and Mark Udall, all from Colorado, and Tom Evans, from Delaware. Tennessee Senator Al Gore also stayed with us, before he became Vice-President, in no-frills room #14. Gore gave an informal presentation at the Aspen Center for Environmental Studies during his time in Aspen about his book *Earth in the Balance: Forging a New Common Purpose*. We also hosted Supreme Court Justice Bryon White and his wife, and IBM's Tom Watson; all were charming and unassuming.

Several other notable guests were involved in Hollywood. In 1962, one of our first guests at the new Boomerang was Rod Serling, creator of the television series *The Twilight Zone*. In the 1960's, director Steven Spielberg's parents became frequent guests: his father Arnold [7] told us about his son's interest in film, and later he reported that Steven was in Hollywood. When actor John Rubinstein stayed with us, it was a pleasure to introduce him to Franz Berko who had photographed his famous pianist father, Arthur Rubinstein, riding the number one Aspen chairlift in 1949 during the Goethe Bicentennial, a photo of which he was previously unaware.

In 1968, I hired two bright and attractive girls just out of college for my front desk, and my life took another important turn. Their names were Fonda Dehne and Carol Boyd. It was early June, the beginning of the summer, and not too busy yet. They found me at the recommendation of my friend Jim Bulkley, who had been swimming in my pool with his son, Jimmy. I was at my annex, The Paintbrush Chalet, only a few blocks away on Bleeker Street, shampooing the hallway carpet. Little did I know that the following spring, Fonda would become my wife, best friend, and delightful life companion.

Cutting our wedding cake at the Bulkley house with my father Steve looking on, April 12, 1969. PHOTO: FERENC BERKO.

Upon our engagement we sent a card to my father, who was at that time visiting my sister Doris and her family in New Jersey, before he departed on a Caribbean cruise.

Aspen   January 5, 1969

Dear Pop,

Thought you might enjoy knowing that Fonda and I are engaged as of January first. We are getting along marvelously and I think that the best time to be married will be in the spring after the ski season. Hope you are having a good trip.

Love, Charles

Dear Steve,

Now I understand why you wanted to leave at Christmas time! I've been doing more working than skiing, but this should change now that things are slowing down a little. The ring is beautiful, and of course, I couldn't be happier.

Love, Fonda

Fonda's engagement ring was a family heirloom that we had thanks to the Langs in Paris who, during the war, safeguarded the few jewelry pieces my father had smuggled out of Austria. This ring is a pear-shaped diamond that my father inherited from his father Karl's second cousin, Baron Gustav Springer. It was originally from a pair of earrings that belonged to Gustav's mother, Countess Amalie Löwenstein. Our wedding was a private ceremony. It took place appropriately on the beautiful property of our friends Kit and Jim Bulkley, which overlooks the Maroon Creek valley with the snow-covered and craggy Pyramid Peak rising majestically in the background. There were twelve family members and friends, including the Bulkley family, in attendance.

Fonda's father Clarence Dehne and mother Lillian came from Iowa, along with Fonda's younger sister Carol, and Agnes Nakayenga from Uganda, the foreign exchange student living with the Dehne family that year. Clarence, a Presbyterian minister, performed the ceremony. After a lovely reception at the Bulkley's house and a small family dinner at the original Steak Pit located under City Market, Fonda and I retired to our honeymoon suite—the Bulkleys' guesthouse, which I had designed two years earlier in 1966. It was built like a mountain chalet, with generous eaves and a second floor balcony sheltered by a protruding prow. I included a Loosian fireplace, light shelves, and a built-in seating area.

Then the cards poured in. I never knew how many people were hoping for me to finally get married.

Bangkok   May 15, 1969

Dear Charles and Fonda,

Congratulations Charlie; there were some of little faith like me
who didn't think you would ever make it to the altar. Strange
as it may seem we ran into a fellow who attended your wedding.
Nona works in a gift shop here in Bangkok and got to talking to
a man who was a member of a tour group only to find out he was
from Aspen. She forgot the name, but he owns Alpine Jewelers.

Best regards,

Jim Dawson

Of course, this was none other than my father's friend Kurt Bresnitz. I can hardly believe he and his wife Lotte were able to bring news of our wedding to my M&CWTC buddy Jim Dawson in Thailand. Somehow the important people in my life have always managed to find each other, even in far off places.

From my old ship companion, Will Semler, I received a letter a few months later. The news of our marriage had been broadcast by my father around the world.

Melbourne   August 14, 1969

Dear Charlie,

It is only now that the card announcing your abolition of freedom has turned up in my place from Mum.

I, as a former cohabiter in interstate Ocean Steamers, congratulate you on this step and I sincerely hope that you will soon be able to fill a cabin right up to the ceiling full of screaming earthly mortals.

It is a shame that in all these years we have not met again but rumour has it that you have grown in the meantime (I hope not a moustache). There is always the danger that one of these days I will invade Aspen and make a thorough nuisance of myself.

In the meantime kindest regards and all the best,

Will

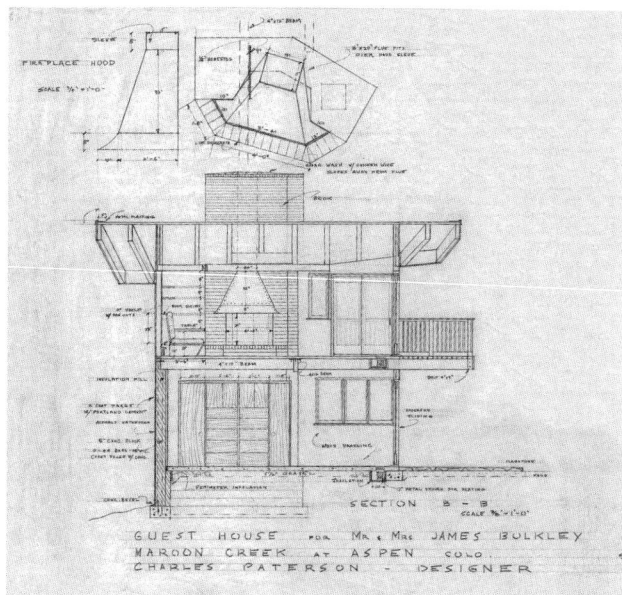

*Guest house for Kit and Jim Bulkley designed by Charles Paterson, 1966.
Cross-section showing Loosian fireplace.*

*Leaving for our Mexico honeymoon, April 1969. Boomerang limousine
"Golden Dachl" ("gold roof") converted Cadillac hearse in background.
My favorite dog Nicky in foreground.* PHOTO: STEVE SCHANZER.

Pencil to Paper

R iding the ski lift in Aspen in February 1968 with one of my pupils, Stanley Glen, I was told he was selling a six-unit building located behind the library on Bleeker Street. I knew the building well since by coincidence I had worked on it as a carpenter in 1952. It was called the Paintbrush Chalet and had been built as a prototype for the Aspen Institute's future Aspen Meadows complex, which opened in 1954. It had south facing balconies, was well built, and honest. Walter Paepcke had hired Wrightean-trained Fritz Benedict and the Bauhaus architect and artist Herbert Bayer (Benedict's brother-in-law) as the designers. They were also responsible for the Paintbrush's then modern features, such as tiled bathrooms, hot water baseboard heating, and a butterfly roof reminiscent of the roof I had designed at Taliesin for the Boomerang Lodge. By the time Stanley and I got to the top of Aspen Mountain, I had made a deal, almost on a whim, to buy the Paintbrush as an annex. What was instinct at the time set the course for my future building plans.

In 1970, a stranger approached me about buying the Paintbrush Chalet, but I had no desire to sell. As it turned out, he was a front man for Mountain Bell, the telephone company, who needed our land to expand Aspen's telephone exchange building, adjacent and east of the Paintbrush. Ultimately, the phone company informed us that as a public utility, they had the right of eminent domain and could condemn the land. With that, and as the offers became better, I reconsidered.

Not wanting to see the building destroyed, I imagined reusing it. The rooms were well designed, and for years I had wanted to expand The Boomerang onto my remaining three vacant west-end lots. At ninety feet, the length of the building was perfect. Aspen was radically down zoning, cutting allowable lodge density in half, and also reducing the heights of buildings. The new zoning regulations would soon make it almost impossible to build onto the existing lodge.

If we submitted plans right then, just under the wire, we would be allowed to have three stories on The Boomerang's west end. So—back to the drafting board and another deadline!

The first story would need to start a half-level below grade. With landscaping, the rooms facing the mountain on the lower level would have expansive garden terraces onto a lawn facing the mountain. This expansion was also a desperate move to increase The Boomerang's capacity. Aspen's rental market was changing, and we needed multi-bedroom apartments to compete with the emerging condominium market.

We sold the land reluctantly—there was no choice. The contract with the phone company stipulated the building would remain ours, but only if it was removed by the beginning of summer. Otherwise they would demolish it.

I was in a serious time crunch.

Fonda took the preliminary plans to Denver and met with the SBA. She explained the drawings, our financial stability as a business, and the worthiness of the project. With The Boomerang's credibility, and Aspen's, we secured a quarter of a million dollar loan, and I finished the working drawings in the following few weeks.

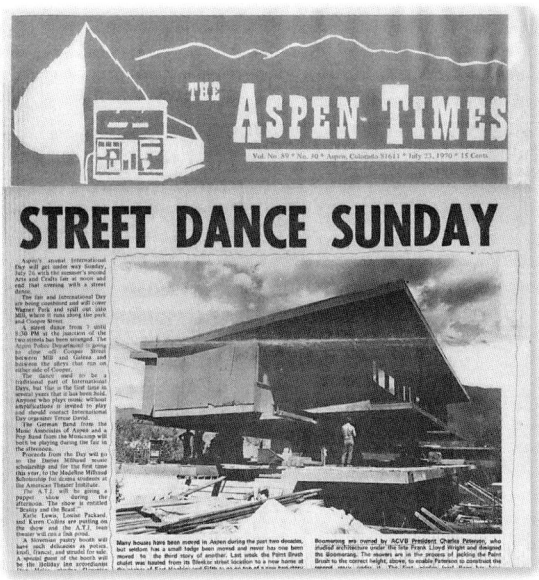

July 23, 1970 front page of The Aspen Times *showing the relocation of the "Paintbrush Chalet."*

Over the course of May and June 1970, we excavated The Boomerang property and quickly built the garden level floor. I hired Thomas House Movers, who placed the ninety-foot, one-story building on two long steel "I" beams, then onto a truck and drove the whole building up Main Street. They backed the truck into our alley and slid the building across onto the top of the first-floor structure that had been completed just in time. Next, we proceeded to jack up the Paintbrush one complete story, with all the furniture intact, the beds made, and the dishes and glasses still in the cupboards. The building looked so strange hanging in the air supported on four columns of railroad tie pylons that we made the front page of *The Aspen Times*.

At one point we almost lost everything when the south walls of the first floor began moving south. The whole building would have collapsed had not one of the workers noticed the walls beginning to lean outward. We rushed in with supporting timbers and managed to move the wall back. The entire lower floor had been heavily supported, which also helped save the day. We had been unable to get insurance (not even Lloyd's of London), so we would have made firewood of the whole project.

But luck was with me, and we completed the middle floor of the "sandwich," pulled the steel beams out, and lowered the top floor a half-foot—we now had our three-story building and thirty-five units. Bayer and Benedict's butterfly roof melded seamlessly with the rest of the lodge.

Kept busy with constant designing and construction on the main Boomerang in the 1960's as well as building the pool, and then a second floor over the original units, I was also contracted for other architectural commissions from my friends and contacts in the ski industry. The realization that I had learned a great deal by my experience of designing and building the lodge, and staying in business with good financial sense, gave me the courage to accept that commission work in addition to doing what I loved—being an entrepreneur, while also outdoors daily on the mountain teaching skiing. Inspirations for my clients were often coming from Wright's work and were adapted to our climate, conditions, and way of living in the mountains.

I have looked down my share of steep snow bowls, but nothing is more terrifying than an empty sheet of paper in front of you. To get started, it helped to become more acquainted with my clients, under-

At my drafting board in the cabin, Aspen, 1965.
PHOTO: FERENC BERKO.

stand their aspirations and finances, and if I would get along with them.

It always helped if they were friends from the lodge or skiing, which many were. After meeting with my clients, I would spend time on their land, initially with them and a map of the topography, and then in solitary on different days and times of day to observe the sun and the wind, the surrounding nature, and even the neighbors. After this, I could sense the placement of a building. At this stage, a pencil may not have even touched the paper. Often I would ruminate for days or even weeks, with only a few rough sketches for my pains. As Mr. Wright taught, it helps to place the logo and captions to get started on any project, and then the work must begin in earnest with the plot plan and orienting the building toward the appropriate features of the land.

On occasion I have been asked to renovate a dwelling. I believe in saving houses that already exist and reinventing their vernacular when the possibility presents itself. However, if the house is not worth saving, it is far better to start all over. Sometimes, design is not even the issue— but rather the management of life. Once I talked a couple out of buying an empty lot where they wanted me to design a home. They could not agree on anything and argued constantly over the smallest details. When they bought an existing home instead, peace reigned again.

Skiing friends and past guests, Pike and Jan Peterson—he a paper-mill executive and she a painter—bought a simple flat roofed house in Fox Run, a small development of the Snowmass ski area, and asked me to jazz it up. It was an elongated rectangle without charm or verve. The concept came quickly to make peaked roofs, redesign the kitchen, and add a built-in dining nook as well as a small balcony. A significant change was made to the upper section of the living room ceiling, which I specified be painted a Taliesin red and the paint brought down a foot onto the walls. We put molding as a band at the edge of the paint to give definition and character to the room. This was an economical solution to create a cozier feeling in what was otherwise a visually uncomfortable space, and which required no extra construction. The final touch was to define the dining area in this large living room and to make it more intimate. I designed a white soffit with brighter lighting to float over the table area. This technique from Loos and Wright focused light over the table and also dropped the apparent height of the ceiling.

Similarly transformative, a kitchen remodel I did for Ferenc (Franz) and Mirte Berko gave the family an inglenook in the style of Loos so they could cook, eat, and be together with their daughters Nora and Gina. The kitchen was too small for a regular table, but the inglenook provided a cozy corner similar to ski chalets in Europe that were familiar to them. Hungarian-born, but raised in Germany, Franz was a pioneer of abstract color photography, who was introduced to Bauhaus legendaries Walter Gropius and Lázló Moholy-Nagy—meetings which circuitously led to his employment by Walter Paepcke to photograph the Goethe Bicentennial in 1949.[1] The Berko children and some of the grandchildren have remained in town, and like our family, have archives of material. Franz's noteworthy photography now fills a number of books.

Many other of my architecture projects were never built. One of the most extensive dates from 1981, a large house overlooking Castle Creek on a bluff, with solar windows stepped back for maximum efficiency of solar gain. These windows would have had two different types of glass and pivoted to deflect heat in summer and absorb heat from the sun in winter. I visited these clients in their home on the West Coast before beginning my design in order to better understand their lives and habits. They love nature and are also passionate about animals, so a feature in the Aspen house was a semi-circular shelter built into the bank for their huskies that included a dog run to be seen from their kitchen. Ling Po created a beautiful rendering of the design, and I still have it hanging in my drafting room. However, this project went to another architect who had a staff and a working office, not a lodge to run.

Also from the "unbuilt" file is a condominium project for my father's cousin, Hannes Parnegg, in Taos Ski Valley. I went to New Mexico to see Hannes' land, an excuse for a ski vacation with a local guide. I have a black and white photo taken of us on top of Kachina Peak, where we hiked up, carrying our skis to survey a new lift location. In fact, I used a circular cut-out from this photo on my brochure for the new 1960's Boomerang. Hannes would joke about the cropped photo saying, "Ah, yes, 'cut out of the picture,' as usual!" Ernie Blake, founder of Taos, also talked to me about a master plan for the Taos ski area—he felt the village was growing without a central direction. That job never materialized, and unfortunately neither did my building for Hannes, the design for which had Alpine style roofs made of timber and fireplaces to be built from local stone that could be quarried from the nearby hillside. The condominiums were configured as duplex buildings and scattered throughout the plot plan of more than an acre. Hannes' financial partners, however, wished to go with the more conventional, long rectangular buildings with shed-like roofs and stucco exterior walls. Only one building of their first phase was constructed.

I loved designing and did it even when I did not expect projects to be realized, as I enjoyed the challenge and to have a creative outlet. Another unbuilt condominium project was for Lowell Koenig, a ski pupil of mine in the 1950's, who asked me to envision one for Aspen on an east side property he owned on the Roaring Fork River. I had already supervised the rebuilding of the Limelite for Lowell (the old Ski and Spur) in the summer of 1956 to include a nightclub. We had a good relationship and were friends. The condominium project I designed for him in 1969 had a futuristic edge, an arc of three tall hexagonal linked towers, like a honeycomb. I maximized the river exposure and the mountain views opposite, and each condominium had its own floor. Even when I look at it now, I would still like to build it.[2]

Another, titled "Small House on a Mountain," maybe to be built by one of my children someday, features a square plan with two bedrooms. The balconies surround three sides of the dwelling in a diamond shape

"Small House on a Mountain" designed by Charles Paterson at Taliesin, 1959.

and the footprint is another square rotated at ninety degrees to the house in parallel with the roof. In the rendering, the house is floating in the white space of the large page, as if suspended by snow on a steep slope and one is looking up at it, a castle in the air.

One project that I was disappointed not to see come to fruition is from 1966, a base lodge for the Dutchess Ski Area in Beacon, New York. Located in the Mid-Hudson region, it had a beautiful view of the river with eleven runs, three ski lifts, and all trails lit for night skiing. The enterprise was to be managed by a skiing compatriot, John Bailey from Dillon. For the Dutchess base lodge, I designed a cafeteria at ground level and placed a more expensive dining area on an upper floor, which overlooked the lower via a balcony and was reached by a grand semi-circular stairway with skylights. The entire building was covered by a great peaked roof that reached almost to the ground. When John finally did not get the management job, my design lost out as well. Dutchess Ski Area was only open until 1975,[3] so the cafeteria they did install inside a low barn like structure—the Rustic Snowflake Lounge—did not have such a long life.

The programmatic requirements for architecture in skiing and cultural areas are unique in that, in my experience, many clients desire buildings that challenge them and help realize their dreams. Often the structures I imagined with my clients were directed to enable a change

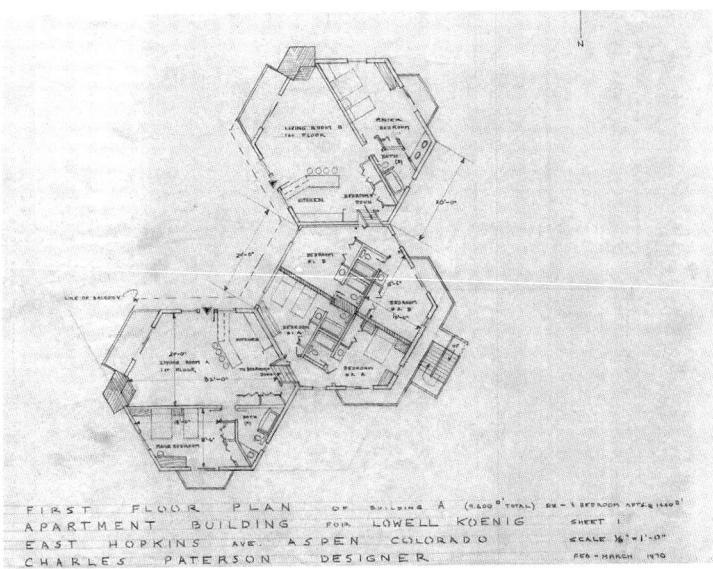

Hexagonal towers for Lowell Koenig, plan view, designed by
Charles Paterson, Aspen, 1970.

in their lives and support their new aspirations. In 1964 I completed a house for Howard and Aline Kaiser in Vail. It was featured in a French magazine the following year as a "Contemporary Mountain House" and had large, cantilevered hip roofs in the Wright Prairie style and an expanse of balconies overlooking the Vail Valley.[4] Aline was an artist and created an additional element in the house. The many large windows meant a lack of wall space for her paintings. She solved the problem by suspending them with fishing lines in front of the windows. The site of the house and its wonderful mountain views then became a perfect backdrop for her artwork. The Kaisers loved the house, which still stands today though with different owners.

In 1961, Stanley Glen, my ski pupil and friend who later sold me the Paintbrush, commissioned me for a painting studio to be located on a rise at the base of Red Mountain on Pitkin Green. I designed a small chalet, tucked into the hillside overlooking Aspen and framing Aspen Mountain. One of my favorite small projects, I had completed a color presentation drawing and an eighth-inch scale plan with elevations. But Stanley eventually decided to sell the land, quit skiing, and retire to Florida to paint.

Then in 1975, I met an important future client, Karl Wallach. I was introduced to him at the Sundeck on Aspen Mountain by my old ski buddy, Max Marolt, a third generation Aspenite. Karl owned Beconta, a successful ski company, and was importer of Nordica Boots and Kastle skis; Max was one of his best reps. Karl wanted a low profile Wrightean house for a property he had just purchased on the Ridge of Red Mountain. It had a dramatic overlook of the town.

Karl and I got along well, and he liked my proposed design. The house was "prairie style for the mountains," long and low, making a minimal visual impact but providing dramatic views of Aspen and the mountain ranges beyond. Designed for entertaining, it had a grand living room with a sunken, built-in seating area surrounding the fireplace and above it, a raised clerestory section. Karl loved watching movies, especially, as I remember, the 1966 movie "Born Free," which was about reeducating a lion cub raised in captivity to survive in the wild. He also used the projector to show ski movies. Before the days of home theaters in Aspen, Karl requested a movie screen that came down from the ceiling and required a fireproof enclosed room for a full size commercial movie projector, which was hidden in a booth behind a wooden door that matched the living room paneling.

The Wallach house also featured a great indoor thirty-four-foot long pool in its own wing off the living room. It was sixteen-feet wide and was surrounded by a white tile floor area that generously allowed for seating areas. Glazed French doors twelve-feet tall opened on three sides to a surrounding cement deck. The wing was at an angle to the main house and carefully sited to take advantage of the natural down-ward topography, which further reduced the visual impact of the house by seamlessly merging the two rooflines. The pool had an unobstructed view down valley toward the dramatic thirteen-thousand-foot Mount Sopris. A raised section the length of the pool, echoing the clerestories above the living room and capped by a glass skylight, allowed one to float and watch the clouds overhead. At the back end of the pool, a rock wall featured a small waterfall. The kitchen was developed to overlook the pool since Karl was a gourmet cook and wanted to watch over his sons Charlie and Eddie while they swam.

The wing on the other side of the house had three bedrooms, including a grand master suite with his and hers walk-in closets, a white Italian-tiled bathroom that had an imported circular shower with skylight, a sauna, and whirlpool. Half a level down from the pool area was a wine cellar and large gymnasium with exercise equipment. It was the most luxurious house that I had ever designed. In future years when everybody started to build their Aspen mansions, these luxuries were all considered standard. It was the beginning of a new era.

The construction of the Wallach house was on schedule when at the end of the summer, disaster struck on Labor Day weekend. I was driving down Main Street one morning to pick up donuts for the lodge breakfast, when I noticed huge flames shooting up from a building on Red Mountain. I soon learned it was Karl's house and had to interrupt his tennis game back east to deliver the bad news.

The investigations concluded that a series of events caused the fire following the week when the painters had been staining all the beams. The windows had been installed, and the house was ready for sheetrock. But the painters had stored all the paint cans in one room and left the paint sprayer compressor plugged into an electrical outlet. It had been giving them some trouble before they left for the weekend, and somehow it restarted, overheating and bursting into flames. When it burned a hole in the floor, it took all the paint cans down to a storage room that was filled with empty cardboard crates. With all of this fuel the fire took off, blowing out all the windows in a huge explosion. The house burned to the ground. All that was left was the pool area and wine cellar.

Undaunted, we cleaned up the mess and started to rebuild as winter was approaching. I was on the job almost daily as the architect and owner's representative and really had my hands full, when suddenly the contractor fell ill and within weeks sadly died of cancer. The foreman with his crew and I were left to finish the house.

It was the 23rd of September 1976, while consulting with the pool contractor for the new pool, that I was urgently summoned to the hospital. Fonda had gone into labor. As I rushed in, a nurse quickly ushered me into a gown. Jenny, our second daughter, had just been born. A beautiful baby and a beautiful mother. What a memorable day.

Fonda and I were still living in the Boomerang cabin, but now the family had grown by one with Jenny. Carrie was then already four years old, and my father also lived with us, so we had to spread our living quarters out into two of the original rental rooms with which I had started the lodge.

Ling Po rendering a house I designed overlooking Castle Creek in Aspen, 1981.
PHOTO: FONDA PATERSON.

In 1968, I was lucky to find a small trapezoid shaped lot for our new house on Waters Avenue while I was looking for employee housing for The Boomerang. There was a very serious housing shortage for seasonal workers in Aspen at that time. Our employees came from many parts of the world, including Australia, New Zealand, Europe, South Africa, and South America, as well as others. When I bought a two-unit complex on Waters Avenue in 1968 I was able to house four or five people in each apartment, and then as my housing needs grew, I built a third unit. The place got a bit raucous in later years.

Asking people who did not know each other to live and work together was a test of everyone's patience and diplomatic skills. I remember one winter in 1981 a group was especially cohesive. The employees had the unique idea to combine their talents at dinner time—all twelve of them, including young Thomas Sichrovsky,[5] a Viennese cousin from my mother's side of the family, and Katy Connolly (now Common), the Patersons' granddaughter from Sydney. Throughout the season, this employee group took turns making many of their meals—one apartment would do the cocktails and hors d'oeuvres, the second the main dinner dishes, the third the desserts. Also their costume parties were outrageous, usually organized by Australians Peter Altman, his girlfriend and later wife, Frankie, and his friends, Redmond and Paul. I was invited to one of these and dressed as a gangster in a trench coat. Meanwhile Peter and Paul (they used to joke they were "the disciples") dressed half-male, half-female, having sewn together opposite halves of a dress and a suit, each wearing half a moustache and one eye with heavy make-up.[6]

A little further up the street from what I still call "The Duplex," I began to build our house, which had taken me many years to conceptualize. It was 1976, the same time the Wallach house was under construction on Red Mountain. I was truly tearing around—a baby, a hotel business, and two architectural projects under construction. I had thought in 1949 I was retiring from the busy madness of New York by coming to live in this beautiful and peaceful setting. Luckily by the time I started to build our house, I was not a ski instructor anymore, and the lodge was organized with a capable staff.

Our lot on Waters Avenue was a perfect location, right on the Roaring Fork River. By coincidence, two other lots—one further upstream and one several blocks downstream from ours along the west bank of the Roaring Fork—were chosen by fellow Taliesin apprentices Fritz Benedict and Robin Molny when they built their homes. The challenge in my case had been to place a home of any scale on the lot because it is quite narrow.

I completed the working drawings in less than three weeks after being stumped for years on the design. I had finally found a solution in the November 1971 issue of *Architectural Record*, adapting a ski vacation house built in Vermont's White Mountains by the architecture firm Huygens and Tappe. The 1976 Aspen building code setbacks for the lot made building impossible and would have placed the house either in the river or the road. But since the Waters lot was platted, the city was required to grant us the right to build and had to compromise on both setback requirements. I sited the house plan on the water, altered the interior flow, and expanded it into three floors. I laid out the floor plan using a Wrightean square module, which when cut in half diagonally to make two isosceles triangles allowed for interesting angles in the resulting architecture. The plan of the house has a shape reminiscent of a Viking longship, with the roofs on east and west sides like prows. The balconies wrap east to west on two stories of the river side.

*Painting studio for Stanley Glen on Red Mountain in Aspen,
designed by Charles Paterson, 1961.*

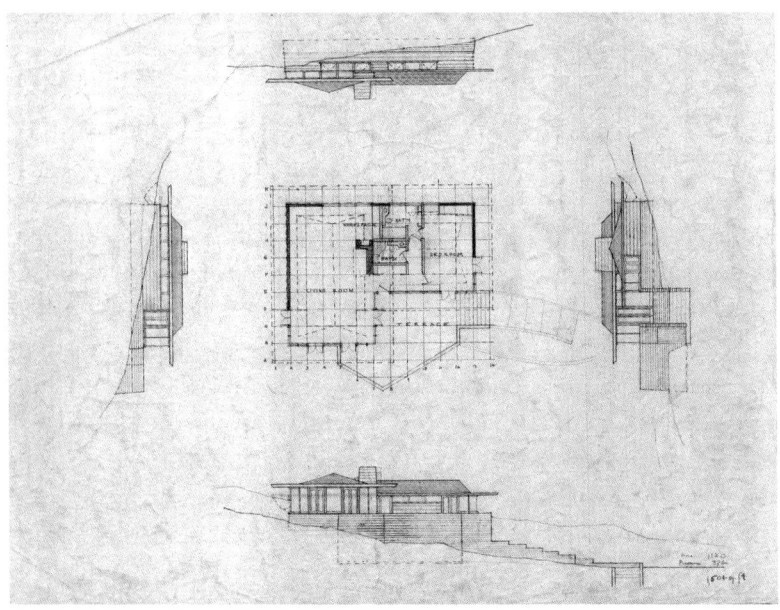

*Painting studio for Stanley Glen, showing Wright's practical solution to
visualize each preliminary perspective of the building using corresponding
elevations on the plan. One simply turned the paper ninety-degrees
to get the next view.*

Having spent so much of my youth being sent from place to place by ship, to safety, perhaps I was attracted to anchoring us right on the river, just as was the Paterson house in Australia.

Except for the bedrooms, all the spaces in the Waters house flow into each other, separated only in certain areas by chest-high cabinets upstairs between the kitchen and dining areas, or on the ground floor, by a sliding panel separating the entrance from my office. I have situated my desk at "the helm," with a panoramic view of the river in a room that shares space with a baby grand piano and a wall of children's books. The river-level below has my drafting studio, a guest area where the children played, and also, all the cabinet space we seem to require for the family archives. At first we thought to leave this floor undeveloped, however, to grow gourmet mushrooms.

I love to come home. Our house for me is like a retreat. From the street one crosses an arched Japanese footbridge that leads to the entrance across a small irrigation ditch feeding the cottonwoods. Willows and Aspen trees also line the edges and shelter the door that is reached by an angled path, at the end of which, on a low wall, is a Japanese stone lantern like Mr. Wright had at Taliesin. To reach our entry one doesn't approach directly but has to make a small journey along a bend in the path. Our entryway foyer has black tile and leads to a wide carpeted stairway that ascends to the second story and is open to the fourteen-foot high ceiling. We love the stairway, and even sit there sometimes, like greeters, to read or look at the mail with our faces in the afternoon sun, leaning up against the fireplace mass that runs in a central column through the house.

The stair is reminiscent of a raked gangway—wider at the bottom than the top—an invitation to ascend to the living and dining spaces. At the top of the stair, one reaches the river side of the house. The result is a towering sensation when one looks forty feet below onto the Roaring Fork River. The two stories visible from the road float over the third, which has been carved into the riverbank. With floor to ceiling glass added in a 1990 remodel, we feel we are almost on the water.[7]

Throughout the seasons, we live with the river, and it is the dominant feature and view in the house. In the winter, we look out and see our own weather report and an astonishing number of animals or their tracks on the frozen and snow covered stream. All year long, it is not

Paterson house, showing prow with east facing deck, 1976.

uncommon to look from the living room and see a fox, a coyote, or a bear.

In the spring, the river is raging with the snowmelt, and the occasional daring person makes the downstream float by inner tube or kayak, dodging the large boulders. By summer, fishermen appear wading in the river. We often observe a pair of mallard ducks who visit yearly and ride the swift water through the rocks, flying back upstream many times to repeat the fun. American Dippers—small birds that also swim—can be seen diving through the air above the river hunting for insects and are very entertaining to watch.[8] Ravens and magpies are year-round neighbors, and migrant songbirds along with red-breasted robins visit the river in spring. During the autumn days the air turns brisk, and the low river runs quietly. It is colored deep brown by moss, rock, and its sandy bottom. The river is so low sometimes one can crawl rock to rock out to little islands of willows, as our daughters and their friends used to enjoy doing in the last warm days in September, the Indian summer. Now that I'm retired I spend mornings in the sun reading out on the eastern balcony, which now has glass sides looking down on the rippling boulder-strewn stream.

The other side of the house faces Aspen Mountain. In the summer, gold flecks of sun speckle the windows through leafy branches. The feeling

Paterson house, south-west facing view toward Aspen Mountain, 1990.
PHOTO: DOUG RAGER.

in the enclosed sun porch off the open kitchen area is of being in a tree house floating in the air like the gondolas we see a few blocks away on Aspen Mountain. In winter one can make out skiers as small as ants whizzing down the slope on Aspen Mountain's Little Nell ski run.

We have thought the house a great success over the years, especially when we first moved and were separated from the lodge business after the many years of being at the beck and call of any guest's whim, the late arrivals, and forgotten keys. But there were wonderful things about it when the children were growing up. When we lived in the cabin, Carrie used to join my father and me in the Upper Lounge at breakfast, entertaining and making friends with the guests. Both our children Carrie and Jenny learned the joys and frustrations of the hospitality business from the ground up, setting up and checking the breakfast, working the front desk, being part of the maintenance crew in their twenties, and then Carrie acting as the manager in 1999 during the summer of my open-heart surgery. Although living in the log cabin in the midst of the lodge operation was convenient in the early days, we realized it was not the best for family life, and we were glad for the escape our Waters Avenue house afforded us. ▪

Silversmithing

My father's move to Colorado from New York was a kind of solace. He found new friends, also émigrés, but also made connections with America's native people. He used to take trips to Indian Country with friends Kurt Bresnitz, Franz Berko, or European visitors, driving his Mustang southwest from Aspen across the desert plateaus to visit various reservations. He would buy Navajo rugs and often meet with people involved in the jewelry trade. He brought that knowledge back to his silversmithing classes at Colorado Rocky Mountain School.

My father had a strong commitment to the Native American students at CRMS, some of whom have talked to us about hearing his stories and the positive example he set. One of my father's friends was the Hopi chief of Second Mesa in Arizona, whose granddaughter, Loretta Secakuku, took my father's jewelry classes. We still have a belt buckle that my father made from a special stone given to him by the chief, an unusual piece of sandstone that has striated colors in black, pink, and orange, and which looks like a desert landscape at dusk.

My father's jewelry classes were very popular, not only because he was skilled, but because he was a good storyteller. From people on his trips to the Southwest he learned Native American mythology, and he also loved to read relevant books like *The Book of Indian Crafts and Indian Lore* by Julian Harris Salomon, which he had sent to me for my birthday in 1944. In addition to these, of course, he often captivated his students with his adventures in Siberia and World War II. He told these stories to the history classes and around the French and German language tables he held in the cafeteria, as well as on the annual school field trips in the Southwest. He was known as the school's "walking history lesson."

When he taught Viennese cooking, other types of stories would emerge. We found a 1960's mimeographed recipe for Linzertorte and Ischlerkrapfen that he made as a class handout with a history of these

My father and Kurt Bresnitz purchasing Navajo rugs at Oljeto Trading Post,
Monument Valley, Utah, early 1970's.

two desserts.

"For both you use the same dough," he wrote. "The Linzertorte is named after the capital of upper Austria, Linz. In the old times they sold Linzertorte on the railroad station of Linz to the passengers of the passing trains, especially on their way to Ischl. This was the worst I ever ate. Linzertorte was also sold during the intermissions of the Vienna Opera House. Probably they do it still today." For birthdays, special occasions, and visitors, we always made this cake, my father's favorite dessert.

"The Ischlerkrapfen," he wrote, "which you get in different forms even today in Aspen, were the invention of the owner of the pastry shop in Ischl, [Mr.] Zauner. Probably it was the father of Zauner whom I knew who invented it. The young Zauner was in 1910 my lieutenant at officer's school in Vienna. A very slim man I have him in my memory. After the First World War I met him in his pastry shop in Ischl as a paunchy man. In those times you got Ischlerkrapfen only at his shop, which was not far from the summer residence of Emperor Franz Joseph, and in Vienna at the pastry shop 'Demel', right next to the Imperial Castle."

Several anecdotes like this are written on his menu-lessons. We also discovered a folded mimeographed menu for a Fourth of July barbecue in this stack. The menu is hand written by a student, with a drawing of an exploding firecracker and small stick figure standing on a rocket holding its "reins," riding it into the sky like a horse. Only a small American flag decorates the bottom inside corner, where the food is listed: "Roast Lamb—Home Fried Potatoes—Cabbage, Viennese Style—American Indian Cream Puffs." [1] On the back, in the same handwriting as the menu, "We never heard of American Indian Cream Puffs," signed "Everett Bear." In my father's writing, he wrote after Everett's name, "Sioux" and added another student who contributed to the menu, "Dan Barney, Navajo."

In the 1960's I designed a "jewelry hogan" at CRMS to my father's specifications. It was built like our cabin, but eight-sided, and was inspired by Navajo log adaptations of their traditional, sacred architecture that we had seen in the Indian country. A ribbon of clerestory windows lit the space, and wrap-around workbenches and cabinets encircled the interior walls. In the heart of the hogan stood the octagon soldering station with eight gas torches.

We attended a school reunion in 2005 where the alumni paid tribute to my father in the hogan. The building had been dedicated in his honor and features a black and white portrait of him by Franz Berko. A broad

My father teaching jewelry at CRMS, 1963.
PHOTO: WES HORNER.

smile lights his round face and his bushy eyebrows stand out. That night the soldering torches were lit in the center of the workstation and cast shadows around the room. Laughter and tears accompanied our reminiscences of his strong presence.

I found a clipping from the twenty-fifth anniversary of the CRMS school newspaper, printed in 1979. It was a brief biography of him written by art teacher and newspaper editor Sharon Wooding:

> "Steve Shanzer has the distinction of being the only person at the school to have made every single CRMS catalog. He was originally hired by the Holdens as a teacher of French and German, a retirement job, for Steve was, at that time, 64 years of age.

> "Steve introduced fold-boating [folboating] and jewelry making to the students. Many former students will remember him as a boating enthusiast who never missed a spring trip. Steve, with his Austrian fold-boats [folboats] of wood and rubberized canvas, was the one who introduced the sport to CRMS.

> "When I asked Steve if I might write about him for the 25th anniversary of the school, he replied, 'My life story, there is too much. No one wants to know all that.' It would take volumes to retell even the more exciting events of Steve's life but there is no question in my mind that many people will want to read about him. The lounges crowded with students and faculty during interim listening to Steve tell about Siberian prison camps during World War I or about trading in the Near East is evidence that this is true.

> Of course, there was always the lure of Steve's Viennese pastries at these sessions. The 25th anniversary newspaper will have to settle for something abbreviated but hopefully informative for those who haven't had the good fortune to hear any of his talks in person or on tape."

All the while in this book I've been saving out two episodes from my father's time in Siberia. They seem appropriate to print here. The first is about how he learned to make jewelry in Vladivostok in 1918 and 1919. At the time, he lived in a prison camp guarded by Japanese soldiers, but was allowed to go into town occasionally with his pass as the camp buyer of provisions. The second tells of his experiences with the Russian black market, which provided him unique liberties and allowed him to escape. These stories, like his others from Siberia, were recorded in 1952 at the Holiday House by Frank Day, Jr. They, in particular, had good traction at Colorado Rocky Mountain School.

JEWELRY MAKING IN VLADIVOSTOK, SIBERIA 1918-1919

We arrived in Vladivostok, Siberia as prisoners. By that time, [after March 1918], a counter-revolution against Lenin's Bolsheviks was taking place. The new party of social revolutionaries lead by Admiral Kolchak was friendlier to the Allies, so there were American, English, French, Italian, and Japanese troops in town, each inhabiting its own section. The Americans had a special dock area where they landed supplies to equip the Kolchak anti-Communist troops. We learned that these troops, outfitted with American equipment, would arrive at the front, kill their officers, and go over to the Bolsheviks with the good military equipment.

One day an American soldier came to the camp for a visit and saw an Austrian medal on an officer. It was the Angstkreus, the so-called "cross of fear," a medal given to those who partook in the mobilization of 1912-13 as the [Habsburg] monarchy annexed Bosnia and Herzegovina. It was not even a very high decoration, but the American paid twenty dollars for it, mainly because the officer did not want to sell it due to sentimental reasons.[2] One of my friends, a first lieutenant named Christanelli, who later became the head of the Austrian Radio Troop, was also a brilliant mechanic who then had an excellent idea. He set up a galvanic plastic process involving electrolysis and he reproduced medals of all kinds, which he sold to the Americans by the hundreds. These medals were popular because the American soldiers wanted to tell about them at home, as if they had taken them off a prisoner on the battlefield.

There was a Canadian camp nearby our camp in Vladivostok, and some of their officers came over. I spoke to them in French and English, and the officers invited me and my friends—Captain Salcher and Captain Krassich—to their quarters. I was wearing a ring that was made for me by a German officer, Roehling, and one of the Canadians noticed it and offered to buy it from me for five Canadian dollars.

Roehling decided to make another ring, and this time I watched. He had no soldering facilities, and he made the ring out of a silver ruble coin. He had an anvil and hammer that he had found around camp. The anvil was a piece of shrapnel. We made a stove out of a can that we filled with burning charcoal. We would swing the can through the air to make it hot, as it had holes in it. This is how I learned to become a jeweler.

Once the silver ruble was heated in this stove, it got hammered down around the edges on the anvil. The technique was hammer-and-turn, hammer-and-turn, to make it thicker and thicker. When it was the right thickness, a hole was punched in it. Then a

Silver rings and wooden box my father made in his Siberian prison camp.
PHOTO: DAVID O. MARLOW.

reamer was used to make the hole larger until it was the approximately the right size. Then the ring was filed nicely with files
we bought in town at the Chinese market when we went on food
purchasing expeditions. Roehling later started to solder, which
he did with a small lamp that burned white gas. The lamp was
made out of a tin can with a spout and a wick. He would light the
wick and blow into the flame through a tube, directing the heat
onto the ring, which was on a piece of charcoal.

I soon began making rings myself, and my friend Captain Krassich
did the engraving. American soldiers found the rings very appealing,
and for every one they bought, I received two dollars and fifty cents.
There must have been a lot of those rings with the veterans of the
First World War from the Siberian Bear Corps.

I got my first solder from Roehling, who rationed me. But I finally
became independent when I found, after long experiments, that I
could make my own solder with tin from the top of a can and the
silver from rubles. I made a good livelihood from these rings.

Someone came up with the idea of arranging an exposition of the
works of the prisoners in Vladivostok. It took place in a school.
There were many thing to be seen, wooden things, paintings, and
I displayed a small box and the rings. I had my name, Stefan
Schanzer, on this box.

In a few days I got a message from a gentleman named Mr. Pollack.
He wanted to talk to me at the Café Olympus because his wife's
maiden name was also Schanzer. This café was a well known
meeting place in the center of all the black market activities.

I wore my new civilian suit and went to the café. Mr. Pollack
thought that a prisoner would appear in rags, so he was very
surprised to meet someone who was well dressed and cultured.
He introduced me to Mr. Riemers, an Englishman, and to an
American named Mr. Wolfson from New York. Mr. Pollack's wife
was in Changchun, a town on the Siberian Railroad. The wife
of Mr. Riemers was a beautiful Georgian woman. We had a very
pleasant meeting, just a social get-together.

I was assigned twice a week to go to town to buy supplies for the prison camp, so I saw this group many times. Christmas came and Mr. Pollack told me about fifty barrels of cocoa that were in a warehouse in Vladivostok. Cocoa at this time was nearly unobtainable, and these barrels were destined for Germany. A group of people wanted to transport these barrels along the rail-road to the Russian front, through the lines, to the Germans, but this had not happened, and the barrels were still in Vladivostok. The people who owned the cocoa couldn't risk selling it on the Vladivostok market because it would cause a great disturbance in the market and probably lead to confiscation.

I learned all of this from Mr. Pollack who was one of the owners of the cocoa, or more accurately, was acting as the agent for the sale. It was finally decided that the cocoa would be bought very cheap and sold to the prisoners. I told the Austrian commander about this, and we put all our money together from the pris-oners. I went to town with the money and agreed to buy the whole lot. The Japanese commander would not have been told about the deal, except on this occasion we needed his help. It was Christmas-time, and since so much merchandise was bought, we were afraid of being attacked by the Russians, who would take the cocoa, so we asked for a Japanese escort.

Somehow, the Socialist Revolutionaries got wind of the plan and tried to confiscate the stuff. The Japanese escorted us, however, and the cocoa was loaded into carts and brought into camp just before Christmas. Everyone considered it a very big deal.

I continued to have regular meetings with my new friends in the black market, and for the first time in my life I had occasion to speak English with the Englishman, Mr. Riemers. I would come into Vladivostok and buy things at one of two department stores—Kunst & Albers or Tschudi—that had branches all over Russia. The main street of Vladivostok where the department stores were was called Svetlanskaja, which means "road of the light." Along Svetlanskaja there was a trolley car of German make. But, on the branch line, [less modern,] you could see the Chinese sawing

Scrapbook page from my father's photo album of officers in his Siberian prison camp. All images from Siberia are re-photographed from the collection of a fellow prisoner, who he was introduced to in San Francisco in the 1960's.

wood by hand, something that would easily be done with an electric saw.

Merchandise was becoming more and more scarce, and sugar was unobtainable, unless you were a prisoner. We had plenty of sugar that we got through the Japanese, so trade grew. I always brought sugar to Mr. Pollack, who, in turn, took me out to dinner often. I had complete freedom as a buyer, but others always had to ask permission of the Japanese.

As a buyer it was somewhat difficult to function in the Chinese market. Because of inflation, scarcity of food, and general unrest, prices fluctuated every day. It was very necessary to be shrewd because the Chinese tried to take everything they could. I had yen and dollars, both of which had to be converted on the spot to Kolchak rubles. Then I had to buy my goods immediately before there was a damaging fluctuation in the ruble. The main seat of this exchange was the Café Olympus.

The Chinese market consisted of a great mass of tents and wooden shacks, and it took a while before I finally found a man who was relatively honest. At the time in this area of the world, honesty had a certain relativity. A lie was not considered an offense. If someone lies to you, it is not done through malice, but only in an effort at politeness, or at least such was the excuse. Westerners misunderstood and often became upset by this.

The man I found in the market was eager to have me as a regular customer. As a result, bargaining was dropped between us. We talked in a rather Russian-Chinese pidgin. This was the language used for trading all over this part of the world. I always went first to this man. Say I bought three or four thousand eggs twice a week, or dried food, or peas. I would say, "Today, what is the best price on the market?" This man knew that if he told me the lowest price immediately, I would buy from him without further ado. As a result, I had right away the lowest market price, without having to run around and check on other suppliers. His price was usually the lowest. But if I was in a hurry, and he knew it, he would raise the price. I learned to act rather casual so the price would be good.

But I knew that he was honest, and I always stored my merchandise at his store without receipt. Nothing was ever missing. When I finally left Vladivostok to go home to Austria, he gave me a pair of very expensive Chinese cufflinks.

At that time, my father and his friend Captain Krassich, became commanders of six hundred men suffering from tuberculosis. My father said, "They were all that was left from crews working on the Murmansk railroad, where the saying was that under each railroad tie a man was buried." My father used his regular food purchasing trips to buy additional food for the soldiers, and so did other officers who had passes to go from the camp to town. They each took five yen a month out of their wages to give to the tubercular men, and many were saved by this charity. His group of officers also pooled money later to send to starving Austrian officers in Nikolsk-Ussuriysk who were under Menshevik rule and were suffering severely. Eventually the Austrian officiers were giving away twenty percent of their wages.

My father continued, "As a good will gesture, the YMCA wanted to do something nice for the [tubercular] prisoners, so they offered to show some movies to the TB group to cheer them up. The projector was set up in the barracks, and the films were shown. [But these terrible films] were very goody-goody, and the hard-boiled prisoners nearly rioted."

My father didn't tell much else about his daily life, but he did have a few more little stories. Of the red light district: "This was a part of town called 'Na Carpathy's' ... where most of the women were Japanese geishas and Russian 'captains' widows'; they would always say, 'My husband fell in the war; he was a captain.'" Then there's the story of some Austrians "who had vineyards at home and knew how to prepare wine from almost anything, even from raisins. In the fall there were wild grapes in the woods. They gathered these grapes and made a sort of wine." These Austrians filled empty French wine bottles and sold their "original French wine" at "fantastic prices." Wine was scarce in Vladivostok, and the whole group of Austrian prisoners benefitted from this venture.

Prisoners from all nations were stuck in Vladivostok for many years after Russia exited the war. The Brest-Litovsk treaty, signed on March 3, 1918 by Russia and the Central Powers, had very few details or stipulations

Prison camp, Vladivostok, circa 1919.

about how the exchange of war prisoners would occur. None of the parties could agree on the terms of repatriation of POWs until the end of June 1918. When the Austro-Hungarian monarchy collapsed a few months later on October 18, 1918, only some of the Austro-Hungarian POWs had managed to return. Restrictions had been put on the soldiers returning for many reasons, including the reality of not having enough supplies to support thousands of men entering back into the nation of Austria daily (ten thousand plus recorded on one day alone) as well as the fear of unrest—the spread of Russian influence, "the Bolshevik bacillus."[3]

My father was virtually cut off from Vienna. Mail service throughout the war had been possible, though heavily and, surprisingly, efficiently censored, but by summer 1918 it was interrupted by unpredictable conditions in Russia.[4] My father's family and friends had presumed he was dead. It was to everyone's surprise, after more than a year of silence, that he wired notification of his homecoming. How he returned to the city and began to pick up the pieces of his old life is yet another story.... ■

ARCTIC OCEAN

STEFAN SCHANZER
POW IN SIBERIA
MAY 1914—JANUARY 1920

LAPTEV
SEA

SIBERIA

RE 1721–1917

LIST REPUBLICS 1917

SEA OF
OKHOTSK

noyarsk

Lake
Baikal

Mogocha

Trans-Siberian Railroad

**Khabarovsk
(Krasnaya Rechka)**
January–October 1915

Chita

Antipikha
April–November 1918

ad   Irkutsk

Harbin   **Nikolsk–Ussuriysk**
December 1914

Dauria
November 1915–
March 1918

Trans-Manchurian Railroad

Vladivostok
December 1918–
Escaped January 1920

Ulaanbaatar

SEA OF
JAPAN

JAPAN

Tokyo

GOBI DESERT

MONGOLIA

Ship

Beijing

Seoul

PACIFIC
OCEAN

CHINA

YELLOW
SEA

Still Escaping

O ne night in the mid-1970's in Carbondale, Colorado after all the jewelry students had left my father's evening activity class at Colorado Rocky Mountain School, he experienced a flashback to the First World War.

He had just turned off the lights and exited. Hanging the padlock on the outside hasp, he was ready to lock the hogan for the night. On a second thought, he went back inside to double check that the gas was shut off. Meanwhile, the school's night watchman noticed the lights off, the door closed, but not locked. Correcting this oversight, he padlocked the hogan with my father inside.

Not discovering his predicament until after he had checked all the valves around the classroom, my father came to the sinking realization that the night watchman was well out of earshot. Already in his mid-eighties by then, he decided to climb on a workbench, open the window over a cupboard and jump to freedom through the narrow clerestory window. When he told people about this latest adventure, he always ended it with a hearty laugh, "Ja, and still I have to be escaping, just like my whole life!"

The year of my father's first escape was 1919. By that time, he had been imprisoned five years when the first prisoners, Polish legionnaires, succeeded in getting home. It was known that they would be sailing on a Japanese ship. According to my father, "This really stirred up all the prisoners. Anybody who had the slightest connection with Polish territory tried to get on that ship, but only a very few Austrians succeeded." Then another ship was announced, and it was learned that the Italians would be going home. My father went to town to see if he could find someone to help him get onto that ship.

ESCAPE FROM VLADIVOSTOK, 1919-1920

I discussed my chances for escape with Mr. Pollack and Mr. Riemers. We decided that the Italians [were my best option] because Mrs. Riemers was having an affair with an Italian count, Phillipi, the commander. She was a very beautiful woman, and her husband, Mr. Riemers, tolerated the situation because of [his] business.

At this time, I had an interesting offer. Mr. Wolfson was the delegate of a New York fur firm, Wolfson & Co., which bought furs in Siberia. In Chita, he had assembled one million dollars worth of furs, but could not get them out because of the war. Mr. Pollack was trying to help Mr. Wolfson persuade the American commander to help them. They offered me all the necessary papers to go to Chita by train to get the furs to Vladivostok, and I was at first very much inclined to go on this adventure.

As the possibility of going home with the Italians was shaping up through Mr. Riemers, however, I turned down the offer. Instead, I recommended a friend, Curt Lass, who took the job and traveled to Chita. He got the train with the furs as far as the Manchurian border, but as the train arrived at the border, Ataman Semenov,[1] [the self-proclaimed chief of the anti-Bolshevik Cossacks], confiscated the shipment. Since the furs were worthless to him, he offered to sell them back to Mr. Wolfson for a large sum of money. Semenov got away with it, and it caused Mr. Wolfson's firm to go broke.

Even though I had a connection with Count Phillipi through my friends the Riemers, it was very difficult for him to put me on the ship. The reason was because during the Empire, there existed a movement against the Austro-Hungarian monarchy by the Italians under Austrian rule, many of whom had been fighting in the Austrian army. These men had been separated from the Austrian prisoners and were known as "Redenti." They wore yellow uniforms, and the local populace in Vladivostok nicknamed them "canaries." They were given preferential treatment and were to be sent back home first. Two of my fellow prisoners—Captain Krassich, from Fiume, and Captain Salcher, from Trieste—were Redenti. I also wanted to get into this group, but the Count couldn't make up his mind, so I finally told him that he should consider my last name.

At this time the minister of finance of Italy was named Carlo Schanzer.[2] He was my father Karl Schanzer's second cousin. This was a happy moment for the Count, who wanted to please my friend Mrs. Riemers, who had been hounding him on my behalf. Perhaps he was also a bit jealous of the friendship between Mrs. Riemers and me.

The Count finally agreed to put me on board, but he told me that if I went on one of the ships I might be arrested when we docked in Trieste. Then came another problem when the leader of the second Redenti group scratched my name from his list, knowing that the set up was on account of a woman. The Count told me not to go on the second ship, but to go on the third. This was the Japanese ship called *Texas Maru*.

Gate of my father's prison camp in Vladivostok, circa 1919.

Before I could leave the camp, there was a question of what to do about my fifty-yen monthly pay, which was a valuable sum.[3] There was also the matter of how to cover up my disappearance. When one of the Redenti, like Captain Krassich, was sent home, he was taken from the camp by the Italians, who contacted the Japanese and said he was leaving. That way, the Japanese marked him off the camp list. The Count didn't want to put the business about me on record, so the Japanese wouldn't know that I was leaving.

About that time I received a letter from an old friend, Scharsach, who had been in the same battalion with me, but who had been stranded in Nikolsk-Ussuriysk, west of Vladivostok, on the railroad. The poor fellow was suffering under the yoke of the Mensheviks. I wrote him, urging that he should somehow escape to Vladivostok.

Somehow he arrived at Mr. Pollack's apartment, where I laid out my plan: the day I moved out of the camp, my friend would move in and take my place, unbeknownst to the Japanese. Scharsach gladly took over my fifty-yen monthly income. He also took over selling the rest of the rings I had made in my jewelry business.

Knowing that Scharsach would make good on his end, I gathered my possessions and hired two Chinese laborers to carry my luggage. We went to the Japanese post at the entrance to the camp, I handed the guard my usual pass, the one I used on buying trips for the Austrian prisoners, and left the camp with the two Chinese and all my things. The Japanese soldier probably knew what was going on, but he didn't have enough nerve to stop me because the buying pass was supposedly valid at any entrance or exit.

I went straight to Mr. Pollack's, where I met Scharsach, who then used my buying pass to go back into the camp that evening. He stayed there for nearly a year under my name. The Japanese never had the slightest suspicion, and he got along very well with the rest of the officers. I stayed with Mr. Pollack for a few days until the ship left.

By now it was late January 1920, and word came from Count Philippi that the *Texas Maru* was ready to sail. My two "Italian" friends—Krassich and Salcher—had already left on ship number two. The *Texas Maru* was the third and last.

Many friends from the camp came to Vladivostok to say good-bye to me. I was dressed in civilian garb. My friends were in Austrian uniforms, and they had the nerve to accompany me to the dock. The ship was on her maiden voyage, a six-thousand-ton coal freighter. She was very clean, and the holds were prepared for troop transport with three- and four-layer bunks. I presented a little slip of paper signed by the Count to the Italian sentry at the entrance of the ship, and I went aboard. I was assigned a very nice bunk on the upper deck amid a group of Turkish officers, who had claimed they were Albanians, since at this time Albania was under Italian control. I was able to speak fluent Italian, which was a great advantage.

At this time, a group of Japanese officers arrived in a car and went aboard to see the captain. My Austrian friends fled, and I thought the soldiers had come after me, that something had slipped up. This broke my great over-confidence.

Finally, the Japanese officers left. It turned out they had only come on a polite visit to bid the Italian commander farewell. The ship finally sailed, and as the harbor of Vladivostok is usually frozen, an ice breaker had to lead the way to open water.

Life on ships was conducted in military fashion, but there was no discipline for the Redenti, only for the regular Italian troops. The Redenti even brought along live chickens and cows for food, which were penned on deck. I remember the food was [otherwise] normal Italian food, mostly spaghetti. After some days we arrived in Shanghai, where the ship had to wait overnight for high tide so that it could go over the sandbar. The harbor and river were full of sampans, long Chinese wooden boats. Along the shore there was one textile factory after another, mostly cotton spinning mills. I was amazed to find such an industrial town in Asia. Siberia had given me a wrong impression.

Parade in Vladivostok showing the five flags of the occupying armies (right)
with the Imperial Japanese flag hung prominently (left), circa 1919.

The ship stayed three days in Shanghai, and the Redenti
received permission to go ashore, most of them dressed in their
yellow uniforms. I made friends with an Italian lieutenant,
who happened to be an Austrian from south Tyrol. The Turks
who were with us also went ashore, where we toured the city
and visited all the international quarters. I was well supplied
with money—four hundred dollars in American and Canadian
currencies—and felt rather prosperous. I was also elated by the
idea that I was going home.

After three days the ship sailed again, this time south toward
Singapore. Even though it was January, the sea had been
extremely calm, and only a few on board were seasick. The
weather grew more pleasant as we went south and stayed that
way for most of the voyage. Life on board was idyllic. The men
were very happy to be on their way home, and they just loafed.
We arrived in Singapore, and after some difficulties, the Redenti
were again allowed to go to town. The British hadn't wanted
anyone to land because they feared many would want to stay
in Singapore. I was very anxious to swim, so I jumped into the
harbor from the dock. The water was extremely filthy.

We left Singapore and sailed to Colombo, Ceylon [now Sri Lanka]. One of the Redenti had acquired a pet monkey in Singapore and, as land came into sight, the little monkey got so excited that he jumped overboard and drowned.

At Colombo, the orders of the English were that no one but the Italian officers could leave the ship. I wanted to go on shore very badly, so my friend, the Italian lieutenant, gave me one of his uniforms, and we both went ashore. No one asked for papers. The yellow uniform was enough.

The ship went from Colombo to Suez, past Aden and into the Red Sea. This crossing was the hottest thing I had ever endured. Arriving in Suez, life seemed much the same as in the rest of Asia, though European influence there was much stronger. Some people went ashore again, but for some reason, I did not go.

The next day there was big excitement on the ship as we heard the news that all the Turkish officers—there were ten—had disappeared from the ship. They had gone off into the desert, where they had made a connection with the Arabs for an escape. They could not go further on the ship because they would have been discovered as regular Turkish officers and not Albanians as they had pretended. The Italian lieutenant told me that his commander was terribly upset about this because he was the victim of the fraud.

That night, we passed through the Suez Canal. A big searchlight on the front of the ship guided the way. Progress through the canal was very slow because ships had to wait for each other to pass. In the middle of the night, we reached one of the salt lakes between Suez and Port Said. The last half of the journey was made during the daylight when we could see. On the right side of the canal were the trenches that the Turks had built under German command.

We sailed through Port Said, past the statue of [Ferdinand de] Lesseps,[4] one of his arms pointing to the entrance of the canal, then we sailed out into the Mediterranean. The next day, Crete came into sight. There the first real storm of the whole voyage struck us, and many were seasick. This was quite a shock after having such a peaceful voyage since leaving Vladivostok. Next, we sailed along the Dalmatian Coast, and finally, we entered the harbor of Lussin-Piccolo, a former Austrian territory now under Italian control. We stayed overnight in the harbor, and nobody was allowed to go ashore.

The next morning, the ship started the most dangerous part of the journey, to Trieste along the Istrian Coast, which the Austrians had mined from Pola, the harbor for the Austrian fleet. No one knew exactly where these mines were located.

We traveled without incident past Brioni, a well-known resort island off the coast of what is now Yugoslavia. As we approached the Capo d'Istria, the Italian commander summoned together everyone on board. As the ship slowly rounded the cape the commander said, "*Redenti, soldati, i lavoratori, qui la sua patria redenta.*" ("Redeemed soldiers and workers, here is your fatherland returned to you.") A long speech followed. I watched this spectacle with mixed feelings, but kept my mouth shut. The ship then landed in Trieste.

As we landed, we saw that ship number two was still in the harbor. As the men disembarked, I waited anxiously for my arrest as Count Phillipi had predicted. I had no papers whatso-ever, and I was not supposed to use the paper that Count Phillipi had given me.

As I looked over the ship's rail, a very charming woman called from the dock: "Are there any Austrians on board?" I cautiously waved my hand to her. The woman passed the sentry at the gangplank, came onto the ship, and talked to me. She was a Yugoslav woman attached to a mission from Austria headed by a man named Hofrat Spitzer, who was later president of the Österreichische Touring Club. They had unofficial permission to take care of prisoners from Austria. She took me from the ship and introduced me to Mr. Spitzer, then passed me through customs. She told me she would make some arrangement to get me safely to the Austrian frontier.

Most of the Austrian prisoners captured by the Italians were still held in camps, and there was great danger that I would again be interned in a camp. I spent the rest of the day walking around in Trieste, where I met my two old friends, Captain Krassich and Captain Salcher, who had arrived on the second ship.

From Trieste, I wired my mother in Vienna, and that evening I went to the railroad station to meet the Yugoslav woman who was to take me to Austria. She was waiting for me with two Italian soldiers who were armed. I thought it was a double-cross, and that I'd be put back in a camp, but she said that the two soldiers would accompany me to the frontier. It appeared to others on the train that they were guarding me very carefully, which they did. They even accompanied me to the toilet and stood guard outside the door.

At Tarvisio, the frontier station between the new boundary of Austria and Italy, I was officially turned over to the Austrian authorities. The camp where I was received by the Austrians was located in Villach, and the reception was very nice and friendly. I was given proper papers, which would give me the retroactive wages due to me, and a ticket to Vienna, where I arrived around midnight. Since I did not want to wake my mother in the middle of the night, I slept until morning on a bench in the station.

The return to Vienna was very sad and very disappointing, for my father had died a year before. The large fortune that my father had accumulated and inherited [as an heir of the Biedermann family] was destroyed by mismanagement and run-away inflation. Upon my arrival, I received a letter from our family banker who said the family fortune and therefore my entire inheritance from my father had been reduced to the value of the postage stamp on the envelope.[5]

I was very happy to see my mother again, but an urge came over me to leave Vienna for good. I stayed only for my mother's sake. The family's textile firm H.P.S. wanted me to take over management of a factory in Germany, where I had worked before the war, but the prospect of going to hated Germany was too much, and I turned the position down.

Later, I received a letter from Scharsach, my replacement at the prison camp, saying he had sold all of my rings and netted eighty dollars. He also had taken a lot of pictures of the camps, ships in the harbor, etc., and had sold these pictures to the Americans. He also took pictures of life in the Japanese war camps and of the Austrian camp. There was a picture taken a year after my escape showing the Japanese commander saluting the departing prisoners. Scharsach sent the money to me, and I sent half of it to Krassich. Scharsach and I continued a very close friendship. Krassich married and settled near Fiume on a pension from the Italian government, but he was quite dissatisfied since much of his property was in Yugoslavia. He was, more or less, a man without a country.

Later, Mrs. Pollack came to Vienna, where she taught English, but soon died of cancer. Mr. Pollack went to Moscow on some kind of business and later died there. About a year after I had returned to Vienna, I received a letter from Mrs. Riemers saying that she had arrived in Europe and wanted to come to Vienna. At that time I still felt so miserable and unadjusted that I could not bear the thought of meeting her. I wrote to her a very polite letter that things were not as good in Vienna as in the old times and that I was not settled at all. I never heard from her again. ▪

Adaptations

My father's Siberia stories leave us on a somber note. It always struck me that his return to Vienna in 1920 must have been alienating, not unlike what reportedly happens to other veterans of war returning home to America after all they have seen and experienced—Korea; Vietnam; Iraq and Afghanistan. The transition is more shocking in the present day in part because the trip back home can be hours instead of what in my father's case was many long weeks, over which time the reality might be allowed to sink in that one would be returning to civil society.

At the beginning of the First World War, the difference between being a POW or fighting on the front contrasted in the most jolting manner with the reality of a Vienna still living in Imperial glory. One wonders how many people frequenting cafés on the Ringstrasse noticed the war at first. Then came the food shortages, the economic depression, and the fall of the Empire in October 1917. By the time my father got home three years later that former life was in ruin.

One writer made heavy critiques of the Viennese lifestyle during wartime—the satirist Karl Kraus (1874-1936). Best friend of Adolf Loos, a Jew who converted to Catholicism with Loos as his witness in 1911, Kraus later rescinded all religious ties whatsoever. His sole devotion in life was his writing. He produced a volume of works unbelievable even by today's standards—over twenty-two thousand pages alone in his (mostly) biweekly journal *Die Fackel* (*The Torch*) in addition to plays and other works. He also lectured, giving more than seven hundred of these monologues, or "spoken recitals," over the course of his lifetime.[1]

Kraus was polemical. He was also a true black sheep of his family and virtually disowned. They never discussed him. That is, *our* extended family never spoke of him—my grandfather Otto Beck's first cousin Rosa Hirsch Kraus had married Karl Kraus' brother, Alfred Kraus. They lived in Vienna in a Loos apartment completed in 1905. It was after seeing

Alfred and Rosa Kraus' interior and another in Pilsen owned by Alfred and Karl's brother, Rudolf Kraus, that the Hirsch family and the Becks brought Loos to do apartments in Pilsen.[2]

Karl Kraus completed a particularly scathing theatrical work in 1922 set during the First World War titled *Die Letzten Tage der Menschheit (The Last Days of Mankind)*, which he had begun in 1915. The epic play of one hundred scenes was translated in full into English in 1999 and aired on the BBC.[3][4] We have only heard it because Alfred Kraus' grandson, John Winterburgh, gave us a CD copy after having met him for the first time in London in 2011 at a Loos retrospective exhibition. *The Last Days of Mankind*, Karl Kraus wrote, "is meant for a theater on Mars," and would, he noted, run for ten evenings on Earth where audiences "would not be able to bear it, for it is blood of their blood, ... and its contents are those years beyond conscious memory, years that live on only in nightmares." His theatrically unperformable masterpiece weaves together conversations he overheard in coffeehouses during the First World War, others he imagined among generals in their favorite restaurants and in cabinet meetings, threading those together with newspaper accounts by naïve reporters, and contrasting all of these in their frivolity, arrogance, or ignorance, with graphic and pained letters home from enlisted men. It is funny and clever, and apt for his concept to suggest the play for Mars, but we won't reveal why. We don't want to spoil the end.

It likely took my father years to absorb all he had seen during that time of the First World War and the following depression in Austria. We continue to find ways that his time as a POW and his escape filtered into his later life. The most amazing thing for us is how subtle its influence was sometimes, like when he made belt buckles out of copper and brass pipe scraps—what thrift.

The era of the First World War also bore the genesis of my father as a storyteller. For his friends and relatives, when he returned home to Vienna, he condensed his endless days in the Siberian prison camps into vignettes, his primary stage being the coffeehouse. Just as with the jokes he told to his friend Kurt Bresnitz in Aspen, as part of their daily coffee klatch, some preparations were needed, and it seems my father scripted the occasional tale before he would tell it.

One of these, found in my father's handwriting on four sides of a large envelope the fashionable color of rust from the later 1960's, is an inventive, whimsical tale of a skiing adventure on the top of Aspen (Ajax) Mountain, just off a trail where there is famous powder snow, out of bounds in the forest. The area is beautiful, with large rock outcroppings above an old mine dump, where in 1955 I had bought an old silver mining claim, the Maude Lode, and always hoped to build another little cabin. I never heard this story; perhaps it was told in CRMS cooking classes to students he inspired with its natural connections between food and history.

TALE FOR COOKING (UNDATED)

BY STEVE SCHANZER

As I was skiing lately on Buckhorn I came a little off the trail and met there a very curious creature. He was a transparent dapper figure with a little gray hat, and we started to talk. He introduced himself as the ghost of the Maude Claim. He said that after his experience immigrating years ago on a ship with the famous movie "The Traveling Ghost" he does not wear old-fashioned iron armor anymore but adapted himself to the local conditions with parka and stretch-pants. He said these people on the mountain don't differ too much from the old knights-errant, because in his opinion they err around the mountains without any visible purpose. So he feels kind of associated with them.

I asked him how he came to Ajax Mountain, so he said, 'As you know perhaps, I was transferred forcibly with enumerated stones of the Scottish castle by ship to Texas. But I didn't like the hot climate there and looked around and finally found Aspen and Ajax Mountain, where I live now. I like Aspen because people here are as crazy as in Scotland, only the craziness is here more friendly. But on the ship I tasted secretly all the goodies they served there. It was all new to me because in Scotland I saw only porridge as the owner of the castle was completely broke—a situation you encounter very often here in Aspen, and through that I feel very much at home.

Now, I am fond of good variated food. But coming to town to

snatch a secret bite in this or that restaurant I found mostly the usual steaks under all kind of different names. So I developed for myself a lot of good recipes, which I cooked in the mineshaft of the Maude Claim, where I scratched together a little experimental kitchen. As I have no money, as usual, I as a ghost can shoplift anytime I want, as I as a ghost can be invisible anytime I want.

I asked him what he is cooking tonight, and he said "Liver Knödel" [liver dumplings], so I said, "That is a very long process." But he gave me a shortcut that is marvelous, and confidentially I'm giving this now to my readers.

He promised me from time to time to introduce me to more of his secrets and disappeared.

I will ski again around there, and I hope that he will appear again.

Confidentially yours.

Skiers looking down on the Maude Lode mining claim, Aspen Mountain, circa 1950. LOEY RINQUIST COLLECTION. ASPEN HISTORICAL SOCIETY.

The unsigned story brought a laugh to everyone in our house, remembering the shortcut. Instead of buying the liver, seasoning, and cooking it, he would simply go to the grocery store and buy Liverwürst to make his dumplings. Being a cook in a French army camp made him unafraid to try anything, and he often invented these kinds of quick, yet epicurean solutions. Another great shortcut was to make the dessert Kaiserschmarrn with left-over glazed doughnuts from the Boomerang breakfasts. He cut them up and mixed them with beaten eggs and raisins, quickly sautéed them, and served them with raspberry syrup and powdered sugar. He called these "Super Goofies," and we loved them.

My father was adaptable to many situations, some of which, I admit, we will never know. Some stories simply were not appropriate for certain listeners, who he gauged before he entered into a tale. In 1940, for example, a story from Marseilles never made it to official record until the 1970's. He considered my nephew Tom Schneider to be old enough to tell this story at that time. My father said to him, "It was not written down on my papers for different reasons. You will see right away."

A STORY NOT WRITTEN

In 1940's Marseilles it was very difficult to move around because the French police collaborated with the Germans and arrested every refugee in sight, and even their own people, and put them in concentration camps. So I lived at this time in a hotel frequented by Arabs. It was not very much controlled by the police—because the Arabs were from Algeria, and they were more or less neutral in the whole war and affairs.

There I met a man, Mr. Löwy, a refugee from Czechoslovakia, whose business had been making candy. He came, as he told me, on a speedboat from Italy. It was a very adventurous flight from Italy to France. But there unfortunately he was drafted into the French Army and was supposed to dig trenches during the time of the war. As everything collapsed [when France was occupied], he left [the Army] and had only on his body a green shirt, a green pair of trousers, and a pair of galoshes. And that was all he had. But in his hands he had a little *sachet*, a little bag. And in this bag were very interesting instruments to cut the corns off the feet. He called that in French *un pedicure*. So he said to me, "That's my business here, and I make a lot of money. But I am very unfortunate. I can't speak French, [only Czech and German]. Until yesterday I had a man who translated for me, but he took a ship to Algeria, and now I am here. I can't talk to my customers. But you speak French very well—so would you perhaps be so kind and translate for me and be the interpreter? I will pay you for it."

So the next morning we went down the Canebière, that is the main street like 5th Avenue in Marseilles, towards the Vieux Port, the old harbor. It is a square basin, and there he turned to the right. I was always on a bike and did not walk on the sidewalk, because there people were arrested. Even going around the corner, I took my bicycle. And I was right; I was never stopped. So he turned slowly to the right. That is a very shady part of the town, which doesn't exist any more. There were the bordellos, and the prostitutes, and the sailors. It was very dangerous especially for the Germans; a lot of them were killed there. The Germans destroyed it later on completely—this whole quarter of the town.

So we went [into the area], and we came to the house. We were very nicely accepted by the *ladies* there. And he started to cut off their corns, and I started to talk to the ladies, and we had a very good time because we were not customers, we were business men there. That is a big difference for them. But they chat amongst themselves, amongst the girls! A writer would have written a whole book, what I heard there. But as I am not a writer I can't tell you very much anymore about what I heard....

The afternoon passed in a very agreeable manner, but at the end the girls started to talk about *razzias* [raids] by the police; they swept through looking for people they wanted to arrest. So I said as we left, "My dear Mr. Löwy, it is very nice of you that you wanted me to have this job. But I will ***not*** be arrested, after all my adventures, by the police in such a spot! So you have to look for another interpreter." And I quit after one afternoon. But the whole story proves I held a job that nobody can top in the whole world— the Interpreter for a Bordello Pedicure!

For the rest of the time in Marseilles, my father remained friends with Mr. Löwy, and in the fall of 1941, when my father was in New York looking for a job, a man approached him on Broadway. A familiar face. As my father told it, the man said,

"Schanzer you are here??!"

I said, "Löwy you are here too!?!"

I said, "Yes, what are you doing?"

"Oh, I am working in a candy factory, what are you doing?"

"I'm looking for a job!"

"Oh, come with me, I work in there, you can go into the union and you can get right away a job there."

So, the next day I was in Brooklyn at the Metro Chocolate Company. And I stayed there a long time as sugar mixer and cooker. And Mr. Löwy worked there too. Then they transferred me to the marshmallow department. But it was so dirty there that I couldn't stand it, and I quit.

A couple of years later on Upper Broadway suddenly a man came toward me, a little bit more fat—Mr. Löwy.

"What are you doing, Mr. Löwy?! How are you?"

"Oh, I have a big factory for brassieres! And I have something in the vicinity of 100 girls working for me!"

He showed me his factory; it was a wonderful factory turning out brassieres. He later introduced me to his wife and his children. He was a very well settled man in New York. But later on I lost him out of sight. ■

A Philosophy of Life

For all the tales my father has written and told I realize they can never relate our entire story. For one, my father's sense of humor, experienced in person, is impossible to render with ink on paper. Also his delight in spinning an amusing tale must be left to the imagination. He lives on with me and is still very much alive in each of us who continue his traditions.

We still have much to learn from our archive. There are files in German that would take many more months to translate. My father also kept a box of the postcards he received from friends all over the world. One we found is from Ilse von Hennig in Vienna with a note from Richard Neutra, their mutual friend and the architect of the neighboring Werkbundsiedlung house.[1] We have yet to read all the shorthand notes made in the journal my father kept in Siberia. The task of finding someone who knows German shorthand and can read the Austrian expressions from that era is daunting.

At some point with family history one has to stop moving backward, researching and reminiscing, and let time go on its forward roll again. I breathe a sigh of relief that we are not going to try to include any more of my father's long and incredible life in this book, save for a few recipes, which we hope can be savored from time to time as a little memory of him by all the readers of these stories. Nevertheless, this process in total has had a salutary effect on me and my family, and it has brought him back to us in memory to enjoy his company again, in an ethereal way perhaps, but real all the same.

My father foretold many events that came to pass in my lifetime. As I think about this I remember that he was a man who made his own destiny by positive thoughts and actions, crafting the story of his life to have an instructive lesson at the end. On the whole, he refused nostalgia and instead, all he experienced pointed forward to the next adventure. He grew into the person he was, and who we treasured, despite his setbacks, his unspoken sadness, and many of the straits he once found himself to be in. Is this kind of storytelling the same as telling one's own future? In hindsight, yes it is.

My wife Fonda reminded me of something told to her by my sister Doris, who remembered that on New Year's Eve our family would swirl molten lead into a bowl of water, an old Austrian-Germanic tradition to foresee the future. People customarily did this, and still do, during the holiday season. One can tell luck, love, wealth, or hardship from the shape of the lead as it returns to a solid form. A horseshoe, for instance, could mean good fortune—a ship could mean a journey. I can imagine all of us in the candlelight at Little Omama's beautiful apartment with the flame casting us as huge shadows on the high ceilings as we waited to see our future in the lead bullion. My father, who was not superstitious, never lingered on this, and it was my sister who kept the memory.

Perhaps he did not talk about this tradition because it is attached to another sad story—a string of tragic deaths that would have affected Little Omama particularly. He did tell me that New Year's Eve was not celebrated in their house because the day was commemorative, but beyond that I had lost why. But according to Fonda, who remembers what my father told her, the family did not celebrate on New Year's Eve because it was the anniversary of Little Omama's mother Katharina's death. Rosa was only twelve years old when her mother died, and out of respect for Katharina's memory, the whole Pollack-Parnegg family kept the turn of the new year as a quiet night of remembrance, a *Yahrzeit*.

Then when my father was five years old, Rosa's older sister Tina Schlesinger died suddenly in France. Rosa, now the only sibling of her generation left, took it upon herself to raise Tina's children—Käthe, then eight years old, and a son, Marcell, about whom we know virtually nothing, save a small reference in a letter about he and my father being in a photograph together. My father always said he was an only child, but really, he wasn't.

When Käthe was only fifteen she sadly died of an illness, also near the New Year, on January 3, 1911. Rosa, who had also been adopted by her grandmother, Theresia Pollack, grieved intensely for Käthe, the only daughter she would ever have. My father would have been twelve years old at the time. He must have remembered Käthe, but we know almost nothing about her either, his cousin/sister.

In that last fact, we have realized a sad truth about of our family history—so many premature deaths of women in our family. It is not an accident this history is a history of men, the survivors. My sister Doris was the rare exception of these generations. She died in 2004, having lived a good life, when she was seventy-six years old. Her own memoir, which she started writing after she and her husband Herb moved to a retirement home, was stored on a computer that suffered a hard drive crash, and all that writing was lost in an instant, frustrating her project. Instead of leaving a written record for history, she returned to her creative artistry. Years before her death she suffered a heart attack; in that moment, she said she saw an open door. This door became a motif in her subsequent paintings, which she began to build out into three dimensions. One painting was of a walkway in a garden under an azure sky. The door leading "home" was no longer a two-dimensional illusion but instead, a space of passage.

History remembered is often history that edifies and buttresses the present.[2] What will this book do? What will it support for my family, when I am gone? What will my drawings represent—of The Boomerang, which is now a memory, or those in the "unbuilt" file, distilled from my waking dreams? I think about all that we have learned in this excavation process. The information has changed all of our perspectives and brought us closer together as a family.

When one crafts the story of one's life, one builds a home in which others may live. Details can become significant and incredibly meaningful when going back in time to learn about people whose traces have nearly disappeared. The smallest turn of phrase, or saying, or habit, becomes a portal into the past. I remember my Little Omama's apartment vividly. Of her personality I have but a few thin paper objects to remind me: her correspondence and a few pictures of her sweet countenance. Yet her voice in her letters resounds clearly with a good heart. Her love for my father also embraces me.

My father crafted two rings when he was making jewelry in Siberia that he kept and I still have—one with an emblem in the shape of a horseshoe, his, and one, which he gave to my mother, crowned by a heart.[3] Lucky to find her, his only love, he never forgot her, and he always

Eva and Stefan, circa 1926.

commemorated April 4, her birthday. A letter my father wrote on June 19, 1944 to Doris and me, shows how he felt her continued presence with him. "Today it is six years that we lost your unforgettable dear mother. It is always for me a very sad day of remembrances of the happy days we were all together. How everything would be else, if she would have lived." On June 21, 1942, he wrote to us that he was always reminded of her in the last days of June "because something special occurs," as if she were watching out for him. "Three years ago we went to Saint-Nazaire, two years ago ... I jumped across the wall in France to liberty, and last year I arrived just in U.S.A. Now this year on this day, the luggage arrived from Paris." We had all survived, but a part of him was still to remain with her, in 1938, though in future years he would not speak of it. I think of how much he must have missed us too, after having sent us away, and the uncertainty of ever seeing us again. "I am as lonely as I was always since your dear mother died and I think it will also remain so."

My father's love for us and his wisdom throughout the years is evinced in a letter of March 28, 1947, which I include here as a kind of coda to his chapters. He sent it to me in Australia a year before we were reunited. I was eighteen, and though I have no memory of it, was deciding between a profession in watch making and pursuing a more adventuresome life in the outdoors.

"Dear Charles, I got your letter and was extremely pleased," the letter started. "I am also very happy you like the fountain pen I sent you.... I would strongly advise you not to consider [the watch making business] at all but to make the decision [about your future] from only one point of view: 'What do I like to do best.' As an example I will cite you myself. I wanted my whole life only to be an automobile mechanic. By H.P.S. and family decisions, and by not having the right connections in the [depressed] country of Austria, I was forced into the textile business, which I never really liked....[4] I wrote you this so that you should avoid the mistakes I made in my youth. If you don't really like the sitting indoor life ... don't touch it. The carpentering line is especially here in America an excellent one.... As you know very much about this now I would stay for the moment in the carpentry line. You could be, later on, a business man in the lumber trade, or could be an architect, because your uncle Loos said always, anyone who wants to be a good architect should first be a good carpenter.... With many, many kisses to you [and Doris] I am—your loving Dad."

In letters such as these I realize my father was building an intentional life for us. And we would go on to build our own lives also with this strong vision for ourselves, doing what we loved to do. He advised us, and through his stories gave us a clear idea about who we were, what our strengths were, and thus suggested what we would become.

The family mythology passed on by him was that our name "Schanzer" meant "fortification builder." The thought was that our ancestors had worked on the walls encircling Vienna, protecting it from invasion. We were immigrants to Vienna, but we helped build it into something great. My father would tell us his speculations, that we were part of the lost "thirteenth tribe," a hypothetical group of people who came north from Turkey in the eighth century and converted to Judaism then. The conversion meant assimilation, and he always prided himself on being able to pick up local customs, no matter where he was. He made friends across cultures

My drawing of a walled city with castle, November 1941, which I made for my father's birthday and sent to him in New York from Australia.

and religions, and felt at home everywhere.[5]

The thirteenth tribe theory advanced my father's feeling of comfort in all areas in the Middle East. He used to say the Viennese croissant came north with the invasion of the Turks—the crescent moon shape reminiscent of the Islamic symbol. Over tales he would share small cups of Turkish coffee with his friends and visitors. He used to brew it in a small, brass conical-shaped pot with a single long armed handle. The mythology was complete—taste buds, genetics, Jewish culture—world traveler and fortification builder of emotional protection for me who never told me how my mother died, but kept alive all the stories of escapes and castles.

In the newspaper article from the twenty-fifth anniversary of CRMS, Sharon Wooding wrote that in an interview with my father he told her that after the First World War, when he became a sales manager for H.P.S. he often went to Greece, Turkey, and Egypt. "When he was in Istanbul for the first time, a company representative said to him, 'I understand you are a graduate of the World Trade University.... Now forget everything you have learned, and let's go to the Bazaar.' It became obvious very quickly that this was not Steve's first time in the East." My father told Sharon, "I already knew how to deal with the Chinese. It was not so different with

My father and I with Carrie (left) and Jenny on Fonda's lap
at his 89th birthday, November 18, 1978.

Turks or Arabs," and indeed when he came to America he bartered well also at the Navajo trading posts, gathering friends along the way.

My mother Eva accompanied him many times on his Middle Eastern sales trips after they were married in 1926. I have a wonderful letter from her, one of the only, saved by my uncle Max as a memory of my mother, his eldest sister. The letter was sent from a trip my mother and father took to Istanbul. She wrote home to her parents Otto and Olga about the stars in the domed ceiling of the former Palace harem, about the Bazaar, the differences in cultures, and the sense she had of her own emancipation compared to the women she saw. It must have been eye opening for her, at the time only twenty-four, to leave Europe and to start seeing other environments. I thank my father that he was able to give her experiences like this and enriched her world with his generous spirit, open heart, and love of adventure and new places. His warm nature and ease in talking to people must have been a wonderful addition to her life.

Even after all this time, in going through my father's files his life seems still so close and present. The emotions this remembrance project has brought up are many and deep. There are so many moments, as I descend through the layers of our lives, which seem like yesterday.

It was early October 1979. The leaves were turning gold, and some had started to fall from the aspen trees. My father had asked for me repeatedly that day. Finally the message reached me at The Boomerang. It was urgent that I go to the hospital. He must have known his life was slipping away, and it was obvious that he wanted me with him because he waited for me before he died. He would not go without me there.

I was inexperienced in these matters of death, and I thought not that these could be our last moments together as I hugged him and held his hand. Our lives had been so closely interwoven that I could not imagine this loss. It was a month before his ninetieth birthday, and almost all his life he had been in vigorous health.

I found out later that he had confided to Dr. Whitcomb at Aspen Valley Hospital that he never imagined it would be "so hard to die," and he stopped taking his pills. I did not resent him for this choice. He felt his body was failing him, and he knew he couldn't survive anymore.[6] Doris and her husband Herb drove from Boulder, four hours away, but when they arrived it was too late.

When my father was hospitalized earlier in Denver in September, he managed to rally enough to be released and get some strength back at my sister's house in Boulder. He stayed with their family for several weeks under Doris and her family's care. He wanted to return to Aspen, and they helped him to be well enough for the short flight. I think in his mind he was truly escaping again, not to be in a Denver hospital, but to die at home.

My father was a man of unflagging love and devotion to Doris and me, his children, and later to our spouses, Herb and Fonda. He was generous and proud of his four grandchildren, Tom, Linda, Carrie, and Jenny. He was a good friend and confidant to many, who trusted him and asked for his advice, and he was a role model for many young people. My father's principles of honesty in everything were uncompromising. If someone wronged him, that person was henceforth ignored. This is a reason why he never wished to return to Vienna; his Vienna simply did not exist anymore. To cut a thread like that is not so easy, but there was no middle ground in his philosophy of life: it was either one way or the other. Simple and straightforward, this philosophy—his truth—has guided me.

At his gravesite at Red Butte Cemetery in Aspen, his ashes, in a ceramic urn that had been imprinted with burlap to create the texture of a fabric's open weave, were placed under a brass plate flush to the ground. Simple

Charlie, Steve, and Doris, 1975. PHOTO: FERENC BERKO.

Masonic rites were performed at his interment just as he requested. His miraculous life ended this way. Afterwards, a circle of friends and family gathered at our house to share Viennese delicacies and tell stories. Adele Hause, a CRMS faculty member with whose family my father stayed part-time during his last years at the school, recounted that when she made a Linzertorte for my father's CRMS memorial service, "I was upset when it burned on the bottom. Then I could hear Steve, 'Ja, it's alright. Vee vill cut off ze burnt part, and it vill be perfect.'"

The early hours of the morning for me are a rich time for thoughts and for retrieving deep memories. I draw architectural plans in my mind. Fonda also in her sleep wanders halls of imaginary buildings she wants us to design together. Her memories of my father's life are like an enormous library, and it is she who has, quietly and with perseverance, recorded what he told her. My wife, my facilitator of translations, my interpreter of dreams—without her having kept these stories and memories close for me, our friends, and our children, this book would never have been possible. What selflessness, a relative and close friend once observed, for Fonda to have adopted all of us, keeping my relatives, people now long gone, alive for this tribute to succeed.

Fonda's father, the minister Clarence Dehne, gave a sermon in the 1960's about the crisis the Holocaust poses to humanity. It was recorded, so we could listen to it, as well as others, on reel-to-reel. Clarence died from pancreatic cancer only two years after we were married, a devastating moment for her. For my father-in-law this book is also a quiet tribute, for it is because of him that she recognized me.

I have now gone back to Central Europe several times, which until my later years I never thought I would. I have met the second, third, and fourth generations who are still living with the results of the conflicts and wars my father and I saw and experienced. People ask me about our family and want to listen and learn about our lives.

Who owns a story? The storyteller, or the listeners? All who choose to tell the story inevitably become part of its chain. A story is an invitation. The listener chooses to possess it and pass it to the next person, and the moral of the story changes as time goes on. My father would be happy there are new people who want to pick up some of the threads he so carefully left for us. We are encouraged to think some may also look deeper into their own lives, to find connections to our shared histories.

The storyteller in exile is never far from home if there are people to listen. The late Argentinian author Roberto Bolaño, addressing a symposium in Vienna in 2000, spoke about a poet friend of his who was arrested in Austria in 1978 on his way to Israel, for reasons left unexplained. The friend was "banished from Austria to the no man's land of the wide world" but in a way, Bolaño continued, it didn't matter to his friend. "He didn't believe in countries, and the only borders he respected were the borders of courage and fear, the golden borders of ethics."[7] I am reminded of my father in Bolaño's words. The borders of courage and fear he speaks of were real for my father—horizon lines with mountains, storm clouds, the ocean, desert, or snow. My father never spoke of being a person in exile. He was firmly grounded, and his philosophy exuded from his present circumstances. ▪

A Cabin Is A Castle

In 2009, a letter arrived from my good friends Tinka and Jim Kurtz, whose family graced The Boomerang pool through many summers. Enclosed was a school essay written that fall term by Slide Kelly, the grandson of one of our most loyal guests, Meta Barton. It was a great pleasure for me to receive his paper, a story of his life at our lodge, with a perspective all his own. When I was Slide's age I was just learning how to build houses in Australia, and the entire Boomerang enterprise was just a possibility in the future's mist. Later when I was building the lodge, it was as if I threw out a boomerang into that place blindly with a faith and positivity inspired by my hearty father. I never imagined the returns that would come back.

The Boomerang south-east corner with Fonda and me on the balcony outside the upper lounge, mid-1990's. PHOTO: DAVID O. MARLOW.

THE BOOMERANG

The Boomerang Lodge, a retro hotel where we stayed with my grandmother, fills my mind with memories and dreams. It was a relatively small building, semicircular, with innumerable entrances and hallways. The Boomerang was always crowded but deserted at the same time, making me feel like I had the whole place to myself. It was a little slice of heaven for an eight-year-old.

My grandmother had a habit of waking up early to go to the early-risers continental breakfast they always had at The Boomerang. The few times I actually woke up we sat at a perfectly tiny table in a small room that had a gigantic window facing snowcapped peaks. Sipping fragrant teas and reading the paper, my grandmother would skim slowly for events down at the music tent. She would drag us there, hours later, coloring books in hand, to listen to angelic music that resonated from somewhere beyond the picture of a train that I was fervently coloring blue.

We would spend hours at the pool, my brother and I, making faces at each other through the glass window that looked into a comfortable underground lounge. We would continue this until an elderly housekeeper would shoo us away, scolding us for being wet in the lounge. Then, defeated, we would soak in the hot tub, enveloped in an aromatic mist, until we became wrinkled as raisins.

One summer The Boomerang was fenced off with large construction signs around the perimeter. Where there used to be a magical pool, shining a luminescent turquoise glow into the lounge below, there is now just a gaping hole. A part of me seemed to be taken out when the hole was dug, a vital part of my childhood missing in the rubble. So I will never forget the Boomerang Lodge, and I hope that I will live to see the hole filled and The Boomerang return.

After fifty years of nurturing and building a business, a heart condition helped make the decision to finally sell the lodge in 2005. We celebrated fifty years in business with a huge garden party to which the whole town was invited. Speeches were made, tears were shed, and many old guests and friends stopped by to drink champagne, eat Viennese pastries, and sign our guestbook. The new developers allowed the Wrightean building to be designated "historic" so that it can be preserved. As I released The Boomerang from my possession, I was gratified to see there might be a new beginning for it, as a landmark.

The other two thirds of the buildings are no more. This includes the cabin—we could not move it off the property because it shared too many walls with the rest of the lodge; its massive fireplace stack, a kind of monument to my first days settling the land, would have fallen to pieces.

I went over to take photos as all the buildings came down. The Boomerang became a pile of logs and stone, the materials returning to a natural state of entropy, just as they were before I came along. It was my life's work—gone in days. The last thing standing on the third building was the elevator shaft, a battered concrete block tower of three stories rising out of the rubble like a temple. As of this writing, the property still waits to be transformed.

We are broken down before we can rebuild. The same is true for all ideals. My father, sister, and I fled Europe as the social-democratic experiment collapsed. We came to America to find new lives, but everything we knew came with us and became elements we wove into all we did. Uncertainty and vulnerability are the given circumstances the Jewish people have lived with for thousands of years of dislocation and resettlement. They are also strengths. The circularity of this history requires a language and an oral history to bring the past to reflect on the future in a meaningful way. Stories can survive even beyond buildings, but they need people to carry the words.

I had a vivid dream in July 2011 about this book. I woke with a start and told it to Fonda, who wrote it down. I was being chased across a graveyard, over earthen mounds, by three Nazi thugs. I felt young and agile, but they were catching up with me nonetheless. Then I spotted a bookstore with a glass front window, and slipped inside. There were people drinking tea and having conversation. The thugs would not come in. The people invited me to sit down in this safe haven, to laugh, and to converse with them. I did. I felt at home there, in that place, a sanctuary.

The vocabulary I chose to tell the journey of my life has for years been architecture—this frame formed around all my stories, which I have written down for the first time here. After watching eight seasons of snow fall on The Boomerang, now quiet, a building I do not enter anymore, I have found a new peace. I read now, write, paint, and draw. I love to cook and prepare the meals. I have many enjoyable occasions with friends and family both in Aspen and in my travels abroad. Concerts throughout the year and skiing in winter fill my life with joy.

I came to Aspen looking for a simple, fulfilling life and found hope, supported by love and confidence in the future, which allowed me to build home. And this has set me free. ▪

March 2013 | Aspen, Colorado

Recipes

The recipes that follow are from my father's cookbook, *Basic Cooking Leading to Creative Cooking*, which he compiled in 1978 for the classes he held at Colorado Rocky Mountain School. We often made these dishes in our early days in Aspen at our home, at the Holiday House, and for friends who we met through The Boomerang. In his words, "Reading of recipes in cooking books should only stimulate inventiveness and should be only a general guide. Always bear in mind that the person who wrote down a recipe was at first an inventive person like you should become. Therefore, sometimes no quantities are given, but only basic ingredients and procedures." He concluded, "This short course will not teach you to be a perfect chef, but will put you on the way to creative cooking."

Einbrennsuppe (Austrian Military Soup)

"The Soup Made from Nothing"

Melt butter or other fat, pour flour over it, and let it brown.

Add caraway seed (if desired).

Add cold water, bouillon cubes, and soy sauce.

Cook.

Serve on top—croutons.

Liverknödel Soup (Liver Dumpling Soup)

Take liverwurst, work in some breadcrumbs, flour, and egg. (Quantity depends on you.)

Form balls approximately ¾" round.

Drop liverwurst balls into bouillon soup and cook until they rise to the surface.

Viennese Cucumber Salad

Peel and slice cucumbers—<u>very</u> thin with a slicer.

Add vinegar, oil, pepper, and a little bit of sugar.

Sprinkle on top—paprika, before serving.

Wiener Schnitzel

For veal, but also beef, pork, lamb, fish, sliced bologna, and large mushrooms.

Flatten out cut veal as much as possible. All fat and bones should be cut off. Salt. (For pork, sprinkle with paprika.)

Put flour in a shallow pan. Roll meat in it.

PREPARATION OF EGG MIXTURE:

In a flat pan, put beaten (scrambled) eggs, a dash of milk, and a dash of water—when you don't have water, eggs will not stick.

Dip meat into egg mixture, next into bread crumbs, which are then packed on. Bread crumbs should be very fine.

Fry breaded meat in deep fat until <u>golden</u> brown.

Serve with lemon cut in six slices. (Don't use ketchup!!)

VARIATION: if you put some anchovies and a slice of lemon on top, you call it **Schnitzel a la Holstein.**

Chicken Paprikash

Chop up onions and fry in sliced bacon.

Put on paprika.

Put chicken in fry pans with fat and onions, lightly brown, put in oven, and cook until soft.

Ten minutes before dinner, put in sour cream or yogurt and some flour, mixed together.

AUTHOR'S VERSION:

One red onion thinly sliced, sautéed in 1 T. of oil till soft in large fry pan.

Add 1 T. paprika—fry two minutes till fragrant. Then push onions to sides.

Add 1 T. oil and lightly brown 4-5 boneless chicken thighs.

Add 1 cup low-sodium chicken broth.

Cover and simmer one half-hour on low-medium heat.

Uncover, cook another half-hour, turn, and mix well.

Remove chicken and cover with foil.

Stir in 1 cup regular or goat's yogurt (plain flavor) with 1 T. flour mixed in, over low heat 4-5 minutes.

Recombine chicken with juice.

Serve immediately over egg noodles cooked *al dente*.

BEST COMPANION DISH: **Red Cabbage**

One head red cabbage thinly sliced and sprinkled with red wine vinegar.

One green apple peeled and thinly sliced.

Sautée in large fry pan 1 T. finely cut onion and 1/3 cup brown sugar in 1/3 cup of vegetable oil or Crisco fat.

Add red cabbage, apple, and 1 cup low-sodium chicken broth. Mix well with tongs as it reduces.

Cook low-medium heat till soft.

Add ½ cup red wine, 3 T. red wine vinegar, and 1 tsp. flour.

Mix well, cook a short time longer, and serve.

Hungarian Goulash

3 lbs. beef

6 medium sized onions

1 tsp. paprika

1-2 cups water or soup stock

Vinegar

Peel onions and chop into pieces.

Place in pan with butter, oil, or best—bacon grease.

Fry onions until golden brown.

Cut meat into 1" inch squares; add to pan and brown in oil.

Add a lot of paprika when golden brown and continue frying for a few minutes.

Add one spoonful of vinegar and soy sauce and salt to mixture, also caraway seed.

Mix well, rinse frying pan, and add water or stock to goulash.

Cook either in pressure cooker or in oven in a pan until soft.

Make mixture of flour and cold water, add to goulash.

Pressure Cooker Cabbage Dish

May be made on paprika or pepper base. If pepper, make recipe without tomatoes.

Pre-cook cabbage so leaves will come off easily—10 minutes.

Pre-cook rice—2 cups water to 1 cup rice with salt. (Or Chinese way, 1 to 1.)

Cook rice in frying pan until glazy—don't ever wash rice—no minute rice.

Fry onions and add paprika—best cut with bacon. Do not burn onions.

Fry ground beef with salt and pepper.

Line bottom and sides of pressure cooker with cabbage leaves. Put several layers on the bottom.

Combine rice and onions with meat and add soy sauce.

Put mixture in cabbage-lined pot and pack down.

Empty can of tomato paste on top of mixture. Fill can with water and pour on mixture.

Fold down leaves on sides and put more small leaf pieces on top.

Rinse skillet in which meat was fried with a little water and add to pressure cooker.

Cook ½ hour in a pressure cooker.

Turn upside down onto broiler and brown for about 15 minutes. Make a small amount of gravy in the pressure cooker and baste as it browns.

VARIATION: Instead of pressure cooker, pat leaves on pre-flattened aluminum foil in pan with meat mixture in middle and leaves on top, then add tomato paste and water.

Kaiserschmarren (Emperor Omelets)

Stir batter of milk and flour.

Beat together: egg yolks, sugar, salt, melted butter, egg whites, and raisins.

Fold in.

Heat some butter in a pan.

Pour in batter 1" high. Mix in raisins.

Fry on both sides until slightly yellow.

Tear into small pieces and sprinkle with sugar. Serve with raspberry syrup, plums, etc.

VARIATION: **Supergoofies**

Mix eggs, milk, salt, raisins, sugar, flour, and vanilla flavoring. (Cut up old donuts can also be used.)

Pour into frying pan.

Bake on both sides.

Goof up with a fork. Put into baking dish into a very low oven or serve right away with plums or raspberry sauce.

Indianerkrapfen (American-Indian Creampuffs)

1 cup water (boiling)

1 cup flour

½ cup butter

4 eggs

Heat water and butter until butter melts. Add all of the flour. Stir until dough forms a ball.

Remove from heat and let stand five minutes.

Add two eggs, beaten, and add two other eggs. Beat until stiff. If it does not set, let stand another 10 minutes.

Shape with tablespoon on baking sheet.

Bake for 40 minutes at 375 degrees.

Fill with whipped cream.

Pour over it chocolate icing that hardens.

CHOCOLATE ICING:

1 cup sugar

½ cup water

4 ½ oz chocolate

1 T. butter

Cook sugar with water until it spins a heavy thread. Melt chocolate in double boiler, add butter. Add hot syrup gradually, stirring constantly until smooth and until mixture coats spoon. Keep soft over hot water.

Ischlerkrapfen

2 cups flour

1 ¼ cups butter

1 cup sugar

1 ½ cups grated almonds

1 dash cinnamon

Raspberry jam

1 Hershey's chocolate bar

Mix dry ingredients and butter to make dough. Cover and chill.

Roll out. Use eggcup to cut cookies. Put on baking sheet.

Bake at 375 degrees 10-15 minutes. Cookies should be a little brown at edge and on the bottom.

Cool.

Put together cookie pairs, bottoms toward each other with the middle layer jam.

Melt Hershey's chocolate bar and put on top.

Linzertorte

1 cup butter

1 cup flour

1 ½ cups grated almonds

½ cup sugar

1 dash cinnamon

2 egg yolks

Raspberry jam

Mix butter, flour, grated almonds, cinnamon, and egg yolks.

Refrigerate dough 30 minutes.

Roll out half of dough ½" thick. Line a shallow pan. Also cover sides.

Spread ½ cup raspberry jam on top.

From leftover dough cut finger-wide strips. Place on torte, making diagonal lines to form diamond grid pattern.

Mix 1 egg white and 1 spoon of sugar and brush onto torte.

Bake at 325 for 1 hour.

Recipes for Turkish Coffee and Cocoa

New York   April 7, 1942

Dear Charlie,

I am really delighted with the detailed report you gave me about your summer vacations, and I thank you very much for it, also in the name of all our friends who read your adventures with the greatest interest. I am really proud of you, because I see that you are on the right way, especially for the time we are living in now. What you were doing I wished always to do during my life, and I would be glad to live the rest of my life on such a cattle farm as you did this summer....

Now, you like to know about the coffee. You must have a pot—you remember they were copper or brass. The upper part must be narrower than the bottom. Then the coffee must be burnt a little lighter than you have it for the ordinary coffee. Now the most essential part is that it is ground so fine as cocoa powder. When you have the pot, you put sugar in it and water, and boil the water and the sugar, till it is really boiling. You add the coffee with a spoon and stir slowly. Then you approach slowly with the pot to the flame and let it boil up once. Then add a little cold water, but only some drops, so that the coffee goes down. Now you can serve the coffee, but in little cups, that is essential. You must see that every person gets some foam. That is the best of it. The cocoa you make in the same manner, only you must put in a lot of cocoa. At the end you add some heavy cream in the cup of each person, if they like.

Perhaps it will be possible to send you such a pot. But I doubt that it is allowed.

With many kisses, I am your loving Dad. ■

Stefan Schanzer's Escape from Nazi-Occupied France

Towns and Villages (in order of passage through)
June 19, 1940 – September 21, 1940

CHAPTER 7 | PAGES 80-82

June 19, 1940 ❶
Escapes French Army camp in **Audierne, Finistère Province,** in **Brittany,** on the west coast of **France.**

June 20, 1940 ❷
Walks toward **Le Guilvinec,** but turns toward **Loctudy,** at the mouth of the **Pont-l'Abbé** river estuary.

June 21, 1940 ❸
Takes ferry from **Loctudy** across the strait to **Île-Tudy,** walks along the beach to **Sainte-Marine.**

June 22, 1940 ❹
Crosses a second strait from **Sainte-Marine**, walks to **La Forêt-Fouesnant.**

CHAPTER 8 | PAGES 83-92

June 23, 1940 ❺
Travels by bicycle from **La Forêt-Fouesnant** to **Baud.**

June 24, 1940 ❻
Travels by bicycle from **Baud** to **Pont-Scorff** in the region of **Lorient.**

Crosses the River **La Vilaine**, travels around impassible salt marshes near **Saint-Nazaire.** Rides toward **Pornichet** to **Sainte-Marguerite,** and on to the farmer Perrin's house in **Saint-Marc-sur-Mer.**

June 25 – June 28, 1940 ❼
Rides from **Saint-Marc-sur-Mer** through the woods of **la Maillardais,** the **Forêt du Gâvre**. Encounters the **Loire River**, rides his bicycle upstream to **Joué-sur-Erdre** and stays the night there.
Nantes, Angers, and **Saumur** have all been occupied.

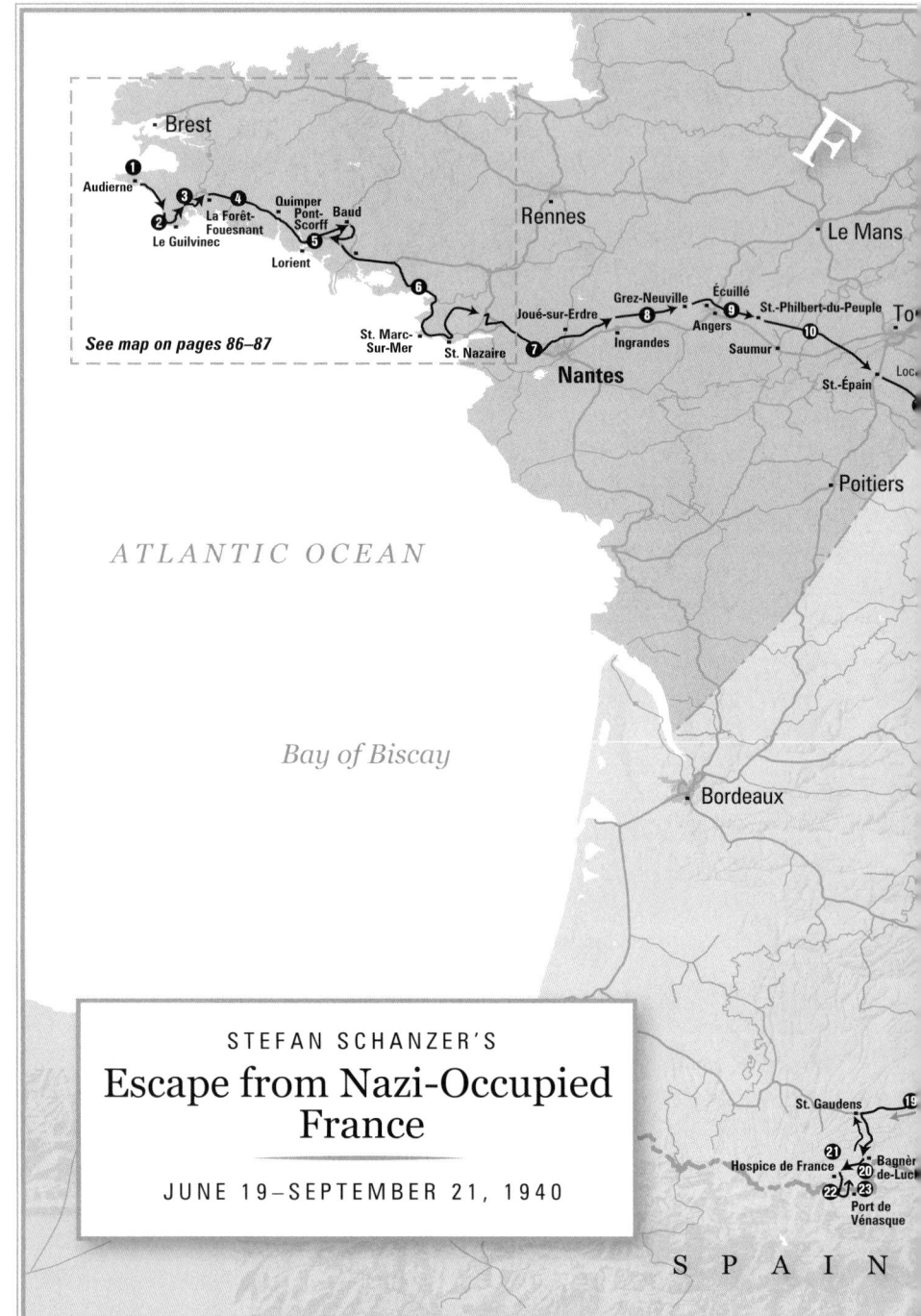

ATLANTIC OCEAN

Bay of Biscay

STEFAN SCHANZER'S
Escape from Nazi-Occupied France
JUNE 19–SEPTEMBER 21, 1940

SPAIN

DESIGN: CURT CARPENTER

OCCUPIED BY GERMANY
JUNE 25, 1940

Tries to cross the **Loire River** at **Ingrandes**, but is not able. Encounters German soldiers at **Chateau du Vauboisseau.**

June 29, 1940 ❽
Decides to try to cross the **Loire River** between **Saumur** and **Tours.** Detours around **Angers** to avoid occupied towns.
Reaches **Grez-Neuville** in the afternoon and then **Écuillé** in the evening. Stays overnight in the **Accueil des Réfugiés** [Refuge Shelter] in **Écuillé.**

June 30, 1940 ❾
Travels with three French soldiers. Stays overnight in **Saint-Philbert-du-Peuple**.

July 1, 1940 ❿
Crosses the **Loire River** with the three French soldiers and goes through the woods near **Camp Militaire du Ruchard.** In **Avon-les-Roches** his bike brake cable breaks. The soldiers leave.

Stays the night in **Saint-Épain.**

July 2, 1940 ⓫
Rides through heavily German-occupied territory, passing through **Preuilly-sur-Claise** and arriving in **Azay-le-Ferron**—unoccupied France.
Stays in the local **Centre d'Accueil** [local shelter].

July 3, 1940 ⓬
Rides through **Mézières-en-Brenne** to **Buzançais.** Met by Mr. Luquet with Les Fils d'Emanuel Lang and Co. and later by cousin Raoul Lang.

CHAPTER 9 | PAGES 93-104

Mid-July, 1940 ⓭
Travels from **Buzançais** to **Pontarion** by bicycle. Stays one night with the family d'Aussy.

From **Pontarion** to **Riom** by bicycle, and then up the **Massif Central (Auvergne Plateau)** by bus to **Alleuze.** Over the **Auvergne Plateau** in one day by bicycle from **Alleuze** through **Alès,** and then to **Saint-Rémy-de-Provence**, where he stays the night in a hotel, but only after taking the wrong bridge over the **Rhône** at **Tarascon** and having to turn back to reach **Saint-Rémy. ⓮**

Wanting to go toward **Aix-en-Provence,** a truck driver gives him a lift 55 miles to the outskirts of **Marseilles** where he finds the Österreichers in **Aubagne.**

Stays three weeks in **Marseilles** ⓖ

> (Often goes to visit the Österreichers in **Aubagne**, and while in **Marseilles** acquires Chinese and Siamese visas, as well as Portuguese and Spanish transit visas, as replacements for his Czech passport.)

Avoids Vichy internment camp at **Les Milles**.

August 25, 1940 ⓰
Travels by train from **Aubagne** via **Marseilles** to **Bédarieux**.

August 26, 1940 ⓱
Rides from **Bédarieux** to **Graissessac** to stay with a friend.

August 27, 1940 ⓲
A truck driver gives him a lift over the high mountain ranges outside of **Carcasonne** to **Limoux**. Stays in a hotel.

August 28, 1940 ⓳
From **Limoux**, rides his bicycle to **Saint-Paul-de-Jarrat** to take a train toward **Toulouse** to **Saint-Gaudens**. After passing a checkpoint, rides thirty miles, passing through the valley of the **Garonne** on his way to **Luchon**. Check points at **Labroquère** and **Cierp-Gaud**. Arrives at **Bagnères-de-Luchon** and stays with uncle and aunt, Paul and Clementine Lang.

August 29 – September 4, 1940 ⓴
Goes back to **Saint-Gaudens** for Visa de Sortie, but it is not possible to get one. Stays in **Luchon** with the Langs.

September 5, 1940 ㉑
Walks to the **Hospice de France** and sleeps in the hay. Many French tourists from **Toulouse** are there.

September 6, 1940 ㉒
Crosses French-Spanish border through **Port de Vénasque**. Glacier range of the **Maledetta** can be seen. Is turned back.

September 7, 1940 ㉓
In **Luchon** with the Langs.

September 8 – 13, 1940 ㉔
Meets with the Inspecteur des Douanes [Customs officier] in **Fos**. Not possible to cross border. Emigrants are being turned around at **Les** (Spain). **Cerbère**, or **Le Perthus** suggested as crossing routes.

Train to **Toulouse** and then to **Perpignan**.

September 14, 1940 ㉕
Travels by bus to **Le Perthus** with Mr. Fischer from Vienna.

September 15, 1940 ㉖
Crosses the French-Spanish border south of **Le Perthus** with Mr. Fischer. They walk all night.

September 16, 1940 ㉗
Arrives in **Figueres, Spain**. Takes train to **Barcelona**.
Takes train to **Madrid.**

September 17 – 19, 1940
From **Madrid** to **Badajoz, Spain**, but no entry into **Badajoz** because of a train derailment.

September 21, 1940
Arrives **Lisbon, Portugal**. ■

Family Trees

The following family trees reflect our own genealogical notes added to a growing, online scanned archive of birth records and wedding registries in Vienna, Pilsen, Bohemia and Moravia; books on Jewish genealogy; *Neue Freie Presse* death notices; and Holocaust lists. They represent what we know as of Spring 2013 and are subject to revision based on new information. Bold font on the family trees indicate people mentioned in this book and points of interest related to this story.

The family trees show our direct Viennese family lines—Sinzheim, Goldstein, Hirschmann, Feigl—and also several relatives by marriage in the Biedermann, Kraus, Todesco, and von Lieben families. Eduard von Todesco, his brother Moritz, and their descendants owned the beautiful Baroque Palais Todesco with hundreds of rooms located on the Kärntnerstrasse across from the Vienna Opera House. The Schanzers, from Galicia, and the Pollacks were textile trade immigrants into the aristocratic Viennese milieu. The Pollacks—later known in Vienna as Pollack-Parnegg or Pollack von Parnau—came from Nikolsburg (Mikulov) in Moravia. The Hirsch, Beck, and Glaser families heralded from different regions in Bohemia.

As a commemoration to those who died in concentration camps, an asterisk has been placed after the date of death; the indication of two asterisks denotes a death related to German occupation or forced emigration.

We thank all the researchers who are part of the many Jewish genealogy projects on Geni.com, and especially our families in England, Australia, Canada, France, Vienna, and the United States for their help in compiling this information and granting permission to be published together. ▪

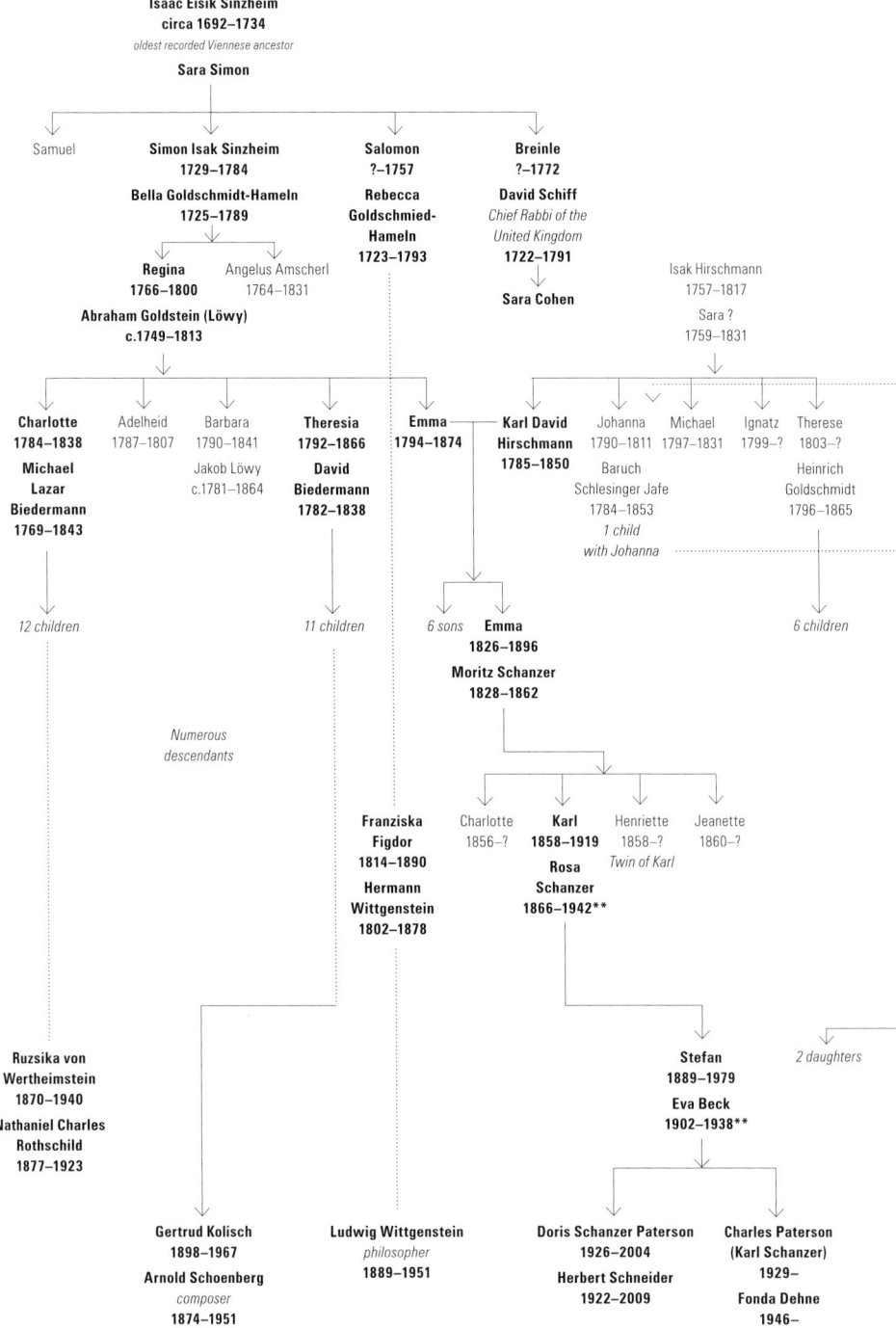

SINZHEIM–HIRSCHMANN–TODESCO

DESCENDANTS

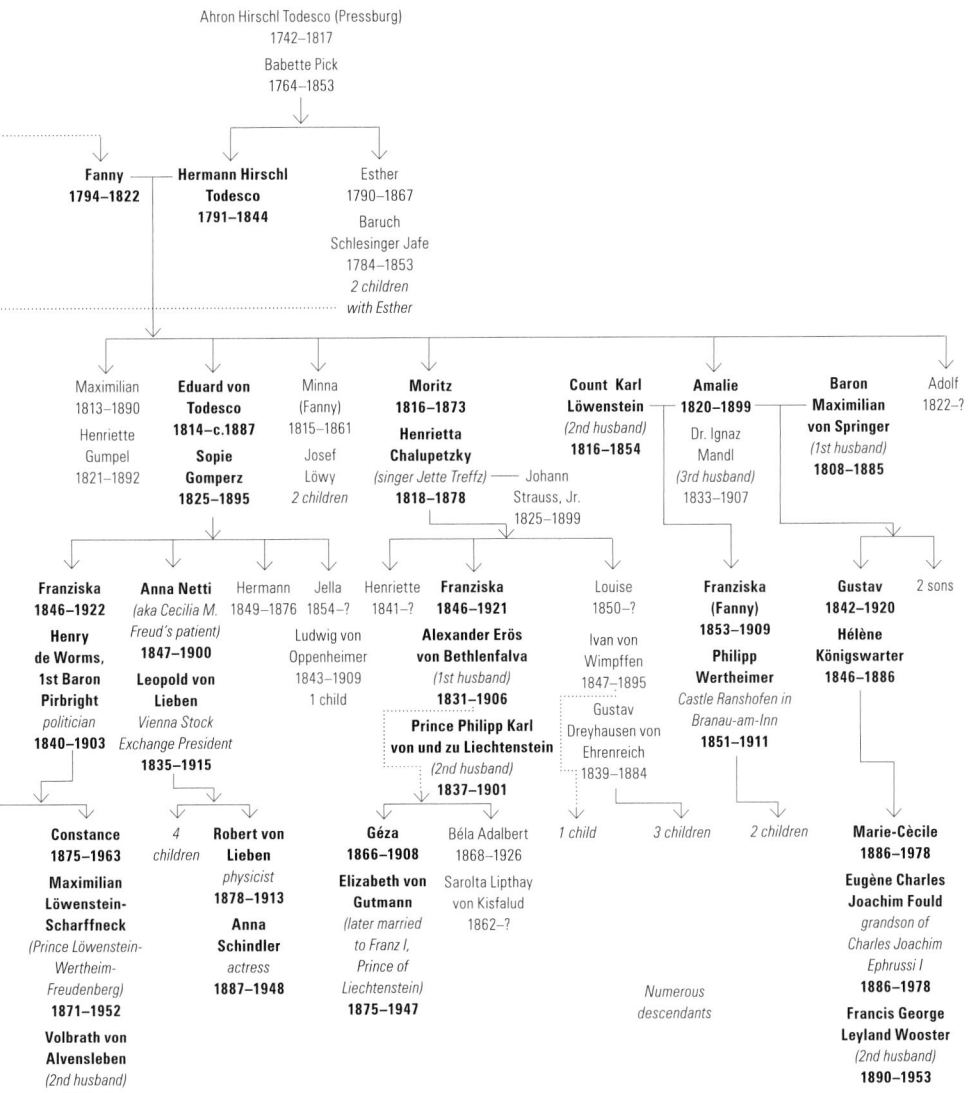

Ahron Hirschl Todesco (Pressburg)
1742–1817

Babette Pick
1764–1853

Fanny — **Hermann Hirschl** — Esther
1794–1822 **Todesco** 1790–1867
1791–1844
Baruch
Schlesinger Jafe
1784–1853
2 children
with Esther

Maximilian — **Eduard von** — Minna — **Moritz** — Count Karl — **Amalie** — **Baron** — Adolf
1813–1890 **Todesco** (Fanny) **1816–1873** Löwenstein **1820–1899** **Maximilian** 1822–?
1814–c.1887 1815–1861 *(2nd husband)* **von Springer**
Henriette **Henrietta** 1816–1854 Dr. Ignaz *(1st husband)*
Gumpel **Sopie** Josef **Chalupetzky** Mandl **1808–1885**
1821–1892 **Gomperz** Löwy *(singer Jette Treffz)* — Johann *(3rd husband)*
1825–1895 *2 children* **1818–1878** Strauss, Jr. 1833–1907
1825–1899

Franziska — **Anna Netti** — Hermann — Jella — Henriette — **Franziska** — Louise — **Franziska** — **Gustav** — 2 sons
1846–1922 *(aka Cecilia M.* 1849–1876 1854–? 1841–? **1846–1921** 1850–? **(Fanny)** **1842–1920**
Henry *Freud's patient)* **1853–1909**
de Worms, **1847–1900** Ludwig von **Alexander Erös** Ivan von **Hélène**
1st Baron Oppenheimer **von Bethlenfalva** Wimpffen **Philipp** **Königswarter**
Pirbright **Leopold von** 1843–1909 *(1st husband)* 1847–1895 **Wertheimer** **1846–1886**
politician **Lieben** 1 child **1831–1906** *Castle Ranshofen in*
1840–1903 *Vienna Stock* Gustav *Branau-am-Inn*
Exchange President **Prince Philipp Karl** Dreyhausen von **1851–1911**
1835–1915 **von und zu Liechtenstein** Ehrenreich
(2nd husband) 1839–1884
1837–1901

Constance — 4 — **Robert von** — **Géza** — Béla Adalbert — 1 child — 3 children — 2 children — **Marie-Cècile**
1875–1963 children **Lieben** **1866–1908** 1868–1926 **1886–1978**
physicist
Maximilian **1878–1913** **Elizabeth von** Sarolta Lipthay **Eugène Charles**
Löwenstein- **Gutmann** von Kisfalud **Joachim Fould**
Scharffneck **Anna** *(later married* 1862–? *grandson of*
(Prince Löwenstein- **Schindler** *to Franz I,* *Charles Joachim*
Wertheim- *actress* *Prince of* *Ephrussi I*
Freudenberg) **1887–1948** *Liechtenstein)* **1886–1978**
1871–1952 **1875–1947**
Numerous **Francis George**
Volbrath von *descendants* **Leyland Wooster**
Alvensleben *(2nd husband)*
(2nd husband) **1890–1953**
1869–?

POLLACK-PARNEGG AND POLLACK VON PARNAU

DESCENDANTS

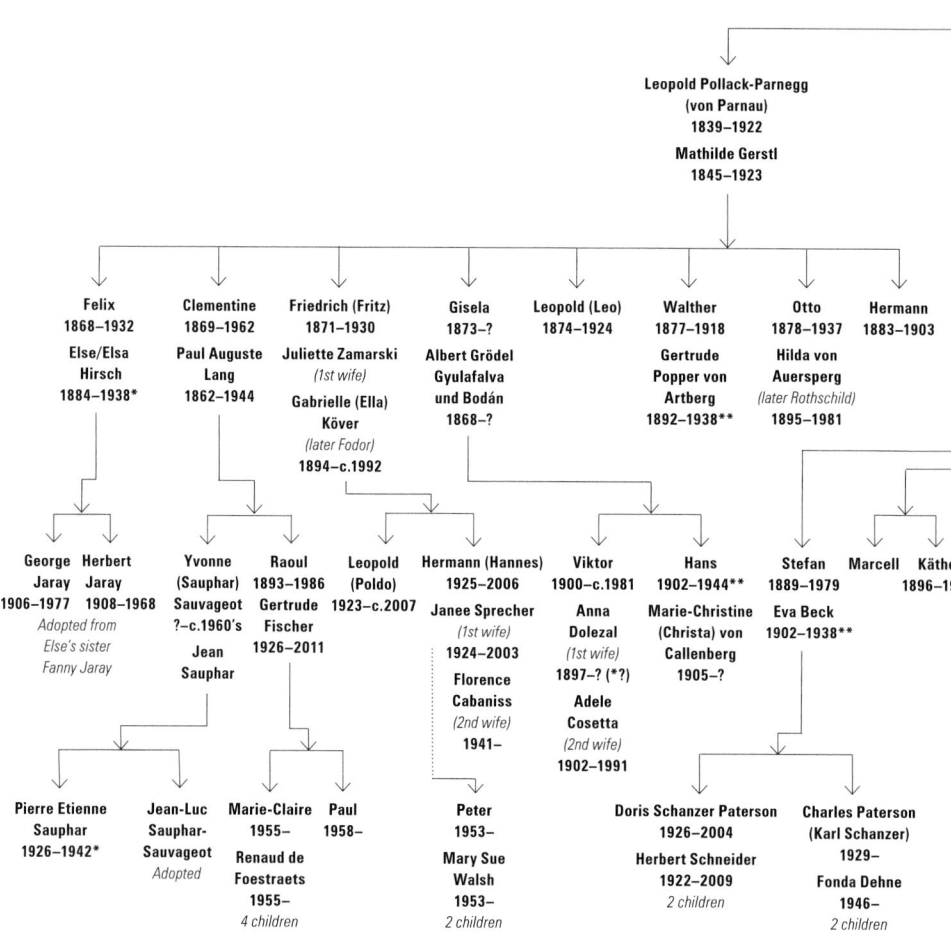

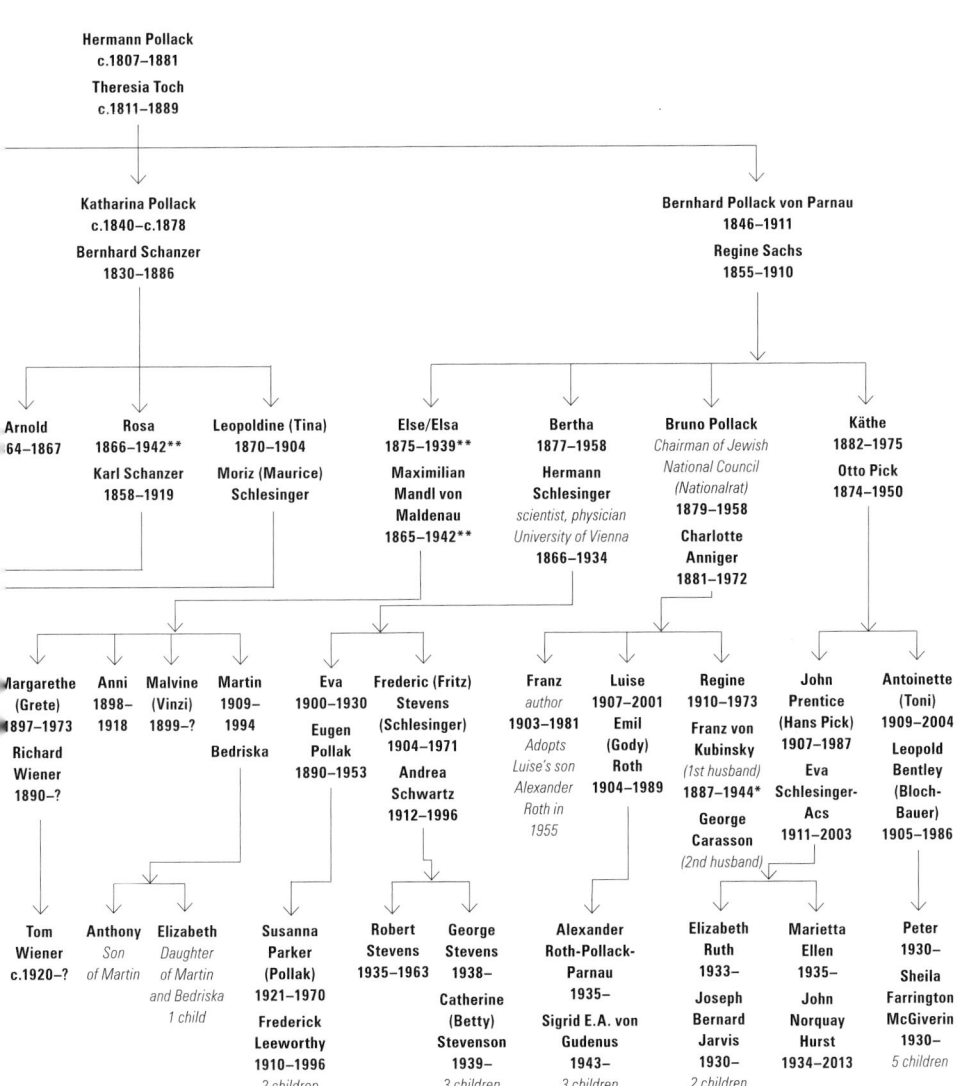

Hermann Pollack
c.1807–1881

Theresia Toch
c.1811–1889

Katharina Pollack
c.1840–c.1878

Bernhard Schanzer
1830–1886

Bernhard Pollack von Parnau
1846–1911

Regine Sachs
1855–1910

Arnold
?64–1867

Rosa
1866–1942**

Karl Schanzer
1858–1919

Leopoldine (Tina)
1870–1904

Moriz (Maurice)
Schlesinger

Else/Elsa
1875–1939**

Maximilian
Mandl von
Maldenau
1865–1942**

Bertha
1877–1958

Hermann
Schlesinger
scientist, physician
University of Vienna
1866–1934

Bruno Pollack
Chairman of Jewish
National Council
(Nationalrat)
1879–1958

Charlotte
Anniger
1881–1972

Käthe
1882–1975

Otto Pick
1874–1950

Margarethe
(Grete)
897–1973

Richard
Wiener
1890–?

Anni
1898–
1918

Malvine
(Vinzi)
1899–?

Martin
1909–
1994

Bedriska

Eva
1900–1930

Eugen
Pollak
1890–1953

Frederic (Fritz)
Stevens
(Schlesinger)
1904–1971

Andrea
Schwartz
1912–1996

Franz
author
1903–1981

Adopts
Luise's son
Alexander
Roth in
1955

Luise
1907–2001

Emil
(Gody)
Roth
1904–1989

Regine
1910–1973

Franz von
Kubinsky
(1st husband)
1887–1944*

George
Carasson
(2nd husband)

John
Prentice
(Hans Pick)
1907–1987

Eva
Schlesinger-
Acs
1911–2003

Antoinette
(Toni)
1909–2004

Leopold
Bentley
(Bloch-
Bauer)
1905–1986

Tom
Wiener
c.1920–?

Anthony
Son
of Martin

Elizabeth
Daughter
of Martin
and Bedriska
1 child

Susanna
Parker
(Pollak)
1921–1970

Frederick
Leeworthy
1910–1996
2 children

Robert
Stevens
1935–1963

George
Stevens
1938–

Catherine
(Betty)
Stevenson
1939–
3 children

Alexander
Roth-Pollack-
Parnau
1935–

Sigrid E.A. von
Gudenus
1943–
3 children

Elizabeth
Ruth
1933–

Joseph
Bernard
Jarvis
1930–
2 children

Marietta
Ellen
1935–

John
Norquay
Hurst
1934–2013

Peter
1930–

Sheila
Farrington
McGiverin
1930–
5 children

KRAUS–HIRSCH–WINTERBURGH DESCENDANTS

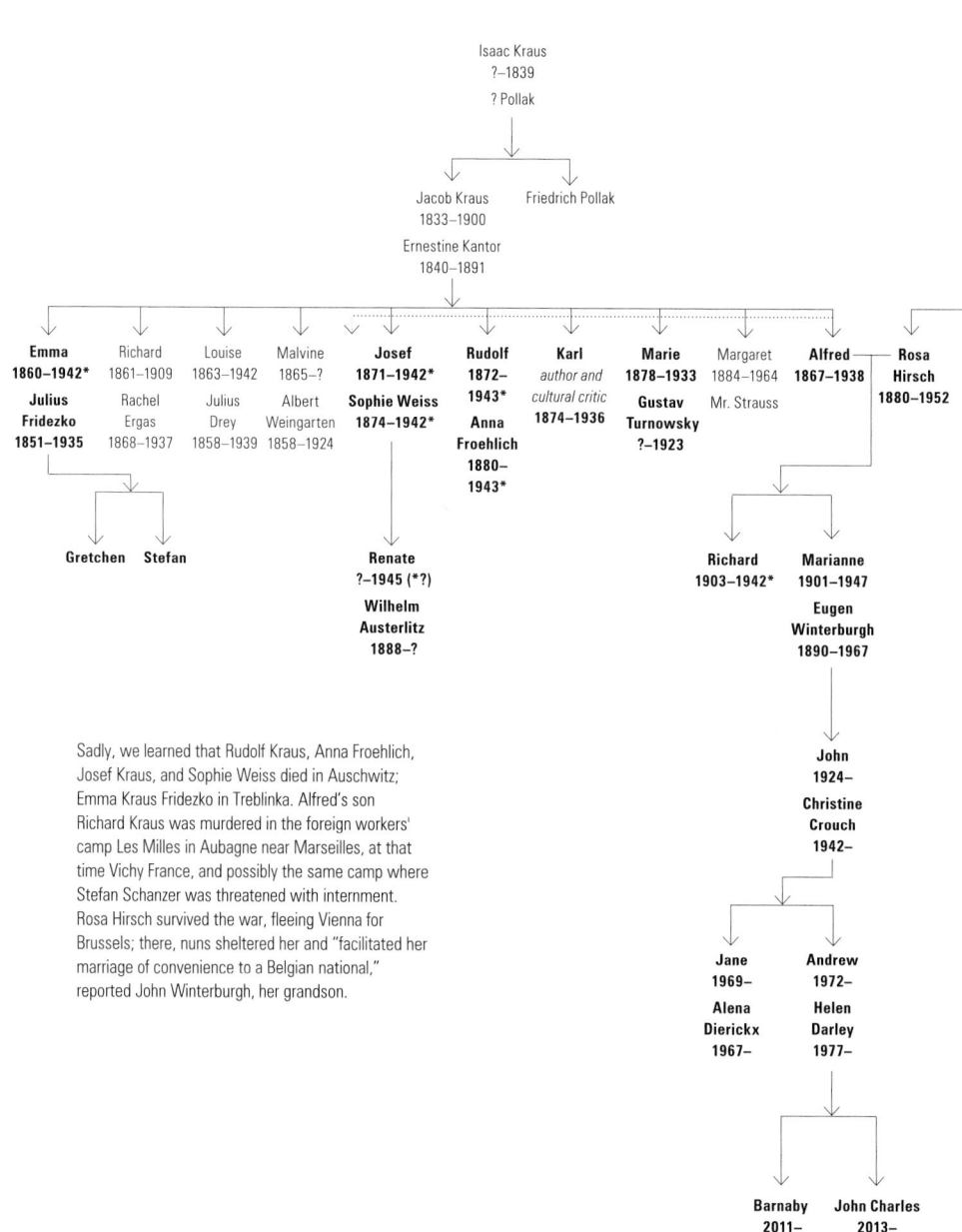

Isaac Kraus
?–1839
? Pollak

Jacob Kraus   Friedrich Pollak
1833–1900
Ernestine Kantor
1840–1891

Emma — Richard — **Louise** — Malvine — **Josef** — **Rudolf** — **Karl** — **Marie** — Margaret — **Alfred** — **Rosa**
1860–1942* — 1861–1909 — 1863–1942 — 1865–? — **1871–1942*** — **1872–** — author and — **1878–1933** — 1884–1964 — **1867–1938** — **Hirsch**
Julius — Rachel — Julius — Albert — **Sophie Weiss** — **1943*** — cultural critic — **Gustav** — Mr. Strauss — — **1880–1952**
Fridezko — Ergas — Drey — Weingarten — **1874–1942*** — **Anna** — **1874–1936** — **Turnowsky**
1851–1935 — 1868–1937 — 1858–1939 — 1858–1924 — — **Froehlich** — — **?–1923**
— — — — — **1880–**
— — — — — **1943***

Gretchen **Stefan**

Renate
?–1945 (*?)
Wilhelm
Austerlitz
1888–?

Richard **Marianne**
1903–1942* **1901–1947**
Eugen
Winterburgh
1890–1967

John
1924–
Christine
Crouch
1942–

Sadly, we learned that Rudolf Kraus, Anna Froehlich, Josef Kraus, and Sophie Weiss died in Auschwitz; Emma Kraus Fridezko in Treblinka. Alfred's son Richard Kraus was murdered in the foreign workers' camp Les Milles in Aubagne near Marseilles, at that time Vichy France, and possibly the same camp where Stefan Schanzer was threatened with internment. Rosa Hirsch survived the war, fleeing Vienna for Brussels; there, nuns sheltered her and "facilitated her marriage of convenience to a Belgian national," reported John Winterburgh, her grandson.

Jane **Andrew**
1969– **1972–**
Alena **Helen**
Dierickx **Darley**
1967– **1977–**

Barnaby **John Charles**
2011– **2013–**

HIRSCH–BECK DESCENDANTS

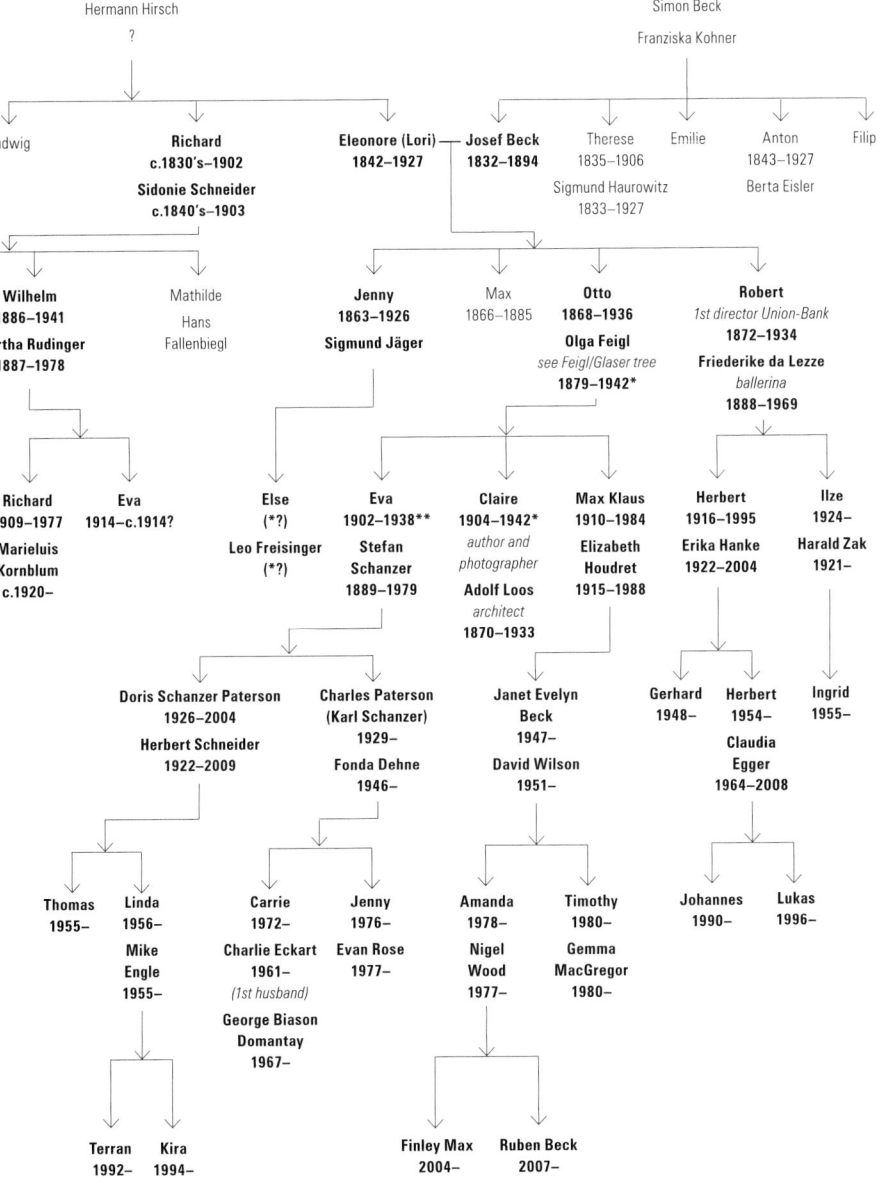

GLASER–FEIGL DESCENDANTS

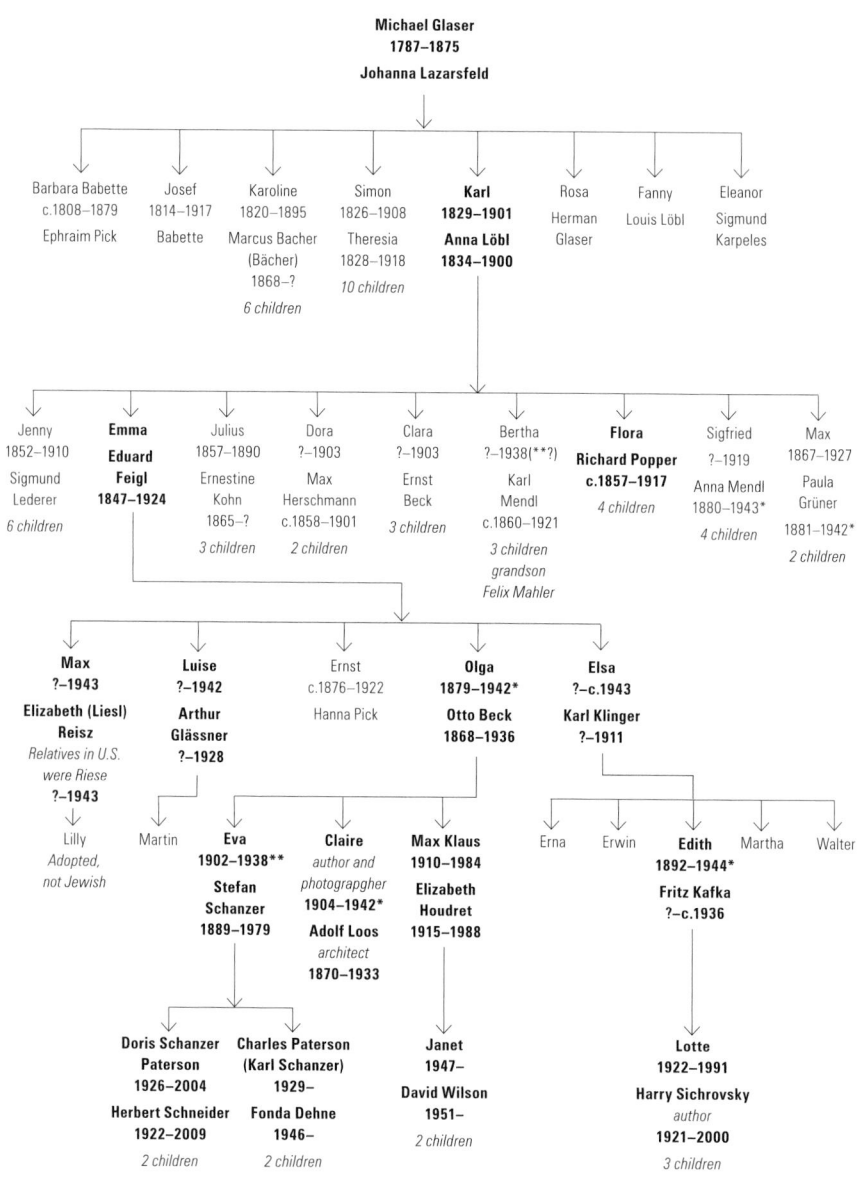

Endnotes

CHAPTER ONE **Foundations**

1. Jenks, William A. *Vienna and the Young Hitler*. New York: Columbia University Press, 1960.

2. Gaugusch, Georg. *Wer einmal war—Das jüdische Großbürgertum Wiens 1800-1938 A-K* [Who was who—The Jewish grand bourgeoisie of Vienna 1800-1938 A-K]. Vienna: Amalthea-Publishing House, 2011. 964.
   "When Maria Theresa came to the throne in 1740, only twelve Jewish families were allowed to live regularly in the capital, though some of these had fairly large households and all were allowed to receive visitors," writes historian William O. McCagg. "By 1780, however, the number of families was fifty-three, of whom twenty-five enjoyed a special 'toleration,' and the total number of regularly resident Jewish individuals had reached five hundred and seventy. In the ten years of Josef's II reign, the number of families went up to about seventy and the registered household members increased to eight hundred and forty." (*A History of Habsburg Jews, 1670-1918*. Bloomington: Indiana University Press, 1989. 48-49.)

3. Bresnitz, Kurt. Interview with Charles and Fonda Paterson. May 1, 2012. Kurt was born in Vienna on February 18, 1919 and has resided in Aspen, Colorado since 1950. Like our family, he is also a descendant of one of the early Habsburg court jewelers.

4. "Jewish Records Indexing—Poland." jewishgen.org. Accessed June 1, 2012.

5. Landaw, Elizabeth. "The Jews of Krakow and Its Surrounding Towns." kehilalinks. jewishgen.org. Accessed March 22, 2012.

6. Wachstein, Bernhard. *Die Statuten der Wiener Kultusgemeinde* [Statutes of the Viennese Jewish Community]. March 18, 1829. S. 12f; Wachstein, Bernhard. *Die Grabschriften des Alten Judenfriedhofes in Wien, Volume II* [Inscriptions in the Old Jewish Cemetery in Vienna, Volume II]. 514. Wachstein was the librarian for the archives at the Israelitische Kultusgemeinde Wien. Seitenstettengasse 4. A-1010 Vienna. Austria. Michael Lazar Biedermann married Charlotte Goldstein, daughter of Abraham Goldstein. (Gaugusch 964.)

7. "Emma Hirschmann married Moriz [Moritz] Schanzer, Kaufmann [merchandiser] on May 16, 1854 in Vienna. He was born February 8, 1828 in Lipnik bei Biala (Galicia) and died October 7, 1862 of tuberculosis in Vienna.... Buried in Unter-Döbling bei Wien.... Son of Jacob Schanzer and Jette Fränkel." (Gaugusch 965.)

8. O'Connor, Anne-Marie. *The Lady in Gold: The Extraordinary Tale of Gustav Klimt's Masterpiece, Portrait of Adele Bloch-Bauer*. New York: Knopf, 2012. 11.

9. Schanzer, Steve. Inscription in *This is Venice* by Miroslav Sasek (born Prague 1916,

died Wettingen, Switzerland 1980). "To Carrie from Granpa Steve, 1975." The book is a first edition. Milan: Fabbristampa, 1961.

10. Kodek, Günter K. *Unsere Bausteine sind die Menschen: Die Mitglieder der Wiener Freimaurerlogen (1869-1938)* [Our Building Blocks are the People: Members of Vienna's Freemason Lodges (1869-1938)]. Vienna: Löker Verlag, 2009. 300.

11. Permanent exhibit. Prague City Museum, Loos' Villa Müller. Nad Hradním vodojemem 14/642, Prague 6—Střešovice. Czech Republic.

12. Quoted in Foster, Hal. *Prosthetic Gods*. Cambridge, Mass: MIT Press, 2004. 72.

13. Loos, Adolf. "Ornament and Crime [1929]." *Adolf Loos Ornament and Crime: Selected Essays*. Adolf Opel, ed. Michael Mitchell, trans. Riverside, Calif.: Ariadne Press, 1998. 39-44.

14. The first English translation of Claire's book did not appear until 2011. *Adolf Loos—A Private Portrait* has interested scholars and researchers looking not only into Loos' history, but also the lives of Jewish families like ours from Pilsen (Beck-Hirsch-Kraus) who helped the architect Loos get his start. (Carrie Paterson, ed. Constance C. Pontasch and Nicholas Saunders, trans. Los Angeles: DoppelHouse Press, 2011.)

15. Domanický, Petr. "People-Clients" *Loos-Pilsen-Connections*. Petr Domanický and Petr Jindra, eds. Pilsen: Západočeská Galerie, 2011.61.

16. Originally called "King's Square," Beneš Platz was dedicated in 1921 in honor of Edvard Beneš, the First Czechoslovak Republic's Minister of Foreign Affairs. The name change reflected the new democratic mood of the country under Tomáš Garrigue Masaryk, its first President, who was elected in 1918. The Nazis renamed the park "Schiller Square" after the German writer Friedrich Schiller in 1940, with the name "Beneš Platz" restored at the end of World War II in 1945. But by 1951 another name change occurred when Communists called it "Náměstí Míru"—"The Square of Peace"—an irony considering the human rights abuses in the country at that time. In 1967 a memorial was placed at the square honoring "fighters and victims of war." (Jindra, Petr. Email to Carrie Paterson. August 17, 2012.)

As for Edvard Beneš, his political history is varied and has had a lasting legacy. During the First World War, Beneš led an independence movement to break from the Austro-Hungarian Empire. In the interwar years he became Foreign Minister, then a member of Parliament, then Prime Minister, and at the end of 1935, succeeded Masaryk as President

Beneš Platz 2, Otto and Olga Beck's apartment, located on middle floor, left side.
Photo taken by their nephew Herbert Beck, Sr., 1935.
COURTESY: HERBERT BECK, JR. AND LUKAS BECK.

of the Czechoslovak Republic. On October 5, 1938 Beneš' government went into exile after making concessions to the Nazis resulting in their occupation of the Sudetenland. ("Edvard Beneš." Encyclopedia Britannica. britannica.com. Accessed July 1, 2012.) As former U.S. Secretary of State Madeleine Albright points out in her memoir *Prague Winter*, history has shown Beneš had no choice but to accept the ultimatum because he had no international support, specifically from France or Britain, who both pressured him to appease Hitler for the sake of peace in Europe. (*Prague Winter: A Personal Story of Remembrance and War, 1937-1948.* New York: Harper, 2012. 90-92.)

When Beneš was reinstated as President of the Czechoslovak Republic in 1945, he instituted an expulsion order for ethnic Germans and their families who were suspected of being Nazi-collaborators. Anyone persecuted by the Nazis or with clear anti-fascist credentials could, however, stay. The decision to punish people collectively for war crimes rather than conduct tribunals to determine individual responsibility is a dark chapter in Czech history. (336-340.) As Czech President Václav Havel asserted in 1992, "The disease of violence and evil spread by Nazism ultimately afflicted even its victims.... We accepted the principle of collective guilt instead of punishing individuals, [and] opted for collective revenge. For decades we were not allowed to admit this, and even now we do so with great reluctance." (Quoted on 339-340.)

Relayed in an article in *The Prague Post,* which we saw on a trip to the Czech Republic in November 2011, evidence of extra-judicial killings of Sudeten Germans are still coming to light and show the terrible aftermath of World War II for people in Central Europe. The politics surrounding the Beneš decrees, which remain in effect today with respect to ownership of property, restitution, and citizenship, remain explosive. (Cunningham, Benjamin and Filip Šenk. "Mass Grave Vandalism Opens Old Wounds: Nationalists again bring post-WWII atrocities into focus." *The Prague Post.* praguepost.com. November 2, 2011. Accessed July 29, 2012.)

17. An Oskar Kokoschka painting used to hang in my grandparents' apartment located on Beneš Platz. Loos and Kokoschka were close friends, and it was common that the architect recommended his architectural clients to buy a painting from Kokoschka's studio. The fate of the painting remains unknown.

CHAPTER TWO **The Werkbundsiedlung 1932-1938**

1. Blau, Eve. *The Architecture of Red Vienna 1919-1934.* Cambridge, Mass.: MIT Press, 1999. 154.
Blau's fifth chapter, "*Grossstadt* and Proletariat: Conceptualizing the Socialist City," details effects of these two very different approaches to socialized housing on the development of Vienna (154-161), and makes connections to the dialectic of power relations established by the large tenement blocks (*Gemeindebauten*) within the fabric of the city, its building codes, and past generations of urban planning (172-173).

2. Blau 154.

3. Historical context for the *Siedlungen* also provided by Otto Kapfinger, who is an architectural scholar, author of many books on architecture, a professor, and has served as curatorial advisor and organizer for several international architectural symposiums and exhibitions. He was an external curatorial consultant for the exhibition "Werkbundsiedlung Wien 1932. Ein Manifest des Neuen Wohnens." [Vienna's Werkbundsiedlung 1932. A Model for New Living.] at the Wien Museum. With Adolf Krischanitz he conducted a renovation of the Wiener Werkbundsiedlung in the early 1980's and in 1985 published a comprehensive book with Krischanitz on this subject, *Die Wiener Werkbundsiedlung:*

Dokumentation Einer Erneuerung [The Vienna Werkbundsiedlung: Documentation of a Renovation] (Vienna: Compress Verlag, 1985).

4. Blau 327.

5. Ibid. 99.

6. Ibid. 98-109.
Demonstrating Loos' interest that workers become autonomous, the "System Loos," a method of wall construction he patented in 1921, could be built easily (109) and reduced cost and materials by not requiring a foundation under front and back external walls of a house. Rather, they were suspended from the lateral walls of attached units, as seen in his 1921 Heuberg settlement houses (107). Loos considered employing this economic solution in his very first Werkbundsiedlung plan for six row houses before the housing authority changed the site and general scheme of the settlement in the spring of 1930. (Kapfinger, Otto. Email to Carrie Paterson. March 14, 2012.)

7. Loos, Adolf. *"Der Tag der Siedler." Neue Freie Presse.* April 3, 1921. 111. From Blau 101.
Blau tells the story that when Loos attended the first movement of the settlers in 1920, "Loos saluted the crowd, '*Hut ab vor den Siedlern!*' ('Hats off to the settlers!'), and called for a new '*Siedlung*-oriented' development plan for Vienna" (98).

8. Krischanitz, Adolf and Otto Kapfinger 128.

9. The garden at our Werkbundsiedlung house was designed by Grete Salzer, who also designed the garden and surroundings at Loos' Khuner house. (Meder, Iris. Email to Carrie Paterson. May 2, 2012.)
Salzer was one of the first women Austrian landscape architects and one of only a few women in the field in Austria during the 1920's-1930's. She also ran a nursery and a coeducational horticulture school in Vienna. In March 1938 after the *Anschluss*, being Jewish, she fled to England. (Krippner, Ulrike and Iris Meder. "Cultivating, Designing, and Teaching: Jewish Women in Modern Viennese Garden Architecture." *Landscape Research*. Vol. 36: 6. 2011. 661.)
In part due to conditions in Austria during World War II, and in part because most of the women working in landscape architecture were Jewish, contributions to the profession of women like Salzer and other female pioneer landscape architects are lost (657-658).

10. Schanzer, Stefan. Letter to Ilse Günther von Hennig. January 1939.

11. Kapfinger, Otto. Email to Carrie Paterson. February 5, 2012.

12. Von Hennig, Oskar. Letter to Stefan Schanzer. May 1, 1956.

13. Kapfinger, Otto. Email to Carrie Paterson. February 5, 2012.

14. "Wien: Sanierung der Werkbundsiedlung beginnt" [Vienna: Restoration of the Werkbundsiedlung begins]. *Die Presse*. diepresse.com. August 18, 2011. Accessed March 22, 2012.

15. In 2010 the World Monuments Fund in New York put the Vienna Werkbundsiedlung on its World Monuments Watch list. ("Wiener Werkbundsiedlung." wmf.org. Accessed July 22, 2012.) The effort spurred on renovation efforts and calls in 2011 for the creation of a full-fledged museum onsite. The latter was specifically promoted by DOCOMOMO Austria, the local chapter of the International Committee for Documentation and Conservation of buildings, sites, and neighborhoods of the Modern Movement. ("A Museum for the Viennese Werkbundsiedlung." docomomo.com. June 2011. Accessed July 22, 2012.)

16. Kapfinger, Otto. Email to Carrie Paterson. January 11, 2012.

17. Kapfinger, Otto. Email to Carrie Paterson. June 19, 2012.

CHAPTER THREE **Weaving**

1. "Stavební vývoj Pollackovy parnické textilní továrny." [Building and development of the Pollack-Parnegg textile factory]. zpravodaj.ceskatrebova.cz/7_04web/Stavebni_vyvoj_HPS.htm. Accessed March 22, 2012.

2. Schanzer, Steve. Inscription in *This is Venice* by Miroslav Sasek.

3. James, Harold. *The Deutsche Bank and the Nazi Economic War Against the Jews.* Cambridge: Cambridge University Press, 2001. 163-164.

4. "Laudon (Hadersdorf)." burgen-austria.com. Accessed July 22, 2012.

5. "Pollack (Polak, Pollak), Leopold Freiherr von Parnegg (österreichischer Adel mit Prädikat [Austrian nobility title] 'von Parnegg' 1903, Freiherr [Baron] 1918)." Deutsche Biographie. deutsche-biographie.de. Accessed February 1, 2012.

6. Ibid.

7. Ibid.

8. Nobility titles were abolished in 1919, but many Viennese continue to use them. (O'Connor 280.) Interestingly, my father's genealogical notes indicate my maternal grandmother Olga Beck's cousin, Ritter (knight) von Lustig, who died in London presumably in exile, "was made a knight by [Franz Josef's grand-nephew] Emperor Karl von Habsburg for weapons Lustig delivered. This was the last document signed before Emperor Karl's abdication."

9. *Hoppe hoppe Reiter*
wenn er fällt, dann schreit er,
fällt er in den Teich,
find't ihn keiner gleich.

Hoppe hoppe Reiter
wenn er fällt, dann schreit er,
fällt er in den Graben,
fressen ihn die Raben.

Hoppe hoppe Reiter
wenn er fällt, dann schreit er,
fällt er in den Sumpf,
dann macht der Reiter... Plumps!

Bump bump goes the rider
he might fall, he cries out,
if he falls in the pond,
no one will find him.

Bump bump goes the rider
he might fall, he cries out,
if he falls in the ditch,
the ravens will devour him.

Bump bump goes the rider
if he falls, he cries out,
if he falls in the swamp,
the rider goes... Plomp!

"Hoppe Hoppe Reiter" with Hannes Parnegg and Carrie, Aspen, 1975.
PHOTO: FONDA PATERSON.

CHAPTER FOUR **Childhood**

1. Blau 401. Pages 4 and 5 of Blau's book also show propaganda posters against "Red Vienna" housing blocks and a photograph of the shell damage done to the Karl-Marx-Hof.

2. I learned of Vienna's 1933-34 political turmoil through two books I read after I retired in 2005, *Night Falls on the City: A Novel about Vienna* by Sarah Gainham (New York: Henry Holt & Company, 1967) and *The Lost City* by John Gunther (New York: Harper & Row, 1964).

3. It was moving for me to read de Waal's masterful family history. After, I was surprised to learn that the Ephrussis are connected to our own family line by marriage in at least four ways that we can trace in the nineteenth century, all through the descendants of the banker Michael Biedermann or through the family trees of Countess Amalie Löwenstein, her son Baron Gustav Springer (Director of the Creditanstalt), and the Wertheimer family. These relations are through marriage to children and grandchildren of Charles Ephrussi the elder (b. Odessa 1792, d. Vienna 1864) through his second marriage to Henriette Halperson. (Geni.com. Accessed June 1, 2012. Database compiled through private family trees and using obituaries published in Vienna's *Neue Freie Presse*.)

4. This information is based on research conducted by Dr. Barbara Sauer in the Austrian National Archives regarding post-*Anschluss* Jewish property registration for houses at the Werkbundsiedlung. ("ÖStA/AdR/6/VA42989 Unbekannt Werkbundsiedlung, Vermögensanmeldung Stefan Schanzer [Haus 46]." Österreichisches Staatsarchiv. Nottendorfergasse 2. A-1030 Vienna, Austria.)

Sauer conducted her research for "Werkbundsiedlung Wien 1932. Ein Manifest des Neuen Wohnens." [Vienna's Werkbundsiedlung 1932. A Model for New Living.] Eva-Maria Orosz and Andreas Nierhaus, Curators. Wien Museum. Karlsplatz. A-1040 Vienna. Austria. September 4, 2012 – January 13, 2013.

5. Wooding, Sharon. "Steve Shanzer." *The First Twenty-Five Years*. Carbondale, Colo.: Colorado Rocky Mountain School twenty-fifth anniversary newsletter, July 1979.

6. The Austrian and the Czechoslovak soldiers were actually more enemies than compatriots. After the dissolution of the Austro-Hungarian Empire, the Russians tried to enlist Czechoslovak POWs by liberating them to fight as an anti-Bolshevik force.

7. In September 1938 Britain and France were unwilling to go to war to defend the Sudetenland against imminent Nazi invasion. To avoid war, the two governments signed an agreement with Germany and Italy that was introduced by Mussolini, and thus the contested area of Czechoslovakia was ceded to Nazi Germany. The intention to avoid war and save lives had the disastrous result of allowing Hitler to expand his territory while at the same time disenfranchising Stalin's Russia from the negotiation process. "The Munich Agreement became a byword for the futility of appeasing expansionist totalitarian states, although it did buy time for the Allies to increase their military preparedness." ("Munich Agreement." The Encyclopedia Britannica. britannica.com. Accessed June 4, 2012.)

8. Quoted in Margolius, Ivan. *Reflections of Prague: Journeys through the 20th Century*. Chichester, West Sussex: Wiley, 2006. 82.

9. "Kristallnacht: The November 1938 Pogroms." United States Holocaust Memorial Museum. ushmm.org. Accessed June 4, 2012.

10. Margolius 83; Albright 13-14.

11. Rothkirchen, Livia. "The Jews of Bohemia and Moravia: 1938-1945." *The Jews of Czechoslovakia*. Philadelphia: Jewish Publication Society, 1984. 9-10.

12. Ibid. 14-15.

13. Ibid. 19.

14. Ibid. 21.

15. Ibid. 13.

16. Ibid. 7.

17. Ibid. 13.

18. Ibid. 21.

19. "Julius Street Flats New Farm." Queensland Heritage Register. epa.qld.gov.au. Accessed January 31, 2012. In 1934 "Julius Street" was dedicated by the Brisbane City Council at the site of the former Rosenfeld Sawmill.

Julius Rosenfeld's granddaughter, Ellie Rosenfeld, contacted me in March 2012 after we searched for her through the Patersons' granddaughter, Jane Wyatt Holmes—a childhood friend of Ellie's. It was a joyous exchange of emails and catch up of families, as she had heard of our stories from her father, Eric. She was brought up in Cairns where both her grandfather Julius Rosenfeld and Charles Paterson had lumber businesses, and from where her father, Eric Rosenfeld, also exported timber from other sawmills to London.

20. Rothkirchen 27.

21. Ibid. 23.

22. Ibid. 42.

23. These collectible stamps were as good as money. Actual currency could not be sent out of Nazi-occupied Czechoslovakia. According to philatelist Lubor Kunc, between March 1939 and February 1940, all letters coming from the Protectorate were examined without public knowledge by the Foreign Money Control (*Devisová kontrola*), which had an office in Pilsen. ("Censorship in Czech Lands 1938-1945." czechphilatelist.tripod.com/cenzury. Circa 2002. Accessed January 15, 2012.) As I still have these stamps, it seems the censor overlooked their potential value.

24. We learned from Edith's grandson Peter Sichrovsky that in 1939 Edith did not want to leave Prague or the grave of her late husband, Fritz Kafka, who had died circa 1936. Because she did not take the opportunity to travel to Australia when she could, sadly she became a victim of the Holocaust. According to testimony submitted to Yad Vashem by her daughter Lotte Kafka Sichrovsky, Edith Kafka died in Auschwitz in 1944.

CHAPTER FIVE **Mutti**

1. The American requirement for an affidavit came from the "LPC clause" ("Likely to become a Public Charge") in the 1917 Immigration Act, which had been reinstated in 1930 by the Hoover administration. A recent revealing book by Erik Larson discusses barriers to American immigration in the 1930's. He writes, "Immigration law also required that applicants provide a police affidavit attesting to their good character, along with duplicate copies of birth certificates and other government records. 'It seems preposterous,' one Jewish memoirist wrote, 'to have to go to your enemy and ask for a character reference.'" (*In the Garden of Beasts: Love, Terror, and an American Family in Hitler's Berlin*. New York: Crown Publishing, Random House, Inc., 2011. 31.)

2. Kwiet, Konrad. "The Ultimate Refuge: Suicide in the Jewish Community under the Nazis." *Leo Baeck Institute Yearbook*. London: Martin Secker & Warburg Ltd., 1984. 148-149.

3. Eva Frodl-Kraft mentions Gertrude Pollack-Parnegg's suicide in *Gefährdetes Erbe: Österreichs Denkmalschutz und Denkmalpflege... [Endangered Heritage: Austria's Monument Conservation...]* (Vienna: Böhlau, 1997. 146). She may have not jumped, however, but been murdered by defenestration.

4. Scholars think that my aunt Claire very well may have influenced the design of the tombstone. (Jindra, Petr. Email to Carrie Paterson. May 18, 2012.) Claire drew something similar in 1931—Adolf Loos' self-specified, architectural *Ehrengrab*, literally his own "grave of honor." (Rukschcio, Burkhardt and Roland L. Schachel. *Adolf Loos—Leben und Werke*. Vienna: Residenz Verlag, 1982. 354.)

5. My cousin Janet Beck Wilson, her husband David, Fonda, and I searched in the Pilsen Jewish cemetery for the family graves when we visited in 1994 but only found a headstone that said Max Beck and Olga Beck—Terezín. As we did not have our grandparents' dates of birth or deaths, we thought perhaps Otto had a different birth name, but if these were our grandparents, who inscribed upon the stone "Terezín"? We took photos, puzzled, but it was as close as we could come. When we visited in November 2011, we walked the same route and realized that in 1994, we had passed our Beck family tombstone with the names of my grandfather Otto and mother Eva, but our eyes had left it unseen.

CHAPTER SIX **A Boy of Ten Is Already Grown**

1. Princess Plump was a character in a hand-made, illustrated book my sister and I created in July 1939 from a story about a very fat princess told to us by Aunt Claire. She helped us make the book as well. It was lost for several years but recently turned up, to our delight. We realized the book was an allegory for my sister about the way a little girl becomes a woman. The princess never listens to anyone and just eats, but soon realizes that if she wants to find her prince and marry she must behave and have self-control. She goes to see a witch who instructs her to spend two years in the forest alone gathering wood and binding fagots. The princess becomes a beautiful woman and soon meets her "prince," a local shepherd.

2. Article from an unknown French newspaper. Summer, 1939. UJM Clarté still exists to this day providing summer camp experiences for children of Freemasons and their friends. The first camp was held in Saint-Nazaire in 1935. ("Espace Colons: L'Histoire." ujmclarte.asso.fr. Accessed July 31, 2012.)

3. An enlightening book review by Holly Case for *The Lost Children: Reconstructing Europe's Families After World War II* (Cambridge, Mass.: Harvard University Press, 2011) details how Czechoslovak pacifist Premysl Pitter set up camps he called "castles" to teach war-orphaned children tolerance. He saw a dire need for these children's socialization because of the violence they experienced and internalized. European children who had experienced World War II became, in the words of the author of the book Tara Zahra, "disturbingly independent, mature, and unchildlike." The review continues, "Most of the remaining survivors of that conflict were children at the time, so children are all we have left of the war.... The danger is ... we will stumble out of the gloom of the past none the wiser, mistaking our obliviousness for innocence restored." (Case, Holly. "Innocents Lost." *The Nation*. October 31, 2011. 32-35.)

4. Blakeney, Michael. *Australia and the Jewish Refugees 1933-1948*. Sydney: Croom Helm, 1985. 147.

5. Ibid. 102.

6. Ibid. 47.

7. Ibid. 122.

8. Ibid. 102.

9. Historically, baptism had been one solution to the intolerance Jews faced in Europe. We know from my father's family history documents that over the generations, often for business or marital reasons, many members of our family converted.

10. Heinrich Kulka was Jewish and emigrated with his family to New Zealand in 1938 with the help of Oskar and Jana Semler. (Domanický 195.) Until his death in 1971, Kulka designed and realized dozens of buildings and is considered one of the progenitors of modern architecture in that country. (Leach, Andrew. "Helmut Einhorn: Dislocation and modern architecture in New Zealand." *Fabrications: The Journal of the Society of Architectural Historians, Australia and New Zealand.* Brisbane: University of Queensland Press, 2004. 59.)

11. Semler, Will. Email to Carrie Paterson. June 7, 2012.
    From Will Semler: "There is a lovely story about [Loos and Heinrich Kulka] whilst in Kulka's home office in Vienna. The two of them were having a marvelous time tearing other people's reputations into smithereens and [making] other jokes. Kulka's wife [Hilda] had her feet on the ground and gave them an ultimatum: 'I am locking this door and will not open it or give you any more coffee or real food until you make some drawings so we can afford to pay for food.' Under the door came a long love poem by [Heinrich] about how he loves her, how he is convinced that she could never do such a thing, etc. She persisted and the drawings appeared below the door."

12. Pearman, Hugh. "In From the Cold." *RIBA Journal.* February 2011. 24.

13. Štěpán Semler eventually escaped military duty in France, went back to England, and joined the Czechoslovak army, but was then thrown out two years later because it was discovered he could only see with one eye. Eventually he made it to Australia to join the family. Will's other brother Oldřich ended up in Switzerland "in the hands of an international crook"—a story, wrote Will, too long to tell. (Semler, Will. Email to Carrie Paterson. February 3, 2012.)

14. Domanický 152.

15. Semler, Will. Email to Carrie Paterson. February 3, 2012.

16. Ibid.

17. Semler, Will. Email to Charles Paterson. February 20, 2012.

18. Semler, Will. Email to Carrie Paterson. February 3, 2012.

19. In Czech, the song is as follows: *"Bejvavalo dobre, Bejvavalo dobre, za nasich mladejch let, bejval svet jako kvet."* (Semler, Will. Email to Carrie Paterson. April 1, 2012.)

CHAPTER SEVEN **My Dear Children**

1. Schanzer, Steve. Interview with Thomas Dana Schneider. June 21/22, 1971. Tape recording. My father noted during the interview that it was the thirty-first anniversary of his escape. Tom is my nephew, my sister Doris' son.
    Additional details that my father remembered about the escape and communicated to us verbally have been incorporated into the story. Where appropriate we have adjusted the language from Tommy Wiener's translation of the text to fit with my father's manner of speech, and in other places, for readability and continuity. From 2006 to 2007, my

niece Linda Schneider Engle transcribed her brother Tom Schneider's recordings of my father's interviews and retraced my father's escape routes in both World Wars. Linda's site research has contributed to the map we have been able to assemble of my father's escape. Many town names are duplicated in France; with Linda's help we have been able to distinguish the regions and thus the exact villages through which my father passed.

2. "Aryans are the so-called selected people of the Germans. And the French had a very good proverb. *Il était un bon arien.—Un 'bon á rien.'* A good for nothing." (Schanzer, Steve. Interview with Thomas Dana Schneider. June 21/22, 1971.)

3. Ibid.

CHAPTER EIGHT **Prisoners Don't Ride Bicycles**

1. Raoul Lang was the son of my father's aunt Clementine and Paul Lang, who owned Les Fils d'Emanuel Lang Co. (Emanuel Lang and Sons), a textile company that had formed a partnership with the Viennese branch of Hermann Pollack's Söhne through Paul's marriage to Clementine.

2. Schanzer, Steve. Interview with Thomas Dana Schneider. June 21/22, 1971.

3. I have some additional insight into my father's despondence—the date on the newspaper was the second anniversary of my mother's death. In 1976 he told my sister that our mother's last letter to him had been left in Audierne with the rest of his papers as he jumped over the wall of the internment camp. Now that I think about it, my sister and I must have recognized the date on the newspaper in this story as well. Perhaps he was trying to communicate to us the depth of this sorrow, along with the gravity of his situation. But maybe it was also the thought of her, and of us, that kept him going.

CHAPTER NINE **Sauf Conduit**

1. The Siberian beds my father refers to consisted of wooden slats braced between two sets of planks that were elevated from the floor on bricks or stone blocks. This made the bed springy when a blanket or mattress was placed on it because it would give slightly under a person's weight. My father learned how to construct these as a POW in Siberia during the First World War and later taught me how to build them. At the Siberian prison camp where men were sleeping on straw mats on cold concrete floors, the man who first figured out how to make these beds must have become a hero.

2. The d'Aussys were relatives of my father's friend, whose first name I do not know. He was a Parisian movie theater owner and fellow Mason who used to let my sister and me in to see the pictures.

3. This man may have been related to our Jewish friends and neighbors in Vienna, the Österreichers, who emigrated to Seattle, Washington a few years later.

4. My father emphasized the danger of the Sécreté, the secret police. (Schanzer, Steve. Interview with Thomas Dana Schneider. June 21/22, 1971.)

5. Ibid.

6. I am amused that my father listened to the official's advice but went another way. He was like that even through his later years, always courteous but of a singular mind. His unconventional thinking was illustrated to me when he spoke about bureaucrats in Vienna. He told me that he would go into a door that had a sign on it "*Eintrag Streng*

Verboten" [Entrance Strictly Forbidden] to find the person he was looking for. One also has to consider his survival instincts: in Marseilles at that time, according to my father's interview with my nephew Tom Schneider, "It was very difficult just to move around because the French police collaborated with the Germans and arrested every refugee in sight, even their own people, and put them in internment camps."

7. My father always said that in Floridsdorf, where one Hermann Pollack's Söhne branch was located, a specific mineral content in the water resulted in textiles that could be dyed a particular red very desirable for the Turkish fez, such that H.P.S. became a major supplier of the felt.

8. The old tile factory at Les Milles, outside of Aix-en-Provence, was being used as a transit camp where several thousand people were interned. Many were later deported from Les Milles to concentration camps such as Auschwitz. Indeed, in his interview with my nephew Tom Schneider, he emphasizes, "*Ja,* it would have meant concentration camp."

9. The Hospice de France is about five miles south of Luchon, an assemblage of buildings formerly part of a trading route in medieval times, where Hannibal is thought to have crossed the Port (Pass) de Vénasque (Benasque in Spain) with his elephants. (Baedeker, Karl. *Southern France Including Corsica.* London: Leipsic, 1902. 175.)

To get to the Hospice, my father hiked from about 1900 feet elevation to 4155 feet. From there it is approximately three miles to the Port de Vénasque at 7917 feet above sea level. When one sees a saddle like this between two mountains, it is usually the case that there will be an easy way to get to the other side.

10. Should my father have remained with the Langs, he would have had to go into hiding, just as they did. Paul and Clementine's granddaughter, Marie-Claire de Foestraets, told me that they were in hiding throughout the war, once even in a surgery ward.

11. "On the way I met the same *gendarme* who held me up six miles from the frontier [in Cierp]. And we greeted each other, very friendly, and he said, 'Oh, you make some [hiking] trips in the mountains.' I said, 'Yes, yes.'—'Very nice,' [he replied.]" (Schanzer, Steve. Interview with Thomas Dana Schneider. June 21/22, 1971.)

12. *Gendarmes* were checking everyone's papers at the railroad station. On the train my father made friends with a young woman who had two children and was also traveling through Perpignan. He told me much later that he offered to carry one of the children in his arms as she showed her passport, thus passing as her husband. He edited this experience out of his letter to us. It is painfully ironic that after losing his children he would have to adopt a family as a disguise.

CHAPTER TEN **Australia**

No endnotes.

CHAPTER ELEVEN **War Cry**

1. In this episode I seem to have regressed to German in that all my nouns are capitalized. In fact, I still do this sometimes, a slight trace that all my good early schooling in my native language did not go to waste!

2. In fact we were at Place de la République and our hotel was just south of us.

CHAPTER TWELVE **Resurfacing**

1. "The [U.S.] Labor Department's solicitor, Charles E. Wyzanski, discovered in 1933 that consuls had been given informal oral instruction to limit the number of immigration visas they approved to 10 percent of the total allowed by each nation's quota." (Larson 31-32.)

2. One little known fact is that Ilse Günther von Hennig worked on the interior details and drawings for the apartment on behalf of Adolf Loos in the late 1920's—her first solo responsibility under the architect, according to an interview she did in the 1980's. Loos apparently assigned Ilse the job because she and Richard had known each other growing up together in Pilsen. In the interview Ilse also recounted how she met Loos through Claire. The two Pilsen friends reunited in Vienna sometime around 1928, and Claire brought Ilse to one of Loos' famous lunches at his house, where friends, artists, architects, members of Viennese high society, and Loos' various journeyman would all convene. According to Ilse, Loos invited her to work with him, but she told Loos that she had already applied to work for the Viennese architect Josef Frank (progenitor of the Werkbundsiedlung); Loos, being nearly deaf, did not hear what Ilse said and told her she could start working for him forthwith. And she did. ("Ilse von Hennig," interview with editor Burkhardt Rukschcio. *Der Künstlerkreis um Adolf Loos. Aufbruch zur Jahrhundertwende* [The Artist Circle of Adolf Loos at the Turn of the Century]. Sonderheft 2. Vienna: Parnass Verlag, 1985. 22-23.)

3. Richard Hirsch's bedroom interior remained unknown to architectural historians until 2012. (V Plzni objevili nové interiéry architekta Aldolfa Loose [A new interior by architect Adolf Loos is discovered in Pilsen]. March 3, 2012. Česká televize [Czech TV], ceskatelevize.cz. Accessed May 15, 2012.)

4. We visited Richard Hirsch's apartment in 2011 and saw the meticulous care Vladimír Lekeš took in the apartment's recreation and the restoration of the surviving furnishings. His consultant on the project was Burkhardt Rukschcio, a Loos scholar who was the curator for architectural drawings at the Albertina in Vienna from 1968-1974. To make the interior of Richard Hirsch's apartment complete, Lekeš bought original furniture designed by Loos: a chair and table by Friedrich Otto Schmidt (1900 and 1912), a table and chairs from another Loos-designed apartment in Vienna (for Valentin Rosenfeld, 1912, which Sigmund Freud would sit on when visiting), and a wall clock from the Strasser house (1918-1919). (Margolius, Ivan. "Journey to the Interior: Hidden Treasures." Building Design. March 4, 2011.) A wardrobe designed by Loos for Leschka and Co. on Spiegelgasse in Vienna (1923) and one of the first sets of Loos' Lobmeyr drinking glasses (1931), whose first owner was architect and Loos pupil Paul Engelmann, completes the collection.

CHAPTER THIRTEEN **The Goldens**

1. Even in the Australian outback, the name of the Golden's cattle station "Spion Kop" was an echo of war. The Battle of Spion Kop was fought for two days, January 23-24, 1900 on the Tugela River in South Africa. It was possibly one of the bloodiest battles of the Anglo-Boer Wars, which lasted three years. At Spion Kop, Winston Churchill was a twenty-three year-old war correspondent, and Mahatma Ghandi served as a stretcher-bearer with the Indian Ambulance Corps. ("Boers, Brits, and Battlefields." fodors.com; spioncop.co.za. Both Accessed August 6, 2012.)

2. *The Australian Women's Weekly.* December 29, 1971.

CHAPTER FOURTEEN **When War Is Over**

1. Elkins, James R. "Strangers to Us All—Lawyers and Poetry: Abraham Felt." mywebwvnet. edu. Accessed July 20, 2012.

Abraham Felt (1881-1957) was born in New Jersey. He gave a radio address in 1944 for the 5th War Loan Bond Drive that was printed later that year as a small leaflet titled "They Shall Remember Us." Among his books of poetry is *Poetic Gems* (New York: Humanitas Lodge No. 123 F. & A.M., 1948). When we acquired a copy from a rare books store, we were interested to find the following on page 62, entitled "Tomorrow May Be Too Late."

Whenever you have something good to do
Please don't ever let it wait
The one who's in need may be counting on you
And tomorrow might be too late.

The best of intentions oftimes go astray.
Good wishes and thoughts by themselves don't avail
Unless followed by actions they soon fade away.
Yes, they're "Gone With The Wind" swept away with the gale.

So why not get going—there's so much to do
Remember delays often bring on ill fate
There's somebody watching and waiting for you.
Don't wait for tomorrow—it may be too late.

2. I have learned more about Charles Raff Paterson's family only recently. Charles came from a family of ten children, two of whom died in infancy. His father, William Hunter Paterson, emigrated from Glasgow, Scotland in 1862. ("Family of William Hunter Paterson and Edith Jeffery." ancestry.com. Accessed August 1, 2012.)

A book by Ross Fitzgerald called *The People's Champion* (Brisbane: University of Queensland Press, 1997) takes up the subject of Charles Paterson's next youngest brother Fred, who was Australia's only Communist Party member of Parliament, serving from 1944 to 1950. Fred had been a lawyer and a theology student. As is obvious from the book, the brothers were both brilliant scholars with Fred gaining a Rhodes scholarship (16-17). It seems they drifted apart about the time of my stay with the family, and the Patersons never spoke about him at our house. In Fitzgerald's book I read that Fred Paterson had been greatly offended when his brother Charles attacked Communism in a public broadcast on the radio (141). Although the brothers may not have seen it this way at the time, it seems the family was split along a hairline about how to deal with fascism. Charles' effort, witnessed in the adoption of my sister and me, was philanthropic and resulted from his business connections while Fred's was idealistic and labor-oriented, which took him into public office.

CHAPTER FIFTEEN **To America**

1. In 1999, my sister and I, together with our spouses, went on a cruise of the Greek Isles. We met our cousin Janet Beck Wilson in Istanbul and visited my father's favorite hotel, the Pera Palais, the first European style luxury hotel in Istanbul, which was built in 1892 to host the passengers of the *Orient Express*. The menu still offered Viennese fare. The five of us ate Wiener Schnitzel, creamed spinach, and crepes—all my father's favorites. As we finished the meal, the orchestra began to play a Strauss waltz.

At Tuckerman's Ravine, Mt. Washington,
New Hampshire, 1950.

Wedding photo of Doris Schanzer Paterson
and Herbert Schneider, 1953.

CHAPTER SIXTEEN **Finding Home**

1. Doris met Herb Schneider in 1951 at a wedding through the same lovely woman who introduced my parents to each other years before, Hilde (Altschul) Mellion, at that time living in New York. Herb was an electrical engineer for Bell Labs. By the time he retired in 1988 he had twenty-six patents in his name and helped create, among other technology, transistor computers. For many years after the war, Herb supported his uncle Pali, returning the lifesaving gesture made for his school sponsorship in Istanbul from 1938-1940. Most of Herb's family survived World War II; two exceptions are his aunt Dora Schneider and grandmother Rosa Schneider, whose fates he was never able to confirm. Herb was drafted into the U.S. Army in 1943. He helped set up communications for the D-Day invasion of June 6, 1944 and then followed General Patton's swift assault from Normandy toward Czechoslovakia.

For much of his life, Herb volunteered on the ski patrol at Eldora Mountain near his home in Boulder, Colorado, working there until age eighty-four. (My sister Doris was also on the patrol, for thirty years.) He was also a voracious reader of politics and philosophy. After he passed away on May 6, 2009, at the age of eighty-six, a long quote by Albert Einstein was found in his wallet. This quote he had always carried with him: "... Many times a day I realize how much my own outer and inner life is built upon the labors of my fellow men, both living and dead, and how earnestly I must exert myself in order to give in return as much as I have received." ("Herbert Anton Schneider, Obituary." *Denver Post*. August 2, 2009; Schneider, Herbert. "A Fortunate Life." Memoir dictated to Linda R. Schneider Engle. November 7, 2006; Schneider, Thomas Dana. "Herb Schneider Memorial." August 8, 2009. www.fred.net/tds/. Accessed July 15, 2012.)

2. Anton (Toni) Matt (1920-1989) was a top racer from St. Anton, Austria who was able to leave Nazi-occupied Austria with an invitation from legendary ski instructor Hannes Schneider. Recently arrived in the United States, Schneider set up a ski school in North Conway, New Hampshire and wanted an eminent racer on his staff. Matt skied his famous Tuckerman's run in April 1939 during a ski race called the "Inferno," breaking the previous record in half with his run that included a straight descent down the one thousand foot headwall. (*Legacy: Austria's Influence on American Skiing—Hannes Schneider and His Disciples*. Dir. Ian Scully. 2006. Film.)

Toni Matt is also part of one of my own survival stories in a way. While I was still at City College on my return to New York studying civil engineering, some friends and I decided to ski Tuckerman's Ravine. It was in the spring of 1950. We hiked a beautiful trail and then proceeded up the more difficult climb, ascending the hard pack with our skis. As I reached the top of the ravine, I experienced sharp stomach pains, but somehow managed to ski the steep pitch down. I could appreciate how Toni Matt felt when he had to schuss the entire bowl. It was hair-raising. Somehow, I got myself back to New York and to the hospital with acute appendicitis. I had my appendix removed just in time.

3. On tips, I noted I made $2 to $7.50, sometimes as much as fifty cents per suitcase.

4. "F.I.S." came from the French, "*Fédération Internationale de Ski.*"

5. Walter Paepcke (1896-1960) was an industrialist, entrepreneur, and philanthropist. He was president of the Container Corporation of America in Chicago, which manufactured corrugated cardboard boxes. His wife Elizabeth (1902-1994) first visited Aspen in 1939 after the pipes froze at their ranch in Perry Park, Colorado, and she brought her guests for a ski trip. Aspen was still a sleepy former silver mining town following the collapse of silver currency and the panic of 1893 when the United States converted to the gold standard.

Walter and Elizabeth Paepcke promoted Aspen's revival in 1949 by creating the Goethe Bicentennial Convocation and Music Festival, which grew into the Aspen Music Festival and School. Walter Paepcke also founded the Aspen Institute for Humanistic Studies and the Aspen Skiing Corporation in the early 1950's. Elizabeth Paepcke founded the Aspen Center for Environmental Studies in 1969. The Paepckes are considered two of the pillars of modern Aspen.

CHAPTER SEVENTEEN **Summer of '49**

1. Herbert Kellman is now Professor Emeritus of Music and Medieval Studies and Director of the Renaissance Archives at the School of Music, University of Illinois at Urbana-Champaign. I reconnected with him after sixty years in 2012. He was still working with graduate students at age eighty-one. Herbert wrote me, "I used to hear about you from time to time from Madeline (Mahr) Day, who told me that you were a very successful hotelier. Bravo! What a place [Aspen] became—not just the old ski-bum and summer festival village, where we climbed in and out of the student-dorm windows, you carpentered for a film company, and I cleaned windows for Gary Cooper." (Kellman, Herbert. Email to Charles Paterson. March 28, 2012.)

Kellman's accomplishments during his tenure as professor at the University of Illinois include the founding of the Musicological Archives for Renaissance Manuscript Studies at the University Library in 1968 with Charles Hamm. Kellman also edited the five-volume *Census-Catalogue of Manuscript Sources of Polyphonic Music, 1400-1550* (Rome: American Institute of Musicology, 1979-1988). A scholar and writer with an impressive career, Kellman has inspired many students and colleagues and was honored with the publication of *Essays on Music and Culture in Honor of Herbert Kellman* by Barbara Haggh (Turnhout, Belgium: Brepols, 2001). ("Musicological Archive for Renaissance Manuscript Studies." library.illinois.edu. Accessed June 20, 2012; Oettinger. Rebecca Wagner. Book review for *Essays on Music and Culture of Herbert Kellman. The Sixteenth Century Journal.* Vol. 35: 3. Fall 2004. 900-902.)

2. Friedl Pfeifer (1911-1995) was born in St. Anton, the Arlberg region of Austria, where he learned and first taught skiing. In 1936, he won the Arlberg-Kandahar downhill and was presented the Kandahar Cup by Hannes Schneider. Observing the race, New Yorker Alice Kaier hired him as the new Olympic coach for her 'Red Stocking Girls,' the U.S. Women's Ski Team. (Pfeifer, Friedl. *Nice Goin'—My Life on Skis.* Missoula, Mont.: Pictoral Histories Publishing Co., 1994. 51-52.) In 1936 he also won the Hahnenkamm ski race in

Kitzbühel. The course is still regarded as the steepest and most difficult on the World Cup circuit.

According to an interview Friedl did on July 21, 1994 with ski country historian Annie Gilbert, he left Austria two days after the *Anschluss* of 1938. (cdp.coalliance.org. Accessed June 21, 2012.) He had an offer to start Charlotte's Pass ski school on Kosciusco, the highest mountain in Australia, but he came shortly after to the United States whereupon he was invited by Kaier to coach the U.S. Women at Sun Valley, Idaho; he also became the director of the ski school at Sun Valley at the age of twenty-eight. (Pfeifer 58-60, 70.) Following a September 1945 meeting with the Paepckes at their ranch in Perry Park near Larkspur, Colorado—where they agreed skiing was a key component of Aspen's vitality— Pfeifer started the first Aspen Ski School in 1945 with two other co-directors (129), Percy Rideout (1918–2013) and Johnny Litchfield (1917–2011).

3. Paterson, Charles and Peter Pfeifer. Interviews with Marie-Claire Messinger. *The Sound of Skiing*. Österreichischer Rundfunk. February 13, 2010. Radio broadcast. Marie-Claire Messinger is Friedl Pfeifer's granddaughter.

CHAPTER EIGHTEEN **Manna from Heaven**

1. Fred R. Lazarus, Jr. (1884-1973) was the founder and owner of the largest department store chain in the United States—Federated Department Stores, which eventually became Macy's. In 1939 he convinced President Franklin Delano Roosevelt to move Thanksgiving from the fourth Thursday in November a week earlier in order to make the Christmas shopping period longer. ("Fred Lazarus Jr." en.wikipedia.org. Accessed May 14, 2012.)

2. My father's job with Fordom Trading Company drew upon his experience working as a representative of H.P.S. in the 1920's and as the general manager of the Vienna branch in the 1930's.

In 1947 he put forward an import business proposition to Otto Pick, that they revive H.P.S. as a textile firm using Austrian cotton mills owned by Mr. Pick in Wiener Neustadt when the country was no longer occupied by foreign armies, and the area was released from the Russian Zone. But the factory had been destroyed and was operating only with salvaged machinery. An investment back into Austria, especially with the unstable political climate, seemed too big a risk. It is unfortunate, as my father's network of textile representatives included people in Argentina, Uruguay, Chile, South Africa, Australia, Philippines, and the Dutch West Indies. Fordom Trading Company was prepared to set up a textile division if my father could bring everyone back together. But in the end, it was better to let it go.

My father intended to buy the trademark from Christa Grödel, the wife of my father's cousin Baron Hans Grödel. By 1947 the company had changed names and was then a much smaller operation. Very sadly, Hans Grödel had committed suicide in Canada at the end of February 1945 as an émigré dispossessed of his ownership of H.P.S. branches in Germany and Austria as well as all incorporated portions of the company. (Pick, Otto. Letter to Stefan Schanzer. March 8, 1945.) We learned Hans had suffered a nervous breakdown after he was misinformed about the viability of his newly acquired Canadian sawmill operation, where he had invested all his remaining funds left from Europe. In the summer of 2012 we learned that the responsibility for the destruction of the Jewish-owned-and-operated H.P.S. enterprise was the focus of ongoing litigation against the Austrian and Swiss banks that perpetrated and abetted Nazi crimes. (Claims Resolution Tribunal In Holocaust Victims Assets Litigation, Case No. CV96-4849. June 6, 2011. crt-ii.org. Accessed August 15, 2012.)

CHAPTER NINETEEN **Dispossession**

1. Gottwaldt, Alfred and Diana Schulle. *Die "Judendeportationen" aus dem Deutschen Reich 1941-1945* [Deportation of Jews from the German Reich 1941-1945]. Wiesbaden: Marix Verlag, 2005. 132, 256.

Claire was sent on a four-day transport to Riga on January 15, 1942. It was mid-winter, and there was no water, food, or heat on the journey. Details about the ultimate fates of people on Claire and Olga's transports are documented in Gottwaldt and Schulle's book.

2. Ivan Margolius is an author and architeture historian who was born in Prague. Many of his family members were also killed in the Holocaust. Ivan was researching the fate of his paternal grandparents, Vítězslav and Berta Margolius, when he found the name "Klara Loosova" (Claire Loos) in the *Terezín Memorial Book*, published in 1995 (Karny, Miroslav, ed. *Terezinska pametni kniha*. Prague: Melantrich). It is truly serendipitous to have met Ivan, even though as a result of such sad circumstances. He was coincidentally working on a paper about Adolf Loos, and when he saw Claire's name, he traced Claire back to my cousin Janet to learn more about Loos' third wife. This contact was the beginning of our family's continuing friendship with him.

3. Lederer, Zedenek. "Terezín." *The Jews of Czechoslovakia*. Philadelphia: Jewish Publication Society, 1984. 110.

4. Lexa, John G. "Anti-Jewish Laws and Regulations in the Protectorate of Bohemia and Moravia." *The Jews of Czechoslovakia*. Philadelphia: Jewish Publication Society, 1984. 80.

5. Lederer 104.

6. Rothkirchen 32-33.

7. Lederer 114, 120.

8. Permanent exhibit. Los Angeles Museum of the Holocaust. 100 The Grove Drive. Los Angeles, CA. 90036. United States; Rothkirchen 50-60.

9. The murderous campaign against the Jews of Czechoslovakia was primarily the result of one man's ambition. Reinhard Heydrich was newly appointed in September 1941 as the acting Reich Protector of the occupied territories and was quickly proving to be one of Hitler's most efficient and ruthless right-hand men, poised to be Hitler's eventual successor. Within a year of Heydrich's appointment to head the Nazi dictatorship of Bohemia and Moravia, things drastically changed in the country. (Roberts, Andrew. *The Storm of War: A New History of the Second World War*. Allen Lane: London, 2009. 242-243.)

A leading director of the pogroms of *Kristallnacht* and killing methods in Nazi death camps, Heydrich would have come close to completing the task he promised Hitler—to remake Prague into one of the great future Aryan cities, modeled on Berlin—were it not for an assassination attempt on his life May 27, 1942 by Czechoslovak resistance fighters. (Ibid.; Margolius 89.)

The government in exile of Edvard Beneš supported these actions. Beneš spoke in London shortly before the attack on Heydrich: "A proof of strength even in our own country—rebellion, open action, acts of sabotage, and demonstrations, may be desirable or necessary. On the international plane, action of this kind would contribute to the preservation of a nation itself, even if it had to be paid for by a great many sacrifices." (Albright 215-219.)

Heydrich—the man who renamed after himself Pilsen's Klatovy Avenue (Domanický 231), the beautiful tree lined boulevard on which my grandparents' first Loos apartment faced—died of a painful septicemia within a week of the attempt on his life. His death did not stop the Nazis' plans for genocide, but in fact, there were atrocious retributive acts— thousands in concentration camps sent to their deaths and terrors committed against the Czech people: targeting killings, massacres, and the razing of the entire towns of Lidice and Ležáky. (Roberts 242-243; Margolius 90.)

10. Lederer 120.

11. Terezín was the setting for Nazi propaganda films including *Theresienstadt: ein Dokumentarfilm aus dem Juedischen Siedlungsgebiet* [Theresienstadt: a documentary film about the Jewish settlement], which was filmed most likely in 1943. The director, Kurt Gerron, was an inmate, as were virtually all actors, writers, and many of the musicians. The ghetto had been set up as a "model Jewish settlement" by the end of 1942 for Nazis to feign to humanitarian agencies like the International Red Cross that Jews were being well treated. But this was far from the truth. Behind the film cameras, people were starving, sick, and untreated for illness. No guards or suffering were shown. ("Nazi propaganda film about Theresienstadt/Terezín." ushmm.org. Accessed August 1, 2012.)

The leader of several artists who managed in secret to document the true realities of the camp was artist Fritta (Fritz) Taussig, aka. Bedřich Fritta, the famous cartoonist and graphic artist from Prague. He was the set designer for the above-mentioned film, which only exists in fragments, as do other films shot earlier. After Taussig's work was discovered he and others were sent to Auschwitz. (Strusková, Eva. "Ghetto *Theresienstadt 1942*: The Message of the Film Fragments." *Journal of Film Preservation*. Vol. 79/80. 2009. 65.)

Film fragments from 1942 hint at collaborations by inmates with the filmmakers. The fragments reveal efforts of resistance within the camp as some images were shot quickly and, it is supposed, excised in secret by Jewish workers who intended to smuggle them out of the camp at great personal risk. One shot shows Taussig/Fritta smiling at the camera suggesting he recognizes and is cooperating with the person behind it. (74-77.)

12. Lederer 123.

13. "Theresienstadt: Spiritual Resistance and Historical Context." ushmm.org. Accessed January 16, 2012.

14. Makarova, Elena. *Friedl Dicker-Brandeis Vienna 1898-Auschwitz 1944: The Artist Who Inspired the Children's Drawings of Terezín*. Tallfellow/Every Picture Press: Los Angeles, 1999. 29.

15. On our visit in 1994, Fonda and I searched for Olga and Claire's names on the interior walls of the Klausen Synagogue, which are covered in red hand-painted names. This original memorial to Czechoslovak Holocaust victims was whitewashed over during the Communist era but at the time of our visit was being painstakingly restored.

16. "The Song of Terezín: the remarkable story of how poems written by children in the Terezín ghetto became a moving oratorio." Transcript of interview with Alena Munkova-Synkova, child survivor of Terezín, by Ian Willoughby on Radio Prague. January 30, 2004. radio.cz. Accessed March 29, 2012.

17. Olga's first apartment was at Belcrediho 6, in the same area. During the occupation the street where her second apartment was located was named Sonnenbergstrasse and is now Milady Horákové.

18. "Aunt Elsa" is most likely my mother's cousin Else Jäger Freisinger.

19. A regulation passed September 13, 1940 disallowed Jews from renting vacant apartments; they could only move into apartments already rented by other Jews. Leases

could be broken by apartment building owners at will with no legal protection for Jewish tenants. (Lexa 86.)

20. "Eva's brother" is code for my uncle Max, at that time already in England. It is a reminder that all of these letters were being read and censored. Divulging Max's whereabouts might have unintended consequences.

21. Claire's description of German efficiency, "*der grossartigen Organisation der Deutschen*" is an ironic statement, "*grossartigen*" meaning something close to "superb." With this statement she was able to pass the censors.

22. Lexa 85.

23. Margolius 87-88.

24. Lexa 85.

25. Ibid. 81-82.

26. Ibid. 81.

27. Ibid. 82-83.

28. Olga's following letter on November 29, 1940 reports that a carpenter whose name is possibly spelled "Vrazek" had Claire's furniture and other items taken away to make room, presumably in his shop. It is likely they were lost at this point.

29. The restrictions placed on Jews can be seen to quickly worsen and accelerate. In September 1939 there was a curfew imposed starting at 8 p.m. By November 1940, Jews needed special permission to leave their city or town of residence. In January 1941, all Jews in Prague and Brno had to turn in their driver's licenses. In September 1941, when Heydrich ordered all Jews to wear the yellow Star of David, Jews needed permission to go anywhere outside their immediate neighborhoods. (Lexa 79.)

30. "This Month's Small House." *Ideal Home and Gardening* [London]. Vol LIII, No. III. March 1946. 33; "Furnishing for Freedom: In This Month's Small House." Ibid. 34-35.

31. Russell, Gordon and Jacques Groag. *The Story of Furniture*. No. 50 of the Puffin Picture Books. Harmondsworth, Middlesex: Penguin Books Limited, 1947. 3.

CHAPTER TWENTY **What Traces Are Left**

1. My sister's birthday was the same as my father's, November 18.

2. Plattnergasse is now Platnéřská.

3. In this passage my grandmother Olga uses "Evchen," the diminutive form of my mother Eva's name.

4. The Leica was a revolutionary advancement in the portability of cameras and is associated with the rise of photojournalism. The 35 mm camera was invented by Oskar Barnack and introduced to the public in 1925. "The Leica became an indispensable companion for all situations, an 'integral part of the eye' or an 'extension of the hand.'" ("Oskar Barnack: His genius revolutionized photography." us.leica-camera.com. Accessed June 14, 2012.) With its small size but cinema screen ratio of 2:3, the Leica forever changed the way people approached the art of taking pictures. It was used notably, for example, by artist and street photographer Henri Cartier-Bresson (1908-2004) and also by Ilse Bing (1899-1998), one of the most important women photographers of the inter-

war period. Hungarian born photographer Ferenc (Franz) Berko (1916-2000), who fled Europe in 1938 and in 1949 came to Aspen at the request of Walter Paepcke, also was a Leica devotee.

5. For this information I thank editor Adolf Opel. His further research also indicates that Claire became involved with Max Thun-Hohenstein and his theories of movement. (Loos, Claire Beck. *Adolf Loos Privat*. Adolf Opel, ed. Vienna: Verlag Hermann Böhlaus Nachfolger, 1985. x-xi.)

6. Meder, Iris. Email to Carrie Paterson. June 19, 2012.

7. Loos, Claire Beck. *Adolf Loos Privat*. 1985. xi.

8. Olga identifies this person as Claire's *Erhalter*—literally "sustainer"—which we assume meant Claire had a trustee, perhaps who at this time was already a refugee.

9. A later card from Walter von Schuschnigg addressed to my father on December 22, 1942 thanked my father for his season's greetings and asked my father to visit at the offices of the Military Committee for the Liberation of Austria in the General Motors building near Columbus Circle in New York. Clearly upon emigration to the United States my father was looking for further assistance or to do whatever he could personally to help the war effort. He also applied to the OSS, forerunner of the CIA, but told me he was turned down because he had the future responsibility of two children.

10. Lexa 89.

11. Margolius 86.

12. Kovály, Heda Margolius. *Under a Cruel Star: A Life in Prague 1941-1968*. Helen Epstein, trans. New York: Holmes & Meier Publishers, Inc., 1997. 102-103.

13. Korngasse is now Žitná ulice, in Nové Město, Prague II.

14. *Liwanzen*—yeast pancakes, a Bohemian dish.

15. *Mehlspeisen*—an Austrian term for any dish made mainly with flour; this can be anything from cakes to dumplings.

CHAPTER TWENTY-ONE **Stefan and Max 1939-1947**

1. As per the archives available online of The American Presidency Project at the University of California, Santa Barbara, President Roosevelt's Proclamation 2348 on September 5, 1939 declared the neutrality of the United States of America in the war existing between "Germany and France; Poland; and the United Kingdom, India, Australia, and New Zealand." By May 11, 1940, Roosevelt had extended America's isolationist policies through Proclamation 2405 to the war with Germany conducted by Belgium, Luxembourg, and the Netherlands. On November 15, 1940, he extended it again via Proclamation 2444 to include Greece in its war against fascist Italy. But on May 27, 1941, global war was clearly on the horizon. On that date, Roosevelt issued Proclamation 2487, which recognized America faced "an unlimited national emergency" and required American "military, naval, air, and civilian defenses be put on the basis of readiness to repel any and all acts or threats of aggression directed toward any part of the Western Hemisphere."

2. "Lend-Lease Act (1941)." ourdocuments.gov. Accessed June 15, 2012.

3. Gerwarth, Robert. *Hitler's Hangman: The Life of Heydrich*. New Haven, Conn.: Yale University Press, 2011. 208.

4. Rothkirchen 29.

5. Gerwarth 211-219.

6. Beck, Max. Letter to Stefan Schanzer. February 24, 1942.

7. Domanický 80.

8. Even with our family tree nearly complete on Rosa's side, the author of this letter is still a mystery. We thought it might have been Regine von Kubinsky or her sister Luise Pollack von Parnau. Their father Bruno Pollack von Parnau was Rosa Schanzer's cousin—both of them grandchildren of Theresia and Hermann Pollack. But upon making contact with Luise's only son Alexander and her grandson Johannes just weeks before publication of this book, we learned Bruno, his wife Charlotte (born Anninger), their son Franz, and daughter Regine emigrated from Vienna to Oxford in 1938 and were not in Portugal in 1942. Luise went to Budapest. We only found this branch of what is now the Roth-Pollack-Parnau family through several rare books for sale online belonging to Franz, who was an author and collector. Franz and Bruno, owners of a large textile enterprise (different than H.P.S.) were arrested in 1938 by the Gestapo and allowed to emigrate only after they signed over all their wealth. This included the family's large palace on Schwarzenbergplatz that the Nazis then made into Vienna headquarters. In the Nazi remodel ionic columns on the palace were replaced with harsh angular ones, the upper balconies removed, a large imperial eagle installed, and three dark gates imposed onto the street-side where elegant windows with window boxes had been. In 1944 the Allies bombed the building, and so when Bruno and Charlotte returned after the war and the property was restituted, they decided to sell it. By 1958 the new owner was Steyr-Daimler-Puch, the makers of none other than my father's favorite motorcycle. Alexander married Sigrid von Gudenus and they have three children. Their son Johannes wrote that the family remained in textiles, with spinning mills in Austria and France up until 1999/2000.

9. Rosa Schanzer was buried south of Vienna's city center in the new Jewish cemetery. The "pensioner's home" on Seegasse referred to in the letter is interestingly on the site of the oldest Jewish cemetery in Vienna, dating back to the mid-sixteenth century. In 1943, the Nazis decided to raze it, but the outraged Jewish community moved many gravestones preemptively. ("Jewish cemetery in Roßau." en.wikipedia.org. Accessed June 15, 2012.)

10. We know now this was in fact another Olga Beck who appeared on the list.

11. My father wrote to my uncle Max on August 25, 1947, "I want to congratulate you on the birth of my newest niece Janet Evelyn, and I thank you very much too for naming her after my wife [Eva]." Janet was also given the middle name Evelyn after her maternal grandmother. (Wilson, Janet Beck. Email to Carrie Paterson. July 15, 2012.)

CHAPTER TWENTY-TWO **Aspen, Early 1950's**

1. Daily, Kathleen Kreiger and Gaylord T. Guenin. *Aspen—The Quiet Years*. Aspen: Red Ink, Inc., 1994. Photos taken by my father of me unloading logs for my cabin at 512 West Hopkins Ave., Aspen in 1951 appear on page 278 (without attribution) as well as another on page 489 my father took of John Strong and me at Lenado.

2. Katie Gantzel, the daughter of Steen and Joan Gantzel running the Christiania, became a childhood playmate and forever friend of my daughter Carrie. The Gantzel family frequently spent time on The Boomerang grounds, as we did at the Christiania. The entire block was like one family. Steen is one of the longest-term ski instructors, still teaching beginners at Buttermilk Mountain after over fifty years! Years ago, Steen was known to take his accordion out on the slopes to inspire his students.

3. The Copper Kettle restaurant was started in the early 1950's by the talented team of Sara and Army Armstrong. They opened their first restaurant in a small Victorian on West Hopkins Avenue between 1ˢᵗ and 2ⁿᵈ Streets with Patricia Moore, six-foot tall "little Patsy." They had all served together in the Foreign Service. (Armstrong, E. F. and Sara Armstrong. *In a Copper Kettle*. Denver: The Golden Bell Press, 1958.) Their idea was to present foods from around the world with a fixed price, five course gourmet meal featuring a country or a region with a menu that changed nightly. Later the Copper Kettle moved to the Four Seasons Club on Castle Creek (now the campus shared by Aspen Music Festival and School and Aspen Country Day School), and then a third and final time into Ken and Betty Moore's Tippler complex. For that location the Armstrongs commissioned Aspen artist Irvin Burkee to create the restaurant's iconic copper *repoussé* panels that depicted animal, fish, and fowl in global agriculture practices. He also designed and built the restaurant's copper room dividers, doors, fountains, and fireplaces. Burkee's oil paintings hung on the entry stairway.

4. Suffering the same fate as a lot of old buildings in Aspen, the Tippler was demolished. The multi-million dollar Residences of Little Nell and the upscale Mulino Restaurant currently are located on the site.

5. In the 1980's my sister Doris opened and ran a jewelry store in the Hotel Boulderado until she retired in 1990. "Design Sphere" was a small elegant store that featured designs she crafted. It had been her dream for decades, ever since she was a teenager in Australia. Even though Doris started as a dressmaker and then designer in New York, she eventually chose this as her career and her primary artistic outlet. It is a good indication of the influence my father had on her after we reunited. Her aesthetic was a mix of traditional and experimental, often using the lost wax casting process to sculpt elements in metal that looked organic.

6. Digitized files have been uploaded to the Internet by my niece Linda Schneider Engle. They are on a website she made to tell my father's stories during the two world wars, which can be found with a simple search using both their names. Listening to my father tell his own stories may be of interest, especially by those who knew and loved him.

CHAPTER TWENTY-THREE **Prisoner of Fortune, Prisoner of War**

1. De Waal, Edmund. *The Hare with Amber Eyes*. London: Vintage, 2011. 181-182.

2. The huge prisoner sweeps on the Russian front left Austrian officers feeling abandoned and betrayed by their Czechoslovak, Hungarian, and Ruthenian soldiers. Many journals by Austrian officers captured on the Russian front during the First World War include the speculation that their soldiers deserted, and this proceeded to be recorded in official Austrian history. A page on my niece Linda Engle's website ("The Austro-Hungarian Empire") shows my father Steve clearly retained this version of the First World War. In Alon Rachamimov's book *POWs and The Great War*, Rachamimov argues comprehensively that the notion of disloyalty needs to be reexamined and provides evidence from first person documents by rank and file infantry to show that many other factors led to the massive captures, including unpreparedness and strategic missteps on the part of the Austro-Hungarian regiments. (*POWs and The Great War*. Oxford: Berg, 2002. 32-34).

3. There were over fifty-four thousand Austro-Hungarian officer prisoners, but this amounted to only 2.5% of total prisoners taken on the Eastern Front. (Rachamimov 9.) The total number of prisoners taken from that region numbered six million, of which 2.77 million were Austro-Hungarians—one third of all the men mobilized for the war (3-4), or eleven percent of all men in the Dual Monarchy (31).

4. Ibid. 60.

5. Ibid. 46.

6. Ibid. 48.

7. Ibid. 49-50.

8. *Das Geheimnis des Reichs* [The Secret of the Empire] by Heimito von Doderer describes the conditions in Siberian prison camps and how they varied between officers' barracks and enlisted men. The novel is based on the author's experiences between 1916-1920 as an Austrian prisoner of war.

9. This special treatment of officers and the language of the Hague Convention is confirmed and elaborated upon by Rachamimov on pages 55-57.

10. Schanzer, Steve. Interview with Thomas Dana Schneider. December 1970/January 1971.

11. There were many of these "duel protocols" by the spring of 1918. In the Central Siberian camp of Kasanoyarsk, for example, a request was sent for extra boxcars to transmit the "piles and mountains" of paperwork back to Austria. This request was refused on grounds the duels were small and petty—the result of men living in tight and uncomfortable circumstances—and the boxcars were needed for food and supplies. (Rachamimov 101-102.)

12. The Semenovs led the "White resistance" movement against the Bolshevik forces primarily in the Trans-Baikal region with the aid of the Czechoslovak Legionnaires, who had been released as prisoners to fight with the Bolsheviks. ("Grigory Semyonov." en.wikipedia.org. Accessed June 18, 2012.) The Czechoslovak Legion was an anti-Habsburg unit comprising a relatively small number of the total number of Czechoslovak POWs. (Rachamimov 195.)

13. Beginning in 1904, the Mensheviks were the minority faction of the Russian Social Democratic Labor Party, the Bolsheviks forming the majority of the party.

14. The Internationalists fought for the Bolsheviks and, before 1918, were formed of POWs who were primarily Magyar (the region of today's Hungary). (Rachamimov 121.)

15. The "Kolomejka" is a fast-paced dance from the Galician region of what is now Poland where among other moves, dancers spin while kicking their heels.

CHAPTER TWENTY-FOUR **At the End of Empire**

1. Albright 41.

2. The Czechoslovak Legion had been granted safe passage out of Russia, but after the Bolshevik revolution, talks broke down between the Communists and Czechoslovakia's president Tomáš Garrigue Masaryk. The legionnaires had to fight their way for five thousand miles across Russia to Vladivostok along the Trans-Siberian Railroad, station by station. After fighting another year, the Allies finally allowed them to leave the country, but "not before many had had to walk the last several hundred miles to Vladivostok." (Albright 41-42.)

CHAPTER TWENTY-FIVE **Money Matters**

1. Lenny Woods, then husband of the Paepckes' oldest daughter Nina, was Vice President of the Aspen Company, which ran the Hotel Jerome and other properties.

2. Hannes Heer et al., eds., *The Discursive Construction of History: Remembering the Wehrmacht's War of Annihilation*. New York: Palgrave Macmillan, 2008. 103, 108.

3. Hubertus Czernin (b. Vienna 1956-2006) also helped expose Austrian President and U.N. Secretary General Kurt Waldheim as a former Nazi. Czernin founded a press—Czernin Verlag—that republished Claire Beck Loos' 1936 book *Adolf Loos Privat* in 2007 as part of their literature project *Bibliotek der Erinnerung* [Library of Memory], encompassing authors who had to emigrate due to Nazi persecution or who died in the Holocaust.

4. The lawyer for the case was E. Randol Schoenberg, who has been recognized by several legal and Jewish organizations for his jurisprudence, and who is currently serving as President of the Los Angeles Museum of the Holocaust. He also manages an enormous genealogical tree and has been a life-long avid genealogist. When we contacted him in 2011 about the first English translation of my aunt Claire's book *Adolf Loos—A Private Portrait*, which features a story about his grandfather Arnold Schoenberg's *Gurrelieder*, Randol noticed his grandmother, Gertrud (Kolisch) Schoenberg, is my fourth cousin, related through the Biedermann family.

5. "The Tale of a Masterpiece: Gustav Klimt, Adele Bloch-Bauer and the Stolen Portrait That Shook The Art World." Los Angeles County Museum of Art. lacma.org. Circa January 2012. Accessed February 1, 2012.

6. Glaberson, William. "For Betrayal by Swiss Bank and Nazis, $21 Million." *New York Times*. April 4, 2005.

7. Ibid.

8. Hermann Göring is quoted speaking to a conference of Reich Commissioners in Berlin on August 6, 1942, "It used to be called plundering. But today things have become more humane. In spite of that, I intend to plunder, and to do it thoroughly." (Edsel, Robert M. and Bret Witter. *The Monuments Men: Allied Heroes, Nazi Thieves and the Greatest Treasure Hunt in History*. New York: Center Street, 2009. vii.) After Hitler made his first choices for his private museum, Göring got second pick from all the loot (200).

9. Bennett, Magnus. "Heir to Stolen Jewish Property Foiled by Czech Restitution Law." *Jewish Telegraphic Agency*. Reposted on highbeam.com. April 25, 2001. Accessed June 18, 2012; O'Connor, Anne-Marie. "[Maria Altmann:] Fighting for Her Past." *LA Times*. articles. latimes.com. March 20, 2001. Accessed June 18. 2012.

10. Göring and Heydrich were only two of the many Nazi officials who took advantage of their positions of power to appropriate cultural objects for themselves, and there were still much larger caches of treasure amassed by Nazis over the period of the war. The collections of stolen items: artwork, heirlooms, and rare artifacts—some of which are still missing—were often gathered in enormous underground vaults, as in Hitler's collection, which was stored in the cavernous salt mines at Altaussee. A map can be seen on the Internet. (Edsel and Witter; "Documents and Photos." monumentsmen.com. Accessed June 1, 2012.)

11. Glaberson. "For Betrayal by Swiss Bank and Nazis, $21 Million."

CHAPTER TWENTY-SIX **Basic Training**

No endnotes.

CHAPTER TWENTY-SEVEN **The *Tachinierer***

1. *K2—The Savage Mountain* by Robert Bates and Dr. Charles Houston (New York: McGraw-Hill, 1954) chronicles the climb, which Houston led. They were the first Americans ever to ascend the peak. Dr. Houston was also my father's physician for many years and studied effects of high altitude exposures while in the Himalayas.

2. "Österreichisch 'Tachinierer.'" ostarrichi.org. Accessed March 30, 2012.

3. The 10th Mountain Division in effect brought Friedl Pfeifer to Aspen as he had trained in the area doing maneuvers with troops from Camp Hale. (Pfeifer, Friedl with Morten Lund. *Nice Goin': My Life on Skis*. Missoula, Mont.: Pictorial Histories Publishing Company, Inc., 1993. 111-115.)

4. Uyehara, Annie. "10th Mountain Redux." *Skiing Heritage*. May/June 2012. 20-21.

5. Today there is little left of Camp Hale but concrete foundations, overgrown roads, and the numerous plaques at an overlook on Highway 24 describing its history with interpretive displays. The streams that had been diverted throughout the camp have been returned to their natural state.

6. In a 2007 interview when he was eighty-four years old, Sergeant Brown said, "We used to say that combat was easier than the training at Camp Hale.... It was very challenging.... In my 25 years in the Army and through two wars, I have to say these are the finest group of kids I have ever trained in my life. But they always tried to outsmart me...." (Addison, Annie. "Camp Hale's Second Generation: It's been 50 years since the Mountain & Cold Weather Training Command." *Aspen Times*. March 24, 2007.)

7. Friederike da Lezze was a ballerina with the Vienna Opera and came from a senatorial family in Venice. It is thought that the da Lezzes (da Legges) trace back to a scribal family in the Roman Empire and through the female line to Julius Ceasar's family. ("DNA conclusions... From Adam to Oisin and Woden...." Macaodhagain.weebly.com/dna-conclusions.html. Accessed March 30, 2012; De Pellegrini, Giovanni & Co, Venice. *Notes and documents relating to the family of da Lezze*. J.A. Herbert, trans. Norwich, England: A.H. Goose, 1900. archive.org. Accessed March 30, 2012.)

8. Gerwarth 214-215; "Mischling." en.wikipedia.org; Uygur, Selçuk. "Second World War Studies: Mischlinge and the Question of Hybridity in the Third Reich." *Yer Altindan Notlar*. selcukuyger.com. August 26, 2011. Latter two sources accessed February 23, 2012.

CHAPTER TWENTY-EIGHT **Breaking Ground**

1. Leopold Bentley (formerly Bloch-Bauer) married Otto and Käthe Pick's daughter Antoinette. Their son Peter Bentley, a philanthropic and nationally recognized industrialist as well as past Chancellor of the University of British Columbia from 2004-2007, has recently published a history of Canadian Forest Products, Ltd. and CANFOR. Otto and Käthe Pick figure significantly in the family history background. (Bentley, Peter with Robin Fowler. *One Family's Journey: CANFOR and the Transformation of B.C.'s Forest Industry*. Vancouver: Douglas & McIntyre, 2012.)

CHAPTER TWENTY-NINE **Taliesin**

1. In Welsh mythology Taliesin was a poet, priest, and magician. Edward Williams (1747-1826)—the Romantic-era, neo-druid Welsh poet and political radical best known by his

bardic name, Iolo Morganwg—also named his son Taliesin.

Frank Lloyd Wright's mother's family was from Wales, and through her came the Jones family motto "Y Gwir yn Erbyn y Byd," translated and inscribed on the fireplace mantel in Frank Lloyd Wright's Taliesin as "Truth Against the World." ("Gorsedd." en.wikipedia.org; "Iolo Morganwg on Primrose Hill." royalparks.org. Both accessed February 1, 2012.)

2. Nemtin, Frances. *Midway Farm at Taliesin.* 2003. 9.

3. *The Valley of the God-Almighty Joneses: Remembrances of Frank Lloyd Wright's Sister Maginel Wright Barney.* First edition published by Appleton-Century, 1965 and reprinted in 1986 as a limited paperback edition by permission of the grandsons of Maginel Wright Barney to commemorate the Centennial of Unity Chapel in "The Valley" (Spring Green, Wisc.: Unity Chapel Publications).

4. Olga (Olgivanna) Ivanovna Lazovich (1898-1985) and Frank Lloyd Wright married in 1928. She was his third and last wife.

5. Berendtson, Indira. "Olgivanna Lloyd Wright—A 'Vivid Inspiration.'" *Frank Lloyd Wright Quarterly.* Vol. 23: 2. Spring 2012. 6.

6. *Frank Lloyd Wright.* Dirs. Ken Burns and Lynn Novik. PBS. 1998. Film.

7. The Theater's curtain was hand made by the Taliesin Fellowship and presented to Mr. Wright on his eighty-seventh birthday in 1956. It was a highlight of the Wright exhibition at the Guggenheim in 2009, which marked the fiftieth anniversaries of Wright's death (April 9, 1959) and the opening of the Museum (October 21, 1959).

8. Wright, Frank Lloyd. *An Autobiography.* New York: Duell, Sloan, and Pearce, 1943. 225.

9. Discovered by fellow apprentices Vern Knutson and Dan Novak during a clean-up campaign in the Taliesin basement after Mr. Wright's death, the photograph required special permission from Mrs. Wright to be duplicated.

10. Heffner wrote a memo to Spectorsky on September 8, 1958, "Very nice job on the ski piece... you worked it out beautifully." Then Spectorsky wrote to Lownes that same day, "Vic, I can't tell you how valuable this letter was to me.... I shamelessly borrowed the entire. Should you be writing to Paterson, please thank him for me." Lownes wrote to me two days later, "Your letter was a masterpiece, and you will be able to see from the enclosed memos just how invaluable your assistance was. I don't exactly know how to thank you, but I will see to it that you get an autographed copy of Spec's new book on skiing as soon as it is published." (In addition to the promise of Spectorsky's book, they also gave me a free *Playboy* subscription for years.) The cover illustration for the Aspen write-up featured a blonde in a sweater with a *Playboy* logo on her sleeve and riding an Aspen ski lift, whose companion was wearing a white bunny head, completed by a moustache.

CHAPTER THIRTY **A Critical Mix**

1. In the years following Mr. Wright's death, Mrs. Wright replaced this rug with a large colorful one that Mr. Wright designed, and there are several photographs that show the living room this way. The more subdued floor covering was returned years later, however, in keeping with Mr. Wright's original design for the house interior.

2. Ironically, although I love spinach now, my father used to tell a story that when I was little, I refused to eat it. Our pediatrician assured my mother that he could make me. So the doctor took a spoonful of the creamed spinach and put it in my mouth. I managed to give it back—promptly spraying it all over him. In my early years I must have been a

bit of handful in the tradition of Viennese manners, where children were expected to be seen, not heard. Dinnertime meant a lesson in keeping one's elbows down, and we were required to hold a napkin across our chest for the whole meal, pinning it to our sides, keeping our arms still.

3. Auer, James. "Home" section. *Milwaukee Journal.* January 30, 1983. 1, 4. As of this writing, the Bogk House is still owned by Barbara and Robert Elsner.

4. Mead, Rebecca. "Winged Victories: The Soaring Ambition of Santiago Calatrava." *The New Yorker*. newyorker.com. September 1, 2008. Accessed April 15, 2012.

CHAPTER THIRTY-ONE **A Sympathetic Chord**

1. A coup on July 14, 1958 led by Abd al-Karim Qasim ended the Hashemite Monarchy, with King Faisal II, Prime Minister Nuri al-Said, and Crown Prince Abd al-Ilah all being assassinated. (Tripp, Charles. *A History of Iraq.* New York: Cambridge University Press, 2007. 142; and quoted in "14 July Revolution." en.wikipedia.org. Accessed June 26, 2012.)

2. Interestingly, after the 2003 invasion of Iraq by the United States, and Saddam Hussein's ouster from power, Wright's plans for "rebuilding Baghdad" created new interest. (Ringle, Ken. "The Genie in an Architect's Lamp: Frank Lloyd Wright's '57 Plan for Baghdad May Be Key to Its Future." *Washington Post.* washingtonpost.com. June 29, 2003; Cohen, Adam. "Frank Lloyd Wright 'Builds' Baghdad ..." *Wall Street Journal.* online.wsj.com. August 20, 2003. Both accessed January 15, 2012.)

3. "Learning to Dwell: Adolf Loos' Works in the Czech Lands." Maria Szadkowska, Curator. Royal Institute of British Architects (RIBA). 66 Portland Place, London W1B 1AD, England. February 24 – May 3, 2011.

4. *Frank Lloyd Wright.* Dirs. Ken Burns and Lynn Novik.

5. Rukschcio and Schachel 385.

6. Ibid. 384.

7. Marie Kraus Turnowsky was the sister-in-law of my grandfather Otto's cousin, Rosa Hirsch Kraus. Marie's brother was Karl Kraus, the Viennese satirist and a friend of Loos.

8. *Guide to the Musée d'Orsay.* Anthony Roberts, trans. Paris: Ministere de la Culture et de la Communication Editions de la Réunion de muses nationaux, 1987. 244.

9. Rukschcio and Schachel 24.

10. It was this autobiography, which included Wright's philosophies not only about radical design but life that initially inspired and reinforced my resolve to be at Taliesin. In fact, the book brought many to apprentice at Taliesin with the master architect.

11. Wright, Frank Lloyd. *A Testament.* New York: Horizon Press, 1957. 18.

12. Manson, Grant Carpenter. *Frank Lloyd Wright to 1910: The First Golden Age.* New York: Wiley, 1979. 9-10.

13. The Prague-born Dr. Irena Murray, Director of British Architectural Library at the Royal Institute of British Architects (RIBA), wrote, "The theatrical nature of Claire Beck Loos' narrative, her ultimately tragic journey and her artist's way of encapsulating the essential about Loos in a mixture of camera-sharp observations [is] mitigated by an affectionate regard for the brilliant, but deeply flawed man that [Loos] was." (Murray, Irena. Email to Carrie Paterson. March 17, 2011.) In the *Neue Freie Presse* in 1935, the

composer Ernst Krenek characterized Claire's book as "snapshots, told without any false pretentions, which permit the reader to permeate the external image of Loos as a fanatical prophet of human dignity. Here, a genuine reformist was at work trying to improve the world." (Loos, Claire Beck. *Adolf Loos Privat*. Adolf Opel, ed. Vienna: Verlag Hermann Böhlaus Nachfolger, 1985. xiii. Translation of this segment by Constance C. Pontasch.)

14. Cohen. "Frank Lloyd Wright 'Builds' Baghdad..."

15. *Frank Lloyd Wright*. Dirs. Ken Burns and Lynn Novik.

16. Loos blasphemously compared nineteenth-century Austro-Hungarian imperial styles to the tattoos of degenerates and criminals in prisons. In elaborate rhetorical turns, he suggested Austria go forward into modernity rather than submitting to an endless parade of nineteenth-century tradition. (Loos, Adolf. 167-176.)

Scholars have compared Loos' rhetorical approach itself to his practice of architecture. He used aphorisms and other linguistic devices as a demolition force in language. John Maciuika writes that Loos applied his craft with an architect's vision—the effect, to "dismantle the usual structure of sense by which ... [we] relate to the world." ("Adolf Loos and Aphoristic Style: Rhetorical Practice in Early Twentieth-Century Design Criticism." *Design Issues*. Vol. 16: 2. Summer 2000. 84.)

On the other hand, Janet Stewart shows "Ornament and Crime" to be "a masterly example of Loos' cultural criticism" that is "woven together" from "disparate threads" that include "interlocking remarks and conjectures, jumping from Socrates, Voltaire, and Beethoven, to the tattooed people of Papua New Guinea, Goethe's use of language, and the uniform of the Austro-Hungarian infantry." ("Talking of Modernity: The Viennese 'Vortrag' as Form." *German Life and Letters*. Vol. 51: 4. October 1998. 459.)

One can also read the second chapter of art critic and historian Hal Foster's *Prosthetic Gods* on Loos' construction of the Modern persona through "Ornament and Crime." Foster overlooks some uniquely cultural aspects to Loos' rhetoric, but he details very well Loos' iconoclasm.

17. Scheine, Judith. *R.M. Schindler*. London: Phaidon Press Ltd., 2001. 15.

18. At the first reunion of the Taliesin Fellowship in 1987 at Taliesin West in Scottsdale, Arizona, I recall Fritz Benedict touching one of the rocks in the wall outside the drafting room, telling us, "I placed this rock here." Fifty years after he had been an apprentice, he still felt a strong connection to Taliesin through the physical labor it took to transform the desert into architecture.

19. Quoted in Elman, Kimberly. "Frank Lloyd Wright and the Principles of Organic Architecture." pbs.org. Undated. Accessed March 1, 2012.

20. Loos, Claire Beck. *Adolf Loos—A Private Portrait*. 63.

21. Jan and Jana Brummel survived Auschwitz and Bergen-Belsen. Jana escaped from the Death March in 1945, and Jan lived out the war in a labor camp in Friedland, Silesia. Their niece Eva Brummel, who was a teenager in 1939 on the last of the *Kindertransports*, is the only surviving member of her branch of the Brummel family. Eva's parents Leo and Gertruda Brummel (also Loos clients), her sister Lilka, and aunt Markéta (Eisenschiml) were killed at Auschwitz, and other relatives at Birkenau or Terezín. ("Neighbors Who Disappeared." Prague Jewish Museum. zmizeli-sousede.cz. Accessed June 21, 2012.) Eva was saved through emigration to England by the generosity of Sir Nicholas Winton (Domanický 120); Winton saved the lives of six hundred and sixty-nine Jewish Czecho-slovak children by his philanthropy. (*In the Presence of Good: Sir Nicholas Winton*. Bratislava History Project. 2008. Video.)

22. Loos, Claire Beck. *Adolf Loos—A Private Portrait*. 68.

23. Sarnitz, August. *Adolf Loos 1870-1933: Architect, Cultural Critic, Dandy*. Cologne: Taschen, 2003. 15.

24. Colomina, Beatriz. "Intimacy and Spectacle: The Interiors of Adolf Loos." *AA files: annals of the Architectural Association School of Architecture*. Volume 1. 1990. 5.
    Colomina argues that Loos' arrangements emphasized the control of the seated figure silhouetted against the window, as "she" would be able to see the faces of people who entered into the space first, before they themselves would be recognized. Our cabin, however different in this respect—it was a bachelor pad—did have a similar feeling, in that the arrangement allowed us our privacy.

25. Sarnitz 15.

26. Adolf Loos designed the Paris branch of Kniže men's haberdashery in 1927-1928, after he did the Vienna store in the years of 1910-1913. The Paris branch closed in 1972.

27. Rukschcio and Schachel 632-633.

28. Ibid. 632.

29. "The precise link to the Schanzer-family still being the clients for this small version appears on one plan at the Adolf Loos archive of the Albertina in Vienna: ALA 620—Adolf Loos, Einfamilien-Doppelhaus (Werkbundsiedlung Wien), Fassaden, 1931; Transparentpapier; Bleistift; 297 x 420 mm—and on the backside in handwriting in pencil: Haus Schanzer. The Loos Archive has 11 numbers concerning this last version of Loos/ Unger for the WBS [Werkbundsiedlung]." (Kapfinger, Otto. Email to Carrie Paterson and Charles Paterson. March 25, 2012.)

30. Ibid.

31. "This research for the WBS [Werkbundsiedlung] and especially for the story of Loos' different proposals for your grandparents was fascinating—sometimes a dead-end-street, sometimes thrilling like Hitchcock. But now all the facts I came to know and moreover all facts that you and your father know fit together perfectly into a new picture of the whole matter—clarifying and enlightening all the obscure speculations and myths that surrounded it previously." (Kapfinger, Otto. Email to Carrie Paterson. April 7, 2012.)
    From Burkhardt Rukschcio, author of *Adolf Loos—Leben und Werke*: "I know faintly about the Werkbund House and [Stefan Schanzer] but never had evidence. Good if this changes now. There is still a lot to discover." (Email to Carrie Paterson. May 12, 2012.)

32. Rukschcio and Schachel 381.

33. Now the story is much more clear. As Otto Kapfinger explained to us, "Loos himself changed the original 9 x 9 meter plan ['The 1930 Paris Plan'] for Stefan Schanzer to ... [the] 8 x 6 meter spilt-level ... [while] in contact with him—but this plan came too late. Kulka had independently continued with his version of the gallery-type-house [known as] 'Type B' from spring 1930.... [The 'Type B' plan has] remarks in red: '*von Loos genehmigt*'! = 'approved by Loos'—and this was before Loos himself made the 9 x 9 meter plan in August 1930 in Paris. In letters of the archive: Loos was very '*wütend*' ['infuriated'] in late spring 1931 that not his final version, but the Kulka/Loos gallery type was under construction. [It] also indicates that very surely he still meant it for [the] Schanzer[s] and they still hoped to have this house. So in summer 1931 the Schanzers at the latest must have realized that 'their house,' although [desired to be built by] Loos and over a period of months in some steps [reconfigured] to the final smaller version, was not to be built. And so they changed [their architect] to Groag." (Kapfinger, Otto. Email to Carrie Paterson. March 22, 2012.)

CHAPTER THIRTY-TWO **Architecture in Evolution**

1. At Christmas 1973 in the first annual letter to past Fellows and the "Friends of Taliesin," Mrs. Wright gave us all "a rough sketch" on their continual work to bring Mr. Wright's unbuilt projects to fruition. "It is wonderful to see these buildings of Mr. Wright's come to life out of paper and into the third dimension. There are many more that can be built, and we intend to see them all constructed…. Once more, with all best wishes for the coming year. For all of Taliesin, Olgivanna Lloyd Wright."

2. In the mid-1950's my father and his New York friend Herb Ortman considered buying Waterman's Aspen complex. Next to the gas station and grocery store, the guest accommodations there were called "Castle Creek Cabins" (later called "The Agate"). However, that scheme never came to fruition because Ortman, the financier, decided against moving to town, thus saving me from either being in competition with my father, or having to run more than one property.

3. The Beth Sholom ("House of Peace") Congregation synagogue was designed in close consultation with Rabbi Mortimer J. Cohen (1894-1972). According to Joseph M. Siry's *Beth Sholom Synagogue: Frank Lloyd Wright and Religious Architecture*, both Wright and Cohen attributed to each other the central idea of the synagogue being Mount Sinai (370). Rabbi Cohen was also interested in the historic architecture of synagogues for two main reasons. First, to give, as Cohen said, "immortality" to the Jewish spirit after the widespread destruction of synagogues in Europe, and second, to reflect upon recent archeological evidence of ancient artifacts and art, showing their importance within the oldest form of synagogues in the Middle East (358). Yet Cohen, like Wright, decried historicism and equally wanted to avoid trends toward the decorative; for him, modernism was the way toward his desire to commission "a sacred architecture that elevated spiritual awareness to a poetic level" (389). He envisioned the synagogue as a place for teaching, where the rabbi was an educator, the Torah held a central place, and "the leader is of the people, in the midst of the people." (Cohen quoted in Siry 360.) As of 2007 the Beth Sholom Congregation synagogue has become a National Historic Landmark. ("Beth Sholom Synagogue, Elkin Park, PA." nps. gov. Accessed March 13, 2012.)

4. Sections are architectural drawings that show the interior layers of construction, as if cutting through a multi-layered cake.

5. In our Boomerang files, we kept a list of Taliesin Fellows who visited us. The following people gave us a beautiful collection of 18 x 23 inch Frank Lloyd Wright portfolios with this insert, "To our dear friends Charles & Fonda: May Happiness & Prosperity forever increase around your hearth, where we throughout the years have enjoyed your very warm hospitality." It was signed "Rodnee & Margy Volden, Keith Kennedy, Tony Putman, Greg Williams, Susan Wagner, Frances Nemtin, Stephen M. Nemtin, Ling Po, Joe Fabris, Charles Montooth, Arnold & Dori Roy, Ken Lockhart, Anna Coor, Susan Lockhart, Sally Logue, Minerva Montooth, David Oliver, Indira Balak [now Berendtson], Julian Cox, Eric Maule, Roger Coor, Alan Daune Olin, Heloise Swaback [now Christa]. November 1977, Taliesin West."

We also enjoyed seeing Tom and Effie Casey frequently, with their daughter Golnar. Wenchin (Wendy) and Bing Hu from China also paid us several visits; he was at Taliesin in 1988 and 1989, and is now a successful architect and developer in Scottsdale, Arizona. His firm H&S International is best known for the creation of custom dream homes.

For many years we saw Frances Nemtin and her husband Stephen, an architect at Taliesin since a year after I arrived. Frances (who I originally knew as Polly Lockhart with her children Leslie and Brian) was the director of the Milwaukee Art Institute before she joined the Fellowship in February 1946 and became the master gardener at Taliesin in 1980. She has written a dozen small books on Taliesin that each concentrate on one theme at a time in the life at Taliesin; for example, one specifically on music, another on the history of the famous water tower Romeo and Juliet, a third on Midway Farm, and many others. In 2011 she asked many of us past Taliesin Fellows as well as current to write tribute letters to Frank Lloyd Wright, which she compiled into a book in 2012.

CHAPTER THIRTY-THREE **Building**

1. Markalunas, Jim. *Aspen Memories: Recollections of Aspen.* Glenwood Springs, Colo.: Gran Farnum Printing & Publishing, Inc., 2010. 298, graphic: "The Big Snows of Sixty Years 1950 to 2010."

2. "Battered Block Walls of Boomerang Lodge Reflect Changing Play of Light and Shadow." *Modern Concrete.* January 1965. 24. The article also detailed the technical aspects of the battered block wall construction: "Each course was set out a half inch above grade, which is about the maximum offset. The total offset between bottom and top course was 12 inches. The 8 x 8 x 16 lightweight concrete blocks were reinforced with three-eighths steel bars vertically every 32 inches, filled with concrete, and placed horizontally as a bond beam, every third course."

3. Ibid.

4. In 1996 when I first read a translation of my aunt Claire's book *Adolf Loos Privat*, it was surprising to find a short chapter that Claire wrote about the Villa Müller in Prague entitled "Shimmering Fish." It is as follows: "The construction of the Müller house is still in the very early stages. Dr. Müller has taken Loos to the construction site for a meeting. Loos stands between some beams and points to a location. 'Here,' he says, 'is where the illuminated aquarium with the fish will be.' No one understands him. The client wants to move on— there are so many important things to discuss. But Loos remains still, unconcerned, and continues: 'This will be the favorite place of the master of the house; when he comes home in the evening tired from work, he will watch the fish silently playing. In the light of the lamps they will shimmer in all colors.' The client is already getting very annoyed, but Loos does not let it bother him. He—the only one who does not see the boards and scaffolds but rather the finished house—talks today only of the shimmering fish." (Loos, Claire Beck. *Adolf Loos—A Private Portrait.* 15.)

5. Lindbergh's isolationist America First Committee maintained that America could not assist Britain in winning the war against Hitler, having examined the situation "from the standpoint of aviation." He stated on April 23, 1941, in response to Roosevelt's Lend-Lease Act, "I do not believe we should be too quick to criticize the actions of a belligerent nation. There is always the question whether we, ourselves, would do better under similar circumstances. But we in this country have a right to think of the welfare of America first.... It is not only our right, but it is our obligation as American citizens to look at this war objectively." In a speech given on September 11, 1941 in Des Moines, Iowa, his plea became more targeted, singling out the British, the Roosevelt administration, and Jewish "propaganda" for driving the nation to war. Many were outraged by his characterizations. ("More about the Film *Lindbergh.*" pbs.org. Accessed June 27, 2012.)

6. In fact, McNamara struggled to make sense of the war for the rest of his life. (*The Fog of War: Eleven Lessons from the Life of Robert S. McNamara.* Dir. Errol Morris. 2003. Film.)

7. At age ninety-five, in 2012, Arnold Spielberg was given the inaugural Inspiration Award by the USC Shoah Foundation Institute, founded by his son Steven, which now holds over one hundred thousand hours of video testimonies from Holocaust survivors. A retired electrical engineer, Arnold took a leadership role in developing the archive's technology

and making it usable for scholars and the general public. Attributed to him are a range of important designs from his career, including the first electronic library system, the first electronic cash register, and the first business computer. The Inspiration Award will carry his name in perpetuity. (Tugend, Tom. "Shoah foundation presents inspiration award to Steven Spielberg's father." May 2, 2012. jewishjournal.com. Accessed October 20, 2012.)

CHAPTER THIRTY-FOUR **Pencil to Paper**

1. On invitation from Moholy-Nagy in 1947, Ferenc (Franz) Berko moved from India, where he and his wife Mirte Berko had been living for nine years, to teach photography and film at the Chicago Institute of Design. Berko had an international career, spanning Berlin, London, Bombay, Chicago, and later, Aspen, with exhibitions in the United States and Europe. Berko is considered as one of the twentieth century's one hundred top photographers. In addition to his creative work, he is known for documenting the growth of skiing in Aspen and its unique cultural life as the official photographer of Paepcke's Aspen Institute. (Mallory, Mirte Berko. Email to Carrie Paterson. August 12, 2012.)

2. Later I designed a house for the Koenigs in Hunter Creek that was not built because sadly, he died. The widow of my friend Lowell, Betty Greenwald, commissioned me for a remodel on Red Mountain that had been declared a teardown by the tax assessor's office. Adding a garage and driveway, a new entrance addition, and remodeling a funky paneled bedroom by removing a dated atrium were improvements that created light filled spaces and transformed the house.

3. Dutchess Ski Area has a small but fanatical following on the Internet, and there are calls to reopen it. ("Ski Dutchess!" slackpacker.com/dutchess.html. Accessed February 15, 2012.) The area now hosts one of the world's largest contemporary art museums, Dia: Beacon.

4. The piece was a conversation between architect/ski resort designer Laurent Chappis (b. 1915) and a staff writer for the ski industry magazine. They discuss, among other topics, the need to reconcile environmental awareness and the pleasures of nature with the social needs of humans. The Kaiser house was the only American illustration included in the article. The photograph of the house is captioned, "We must think in contemporary terms." ("In Search of Mountain Architecture." *Economie et Prospective de la Montagne* [E.P.M.]. 1965. 48.) A side note: Chappis planned the development of the *Trois Vallées*, the seven linked French resorts including Courchevel, while he was a POW in Austria in 1943. Throughout his career, he advocated for the environmental use of mountains rather than economic exploitation, and in the 1960's he was honored by the United Nations as an expert on mountain development. ("Laurent Chappis." pistehors.com; "Laurent Chappis." en.wikipedia.org. Both accessed December 27, 2012.)

5. Thomas Sichrovsky is the great-grandson of my great-aunt Elsa Feigl Klinger, sister of my grandmother Olga Beck. We met Thomas and his father Harry Sichrovsky, a wonderful man, when my wife Fonda and I traveled to Vienna with our daughters Carrie and Jenny in 1996. I recall we enjoyed an evening with them in a biergarten. Harry was a professor and an author who survived the war in England with his wife Lotte and even fought for the British Army. Another of Harry's sons, Peter Sichrovsky, is a well-known author and playwright who had a stint in politics and served two terms in the European Parliament. He was also a co-founder in 1988 of *Der Standard*, a liberal Austrian newspaper. It was a surprise when he joined Jorg Haider's demagogic, far-right "Freedom Party" in the 1990's, and it was equally interesting when it was revealed in 2005 that he had been collaborating with Israel's secret service, the Mossad, up until he left politics in

2002. (Boyes, Roger. "Mossad spied on far-right Austrian." *The Times* [London]. June 2, 2005. 42.)

6. During Wintersköl that year the Australians in this group had a very outrageous float from The Boomerang that consisted of a rough shelter built of pine branches to portray living in the outback. Dressed as Aborigines, they made war on other floats and threatened to throw boomerangs, which was not appreciated, especially by the people on the float from the Aspen Hospital. One of them with his boomerang disappeared into a limousine not to return for quite some time.

7. In the early 1990's a plan came together for a garage with a new deck and expanded breakfast room and entry, as well as a complete makeover of the exterior wood walls. New balconies were built out like the battered block at The Boomerang only made out of foam panels covered over in textured light grey stucco. Fonda and I collaborated on the design with interior designer Ray Lavender and his architect Doug Rager, who did all the working drawings for remodel and addition. (I decided that I should concentrate more on the hotel business rather than doing details—a good decision!) Copper cladding of all exterior railings and fascias added elegance and a finishing touch to the house. Fonda had key input, requesting a garage after we had had twenty plus years of shoveling cars out of the snow and scraping ice off the windshields. We also wanted to create more visual access to the river. This updated version of the original design makes the house feel palatial—in the 1970's the color palette was more like the log cabin, with warm wood tones.

8. A "Wilderness Workshop" lecture by Dee Malone given at the Aspen Center for Environmental Studies, April 5, 2012—"The American Dipper as an Indicator of River Health"—indicates that Dippers (also known as Water Ouzels) have made several anatomical adaptations to mountain streams including large feet for walking on slippery river rocks and the ability to communicate with other Dippers by blinking out signals with their highly visible eyelids of white feathers.

CHAPTER THIRTY-FIVE **Silversmithing**

1. The credits on the CRMS Fourth of July menu: "Baking—Dan Black, Abby Miller; Cooking—Kirk McAllister, Elizabeth Delgado, Kate Sontag, Shelley Arlen, Gregor Smith, and Steve Shanzer."

"American Indian Creampuffs" are my father's version of Indianerkrapfen, an invention by an unknown Hungarian pastry chef. The story goes that the experiment was initiated by Count Palffy, a Hungarian aristocrat, whose Theater an der Wien's musical operettas were failing to bring in large crowds in Vienna despite juggling acts and stunts by an American-Indian "chief" with a blowgun. The pastry chef reportedly made chocolate buns in the shape of the chief's head and filled it with whipped cream, the first time whipped cream had been used in a dessert. Soon Palffy's Theater had long lines, and all the pastry shops in Vienna were selling their own versions of the "Indianer," or *Mohrenkopf*, which you can still find today. (Lang, George. Milton Glaser, illus. *Lang's Compendium of Culinary Nonsense and Trivia*. New York: Clarkson N. Potter, Inc./ Publishers, 1980. 72-73.)

2. My father had another story about the different ways the international players in Vladivostok dealt with the issue of money and goods. He said, "In the camp, the Austro-Hungarian men were commanded to assist Americans in unloading the supplies from ships. Much of this was clothing, and soon half the town wore American uniforms. The reason lay in the fact that many of the shipping cases were dropped on purpose by the

Austrian men unloading them onto the docks, where the cases broke open and everyone helped themselves. The Austrians then sold the goods to the Chinese, who were waiting outside.

"I was asked to look into this matter for the Austro-Hungarian commanding officer. This was strange in itself because the monarchy did not exist anymore, and yet there he was, this Austro-Hungarian Kommandant. The officers were never permitted to go to work at the docks—that was left to the [enlisted] men—so I dressed more shabbily than usual and masqueraded as one of the men of my company. The Czechoslovak who commanded them looked suspiciously at me, but on the day I went, only chemicals were unloaded. Nothing was dropped, so I could make no report. Soon after that, dock duty was deemed unsafe, and volunteers were no longer taken.

"The Austrians were allowed to buy things at the Japanese exchange. The merchandise there was of very bad quality; the matches didn't light, and the pencils didn't write. Nevertheless they looked like the real thing. The most important item was sake, the Japanese rice whiskey. The men bought it for one yen and sold it again for one dollar, which meant a profit of one hundred per cent." (Schanzer, Steve. Interview with Frank Day, Jr. Circa July/August 1952.)

3. Rachamimov 192-193.

4. Rachamimov 136-137, 155.

CHAPTER THIRTY-SIX **Still Escaping**

1. Self-proclaimed Ataman ("Chief") Grigory Mikhaylovich Semenov (1890-1946) was the General of the anti-Bolshevik Cossacks and the Commissar of the Provisional Government in the Baikal region from December 1917 to November 1920. The so-called Siberian Provisional Government had appointed Semenov commander of a detached unit with headquarters in Chita. Supported by the Japanese, the "White resistance" leader imposed his ruthless regime, while his troops marauded, stole railcars, and made a bloodbath of the Eastern Siberia region. ("Grigory Semyonov." en.wikipedia.org. Accessed June 28, 2012.)

2. The grandfather of Carlo Schanzer (1865-1953) was Maximilian Schanzer, brother of Jacob, my second great grandfather. Carlo Schanzer was not only Italy's finance minister during the First World War, but after, he became a senator. He was a registered Italian Fascist starting in 1926, but he retired from politics at age sixty-three in 1928. His grandson is the Italian statesman Carlo Ripa di Meana (born 1929), a Socialist who has become an environmental leader and is also former president of the Venice Biennale (1974-1978). ("Carlo Schanzer." it.wikipedia.org. Accessed July 12, 2012.)

3. To have a salary at that time was unusual. The Bolsheviks cut officers off immediately after the revolution because they saw them as "class enemies" (Rachamimov 102).

4. Viscount Ferdinand de Lesseps (1805-1894) was a French diplomat at the time of Napoleon and was also the French developer of the Suez Canal. Later he was involved in a scandal when his Panama Canal Company was found to have bribed French deputies to secure funding for that project. ("Ferdinand, viscount de Lesseps." Britannica.com. Accessed June 28, 2012.) Thus, the Panama Canal was never built by him but rather by the United States.

5. The family fortune disappeared supposedly under the mismanagement of a relative of the German playwright Berthold Brecht, who we can trace as a relation through several marriages to my mother's side of the family. As it was, my father returned from Siberia to Vienna to survive on his primary resources—ingenuity, thrift, and will.

CHAPTER THIRTY-SEVEN **Adaptations**

1. *Who Was Karl Kraus?* BBC-3. Circa December 7, 1999. Radio broadcast.

2. Domanický 60.

3. *The Last Days of Mankind.* Written by Karl Kraus, adapted and directed by Giles Havergal. BBC-3. Circa December 7, 1999. Radio.

4. Seeds of *The Last Days of Mankind* are seen in Kraus' editorial from February 23, 1915 published in *Die Fackel*, "*Ein Tag aus der Grossen Zeit* [A Day in the Great Age]," where he ran, side by side, two accounts of one day in the Empire. The first, an eye-witness report from the battle lines, and the second from the opening of the new Kaiser Wilhelm Café. (Vergo, Peter. *Art in Vienna 1898-1918: Klimt, Kokoschka, Schiele and Their Contemporaries.* London: Phaidon Press, Ltd, 1975. 220-223.) This shocking duality is worth reading and reflecting upon in our own day and time after America's decade-long engagement in foreign wars, which were largely invisible to the populace at home.

CHAPTER THIRTY-EIGHT **A Philosophy of Life**

1. The house at the Werkbundsiedlung was Neutra's only realized project in his native Vienna. (Mac Lamprecht, Barbara. *Neutra: Complete Works.* Köln: Taschen, 2010. 98.)

2. In late-May 1945 the former architect and author Simon Wiesenthal (1908-2005), upon his release from the Austrian concentration camp Mauthausen, one of the last to be liberated by the Allies, was told he could go back to building houses. Wiesenthal, weighing less than one hundred pounds from near starvation, said, "Build houses? You think you can continue in the same place where the life was interrupted? We have not only lost people and houses, but everything [we] believe in." Instead of pursuing architecture, he founded a documentation center for war crimes in Vienna that changed history and helped bring many Nazis to face war criminal tribunals over the course of his lifetime. But Wiesenthal was indeed still an architect—he made his life into a memorial, remembering all the people, including almost ninety members of his own family, who perished in the monstrous Nazi camps. He helped crack the stoic face of Vienna after the war, where many people were trying to put everything behind them in a collective and systematic effort of active forgetting. Wiesenthal went on to integrate the lessons he learned from his own history to advocate for tolerance and justice in all parts of the world, speaking out against genocides in the former Yugoslavia, Cambodia, and Rwanda. (*I Have Never Forgotten You: The Life and Legacy of Simon Wiesenthal.* Dir. Richard Trank. Narrated by Nicole Kidman. Moriah Films of the Simon Wiesenthal Center, 2006.)

3. The rings are pictured on page 419.

4. My sixth cousin, the Viennese philosopher and architect Ludwig Wittgenstein advised that to be a good philosopher, one should become an auto mechanic. (Martin, Andy. "Beyond Understanding." *New York Times.* opinionator.blogs.nytimes.com. November 21, 2010. Accessed January 15, 2011.) (Wittgenstein is related to us through another branch of the Sinzheim family than ours and was born the same year as my father, 1889.)

Wittgenstein was not only a philosopher, but he was also an architect. The distance in our family tree to Wittgenstein is paralleled by distinct ideas about architecture, as seen in our relationship to the architect of our Werkbundsiedlung house, Jacques Groag. Though Wittgenstein had been working with Loos' former student, architect Paul Engelmann, he hired Groag to do the final technical drawings and engineering on a large villa commissioned by Wittgenstein's sister Margaret Stonborough; it was a demanding position for Groag in what was Vienna's most structurally and technically complex villa of the time, not to mention the most expensive. (Kapfinger, Otto. Email to Carrie Paterson. August 30, 2012.) Groag had worked in the same manner for Loos at the textile businessman Moller's house (finished in that same year, 1928). Because of Groag's experience on both projects, the architecture of Groag is considered somewhere between Wittgenstein and Loos (Wijdeveld, Paul. Ludwig Wittgenstein Architect. Amsterdam: Pepin Press, 1993. 145). Of the Werkbundsiedlung, where Groag built one of his later and more refined projects—our house, which we loved—Wittgenstein criticized the openness of its "bloody modern houses" as "indecent" and remarked, "Look at all these houses. They are grinning at you." (Quoted on 161-162.)

5. As shown in the book *Reclaiming Heimat: Trauma and Mourning in Memoirs by Jewish Austrian Reémigres* by Jacqueline Vansant (Detroit, Mich.: Wayne State University Press, 2001), for many Jewish-Austrians facing the loss of their "homeland" (*Heimat*) after the *Anschluss*, exile meant the loss of self and community, language and identity. Acquiring a second language in a new place could never restore the "intimacy" and "spatial ties" found at home (38). Going "home" was actually impossible and disillusioning, because lost time could never be recovered, environments were forever altered, and relationships were drastically shifted by divergent experiences and suffering during the war. According to Vansant, one of the authors profiled named Jean Améry, a survivor of Auschwitz, viewed "his relationship to the land and his fellow (but non-Jewish) Austrians as an illusion." She quotes Améry, "We had not lost our country, but had to realize that it had never been ours. For us, whatever was linked with this land and its people was an existential misunderstanding" (39).

In the face of our own crisis, we realize now that my father, my sister, and I as émigrés resolved to bring all our spatial identifiers with us—the maps, the phone book, architecture plans, pictures, letters, all the smells in the kitchen, the coffee rituals, genealogical notes, modes of travel from skiing to folboating, and a leaf from our cherry tree to remember my mother—to try not to be homesick, but suspended in the exercise of constantly recreating home as an idea, and being "at home" as a state of mind.

6. On October 6, 1979, two days after my father's death, among the mountain of sympathy cards and letters we received, came a letter from Margaret Day, our old friend from the Holiday House. She wrote, "Steve is gone and even though you knew that the end was imminent, it hurts, deep and long. I sat out alone on the patio tonight, looking at the moon on the water, and thinking about the happy times we had with your father. When we sat around talking late into the night, with the 'grog' he had concocted. Of the long talks, when he recounted his adventures in Siberia. What a man. With such a will to survive. He had force, [a] determined purpose, but withal, such a loving, gentle, tender nature.... He put up a good fight, and that is something to remember with respect, too. Extend my love to Doris. I know it will hit her very hard. And to the whole family.... Sorrow is sorrow; no escape."

7. Bolaño, Roberto. "Literature and Exile." *The Nation.* January 31, 2011. 32.

CHAPTER THIRTY-NINE **A Cabin Is A Castle**

No endnotes. ■

Selected Bibliography

BOOKS

Albright, Madeleine Korbel. *Prague Winter: A Personal Story of Remembrance and War, 1937-1948*. New York: Harper, 2012.

Blakeney, Michael. *Australia and the Jewish Refugees 1933-1948*. Sydney: Croom Helm, 1985.

Blau, Eve. *The Architecture of Red Vienna 1919-1934*. Cambridge, Mass.: MIT Press, 1999.

De Waal, Edmund. *The Hare with Amber Eyes*. London: Vintage, 2011.

Felt, R. W. Abraham. *Poetic Gems*. New York: Humanitas Lodge No. 123 F. & A.M., 1948.

Fitzgerald, Ross. *The People's Champion*. Brisbane: University of Queensland Press, 1997.

Foster, Hal. *Prosthetic Gods*. Cambridge, Mass: MIT Press, 2004.

Gainham, Sarah. *Night Falls on the City: A Novel about Vienna*. New York: Henry Holt & Company, 1967.

Gaugusch, Georg. *Wer einmal war—Das jüdische Großbürgertum Wiens 1800-1938* A-K [Who was who—The Jewish grand bourgeoisie of Vienna 1800-1938 A-K]. Vienna: Amalthea-Publishing House, 2011.

Gerwarth, Robert. *Hitler's Hangman: The Life of Heydrich*. New Haven, Conn.: Yale University Press, 2011.

Gottwaldt, Alfred and Diana Schulle. *Die "Judendeportationen" aus dem Deutschen Reich 1941-1945* [Deportation of Jews from the German Reich 1941-1945]. Wiesbaden: Marix Verlag, 2005.

Guide to the Musée d'Orsay. Anthony Roberts, trans. Paris: Ministère de la Culture et de la Communication Éditions de la Réunion de muses nationaux, 1987.

Gunther, John. *The Lost City*. New York: Harper & Row, 1964.

"Habsburg" (Vienna) Phone Book. 1936.

Hašek, Jaroslav. *The Good Soldier Švejk and His Fortunes in the World War.* Cecil Parrott, trans. Josef Lada, illustr. Bungay, Suffolk: Penguin Books, in association with William Heinemann, 1975.

Heer, Hannes, Walter Manoschek, Alexander Pollak, Ruth Wodak, eds. *The Discursive Construction of History: Remembering the Wehrmacht's War of Annihilation.* New York: Palgrave Macmillan, 2008.

James, Harold. *The Deutsche Bank and the Nazi Economic War Against the Jews.* Cambridge: Cambridge University Press, 2001.

Jenks, William A. *Vienna and the Young Hitler.* New York: Columbia University Press, 1960.

Karny, Miroslav, ed. *Terezinska pametni kniha* [Terezín Memorial Book]. Prague: Melantrich, 1995.

Kodek, Günter K. *Unsere Bausteine sind die Menschen: Die Mitglieder der Wiener Freimaurerlogen (1869-1938)* [Our Building Blocks are the People: Members of the Viennese Masonic Lodges (1869-1938)]. Vienna: Löker Verlag, 2009.

Kovály, Heda Margolius. *Under a Cruel Star: A Life in Prague 1941-1968.* Helen Epstein, trans. New York: Holmes & Meier Publishers, Inc., 1997.

Krischanitz, Adolf and Otto Kapfinger. *Die Wiener Werkbundsiedlung— Dokumentation Einer Erneuerung* [The Vienna Werkbundsiedlung— Documentation of a Renovation]. Vienna: Compress Verlag, 1985.

Larson, Erik. *In the Garden of Beasts: Love, Terror, and an American Family in Hitler's Berlin.* New York: Crown Publishing, Random House, Inc., 2011.

Loos, Claire Beck. *Adolf Loos—A Private Portrait.* Carrie Paterson ed., Constance C. Pontasch and Nicholas Saunders, trans. Los Angeles: DoppelHouse Press, 2011.

———. *Adolf Loos Privat.* Vienna: Czernin Verlag, 2007.

———. *Adolf Loos Privat.* Adolf Opel, ed. Vienna: Verlag Hermann Böhlaus Nachfolger, 1985.

———. *Adolf Loos Privat.* Vienna: Johannes-Presse, 1936.

Mac Lamprecht, Barbara. *Neutra: Complete Works.* Köln: Taschen, 2010.

Makarova, Elena. *Friedl Dicker-Brandeis Vienna 1898-Auschwitz 1944: The Artist Who Inspired the Children's Drawings of Terezín.* Los Angeles: Tallfellow/Every Picture Press, 1999.

Manson, Grant Carpenter. *Frank Lloyd Wright to 1910: The First Golden Age.* New York: Wiley, 1979.

Margolius, Ivan. *Reflections of Prague: Journeys through the 20th Century.* Chichester, West Sussex: Wiley, 2006.

Markalunas, Jim. *Aspen Memories: Recollections of Aspen.* Glenwood Springs, Colo.: Gran Farnum Printing & Publishing, Inc., 2010.

McCagg, William O. *A History of Habsburg Jews, 1670-1918.* Bloomington: Indiana University Press, 1989.

Nemtin, Frances. *Midway Farm at Taliesin.* 2003.

O'Connor, Anne-Marie. *The Lady in Gold: The Extraordinary Tale of Gustav Klimt's Masterpiece, Portrait of Adele Bloch-Bauer.* New York: Knopf, 2012.

Pfeifer, Friedl with Morten Lund. *Nice Goin': My Life on Skis.* Missoula, Mont.: Pictorial Histories Publishing Company, Inc., 1993.

Rachamimov, Alon. *POWs and the Great War: Captivity on the Eastern Front.* Oxford: Berg, 2002.

Roberts, Andrew. *The Storm of War: A New History of the Second World War.* London: Allen Lane, 2009.

Rukschcio, Burkhardt. *Adolf Loos: Apartment for Richard Hirsch.* Prague: Adolf Loos Apartment & Gallery, 2012.

Rukschcio, Burkhardt and Roland L. Schachel. *Adolf Loos—Leben und Werke.* Vienna: Residenz Verlag, 1982.

Russell, Gordon and Jacques Groag. *The Story of Furniture.* No. 50 of the Puffin Picture Books. Harmondsworth, Middlesex: Penguin Books Limited, 1947.

Sarnitz, August. *Adolf Loos 1870-1933: Architect, Cultural Critic, Dandy.* Cologne: Taschen, 2003.

Scheine, Judith. *R.M. Schindler.* London: Phaidon Press Ltd., 2001.

Siry, Joseph M. *Beth Sholom Synagogue: Frank Lloyd Wright and Modern Religious Architecture.* Chicago and London: University of Chicago Press, 2012.

The Valley of the God-Almighty Joneses: Remembrances of Frank Lloyd Wright's Sister Maginel Wright Barney. Spring Green, Wisc.: Unity Chapel Publications, 1985.

Vansant, Jacqueline. *Reclaiming Heimat: Trauma and Mourning in Memoirs by Jewish Austrian Reémigres.* Detroit, Mich.: Wayne State University Press, 2001.

Vergo, Peter. *Art in Vienna 1898-1918: Klimt, Kokoschka, Schiele and Their Contemporaries*. London: Phaidon Press, Ltd., 1975.

Von Doderer, Heimito. *Das Geheimnis des Reichs* [The Secret of the Empire]. John S. Barrett, trans. Riverside, Calif.: Ariadne Press, 1998.

Wijdeveld, Paul. *Ludwig Wittgenstein Architect*. Amsterdam: Pepin Press, 1993.

Wright, Frank Lloyd. *A Testament*. New York: Horizon Press, 1957.

———. *An Autobiography*. New York: Duell, Sloan, and Pearce, 1943.

ARTICLES IN BOOKS

Domanický, Petr. "Loos-Pilsen-Connections." *Loos-Pilsen-Connections*. Domanický, Petr and Petr Jindra, eds. Pilsen: Západočeská Galerie, 2011.

Kwiet, Konrad. "The Ultimate Refuge: Suicide in the Jewish Community under the Nazis." *Leo Baeck Institute Yearbook*. London: Martin Secker & Warburg Ltd., 1984.

Leach, Andrew. "Helmut Einhorn: Dislocation and modern architecture in New Zealand." *Fabrications: The Journal of the Society of Architectural Historians, Australia and New Zealand*. Brisbane: University of Queensland Press, 2004.

Lederer, Zedenek. "Terezín." *The Jews of Czechoslovakia*. Philadelphia: Jewish Publication Society, 1984.

Lexa, John G. "Anti-Jewish Laws and Regulations in the Protectorate of Bohemia and Moravia." *The Jews of Czechoslovakia*. Philadelphia: Jewish Publication Society, 1984.

Loos, Adolf. "Ornament and Crime (1929)." *Adolf Loos Ornament and Crime: Selected Essays*. Adolf Opel, ed. Michael Mitchell, trans. Riverside, Calif.: Ariadne Press, 1998.

Rothkirchen, Livia. "The Jews of Bohemia and Moravia: 1938-1945." *The Jews of Czechoslovakia*. Jewish Publication Society: Philadelphia: Jewish Publication Society, 1984.

ARTICLES IN PERIODICALS, PRINT

Addison, Annie. "Camp Hale's Second Generation: It's been 50 years since the Mountain & Cold Weather Training Command." *Aspen Times*. March 24, 2007.

Anonymous ("A Brisbane Reader"). "By Train and Buggy to 'Bundi' Station, in 1913." *The Australian Women's Weekly*. December 29, 1971.

Auer, James. "Home" section (Frederick C. Bogk House). *Milwaukee Journal*. January 30, 1983.

"Battered Block Walls of Boomerang Lodge Reflect Changing Play of Light and Shadow." *Modern Concrete.* January 1965.

Berendtson, Indira. "Olgivanna Lloyd Wright—A 'Vivid Inspiration.'" *Frank Lloyd Wright Quarterly.* Vol. 23: 2. Spring 2012.

Bolaño, Roberto. "Literature and Exile." *The Nation.* January 31, 2011.

Burke, Ted. "Burke's Guide: The World's Leading Winter Resorts." *Town & Country.* Vol. 123, No. 4563. October 1969; Vol. 126, No. 4596. July 1972.

Case, Holly. "Innocents Lost." *The Nation.* October 31, 2011.

Colomina, Beatriz. "Intimacy and Spectacle: The Interiors of Adolf Loos." *AA files: annals of the Architectural Association School of Architecture.* Volume 1. 1990.

Glaberson, William. "For Betrayal by Swiss Bank and Nazis, $21 Million." *New York Times.* April 4, 2005.

"In Search of Mountain Architecture." *Economie et Prospective de la Montagne* [E.P.M.]. 1965.

Krippner, Ulrike and Iris Meder. "Cultivating, Designing, and Teaching: Jewish Women in Modern Viennese Garden Architecture." *Landscape Research.* Vol. 36: 6. 2011.

Maciuika, John. "Adolf Loos and Aphoristic Style: Rhetorical Practice in Early Twentieth-Century Design Criticism." *Design Issues.* Vol. 16: 2. Summer 2000.

Margolius, Ivan. "Journey to the Interior: Hidden Treasures." *Building Design.* March 4, 2011.

Oettinger. Rebecca Wagner. Book review for *Essays on Music and Culture of Herbert Kellman. The Sixteenth Century Journal.* Vol. 35: 3. Fall 2004.

Smith, Margaret Supplee. *Aspen's Twentieth Century Architecture: Modernism 1945-1975.* Aspen: Historical Preservation Commission, 2010.

Stewart, Janet. "Talking of Modernity: The Viennese 'Vortrag' as Form." *German Life and Letters.* Vol. 51: 4. October 1998.

Strusková, Eva. "Ghetto *Theresienstadt 1942*: The Message of the Film Fragments." *Journal of Film Preservation.* Vol. 79/80. 2009.

"This Month's Small House." *Ideal Home and Gardening.* Vol. LIII, No. III. March 1946.

Uyehara, Annie. "10th Mountain Redux." *Skiing Heritage.* May/June 2012.

Wooding, Sharon. "Steve Shanzer." *The First Twenty-Five Years.* Carbondale, Colo.: Colorado Rocky Mountain School, July 1979.

ARTICLES IN PERIODICALS, ACCESSED ONLINE

Bennett, Magnus. "Heir to Stolen Jewish Property Foiled by Czech Restitution Law." *Jewish Telegraphic Agency*. Reposted on highbeam.com. April 25, 2001.

Cohen, Adam. "Frank Lloyd Wright 'Builds' Baghdad ..." *Wall Street Journal*. online.wsj.com. August 20, 2003.

Cunningham, Benjamin and Filip Šenk. "Mass Grave Vandalism Opens Old Wounds: Nationalists again bring post-WWII atrocities into focus." *The Prague Post*. praguepost.com. November 2, 2011.

Elkins, James R. "Strangers to Us All—Lawyers and Poetry: Abraham Felt." mywebwvnet.edu. Undated.

Elman, Kimberly. "Frank Lloyd Wright and the Principles of Organic Architecture." pbs.org. Undated.

Kunc, Lubor. "Censorship in Czech Lands 1938-1945." czechphilatelist.tripod. com/cenzury. Circa 2002.

Martin, Andy. "Beyond Understanding." *New York Times*. opinionator.blogs. nytimes.com. November 21, 2010.

Mead, Rebecca. "Winged Victories: The Soaring Ambition of Santiago Calatrava." *The New Yorker*. newyorker.com. September 1, 2008.

O'Connor, Anne-Marie. "Fighting for Her Past." *LA Times*. articles.latimes.com. March 20, 2001.

Ringle, Ken. "The Genie in an Architect's Lamp: Frank Lloyd Wright's '57 Plan for Baghdad May Be Key to Its Future." *Washington Post*. washingtonpost.com. June 29, 2003.

Uygur, Selçuk. "Second World War Studies: Mischlinge and the Question of Hybridity in the Third Reich." *Yer Altindan Notlar*. selcukuyger.com. August 26, 2011.

"Wien: Sanierung der Werkbundsiedlung beginnt [Vienna: Rennovation of the Werkbundsiedlung begins]." *Die Presse*. diepresse.com. August 18, 2011.

ARCHIVES

Adolf Loos Archive. Albertina. Augustinerstraße 1. A-1010. Vienna. Austria.

Beck, Max. Personal archives. York. England.

Österreichisches Staatsarchiv. Nottendorfergasse 2. A-1030 Vienna. Austria.

Paterson, Charles. Personal archives. Aspen. Colorado.

Schanzer, Steve. Personal archives. Aspen. Colorado.

MEMOIRS

Parnegg, Hannes.

Schneider, Herbert Anton Maxemilian. *A Fortunate Life.*

Semler, Will. *The Family Paperweight.*

INTERVIEWS AND TRANSCRIPTS OF INTERVIEWS

Day, Frank Jr. Transcript of interview with Steve Schanzer. July/August 1952.

Engle, Linda R. Schneider. "Journey to Freedom: Steven B. Schanzer's WWII Bicycle Escape across France." Transcription of Steve Schanzer's interview with Thomas Dana Schneider. June 21/22, 1971.

Pfeifer, Friedl. Interview with Annie Gilbert. *Heritage West.* cdp.coalliance.org. July 21, 1994.

Schanzer, Steve. Interviews with Thomas Dana Schneider. December 1970/ January 1971; June 21/22, 1971. Tape recordings.

Von Hennig, Ilse. Interview with Burkhardt Rukschcio. *Der Künstlerkreis um Adolf Loos. Aufbruch zur Jahrhundertwende* [The Artist Circle of Adolf Loos at the Turn of the Century]. Sonderheft 2. Vienna: Parnass Verlag, 1985.

Willoughby, Ian. "The Song of Terezín: the remarkable story of how poems written by children in the Terezín ghetto became a moving oratorio." Transcript of interview with Alena Munkova-Synkova, child survivor of Terezín. Radio Prague. radio.cz. January 30, 2004.

EXHIBITIONS

"Learning to Dwell: Adolf Loos' Works in the Czech Lands." Maria Szadkowska, Curator. Royal Institute of British Architects (RIBA). 66 Portland Place, London W1B 1AD. England. February 24 – May 3, 2011.

"Loos-Pilsen-Connections: Places, People, Events—Loos' Work for Pilsen in Context." Petr Domanický and Petr Jindra, Curators. Západočeská Galerie Exhibition Hall "13." Pražská 13, 2. patro. 301 00 Pilsen. Czech Republic. November 7, 2011 – February 12, 2012

Los Angeles Museum of the Holocaust. Permanent exhibit. 100 The Grove Drive. Los Angeles, CA 90041. United States.

"Vienna's Shooting Girls: Female Jewish Photographers in Vienna." Iris Meder and Andrea Winklbauer, Curators. Jewish Museum Vienna. Dorotheergasse 11. A-1010 Vienna. Austria. October 23, 2012 – March 3, 2013.

Villa Müller (Prague City Museum). Permanent exhibit. Nad Hradním vodojemem 14,CZ 162 00 Prague 6—Střešovice. Czech Republic.

"Werkbundsiedlung Wien 1932—Ein Manifest des Neuen Wohnens" [Werkbundsiedlung Vienna 1932—A Model for New Living]. Eva-Maria Orosz and Andreas Nierhaus, Curators. Wien Museum. Karlsplatz. A-1040 Vienna. Austria. September 4, 2012 – January 13, 2013.

RADIO, FILM, AND TELEVISION

Cheyenne Autumn. Dir. John Ford. Warner Brothers, 1964. Film.

Devil's Doorway. Dir. Anthony Mann. Perf. Robert Taylor, Louis Calhern, Paula Raymond. Metro-Goldwyn-Mayer, 1950. Film.

The Fog of War: Eleven Lessons from the Life of Robert S. McNamara. Dir. Errol Morris. Sony Pictures Classics, 2003. Film.

Frank Lloyd Wright. Dirs. Ken Burns and Lynn Novik. PBS, 1998. Film.

I Have Never Forgotten You: The Life and Legacy of Simon Wiesenthal. Dir. Richard Trank. Narrated by Nicole Kidman. Moriah Films of the Simon Wiesenthal Center, 2006. Film.

In the Presence of Good: Sir Nicholas Winton. Bratislava History Project, 2008. Video.

The Last Days of Mankind. Written by Karl Kraus, adapted and directed by Giles Havergal. BBC-3. Circa December 7, 1999. Radio.

Legacy: Austria's Influence on American Skiing–Hannes Schneider and His Disciples. Dir. Ian Scully, 2006. Film.

Little Skier's Big Day. Dir. Fred Iselin. H. J. Heinz Company, 1956. Film.

The Sound of Skiing. Messinger, Marie-Claire and Nicole Dietrich. Österreichischer Rundfunk. February 13, 2010. Radio.

V Plzni objevili nové interiéry architekta Aldolfa Loose [A new interior by architect Adolf Loos is discovered in Pilsen]. Česká televize [Czech TV], March 3, 2012. Television and Webcast. ceskatelevize.cz.

Who Was Karl Kraus? BBC-3. Circa December 7, 1999. Radio.

Acknowledgments

We thank our editor Hensley Peterson for her dedication to the project of *Escape Home*. She has been part of this book from beginning to end, and it reads as it does because of her nuanced understanding of all that is bound within these pages. She has carefully considered the way these stories reflect onto the world, which demonstrates her fine ability to listen and to deeply engage with the material she is editing and reading. We could not have produced this book without her guidance and friendship, astute responses and observations, her compassion, vision, and kindness.

Fonda Paterson entered into this story in 1968 when she came to work at The Boomerang and began eliciting stories from her future father-in-law Steve, recording them, and researching historical facts. Her desire to understand and willingness to ask questions have not abated. She worked diligently with the authors and editors reading every word in this book, continuing to find parallels and connections across families and time. Her contributions and fine-tuning have made this book into more than a meaningful family endeavor, but also a historical memoir.

Author and editor Paul Andersen has been an important contributor to this project. He spent many hours doing interviews with us and helping us organize our thoughts, as well as working with Steve's dictated histories to make them more easily read, meeting with Hensley and our family, and editing long letters. Paul asked questions and made suggestions that sent us down fruitful paths of inquiry both into our history and into the book's structure.

Beatrice Lang has accompanied us through the book in many respects with her insightful comments and knowledge of family history. Beatrice, who is the daughter of Philippe Lang, Raoul Lang's cousin, also found the small plaque memorializing those interned like my father at the camp in Audierne, Brittany and took Carrie there in 2011, just as

Philippe had done thirty years earlier with Steve, before the location was commemorated with a marker.

Janet Beck Wilson has been a great personal support and generous with her time, advising us and allowing us access to papers and photographs she inherited from her father Max Beck. Through Janet's extensive family research over the past two decades we have come closer to understanding the lives of Otto and Olga Beck and their children.

Australians Katy Connolly Common and her cousin Jane Wyatt Holmes, granddaughters of the Patersons, graciously provided additional information for us about the Paterson family.

For both Claire Beck Loos' book *Adolf Loos—A Private Portrait* and this one, we worked with the multi-talented graphic designer Curt Carpenter. We thank him for his patience, advice, guidance, and expertise. We thank Bobette Host for the creation of our detailed index.

E. Randol Schoenberg helped connect many of the dots on our shared family tree. He discovered the extensive Schanzer clan in Żywiec (Galicia) as well as the relation of Bernhard and Moriz Schanzer. His curatorial work with Geni and JewishGen, among other genealogical projects, has facilitated a network of researchers around the world who are putting back together a picture of Jewish life in Europe before the Holocaust. Through these sites we have been able to see scanned pages from archival records and newspapers, allowing us to trace lost family.

Other family history we were happy to find through writer Ivan Margolius. We thank him for his friendship and intellectual curiosity, his fact-checking, and willingness to translate documents and letters from Czech. He found street names in Prague whose German names no longer exist and pointed us to helpful articles by the Jewish Publication Society to contextualize and reconstruct Claire and Olga's lives in Czechoslovakia during the war.

Architectural scholar Otto Kapfinger advised us on the Viennese architecture sections of this book. We appreciate his enthusiasm, expertise, intuition, and kind responses to all our inquiries, as well as his footwork in archives and bookstores finding sources in German and uncovering mysteries.

Constance Pontasch, Beatrice Lang, Margo Gubser, Nora Berko, Kurt Bresnitz, Lukas Beck, and Benoit de Lavassier translated documents from French and German printed here. Will Casey and Ashley

Nowygrod assured our documents' preservation through their long hours of scanning and transcribing.

Linda Schneider Engle helped us clarify key details about the paths of travel Steve took through France and through Siberia. Her transcripts of Steve's adventures recorded by her brother Tom Schneider, along with her research and photographs taken as she traced Steve's routes contributed to our understanding of geography and context.

We want to thank our readers—Paul Andersen, Tom Shakow, Seph Rodney, Jenny Paterson Rose, her husband Evan Rose, Linda Schneider Engle, Beatrice Lang, and Su Lum, columnist for *The Aspen Times.* As well we extend our gratitude to those people we have met on recent trips to London, Vienna, Pilsen, and Prague, who have enlightened us to important architectural history and to our families' lives. Among these are editor, playwright, and filmmaker Adolf Opel; the late architect Brigitte Heinz, daughter of Ilse and Oskar von Hennig, her husband Ing. Mag. Arch. Raimund Heinz, and two of her sons, Philipp and Lukas; our Viennese relatives Herbert Beck, Jr., his son Lukas Beck, Ilse Zak, and her daughter Ingrid Zak; Marie-Claire de Foestraets and her husband Renaud de Foestraets; Dr. Peter Csoklich and his mother, Effi Csoklich; Dr. Irena Murray at the Royal Institute of British Architects; John and Christine Winterburgh; Prof. Otto Kapfinger; Dr. Andreas Nierhaus and Mag. Eva-Maria Orosz of the Wien Museum; Dr. Iris Meder; Mgr. Vladimír Lekeš; Dr. Burkhardt Rukschcio, through his correspondence with us; and Mgr. Maria Szadkowska, curator and director of the foundation that runs Loos' Villa Müller as part of the Prague City Museum.

Of special mention are Mgrs. Petr Jindra and Petr Domanický of Pilsen's Západočeská Galerie. They engaged in detailed research putting together the exhibition on Loos clients that included the Beck-Hirsch-Kraus extended family. We thank Petr Domanický for finding the Beck family headstone in Pilsen's Jewish cemetery, and we appreciate Petr Jindra's kind coordination with the Jewish community there to have the stone refurbished and a plaque added for Olga and Claire. We also thank Petr Jindra for his continued correspondence with us, his fact-checking, and his scholarly insight into Oskar Kokoschka's paintings of our relatives Martha and Wilhelm Hirsch.

The delightful wedding poem sent by my great-uncle Robert Beck to my parents was retrieved from the Vienna Beck's family archives by Robert's great-grandson Lukas Beck. Not leaving a stone unturned, Lukas has spent many hours scanning photographs and documents, as well as joining us on several research expeditions and performing his own detailed family history investigations.

Professor Hans Puchhammer generously shared his and his students' visualization of Loos' "1930 Paris Plan," the 9 x 9 meter house that is the precursor to the newly identified "Haus Schanzer" intended for the Werkbundsiedlung.

We thank former and current members of the Aspen Music Festival and School: Ara Guzelimian, Mark Ludwig, Asadour Santourian, Murray Sidlin, and Nancy Thomas; also Andreas Haefliger, for a detailed etymological understanding of the "Pleite Geier."

For allowing us to publish articles, letters, family portraits, stories, poems, photographs, and transcripts, we thank Herbert Beck and Lukas Beck, Perry Curtis, Frank Day Jr., Marie-Claire de Foestraets, Linda Schneider Engle, Evol Ferguson at the *Australian Women's Weekly*, Mohsen Ghajari of Humanitas Lodge, The Aspen Historical Society, Wes Horner, Dr. Ingrid Kastel of the Albertina, Slide Kelly, Herbert Kellman, Dr. Markus Kristan of the Albertina, Bob Krueger, H. Stephen Lieb of Humanitas Lodge, David O. Marlow, Dave Olson, Peter Parnegg, Eva Popper, Doug Rager, Tom Schneider, Will Semler, Janet Beck Wilson, and Sharon Wooding.

Steve's friend, who shared his Vladivostok prison camp photos in San Francisco after they met for the first time in the 1960's, will unfortunately remain nameless, but appreciated nonetheless.

ADDITIONAL ACKNOWLEDGMENTS

By Charles Paterson

I would like to specially thank the CRMS community, including particularly the Holdens and the Hause family, for giving my father a second home during his twenty-five years of teaching at the school.

Kit and Jim Bulkley, some of my early guests at The Boomerang and special friends, took in my father and me—two bachelors then—and included our family at their holiday dinners for over fifty years, soon with our daughters, their husbands, other visiting relatives, and with the Bulkley's son Jim Flint, daughter Kate Bulkley, and son-in-law Ross Biddiscombe. Many stories were told at these events and will continue to be. We all mourn the loss of Jim senior in the spring of 2012.

And to my sister Doris, though she is no longer with us, I am grateful for her letters and that we journeyed together through travails, but also shared each other's happiness at founding new lives in the United States.

Finally, and most significantly, I am grateful to my wife Fonda and to my daughter Carrie. I extend warm thanks to all our friends for their ongoing encouragement and for waiting decades to see these stories compiled into a book.

ADDITIONAL ACKNOWLEDGMENTS

By Carrie Paterson

In addition to the above, I would like to thank Casady Henry, Krissy Henry, Ben Madley, Rick Magnuson, Joanna Roche, Evan Rose, Judy Ross, Elham Shoja, and Liat Yossifor. I extend special thanks to my sister Jenny Paterson Rose and above all, to my partner George Biason Domantay.

I also want to acknowledge several individuals who played a role in the structure of this book. Mike Masatsugu suggested I read *Dictée* by Theresa Hak-Kyung Cha regarding the role of language in a life of exile. Tom Shakow gave my parents *The Emigrants* by W.G. Sebald, published in 1992. In 2008, I read this miraculous piece of literature and subsequently much of Sebald's body of work. It, as well as *Searching for Sebald: Photography after W.G. Sebald*, edited by Lise Patt and with contributions by the lead designer and associate editor Antoinette La Farge, informed our selection of photographs and enlightened us to the central role photography and objects play in our family's archives. Professor Michael Levine introduced me to Holocaust literature and poetry in the early 1990's at Yale University, including the first work I ever read by a second generation survivor—the astounding and brave personal exposition *Maus* by Art Spiegelman—as well as to issues in literary translation, and importantly, to literature of witnessing.

I am grateful to the visual art professors at University of California, Irvine who were there during my graduate studies. They emphasized philosophy and intuition as a complement to critique, which helped me integrate art and writing—the poetry that reflect the world.

It has been a great pleasure to finally complete this book with my parents, who I thank with all my heart for their perseverance, dedication, and for encouraging me to be involved in this meaningful project. Together we have tried to integrate oral histories about war, displacement, and some of their effects, with the shared resolution to pursue and live full lives. I am happy to have found that we have many friends old and new who together formed a network of enthusiasm and support around us. Additionally, discovering the extent of our large family has produced for us hope and joy. This book involved a concerted effort by many who understood its import, not just to our family, but to others whose stories are as unique as they are similar. ■

Index

NOTE: In subheadings, references to author Charles Paterson (formerly Karl Schanzer) are shown with the initials CP. Subheadings referring to the author's father, Steven B. Shanzer (formerly Stefan B. Schanzer), are shown as SBS. The author's sister, Doris Schanzer Paterson Schneider, is referred to as Doris in subheadings and co-author Carrie Paterson is referred to as Carrie.